COLLECTED ESSAYS

H. P. LOVECRAFT: COLLECTED ESSAYS

Volume 1: Amateur Journalism (2004)
Volume 2: Literary Criticism (2004)
Volume 3: Science (2005)
Volume 4: Travel (2005)
Volume 5: Philosophy; Autobiography and Miscellany (2006)

COLLECTED ESSAYS:
VOLUME 4: TRAVEL

H. P. Lovecraft

Edited by S. T. Joshi

Hippocampus Press

New York

Library of Congress Cataloging-in-Publication Data

Lovecraft, H. P. (Howard Phillips), 1890–1937
  [Essays]
  Collected essays / H.P. Lovecraft ; edited by S.T. Joshi. --
1st ed.
    v. cm.
  Includes bibliographical references and indexes.
  Contents: v. 1. Amateur journalism -- v. 2. Literary criticism.
  ISBN 0-9721644-1-3 (v. 1 : hardcover) -- ISBN 0-9721644-2-1
(v. 1 : pbk.) -- ISBN 0-9721644-4-8 (v. 2 : hardcover) -- ISBN
0-9721644-9-9 (v. 2 : pbk.)
  I. Joshi, S. T., 1958–   . II. Title.
  PS3523.O833A6 2004b
  814'.52--dc22

2004000766

Select unpublished texts have been published by permission of the Estate of
H. P. Lovecraft and John Hay Library, Brown University.

Published by Hippocampus Press
P.O. Box 641, New York, NY 10156.
http://www.hippocampuspress.com

Cover art by Virgil Finlay, used by permission of Lail Finlay.
Hippocampus Press logo by Anastasia Damianakos.
Cover design by Barbara Briggs Silbert.

First Edition
1 3 5 7 9 8 6 4 2

Cloth: ISBN 0-9761592-0-1
Paper: ISBN 0-9761592-1-X

CONTENTS

INTRODUCTION

Some of the most heart-warming pages in Lovecraft's letters are those in which he describes the surprisingly far-flung travels in which he engaged over the last decade of his life. The man who, in 1915, could state with a certain perverse pride that "in all my life I have never been beyond the limits of the three states of Rhode Island, Massachusetts, & Connecticut"[1] would later take equal pride in the extent of his traversing of the American continent—from as far north as Quebec to as far south as Key West, from as far west as Cleveland and New Orleans to as far east as Cape Cod and Nantucket. It may well be that this range is not as impressive as might be imagined today, and Lovecraft unconsciously reflects his own rootedness in New England when a Vermonter in "The Whisperer in Darkness" (1930) refers to an Ohio man as a "Westerner." But for someone of Lovecraft's slender means, it was a noteworthy achievement. He keenly regretted his inability to cross the ocean to England, and perhaps his assertion that, after any such visit to a land where he felt such deep ancestral and cultural ties, he would never be able to return was merely a kind of defence mechanism.

Lovecraft's travels, even within the circumscribed area of New England, only got underway with the illness of his mother in 1919, which appeared to liberate him both physically and emotionally from her apron-strings. The two aunts, Lillian D. Clark and Annie E. P. Gamwell, with whom he successively lived for the rest of his life in Providence (barring the two years of his marriage in New York, 1924–26) were certainly dear to him, but he showed little compunction in leaving them for extended periods while he gallivanted up and down the Eastern Seaboard. To be sure, it is touching to read, as early as the summer of 1922, Lillian's confession that she missed him,[2] but this did not curtail his lengthy visit to Cleveland and New York.

It was, however, during those wide travels of 1922, which encompassed a full three months, that Lovecraft began what he referred to as a "diary" of his travels.[3] At this time, the comment appears to have referred merely to the chronicle of daily events that he would habitually include in his letters to his aunts, but later—perhaps as early as his New York years, when he undertook extensive explorations of antiquarian oases in the area—Lovecraft appears to have written an actual diary, probably similar to the surviving diary of 1925[4] that contains very tersely recorded details of his daily life and activities. In 1929 he reports losing such a diary, describing it as a "record of all my spring travels."[5] It becomes clear that Lovecraft used this diary to write not only accounts of his travels in letters to his aunts, but also the formal (or informal) travel essays that became a regular feature of his final decade.

---

1. HPL to Rheinhart Kleiner, 29 June 1915, *Letters to Rheinhart Kleiner* (New York: Hippocampus Press, 2005), p. 16.

2. HPL to Lillian D. Clark, 9 August 1922 (ms., JHL [written from Cleveland]).

3. "This is a letter & a diary combined!" HPL to Lillian D. Clark, 13–16 September 1922 (ms., JHL).

4. The unpublished work (ms., JHL) will appear in CE 5.

5. HPL to Lillian D. Clark, 13–14 May 1929 (ms., JHL).

The first such essay, "The Trip of Theobald" (1927), is by no means the most impressive of these works, and perhaps we should look back a few years to his whirlwind one-day visit to Washington, D.C., on 11–12 April 1925 for the true commencement of his travel writing; for this trip was shortly thereafter written up in what purported to be a letter to his aunt Lillian (dated 21 April), but which exists as a single-spaced typescript, in contrast to the autograph manuscripts of most of his other letters to Lillian or Annie. We can therefore assume that Lovecraft prepared at least one carbon copy of this document, to circulate among other colleagues, so that he would not have to recount the details of his trip individually to his many correspondents. Two of his finest travelogues, "Observations on Several Parts of America" (1928) and "Travels in the Provinces of America" (1929), exist in such single-spaced typescripts.

It is, however, a bit anomalous that the two documents that may stand at the very pinnacle of his travel writing, "An Account of Charleston" (1930) and "A Description of the Town of Quebec" (1930–31), exist only in autograph manuscripts. No doubt the heroic effort of typing up the latter (a mammoth work in 136 foolscap pages) proved too much for Lovecraft; and it was only in 1936, when H. C. Koenig requested tips on Charleston sites, that Lovecraft radically rewrote "An Account of Charleston" into what Koenig published as *Charleston*. Those practical souls who shed bitter tears at Lovecraft's "wasting" his time in writing these substantial works with no other intended audience but himself might do well to consider that their mere writing was a kind of therapeutic—a means of expressing the deep and overwhelming impressions that these and other locales made on a man whose receptivity to landscape and architecture was in every way exceptional. "I am above all *scenic and architectural* in my tastes," he wrote in 1928 (*SL* 2.229); and a few years earlier, as part of his plea to return to Providence from the hated New York:

> To all intents & purposes I am more naturally isolated from mankind than Nathaniel Hawthorne himself, who dwelt alone in the midst of crowds, & whom Salem knew only after he died. Therefore, it may be taken as axiomatic that the people of a place matter absolutely nothing to me except as components of the general landscape & scenery. . . . My life lies not among *people* but among *scenes*—my local affections are not personal, but topographical & architectural.[6]

It is therefore no surprise that Lovecraft required continual new doses of antiquity (if that is not an oxymoron) in order to sustain his mental equilibrium. From 1926 onward, with Providence as a secure base of operations, he could extend his reach farther and farther afield, willingly undergoing the hardships necessitated by poverty (sleeping on buses to avoid hotel charges, staying at cheap and not always salubrious Y.M.C.A.'s, exploring locales on foot rather than on expensive guided tours) to absorb the antiquity he needed to feel a part of the massed heritage of his nation and his race.

Some may find the habitual use of eighteenth-century diction in several of the travelogues a bit wearisome, but it is more than a harmless affectation. At a minimum, we must admire the accuracy and faithfulness of his imitation of the language of two centuries before, a pointed contrast to the many writers (from William Hope Hodgson to several *Weird Tales* hacks) whose attempts at seventeenth- and eighteenth-century prose produced comically mediaeval effects. But more than that, this archaic diction allowed

---

6. HPL to Lillian D. Clark, 29 March 1926 (ms., JHL).

Lovecraft to merge himself psychologically in the era in which he felt most at home, and which the locales he visited evoked with especial emphasis because of their miraculous historic preservation. One of the chief reasons why he found Charleston and Quebec so entrancing was the *completeness* of their antiquity: even today there are places in both cities where one can become half-convinced that the twentieth or twenty-first century does not exist, or is merely a mad dream of the future.

After 1931 Lovecraft wrote no travel essays of the scope of the Charleston or Quebec treatises; his best travel writing for the last five years of his life is embodied in letters to his aunts or to others. We must regret the absence of a formal travelogue of his travels of 1932 (Chattanooga, Natchez, New Orleans, Mobile), but letters help to supply the loss. In 1933 aunt Annie broke her ankle shortly after she and Lovecraft moved into 66 College Street, so no extensive travels occurred that year. As is well known, the bulk of his travels of 1934 and 1935 consisted of lengthy stays in Florida with R. H. Barlow, and it is surprising how little time Lovecraft spends in letters to various correspondents telling of his activities or the places he visited. In the summer of 1936 he was too ill and too busy with revision work to undertake any travels at all, except brief day-trips to Newport. The few travel essays Lovecraft wrote during these years are routine exercises in description ("Homes and Shrines of Poe") or history ("Some Dutch Footprints in New England").

Nevertheless, the gathering of all Lovecraft's travel essays is the fulfilment of a dream of at least a few scholars and critics who believe that they embody some of his best, most heartfelt writing. Travel was the chief, perhaps the only, form of relaxation Lovecraft allowed himself, and the fact that he would carefully save up his pennies for the better part of a year simply in order to spend them on excursions that seem to us almost appallingly crowded and arduous bespeaks the psychological importance of travel to Lovecraft's spirit. The nervous energy that he brought to travel paid its dividends not only in the topographical and philosophical expansion of his later fiction, but in the balm that it evidently brought to his antique temperament. He seemed to have little choice but to express his rapture in essays that may have had few if any readers in their own time, but which now deserve the keenest attention of his many devotees.

A NOTE ON THIS EDITION

This edition is based upon rigorous examination of the manuscripts of Lovecraft's essays, as well as first publications and relevant later appearances; the texts are based upon the manuscript or first appearance unless otherwise specified. At the end of each essay, an editor's note supplies bibliographical and other information that readers might find useful for placing the item within the context of Lovecraft's life and work; footnotes elucidating specific literary, historical, and other data in the essay follow the editor's note.

Manuscripts exist for nearly all the essays in this volume, and they have been followed as carefully as possible, with the understanding that some (e.g., "An Account of Charleston") are in essence first drafts not intended for publication. Some of Lovecraft's inconsistent renderings of French names in his Quebec travelogue have been systematized. Several essays are accompanied by hand-drawn sketches or maps by Lovecraft, and these have been placed as close to their locations in the original manuscripts as is feasible. Many of them have captions written by Lovecraft in archaic English. No attempt has been made to correct or expand upon Lovecraft's historical comments in the essays, or his discussions of specific structures. In some cases, further research by local historians has revealed that Lovecraft's dating of certain structures (derived, probably, from contemporary guidebooks) is slightly erroneous. Footnotes have been restricted to clarifications of historical or other points that cannot otherwise be easily ascertained by consulting standard reference works.

Abbreviations used in the notes are as follows:

AHT	Arkham House transcripts
AMS	autograph manuscript, signed
AT	*The Ancient Track: Complete Poetical Works* (Night Shade Books, 2001)
CE	*Collected Essays* (Hippocampus Press, 2004–06)
D	*Dagon and Other Macabre Tales* (Arkham House, 1986)
DH	*The Dunwich Horror and Others* (Arkham House, 1984)
FP	first publication
JHL	John Hay Library, Brown University (Providence, RI)
LL	*Lovecraft's Library: A Catalogue*, rev. ed. (Hippocampus Press, 2002)
LR	*Lovecraft Remembered*, ed. Peter Cannon (Arkham House, 1998)
MM	*At the Mountains of Madness and Other Novels* (Arkham House, 1985)
MW	*Miscellaneous Writings* (Arkham House, 1995)
SL	*Selected Letters* (Arkham House, 1965–76; 5 vols.)
TMS	typed manuscript, signed

I am grateful to Esther Rochon, Marc A. Michaud, David E. Schultz, Scott Connors, James C. Sanford, and Dan Lorraine for their assistance in the preparation of this volume. I have done most of my research for this volume at the John Hay and John D. Rockefeller Libraries of Brown University (Providence, RI), the Rhode Island Historical Society (Providence, RI), the Providence Public Library, the New York Public Library, and the University of Washington Library (Seattle, WA).

—S. T. Joshi

First, August 19, Worcester by 'bus, where W. Paul Cook[1] met me with his car. Thence to Athol. On Aug. 20 took a side trip to Deerfield; which is a marvellous old colonial town. On Sunday the 21st, we went on a trip to Vermont and New Hampshire—stopping at West Brattleboro to see Goodenough,[2] who lives in a quaint old farmhouse on a hillside amidst some of the most beautiful unspoiled country in New England. Goodenough is a modest, hospitable, altogether admirable and dutiful man—an old-time Yankee Puritan, untouched by the centuries. From Brattleboro we went to Lake Sunapee, and thence back to Athol. On Monday I climbed a high hill west of Athol and had an admirable view.

Wednesday I left for Boston. Stayed over night in the Y.M.C.A. and took the Portland 'bus in the morning. Got to Portland Thursday afternoon, and explored the town, taking a side trip to the old colonial village of Stroudwater. Also went up in the observation tower, built in 1807, for signalling ships. Just the same today—splendid view of town and harbour.

Portland is too modern and large to be really quaint, but it is a beautiful hill city with magnificent views and promenades. Friday took a side trip to ancient Yarmouth, 13 miles from Portland, and another to Portland Head Lighthouse, built in 1791. Went through both Longfellow houses—birthplace and principal residence. Saturday took a cheap excursion to the White Mountains—saw real mountains for the first time in my life, and had some superb views at Crawford Notch. Ascended Mt. Washington by cogwheel railway, and had some splendid views on the way up, though it rained just as I reached the summit.

Sunday moved on to Portsmouth, where I revisited all the ancient scenes I had [seen] four years previously. Also hiked out to the Old Benning Wentworth[3] House at Little Hampton, which I had never seen before, but which is the scene of Longfellow's poem, "Lady Wentworth". The house was a disappointment, for it was a rambling farmhouse now made over into a summer estate. Doubt if Longfellow had ever seen it when he wrote his poem. Monday moved on to Newburyport[4] which is fully as colonial as Portsmouth. These two towns are probably the most ancient-looking places of large size in America. Both of them have a whole network of narrow unpaved streets without sidewalks in the poorer sections—just as they were before the Revolution, same houses and all. In Newburyport the whole business section, outside of buildings erected about 1812 just after the great fire of 1811, [. . .] Stopped at the Y.M.C.A. In all these places except Portsmouth, where it was closed Sunday. So stopped at the Kearsage House there.

Tuesday, explored Newburyport further, and took a side trip to Parker River, climbing a great hill getting one of the finest views in New England.

In the evening went to Amesbury and Haverhill, putting up at Y.M.C.A and making a trip to Tryout office where I am now. Hope to get to Ipswich and Gloucester tomorrow, if I can get good transportation. Then Salem, Marblehead, Boston, and home.

After leaving Haverhill Wednesday morning, I returned to Newburyport via West Newbury, giving this ancient town of "Lord" Timothy Dexter[5] a final survey. I then took the train for Ipswich, where I thoroughly explored the ancient Whipple House, built in 1640, and housing one line of my ancestry. Obtaining transportation to Essex I there took a 'bus for Gloucester, which I reached in the afternoon. Registering at the Y.M.C.A. I purchased a guide-book and proceeded to explore the town much more thoroughly than on my former visit five years ago.[6] This time I left nothing unseen, including the fine 1896 church, the stately old mansion on Middle Street, the hidden graveyard on Church Street, [and] a fine panorama view from Governor's Hill.

The perennial colour and atmosphere of the waterfront, where the last of New England's maritime still survives, [. . .] The next day I devoted to interiors, notably the fine Sargent-Murray-Gilman House (1768) and the ancient Ellery House (1704), and a side trip to quaint Rockport, where old Main St. stretches beside the sea. On the final day I visited the Riggs House, oldest on Cape Ann—at Annisquam, and explored the cliffs of Magnolia, overlooking Norman's Woe, and containing the celebrated Rafe's Chasm. At noon I proceeded southwest through picturesque Manchester and bustling Beverly to Salem, where I steeped myself in the usual quota of historical sights. Then crossing by trolley to Marblehead I devoted the glorious sunset hours to that finest of colonial survivals, imbibing the spirit of Georgian antiquity to its fullest extent.

In the evening I returned to Providence by way of Lynn and Boston, reaching home at midnight, after exactly two weeks of scenic and antiquarian travelling. The trip, as a whole, exceeded all others I have taken in general pleasure and picturesqueness, and will surely be difficult to improve upon in future years.

EDITOR'S NOTE FP: *Tryout* 11, No. 8 (September 1927): [27–30] (as by "Theobald"). The first and least interesting of HPL's travelogues. As HPL states in the sixth paragraph, he wrote at least part of the article (in apparent haste) while at the "office" of Charles W. Smith, editor of the *Tryout*, in Haverhill, Mass. It recounts HPL's travels in the summer of 1927, the first occasion when he spent part of the summer in travel (although this visit was only of two weeks' duration). HPL's visits covered points in Massachusetts (Athol, Deerfield, Newburyport, Amesbury, Haverhill, Ipswich), Vermont (Brattleboro), Maine (Portland, Yarmouth), and New Hampshire (Portsmouth). The text is printed very poorly and in parts is incoherent; editorial insertions are indicated in square brackets.

Notes

1. W. Paul Cook (1881–1948), amateur publisher who resided in Athol, Mass., and one of HPL's oldest friends.

2. Arthur Goodenough (1871–1936), amateur poet who had written a poem on HPL in 1918, to which HPL replied with "To Arthur Goodenough, Esq." (*Tryout*, September 1918; AT 344–45). Goodenough's home, seen again in 1928, along with Vrest Orton's home outside Brattleboro (seen in 1928), served as the prototype for Henry Wentworth Akeley's house in "The Whisperer in Darkness" (1930).

3. Benning Wentworth (1696–1770) was a provincial governor of New Hampshire (1741–66). His last name is probably the source for Henry Wentworth Akeley's middle name.

4. HPL had first seen Newburyport, in the company of Edgar J. Davis, in 1923. A later visit, in the fall of 1931, led to the writing of "The Shadow over Innsmouth" (1931).

5. For "Lord" Timothy Dexter, see SL 1.225.

6. HPL had visited Gloucester, in the company of Sonia H. Greene, in June–July 1922.

VERMONT—A FIRST IMPRESSION

To the southern New-Englander entering Vermont for the first time there is a sense of mystic revivification. On the towns of the lower coast the blight of mutation and modernity has descended. Weird metamorphoses and excrescences, architectural and topographical, mark a menacing tyranny of mechanism and viceroyalty of engineering which are fast hurrying the present scene out of all linkage with its historic antecedents and setting it adrift anchorless and all but traditionless in alien oceans. Swart foreign forms, heirs to moods and impulses antipodal to those which moulded our heritage, surge in endless streams along smoke-clouded and lamp-dazzled streets; moving to strange measures and inculcating strange customs. All through the nearer countryside the stigmata of change are spreading. Reservoirs, billboards, and concrete roads, power lines, garages, and flamboyant inns, squalid immigrant nests and grimy mill villages; these things and things like them have brought ugliness, tawdriness, and commonplaceness to the urban penumbra. Only in the remoter backwoods can one find the pristine and ancestral beauty which was southern New-England's, or the unmixed signs of that continuous native life whose deep roots make it the one authentic outgrowth of the landscape. There are traces enough to allure and tantalise, but not enough to satisfy. With our keenest pleasure and satisfaction is mixed a certain melancholy; for it is upon the ghost of something beloved and departed, rather than upon the thing itself, that we gaze. Our own country and history seem subtly dissolving away from us, and we clutch frantically at the straws and symbols through which our imaginations may momentarily recall and recapture a past which is really our own.

With such a mood, softened perhaps by the beauty of the hills and river-bends which flank the gateway, the southern New-Englander enters Vermont. He has seen its hills for some time across the Connecticut, domed and undulant, and shining with a clear emerald light unmarred by vapour or defacement. Then comes a sweeping downward curve, and beyond limpid water the climbing terraces of an old town loom into sight, as a loved, remembered picture might appear when the leaves of a childhood volume are slowly turned. It is plain from the first that this town is not quite like those one has left behind. Roofs and steeples and chimneys, prosaic enough in the telling, here cluster together on the green river-bluff in some magical collocation that stirs dim memories. Something in the contours, something in the setting, has power to touch deep viol-strings of feeling which are ancestral if one be young and personal if one be old. The whole scene vaguely brings us a fleeting quality we have known before. We have seen such towns long ago, climbing above deep river-valleys and rearing their old brick walls beside sloping, cobbled streets. Grandeur may be wanting, but the marvel of rekindled vision is there. Something is alive that is dead elsewhere; something that we, or the blood that is in us, can recognise as more closely akin to ourselves than anything in the busy cosmopolis to the southward. This, in fine, is a surviving fragment of the old America; it is what our other towns used to be in the days when they were most themselves, the days when they housed their own people and gave birth to all the little legends and bits of lore which make them glamorous and significant in the eyes of their children.

By an ancient covered bridge we ride back through decades and enter the enchanted city of our fathers' world. We had not thought such bridges still existed, for southward the last of them was demolished years ago. The river-valley is deep, and as we come from the wooden tunnel we feel the kind guardianship of the ancient hills and the eternal streams from unknown fountains of the north. On past an island stepping-stone we go, and up the homely slopes of the dawn-fresh town. There is life here, and the clatter of modern industry; but somehow the life and industry are more our own than the febrile bustle to the southward. It is the fresher, more coherent vitality that springs from continuity with ancestral sources; the vitality our own coastal region might have had under different dispensations of history. This, then, is Brattleboro; the town where Kipling wrote and Royall Tyler rhymed.[1] Say what you will of changing Vermont life, the outsider can still find in it far more basic worth, far more of the unmixed primal fund of mood and fibre which was New-England's supreme heritage, than the commerce-plagued cities to the south can shew. Into this hive of half-concealed glamour we ascend, stirred and rejuvenated by memories and influences too ethereal to define. The kinship and hospitality of the Main Street spread over us, and encourage us to climb higher into the charmed sea of westerly greenness to which these atavistic bricks form pylon and peristyle. The wild hills are before us, where song and witchery lurk.

And now we cast off all allegiance to modern things; to change, and the rule of steel and steam, and the crumbling of ancient visions and simple impulses. The tar and concrete roads, and the vulgar world that bred them, have ended; and we wind rapt and wondering over elder and familiar ribbons of rutted whiteness which curl past alluring valleys and traverse old wooden bridges in the lee of green slopes. The nearness and intimacy of the little domed hills have become almost breath-taking. Their steepness and abruptness hold nothing in common with the humdrum, standardised world we know, and we cannot help feeling that their outlines have some strange and almost-forgotten meaning, like vast hieroglyphs left by a rumoured titan race whose glories live only in rare, deep dreams. We climb and plunge fantastically as we thread this hypnotic landscape. Time has lost itself in the labyrinths behind, and around us stretch only the flowering waves of faery. Tawdriness is not there, but instead, the recaptured beauty of vanished centuries—the hoary groves, the untainted pastures hedged with gay blossoms and the small brown farmsteads nestling amidst huge trees beneath vertical precipices of fragrant brier and meadow-grass. Even the sunlight assumes a supernal glamour, as if some special atmosphere or exaltation mantled the whole region. There is nothing like it save in the magic vistas that sometimes form the backgrounds of Italian primitives. Sodoma and Leonardo[2] saw such expanses, but only in the distance, and through the vaultings of Renaissance arcades. We rove at will through the midst of the picture; and find in its necromancy a thing we have known or inherited, and for which we have always been vainly searching.

At the heart of this weirdly beautiful Arcadia Vermont's gentle poet dwells. One with his hereditary hills and groves, with the spreading, venerable trees and the ancient peaked roofs of the vine-banked cottages, lives Arthur Goodenough; singer of the olden strain and last of the long line of New-England's Puritan oracles. Tilling ancestral acres in the good old way, and keeping alive beside his daily hearth the well-loved thoughts and customs of our Golden Age, he is vastly more than a retrospective teller of bygone tales. Alone amongst the surviving choir he truly leads the pastoral life he breathes; so that we need not wonder at the flawless authenticity of his message. He has prolonged our old New-England in himself, and his stately charm and genial hospitality are as truly poems as anything the pen could write. Lovely beyond words is the realm over which the poet holds agrestic sway. The ancient house on the hillside, embowered in greenery and shadowed by a lone leafy monarch; the dream-stirring slope to the westward, where earth's beauty melts into the cosmic glory of sunset; the narrow, beckoning road, the outspread, dew-glistening meadows, and the hint of spectral woodlands and valleys in the background—all these mark out a perfect poet's seat, and cause us to thank Fate that for once in history a man and his setting are well matched.

Northward from Brattleboro the charm still holds. There are glorious sweeps of vivid valley where great cliffs rise, New-England's virgin granite shewing grey and austere through the verdure that scales the crests. There are gorges where untamed streams leap, bearing down toward the river the unimagined secrets of a thousand pathless peaks. Narrow, half-hidden roads bore their way through solid, luxuriant masses of forest, among whose primal trees whole armies of elemental spirits lurk. Archaic covered bridges linger fearsomely out of the past in pockets of the hills, and here and there a summit bears a tiny hamlet of trim, clean old houses and steeples that Time has never been able to sully.

Now to the right the river shimmers mystically around its bends, while New-Hampshire's granite vistas stretch panoramically toward the unknown East, whence far birds bring legends of the sea's wonder. Putney, East Putney, Grout, Westminster—one by one new piquancies unfold and retire as the traveller fares northward. The steep river-bank quaintness and ancient Yankeedom of Bellows Falls appears, a bridge is crossed, and suddenly one realises that Vermont has been left behind.

But it is still visible for leagues across the river, veiled in distance and golden with elfin light. The spell of the past has not departed, for Vermont has given us something that we have always sought, and that can never be effaced from our spirit. Dim on the horizon the purpling hills rise, Ascutney towering in lordship above its neighbours. A bend shuts it from sight, and we are alone with our meditations.

EDITOR'S NOTE FP: *Driftwind* 2, No. 3 (March 1928): [5–9]. Text based on the TMS (JHL), dated 29 September 1927. HPL's rhapsody on first seeing Vermont, albeit only the extreme southern part of the state. The article was published in *Driftwind*, a Vermont magazine founded the previous year by HPL's colleague Walter J. Coates (1880–1941). Portions of the second, third, fourth, and sixth paragraphs, significantly revised, were incorporated into "The Whisperer in Darkness" (1930; see esp. *DH* 246–47).

Notes

1. British author Rudyard Kipling (1865–1936) stayed in Brattleboro from 1892 to 1896. Royall Tyler (1757–1826), Colonial American poet, was born in Boston but moved to Guilford, Vermont, shortly after the Revolution, where he began a law practice. He was chief justice of the Supreme Court of Vermont (1807–13) and also a professor of jurisprudence at the University of Vermont (1811–14).

2. HPL refers to the Italian painters Giovanni Antonio Bazzi Sodoma (1477–1549) and Leonardo da Vinci (1452–1519). The term "Italian primitives" is a now outmoded term for Italian tempera painters of the 13th and 14th centuries who broke from mediaeval traditions of painting and helped to usher in the Renaissance.

OBSERVATIONS ON SEVERAL PARTS OF AMERICA

Being the Journey of H. Lovecraft, Gent., into His Majesty's Colonies of New-York and the Massachusetts-Bay; the New-Hampshire Grants; the Towns of Philadelphia and Baltimore; Annapolis, Georgetown, Alexandria, and the rebel Federal City call'd Washington; and certain Parts of Virginia, westward to the Endless Caverns.

PROVIDENCE, RHODE-ISLAND
Printed and Sold by John Carter, at Shakespear's-Head
in King-Street, over-against the Court House, and Sold
by Merchants generally.
1728

Being oblig'd by circumstances to spend above a month and a half, last spring, in the town of Flatbush, near New-York,[1] in the province of that name, I resolv'd to make my sojourn pleasant by means of such observations of good scenery and historick monuments as the nature of the region permitted. By good fortune I came upon not a few things of lively interest and agreeableness; both close to the town, and on short coach journeys out of it. These things, however, turn'd out to be no more than a prologue to the wider travels and sprightlier sights that follow'd them; so that a compleat record of my late wanderings must embrace near three months of time, and a territory of extream bigness, extending from His Majesty's New-Hampshire Grants (lately known to the rebels as the Federal State of Ver-mont)[2] to the antient and civilised Province of Virginia.

My stay in Flatbush was chiefly notable for my discovery, thro' diligent searching of many books, of several objects of much antiquity which I had never discover'd before. The western end of Long-Island, in which the village is situate, was settled by Hollanders at a very early date; and so widely scatter'd were their architectural constructions, that a surprising number have surviv'd to the present time amidst surroundings more and more incongruous. On this occasion it may be imagin'd that I did not neglect the old church whose steeple, put up in 1796, still dominates the village so agreeably. It is to be lamented, that a recent sprucing-up of the churchyard hath depriv'd the place of some of that air of picturesque neglect which so much captivated me six years ago; but despite all changes there remains an air of loveliness and mellow repose which nothing can take away. To behold this venerable fane in the golden light of a setting sun is an experience not to be scoff'd at; and having once done this, the visitor is dispos'd to forget the constant decay which is debasing a quiet and beautiful village little by little to the state of a crowded mongrel suburb.

But most of my late explorations dealt with those parts of the country south of the village; once very open and sparsely settled, but now fast spoilt by cheap streets and the cottages of an hybrid foreign rabble. On the 19th of May I made a trip to that part of Jamaica Bay call'd the Mill Basin, there seeing for the first time the Jan Schenck house, built in 1656 from the timbers of a privateer, and reputed to be the oldest house in the entire province of New-York. This house, an old Dutch cottage with steep peaked roof, is situate on a flat tidal marsh near the shoar, and is now being crowded by the growth of an ugly manufactory district. Its condition is still very good, and the trees and buildings immediately around it help to save it from the squalor so close upon it. It is very little alter'd from its original state, and such alterations as have been made, are all of the eighteenth century. Many newspaper articles attribute a very romantick history to the house, but I do not find these tales sustain'd by such guide-books as I deem responsible. The Schencks, in general, came from Holland in 1650 and establisht many homesteads near the south shoar of western Long-Island, where the numerous creeks and salt marshes gave the country something of the home-like aspect of the Netherlands. On another trip I beheld the Nicholas Schenck house in Canarsie, only second to the Jan Schenck house in age, but sunk into a frightful state of disrepair. On still another occasion I visited the old Gerritsen Tide Mill on a creek south of Flatbush. This was built in 1688, and a dam made at the same time still confines the rising waters of the sea. The wheel is in a good state, though the building itself hath suffer'd considerably since its abandonment near forty years ago.

I vary'd these excursions into Hollandish history by a trip to a forgotten village which, tho' close at hand, is of as truly ENGLISH an origin as any town on the sacred soil of my own NEW-ENGLAND. This is the hamlet of Gravesend, south of Flatbush on the road to Coney-Island, and at no great distance from that plebeian watering-place. Gravesend was settled in 1643 by an English gentlewoman of non-conformist persuasion, one Lady Moody, who like the people of New-England, dislik'd the usages of the establisht church and sought a retreat therefrom. Tho' her settlement was within the domain of the Holland States-General, she was allow'd perfect freedom to live in the English way, and gather around her a British population; so that the region was fully prepar'd for the change which came in 1664, when Col. Nicholls and His Majesty's fleet took over the province to add to our empire. There were, of course, a sensible number of Dutch residents, as is manifest to this day in many family names. I had never seen Gravesend before, but came upon it without difficulty. Its present situation is very unfavourable, insomuch as the thickest part of it is buried beneath the trestles of an elevated rail-road; but the number of buildings still standing is singularly large. Near on a dozen cottages in plain sight date from before 1700, and not even the spreading of a vast colony of Italians can destroy the air of antiquity that hangs over the place. The Hicks-Platt house, a low cottage cover'd with thick ivy, was built in the time of Lady Moody; and within its walls the Holland governors, Willem Kieft and Petrus Stuyvesant, are known to have been entertain'd.

Further explorations in Flatbush, Flatlands, New Utrecht, and related regions yielded many highly picturesque glimpses of old farmhouses, churches, churchyards, and other reliques of better days. In some cases these were wholly surrounded by the incursions of decadent modernity, whilst in other cases small bits of contiguous farm-yard or boskage lent a touch of redeeming congruity to the background. The region, as a whole, is doomed; for it is slowly being bought out by oily Jews fat with ill-got money, who are flocking out from the New-York Ghetto. Only certain parts in Flatbush proper, now zoned with fanatical strictness and held by families who have long liv'd there, will remain as a civilised oasis amidst this flood of ethnick and social putrefaction.

More striking, perhaps, than these Flatbush excursions, were those long coach journeys made once or twice each week with the family of my small foster-grandchild Frank Belknap Long, Jun.[3] I was by this means made familiar with the pleasing rolling country north of New-York, wherein are many attractive farmsteads and villages not greatly inferior to those of New-England. The Croton reservoir region on the east side of the Hudson is mark'd by many noble hills and valleys, and I can still recall a multitude of vivid prospects very like those to be had from the hills of the Connecticut Valley. Our trips on this side of the river extended as far north as Peekskill and Lake Mahopac, and as far east as Stamford and Ridgefield, in His Majesty's Colony of Connecticut, in New-England. It was an almost unbearably tantalising experience to dip within the edge of my native country of New-England, only to emerge again into the desart of New-York. We also crossed the Bear Mountain Bridge, and enjoy'd the truly magnificent spectacle of the domed hills along the Hudson's margin. On one occasion we visited the fortress and school of West-Point, witnessing a highly impressive dress-parade from a bench beside an elderly gentleman in uniform who turn'd out to be the commandant of the Academy. Another trip on the west shoar extended to that impressive hill country wherein Tuxedo is situate, and where the Ramapaugh mountains assume an agreeable diversity of aspects. We return'd across the hills, by a winding road which travers'd the so-call'd Seven Lakes country; emerging on the shoar of the Hudson at Haverstraw.

Naturally I did not omit the town of Paterson from my itinerary, but was very congenially entertain'd by the head of the local Musaeum there; a fat, shock-headed gentleman named Morton, with whom I had had considerable previous acquaintance.[4] James Ferdinand, I may remark, is an ideal host; and his establishment is a marvel of accomplishment and effective administration. A building all too small is utilis'd with the greatest ingenuity conceivable, and the system of arrangement and labelling wou'd do credit to the most veteran practitioner of the curatorial art. The mineral collection, which covers the entire exhibition part of the second floor, is one of the most ample and well-classify'd in these colonies; and is due entirely to the keen skill and unremitting vigilance and activity of our genial colleague. Mortonius also shew'd me as much of the local scenery as limited time wou'd permit; taking me to the top of Garrett Mountain, whence is observable as fine a prospect of Paterson on one cou'd ask—a prospect which removes much of the grimy sordidness habitual to the town as seen closely.

Another trip of interest was with our young fellow-amateur Wilfred B. Talman, Esq.,[5] to his ancestral region of Spring Valley, on the west of the river. I here beheld an unspoilt Dutch countryside still in the hands of its original families, of whom young Talman is an unmixt descendant. Tho' the village is ugly, the farm lands adjacent are very fine; and the number of old Dutch houses and burying places is almost past counting. We concluded the day with a full survey of the village of Tappan, where the unfortunate Major André was confin'd, try'd, and put to death by the rebel army in 1780. The tavern which form'd his prison (in 1780 kept by an ancestor of Talman's), and the headquarters of Genl. Washington (in which Talman's own mother was born), are still in unimpair'd condition; and the old church and churchyard (fill'd with Talman's forbears) form a spectacle worth a long journey to see. Sparkill, near by, is another antient village affording many fine specimens of Georgian architecture; but it is unfortunately given over altogether to Italians. Piermont, a river port adjacent to Sparkill, has a vast negro settlement; and affords a sinister study in decadence.

Not the least of my pleasures was a trip up the Hudson's east bank to Tarrytown, Sleepy Hollow, and the Washington Irving country in general. Tarrytown is an exquisite village perched on a cliff whose steepness and height make Providence's hill seem like a prairie. At Sleepy Hollow is an antient Dutch church built in 1685, which with the exception of the Old Ship Church at Hingham (1681) is the oldest house of publick worship, continuously us'd, in these colonies. It stands high on a terrace dominating the post road, and its churchyard has expanded into that enormous Sleepy Hollow Cemetery where the mortal remains of Mr. Irving repose. Sleepy Hollow itself, one of the finest wooded river gorges I have ever seen, is within the domain of the cemetery; no doubt forming a place of convocation for the numerous ghouls attendant upon the subterraneous population. I was every moment on the watch for the Headless Horseman, but was deny'd that sight by reason of the strength of the daylight. In returning to Flatbush, I stopt off the stage-coach at Irvington from a desire to visit Mr. Irving's country-seat of Sunnyside. Here, however, I met with disappointment; for though I descended the bank to the level of the grounds, I was inform'd by a lodge keeper that the present proprietors do not admit spectators.[6]

Another field of exploration near New-York was the extensive county of Queens, now a borough of the greater city, and fast being ruin'd by cheap suburban villas. I made several trips thro' the still unspoilt parts of this territory, and found on its north shoar several old Dutch bouweries in much their original condition—pleasing reliques of healthier days, that will soon fall victims to the blight of vulgar land-agents. Some of the old Rapalye homesteads in this part of the county are among the best kept of all Dutch colonial specimens. In central Queens a sad transition is occurring; new rows of cheap houses being flung out across once lovely meadows where still an elder farmhouse may now and then be seen. I shall never forget my experience on the 31st day of May, when, at a point not far from Northern Boulevard, and at the very edge of a depressing line of flimsy stucco'd rookeries, I beheld a peaceful antient farmhouse with barns, byres, orchards, and plough'd fields about it; dreaming in compleat changelessness amidst so much of change. Westward, in fantastical outline against a glamorous sunset, tower'd the grotesque spires of Manhattan like a mirage of doom. Eastward the drab rows of sordid villas stretcht. But between the two the old farm still dream'd on, and the sturdy hind still bent behind the plough as the kine came in to rest at evening. It was of particular interest to me to learn, that this was not a Dutch place at all, but the farm of a New-England settler of early date, by the name of Hazard. Since all the colonial Hazards are descended from that Thomas Hazard or Hassard whose principal posterity settled in the Narragansett Country, and since I my self have a double line of Hazard ancestry in me, I felt that this place was indeed of a personal significance; and in truth it does very aptly typify the state of an archaick old gentleman left over from former times, and soon to be crowded into oblivion by the rise of a new aera to which he hath no resemblance, and with which he hath nothing in common. I need not say that my explorations of Queens included a revisiting of those spots formerly known to me; namely, the still pleasing old villages of Jamaica and Flushing. These towns were settled by gentlemen and yeomen from New-England, and were especial seats of the Quaker sect. Flushing contains the antient Bowne House, built in 1661, where George Fox once slept, and across the road from which he once preach'd.[7] The meeting house of the Friends, built in 1694, has a very odd hay-cap roof, and is surrounded by a pleasing churchyard. I also explor'd antient Newtown, now call'd Elmhurst, with its quaint streets, old churches, and historick homesteads.

Nor must I overlook that one last bit of truly untainted countryside near New-York—the rolling agrestick reaches of Staten-Island. I saw much more of it than I ever had before, visiting in particular the tangled colonial alleys of Stapleton, the archaick lanes of New-Dorp, and the steep streets of Richmond, which rests in a picturesque valley. In New-Dorp is the antient Britton-Cubberly house, a hoary moss-grown pile now employ'd as a Musaeum; whilst at Richmond are the finest hilltop court-house and valley churchyard that the length and breadth of the island can afford. I shall

never forget my sight of Richmond in a glorious sunset, when I stood on a neighbouring hill behind the churchyard and saw the spires and roofs of the drowsy village below
tipp'd with a magick and trans-figuring flame.

I once remarked, that Flatbush forms the only habitable oasis in the immediate vicinity of New-York; and my late sojourn disclos'd to me but one exception. That exception is the strip of land just north of Manhattan Island, betwixt Van Cortlandt Park
and the Hudson, and known by the name of Riverdale. It is here that the modern line
of Broadway diverges from the course of the old Albany Post Road for a space, leaving
the antient thoroughfare as a bend of hillside bye-street curving toward the bluffs
above the river. Along this road many quaint houses of Georgian times still remain,
whilst in the hills beyond it nestle the fine modern houses of such gentlemen of taste as
appreciate the region and study to preserve its unspoil'd character. I spent a memorable day here, as a guest of my esteem'd friend, Vrest Orton, Esq.,[8] a gentleman of Vermont birth, rear'd in Athol, in the Massachusetts-Bay, and now enduring New-York
from reasons of business necessity involving a connexion with the *Saturday Review of
Literature*. Ortonius naturally took care not to settle in any but the least offensive parts
of the metropolitan area, and he surely succeeded in choosing that section with the
greatest number of mitigating points. I wander'd with pleasure over the quaint, shady
roads, and lookt down with agreeable awe into the many pine ravines and graceful
wooded gorges. Some of the antient houses were deserving of close study, whilst none
of the newer ones was beneath contempt.

It was this same Vrest Orton, Esq., who was responsible for the first part of my
subsequent wanderings. With the close of the Flatbush period I had design'd to go
south at once, but by coincidence Ortonius also chose this precise season for a rural
escape. Opprest by the noxious atmosphere of town, he had hired a delightful farm
some miles out of Brattleboro, in Vermont, for the summer; and hither he insisted on
my accompanying him for as long a period as I car'd to remain. It will be recall'd, how
fervent was my admiration for Vermont when I beheld it so briefly last summer. This
year my sentiments were in no wise chang'd, hence I did not waste time in hesitancy
upon receiving this invitation. I had been away from my native New-England a month
and a half. Now, in one glorious sweep of the rail-road coach, I left all decay behind me
and was plung'd into an extatick delirium of familiar rolling hills, stone walls, embower'd white steeples, and slope-nestling farmhouse roofs. Home soil—antient New-
England—loveliest land of all!

In one day I pass'd over the soil of no less than four of His Majesty's New-England
Provinces—Connecticut, the Massachusetts-Bay, New-Hampshire, and that region of
the New-Hampshire Grants which hath lately been given the name of "Vermont".
New-Haven and Hartford were pass'd in the daylight. Springfield came at twilight.
Greenfield was glimps'd in the dark, whilst Brattleboro came in the dead of midnight.
The rail journey was at an end, and five miles of narrow hill road in a Detroit chaise
brought me to the isolated Orton dwelling.

The history of the region whither I had come is known to most persons in rough
outline. It is the last settled part of New-England, and remains the closest of any section to the ways of our ancestors. Before the period of its settlement it was but loosely
allocated with respect to the other colonies, both New-Hampshire and New-York having vague claims of sovereignty. Colonisation began in 1724, and in times subsequent
to that grants of land were made by His Majesty's Governor of New-Hampshire, the
Honourable Benning Wentworth, Esq. (whose rambling country-seat near Portsmouth

I saw a year ago), notwithstanding a verdict of the Crown in favour of the New-York claims. Until and during the late unfortunate revolution the region was subject to dispute, but generally known as the New-Hampshire Grants. The settlers themselves were inclin'd to oppose the New-York claims, by reason of the arbitrary acts of New-York agents who sought to invalidate the land titles obtain'd from New-Hampshire; and to resist these New-Yorkers was form'd the organisation call'd the Green Mountain Boys, who later turn'd arms against His Majesty's government as a whole. Upon the collapse of the lawful sovereignty in these parts, New-York still continued to assert her claim as a Federal State, as she had once asserted it as a British province. Vermont, resisting, maintained the status of an independent republick; disjoin'd from Great-Britain, but separate from the Federal union of the late colonies. This anomalous condition prevail'd until 1791, when after much debate Vermont was admitted to the new union— the first non-original State to be so included. The inhabitants of Vermont, of a hardier and more frugal sort than those of the rest of New-England, have never changed in character or habits to any large extent. They have stuck close to the soil, building but few large houses and founding but few large towns; and retain to this day the peculiar accents of other times, having a dialect of great singularity, unlike any to be found in other parts of New-England. Pleasingly few foreigners are amongst them, and the survival of old traditions is a common and gratifying spectacle. A few of the lower orders have fallen into a kind of gentle decay through poverty and isolation, relaxing those standards of enterprise and neat housekeeping which typified their ancestors. This decay, however, is very unlike the deep and insidious decay of central and western Massachusetts; where the moral and social order fall into odd perversions despite a maintenance of household neatness. The gentry, as in Massachusetts, maintain a very high level of life and thought; and indulge in a literary and aesthetick activity which is quite remarkable in view of their remote situation.

The country, as indeed my reports of last year attest, is of almost miraculous beauty and picturesqueness. It is a veritable fairyland of closely ranged green hillsides, multitudinous murmuring brooks, deep, wooded glens with many a cavern and waterfall, and steep, winding, rutted roads free from all trace of billboards and other defacements. Covered bridges of the antient sort abound, and the houses are old, simple, and ineffably lovely in their traditional hillside setting with rambling stone walls and gigantic elms in the background. The omnipresent vividness and poignancy of the landscape, in which every turn means a fresh hillside, glen, woodland rise, or steeple-filled valley vista, almost spoils one for any other kind of scenery; and gives a persistent impression of picturesque unreality. The mind vows that so much of breathless loveliness simply cannot be—and lays the sight to some subtle spell, emanating perhaps from the special aura or enveloping local atmosphere of the region. Hills and brooks—brooks and hills—these are the impressions that persist after all others become merged into the general background.

The farmhouse leased by Orton is of colonial date and idyllick setting; far from the nearest neighbour, and at the edge of an exquisite brook-filled ravine. It is of the familiar New-England story-and-a-half type, and is furnished entirely with eighteenth-century material, carefully selected by the antiquarian taste of the owner. There is no plumbing save a leaden pipe to lead in the spring water (a system which hath always serv'd the hilly Vermont to replace the wells common to flatter regions), and no illumination save oil lamps and candles. Orton is himself a stickler for the antient ways, and arranges all things with great care in the ancestral manner. The sitting-room of the house, with its great fireplace, crane, kettle, and andirons, is an object of admiration to all visitors; and the whole place form'd as appropriate a setting for an old country-gentleman like myself, as cou'd possibly be imagin'd.

In this elder paradise I remain'd two weeks, assisting in some of the rural activities of the locality—at least, to the extent of helping the neighbours' boys[9] hunt stray kine, helping Orton dam up his brook to alter the channel, and looking on whilst Orton fished. I also took long solitary expeditions of scenick appreciation, ascending the highest peaks of the region, and exploring many a brook-murmurous ravine that led out to some open space where the setting sun lit up unexpected village spires or spread elfin glamour over some remote upper slope. I cou'd write a whole volume of verse about the vary'd prospects of ineffable loveliness which that region afforded me. Even a bald catalogue wou'd be a poem. The brook winding sinuously through the sunlit meadow—the great rock falls in the forest—the curve of great green terraces against the sky at Hinesburg—the hushed dip of the wood-bordered road beyond Watson's house—but Lud, Sir, this is prose! Be it sufficient to say, that I believe I did the region fair justice. The homely Yankee villages of Brattleboro and West Brattleboro I found very charming, and obtain'd what might be term'd the culminating view of both town and country from the top of wooded Mount Wantastiquet, across the river in New-Hampshire; whither I climb'd despite the grave warnings of villagers regarding rattle-snakes. From this eminence all of Brattleboro and West Brattleboro lie outspread—they, and the country and hills beyond them even unto the Green Mountains, and the curving reaches of the broad Connecticut that glimmer blue northward and southward as far as the eye can see.

Naturally enough, I saw considerable of the poet Goodenough, who dwells not much above a mile from Orton's; and again I took occasion to admire the exquisite scenick setting of his antient farmhouse with its giant elms and hillside vistas. On Sunday, June 17th, there was a literary assemblage of much interest at the poet's abode, to which came not only Orton and myself, but good old Cook from Athol, and the Vermont editor Walter J. Coates, all the vast way down from the Montpelier region. Local literati, including a man from the Brattleboro paper, also attended; and the event received considerable publicity in the publick press.[10] Orton and I were also the subject of newspaper articles, adulatory in the usual rural vein.[11]

On Monday the 18th of June I took a trip south to the Province of the Massachu-setts-Bay, visiting the drowsy and beautiful town of Greenfield, and the well-remember'd shades of hoary and portentous Deerfield. In the latter place I revived all my pleasing memories of last year; studying the century-lashed houses and living over again the frightful massacre of French-led Indians in 1704, which forms this town's chief claim to historick notice.

On June 24th the genial Cook, having come up in his coach, bore me away to Athol for another delectable sojourn. The ride was agreeable, and in the evening I was gratify'd to renew my acquaintance with that sightly town whence I deriv'd so much enjoyment last year. I visited the site of the original Pequoig settlement of 1735, and mark'd the older village common with its colonial houses and steeples, which towers so high on the bank above the river-valley in which the industrial and Victorian part of the town hath grown. My Athol days were spent in rural rambling, and in conversation with Cook and young Munn, the *Weird Tales* contributor.[12] Munn took me out by coach to his residence, a farm some distance from town; and on another occasion shew'd me one of the finest woodland sights of my whole experience—a glen with high rock falls and a remarkable series of narrow caves or fissures. In Athol I was oblig'd to purchase a new suit of cloaths—a plain elderly outfit of blue serge—to replace one which wild Vermont had reduc'd beyond the limit of hasty repair.

Meanwhile I was receiving urgent invitations from the learned Mrs. Miniter,[13] now residing with a cousin on her ancestral rural soil of Wilbraham, to extend my round of visiting to her part of the Province; which is but a little south of Athol, across that lovely Swift River Valley now doom'd to extinction for reservoir purposes. Accepting without reluctance, I proceeded thither on Friday the 29th of June; going by railroad and being met by the chaise of Mrs. Miniter's next-door neighbour. I found Mrs. Miniter not in the least aged by the five intervening years since I last beheld her; her defiance of time being somewhat akin to that of Tryout Smith, whom I last year found unchang'd after a similar stretch of time. Wilbraham is a very lovely country—in the rich, gentle way of Massachusetts as opposed to the bold, dramatick quality of Vermont scenery. The vegetation is thicker and greener; and the hills, tho' high and numerous, are more widely spread. Mrs. Miniter's cousin, a stout, important gentlewoman of 73, resides on an antient farm just across the marsh-meadows from Wilbraham Mountain; at a bend and dip of the road where giant maples form a green, mystical arcade. She is head of the local school committee, a member of the taown caouncil, and several other important official things; and is one of the Beebes ancestrally domiciled there. Curiously enough, she herself happened to be born in Wisconsin, during a pioneering venture which did not prove permanent in her family's case. Miss Beebe is one of the foremost private collectors of antiques in the country, and has her house packed with antient material of the most valuable sort; with only narrow lanes remaining to accommodate the seven cats, two dogs,[14] and incidental human beings who sometimes traverse the rooms. Her farm also contains several poultry, two kine, two aged horses, and one hired boy. Her collection will be left to the museum in Springfield (the nearest city) upon her death.

I tarried eight days in Wilbraham, picking up many strange legends of great interest to me, since both Mrs. Miniter and Miss Beebe are expert in the curious folklore of that archaick region. I am at this very moment introducing one, as subsidiary colour, into a weird novelette I am writing.[15] The peasantry hereabouts are somewhat decadent, and their odd beliefs and doings would fill volumes. Of the encroaching Polish element, Mrs. Miniter's novel of a decade ago treats very fully and cleverly.[16] Old witchcraft whispers are remembered, and people nowadays wonder why so many people in a certain part of the neighbouring village of Monson go mad or kill themselves. I visited all the churchyards and burying places, and inspected the pleasing village of Wilbraham proper, where still flourishes the old academy founded in 1825. I was taken to Monson in a chaise, and walk'd myself to Hampden—a delightful old town at the bend of a stream, where all the houses are strung at length along a road winding up the side of a mountain from the valley. I also visited the other side of Wilbraham Mountain, where the vistas are vary'd and exquisite, and where a strangely blasted slope, supporting no living vegetation, is found.

On Sat'day, July 7th, I prepar'd to resume my journey, proceeding by chaise to the sizeable city of Springfield, which I had never seen before except from a train window. I found it not unbeautiful, tho' not sufficiently colonial to arrest my imagination. There is a pleasing old church on the green, and a museum of some interest; but it is not a place in which an antiquarian wou'd linger. Accordingly I started northward at once, with a design of ascending the Connecticut to Greenfield, and the next day going west to Albany over the famous Mohawk Trail. Towns along the coach route were Holyoke, a dingy mill city, Northampton, a pleasant, quiet town, and the residence of His Majesty's Viceroy, Sir Calvin Coolidge, and the antient Deerfield, already so favourably known to me. I arriv'd in Greenfield in the late afternoon, put up at a tavern, and saw the sunset from a neighbouring peak call'd the Poet's Seat, whence I obtain'd one of the most extensive prospects I have ever beheld. I also had my tye-wig put in shape by a good perruquier; it being very badly in need of such attention.

The following day dawn'd fair, and I embarkt upon the coach for Albany. To describe a route so well known as the Mohawk Trail wou'd savour of triteness; hence I can only say, that its marvels did not come below my expectations. The stupendous panorama of the Deerfield Valley from the eastern slope, and the dramatick vividness of such valley towns as Shelburne Falls, form a good preparation for the culminating sweep of limitless hill country to be seen from the very top, where tall observation towers have been erected. I ascended one of these, beholding at once I know not how many states. As one descends the western slope the scenery is even more wondrous. The rugged Berkshires here open out in all their majesty, and the precipitous descent into the valley town of North Adams, preceded by a distant view of it, is one of the experiences of a lifetime. North Adams itself is a place of great quaintness and attractiveness, wall'd in as it is on all sides by towering precipices of green. Beyond this point came the tranquil collegiate settlement of Williamstown, whose college edifices are all new Georgian structures of the greatest possible attractiveness. After this the coach cross'd a corner of Vermont, passing thro' the quaint town of Pownal, nam'd from Tho: Pownall, Esq., His Majesty's Governor of the Massachusetts-Bay from 1757 to 1759.

Now came the melancholy circumstance of quitting my native country of New-England once more; tho' I knew it wou'd be needful if I was to behold Philad'a, Baltimore, and the South. The scenery instantly became less attractive as the coach pass'd into the Province of New-York, tho' I was interested to reflect, that I was now in the general region inhabited by my good old friend Mr. Hoag, whose departure from earth scarce yet seems a reality.[17] Troy is a detestably dingy place, but Albany is less repulsive. I did not relish Albany, since it is overwhelmingly Victorian; but I own'd a certain rococo glamour in the vast size and striking situation of the State House, which lyes at the head of a very broad uphill street, outlined boldly and picturesquely against the sunset sky. The bastard Renaissance architecture of Victorian times is in Albany carried out to greater extreams of size and grandeur than in any other place I have ever beheld; and for that reason it will be perniciously hard to get rid of. The older houses of Albany closely resemble those of a similar period in New-York, tho' the stoops tend uniformly to be lower. Albany, of course, is of Dutch settlement; though it is now wholly English'd. It appears commendably free from foreigners; most of these no doubt being the Manhattan delegates at the State House.

I stay'd in Albany only one night, embarking on a river packet the following morning and spending all that day amidst the imposing scenery of the hill-lined banks. Here again I will spare detail lest I be trite; for there is no one but knows of the great domed eminences and majestick bends which make the Hudson voyage one of the ultimate peaks of observational travel. The best part is that below Newburgh, along which I sail'd once before, in the year 1925.

Stopping in New-York only for brief calls on small Belknap and young Wandrei[18] (who is now seeking his fortune there, having graduated from the U. of Minn. in June), I proceeded at once to the colonial shades of old Philadelphia, which I survey'd with undiminished affection. Since this town hath form'd the subject of two former treatises of mine,[19] I will touch upon it but briefly; relating that I travers'd all my accustom'd routes in the city proper, and that I saw all the Georgian houses, churchyards, and lanes which have been wont to captivate me in the past. I spent the longest time in the churchyard of Gloria Dei Church, built in 1699 by the Swedes settled at the mouth of the Delaware.

That afternoon I took coach for Baltimore, finding the route sadly devoid of good scenery. The only spots I lik'd were a small village just beyond Wilmington, and the towns of Elkton and Havre-de-Grace, in Maryland. Baltimore was attain'd about sunset, and I had time only to survey its boldest central outlines before putting up at a tavern. The following day I survey'd the city in much detail, and receiv'd a very pleasing impression.

Baltimore, for a colonial town, is very new; having been founded in 1729, at a time when Annapolis was the metropolis of the province. Its original site was 60 acres of land on the north side of the Patapsco River—a stream which the present lower-class inhabitants insist on pronouncing "Pat-ap-si-co". Its growth was slow, and it did not outdistance Annapolis till just before the Revolution; this phenomenon of replacement being curiously like the passing of Newport by Providence, in my own colony, at about the same time. In 1776 the population was 6700. It is now about 750,000, including the niggers, who are segregated from the regular inhabitants in parks, schools, and places of publick conveyance or assemblage. It is one of the few really great seaports of the country, and has a very mature civilisation despite its loss of genuine southern quaintness. Its foreign population is unfortunately quite large, and not so well segregable as its niggers. The bulk of the town is unmistakably Victorian, though the slums near the Patapsco teem with brick colonial houses precisely like those of Philadelphia, after which they presumably pattern'd themselves. All the old houses have white marble steps, which are kept spotless by dint of constant labour.

The Popish cathedral, erected in 1808, is the most impressive of the edifices; crowning as it does the principal hill in a rather hilly town. The great column of 1815, with its surmounting statue of Gen. Washington, is another landmark of importance; and the source of the popular sobriquet "Monumental City", as apply'd to Baltimore. The country-seat of Charles Carroll, Esq., now in Carroll Park, is the oldest building in the city; dating from 1754. This and its congeners are not so much of the southern as of the middle-colonies type of architecture; favouring Philadelphian usage as do the town houses. Very interesting to behold was Fort McHenry, on a peninsula some distance from the centre of the town. This, as all are aware, was the fortress whose ensign mov'd Mr. Key to compose his spirited verses to the tune of "Anacreon in Heav'n" in 1814.[20] The place is in excellent condition, with walls, gun emplacements, and soldiers' quarters precisely as they were at the beginning of the nineteenth century. It and the land around it form a publick government park, at whose entrance is an heroick bronze statue of Orpheus, dedicated to Mr. Key and set up only a few years ago. But to me the culminating thing in Baltimore was a dingy monument in a corner of Westminster Presbyterian Churchyard, which the slums have long overtaken. It is near a high wall, and a willow weeps over it. Melancholy broods around it, and black wings brush it in the night—for it is the grave of Edgar Allan Poe.

From Baltimore I took coach to Annapolis, that gorgeous centre of bygone taste and gaiety which still remains the capital of the province. It was founded in 1649 by Virginia Puritans who misliked the rule of the establisht church in that province, and was named at first PROVIDENCE, in view of the circumstances of its settlement. In 1694 it became the capital of Maryland in place of St. Mary's, and in 1708 it was incorporated as a city, having assum'd its present name in honour of Queen Anne. From 1694 on, its growth was very rapid; and it soon boasted one of the most brilliant and accomplisht societies of any town in the colonies. It fell within the truly southern area of the country, and follows the South rather than Philadelphia in architecture. This means that the country-seats have a large central portion flanked by two wings, and that the chimneys are wide and flat, and situate on the ends of the house. The street names well typify the conservatism of the South as oppos'd to the sadly seditious spirit of many parts of my own New-England. Here King St., Prince George St., Duke of Gloucester St., and so on, retain their original appellations despite disaster and rebellion. The naval academy is very pleasing, and I visited most parts of it; but to me it was not the really dominant feature of the place. The river Severn, on which the town is situate, shews a distinct yellowish tinge; which indeed is characteristick of all the southern streams I have seen.

The old houses and narrow streets are the real glory of Annapolis. At the centre of all is the fine old state house, built in 1772–74, but having a rather ugly dome added soon after the Revolution. As domes go, I prefer the modern Renaissance dome of gold surmounting the naval academy chapel. This dominates the skyline, and covers the ashes of that picaresque marine adventurer, John Paul Jones, whose elaborate bier is shewn in much detail to all visitors. The state house lyes atop an eminence near the centre of the town, all the streets tending to converge toward the circular street which wholly surrounds it. The building proper is in very good Georgian taste, and has an interior of singular grace and majesty. Not very far away is St. John's College, whose oldest building dates from 1789, and on whose campus is situate the great poplar tree under which the settlers treated with the friendly Susquehannock Indians in 1652. The tangle of ancient lanes down the hill east of the state house may be said to contain the greatest number of picturesque antiquarian effects. They make Annapolis the Marblehead of the South, and suggest an explanation for the old city by-law of Queen Anne's day:

> "Any person residing within this City or the Precincts thereof who shall by galloping or otherwise force any Horse, Mare, or Gelding through any of the Streets, Lanes, or Alleys of this City, or carry any Fire uncover'd through the same, shall if a Freeman forfeit and pay for every such Offence the sum of Ten Shillings Sterling to the use of this Corporation."

At least two houses in Annapolis, an official building on the state house grounds and a residence in Prince George Street nearby, date from the year of the transference of the capital—1694. They are both of brick, and marked by that peakedness typical of seventeenth-century architecture throughout the colonies. Fine houses of the eighteenth century, both late and early, are very common; both town houses and country-seats being represented. Houses of the rural type were built curiously close to the town, so that the two types are seen in rather singular juxtaposition. The Brice (1740), Paca (1763), Hammond (1750), Harwood (1770), Ogle (1742), and Randall (1730) houses are all worthy of detailed attention. A little out of the main section is a large colonial mansion said to have been used by Winston Churchill (who attended the naval academy and knew Annapolis well) as a prototype for his Carvel Hall.[21] The application of the name "Carvel Hall" to the fashionable hotel housed in the old Paca mansion is purely fanciful.

The Stewart house (1763) in Hanover Street reminds one of a curious Revolutionary incident. During the tea agitation Mr. Anthony Stewart paid the duty on some tea which occurred in the mixt cargo of one of his brigs, the "Peggy Stewart"; thus antagonising the local rebels, who had resolv'd to exclude the commodity from the colony. Seeing that the popular hate was not to be appeas'd even by a burning of the offending cargo, Mr. Stewart was induc'd by the celebrated Charles Carroll (who was born in a mansion overlooking Spa Creek, which I beheld) to perform the still more dramatick gesture of burning the entire brig himself. This he carry'd out off Windmill Point, and was thereupon voted a "loyal" citizen by the rebels whom he had found it commercially and socially advantageous to please. Ever afterward the "Peggy Stewart" form'd a basis for local tradition.

Annapolis is one of those places which I surely must behold again. I left it with reluctance, but at last felt constrain'd to move onward to Washington. The coach was swift, and I arriv'd in the Federal capital late at night on July 12th; securing a cheap room recommended by the Y.M.C.A. and preparing to linger several days. The city itself I had seen, as former treatises attest; but I wish'd to make it a base for excursions into the surrounding territory.

On the 13th I revisited Alexandria, and renewed all the glowing colonial impressions describ'd in 1925. The town is much larger than Annapolis (25,000 as contrasted with 13,000), and is much less quaint owing to the regularity of the streets. It was lay'd out in 1749 under the name of Bellhaven, but soon changed its appellation to the present one. The oldest parts are those nearest the Potomac. Christ Church, which Gen. Washington attended, is undoubtedly the greatest single attraction of the place. It was built in the 1770's, and has one of the quaintest churchyards conceivable. But the whole town is fascinating, and abounds in brick Georgian houses of neat and tasteful outline. It calls up at once the picture of bygone times, and has much of the genial grace and well-bred somnolence of old Virginia life.

On the 14th I visited Gen. Washington's country-seat of Mt. Vernon, on the river below Alexandria, and left not a corner of house or grounds unexamin'd. It were trite to speak in detail of this well-known scene, but I may mention that the house was built in 1743 by Lawrence Washington, half-brother to the General, and that the latter inherited it in 1752, upon the death of Lawrence and his daughter. It was call'd Hunting Creek Estate till its builder renam'd it in honour of Admiral Vernon, the inventor of "grog", under whom he had serv'd against Spain. The house is low and spacious, most of the rooms being rather smaller than one wou'd expect in an edifice of such pretensions. The grounds, sloping down from a high bluff to the river with many a wooded ravine and willow-lin'd path, display the finest taste in selection. Stables and other outbuildings comport with the mansion house in style and beauty; the whole forming as sightly a plantation as any gentleman in Virginia cou'd reasonably demand. The elegance of the lower rooms, in point of architectural ornament, is carry'd almost to excess; but the upper rooms are singularly austere. I beheld the bed upon which the General dy'd, together with innumerable other objects connected with him. In walking thro' the grounds I came upon his tomb, and stood but a few feet from the body (in its sarcophagus beyond the grating) which even now must bear some resemblance to the living gentleman, so perfectly was it embalm'd. In the 1830's, when it was transferr'd from its original resting-place on the river bluff to this mausoleum, a person who gaz'd upon the features declar'd them but little impaired by the more than three decades of interment. I descended to the river, view'd all the buildings, and in general familiaris'd myself with the whole estate. I cannot praise it too highly, or hope too strongly that it may always be preserv'd with unremitting diligence as a specimen of good architecture and ideal type of a southern gentleman's seat.

Upon my return from Mt. Vernon I repair'd to Georgetown, the old city on the heights above Washington; far antedating the Federal City, but now included within it as Germantown is within Philadelphia. It was formerly part of Maryland, and has a pleasing irregularity lack'd by the too symmetrical artificial capital. I saw nothing I had not seen before, but upon re-crossing to Washington proper I visited the newer north-western parts which I had never previously been over. Here I was arrested mainly by the great temple of the Scottish Rite Masons, whose striking architecture* lifts it out of the commonplace and mundane into the realm of the cosmick and mystical. Gazing upon it, I could well believe all the vague legends connected with the Masonick order; for here surely dwelt arcana whose sources are not of this earth. I saw it first at night, when only the twin cryptick braziers beside the great bronze door lit up the grim guard-ian sphinxes and the huge windowless facade. Mystery dwelt there—and I departed full of vague thoughts hinging upon the obscurest of dream-memories.

Other Washington sights which I imbib'd at spare moments included the great new cathedral now building upon Mt. St. Alban. This gigantick fane, completed only at the apse end, is of the most exquisite Gothick beauty; and such is its design and set-ting, that I believe it will in time surpass its only American rival, St. John the Divine in New-York. I might likewise mention a brief pleasant trip to Falls Church, in Virginia, where I beheld a tasteful square edifice set in a grove, that once own'd Gen. Washing-ton amongst its vestrymen. The village of Falls Church is in a beautiful valley, and is of extream quaintness. Virginia, in the direction of Fairfax Court House and Falls Church, has a scenick beauty comparable to that of New-England; and contrasting strongly with monotonous scenery higher up the Chesapeake coast.

On Sunday, June 15, came the culminating event of the trip—the long railway excursion to the Endless Caverns, near New Market, in Virginia's exquisite Shenan-doah Valley. The train pass'd thro' some of the most historick battlefields of the Civil War, beginning with Manassas and ending with the scenes of Sheridan's Ride; but the scenery did not become vivid till the latter half of the trip, when the mountains were reacht. Then I observ'd much the same kind of scenery that one finds around Athol, or the Connecticut Valley generally—bold ridges of hills, and splendid prospects of val-leys and distant towns. The agricultural state of the country seems more prosperous than that of New-England, though none of the farms even begin to approach ours in neatness and beauty. Zigzag rail fences of the southern type serve generally, instead of stone walls, to divide the fields. A few stone walls, however, do exist; shewing the op-erations of New-England influences at a great distance. Foreigners seem altogether ab-sent, an happy condition which I hope will be of permanent duration. Niggers are everywhere segregated, even in the smallest railway stations.

New Market was reacht after a four-hour ride, and a coach took the sightseers to the mouth of the actual caverns, some six miles away. These open from a pleasant spot just at the base of a great hill, where the owners have built an office and lay'd out grounds for the benefit of visitors. I purchas'd my ticket, enter'd the building covering the mouth, fell into a party, and was soon guided down steep stone steps into a region whose coolness contrasted oddly with the oven-hot day outside. I knew that I was at last in a real cavern—the first I had ever seen—and that I was about to sample in ac-tuality those secrets of earth's ultimate abysses which heretofore I had traversed only in dreams and in literature. It was a great moment—and as the first of the wide gulfs opened out before me I felt that something out of fantasy had come earthward to meet me and give substance to my profoundest imaginings.

---

*Modell'd upon that of the celebrated Mausoleum at Halicarnassus, which the Antients reckon'd amongst the Seven Wonders of the World.

After the booklets to which I have given such wide circulation, I need say nothing in detail about the marvellous caves themselves. All I need do is to endorse with fervour each word of the printed text. There is no exaggeration! As deep gave place to deep, gallery to gallery, and chamber to chamber, I felt transported to the strangest regions of nocturnal fancy. Grotesque formations leer'd on every hand, and the ever-sinking level appris'd me of the stupendous depth I was attaining. Glimpses of far black vistas beyond the radius of the lights—sheer drops of incalculable depth to unknown chasms, or arcades beckoning laterally to mysteries yet untasted by human eye—brought my soul close to the frightful and obscure frontiers of the material world, and conjured up suspicions of vague and unhallowed dimensions whose formless beings lurk ever close to the visible world of man's five senses. Buried aeras—submerged civilisations—subterraneous universes and unsuspected orders of beings and influences that haunt the sightless depths—all these flitted thro' an imagination confronted by the actual presence of soundless and eternal night. I regretted the uniform illumination of the visited parts of the cave, and lagged behind the party as much as the rear guide would let me, in order to imbibe the stupendous spectacle without excessive human cluttering. I thought, above all else, of that strange old novel "Etidorhpa" once pass'd around our Kleicomolo circle and perus'd with such varying reactions.[22] Dost recall it, O Sage? The Endless Caverns are amongst the best known in point of picturesque formations, though for great spaces they cannot compete with Kentucky's Mammoth Cave.[23] I wished that I might visit the Luray and Shenandoah Caverns, not far from New Market; but the schedule of the excursion did not permit of it. Still—the sample I receiv'd was surely enough for a beginning. It was a glorious tangible introduction to that tenebrous nether world whereof I have scribbled so much, and I shall never forget the least particular of it. The crystal formations at several points were of a fantastick beauty so poignant that all sensations of horror were momentarily forgot. Words cannot describe the utter, supernal loveliness of those formations known as the Diamond Lake and Oriental Room. And at the bottom of all—far, far down, still trickles the water that carv'd the whole chain of gulfs out of the primal soluble limestone. Whence it comes and whither it trickles—to what awesome deeps of Tartarean nighted horror it bears the doom-fraught messages of the hoary hills—no being of human mould can say. Only They which gibber Down There can answer.[24]

This was the climax of my spring and summer wanderings. After that, anything but a return home wou'd have been an anticlimax. The next day I took coach for Philadelphia, changed for New-York, and arrived in that pest spot in the dawn twilight of the 17th. Collecting mail from home, I learnt that my elder aunt was ill with lumbago and forc'd to employ a nurse; so that I gave over my design for a leisurely return by coach thro' rural Connecticut and at once hasten'd to Providence on the rail-road. On the morning of the 18th I saw in the distance the spires of my native town, and ere long I walked in the lee of the great green hill, crowned with its ancient domes and steeples, whereon I was born. The old village streets were quiet and mystical with dawn-haze and elder memories, and up the hill there beckoned long vistas of carven doorways and rayed fanlights, and iron-railed flights of steps such as I had not seen since I left there in the April before—things such as only Providence knows. A fresh salt wind came up from the harbour, over the roofs of the centuried warehouses and the Old Market House of 1773; and down the narrow, curving line of the old town street by the shoar I glimpsed the chimneys and gambrel roofs of mouldering houses known to ancient captains and tarry West Indian seamen. I was home again—in the old New-England seaport that is not quite like any other New-England seaport;

in the old maritime New-England that is so different in its soul from even the inland New-England of Brattleboro or Athol or Wilbraham or Greenfield. Home—amongst the unnumber'd influences and sights and sounds which, operating through a full half of my heredity for three hundred years and through all my life from infant memories onward, has little by little moulded my germ-plasm and my spirit, and created out of formless protoplasm the individual entity that is I. For what is any man but the impress of his home and lineage? What is in us, that our pasts have not placed there? Truly, no man is himself save among the scenes that have shaped him and his fathers; nor cou'd I ever hope to find a lasting peace save close to the ancient monuments of green-leaved, hill-crowning Providence—Providence, of the old brick sidewalks and the Georgian spires and the curving lanes of the hill, and the salt winds from over mouldering wharves where strange-cargoed ships of eld have swung at anchor. Providence is I, and I am Providence. One and inseparable! So after all my wanderings I came back to a wonder and beauty greater and always stranger than any I sought in distant ports or found amidst the marvel of alien roofs and exotick mountains. GOD SAVE HIS MAJESTY'S COLONY OF RHODE-ISLAND AND PROVIDENCE-PLANTATIONS!

EDITOR'S NOTE FP: In *Marginalia* (Sauk City, WI: Arkham House, 1944), pp. 238–67 (as "Observations on Several Parts of North America"). Text based on the TMS (JHL). The essay, describing HPL's travels in the summer of 1928, was in effect a letter to Maurice W. Moe (see the reference to "O Sage" [p. 29], one of HPL's nicknames for Moe), but he no doubt assumed that other associates would also like to read of his travels, so he typed up the letter (single-spaced) and presumably circulated it among his colleagues. It was the first of HPL's travelogues to be written in archaic English, a technique utilised even more exhaustively in "Travels in the Provinces of America" (1929), "An Account of Charleston" (1930), and "A Description of the Town of Quebeck" (1930–31). The publication in *Marginalia*, aside from printing the title erroneously, deliberately omitted or altered some of the racist sentiments expressed by HPL in the essay.

Notes

1. HPL had to go because his wife Sonia had asked him to come to Brooklyn to assist her in setting up a hat shop. During his stay in the Flatbush district of Brooklyn (24 April–8 June), he stayed in Sonia's apartment at 395 East 16th Street.

2. Vermont was not separated from the state of New Hampshire until 1791. HPL gives a history of British colonisation of the region below (pp. 20–21).

3. HPL had become acquainted with Frank Belknap Long in 1920, and they met on many occasions during HPL's New York stay of 1924–26.

4. James Ferdinand Morton (1870–1941) had been appointed curator of the Paterson (N.J.) Museum in early 1925.

5. Wilfred B. Talman (1904–1986) was a later member of the Kalem Club whom HPL had met in late 1925. Of Dutch ancestry, he later encouraged HPL to write "Some Dutch Footprints in New England" (p. 253).

6. This paragraph was excerpted by Maurice W. Moe as "Sleepy Hollow To-day" (see p. 288).

7. British religious leader George Fox (1624–1691) founded the Society of Friends, or Quakers, in 1648. He visited Flushing in 1672–73 in the course of an extensive tour of the Eastern Seaboard, from Portsmouth, N.H., to Cape Hatteras, N.C.

8. HPL became acquainted with Vrest Orton (1897–1986) in late 1925. He compiled *Dreiserana* (1929), the first bibliography of Theodore Dreiser, and later founded the Vermont Country Store.

9. This was the Lee family, later commemorated in "The Whisperer in Darkness" in the name Lee's Swamp (*DH* 225). For a photograph of them, see *MW* (facing p. 307).

10. See [Unsigned], "Literary Persons Meet in Guilford," *Brattleboro Reformer* (18 June 1928).

11. See Vrest Orton, "A Weird Writer Is in Our Midst," *Brattleboro Reformer* (16 June 1928); rpt. in *LR* 407–9.

12. H[arold] Warner Munn (1903–1981), prolific contributor to *Weird Tales* and later the author of several historical and fantasy novels.

13. Edith Miniter (1869–1934), amateur colleague of HPL's; they had been acquainted since at least 1921. See his memoir, "Mrs. Miniter—Estimates and Recollections" (1934; *CE* 1.378–87). She was residing in Wilbraham, Mass., with her cousin, Evanore Beebe.

14. HPL wrote a succession of poems on these animals under the title "Veteropinguis Redivivus" (1930; *AT* 177–79).

15. HPL alludes to "The Dunwich Horror," written in August 1928.

16. Edith Miniter, *Our Natupski Neighbors* (1916).

17. Jonathan E. Hoag (1831–1927), who resided in the area around Greenwich and Troy, N.Y. HPL had known him since 1918 and had written annual birthday tributes to him until his death on 17 October 1927, whereupon HPL wrote the elegy "Ave atque Vale" (*AT* 382–83).

18. Donald Wandrei (1908–1987), weird fiction writer whose association with HPL began in December 1926. For their joint correspondence, see *Mysteries of Time and Spirit: The Letters of H. P. Lovecraft and Donald Wandrei* (San Francisco: Night Shade Books, 2002).

19. Either these "treatises" do not survive, or HPL is referring to extensive descriptions of Philadelphia included in letters to Moe.

20. HPL refers to "The Star-Spangled Banner," written by Francis Scott Key.

21. HPL refers not to the British statesman but to the popular American author Winston Churchill (1871–1947) and his best-selling novel *Richard Carvel* (1899), an historical novel about the American Revolution.

22. *Etidorhpa* (1895) was written by American author John Uri Lloyd (1849–1936). For HPL's discussion of it, see his letter to Alfred Galpin, 26 January 1918; *Letters to Alfred Galpin* (New York: Hippocampus Press, 2003), p. 13. The novel, dealing with a journey to the hollow centre of the earth, may have influenced *The Dream-Quest of Unknown Kadath* (1926–27).

23. HPL's early story "The Beast in the Cave" (1905) is set in Mammoth Cave.

24. HPL reworked this discussion of the Endless Caverns in the essay "A Descent to Avernus" (p. 287).

TRAVELS IN THE PROVINCES OF AMERICA

Made in the Year 1929 by H. Lovecraft, Gent., and Extending from
Jamestown, in Virginia, to the Southerly Part of His Majesty's New-
Hampshire Grants, Latterly call'd Vermont. With Observations upon
the History, Scenery, and Antiquities of the Several Regions Travers'd.

PROVIDENCE, RHODE-ISLAND
Printed by John Carter, at Shakespear's-Head in King-street,
over-against the Court House, and Sold by Merchants generally.
1929.

My travels for the year 1929 began at a somewhat earlier season than is customary
with me, owing to an extreamly cordial invitation from Vrest Orton, Esq., of
Yonkers, in the Province of New-York; that hospitable gentleman at whose estate in
the New-Hampshire grants I spent so many pleasing days in 1928. I left Providence
early on the 4th of April, arriving at my destination on the same day, and being much
captivated by the charm of the Yonkers countryside, notwithstanding its close nearness
to the ugly and foreign town of New-York. The section inhabited by Mr. Orton is not
any meer suburban "development" of the kind often found on the rim of large cities,[1]
but a genuine open territory with wooded hills, lakes, farms, and glorious vistas. Houses
are few, and no network of streets hath yet come to usurp supremacy from the winding
hill roads, meadows, woods, and country seats. The Orton house, a white gabled relique of Georgian times, is on a picturesque side-hill with grounds, fence, grape-arbour,
and all the appurtenances of a real farm. A rushing, Vermont-like brook flows bub-
blingly beside the front gate, and the whole vicinity is antithetical to the ways and
spirit of New-York. Nor does the house contain any jarring note. Flagstone walks, old
white gate, low ceilings, small-paned windows, wide-boarded floors, white-manteled
fireplace, cobwebb'd attick, rag carpets and hook'd rugs, old furniture, century'd Connecticut clock with wooden works—all things, in truth, bespeak an antient New-
England hearthside. The guest-room to which I was assign'd is situate in the gabled
second storey of the east wing, with windows on three sides—looking north over
meadows and ponds to the hills, south across the flagstoned yard to the front gate and
shady country road, and east to the deep forest that runs down a slope toward the great
highway. Add to these advantages a gracious and congenial host, and a library almost
unexcell'd amongst the members of our circle, and there will be form'd a picture of the
pleasant environment in which I spent above two weeks. During this time I was oblig'd
to visit New-York with frequency in order to look up old acquaintances, but I nevertheless contriv'd to indulge in many of my favourite antiquarian explorations. I need
not speak of the antiquities of New-York proper, insomuch as I have describ'd them in
so many previous volumes of travel; but will meerly mention that I visited most of
them, such as the Van Cortlandt, Dyckman, and Gracie houses, the tangled Georgian
streets of Greenwich, the antient waterfront of Brooklyn and so on. I did not neglect
the various museums and literary facilities of the metropolis, nor did I fail to pay a visit
to Paterson, where my august and curatorial friend James Ferdinand Plantagenet-
Morton was so good as to arrange for me a particularly fine display of the Great Falls of

the Passaick River. On this occasion I beheld the stupendous torrent in all its force, forming a prodigiously impressive spectacle of roaring foam and rising mist, with a delicate rainbow arching over the whole band of scoriack crag and milk-white flood. The chasmal majesty of the enormous gulph was such as to suggest the monstrous scenery of other planets.

Of my New-York suburban trips to places I had never before seen, may be mention'd one to antient Eastchester, now included within the city of Mount-Vernon, where still remains one of the finest old churches in the Province. This archaick fane, known as St. Paul's, was built in 1761 upon the site of an edifice of 1699, and is surrounded by a churchyard with above six-thousand graves. It is of grey stone, with a rather low and unambitious belfry or steeple, and is of highly captivating aspect. During the late uprising of 1775–83 it was us'd as an hospital by His Majesty's forces; many soldiers both British and Hessian being here interr'd. Across the road is an old tavern frequented by His Majesty's officers; from whose signpost a deserter was once hang'd. As a village Eastchester is well-nigh obliterated; there being only one small stretch of rather quaint street some distance away from the church and tavern. Manufactories have brought that curse of smoke and decadence which invariably follows in the wake of machinery and excessive trade.

Another trip of uncommon interest was to the town of New-Rochelle, on whose outskirts is situate the cottage occupy'd by the eccentrick rebel philosopher and œconomist Thomas Paine, author of "Common Sense", "The Age of Reason", and so on. The cottage, mov'd from its original site some years ago, stands on a picturesque slope in a highly pleasing small park, together with other antiquarian reliquiae brought from a distance—an old schoolhouse and a curious Indian idol-stone. The whole group, well arrang'd on a hillside with coursing stream and wooden foot-bridges, forms a landskip of the finest sort. The house, given to Mr. Paine by the grateful rebel nation at whose treasonable birth he so substantially assisted, was built in 1793 and 1794, upon his return from France, to replace an earlier gift-house which had been burnt. The interior is well furnisht with reliques by the New-Rochelle Historical Society, and possesses an admirably quaint and home-like aspect. Among the contents is a Franklin stove given to Mr. Paine by Dr. Franklin himself. New-Rochelle was founded in the seventeenth century by Huguenots from France, but retains lamentably little to remind the traveller of former times.

On the 21st of April I remov'd my visiting headquarters from Yonkers to New-York proper, where my host was my young adopted grandson, the eminent, sophisticated, and disillusion'd poet-critick Frank Belknap Long, Jun. Here, despite my dislike of the metropolis, congenial society serv'd to make my hours pleasant; and many trips on foot and by coach enliven'd a period of above a week. In this interval my host and I made many architectural excursions, surveying and studying the best Gothick edifices in the town, such as the churches of St. John the Divine (now well along toward completion), St. Thomas, the Heavenly Rest (with its barren modern use of Gothick design), and St. Patrick. Of rural trips, that to the town of Bedford was the most pleasing; for I am ever fond of this settled, reposeful old village, whose atmosphere is so greatly enhanc'd by its white church, hillside burying ground, colonial houses, and triangular village green. On the road to New-England, it partakes not a little of the spirit and aspect of that idyllick region.

On the 1st of May I quitted the vicinity of New-York to begin the major part of my historick and antiquarian tour; whose earlier parts were schedul'd to lie in the southern colonies. Securing a stage-coach for Washington (the new Federal City put

up by the rebels near Georgetown), I took a good seat and prepar'd to enjoy the archaick regions thro' which I was to pass. The journey was made amusing by the presence
in the seat beside me of a slightly demented German—a well-drest and respectable-
looking fellow whom I had observ'd at the tavern reading a German paper before the
start of the coach.[2] He shew'd no signs of his affliction till we reach'd a sort of stagnant
mill-pond near Newark, in New-Jersey, when suddenly he burst forth with the question, "Iss diss der Greadt Zalt Lake?" Deeming the inquiry addrest to me, I reply'd that
I scarcely thought his identification correct; whereupon he reliev'd me of all responsi-
bility by remarking in a far-off, sententious voice—"I vassn't talkingk to you; I vass
shoost leddingk my light shine!" Properly rebuk'd for my officious desire to give information, I held my peace and permitted my seatmate to illuminate without hindrance.
After a time he became vocal again, confiding to the empty air ahead, "I'm radiatingk
all der time, und nopotty knows it!" The passengers in general, to say nothing of the
driver, were not insensible to the grotesqueness of the speech, but confin'd their comment to smiles. Apparently this was the proper course, insomuch as the thoughtful ra-
diator shortly afterward signify'd his approval of the mundane scheme by beginning a
series of impersonal ejaculations of the phrase, "Efferythingk iss luffly! Efferythingk iss
luffly!" As the coach near'd Princeton, an exquisite colonial town which I must some
day explore in detail, the mystical fellow-countryman of Kant and Hegel became concretely philosophical; evidently affected by the academick atmosphere of the old college village. "You make money your vay;" he volunteer'd to the circumambient air, "I
make money my vay—diff'rent kinds of money!" After this supreme epitome of worldly
wisdom, the philosopher attempted no further specific radiations. Thereafter his dicta,
when articulate, were confin'd to reiterations of the genial "Efferythingk iss luffly!" He
alighted at antient Philadelphia, and I saw him no more. No doubt he was a leader in
some modern religious or ethical cult, for which post he appear'd especially fitted; or
perhaps he was one of the traditional Quakers, Ephrantans, Dunkards, or Moravians of
the Teutonick and many-faith'd Pennsylvania Colony. I did not stop in Philadelphia
on this southward trip, but kept on to Washington. The afternoon's ride was very
beautiful, and I was glad to pay my respects to the South again as the coach enter'd the
Colony of Maryland. Elkton, Havre-de-Grace, and other villages of this region are of
extream quaintness and charm; and the whole landskip below Baltimore is of a marvellous glamour. I noted the yellowness of the streams—a leading characteristick of
southern rivers, due to the soil thro' which they run—and was gratify'd by the increasing warmth of the air; the vernal scene having all the mildness and luxuriance of summer. The South is in some respects my favourite part of America; its climate,
atmosphere, blood, traditions, and social-political views all being closer to my own liking than those of any other region. But for my ancestral attachment to the landskip,
architecture, and geographick-historick memories of New-England, I wou'd certainly
become an inhabitant of the sane, unhurried, racially pure, and perspective-blest
southern colonies which I love so much to visit. Washington was reacht in the evening, and I took a pleasing twilight walk before putting up at a tavern near the starting-
place of the Richmond coach. I did not design to stop long this time, deferring my
Washington explorations till after my more southerly peregrination.

On the following morning I rose early and took the 6:45 Richmond coach; thereby
embarking for a region I had never before seen. I had an excellent seat and an ideal
day; and was glad to behold again the classick shoars of Virginia, and the ancient
chimneys, gables, and steeples of Alexandria, whose colonial charm I have often describ'd in earlier books of travel. Old Virginia! Here, indeed, flower'd the earliest and

the greatest Anglo-Saxon civilisation on this continent—and one which has perhaps left more tangible reliquiae in this decadent age than has my own almost equally an-tient New-England civilisation. I was glad to see old Pohick church, of which the late Gen. Washington was a parishioner, and enjoy'd such glimpses of great plantation-houses as I had. The dominant type hereabouts is the steep-roof'd brick manor with lateral connecting wings for kitchen and servants' quarters; a form found throughout the upper fringe of the South. I also observ'd with interest the smaller farmhouses of the white freeholders and yeomen, and lesser gentry; narrow, two-storey edifices with chimneys on each end and steeply pitcht roof with dormers. This type is characteristi-cally southern, scarce any example being found north of Maryland, where the Pennsyl-vania influence ends. In this Washington–Richmond interval agriculture is more abundant than in New-England, though the farmsteads are less picturesque. Blacka-moors and mules are omnipresent, and the leisurely tempo of the prevailing life is re-freshing to observe. All the natives are American, and now and then some very quaint and individualised specimens appear. Every rank of the community is markt with a kind of natural courtesy and good-will unknown to the decadent North; so that I verily believe I wou'd have less natural contempt and dislike for mankind if I were to live long in that district. These virtues proceed undoubtedly from the fact that the prevail-ing population *actually belongs here* by heredity and immemorial attachment. Race and landskip fit each other, and life has had an opportunity to crystallise into natural and beautiful forms. Only such an ancient seating of a race upon its terrestrial environment can produce a genuine and endurable civilisation—all other makeshifts and immi-grant-huddles are vile and detestable parodies which are nothing and mean nothing. May Heaven preserve Old Virginia from the industrialisation and mongrelisation which have ruin'd New-England and virtually remov'd the city of New-York from the world of Western civilisation and Aryan thought and feeling! The Virginia soil is yel-low and clayey, and colours all the numerous streams as in other parts of the South. Landskips are broad and rolling; and, until Richmond itself is reach'd, below those of New-England in beauty. High-roads are mostly of very recent construction, and lack the rambling charm which must have pervaded the famously bad clay roads that pre-ceded them. Some of the rural crossroads or court-house villages are quaint beyond anything we have in New-England; being of great primitiveness in design, and great leisureliness in atmosphere. Points of historick interest along the route are carefully markt by the state, for the road traverses some of the most famous battlefields of the Civil War (including Fredericksburg and Spotsylvania) besides lying in a territory of the utmost colonial interest. The apex of charm along this route is the vicinity of the Rappahannock River, where Falmouth and Fredericksburg rear their ancient chimneys and gables. I had deferr'd my exploration of this region till my return trip, so on this occasion noted principally the charm of hilly Falmouth—a sleepy hamlet whose crum-bling brick houses and general irregular plan make it a kind of Virginian Marblehead. Across the shallow, yellow Rappahannock is sedate and Georgian Fredericksburg—my glimpse of which made me eager for the exploration to come on the return trip. To-ward Richmond the scenery became finer, till at length the world seem'd transform'd to a thing of unbelievable aestival beauty. At last the old Confederate capital began to make itself visible—tho' in a very modern way, since the newer boulevard section is thrust out in the general direction of the Washington road. The coach stopt at Mur-phy's antient tavern, near the old-time heart of things, and I there secur'd a room—determin'd to do the city justice, and to make it my headquarters whilst I visited still older and more historick parts of the great peninsula betwixt the James and York Rivers. Hail to Old Richmond! Opulent with memories of John Smith, William Byrd,[3] Edgar Allan Poe, Robert Edward Lee, Jefferson Davis, and the Great Lost Cause! Repository of tradition and headquarters of reposefulness—closest approach to mine own psychological standpoint to be found amongst the sizeable cities of these colonies! I had dream'd of it for thirty years or more—now I was to behold and know it—to know it, and to know its venerable neighbours Williamsburg, Jamestown, and Yorktown! Even the prevailing speech of the town was delightful to me; for of all forms of American dialect, none is more pleasing and genuinely musical than the broad, drawling tones of the South, which here find full embodiment.

Richmond is a subtly delightful town of much poise and background, tho' a machine-age barbarian with false standards might complain that the languid negligence prevents its shops and restaurants from being numerous, sumptuous, and overflowingly stockt. The aristocratick residential districts are magnificent—mansions, broad boulevards, and park-like grounds in the full bloom of summer at May's beginning—but the business section has an air of shabbiness and Victorianism. There is no one vast colonial district, though colonial houses are likely to be found anywhere near the river. A diligent searcher can discover much to enthrall him architecturally, and of course a student of history could ask nothing more than this centre of Civil War operations. It is not as outwardly attractive a city as Washington or Alexandria, but is of the sort which grows on one. It is the most American city I have ever been in. Of a population of 200,000, about 30% are niggers and only 3% foreigners—the latter mostly Jews, who always swarm where money is to be had. The remaining 67%—forming indeed almost 97% of the white inhabitants—are pure-blooded English-Americans whose forbears have dwelt in Virginia from 300 to 325 years. It is this pure native stock which makes up all the crowds and controls all the functions of urban life. Everybody one speaks to is a regular American—hotel clerks, soda-fountain men, conductors, motormen, coach-drivers, and so on. And of course all the workmen and bootblacks and newsboys and lift-men are blacks. Blacks are not segregated as rigorously as in the farther South, because they are not as numerous. Indeed, one sees no more of them than in the upper part of New York City. Oddly enough, the much more northerly city of Baltimore (which is, incidentally, hideously foreignised) has strict segregatory ordinances which are unknown in Richmond.

Richmond lies along the northern bank of the yellow James River, at the falls forming the head of navigation; the oldest parts being naturally those nearest the water, where a bluff of varying steepness, at certain points rising into actual hills, ascends from the shore. Its ancient section was much decimated by the burning of the business district in 1865, to prevent valuable merchandise from falling into the hands of the Federal troops. The original town was built on seven hills like Providence and Rome—Church Hill (containing ancient St. John's), Smith's Hill, Libby Hill (now a park), Gamble's Hill (also a park), Oregon Hill, Hollywood Hill (site of the principal cemetery), and Capitol Hill (containing the fine old state capitol). It has tended, however, to shift westward—building up over the pleasant countryside and leaving the old eastern parts to a state of slumdom. The sections along the waterfront have long been given over to the tobacco industry, and possess at all times the pervasive odour of the weed. Richmond is the foremost tobacco town in the world. Parks are numerous and lovely—William Byrd Park on the western edge of the town being comparable to Providence's Roger Williams Park, tho' by no means rivalling it. Forest Hills Park across the river contains woodland ravines almost equal to New-England's. Richmond flora does not perceptibly differ from that of the North, though it perhaps grows in greater luxuriance. Several bridges connect Richmond with the opposite shore, using islands as stepping-stones. Across the river is the dingy district of South Richmond, formerly Manchester.

The colonial houses of Richmond are small and made of brick, having resemblances to those of Philadelphia and Alexandria. There is also a late-Georgian type quite peculiar to Richmond—square brick facade, and heavy Dorick porch like that on Providence's 1815-type houses. Peaked roofs with dormer windows seem to have been the rule—I have seen only *one* gambrel roof in all my Richmond wanderings! The oldest house—preserv'd as a Poe shrine though Poe never inhabited it—dates behind any of the others (estimates vary from 1685 to 1737!); it being a stone farmhouse preceding the urban settlement of the town.

Richmond—or the land it now covers—has been continuously known to the white man since the voyage of Captains Christopher Newport and John Smith in 1607—29 years before the founding of Providence, 23 before the settlement of Boston, and 13 before the Pilgrims landed on Plymouth Rock. It is thus the oldest civilised region I have ever seen in person so far. A cairn and cross on Gamble's Hill mark the spot where the voyagers debarked—their mission being to treat with the Indian Powhatan. The region, and the settlement founded there by Sir Thomas Dale, were at first call'd *Henricopolis*, in honour of King James the First's eldest son and heir-apparent Prince Henry (who dy'd, however, before succeeding to the throne, thus giving the Crown to his younger brother, the martyr'd Charles the First); a designation which still survives as *Henrico County*, in which Richmond is situate. Henricopolis lay some distance southeast of the present town, and was destroy'd by the Indians in 1622. In rebuilding, a safer site was naturally sought—hence the choice of the seven hills. Richmond proper was not establisht till 1737, when a settlement was made by the great landed proprietor, poet, and cavalier William Byrd, Gent., of Westover on the James— direct lineal ancestor of the present explorer Richard Byrd, and of his brother Harry Flood Byrd, now Governor of Virginia. Westover, a splendid Georgian manor-house built in 1737, lies some distance away; and I regret that I have not yet seen it. In the garden of this estate William Byrd lies buried; he having dy'd in 1744 at the age of seventy. In 1742 Richmond was incorporated as a town, and by 1779 it had so eclips'd the older town of Williamsburg (as Providence eclips'd Newport, and Baltimore eclips'd Annapolis) that it was made the capital of Virginia. In 1782 it was incorporated as a city, and it has since remain'd the metropolis of Virginia, having a population of 200,000 against Norfolk's 160,000. It is a seaport—lying at the James's head of navigation—though it is content to leave chief maritime honours to Norfolk. In the Revolution Richmond sided largely with the rebels, and was harass'd by Benedict Arnold after his transfer of allegiance to Great-Britain. Arnold burn'd dwellings and tobacco warehouses, displaying as savage a spirit as when he burnt New-London, in his own native Connecticut Colony. On June 16, 1781, the town was enter'd without opposition by Lord Cornwallis on his way to the York-James peninsula—the Virginia government having temporarily remov'd to Charlottesville, a great distance westward. The Civil War, however, brought Richmond its greatest and most tragick martial fame. As capital of the Confederate States its capture was always the prime objective of the Federal armies; and at two distinct periods it form'd the focus of some particularly desperate fighting. Constantly in a state of siege, it develop'd defensive fortifications of the utmost effectiveness—some of which may still be seen as grass-grown trenches and embankments. I saw some in the western part of the town, and believe a good number are always pointed out by the drivers of sightseeing coaches. It was around Richmond that the art of balloon observation first rose to prominence, this being the only method whereby the Federals cou'd ascertain the state of things within the Confederate redoubts. In this procedure the leaders were none other than James and Ezra Allen of Providence, with whom the young German attaché Graf von Zeppelin took that first flight which launch'd him upon his memorable career. The battles around Richmond are too well-known to old-timers to need description—Spotsylvania Court-House, the Wilderness, Cold Harbour, Yellow Tavern, Williamsburg, Seven Pines, Mechanicsville, Gaines' Mill, Savage's Station, Frazier's Farm, Malvern Hill, Sharpsburg, Drewry's Bluff, and so on. Grant's "hammering campaign" finally made the city's abandonment necessary, and on the morning of April 3, 1865 (six days before the surrender at Appomattox) the defenders mov'd out. It was decided to destroy all the tobacco and supplies in the warehouse district along the river at the foot of the hills lest it prove of value to the Federals, so sadly and reluctantly the whole section was put to the torch—just as the Yankee rebels in 1776 set fire to New-York when forc'd to surrender it to His Majesty's lawful troops. The fire proved more extensive than had been plann'd—destroying Mayo's Bridge and obliterating nearly a thousand buildings. Reconstruction, however, was very rapid after the war; so that today all the structures in the burn'd district are old and dingy. Richmond will always remember the Civil War, and has erected some splendid monuments to Confederate heroes. Monument Avenue, a gorgeous boulevard with park centre strip and numerous landscaped circles at intersections, contains many noble tributes to vanisht leaders—especially the great equestrian statues of Lee, Jackson, and Stuart, and the mighty Roman column, adorn'd by statuary and surrounded by a semicircular colonnade, sacred to President Jefferson Davis. In Hollywood Cemetery are bury'd Fitzhugh Lee, Stuart, Pickett, the oceanographer and naval officer Maury, and President Davis. On Libby Hill is another vast Roman column (modell'd after the pillar of Cn. Pompeius) dedicated to the Confederate dead.

Richmond's cultural life, like that of Providence, culminated in the 1830's and 1840's—the Poe period. It was then that the *Southern Literary Messenger* flourish'd, giving Philadelphia a close race for the cultural supremacy it was about to lose to Boston. Today the city has not a scholastick mood; at least, there are no museums, art galleries, or historical societies comparable to those of Worcester, Springfield, Providence, or other New-England cities of similar size. There are, however, signs of improvement in this direction—and a new publick library is under construction. There is one college—the University of Richmond.

As for specifick objects of interest—these are very numerous, tho' not beyond the compass of a single day's trip, especially if one avail himself of the excellent Grey Line sightseeing coaches. The splendid State Capitol, crowning a grassy Acropolis-like height whose slopes are a park, was design'd by the architecturally expert Mr. Tho: Jefferson, and forms perhaps the finest of early classick-revival specimens aside from Mr. Jefferson's products at Charlottesville. Its foundation was lay'd in 1785, and it was finish'd in 1792. The two wings—of congruous design—added in 1902 are regrettable, but not as bad as one might fear. Within is the famous Houdon statue of Genl. Washington and other matter of historical interest. The capitol grounds contain several noteworthy items—library and state office buildings, an old bell-tower used as a powder-magazine during the Civil War, a vast equestrian statue of Washington, and a fine Governor's mansion (now housing a true Virginia Byrd) built in 1811. Capitol Park is an ideal place to sit in the sun and read, for no barbarick spirit of haste or regularity obtrudes upon the omnipresent beauty and civilised reposefulness. Pres. Davis's executive mansion, not far away, is now a Confederate Museum. This is a fine old house built in 1819, with a splendid Georgian doorway on the street side, and a pillar'd portico on the garden side. Within, each of the Confederate States is represented by one room. In the yard is an anchor chain from the sunken *Merrimac*. The Valentine Museum, devoted to fine arts, archaeology, anthropology, and history, is noted as the repository of the Poe correspondence only recently made publick.[4] It is housed in a fine mansion built in 1812 and containing notable interior woodwork. The Valentines are among the foremost families of Richmond. A third museum is the John Marshall house, residence of that famous Chief Justice of the U.S. Supreme Court from 1795 to his death in 1835. Most of the reliques are of Marshall himself, tho' there are a few of general nature. The town house of Genl. Robert E. Lee, occupied by the Virginia Historical Society, houses rare books, MSS., and reliques connected with the Old Dominion. Of supreme interest to me, however, was the ancient stone house and its adjuncts lying in the easterly slum reaches of Main Street and now serving as a "Poe Shrine". This house, a farmhouse built perhaps in 1685 (though some identify it with the Jacob Ege house, built in 1737) and overtaken by the growing town, is the oldest edifice in Richmond, and remains in a sound state of preservation. The space near it has been purchas'd by Poe-lovers and developed with great taste and ingenuity; an exquisite garden (suppos'd to represent symbolically that "enchanted garden" in Providence where Poe first glimps'd Mrs. Whitman and of which he wrote so movingly)[5] lying in the rear, and the two adjacent houses on each side being annex'd as part of a three-building unit. Of these added houses that on the west is colonial, whilst that on the east is a fireproof museum in imitation of the Richmond residence of John Allan, Esq., where Poe was rear'd as an adopted son. I spent an hour in this fascinating place, and saw all manner of Poe reliques—far more than are stor'd in the Fordham cottage I know so well. Poe's chair, desk, and various personal belongings are there, as well as many architectural details (mantels, a staircase, etc.) from the two Allan houses and the *Southern Literary Messenger* building, all now demolish'd. One utterly magnificent feature is a gigantick model of the whole town of Richmond as it was during Poe's boyhood—about 1820—in a glass case occupying the entire ground floor space of the colonial house attached to the shrine. This model, made in natural colours and on a scale permitting even the smallest houses to be about an inch square, was constructed a few years ago with the utmost antiquarian accuracy and artistick skill; and is so vivid that one can almost imagine himself in a balloon looking down over the outspread Georgian city. Never have I seen an antient town so miraculously conjured out of the past—I wish someone wou'd do the same for Old Providence! It gave me a short cut to Richmond's topographical and architectural history which at once plac'd that venerable city amongst those I know best. What I had to worry out for myself in connexion with other colonial towns, was all done for me in the case of Richmond. I am convinc'd that models are the very best media for perpetuating the former appearance of old towns, and wou'd advise a widespread adoption of the Richmond idea were I a person of influence in historical circles.

It remains to describe the most historick churches of Richmond, of which antient St. John's, on Church Hill in the eastern part of the town, is easily the foremost. This is a lineal successor to the original Church of England of Henrico Parish—the parish surrounding the first settlement made by Sir Thomas Dale at Henricopolis. A building was under construction at Henricopolis when the Indians destroy'd it in 1622, and of this nothing remains but the baptismal font, which the salvages carry'd off, but which was recover'd from them in slightly damag'd condition. This font still remains in the present church. After the founding of Richmond in 1737 it was decided to rebuild the

church there, and land was given by William Byrd for the purpose. The region—
"Church Hill"—was then quite rural or suburban, on the eastern fringe of the town,
tho' it is now of course urbanly ingulph'd. In 1741 a building was erected, part of which
survives in the present edifice. The fane is very restful and captivating to the eye as it
stands today in its antient churchyard—the whole rais'd above the street level on a
gentle mound and surrounded by an iron railing. The stones in the churchyard date
back to 1751; and among the interments is the unfortunate Mrs. Poe, actress-mother
of the poet, who dy'd in destitution in 1811. A fine monument to Mrs. Poe was set up a
year or two ago by admirers of her great son. During the course of time St. John's un-
derwent such radical alterations and remodellings that almost nothing of the original
church can be distinguisht. What was once the nave, running east and west, is now the
transept of a new nave running north and south—tho' a few of the old pews, and the
antient high pulpit and sounding-board, remain to this day. This church form'd the
meeting-place of Virginia delegates on March 20, 1775, during the early stages of the
treason against His Majesty's lawful government; among them being Genl. Washington, George Mason, of Gunston, Esqr., John Marshall, Tho: Jefferson, of Monticello,
Esqr., Patrick Henry, and other celebrated figures. On this occasion Mr. Henry, standing up in his pew, utter'd those cheaply melodramaticall words which have become
such a favourite saw of schoolboys—"Give me liberty, or give me death!" The pew
from which he spoke is still preserv'd and markt with a tablet, but as a loyal subject of
the King I refus'd to enter it. The whole ensemble of church and churchyard is marvellously fascinating, and I stroll'd thither more than once during my sojourn in the town.
A pleasing mulatto sexton—very intelligent for his race—shews visitors around the
building. Another celebrated fane is the Monumental Church in Broad St., on the site
of the old Richmond Theatre where Mrs. Poe acted and where the Convention of 1788
met to ratify the U.S. Constitution. The theatre was burn'd for the second time on
Decr. 26, 1811—during the performance of a weird-horror play, "The Bleeding Nun",
taken from Lewis's famous Gothic novel, "The Monk". In this disaster, caus'd by the
contact of an oil lamp with the scenery, 72 persons out of an audience of 643 lost their
lives—among the victims being the Governor of Virginia, William Smith, Esq., who
escap'd at the first alarum, but perisht when he reëntered the building in an effort to
save his small son. The magnitude of this calamity was an occasion for general mourn-
ing, and for four months theatrical performances were forbidden in Richmond. Jany. 1,
1812 was sett aside as a day of fasting and prayer. At length it was decided to build a
church on the site of the theatre, dedicated to the victims and forming a tomb for their
mortal remains. The present edifice, finisht in 1814, is a sightly structure with low
dome and portico of two Dorick columns in antis. Old St. Paul's church, near the capitol, has a belfry-tower and Ionick portico, and evidently belongs to the 1830–40 period,
tho' I cannot ascertain the exact date. It was here that Genl. Lee and Pres. Davis both
worshipp'd—and here that Pres. Davis receiv'd, on the morning of April 2, 1865, the
fateful telegram from Lee warning him that Richmond must be evacuated. The Lee
and Davis pews are markt by tablets, and the memorial windows to Lee are the finest
things of their kind in the United States. In Franklin St. near 19th is an austere old
structure which, tho' not a church, has an almost religious significance for many—
being the oldest Masonick hall in the United States; i.e., the oldest edifice built as such
and continuously used for the same purpose. The corner stone was lay'd in 1785 by the
chief Masonick dignitaries of Virginia, and the building has been occupy'd since 1787
by Richmond-Randolph Lodge, No. 19. In the War of 1812 it form'd a military hospital, and Genl. La Fayette was here entertain'd in 1824.

Besides actual old buildings, I beheld many historick sites where famous structures have existed and pass'd away. Among these is the site of the dreaded Libby Prison, at Cary and 20th Streets near the waterfront. The building was originally a tobacco warehouse, and the hospital connected with it (probably a former dwelling-house) is still standing. The prison building existed until 1892, when it was taken down stone by stone to be reassembled and exhibited at the Chicago World's Fair. The intention was to return it later to Richmond, but for some reason this plan was never carry'd out. I do not know whether the building still exists in Chicago or not—but I am sure that Chicago cou'd use it, as well as many other extra gaols, to great advantage!

I quitted Richmond with the greatest reluctance, and only because my waning finances made a longer stay impossible. The place grows on one from day to day—and it gives one an amazing sensation to be in a *really American* city in the year 1929. After all, the old America is not yet truly dead, but simply *contracted in area*—confin'd to the South, and to isolated places like Vermont. This is the real old Richmond—real through the continuous habitancy and supremacy of the same kind of people—that William Byrd and Poe and Jefferson Davis knew. Its great charm is its utter lack of cheap "smartness" and senseless bustle. Like the old-time New-Englander, the Southerner has no false front. Life is divested of affected excrescences, stultifying routines, and meaningless speed, and kept to the significant essentials of the main Anglo-Saxon stream. I wish I liv'd there—tho' personal memories will always bind me to mine own antient town of Providence.

Prior to my departure from Richmond, I had the good fortune to behold the still older and richly historick towns of Williamsburg, Jamestown, and Yorktown in a single afternoon, thanks to the excellent sightseeing coaches of the Grey Line. The trip from Richmond to Williamsburg was made on the regular Norfolk coach—which was met by the sightseeing coach with able lecturer and full Williamsburg–Jamestown–Yorktown historick itinerary. Starting from Richmond, I pass'd over the old Williamsburg Road—or Nine-Mile Road, to use another antient name. This took me past some of the most celebrated battlefields of the Civil War, including Seven Pines and the Chickahominy Swamp. The Chickahominy River was cross'd on a new concrete bridge, and presented a weirdly fascinating swamp-like aspect with trees growing out of the water far back from the open channel. This is the most distinctively southern-looking landskip I have yet seen—for Virginia is not really a southern region except socially and politically. Climatically it is in the same approximate zone as New-England, as fauna, flora, and general atmosphere suggest. It is in the Carolinas and Georgia, I imagine, that the actual climatick South begins. As the coach near'd the drowsy and infinitesimal hamlet of *Providence Forge*, I lookt about with keen interest to see how well my own Providence might be echo'd. The place is too small for a post-office, and does not greatly suggest its Rhodinsular namesake—but I did experience one home touch when, by coincidence, there flasht by the coach a gentleman's private chaise bearing a Rhode-Island licence plate—"25.116—R.I.—29". It was my fortune to see many Rhode-Island and Massachusetts-Bay plates in the South—more, I think, than one commonly sees in New-York. After all, the real white men's parts of the colonies will hang together long after Manhattan is frankly recognis'd as an outpost of the Levant! Providence Forge was nam'd from an old forge used in the making of farm implements; sett up there in 1770 by three men, one of whom was a Presbyterian clergyman. It has given its name to the principal gentleman's seat near by—an eight-room colonial house of the farm type with dormer windows, and a pair of chimneys on each end. A stream, dam, and mill exist at Providence Forge, and remnants of the old forge itself were recently found. Some distance beyond this town I saw the small but famous old Hickory Neck Church, built in 1733 and serving as an academy for some time subsequent to 1825. It is a very small, plain brick structure—like an enlarg'd dog-kennel—of a type fairly frequent in Virginia. Toano next was reach'd—a straggling southern village without distinctive features.

At last came Williamsburg, where a change to the Grey Line sightseeing coach was made. This is one of the best-preserv'd colonial towns in the country, and amply justifies the Rockefeller plan for restoring it to its pre-Revolutionary state. Much restoration has been accomplished even now, but most of it is still to come. Not only will decay'd and alter'd houses be put back into pristine shape, but intrusive modern buildings will be torn down, and vanisht colonial edifices reërected from old plans, prints, descriptions, and so forth—resting in many cases on their original foundation-walls as uncover'd by judicious excavations. In layout and atmosphere, Williamsburg resembles *Deerfield* more than any other New-England town; since it is largely concentrated along a broad main street, and consists of houses widely spaced amidst their grounds. The central thoroughfare, Duke of Gloucester Street, is well shaded with trees (including mulberry trees planted in a fruitless effort to establish the silk culture), and has a strip of park or turf down the centre. Houses vary from quaint peaked-roof affairs of early date (plus a few gambrel specimens) to fine Georgian mansions in the southern style. One by one the non-colonial intruders are coming down, whilst the Phoenix-like rise of the vanisht colonial buildings may soon be expected.

Williamsburg, the oldest incorporated town in Virginia, began in 1633 with a palisade built by Gov. Wyatt as a defence against the Indians. It grew very rapidly, and with the decline and burning of Jamestown (in Bacon's Rebellion of 1676) became the chief settlement in the Colony. It was made the capital in 1699, after the burning of the Jamestown colony-house. During the eighteenth century it was the centre of a brilliant life, as is attested by its many noble mansions. It likewise became the seat of William and Mary College, founded in 1693. The name Williamsburg was first apply'd in 1699—the former designation having been "Middle Plantation". It was made a city in 1722, and has always remain'd such, tho' it is scarce more than a village in population. As Richmond rose, Williamsburg declin'd; till at length (1799) it gave place to its younger rival as capital. This stagnation, akin to that of Newport, in Rhode-Island, is what hath preserv'd its colonial reliquiae so marvellously.

I can describe but a few of the sights of Williamsburg, thro' which the Grey Line party was guided by a very bright young student from the college. Old Bruton Church, built 1710–15, is perhaps the most impressive object; and I was glad of a chance to explore it amply, crypt and all. It contains the antient silver communion service from the early church at Jamestown, as well as other colonial reliques of the highest value. The churchyard is, bar none, the most hauntingly picturesque I have ever seen; with curiously carv'd granite monuments bearing coats-of-arms. William and Mary College, at the west end of Duke of Gloucester Street, has for its original edifice (erected 1697) the only building in America design'd by Sir Christopher Wren. Newer buildings, including several still unfinish'd, all conform to the same type of design. The President's house, built in 1732, is of the steep-roof'd southern Georgian pattern. A chapel attach'd to the Wren building was erected in 1730, and another small building (presented by the eminent man of science Sir Robt. Boyle for use as an Indian school) was built in 1723. In front of the Wren building stands the marble statue of the colonial governor Lord Botetourt, originally set up near the colony-house, and remov'd hither in 1797. Ld. Botetourt himself lyes bury'd beneath the chapel. At the east or opposite end of Duke of Gloucester Street the foundations of the colonial capitol are still visible—or rather, visible again after excavation. This building will rise again from these foundations, a perfect copy of the one erected in 1705, rebuilt after burning in 1750, and abandon'd to decay in 1780. The white-belfried colonial court-house, built in 1769, is still in use as such; but will eventually become a publick library. The old "Powder Horn" is a typical colonial powder-house, like those at Marblehead and Somerville in the Province of the Massachusetts-Bay except that it is octagonal instead of cylindrical or conical. It was built in 1715, and hath been put to a curious variety of uses—market-house, Baptist church, dancing-school, Confederate arsenal, stable, and historical museum. Two interesting old gaols are shewn—the Debtors' Prison, built in 1748, and the Old Colony Prison built in 1705 with especially thick walls. In the latter were confin'd thirteen of the pirate Blackbeard's men—who were subsequently hang'd near by—as well as the royal governor of Detroit, Henry Hamilton, who was captur'd at Vincennes, Indiana, in 1779 by George Rogers Clark. Another interesting object is the pre-Revolutionary apothecary shop, now in process of restoration.

The private dwellings of interest are too numerous to catalogue. Most famous perhaps is the George Wythe house in Palace Green,* built in 1755 and inhabited by the celebrated statesman from 1779 to 1789. It was the headquarters of Genl. Washington in 1781. In 1927 this fine middle-Georgian edifice became the Parish House of antient Bruton Church, and hath been restor'd as a museum. I was glad to be able to give it a thorough exploration. The Paradise house is a splendid Georgian mansion built in 1760 and inhabited in 1788–9 by John Paradise, at one time a member of Dr. Johnson's literary circle in London. The Gov. John Page house (1710), a smallish wooden structure, is the scene of Mary Johnston's novel "Audrey".[6] There are strange inscriptions scratch'd upon two of its window-panes—"S. B. 1796 Nov. 23 O fatal day." and "A. Boush 1734." The Vest house is the largest brick mansion in Williamsburg. The Galt house (1640) is the oldest in Williamsburg and probably the oldest private dwelling in Virginia. It is small, wooden, and steep-roof'd. Besides the existing houses, there are many sites where houses will be rebuilt from surviving foundations—among them the Governor's house, the Masonick Hall, and the famous Raleigh Tavern. I must revisit Williamsburg when the restorations are compleat, perhaps two to five years hence. It will then form, without doubt, one of the most impressive evocations of the colonial past that America can display. One curious fact emphasised by this restoring work is the manner in which Nature tends to give burial to the things which man hath forgotten—a slow, subtle burial inch by inch as the dust of decades drifts and accumulates. It is thus that half the steps of Notre Dame have been cover'd up, and thus that classick Rome lyes many feet below the level of the modern town. In Williamsburg the old foundation-walls of vanisht structures lye severall inches below the present surface; and I observ'd with interest the lost brick driveway of the Governor Dinwiddie house, rediscover'd only two or three weeks before my visit, which is fully a foot lower than the existing sidewalk.

From Williamsburg the coach drove over a lonely road to the island of Jamestown, birthplace of our British civilisation in America. On the way we pass'd several lakes of clear blue, exempt from the general yellow mud colour of southern waters. The reasons for this difference are intricately geologicall, so that only a Mortonius cou'd describe them; and I was soon to find that the great York River shares the

---

*Which extends north of Duke of Gloucester St. So nam'd because the Governor's house or palace stood at the head of it.

happy exemption. The James is yellow, but the York is blue! Incidentally, the whole area travers'd in this town lyes betwixt the York and the James, being hence commonly known as "The Peninsula".

Jamestown is no longer a village, but simply a wind-swept grassy expanse overlooking the river and strown with monuments and melancholy reliques. Yet it is here that our nation took its rise in 1607—thirteen years before the Plymouth landing of the Pilgrims. The fateful expedition sail'd from London on Dec. 30, 1606, in three ships—the *Sarah Constant* under Capt. Sir Chr: Newport, the *Goodspeed* under Capt. Bartholomew Gosnold (who also explor'd our New-England coast), and the *Discovery* under Capt. John Ratcliff. On May 13, 1607, the colonists landed at the spot which became Jamestown, naming their settlement from our Sovereign James the First. There were 105 settlers in all, all men, and mostly of good blood. First preparing a crude shelter for worship, they render'd thanks to Heaven according to the Church of England rite; and subsequently began building their primitive village. The first church was rough and ugly, but a finer brick Gothick specimen was put up in 1638 (not 1617 as often wrongly stated in guide-books), the tower of which yet remains in a ruin'd state, with a modern nave (1907) built on the excavated foundations of the old one. In 1608 Capt. John Smith became President of the Council, and used his distinguisht ability in furthering the fortunes of the settlement. He had sail'd up the James in 1607 with Capt. Newport and erected a cross at the falls and head of navigation where Richmond now stands. Indian troubles follow'd, as is well illustrated by the familiar incident of Pocahontas. In 1609 Capt. Smith was succeeded by Percy, and in that autumn came the great famine which left only sixty out of some 500 settlers. In 1610 the dissatisfy'd colonists all started back for England, but decided to stay when a fresh load of colonists (delay'd by shipwreck) arriv'd. Lord De La Warr now became Governor, and increas'd the general contentment; Sir Tho: Dale succeeding very ably to him. In 1619 wives were sent out for the colonists, and in the same year the first cargo of African blacks arriv'd—proving that troubles never come singly. This was under the governorship of Sir George Yeardley. Industry and agriculture grew, silk culture and glass-making being among the experiments. An Indian massacre in 1622 fail'd to kill off the settlement; and by the time of Bacon's Rebellion against Gov. Berkeley in 1676 the colony had so grown that Jamestown's burning meant only a local loss—Virginia's supremacy passing to Williamsburg, then call'd "Middle Plantation". Many buildings of brick and wood were put up in Jamestown, including several notable colony-houses, the last of which was burn'd in 1699. After 1700 the town was gradually abandon'd, so that fewer and fewer houses remain'd standing—the high winds destroying things rather readily. In the 1830's only one house—the brick Ambler house—existed on the island in addition to the ruin'd church tower; and today even this hath succumb'd save for part of the walls. These reliquiae prove the house to have been of the Gothick design—for it must be remember'd that Jamestown was founded before the original Gothick period had wholly ended. The principal area of Jamestown is today own'd by the Association for the Preservation of Virginia Antiquities, and is strown with monuments and excavated foundation-walls. I cannot here attempt to describe these individually, save to say that the outlines of the old colony-house were unearth'd in 1903, together with those of four private dwellings in a solid block. The brick-pav'd cellar of one of the latter— Colonel Philip Ludwell's house—hath been carefully and compleatly excavated. The colony-house here unearth'd was that of 1686—whose burning led to the transfer of the capital to Williamsburg. There are two small museums in Jamestown, housing some minor excavated reliques and some historical pictures. A sea-wall hath been built around the island to check the constant encroachments of the wind-lash'd river. Part of Jamestown is privately own'd and not open to the publick—some day it will yield up rich archaeological material. The real focus of interest is the ruin'd and ivy'd church-tower of the 1638 edifice. Amidst its antient brick-wall'd churchyard, where curious giant roots weirdly creep and play havock with the slabs, and with its modern nave behind it, it well symbolises both the decay of the town and the permanence of the colony which sprang from it. Jamestown, despite its visual barrenness resulting from its desolation, is one of the most stimulating of all spots to the sensitive imagination. To stand upon the actual seed from which the Anglo-American provinces grew—to tread on soil once peopled by gallant gentlemen-adventurers of the Elizabethan generation—what more hath this continent to offer?

The coach now sett out for Yorktown, a quaint colonial city celebrated as the scene of Ld. Cornwallis's unfortunate surrender to the rebel armies of Genl. Washington and Marquess de La Fayette. This town, now sunk to a sleepy village, was once a port of very great wealth and standing, being a noted port of entry whose custom-house in 1749 recorded an annual trade of £32,000. It lyes on land first patented by one Nicholas Martian, a Walloon, who came to Virginia in 1621. In 1691 Martian's grandson Benj: Reade sold 50 acres of the tract to Messrs. Ring and Ballard to be settled as a town. The venture prosper'd, and in 1698 the new village became the seat of York county. In 1705 a brick custom-house, still standing, was built to accommodate its increasing trade. In 1781 the retreating troops of Ld. Cornwallis reach'd this place, establishing a final line of defence some distance east of the town and surrendering on the 19th of October. This event, deciding the colonial rebellion in favour of the rebels, mark'd the virtual close of hostilities and signalised the practical separation of the colonies from their rightful government; hence is widely celebrated throughout the present United States

"Treason doth never prosper, what's the reason?
Why, if it prosper, none dare call it treason!"[7]

Or as Seneca saith

"—Prosperum ac felix scelus
Virtus vocatur."[8]

The town and field are distinguisht by monuments, and the place much visited by travellers. Some events of the Civil War also took place here, Genl. McClellan employing Yorktown as a Federal base in 1862. There is a cemetery and a monument dedicated to the memory of Union soldiers kill'd in battel and in an accidental explosion.

Yorktown is situate on the south bank of the broad blue York River—a stream curiously exempt from the yellowness of most southern waters. A ferry connects it with Gloucester—which, together with another ferry across the James from Jamestown to Surry, forms a continuous route across the peninsula to the farther south. This is not, however, the main highway southward; the latter passing thro' Richmond and avoiding the peninsula altogether. Yorktown is 12 miles from the mouth of the York, 18 from Jamestown, and 12 from Williamsburg. In proceeding from Jamestown, my coach repass'd thro' Williamsburg, which I was very glad to see again. On the highroad thence to Yorktown I beheld some Civil War and Revolutionary battlefields, and saw in the distance one or two famous colonial estates such as Carter's Grove, built in 1751 by Carter Burwell, Esq. The coach also pass'd thro' the shabby whitewash'd hamlet of Lackey, which is apparently inhabited wholly by blackamoors. It is notable that the blacks are much more numerous on the peninsula than in Richmond. The Richmond–Norfolk coaches require them to sit in the rear, and the stations around Williamsburg, Yorktown, and Lee Hall all have separate white and black waiting-rooms. In Norfolk, of course, the colour-line is necessarily very strictly drawn; for the place teems with niggers.

Yorktown proper is a kind of southern Marblehead, if I may overlook a designation I have worn trite by many applications, for most of the houses are of colonial date. There are no sidewalks, and the only pavement is the concrete of the state road. Its architecture is more typically southern than that of Richmond, steeply pitched roofs and end chimneys being everywhere seen. The Grey Line coach pass'd thro' it, view'd the battlefield, and then return'd to inspect the town at greater leisure. On the east edge of the compact part are the foundation-walls of the Nelson house, used by Ld. Cornwallis as his headquarters till its destruction by shell-fire on Octr. 11, 1781. These were excavated only a month before my visit, and will be very carefully preserv'd. The town as a whole is meerly a double line of straggling brick, stone, and wooden houses along the highway, and most of it can be seen from the coach. I was glad, however, when a stop was made which permitted me to indulge in some pedestrian exploration. The greatest mansion in Yorktown is the imposing Tho: Nelson house—York Hall—a middle-Georgian structure shewing the Pennsylvania-Welsh influence in its architecture. This was own'd by the nephew of Secretary Nelson, owner of the demolish'd house. During the Revolution it was held by His Majesty's officers, and to dislodge them the owner—himself serving as a rebel general under Washington—order'd his own mansion to be fir'd upon. Of this Spartan fusillade, which fortunately fail'd to destroy the splendid house, two cannon balls yet remain imbedded in the eastern gable end. A garden of particular beauty adjoins the edifice, and helps it to form one of the most pleasing gentlemen's seats on the peninsula. The oldest house in Yorktown, built in 1690, stands next to York Hall, and is a modest brick dwelling with antient curb roof and colonial dormers. It was built by Tho: Sessions, and escap'd injury in the Revolution. Its present condition is excellent. Grace Church, built also in 1699 as York-Hampton Church, is of grey marl rock and having a modest white belfry. In the antient churchyard are some interesting slabs. The small brick custom-house put up in 1706 is the oldest custom-house in the U.S., and is now a publick museum operated by the D.A.R. The Yorktown Hotel, put up in 1725, is still in continuous use for its original purpose; rivalling in that respect the celebrated Red Horse Tavern in Sudbury, in the Massachusetts-Bay.[9] It is a small, steep, southern-looking building with end chimneys and dormers, and has been enlarged by a long rear extension which does not mar the original street facade. Other noted old Yorktown houses are the Cole Digges (1705—small brick), the West (1706—small wooden), and the Moore, a farmhouse of early but uncertain date near the village. This latter was antiently the abode of Gov. Spottswood, and in 1781 form'd the scene of Ld. Cornwallis's conference with Genl. Washington as to terms of surrender. It is on that account highly esteem'd by those who sympathise with the revolt against our rightful sovereign.

I was very glad to have seen this village—and indeed, I reckon the whole itinerary of that day among the most pleasant and striking experiences I have ever had. From Yorktown the coach went to Lee Hall, a small town where it connected with the Richmond coach. The return trip to Richmond included one more welcome passage thro' Williamsburg, and a magnificently apocalyptick sunset seen over the Chickahominy Swamp. The scenery here has good isolated embodiments, but scarcely equals that of New-England as a whole.

It being now time to turn my course northward, I look'd forward with much eagerness to a detail'd exploration of that Fredericksburg–Falmouth region whose quaint and colonial picturesqueness I had glimps'd so tantalisingly on the southward trip. Taking an early stage-coach from Richmond, I was given some anxiety by the uncertainty of the weather; but fortunately the afternoon turn'd out clear when I reach'd Fredericksburg, so that I had quite perfect conditions for sightseeing. A very pleasant coach-driver supply'd me with information highly useful in getting about quickly and directly; and was so good as to furnish me with several guide booklets with maps, whereby I grew reasonably familiar with the plan of the town before attempting to wander through it.

Quaint and historick beyond my fondest expectations, Fredericksburg and environs kept me busy for all of the five hours at my disposal; and made me wish I had five more—or rather, five days more—in which to study its numberless antiquities and fascinating Old-Virginia atmosphere. For here is a quiet village which has slept unchang'd thro' the centuries with its shady streets and colonial houses beside the green south bank of the yellow Rappahannock. The Civil War scarr'd it cruelly, but fail'd to impair its century'd charm and continuous tradition. There are very few foreigners, and very few persons of any kind whose ancestors have not dwelt there for centuries. Blacks are not numerous—indeed, they are by no means a conspicuous feature of the northern Virginia landskip. I was very fortunate in encountering a kindly, talkative, well-bred, and scholarly old gentleman who noticed my contemplative mien and frequent guide-book glances, and who volunteer'd to conduct me to the best uncharted colonial reliquiae. He was a connoisseur of Georgian architecture, inhabiting a colonial house himself and being no mean student of furniture, decorative detail, and early brick construction. Under his tutelage—and he tirelessly walkt me thro' street after street, lean and alert despite his years—I absorb'd dozens of sights and atmospherick touches which I wou'd otherwise have miss'd; and he offer'd to shew me interiors on some later visit when I might have more time. This good old man—a Mr. Alexander—is quite typical of nearly everyone I met in the South—including Mr. Strain, the genial coach-driver. Without question, I find southern people more congenial as a class than any other type I have so far seen—despite my devotion to New-England's landskip, architecture, and quiet ways. The Southerner reflects a civilisation of riper mellowness and higher graces than any other on this continent, and I wish this civilisation had a greater chance of spreading and leaving its impress on the culture of the nation as a whole—if indeed the nation as a whole may be said to possess any culture beyond a barbarick devotion to wealth, speed, glitter, and useless magnitude and activity.

Fredericksburg straggles sleepily along the southern bank of the shallow Rappahannock at the original head of navigation, with the green unspoil'd countryside (boasting the full luxuriance of summer early in May) drowsing exquisitely across the stream. Two bridges connect the town with the northern shoar—one from the "civick centre" to the roads of the open Stafford Heights country, and the other (the main Washington–Richmond highway bridge) from the extream westerly fringe to the quaint and somnolent hamlet of Falmouth, which is seven years older than Fredericksburg. The centre of the town before the Revolution lay farther west than at present, but a destructive fire during that period wiped out the business section and caus'd the residential streets farther east to turn to trade. The plan today is the same as in Civil War times. The town was named in honour of George the Third's father—Frederick, Prince of Wales, who dy'd before succeeding to the throne. All the principal streets are named from members of the royal family—Princess Anne St., Prince Edward St.,

Prince George St., William St., Sophia St., Amelia St., Caroline St., and so on. This is the kind of atmosphere in which my Tory soul revels—GOD SAVE THE KING!

The Fredericksburg region—to exclude all apocryphal tales—was first visited by Capt. John Smith with a crew of twelve men and Indian guide in 1608, on a trip during which he had a severe fight with a band of prowling Rappahannocks. Settlement—in the form of farms and gentlemen's plantations—was very gradual, but a fort was maintain'd near the falls of the river, and much sea-trade conducted; for the river was then broader and deeper than at present, and better adapted to navigation. In 1671 land patents were granted to Tho: Royston and John Buckner for the purpose of forming a settlement of forty persons, but this did not prove lasting. The tiny hamlet of Falmouth, on the north bank of the river near the falls, was founded in 1720, and is the earliest continuous settlement. Falmouth still contains many decrepit, steep-roof'd houses which must date back to almost the first decade of its colonisation. All these settlements reflect the desire of the neighbouring country-gentry for a town in their midst to serve as a trading-centre. Virginia was always rural by instinct, and even in 1700 Williamsburg was the only important town. Northern Virginians, wishing a more convenient centre of commerce, encourag'd the trading classes to settle around the Rappahannock region in urban fashion—then, realising the advantages of town houses for themselves, began to build mansions in the village and to develop a town social life in conjunction with their manorial existence. Fredericksburg, as a definite town, was incorporated and named in 1727. It was in this region that most of the Washingtons dwelt in the early eighteenth century; the "Cherry Tree" farm of Genl. Washington's father being just across the river from Fredericksburg. Young George and his brothers and sister went to school in Falmouth and Fredericksburg, and his mother always lived there. The sister, Betty, marry'd Col. Fielding Lewis, who built Kenmore mansion for her. In later years Madam Washington liv'd in a cottage near Kenmore to be close to her daughter, and there she dy'd in 1789. She is bury'd in the vicinity, and I beheld her tomb.

The early houses of Fredericksburg are small, steep-roof'd, wood and brick affairs with dormers and end chimneys—the regular southern type—built along the riverbank and sometimes forming solid blocks of four or five. Later and finer dwellings are on the higher parallel streets farther back from the stream. Kenmore—really a country-seat—is very far from the Rappahannock, in what were open fields at the time of its building. Madam Washington's cottage was connected with it by a flower-border'd path. Both are standing, and in excellent preservation—I gave them a close and appreciative survey. The oldest real mansion, the Charles Dick house, was built in 1745 and is still standing in good shape. I view'd it with much interest. Another thing which imprest me greatly was the Rising Sun Tavern, built in the 1780's by Charles Washington, George's brother, and famous for having harbour'd most of the eminent southern statesmen of the eighteenth century. Still quainter is the little apothecary shop in Caroline Street kept by Col. Hugh Mercer, who was both a physician and a chemist, and who was kill'd in the Revolution. This has been fitted up exactly as it was in Mercer's day, with old-time jars, great brass scales, and all the appurtenances of a colonial pharmacy. Another cherisht sett of Fredericksburg associations is that connected with President James Monroe, who was born near by and who practis'd law there after the Revolution. His old law-office hath been refitted just as it was in his day, so that it forms an admirable companion-piece to the Mercer shop. Of great Masonick interest is the antient brick home of Lodge No. 4, where on Novr. 4, 1752, George Washington was initiated as a Mason. The Masonick order was very strong throughout colonial Virginia, and especially at Fredericksburg, where there is a special Masonick Cemetery.

But the chief charm of Fredericksburg is less in any one house than in its whole pervasive atmosphere of colonial Southernism—a culture which has certainly survived to a much greater extent than colonial New-Englandism. Fredericksburg doorways, whilst by no means equal to New-England specimens, are famous throughout the South. The doors are generally double—that is, *vertically* double like those of Philadelphia— and above them is generally a rectangular *transom* of the colonial New-York type rather than a *fanlight* in the New-England and Philadelphia manner. The traceries on these transoms are often exquisite in the extream, and are worthy of a special study. Only very late Georgian houses (circa 1825) have fanlights and sidelights. One or two of these have doorways very like those design'd by John Holden Greene of Providence for such Providence houses as the Beckwith, Allen, Halsey, Cooke, and Crawford mansions.

Kenmore deserves a chapter all to itself. This celebrated mansion was begun in 1752, on land survey'd on Feby. 20th of that year by young George Washington, brother-in-law of the builder. It is a splendid specimen of the plainer type of middle-Georgian architecture, and seems to follow northern or British models rather than the typical southern style. There is a portico and a garden in the rear, and the grounds are still spacious despite many ruthless subtractions from the original large estate. The doorways and panelling are very notable, and the great recess'd windows lend a charm of memorable poignancy. Massive locks and "Holy Lord" hinges form matters of importance to those interested in structural details. But the chief "show pieces" of Kenmore are, curiously enough, not parts of the original fabrick but additions made more than twenty years later—viz., the marvellous stucco'd ceilings and overmantels. Most of these were done in 1774 and 1775 by the same Frenchman who did the stucco work at Mount Vernon; and he hath left a monument to his national loyalty in the dining-room, the centre of whose ceiling is the head of King Louis XIV, surrounded by solar rays typifying the monarch's boasted function as the bright sun of civilisation. In the "great room" the stucco'd overmantel is of different and perhaps more interesting workmanship. This was done during the Revolution by two Hessian prisoners taken at the battle of Trenton and quarter'd at Falmouth. When Mrs. Lewis learn'd of these artisans and what they cou'd do, she decided to have them compleat the stucco work at Kenmore, and writ her brother Genl. Washington, asking for suggestions as to a good overmantel design. Aesopick fables being then of vast popularity as decorative themes, the General thought that the fable of the fox, the crow, and the piece of cheese would be a good thing to select for the place—both as an ornament and as a didactick lesson to his little nephews to beware of flatterers. Accordingly he sketcht out a rough design for the artists to follow—a design in which the landskip and buildings are typical of the homely rural Virginia scene. The suggestion was duly acted upon, and the result remains to this day in prime condition. Architects agree in praising it as a very fine specimen of its kind. Col. Lewis, his health and fortune wreckt by his unceasing expenditure of money and strength upon the rebel cause—for he was a leader in the intensive manufacture of muskets for the continental troops—dy'd penniless in January 1782, and his widow was forc'd to open a school and sell portions of the estate. Throughout her trials she was ably advised by her illustrious brother, and in 1786 she sold Kenmore and went to live with a marry'd daughter in Culpeper County, where she dy'd March 31st, 1797. She was greatly belov'd and mourn'd by Genl. Washington, who was of about the same age, and whom she so greatly resembled, that it was commonly said she cou'd well pass for him if drest in his cloaths. She had a sprightlier disposition, however, and a greater sense of humour than either her brother or mother. Temperamentally she seems to have been largely a Washington, whilst the General took after the Balls in his disposition. Kenmore remain'd in good hands after its sale, till in 1914 its use as a boarding-house was threaten'd. This peril gave rise to merited alarm, and an association was form'd to preserve it. Success happily crown'd the efforts of the association, and the house is today a publick museum of distinguisht excellence and wide repute. I thoroughly explor'd the house and grounds, and accounted my time well spent. Old Madam Washington's cottage is likewise safely preserv'd and open as a publick museum.

The Civil War history of Fredericksburg was of less interest to me, yet is dramatick in the extream. Its strategick position can be understood when we realise that the whole crux of the war was really the capture of Richmond, south of it. The great battel—a futile and wasteful affair—was precipitated by the rashness of our Rhode-Island Genl. Burnside and by the clamour of the northern press. The Yankees were encamp'd on Stafford Heights across the Rappahannock, and began on Dec. 13, 1862, with a cannonade almost unparallel'd in the annals of warfare prior to the Great War. The townspeople fled, and the Confederate defenders retir'd to Marye's Heights, which overlook the town on the south. Bridges having been burnt by the Confederates, Burnside's men crost the river on hastily lay'd pontoon-bridges, and for a few hours occupy'd the town—not without some vandalism. Notwithstanding the obviously impregnable defences of Lee and Longstreet on Marye's Heights, the brave and reckless Burnside determin'd to attack the Confederate position; and led his men to what was virtually a wholesale suicide. What happen'd to Genl. Meagher's Irish brigade is a sample of what the whole charge was like. Of that unit of 1200 men, 937 were left dead on the field—one officer's body being found within fifteen feet of the Confederate parapet. Utterly beaten, Burnside retir'd back across the river to Stafford Heights when night fell. He had kill'd the best part of his troops absolutely for nothing! Earlier in the war Fredericksburg had been the scene of a more peaceful Yankee occupation—in the spring of 1862, when Genl. McDowell controll'd the Rappahannock region. During that period Pres. Lincoln deliver'd an address from the steps of the (still standing) National Bank—fram'd in its exquisite colonial doorway. The Federal officer then in occupation was Genl. Marsena Patrick, whose kindliness and consideration won him many southern friends. His correspondence with Mayor Slaughter (for Fredericksburg, small as it is, is a real city) was of such courtliness that one historian hath said that the letters "read like the extracts from the correspondence of diplomats". Fredericksburg is also quite near to many other noted Civil War battlefields—such as Salem Church, Chancellorsville, Spotsylvania Court-House, and the Wilderness.

After a thorough survey of urban Fredericksburg, I walkt out along the highroad to quaint Falmouth—about a mile and a half, and across the long Rappahannock bridge. This hamlet is ineffably archaick and half fallen to ruin, and evidently houses a rather poor class of whites in addition to its niggers. It lies picturesquely on a curving hill road which ascends the northerly slope of the river-valley, and most of its houses are of the early eighteenth century. A few late-Georgian houses lye on the lower level near the river-bank—one of them, with a splendid fanlighted doorway, being labell'd as the home of the "first millionaire in America". The interior woodwork of this fine house is announc'd as for sale—symbol of an increasing and very discouraging habit of stripping noble old buildings to enrich museums and the private houses of vulgar money'd parvenus. In returning to Fredericksburg I did not follow the main highway, but ambled along the leisurely, unfrequented old road that skirts the river's northern bank; crossing by the bridge from the foot of Stafford Heights to the centre of the town. I reacht the Princess Anne Tavern in time for the evening stage-coach to Washington, and after a pleasing drive in the twilight—during which I had a second glimpse of the old Pohick Church—was deposited in the Federal capital, where I found quarters at a good inn.

In Washington, owing to my now considerable familiarity with the local antiquities, I spent much time in museums and galleries; including the Smithsonian Institution and its striking collection in every field of learning and technology. Of everything I saw, nothing imprest me more than the Cyclopean stone images from Easter Island in the Pacifick—last mute and terrible survivors of an unknown elder age when the towers of weird Lemurian cities clawed at the sky where now only the trackless waters roll. At the Library of Congress—whose overlavish building was design'd, by the way, by a remote blood-kinsman of mine[10]—I beheld a wealth of interesting exhibits; including a sett of splendid colour'd photographs of the antient parish churches of Virginia. At the Corcoran Gallery I saw a sett of models illustrating coming architectural developments in Washington—developments, I am glad to say, which will involve no departure from classick and traditional designs. At the Freer Gallery the celebrated "Peacock Room" of Whistler was perhaps paramount in interest. On a side-trip I survey'd the results of the past year's progress toward compleating the magnificent Gothick cathedral atop Mount St. Alban. In many of my trips I was ably guided by my friend Edward Lloyd Sechrist, Esq., whose courtesy contributed so much to my Washington trip of 1925.[11]

From Washington I took the coach for Philadelphia, and after a pleasing drive reacht that venerable and favourite town in the golden glamour of sunset. Here, besides renewing my acquaintance with the colonial streets and squares I know and love so well, I devoted some time to the museums—especially that marvellous new art museum near the Schuylkill at the end of the great Parkway. This latter is absolutely the most magnificent museum building in the world—the most exquisite, impressive, and imagination-stirring piece of contemporary architecture I have ever lay'd eyes on—the most gorgeously perfected and crystallised dream of beauty which the modern world hath to give. It is a vast Grecian temple group atop a high elevation (a former reservoir) which terminates the Parkway vista toward the Schuylkill; reacht by broad, spacious flights of steps, flankt by waterfalls, and with a gigantick fountain playing in the centre of the great tessellated courtyard. A veritable Acropolis—I had seen it before, but had never ascended the steps or enter'd the place. This time I did ascend and enter; and tho' the structure is not yet compleat or fully equipt, I found it no disappointment. Colonial and British Georgian rooms are there in infinite profusion; not so many American rooms as in the new decorative wing of the Boston museum or the American wing of the Metropolitan Museum of New-York, but much more British material than in either of those places. A very rare feature is a pair of rooms from an eighteenth-century Pennsylvania-German house—the only things of their kind in any museum I know of. The furniture and paintings occupying these rooms are as rare as the rooms themselves, and include the best work of the corresponding periods. The pictures have amongst them specimens by Reynolds, Gainsborough, Romney, Raeburn, Gilbert Stuart, and so on. The wide assortment of English rooms presented enables one to form a very good comparative estimate of English and American Georgian styles; and curiously enough, I think I prefer the American. The provincial interiors are less lavish in scale and decorative detail, and thereby gain a classick austerity of tone which wou'd be hard to surpass.

From Philadelphia I pass'd northward thro' New-York to a second phase of my travels which was to include the legend-haunted Hudson Valley as its chief seat; and owing to the kindness of my grandchild Belknap and his parents, I was provided with an instant up-river coach transportation which sav'd me from stopping in the metropolitan pest-zone. As the party fared northward, it was curious to reënter an early-spring environment whose delicate freshness contrasted so oddly with the lush summer luxuriance I had been enjoying in the South. This fragile exquisiteness of young foliage and apple-blossoms offers many compensations for the drowsy fulness, peace, and restfulness of my favourite aestival season, and I was well pleas'd to encounter it. It was curious, too, to pass from a purely English region into one where Dutch influences are ancestrally paramount. Crossing the ferry at Rhinebeck, we enter'd antient Kingston—which is truly one of the most delectable places I have ever seen; a sleepy, wide-spreading old city of about 30,000 population, with unbelievably antient stone houses and scores of old wooden buildings in the colonial tradition of northern New-York state. The old Dutch churchyard is ineffably fascinating—full of old red sandstone markers, and redolent of fine traditions and civilised reposefulness. The church now standing is of Victorian date (1852), but in its facade are sett old Dutch Bible texts—stone slabs taken from an earlier church on the same site. Buildings as old as 1680 or so are fairly common, and the graceful court-house was built in 1818. The modern parts are surprisingly tasteful, and the whole town hath the atmosphere of a country village despite the phenomenally large area it covers. In many parts the open country is astonishingly near, and most of the street vistas west and northwest have dim tracings of the violet Catskill foothills at their far, mysterious ends. I can well imagine Rip Van Winkle as flourishing in such a place—in fact, it is still a perfect part of the old America; as authentick a survival as the story'd South which I left behind with so much regret. It has nothing to do with New-York City—all its affiliations being with the wholesome "York State" rustick region to the north. In this town I was the guest of Bernard Austin Dwyer,[12] who is a product of the wild domed hills and hanging woods of the West Shokan hinterland. Most of my writing whilst there was done in a green and sunny country lane just around the corner from a fine residential street—a lane whose vistas are wholly rustick as far as the eye can reach, and from which can be obtain'd glimpses of a charming and mysterious gap in the far-off, vapour-wreath'd purple hills. There birds sang, and the sun filter'd down thro' delicate vernal foliage and trac'd strange faery patterns on the grass and sand of the lane. Near by I cou'd spy the picturesque, ivy-grown ruins of some great stone building as I sate on the tumbled rocks of a low wall evidently belonging to it. I was fortunate enough to be able to tarry long enough at Kingston to imbibe its atmosphere rather fully, besides visiting its two still more antient and glamorous neighbours, Hurley and New Paltz. It is a fine old place—the present city being a fusion of two once separate villages—*Kingston* proper, where my host dwells and which is about a mile inland, and the port of *Rondout* on the hilly Hudson bank where the ferry from Rhinebeck lands and where a somewhat picturesque slumdom now prevails.

The history of the region goes back to the decade of 1620–30, when the Dutch built a fort (*ronduit*) at the mouth of a creek on land call'd by the Indians *Ponckhockie*. The fort became the centre of a settlement call'd *Rondout*, and the creek receiv'd the name of Rondout Creek. About 1652 Kingston proper—the land then call'd *Atkarkton*, northwest of Rondout and inland along Esopus Creek—was settled by Dutchmen and Englishmen from Rensselaerwyck, farther up the river, after disputes regarding land titles had driven them from the latter place. In 1655 serious Indian wars convuls'd the locality, and in 1658 the Atkarkton settlers appeal'd to Gov. Petrus Stuyvesant for aid. "Old Silverleg" was dispos'd to grant the petition only on condition that the colonists form their holdings into a palisaded village, and this requirement was duly and immediately comply'd with. The resulting stockaded town, which was charter'd by Stuyvesant in 1661 under the name of *Wiltwyck*, was embraced in the area bounded by the present Main St., Clinton Ave., North Front St., and Green St. Streets were lay'd out which correspond quite closely to the streets of today. After the transfer of New-Netherland to His Britannick Majesty's domain, the name of Wiltwyck was chang'd to *Kingston;* and the village prosper'd exceedingly. In 1695 the Revd. John Miller, Chaplain of His Majesty's forces and Aide to the Governor of New-York, publisht a book with maps descriptive of the Province, and therein spoke of Kingston as a town of the same area as Albany, but with half as many houses—i.e., as being six furlongs in circumference, and having an hundred buildings in its compass. Many of these buildings are still standing today. Severe Indian warfare harass'd the town throughout its early history—incidents not unprovok'd by the high-handed seizure of lands and cruel treatment of Indians by the Dutch settlers. When the unfortunate sedition against the lawful authority of Great-Britain occurr'd, Kingston had well-nigh 200 houses, a market and brew house, a church, an academy (still standing), a court-house, and two schools. As a storehouse and source of supply for the rebel armies operating in its vicinity, it was a highly dangerous menace to His Majesty's forces; so that in the autumn of 1777 its destruction by fire was found needful. Most of the rebel inhabitants, being forewarn'd, fled to the village of Hurley and other points, and our troops enter'd the place without opposition; setting fire to all the edifices save those inhabited by loyal subjects of His Majesty. This process consum'd only the wooden dwellings, leaving the walls and great beams of the much more numerous stone houses scarcely damag'd. Accordingly the returning rebels later rebuilt their homes, so that large numbers of the early structures still stand. At this time, Octr. 16, 1777, the rebel Senate of New-York was meeting at the Ten Broeck house in Kingston (now pointed out as the "Senate House" and forming a publick museum), and adjourn'd its sessions to the Van Deusen house in Hurley when our troops burn'd the former. The city of New-York was the legal capital of the Province; but it was not at that time in the hands of the rebels, hence their sessions at Kingston, which was the third town in importance in the colony, Albany being second. In the compact part of Kingston not above one or two houses were left undamag'd by flame. Today the Van Steenburgh house, in Wall St. at the head of Franklin (hardly in the village according to the limits of 1777), is pointed out as the only one which was not touch'd. For this exemption various reasons are assign'd—loyalty of the owner being the most probable one. The tenure of Kingston by His Majesty's forces was not of long duration, since powerful rebel detachments under Genl. George Clinton (a native of this Ulster County region, and later Governor of New-York for 21 years) were observ'd to be advancing toward the town. Having destroy'd all possible rebel supplies, the army evacuated without pursuit of the fleeing villagers; and did not again enter. The rebel army soon arriv'd, and with its aid the villagers quickly reëstablisht themselves in their accustom'd haunts. Local progress was by no means retarded, and in 1783 (being us'd to harbouring a legislative body) Kingston offer'd itself as a possible capital of the United States—which offer was declin'd, as the Federal City of Washington had been plann'd. After the Revolution Kingston remain'd a very important town, tho' it did not grow as rapidly as many—Albany and New-York City monopolising the activity along the Hudson. At the Bogardus Tavern, which stood at the corner of Fair St. and Maiden Lane, many persons of the first importance were entertain'd; and it was there that Aaron Burr, observing the clever chalk drawings of a stable-boy on a barn-door, resolv'd to send the lad to Europe for an art education, and thus produced the eminent painter John Vanderlyn. As the nineteenth century wore on, Kingston was more and more rivall'd commercially by the river settlement of

Rondout, at the mouth of the creek, which habitually obtain'd a great share of the region's trade. By the 1840's Rondout was larger than Kingston in population, and was heavily built up along its narrow, hilly streets in contrast to Kingston's straggling houses, broad streets, and level terrain. At the same time it was less select in population and less rich in traditions—a hive of traders and bargemen rather than a settled domain of hereditary agricultural magnates. In the 'fifties Rondout apply'd for a city charter, and seem'd for a while likely to get it; but vested and dignify'd Kingston interven'd, and finally succeeded in disposing of its rival by ingulphing it—i.e., by securing a combin'd city charter for the two neighbouring villages of Kingston and Rondout, *under the name of Kingston.* Thus Kingston became, by one sudden act, a city and a Hudson River port, with two distinct settled areas separated by a sparsely populated zone. So it hath remain'd to this day; save that the sparse zone is gradually filling up with publick and private buildings including the railway station, post-office, publick library, city hall, hospital, and Y.M.C.A. Kingston proper (or "uptown") hath retain'd its social supremacy, and there may be found all the leading dwellings and shops. Hilly Rondout on the river hath become a sort of slum fringe—distinctly declassé, and largely given over to foreigners, from whom Kingston proper is almost wholly free. The city is distinguisht by a reposefulness highly pleasing to observe, and scarce changes in population—having linger'd betwixt 25,000 and 30,000 for the last thirty years. It has a single street-car line from the Hudson Day Line wharf at Kingston Point through Rondout to Kingston proper—which still remains wholly two-man, still uses little single-track cars, and still has open cars in season. I took several rides on the latter. Stage-coach service also exists, both local, and to other towns including New-York City. It must be a delightful place to reside, save for its coldness in winter, for it has all the freshness, charm, and simplicity of a small village.

Of the individual houses in Kingston, some of the most notable are the ancient Hoffmann house (just around the corner from where I slept in Green St.),[13] built not long after 1660; the Ten Broeck or Senate House at North Front St. and Clinton Ave., built in 1676; the Elmendorf Tavern (1726), the Sleght[14] or Capt. Tappan House (mid-Georgian), the Kingston Academy (1774—now housing a newspaper), the De Waal Tavern in N. Front St., and so on. The typical Kingston house is a seventeenth- or early eighteenth-century building of one or two storeys and attick, of solid drest stone, and early Dutch architectural lines. The style is predominantly rural and primitive until the Georgian period; no Dutch town-houses with stept gables, or cottages with curving gambrel roof, having been constructed in this northerly region. With this omnipresence of the plain, sloping roof, it may be seen that Dutch Wiltwyck (or *Esopus,* as it was likewise often call'd) must have been a very different-looking region from the Dutch areas nearer the mouth of the Hudson—New-Amsterdam, Long Island, and the adjacent parts of New-Jersey. I visited the Sleght house, a fine middle-Georgian mansion at the junction of Crown and Green Sts.; preserv'd by the D.A.R. and open as a publick museum. It has an excellent panell'd interior, and shews the spread of cultivated and British influences over the Dutch parts of the Province as the eighteenth century advanc'd. I also inspected the "Senate House"—the Ten Broeck homestead of 1676—which is likewise a museum. In this I was by no means disappointed; for the interior is of the greatest conceivable interest, with low ceilings, hand-hewn beams, Dutch doors with antient hinges, steps up and down caus'd by late seventeenth- and eighteenth-century additions to the original house, bullseyes in interior doors, and other typical earmarks of solid and conservative Dutch colonial craftsmanship. The Historical Society which controls it is building a splendid new museum—in

the exact style of a typical Old Kingston stone house—on the grounds west of the antient edifice; into which the general historical collection will shortly be mov'd. When
this transfer is effected, the Ten Broeck house will be furnisht as a colonial home; thus
forming an analogue of the Pendleton house in Providence, or the Van Cortlandt
house in New-York. In the historical collection are some prodigiously interesting
items—including the wooden sides of the rural wain in which Genl. Burgoyne was
convey'd from the battlefield of Saratoga as a prisoner.

There now remain'd to be cover'd the ineffably quaint and lovely neighbouring villages of Hurley and New Paltz—unspoil'd reliques of the earliest days—and of these I
chose to see Old Hurley (as it is commonly known) first. I rose early on the designated
day and caught the stage-coach at the ancient Van Ross Tavern, despite an unpleasant
drizzle which persisted throughout the day. The road lay thro' an exceeding fine rolling
countryside; with green cultivated fields in a very unspoil'd and un-modern state, and the
foothills of the story'd Catskills as an eternal dominating background. In general, this territory is unchang'd since the colonial period; being still own'd and farm'd by the descendants of the original Dutch and Huguenot settlers. Hurley, some three miles northwest of
Kingston, was not in any way a disappointment. It is a straggling village of antient stone
houses stretcht along the highroad, with plenty of trees and diverging lanes, and with
green fields and blossoming orchards stretching off on either side to where the purple
mountains loom mystically. The houses are of Dutch masonry construction, some of
them with wooden atticks and lean-to's, and a few with projecting porches. All have the
horizontally divided Dutch door with iron knocker and hinges to match, and the average
date is from about 1700 to 1730. It is noteworthy, as previously remarkt, that none of
these Ulster County Dutch houses ever develop'd the gracefully curving roof-line or the
gambrel arrangement so characteristick of the Dutch colonial architecture of southern
New-York. Up here the plain peaked-roof tradition always persisted. The houses of Hurley have seen very little change in the more than two centuries of their existence, for the
place is delectably slow and sleepy, with true Catskill conservatism. All the dwellings are
tenanted by the same old families who built them—an Elmendorf still runs the single village store and post-office and the antient Dutch Reform'd Church still ends the vista at
the bend of the road on the farther side from Kingston—the only church in the hamlet.
The town is very famous among antiquarians, models of the houses being in the museum
of the New-York Historical Society, and a large space being devoted to them in Eberlein's
volume, "The Architecture of Colonial America."[15] A Dutch diplomat has call'd it "more
Dutch than anything left in Holland".

Hurley, at first call'd merely "Nieuw Dorp" or the "New Village", was founded
about 1660 by the overflow population of Wiltwyck, who desir'd to expand in the fertile untimber'd lowlands. A large proportion of the settlers were French Huguenots,
tho' the Dutch element was very numerous. Land grants were made by Gov. Stuyvesant without consent of the Indians who form'd the original population; a circumstance which paved the way for considerable warfare and general harassment. On June
7, 1663, Hurley was burn'd to the ground by salvages, and all the women and children
were carry'd away into captivity. It was not until September that the pursuing forces of
the Dutch succeeded in discovering the unhappy prisoners—who had not been ill-
treated, tho' they were soon to have been burn'd alive in revenge for certain Indians
who had been captur'd by the whites and sold as slaves to traders from Curacao. In the
years that follow'd, Hurley prosper'd exceedingly; perhaps occupying a more important
position in the life of the region than it does today. Its cheeses, milk, cakes, and other
products were famous throughout the New-Netherlands, and became celebrated in

more than one bit of Dutch doggerel folklore, of which the following is a typical specimen, literally translated:

> "What shall we with the wheat-bread do?
> Eat it with the cheese from Hurley!
> What shall we with the pancakes do?
> Dip them in the syrup of Hurley!
> What shall we with the corn-meal do
> That comes from round about Hurley?
> Johnnycake bake, both sweet and brown,
> With green cream cheese from Hurley!"

The resemblance betwixt the Dutch and English languages, both representatives of a
Low-Germanick syntactical system, may be seen by citing the second distich of this
piece with the original:

> "Wat zullen wij met die pannekoeken doen?
> Doop het met die stroop van Horley!"

It was from Hurley that the settlement of New Paltz was made by Huguenots in 1677;
and to Hurley that the fleeing people of Kingston repair'd just a century later, when
the torches of His Majesty's troops menaced their houses. On that latter occasion the
rebel state senate also fled to Hurley, conducting its deliberations in the old Van
Deusen house (1723), which is still standing and colonially furnisht with a view to an-
tique-selling. I enter'd and thoroughly examin'd the Van Deusen house; noting in particular the graceful staircase and hall-panelling, and the marvellously quaint door-
hardware. There has been little change in it since the eighteenth century, and one may
recognise the atmosphere of the past on every hand. The oldest house in the village is
the Elmendorf store, dating from about 1700—the proprietor of which gave me much
valuable information.

On the afternoon of the same day I made the New Paltz trip, thus completing my
long-plann'd circuit of the famous Ulster County triad of colonial survivals. New Paltz
lyes about sixteen miles south of Kingston, by the Wallkill and Shawangunk Creeks,
and in the eternal shadow of the lordly and lovely Shawangunk Hills. It is a thriving
village with shops, hotels, banks, a normal-school, and a newspaper; but the modern
(i.e., post-Revolutionary) town is at some distance from the heart of the antient settlement. This hath tended to preserve the original area in its pristine, Hurley-like state;
so that we may still see the place as it was in the early eighteenth century. To reach the
old town from the modern town one has to walk a considerable space, descending a
steep hill and crossing the railway track. On this occasion the day was dismal, but I ap-
preciated the splendid unspoil'd countryside none the less. Here is the old Hudson valley of Irving's day still flourishing and unalter'd; any of these villages being a suitable
abode for the mellow Dutchmen of "Geoffrey Crayon's" fancy.[16] Lovely valleys abound,
and bends of streams in the lee of mountains produce a scenick effect hard to surpass. I
saw at least one old-fashion'd cover'd bridge. Finally the coach ascended a hill and deliver'd me at the principal tavern of New Paltz—the "modern" part, tho' even that is as
quaint as can be imagin'd, and marvellously native as to population. There are virtually
no foreigners in this idyllick backwater, nearly all the population being descended from
the original Huguenot settlers. Making judicious inquiries, I soon found my way down
to the antient section—Huguenot Street—and there revell'd in the sparse line of old

stone dwellings which hath given the town so great an historical and architectural fame. There are not many—perhaps half a dozen at best—but their fine preservation and isolation from modern influences give them a magnify'd charm. One of them is fitted up as a museum and open to the publick; others remain private dwellings, mostly in the hands of the families that built them more than two centuries ago. The museum—which is the old Jean Hasbrouck[17] house built in 1712—is a large stone house of one full storey and two attick storeys under the immense sloping roof—an ideal storehouse for grain or other rural material. It is a fine type of early colonial construction under Dutch influence (tho' Frenchmen built it), and I examin'd it with the utmost thoroughness and interest; visiting the attick and noting the massive expos'd beams. It is call'd the "Memorial House", and a boulder monument to the town's founders stands on the small triangular green opposite it. Near by is the quaint burying-ground housing these 'rude forefathers of the hamlet'.[18] The other houses—of vary'd types, and having features as unique as transoms with double rows of lights—stretch southward; the DuBois, Elting, Abraham Hasbrouck, Freer, etc. places. All are of about the 1700 period, as can be well seen from every detail of their construction. The interior of the Memorial House hath some highly primitive features such as the great plank doors—some unpanell'd, and some single-panell'd. Oddly enough, there is just one of the antient stone houses in the "modern" village—now us'd as a publick library. In the old times it must have been an isolated farmhouse on the hill.

New Paltz was settled by French Huguenots who had undergone a long and singular course of persecution and migration. Emigrating originally from France, they had settled at Pfalz or Paltz in the Protestant Rhineland; but had eventually been so harass'd by French troops from across the border in their Catholick homeland that they reëmigrated to Holland. There, affected by that longing for a new world which sent so many religious refugees overseas, they took part in the general Dutch migration to New-Netherland—tho' sedulously retaining their French language and customs; a Gallick characteristick which we see today exemplify'd in the French of Quebeck, and in those who have come thence to Rhode-Island. Preferring the rural reaches of the upper Hudson to the crouded and cosmopolitan New-Amsterdam, this band of Huguenots (led by one Louis DuBois, a Pioneer of the utmost solidity and ability) selected Wiltwyck—the Kingston of later times—as an abiding-place; but later transferr'd themselves to the New Village (Hurley), which they considered more favourable to their retention of French speech and ways than the rather uncongenial Dutch trading-post within the palisade. After the burning of Hurley in 1663, Louis DuBois was most imprest by the lovely countryside south of Rondout Creek, which was made familiar to him during his participation in the search for the Indian captives—amongst whom were his own wife and three sons. Especially did he relish the idyllick valley of the Wallkill, nestling amidst the Shawangunks and cut off from the bustling world which had treated him and his kind so ill. During the next fourteen years—a span markt by the transfer of the region from the Holland States-General to the authority of His Britannick Majesty—DuBois interested many of his fellow-Frenchmen in a project for securing land patents and founding a new Huguenot village in the Shawangunk country; a project finally carry'd through with the aid of Abraham Hasbrouck, a young Huguenot having influence with His Majesty's Governor of the Province, Sir Edmund Andros—the same official whose arbitrary measures made him so much hated in New-England. Arrangements were also made to purchase the land lawfully from the Indians—a step which wou'd have delighted Mr. Roger Williams of Rhode-Island—for the patentees were not insensible of the hostility created by the high-handed seizures of the Dutch.

In May, 1677, the Indians formally ceded the land in exchange for much assorted merchandise, and four months later His Majesty's Government granted the legal patent to the settlers—Louis, Abraham, and Isaac DuBois, Abraham and Jan Hasbrouck, Andries and Simon LeFevre, Pierre Deyo, Louis Bevier, Antoine Crispell, and Hugo Frere, ancestor of the Freer family. Homes were built the following spring—rude cabins on the site of the stone houses built during the next generation—and a few other settlers were admitted, including at least one Dutch family. A little stone Huguenot church, with services in French, soon adorn'd the village green; and the hamlet was nam'd *New Paltz* in honour of that place in Germany which had first given the wanderers a haven.

With the years New Paltz attain'd a very comfortable agricultural prosperity, tho' remaining in that unspoiled state which best suited its founders' wishes. Every effort was made to preserve the traditional piety and French ways of the forefathers, yet in the course of time the influence of the surrounding Dutch population cou'd not help being felt. It became harder and harder to secure French-speaking schoolmasters and clergymen, and after a while the younger generation fell into the habit of speaking Dutch. Naturally the elders protested, and there is a well-known tale of a child sent to a relative to borrow some household utility, and refus'd it because she cou'd not speak its name in French. This transition period was likewise markt by ecclesiastical schisms—some church members wishing to adhere to the Reform'd Dutch Church whilst others clung to a French Huguenot independence. By 1750 Dutch had definitely displac'd French as the language of New Paltz, and in 1752 the church commenc'd the use of that tongue. The village was now essentially a part of the Dutch Hudson Valley, tho' still remembering its different traditions. Some of the pathos of the linguistick change is reflected in the will of Monsieur Jean Tebenin, the local schoolmaster who flourisht in the early eighteenth century. He saw the gathering clouds; and when he left his French Bible to the church, provided for its sale for the benefit of the poor if the French language shou'd ever cease to be spoken thereabouts. New Paltz in its Dutch-speaking period enjoy'd a steady growth, and that happy immunity from striking incidents which marks a peaceful community. Branches of its Huguenot stock were represented in the late unfortunate rebellion against His Majesty's authority, yet the war itself left the town serene and unravag'd. As the eighteenth century drew to its close, time took its revenge upon the once conquering Dutch language by pressing it to extinction as French had formerly been prest—the latest conqueror being the all-ingulphing English. Signs of Yankee progress became manifest as an Anglo-Saxon population filter'd in, but the newer element built on the hill above old Huguenot Street; shifting the centre of gravity of the village and leaving the antient part undisturb'd to this day. In 1833 an academy was founded, which survives to the present as a state normal-school. Connected with these educational enterprises was the late Albert K. Smiley, once head of the Friends' School in Providence, Rhode-Island, who with his twin brother conceiv'd a vast liking for the region and develop'd a great estate at Lake Mohonk, in the neighbouring hills—where he founded a series of annual conferences on Indian affairs which endures to this day. New Paltz hath erected a memorial gateway at the entrance of the Smiley estate—thus linking the sleepy Shawangunk valley with the antient town of Providence, in His Majesty's Rhode-Island Colony!

Having completed the exploration of New Paltz, I return'd by stage-coach to Kingston and took the rail-road cars (new-fangled nuisance!) to Albany—my plan being to cross thence into New-England by way of the Berkshires, and pay a long-anticipated visit to the learned and congenial W. Paul Cook, Esq., at Athol, in the

Province of the Massachusetts-Bay, before finally coming back to Providence. The ride to Albany was somewhat marr'd by misty weather, yet was not without picturesqueness; involving many weird glimpses of the vapour-cloakt Catskills. Reaching Albany—a town of no great attractiveness to which I had been before—I sought out but few sights; prominent amongst them being the graceful late-Georgian Albany Academy north of the massive and ugly Victorian state-house.

Having putt up at an inn, I the next day sett out in the rail-road cars (the stage line being out of operation at the time) for the Massachusetts-Bay. The day was good, and the trip pleasing—it being very agreeable to change at Troy into a train of the antient *Boston and Maine* railway; a system wholly bound up with New-England and its associations, and thus furnishing the first touch of concrete symbolism in my gradual homecoming. God Save His Majesty's New-England Colonies!

The ride thro' New-York State was not at all dull; for the landskip is very fine, and includes many sightly mountain vistas and delightful glimpses of river scenes. Then the hills grew wilder and greener and more beautiful—yet less luxuriant in foliage as we receded from the warmth of the South. Finally I saw a station-name which made my heart leap—North-Pownal, in His Majesty's New-Hampshire Grants, latterly call'd Vermont, in NEW-ENGLAND! God Save the King! A town nam'd for Tho: Pownall, Gent., Governor of the Province of the Massachusetts-Bay! Home at last! After all, there is nothing else like home-coming; and it was good to have the scene shift from the exotick to the accustom'd—no more unfamiliar names and sights, but the cherisht, familiar things I have always known. Vanisht were the pillar'd doorways of New-York, the steep roofs and dormers of the South, the marble steps and keystones of Philadelphia, and the old stone dwellings of the Esopus Valley—all these, and the century'd echoes of those who have known them. They were snapt off as by the turning of some new-fangled electrick switch, and thenceforward my eyes and talk were to be fill'd with known and neighbouring things—the eternal hills and stone walls of my native land, the oft-rehears'd legends of familiar tribes and settlements, the homely accents of Puritan speech, the white steeples and farmhouse gables of New-England's countryside, the lov'd, antient names of known places which look back only to English dreams and memories—Pownal, Vermont—Williamstown in the Massachusetts-Bay—North Adams—Zoar—Charlemont—Buckland—Shelburne-Falls—West Deerfield—Greenfield—Orange—and Athol!

A second thrill occurr'd when the cars enter'd the Massachusetts-Bay, for this region, close to Rhode-Island, hath ever been as a second home colony to me—my first conscious memories, indeed, dating from a summer's visit to Dudley in that province, in 1892, when I was one and three-quarters years old. Near North-Adams the Berkshires became highly impressive, and I regretted bitterly that I was to go under them instead of over them. Then came the Hoosack Tunnel, a long period of artificial night, and after that occasional exquisite glimpses of mountain and valley—Charlemont, Shelburne-Falls, and so on. The landskip grew best near the end of the Berkshire region, when the lovely valley of the Deerfield River open'd up in full sunny expansiveness. Then came the now-familiar Greenfield, and the picturesque run along Miller's River thro' Orange to Athol, where I once more, after near a month and a half, sett foot upon my native Novanglian soil! GOD SAVE THE KING!

My visit to Athol was of the most extream pleasantness; Mr. Cook being ever the most gracious of hosts, and the young weird author H. Warner Munn, Esq., being a companion of the greatest charm and congeniality. Mr. Cook's country-seat is in the township of Phillipston, adjoining Athol proper; a region whose beauty and atmosphere make it the very quintessence of traditional New-England. What a place to be in after a long voyage amongst alien scenes! Rolling stony hills, narrow, winding, rutted roads, stone walls, antient apple-orchards, sparsely scatter'd white farmhouses with trim gables peeping above the brier-bushes of wall-travers'd hill-crests—if this be not New-England, what is? My host's estate is a rural dwelling of the traditional kind, sett on high ground with one of the most magnificent agrestick landskip effects conceivable; as regards both foreground and far horizon of hills beyond hills. At one point a blue lakelet glistens among pines. No other estate is in sight—just stone walls, green fields, distant hills, and the rambling, scatter'd buildings of a typical New-England farm. It is a poem in real life—and the interior of the house prov'd quite compatible with the exterior scene; low ceilings, glamorous atticks, and other suitable appurtenances leaving nothing to be desir'd by the lover of century'd beauty and background.

The town of Athol itself I have describ'd many times before, so I need not here dwell upon its pleasing qualities. It remains to be said, that my stay in this region was enliven'd by many coach trips provided by Messrs. Cook and Munn, amongst them being one of the scene of my sojourn of the previous year—the exquisite and magical hills of Brattleboro, in Vermont. The day of this trip was ideal in its conditions, and I found Vermont fully as marvellous in its mystick grace as I found it in 1927 and 1928. We pay'd a call upon the gentle bucolick poet Arthur Goodenough, whose lovely hillside seat I have so often and so rapturously describ'd; finding him at work upon his fences in the wooded hills behind his house, and enjoying the breathlessly marvellous panoramas afforded by every hilltop prospect. The sumptuous rustick fare offer'd us, and the ride back to Athol in the afternoon's golden light, are things not soon to be forgotten. Another trip lay through the Westminster region, where I was a summer visitor in the year 1899,[19] and of which I retain'd many boyhood memories. The scene hath chang'd but little since then, and all the houses were familiar to me. Even the families are the same—tho' of course the old folks are no more.

At length the time arriv'd for me to return to my accustom'd Rhode-Island scenes, and my host very courteously gave me transportation thither in his coach. On a pleasant late-spring day we set out down the lovely Petersham-Barre road, enjoying the typical Massachusetts vistas, and the dense sylvan stretches belonging to the Harvard forestry department. Petersham is a delectable hilltop village abounding in fine old houses of the white-pillar'd classick-revival sort; and maintain'd in especially good state by wealthy persons dwelling there in the summer. It was here that Judge Royall Tyler, the celebrated Vermont statesman and man of letters, led the arm'd force which finally putt down "Shays' Rebellion" in 1786, when the debt-harass'd farmers of western Massachusetts rose to the number of two thousand in an effort to abolish all litigations for indebtedness. They had besieg'd the court-houses at Worcester and Springfield, and were not subdu'd without vast effort on the part of the military. A tablet at Petersham marks the scene of their final stand. Judge Tyler vainly pursu'd the instigator, Daniel Shays, into other states, but did not succeed in capturing him. Eventually Shays was not only pardon'd by the government, but even allow'd a pension for his services in the revolution. He dy'd at Sparta, in New-York State, on the 29th of September, 1825.

Barre is a sightly New-England town with a pleasing green, and the country south of it affords some extreamly imposing vistas. We later pass'd thro' Worcester, a very pleasant city of moderate size, whose inhabitants are noted for taste and scholarship. Then came the towns and terrain of the Blackstone Valley, and finally a crossing of the line into His Majesty's Colony of Rhode-Island and Providence-Plantations! A great moment, at which I remov'd my hat as a token of reverence for my native sod. Avoiding the centre of the border city of Woonsocket, an industrial town of French population, we hit upon the broad Louisquisset Turnpike and were soon spinning southward thro' the loveliest region in the colony. Old Rhode-Island! And where, after all, can greater charm be found? At Break-Neck Hill Road we diverg'd to the eastward and travers'd the winding roads thro' the exquisite sylvan stretches of Quinsnicket, or Lincoln-Woods, my favourite haunt on fine summer afternoons. It seem'd appropriate to return to my native scenes thro' this lovely and typical part of them—and this avenue of approach sett off very ably the occasional glimpses of the distant spires and domes of OLD PROVIDENCE which hilltop moments afforded. PROVIDENCE—my native land! No sensation at any stage of my travels equall'd that with which I was animated as we drew near the scene of my birth and lifelong memories. Pawtucket was a dingy interlude. Then the line of East Avenue and Hope Street—and the PROVIDENCE urban boundary at the end of Blackstone Boulevard, known to me for thirty years and more, and the scene of my choicest bicycle rides of boyhood! Again my three-corner'd hat was rais'd from the powder'd locks of my periwig. HOME! After that but a little space to Barnes Street, then a turn under shady trees, a square or two westward to where the road touches the brink of the antient hill and vanishes into the golden sunset sky betwixt old houses—and then Number Ten! My own hearthstone at last—and all the remember'd books and furniture of my youth! It was the eighteenth of May, and I had been abroad since the fourth of April! A marvellous, pleasing, and vary'd trip in all its parts, yet providing no sight more agreeable than Old Providence, or any moment so delightful as that of my return to my cherish'd doorstep.

GOD SAVE THE KING!

EDITOR'S NOTE FP: MW 319–60. Text based on the TMS (JHL). One of the longest, and perhaps the best, of HPL's travelogues. Written in a flawless eighteenth-century idiom, it recounts HPL's exhaustive travels in April and May of 1929, in which he first visited Vrest Orton in Yonkers, N.Y., then headed south to visit numerous historical sites in Virginia (Richmond, Williamsburg, Jamestown, Yorktown, Fredericksburg), then returned north through Washington, D.C. (which HPL had first visited in 1925 [see n. 11]) and on up to Kingston, Hurley, and New Paltz in upstate New York. He then re-entered New England by way of Athol, Mass. The essay exists as a typescript, so it was presumably circulated among his colleagues, although there is no evidence of this either in HPL's extant letters (where the essay is never mentioned) or in any extant replies by his correspondents. The date of the essay's writing is uncertain, but it was probably written not long after HPL's return home on 18 May.

Notes

1. HPL himself and his wife Sonia had, in 1924, planned to settle in such a "development" in the Bryn Mawr Park region of Yonkers. They had purchased a home lot from the Homeland Company of 28 North Broadway in Yonkers, but their financial difficulties forced them to give it up.

2. Some aspects of this person's character were incorporated into the character of the madman Arthur Feldon in HPL's revision of Adolphe de Castro's "The Electric Executioner" (1929).

3. William Byrd (1674–1744) was a Virginia planter and lawyer who wrote several scientific and historical works, published posthumously as *The Westover Manuscripts* (1841).

4. This is the correspondence to Poe's godfather John Allan, used by Hervey Allen in his biography *Israfel* (1927; *LL* 18).

5. Poe's poem "To Helen" (1848)—not to be confused with the celebrated poem of the same title (1831)—was addressed to Sarah Helen (Power) Whitman (1803–1878), of Providence. The words "enchanted garden" appear in l. 9.

6. Mary Johnston (1870–1936), American novelist and author of *Audrey* (1902). She is best known for *To Have and to Hold* (1900). Most of her novels are set in Virginia.

7. Sir John Harington (1561–1612), "Of Treason," *Epigrams* (1615).

8. "A prosperous and beneficial crime is called virtue." Seneca the Younger (4 B.C.E.–65 C.E.), *Hercules Furens* 251–52.

9. See further "An Account of a Trip to the Antient Fairbanks House . . ." (p. 62).

10. The Library of Congress's Jefferson Building (1888–97) was designed by John L. Smithmeyer, Paul J. Pelz, and Edward Pearce Casey. HPL was related to Casey through his great-grandmother, M. Roby Rathbun.

11. Edward Lloyd Sechrist (1873–1953), beekeeper, amateur journalist, and colleague of HPL. He, along with Anne Tillery Renshaw, had guided HPL and George Kirk on a whirlwind one-day tour of Washington, D.C., on 11 April 1925.

12. Bernard Austin Dwyer (1897–1943), weird fiction fan and artist, had gotten in touch with HPL through *Weird Tales* in early 1927.

13. Dwyer was then living at 177 Green Street, a house that no longer survives.

14. Cf. Adriaen and Trintje Sleght in HPL's revision of William Lumley's "The Diary of Alonzo Typer" (1936). (These and all other character names in this story are of HPL's devising.)

15. Harold Donaldson Eberlein, *The Architecture of Colonial America* (Boston: Little, Brown, 1921; *LL* 290).

16. "Geoffrey Crayon" was the pseudonym under which Washington Irving published *The Sketch Book* (1819) and *The Crayon Miscellany* (1835).

17. A Squire Hasbrouck is mentioned in HPL's revision of Hazel Heald's "The Man of Stone" (1932), set in the upper Adirondacks.

18. Thomas Gray, *Elegy Written in a Country Churchyard* (1751), l. 16.

19. HPL elsewhere reports laconically that "I spent the summer of 1899 with my mother" (*SL* 2.348). The trip was taken after HPL's first year of formal schooling at the Slater Avenue School (1898–99).

AN ACCOUNT OF A TRIP TO THE ANTIENT FAIRBANKS HOUSE, IN DEDHAM, AND TO THE RED HORSE TAVERN IN SUDBURY, IN THE PROVINCE OF THE MASSACHUSETTS-BAY

Taken by H: Lovecraft, Gent., of Providence, In Rhode-Island,
on the 5th of August, 1929, from 9 a.m. to 7 p.m.

Having long wish'd to behold the Red Horse Tavern, in Sudbury, made famous as the "Wayside Inn" in the verses of Prof. Longfellow,[1] I one morning embarkt upon a tour thither, conducted by one A: Johnson, Esq., of Providence, who frequently accommodates paying passengers in his easie-running and capacious chaise. The day cou'd not have been better or sunnier; and it being my good-fortune to sitt upon the front seat of the coach, I soon fell into conversation with Mr. Johnson, the gentleman driver, as we bowl'd along the Pawtucket Turnpike toward the Province of the Massa-chusetts-Bay. By a lucky chance I learn'd that he design'd to keep along the Boston road as far as Roxbury before turning north; which reminded me that we must inevita-bly pass thro' the antient town of Dedham, where lyes the old Fairbanks house, oldest building in New-England, and oldest frame building of English origin on the continent of North-America. Now I had never seen this structure, tho' near as anxious to do so as to see the Red Horse itself; so on this occasion lost no time in recommending to Mr. Johnson that he seek it out and give his sightseeing passengers a glimpse of it. Being no mean judge of antiquities, he attended my discourse with interest, and finally decided to follow out my suggestion.

The road toward Boston is a highly attractive one, and I was glad to renew my ac-quaintance with such sights as Wrentham's village green, with white-steepled New-England church rising gracefully above it. After passing the villages of Pawtucket, North-Attleboro, Plainville, Wrentham, Walpole, and Norwood, we at length reacht Dedham, whose sleepy green and antient buildings make it ever pleasing to my eye. I some time intend to explore this town on foot, and in much detail.

Inquiring the situation of the Fairbanks house from obliging villagers, we diverg'd from the green down a road lin'd with great willows, cross'd the rail-road track, and went a short space among verdant fields. Very soon, beyond a tumbled stone wall on our right, we beheld an infinitely picturesque line of grey, sagging roofs; and knew that we had come upon the object of our quest—the hoary and rambling homestead of the Fairbanks family, built in 1636, the year that Roger Williams landed on the uninhab-ited shoar in the lee of the hill which was to be Providence—only six years after the founding of Boston!

This oldest of all New-England houses, made familiar to the public by many popu-lar pictures, wood-carvings, and clay bas-reliefs, is built of massive timbers from Old England; probably parts of a ship dismantled in Boston Harbour. Stout British oak, des-tined to endure thro' uncounted millennia, and typifying the staunch fibre of the peer-less race that made New-England what it is. GOD SAVE THE KING! The house, which hath been study'd with the minutest care by the eminent Providence antiquar-ian Norman Morrison Isham,[2] is believ'd to have undergone no changes whatever since the early eighteenth century. Wings were added to the original part in 1641 and 1648, and in the early 1700's the peaked roofs of the wings (but not that of the original part) were made gambrel according to the universal fashion of that time. The house hath never been out of the family, and is now own'd and operated as a publick museum by the Fairbanks Family of America, Incorporated. The atmosphere of the place is beyond description—*antiquity—hoary antiquity—immemorial antientness and kinship to elder and forgotten worlds—*

The walls and roof are in places oddly sunken, and present an ineffably picturesque silhouette as seen from the road, but modern engineering skill hath remov'd the possibil-ity of further decay or collapse. Here it stands—unique in its age, fascinating in its col-ourful irregularity—cobwebb'd atticks, staircases everywhere, steps up and down from room to room, vast beams, wooden-pegg'd and markt with vestiges of hand-hewing, great fireplaces, titanick chimney of Old English brick, massive woodwork blacken'd by smoak and long centuries, curiously slanting floors, archaick latches, queer, half-forgotten kinds of furniture and household utilities—in fine, all the subtle earmarks of long continuous living; bringing down to the present the faint, strange, stirring echoes of 1636, when New-England was a frail infant colony clinging to the seacoast, and this house was a bold outpost sett on the edge of black unknown woods, haunted by shadowy daemons and reaching none knew whither. For once I forgot my periwigg'd membership in the rational eighteenth century, and allow'd my self to be ingulph'd by the sinister sorcery of the dark seventeenth. Verily, this was the most poignantly imagination-stirring house I had ever seen. . . . I cou'd hear the sound of the builder's axe in the nighted woods three hundred years ago, when King Charles the First, still unmartyr'd by Roundhead treason, sate on the throne, and the lone, questing canoe of Roger Williams and his companions dug its prow into the sand of Moshassuck's pathless shoar, not four squares downhill from the spot where I now am seated. The custodian of the house is a true Fairbanks, of the ninth generation from Jonathan Fayerbanke of Sowerby, near Halifax, in Yorkshire, who came to the young Massachusetts-Bay and built this sightly edifice. He truly appreciates his charge, and conducts visitors about with a highly erudite courtesy. There are on sale in the parlour many pictures, pieces of chinaware, and diverse reliques, including a fine reprint of the famous New-England Primer, indispensable adjunct of every New-England child of the late seventeenth and eighteenth centuries.[3] I have several copies of this historick work, but purchas'd another to give an adopted grandchild of mine who hath been travelling in the Province of Quebeck and whose soul is in sad need of reclamation from Frenchify'd ways and the cursed snares of Popery.[4] God Save the King! Mr. Johnson, the conductor of the tour, profest the most extream gratitude toward me for acquainting him with this distinguisht shrine of the past; and declar'd he meant to include it in future in all tours extending thro' Dedham. Thus I shall be responsible for an enlargement of the itinerary of one of the most well-regarded coach touring systems in the Providence-Plantations!

From Dedham we proceeded northward toward Sudbury, the seat of the Red Horse Tavern; passing thro' the region call'd Norumbega, on the upper reaches of the Charles. It is here that the late Prof. Horsford conceiv'd the remains of a Northmen's city to exist—professing to trace the Indian name of *Norumbega* to *Norway*, and constructing a whole fantasticall history of the region on the most absurdly groundless evidence.[5] He even went so far as to sett up a stone tower and "historical" tablet there in 1889—on the river-bank, in a beautiful stretch of countryside now preserv'd by the Metropolitan Park Commission of Boston. At my suggestion Mr. Johnson detour'd to inspect this tower, whose naive inscription cou'd not be perus'd without a smile.

At length, after traversing a sunny and tranquil countryside of the most pleasing description, we arriv'd at the celebrated Red Horse Tavern, 23 miles from Boston, which hath lately been cut off from lines of heavy travel by the construction of a new stretch of main highway to divert passing vehicles—a task undertaken by the tavern's present owner, Henry Ford, Esq., a very respectable coach-maker. The antient hostelry, once fronting directly upon the road, is shelter'd from the present avenue of access by a series of paths and gardens; and is densely embower'd by great trees. The fine old colonial doorway hath been barbarously malform'd to make room for a tawdry modern porch, and the neighbouring coach-house is now the seat of a primitive spinning industry, conducted by two venerable gentlewomen of Boston. Across the road is the stable mention'd in Mr. Longfellow's verses, "Tales of a Wayside Inn"; now harbouring sheep, oxen, horses, and some pleasing and curious vehicles of former times— a coach, a calash, and a clos'd sleigh of the eighteenth century. Not far away can be found a fine old stone water-mill with blithely turning wheel, and a small schoolhouse of the late eighteenth century, mov'd from Sterling, in the Massachusetts-Bay, and celebrated as the scene of the incident which created the well-known juvenile doggerel of "Mary's Lamb". This schoolhouse is fitted up with old-fashion'd benches and teacher's desk, and is situate in a pine grove just off a winding bye-road, in a manner very suitable and natural to colonial seats of instruction.

But naturally the tavern itself is the object of chief interest. It is a prodigiously vast structure of three storeys, wings, and attick, and hath a dormer-lined gambrel roof which cannot be part of the original design, since the date of the house is sett variously from 1683 to 1689. It hath since 1714 been a tavern, conducted by various generations of the Howe family till the extinction of that antient and armigerous line (it was common in colonial New-England for gentry to engage in tavern-keeping), and latterly re-open'd by Mr. Ford. Persons of the most distinguisht quality have been its guests, including Genl. Washington, the Marquis de La Fayette, Danl: Webster, Esq., and Prof. Longfellow the poet; and the rooms tenanted by them are markt for the information of posterity. The interior is restor'd as nearly as possible to its colonial condition; and the antient sign of the Red Horse, long mislay'd and forgotten, hath been putt back to that spot where for centuries it creak'd in the wind. Within are display'd some panes of glass originally in the windows, scratcht upon in convivial verse by the diamond ring of that loyal young officer of His Majesty, Major William Molineaux, to whom Prof. Longfellow and Mr. Hawthorne both made reference in their writings.[6]

Entering at the front door, the visitor beholds a long hallway extending to the rear of the building, with a staircase rising on the right. Near the foot of the stairs a door leads into the antient tap-room; where tables, settles, bottles, mantelpiece, wainscoting, adornments, utilities, and great iron safe are still in their accustom'd places; and where the high bar with adjustable grating is used as a vending-place for postcards, publications, and billets of admission. In the narrow passage betwixt tap-room and dining-room the old panell'd wall is nearly hackt to pieces at one spot on the left. This is where colonial landlords used to stick carelessly and conveniently into the wall, as an arrow in the flesh of its victim, the sharp bottle-opener (like a modern ice-pick) which preceded the invention of the corkscrew, and which was frequently call'd upon for employment. The colonial dining-room, an extreamly antient apartment with dark panelling, is all set with pewter plates, knives, forks, and porringers for a party of Georgian gentry—perhaps Major Molineaux and some fellow-roysterers—and forms one of the most attractive spots in the house. Opening off this is the venerable kitchen, with vast fireplace, long wooden table for the servants, and numerous culinary devices of great ingenuity and elaborateness, including a clockwork turnspit of a sort rarely found in the colonies.

On the other side of the great hallway is the famous parlour so exactly describ'd in Prof. Longfellow's poem. All the articles mention'd in those verses have been reclaim'd from the various owners to whom they were sold after the last Howe's death, and have been sett back into place so that the author wou'd think nothing chang'd since the period of his observation. Here may be found all the familiar objects dear to the reader— the How* coat-of-arms, the tall, sombre clock, the portrait of Princess Mary (daughter to George the Second), and so on. Prof. Longfellow and his friends were extreamly fond of the inn, and visited there at various times; tho' they were never assembled all at once under its roof as in the poem. Upstairs all the rooms are appropriately adorn'd (except a Victorian room dedicated to the inventor Mr. Edison), and an old-fashione'd assembly-hall or ball-room extends the whole length of a very capacious wing whose

---

*Earlier spelling of the name Howe.

ground floor is a dining-hall. The third storey and attick are not open except to the guests of the tavern. On the read of the building an immense and very new wing hath been added; its ground floor a dining-hall, and its upper floor an assembly-hall, so that it really duplicates the older wing. This intrusion, owing to the size and tree-girt situation of the building, is fortunately invisible from the front.

Altogether, the Red Horse is as adequate a survival of colonial publick hospitality as it hath ever been my good-fortune to behold; and I rejoice that it is still so well maintain'd. Mr. Ford, the present landlord, employs guides to conduct visitors about and explain the history of the place; whilst food and lodgings can be obtain'd for a proper consideration. Tho' hard to discover from the relocated highroad, and scorning the cheapnesses of advertisement, the tavern is crouded with guests who come in their coaches. Unfortunately it is near no regular line of publick transportation—and the nearest village is some three miles away. It is clos'd upon Sundays, save to guests sleeping under its roof.

Having spent some hours at the Red Horse, the Johnson coaching-party return'd to Providence by the way of Marlboro, Framingham, Holliston, Milford, Franklin, Woonsocket, and Pawtucket; traversing a high country of pleasing aspect, adorn'd with numerous lakes and boasting many imposing prospects of distant hills and vales. I reacht home in the golden sunset, and was courteously deposited at the door of my residence by the obliging Mr. Johnson. As a whole, the excursion was one of singularly delightful nature; enliven'd as it was by the element of surprise and unexpectedness display'd in the inclusion of the Fairbanks house in the itinerary.

EDITOR'S NOTE Unpublished; text based on the TMS (JHL). A brief but piquant travelogue of a one-day trip to two ancient sites in Massachusetts, undertaken about two months after HPL returned from his extensive travels of spring and summer 1929.

Notes

1. Henry Wadsworth Longfellow (1807–1882), *Tales of a Wayside Inn* (1863), a collection of 21 narrative poems built around a framework similar to that of Chaucer's *Canterbury Tales.*

2. Norman Morrison Isham (1864–1943), head of the architectural department at the Rhode Island School of Design (1912–20, 1923–33) and a lecturer on architectural history. HPL owned his booklet, *The Meeting House of the First Baptist Church in Providence: A History of the Fabric* (1925; LL 465).

3. *The New England Primer* was a "little Bible" designed to instruct the young, chiefly in matters of religion. The earliest extant edition dates to 1727, but probably the first edition is much earlier. Its compiler is unknown. HPL quotes its celebrated couplet "In Adam's fall / We sinned all" in a letter of 1931 (SL 3.409), going on to say that his family owned three different editions.

4. Possibly Frank Belknap Long.

5. Eben Norton Horsford (1818–1893), professor of chemistry at Lawrence Scientific School (1847–63). See such works as *Discovery of America by Northmen* (1888) and *The Discovery of the Ancient City of Norumbega* (1890).

6. The proper spelling is Molineux. See Longfellow's "Prelude" to Part I of *Tales of a Wayside Inn* and Nathaniel Hawthorne's "My Kinsman, Major Molineux" (1832; in *The Snow-Image and Other Twice-Told Tales*, 1851).

ACCOUNT OF A VISIT TO CHARLESTON, S.C.

April 28th, 1930, et seq.

Confronted by a dizzying embarrassment of riches which it would be impossible to weave into a suitable travelogue of less than book length, I take my pen in hand to convey at least a microscopic notion of what I beheld upon my late visit to that apex of colonial antiquity—Charleston, South-Carolina. That I was wholly captivated, goes without saying. The place was meant for my old bones—to say nothing of my old tastes and historic yearnings. Truly, I did not know that such miraculous survivals existed!

As I stated on a former postcard, I travelled day and night from New York by motor coach; stopping nowhere save to change vehicles at Washington, Richmond, Winston-Salem, N.C., and Columbia, S.C. This procedure turned out to be very well-advised, insomuch as every moment spent away from Charleston betwixt Septr. 15th and May 15th is a sheer waste of time. Never have I beheld a place which appeals more thoroughly to me. The climate is marvellous and summer-like—palmettos, live-oaks, creeping vines, wisteria, jasmine, azaleas, etc., etc. everywhere, and the thermometer up around 75° and 80° in April and May. Nearly everyone was wearing a straw hat, and it was possible to sit outdoors all day and enjoy it. Most of my reading and writing were done either in ancient Battery Park—looking out across the harbour toward Ft. Sumter of Civil War fame—or in Washington Square, in the lee of a statue of William Pitt set up in 1770. The atmosphere made me feel 20 years younger and 100% better—indeed, I seemed to have a genuine surplus of energy for the first time since the preceding August. The sea-breeze was always blowing, and I became as tanned as an Indian in two days.

But the climate was only the beginning of the miracle from my antiquarian standpoint. The truly important and distinctive thing about the place is its astonishingly eighteenth-century atmosphere—for in all verity I can say that Charleston is the best-preserved colonial city of any size, without exception, that I have ever encountered. Virtually *everything* is just as it was in the reign of George the Third—indeed, it is easier to count the houses which are *not* colonial, than to attempt to count those which *are*. The inhabitants are by nature conservative, and have never changed their major housebuilding fashions through all the years, except for trifling Victorian lapses in extending the northern fringe of the city and in replacing the buildings burnt in the fire of 1861 (an event *not* connected with the Civil War). On account of the climate, these edifices differ somewhat from the structures of the northern colonies; usually having piazzas on all three storeys of the southern or western side. This is a feature developed shortly after 1750; houses before that date being more of the general Colonial or British Georgian type. There are even a few cases of the New England gambrel roof—a design perhaps picked up by Charleston mariners on voyages to Salem or Newport, but soon abandoned because of its unsuitability for a warm region. Houses in Charleston are generally of brick with stucco exterior, and the general details and contours shew more latitude and individuality than elsewhere. Tiled roofs are a distinctive feature, this fashion having been introduced after 1735. Gables and chimney-pots follow odd and varied patterns, and exhibit what is perhaps a Dutch influence transmitted through Huguenot immigrants. In general, the skyline of Charleston is more European in a Continental sense than is that of any other American city.

The public buildings, dating from 1767 to 1800 and after, are of monumental magnificence; nearly all in the classic Grecian manner, and of such solid workmanship as to be well-nigh imperishable. There are likewise many excellent churches and steeples; of which my favourite is St. Michael's, erected in 1762, whose sweet-toned chimes dominate the aural atmosphere of the city. This was visible from my Y.M.C.A. window.[1] The most picturesque of all is the old Unitarian church in Archdale Avenue; one of those very rare specimens of revived Gothick built in Georgian times—perhaps as an echo of the antiquarians which produced Horace Walpole's "Strawberry Hill". It was erected in 1772, yet is in every detail a fine type of English pointed Gothick. The churchyard is the very last word in glamorousness—a perfumed green tropic twilight of twisted-branched, overarching live-oaks and hanging vines, with ancient headstones peeping through a vivid, verdurous undergrowth threaded by curious winding walks. It is really something out of a dream—such things do not belong to the waking world! In this enchanted spot are interred the remains of the Rev. Samuel Gilman, author of the college hymn "Fair Harvard";[2] who was for 40 years pastor of the church, and to whom a Memorial Room in the tower has been established by Harvard alumni. As coincidence would have it, I saw Dr. Gilman's birthplace in 1927—the famous Sargent-Murray-Gilman house in Middle St., Gloucester, Mass.

One of the most famous features of Charleston is its profusion of wrought-iron work—gates, balconies, window grilles, railings, and the like; all of the finest craftsmanship. The gates are especially numerous because or the prevalence of high-walled gardens in this land of luxurious flowers, rambling vines, and opulent trees that weave an omnipresent green twilight redolent of perfume and musical with bird-song when the sun goes down. Charlestonians endeavour to secure privacy and the open air at the same time.

Another phase of Charleston is represented by the sea islands that bound the harbour, one of which—the Isle of Palms—is reputed to possess the finest beach on the Atlantic Coast. Of these, my own chief interest centres in Sullivan's Island, which contains Ft. Moultrie, where Poe served in 1829 as "Corp. Edgar A. Perry". Many of the scenes of "The Gold-Bug" were laid upon this island, and it gave me a thrill to visit in person a region familiar to me in literature for above thirty years.

Of the general history of Charleston, I need here give only the briefest outline. The original settlement was made in 1670 on the west bank of the Ashley river by some colonists under Col. W^m. Sayle. Ten years later they removed to the narrowish, Manhattan-shaped peninsula betwixt the Ashley and Cooper rivers, and founded the still-existing town on its present site. It is this second founding in 1680 whose 250th anniversary is this year commemorated by a special postage stamp.

The colony prospered exceedingly despite wars with pirates, Florida Spaniards, and Indians, and despite several disastrous hurricanes, fires, and yellow-fever epidemics. In the course of time it received many valuable accessions—gentlemen-adventurers from England, Ireland, and Scotland, opprest Huguenots from France, and solid planters from the West Indies. The best settlers established themselves inland as planters; raising rice and indigo, but living much in Charleston because of the malaria infesting the interior lowlands in summer. Their wealth and taste built up an exceedingly rich and mature civilisation; equalling or surpassing any other in the country so far as I can judge. Just before the Revolution Charleston was one of the foremost cities in all America—sharing honours with Boston, Newport, New-York, Phil^a., Annapolis, and Alexandria. During the Revolution the town was besieged by a British fleet, but held out till 1780, when the forces of Sir Henry Clinton and Lord Rawdon moved in and took up headquarters at the Brewton-Pringle house in King St.—a mansion of much splendour, which I explored very thoroughly during my visit.

After the Revolution the town (now chartered as a city and changing its name from *Charles-Town* to the present form *Charleston*) regained its prosperity; having meanwhile suffered but little change in manners and emotions. It was still discriminating and cultivated in temper, notwithstanding the democratic fallacies into which its politics had been betrayed. The invention of the cotton-gin gave the planters a new source of revenue, so that from 1800 to the Civil War there was not a prouder or more cultured city in the Western Hemisphere. But the war produced collapse and stagnation, and since then the material importance of Charleston has been less great. It has, however, retained its eighteenth-century standard of taste and learning; so that I doubt if there be at this moment a more suitable place on this continent for a gentleman to live in. It forms the last stand of our genuine hereditary civilisation—agricultural, individualistic, qualitative, and leisurely—as distinguished from the intrusive mongrel barbarism brought about by the new era of speed, quantity, time-tables, trade, and machinery.

Charleston, as before stated, is on a peninsula shaped somewhat like Manhattan Island, and the arrangement of streets is not dissimilar. King (business) and Meeting (residences and small business) are the principal longitudinal streets from west to east, whilst Tradd, Broad, and Calhoun are the best-known transverse streets from south to north. The best residential section is in Meeting St. below Broad, culminating in the park-like South Battery at the tip of the peninsula. The quaintest streets, alleys, squares, and hidden courtyards are also below Broad. The principal commercial waterfront is on the east side along the Cooper river, where scores of abandoned and ruined warehouses tell a tale of former prosperity. As in Newport and Salem, relatively few of the ancient houses are ever demolisht; and the population appear to appreciate their history and background very keenly. Views and guidebooks are more easily procurable than in most old towns. Besides using these I spent any entire day of historical-architectural research at the public library in order to make my enjoyment as full and comprehending as possible. The odd ramifications to follow up are almost numberless—the subject of *street cries* alone being worth a full volume of close research. Niggers are exceedingly numerous and incredibly black, but know their place to perfection. Foreigners are gratifyingly scarce.

EDITOR'S NOTE Unpublished; text based on the AMS (JHL). A kind of synopsis or rough draft of a travelogue of Charleston, South Carolina, which HPL visited from 28 April to 9 May 1930. It is likely addressed to HPL's aunt, Lillian D. Clark, to whom he customarily sent long letters recounting his travels (although no letters to Lillian for this period survive).

Notes

1. The Y.M.C.A. on George Street is no longer extant.

2. Samuel Gilman (1791–1858), Unitarian minister and poet, wrote "Fair Harvard" in 1836, for the 200th anniversary of Harvard College.

AN ACCOUNT OF *CHARLESTON*, IN HIS MAJ^TY's PROVINCE OF *SOUTH-CAROLINA*,

Design'd for the Information of Travellers to that Place,
And for the Generall Instruction of the Curious.
By
H. Lovecraft, Gent.,
Of *Providence*, in *New-England*
MDCCCCXXX

I. The History and Civilisation of Charleston

In considering the town of Charleston, it is proper to take notice of the generall region to which it belongs, and to survey the events of history that extend behind it. The province of Carolina, lying just north of those parts of Florida settled by the earliest Spanish explorers, was first peopled by white men in the year 1562, when the French Huguenot Jean Ribaut establish'd a colony at Port-Royal, on the southerly part of the coast. The settlers number'd but thirty or less, and were confin'd in a miserable log fort; but great hopes were harbour'd for a vast French commonwealth, and the country was named *Carolina* in honour of King Charles the Ninth. Driven by hardship and home-sickness, the Huguenots in the following year deserted their colony and sett out for Europe in a rudely built vessel; but in 1564 another colony was brought to America by Laudonniere, and establish'd at the mouth of the St. John's River in Florida. This being within the limits of Spanish settlement, it was mov'd against by Spain in the year 1565; the attack led by Pedro Menendez, who during his campaign built the fort of St. Augustine, destin'd to survive as the oldest continuous white settlement north of Mex-ico on this continent. Menendez surpris'd the French garrison and slew all the inhabi-tants of the St. John's colony, disregarding age and sex; later capturing the French arm'd forces under Ribaut and dedicating them to massacre and slavery. This ended the at-tempts of France to colonise the lower Atlantick seaboard, tho' shortly afterward the French Papist Dominic de Gourges led an expedition of revenge which wiped out the Spanish garrison on the St. John's. When Menendez murther'd the French settlers, he had left a placard saying that he had slain them "not as Frenchmen, but as hereticks". De Gourges, having hang'd the Spanish garrison, left a sinister retaliatory note declaring he had punished the men "not as Spaniards, but as assassins".

After this we behold the Spaniards in full possession of Florida, with Carolina largely uncolonis'd to the northward. The true history of the present province begins in the year 1663; when, claiming the region by right of exploration, our English monarch, Charles II, Whom God Save, granted the land betwixt Virginia and Florida to a com-pany of gentlemen-proprietors compos'd of my Ld Clarendon, the High-Chancellor; Genl Monk, Duke of Albemarle; Anthony Ashley Cooper, First Earl of Shaftesbury; my Ld Craven; my Ld Berkeley; Sir J: Collaton; Sir G^o. Carteret; and Sir W: Berkeley, Gov-ernor of Virginia. From two of these gentlemen were nam'd *Albemarle* Sound, and the *Ashley* and *Cooper* Rivers. The name of the country was suffer'd to stand unchang'd, tho' now interpreted to honour the memory of His Martyr'd Britannick Majesty *Charles the First,* rather than the old French King. Vivat *Carolus Secundus,* Rex Britannorum!

At this time there were no white men in Carolina, except the few planters in the northern part who had straggled down from Virginia. These, in 1663, were made provisionally into a colony call'd *Albemarle.* In the year 1664 my Ld Clarendon's name was given to another small colony of gentlemen planters from the West Indies, some 25 miles up the Cape Fear River. All these settlements, of course, were within what is now North-Carolina.

The history of the present *South-Carolina* begins with the very settlement we are about to study, when in 1669 the proprietors sent out two shiploads of colonists to form a town on the Ashley River, near where it joins the sea in an excellent natural harbour. This group of 160, which included several women, were under the leadership of Col. William Sayle; and built their "Towne of Trade" on the Ashley's west bank, where two creeks (since call'd Orange Grove and Old Town Creeks) empty into the larger stream. At this time the two great neighbouring rivers were known by their Indian names of *Kiawah* (Ashley) and *Wando.* The new settlement was call'd at first Albemarle Point, and later Charles-Town, in His reigning Maj$^{ty's}$ honour.

The governance of the new colony was of a very philosophick sort, and may be taken to represent an application of theory to politicks such as Plato, or Sir T. More, wou'd have approved of. The plan of organisation and administration, called *The Grand Model,* was drawn up by My Ld Shaftesbury (then Lord Ashley), under the advice of the eminent philosopher Mr. John Locke, then resident with his L^{d}ship at Exeter House as private secretary; and was believed by its authors to be as perfect a scheme of rule as the human mind is capable of conceiving.

This enlighten'd constitution was of a wholesomely aristocraticall sort, and establish'd the Church of England throughout the Colony, whilst permitting other sects full

Plan Illustrating Early History of Charles-Town.

liberty of worship. Carolina was made a *County Palatine,* wherein the Crown may delegate royall powers to one man for defence against enemies. Rank was apportion'd thro' the ownership of land; severall orders of nobility being fixt and endow'd with appropriate powers. A *landgrave* held 48,000 acres; a *cassique* (taken from yᵉ Indian title *cacique*) 24,000; and a *baron* 12,000. These titles were not, however, commonly us'd as modes of address; the social ranks of the parent country being retain'd in ordinary as distinguisht from political usage. The lower orders, comprising those not granted land by the Lords Proprietors, had no political power, but were consider'd as attach'd to the soil. As years pass'd, and the influence of the non-landed classes increas'd, the provisions of the Grand Model were repeatedly attack'd, and finally fell into desuetude. It is probable that it had never been fully liv'd up to, and the government of proprietors was superseded by direct royall authority; the province being divided into North and South Carolina, and governors being appointed by the Crown. Black slaves were first brought in by the Governor Sir John Yeamans, who came from Barbadoes with his own niggers and sett the fashion for their ownership amongst others. Most of the large, negro-owning planters came from the West Indies and settled on plantations along Goose Creek, an affluent of the Cooper River somewhat above Charles-Town. Other immigrants were of humbler classes, largely dissenters, who arriv'd in large numbers from various places and settled in the town or elsewhere.

The Lords Proprietors were from the first sensible of the poor defencibleness of the original Town of Trade, and as early as 1671 took note of the superior strategick value of the neighbouring narrow peninsula betwixt the Ashley and Cooper Rivers. In that year a new town on this peninsula was propos'd, the site being thus describ'd by Mr. Dalton, Secretary of the Grand Council of Carolina, in a letter to my Lᵈ Ashley (Shaftesbury):

> "It must of necessity be very healthy, being free from any noxious vapours, and all the summer long being refresh'd with continual cool breathings from the sea, which up in the country men are not soe fully sensible of."

This site, already thinly inhabited since 1672, was then call'd Oyster Point, and in 1679 my Lᵈ Ashley order'd Governor West to build and settle on it according to a very fixt and ambitious plan; it being clearly his design to make it the chief town of the colony. In the following year the orders were acted on, and after that the old town fell largely into disuse; being formally abandon'd in 1682, and sinking finally to a meer plantation. It is this founding of the *new town* which, in the eyes of recent historians, forms the true birth of *Charleston* (for the name *Charles-Town* became quickly transferr'd to it); and which is now receiving special celebration upon its 250ᵗʰ anniversary.

In order to secure perfect defence against the Spaniards and Indians, the new Charles-Town of 1680 was very strongly fortify'd by means of breastworks, which soon develop'd into a full line of city walls, with bastions, salients, and guard posts at the gates. According to the plan of the Lords Proprietors, put into effect by Surveyors-General Culpepper and Bull to as great an extent as possible (for the original design was too ambitious for use), the town was to have regular streets; a great street 100 to 120 feet wide, lesser streets not under 60 feet wide, and alleys 8 or 10 feet wide—the whole protected by a palisado and ditch against the Indians. Around the town for half a mile outside the walls was to extend a common without any buildings whatsoever. As it turned out, the town became a narrow parallelogram 4 squares long and 3 wide, fronting on the Cooper River and bounded on the south by Van der Horst's Creek—now fill'd in and forming the line of Water St. The western boundary corresponded to the present Meeting St., having here a wall, gate, and drawbridge. Places were reserv'd

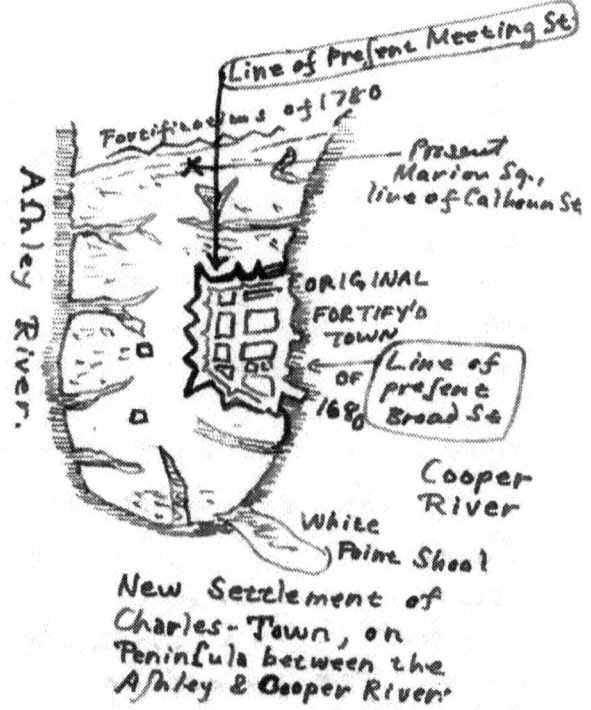

Line of Present Meeting St
Fortification s of 1780
Present Marion Sq., line of Calhoun St
Ashley River.
ORIGINAL FORTIFY'D TOWN OF 1680
Line of present Broad St
Cooper River
White Point Shoal
New Settlement of Charles-Town, on Peninsula between the Ashley & Cooper Rivers.

for a church, a town hall, and a parade-ground. The north-and-south streets, from the river-front inward, were Bay, Church, and Meeting; whilst the east-and-west ones, from the south boundary upward, were Tradd (nam'd from the first white child born in the town), Elliott, Broad, and Dock (afterward Queen).

The town very soon outgrew its original wall'd space, and by 1700 had spread desultorily westward to the Ashley River. Many liv'd outside the walls on small farms, and the peninsula was order'd cleared of heavy vegetation to destroy Indian ambushes. The decade 1679–1689 brought heavy immigration, especially after the accession of James II promoted the exodus of dissenters from England. One dissenting colony of 500 was brought over in a single month by Morton and Axtell, who were made landgraves for their services. Gentlemen planters also flock'd in from Barbadoes and other West-Indian places, together with large numbers of men of every sort from England. Typical surnames, persisting to this day because of Charleston's happy immunity from value-destroying change, were Blake, Drayton, Middleton, Daniel, Moore, Ladson, Grimball, Carter, Boone, Smith, Shenking, and Izard. Lands granted to these gentlemen are still held by their descendants in the year 1930, when the world outside is sunk in chaos and decay. The first settlers were planters and merchants, trading in many cases full 1000 miles inland with the redskin salvages. In 1693 the culture of *rice* was experimentally introduc'd, and so well succeeded, that rice-planting soon became the chief pursuit of the inhabitants. The later introduction of *indigo* (1741) provided another major industry which remain'd dominant till the nineteenth-century age of cotton.

Churches very early appear'd; the Establish'd Church, the Baptists, and the Presbyterians or Congregationalists soon having houses of worship. Not long after came the French Huguenots and the Quakers, both building suitable edifices. All of these sects save the Quakers (who are extinct in Charleston, but whose adherents elsewhere maintain the antient burying-ground in King St.) still worship on their original sites; the Huguenot church being the last of its kind in America.

The Huguenots, who form'd so important an element in Charles-Town's population despite their gradual assimilation into the dominant British fabrick, came mostly betwixt 1680 and 1688, the greatest influx stimulated by the revocation of the Edict of Nantes. About 450 in all arriv'd, coming to a community of some 2500 souls. Some Dutch from New-Netherland likewise appeared, whilst in 1695 there came a body of Puritan Yankees from Dorchester, in the Province of the Massachusetts-Bay. These latter settled 20 miles from town in a place which they call'd "Dorchester"; building a meeting-house and dwelling there for half a century, but finally moving en masse into Central Georgia, whose climate they preferr'd. A small minority of them remain'd and mixt with the general population of the region. At a later date many Germans and Swiss came to Carolina, probably establishing the wrought-iron industry whose products have so added to Charles-Town's beauty. Most of them, however, did not remain on the seabord. All elements got on rather well, and with a minimum of friction except in the case of some of the Huguenots in Craven County who were slow in becoming naturalised. An homogeneous English culture overshadow'd and absorb'd all other fabricks, and the protestant faith was everywhere paramount. The Church of England, proud, select, and officially establish'd, was not numerically strong; English, Scotch, and Irish dissenters claiming in 1706 to form $^2/_3$ of the whole population. Buildings of a good type were erected (tho' none survive from the seventeenth century), and the town began early to have the air of a cultivated metropolis; presaging that later day (1773) when Josiah Quincy of Boston was to say of Charles-Town, 'that in almost every thing it far surpass'd all he ever saw, or ever expected to see, in America'.

But the history of the place was not unmark'd by turbulence. In 1682 a colony of Scotch dissenters, whose position in Scotland was becoming increasingly precarious, was establish'd at Port-Royal, semi-independently of the authorities at Charles-Town, by Henry, Ld Cardross. Disputes concerning power quickly arose with Gov. Joseph Morton of Carolina, and continu'd after Morton had been superseded by Quarry; Cardross finally resigning and returning to Scotland. In 1686 the Florida Spaniards raided the coast and burnt Port-Royal, torturing and killing its 25 inhabitants, robbing plantations, and carrying off prisoners to St. Augustine. Only two or three Scotchmen escaped to carry the news to Charles-Town, where it was receiv'd with varying sentiments. Most of the population wish'd to punish the Spaniards at once, but delay was caus'd by the new Governor, Sir Jas: Collaton, who sided with the papist King James II, and did not wish to attack the Spanish Catholicks on behalf of the murther'd dissenters. This difference led to an encreas'd friction betwixt the general inhabitants and the Lords Proprietors, which culminated in 1719 in the abolishment of the proprietors' government and the establishment of Carolina as a direct Royall province. The year 1699 was marked by an epidemick of yellow fever, and by a vast hurricane and flood. Fever, long the chief scourge of Charleston, has now been largely eradicated by medical science; tho' the gales of late August and September are still to be reckon'd with. Even these, however, are made less disastrous by stouter sea-walls and the better building construction of the eighteenth century.

It was in the eighteenth century that there finally flower'd and crystallis'd that perfect visual and social fabrick which is the Charleston of song and story—the ripe, compleat, and self-contain'd civilisation which has through some miracle been prolong'd to our day, and which is at present probably the only genuine civilisation surviving in the mechanised desert of decadence call'd North-America. The devastating effect of the floods of 1699 and 1700 must have been considerable; for we immediately afterward read of a great wave of building, this time of the type which has survived to the present. The oldest remaining edifice in Charleston is a bastion of the reinforced wall, built in 1703 and now known as "The Old Powder Magazine" in Cumberland St. Of dwelling-houses, the oldest remaining are probably certain specimens in Hasell St. and in an alley off Tradd St., each dating from not much after 1720. Houses as early as the decade of the 1730's are still very numerous; and we still see the town, so far as general impressions go, as it was in the middle and later Georgian period. Block on block of the ancient houses may still be descried in the regions below Broad St.—to an extent not duplicated in any other American city.

In 1702 the Governor of Carolina, an ambitious Irishman nam'd Moore, conceiv'd the notion of developing mines in the western part of the province, and of marching against the Spaniards in Florida. The latter expedition was put into effect, and St. Augustine was for a time taken—though the inhabitants had all retired to the fortress and evaded capture. The expedition was on the whole an indecisive failure, and increas'd the dissatisfaction of the people with the government of the Lords Proprietors. Shortly afterward wars with France and Spain were threatened, and Indian menaces appeared on the horizon. Pirates likewise help'd to make the century's first quarter turbulent. At one time Colonel Rhett hang'd 57 of them at once on a spot near the tip of the peninsula, betwixt the present Church and Meeting Sts., and in 1718 the notorious Capt. Teach, or Blackbeard, caus'd worry along the coast. This year also Colo. Rhett hang'd Capt. Stede Bonnet and 40 men on the Battery near the foot of King St. To this day there are pointed out certain houses in Church St., near Queen, said to have been the rendezvous of pirates in the eighteenth century. Pirate lore is inherent in Charleston tradition, and is well reflected by Poe in "The Gold-Bug".

In 1719 the Province was taken from the Lords Proprietors and given directly (tho' unofficially) to the King, and a decade later—the Royal government being made official and definitive—it was divided into the present provinces of North and South Carolina. By 1720 Charles-Town had largely overflowed its walls, and these barriers now began to be demolish'd bit by bit. 1740 brought evangelical troubles due to the fanatical exhorting of the dissenter George Whitefield, but these were powerless to stay the tide of growing prosperity and culture.

We now see the city assuming very much of its present aspect. Roof-tiling—a rare thing in early American towns—was introduced about 1735, and gave to the steep gables of the houses their characteristick aspect. Early experiments with porches, occasion'd by the warm climate, must likewise have occurred about this time; for before the close of the century we behold Charleston as a town of outdoor living, with great verandahs on all three storeys of the south or west sides of the houses, opening on exquisite walled gardens which passers-by might glimpse through gates of magnificent wrought-iron grille-work. Little by little the inhabitants were achieving that settled and perfect adjustment to the climate and landskip which means a definite civilisation in its mellowest and most genuine sense. The brick and stucco houses generally follow'd the best Georgian models, but in an individual and localised way; so that no other colonial city looks just like Charleston. The climate, vegetation, and general natural conditions encouraged beauty and contentment to a singular degree. Palmettos, live-oaks with writhing branches, festoons of Spanish moss, fragrant magnolias, gorgeous azaleas, and an almost continental clearness of sky, brought out life at its best. At twilight—a very brief subtropical twilight—the birds sang in the gardens, and an insidious perfume of many blossoms floated cryptically over the whole city. Cool breezes sprang up, and those who disliked warmth would walk along the Battery, or White Point Gardens, at the very tip of the peninsula, which fronts the spacious harbour and receives a sweep of air from across the low islands dividing the harbour from the open Atlantick. It is no wonder that a great and gracious civilisation here flower'd, and it is pleasing to reflect that both the natural boons and the civilisation still remain as an oasis in this aera of social and physical ugliness.

We find the *gardens* of Charleston first mention'd about 1740. In 1748 the present proprietary library was founded, attesting to the good scholarship of a people more urban than the Virginians because of the heat and fever which drove them from their island plantations to their town houses during a great part of the summer. Theatres (the first in 1736) appear about the middle of the eighteenth century, the principal one being at the corner of Dock (Queen) and Church Sts. To these came the best companies of players, both British and provincial, presenting all the standard favourites of publick taste. In 1752 much damage was caus'd by a great hurricane, after which came the wave of rebuilding which gave the town—including the Battery—its exact present form. The present St. Michael's Church, whose lovely spire is the choicest object on the local skyline, was finish'd in 1761; and in 1774 receiv'd the famous set of chimes whose sweet musick has regaled the town ever since, save for intervals when the vicissitudes of war and accident made necessary their removal and re-casting.

Charles-Town encounter'd the unfortunate political difficulties of the 1770's with a remarkable amount of poise; tending to sympathise with the rebel cause more than did most towns of equal cultivation, such as Newport, New-York, and Philadelphia; yet preserving so rigidly aristocratick a personal tradition that this seditious radicalism occasion'd no loss of cultural tone. Boston and Newport were socially ruin'd by the disaster, but Charleston pass'd through it almost unscathed. Before the outbreak of overt treason, political debate was conducted in a more than commonly civil fashion; notwithstanding riots over the Stamp Act, and a very savage duel betwixt a loyalist visitor from New York—a Mr. De Lancey, brother-in-law to a Charleston Izard—and the local rebel Dr. Haley, which took place at the South-Carolina Coffee-House, a highly

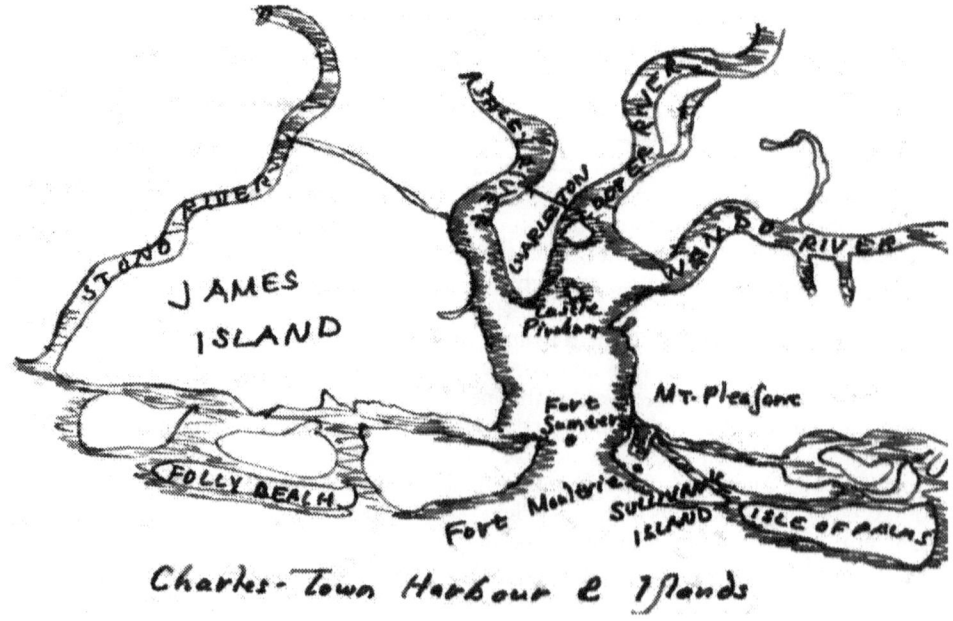

Charles-Town Harbour & Islands

genteel place of entertainment in St. Michael's Alley. Dr. Haley was arrested for Mr. De Lancey's murther, but was acquitted at the next assizes. At this period many tea vessels enter'd Charleston Harbour, but for the most part the cargo was quietly stored in the vaults under the Exchange Building (built 1767—still standing in prime condition), awaiting some later adjustment of the question of duty. In a few later instances, however, seditious mobs dumped bales of tea into the harbour, much like the kindred rabbles of the North. By 1775 the disputes had grown to such an extent that cases of tarring and feathering became common; these indignities being always perpetrated by rebel bands. During the actual hostilities, Charleston was at first neither very strongly attack'd nor very strongly defended. The islands enclosing the harbour were fortify'd with breastworks of earth and palmetto logs, the main defence being old Fort Sullivan on Sullivan's Island, the logical key to the harbour and the city. His Majesty's vessels occasionally made casual attempts to take these fortresses, and on June 28, 1776, began that celebrated engagement with Ft. Sullivan (then commanded by Col. William Moultrie and afterward call'd from him "Fort Moultrie") in which the rebel Sergeant Jasper leapt outside the breastworks and saved his colours under fire.

Charles-Town held out under the rebels until 1780, when the forces of Sir Henry Clinton and my Ld Rawdon mov'd in and took up headquarters at the splendid Brewton-Pringle mansion in lower King St.—a place still standing and open to the publick for a dollar admission fee. Some unpleasantness developed betwixt the troops and the populace, in which the blame seems pretty evenly divided. Charleston was us'd as a base of supplies by His Majesty's troops during most of the southern campaign; a campaign in which the chief obstacles were the Rhode-Island general Nathanael Greene, and the local South-Carolina guerrillas Francis Marion ("The Swamp Fox", at first scorn'd by his fellow-rebels for the rustick uncouthness of his band, but afterward the particular hero of Charleston), Sumter (after whom the celebrated fort in Charleston Harbour was named), and Pickens. After the disaster to Ld Cornwallis's army, the town was evacuated, the troops bearing away the chimes of St. Michael's to London, whence they were afterward regain'd by purchase. When the rebel army enter'd the town late in 1781, some unfortunate atrocities were committed against citizens who had been loyal to his Majesty's rightful cause.

In 1783 the name of the city was officially chang'd from *Charles-Town* to its exact present form of *Charleston*. Its general culture had been very little impair'd by the upheavals of war; and despite the meaningless catchwords of impossible democracy mouthed by the vulgar orators of the day, the same old families continued to flourish and rule amidst an unbrokenly aristocratick social order. In 1792 the negro uprisings in St. Domingo sent to Charleston a great number of French gentlefolk; who were instantly made welcome, and who form'd a highly civilising influence at this stage of the city's growth. About this time Charleston was superseded by the inland town of Columbia as capital of South-Carolina—the new place being lay'd out for that purpose.

This age—the late eighteenth and early nineteenth century—marks the summit and heyday of Charleston's social glory and material prosperity. The local culture which had been crystallising for a hundred years had been singularly undisturbed by the war, and it was now to enjoy a similarly happy immunity from disturbance through mercantile, mechanical, and democratick contamination. For this immunity the depth and tenacity of the existing fabrick was in some degree responsible; but another contributing cause was the extream isolation of the city from the crude life of the commerce-minded colonies, coupled with its frequent marine intercourse with the most cultivated centres of the Old World. Charleston, situate at the coastal edge of a vast lowland plain of rural plantations, was (and still is) near no other town of any size, and did not lie along any trunk line of travel. It was a choice world in itself, and the logical focus of a stable social and intellectual life shared by planter families dwelling on hereditary estates under traditional conditions. The eldest sons of gentlemen went to Oxford and Cambridge for their education, and there was no such lapse of refinement as we find even in Virginia, where a negroid accent invaded common speech and became the typical dialect of the South. In Charleston the perverted accent never became deep or general; the standard of good English speech remaining permanent at all times.

When other regions, deprived of their wholesome linkage with the transatlantick source of culture, began to decline in civilisation and slip into the barbarities and extravagances of the 1830's and 1840's, Charleston remained as a solitary island of sound eighteenth-century taste. This is attested by all open-eyed analysts, and is mention'd with especial force by Samuel Gaillard Stoney, Esq., in his preface to the book on Charleston houses in the Octagon Series. He says:

> "A clue to the character of Charleston and her people is to remember that during this period of growth and greatest importance they were essentially of the eighteenth century. It was then that their culture crystallised; and their mode of thought, their institutions, and their very pronunciation keep the flavour of the age. From that time they preserved the tradition of the classic; with its intellectual freedom, its moral tolerance, its discipline in matters of etiquette, its individualism, and the spirit of logic which elsewhere largely perished in the romantic movement."[1]

One visible instance of this is shewn in the fine series of buildings erected from the decade of 1780 onward; buildings in which the Graeco-Roman tradition is employ'd in its happiest form, and in which an innate native taste crops out in all such adaptive details as wrought-iron work, curved flights of steps, railings, windows, and the like. Among these buildings—worthy successors to old St. Michael's of 1761 and the Exchange of 1767—are the Court House (Broad and Meeting) (1788), the Orphan House (Calhoun St.—1792), the brick Vanderhorst Row (East Bay St.—1800), the City Hall (Broad and Meeting, 1801), the South Carolina Society's Hall (Broad below Meeting—1804), the Second Presbyterian Church (upper Meeting St. 1811), St. Paul's Church (Coming St.—1810–12), the First Presbyterian Church (Meeting St.—1814), St. John's Lutheran Church (Archdale St. 1817), the old Baptist Church (lower Church St. 1822), the Fireproof Record Building (Meeting and Chalmers 1826), the College of Charleston (George St. 1828), St. Philip's magnificent church and steeple (Church St. 1835), St. Mary's Catholick Church (Hasell St. 1838), Hibernian Hall (Meeting—1841), Charleston Market (Meeting and Market 1841), the Jews' Synagogue (Hasell St. 1841), Bethel M. E. Church (Pitt and Calhoun—1850–3), the splendid Custom House (E. Bay St.—1850 et seq.), the chapel of the Circular Congregational Church (Meeting St. 1867), and Trinity M. E. Church (upper Meeting 1875). This late persistence of good architecture is unique in the United States. Other fine buildings, of other schools, are the Gothick Unitarian Church in Archdale St., built in 1772 at a time when Gothick was almost unknown as a creative medium outside the realm of Strawberry-Hill, and the Gothick Huguenot Church at Church and Queen Sts., built in 1845 on the site of earlier fanes. Private houses, it may be added, bear out the picture suggested by the publick buildings. There was no such general lapse of taste in the Victorian age as we find elsewhere; tho' a few bad specimens were put up after the War between the States, on the northerly fringe of the town, and on the site of the burned district of 1861. Broadly speaking, the sound taste of the eighteenth century in architecture and other things has come down unbroken to this day; the Victorian years shewing merely a lessen'd deftness and coarsening of detail (due in part to the substitution of negro for white craftsmanship) instead of the total collapse elsewhere observable. The newest twentieth-century publick buildings are all in the old tradition—the Charleston Museum, Gibbes Art Gallery, and Publick Library being notable among them.

Light on Charleston's great days may be had by reading a few of the many works devoted to the subject, such as the volume by Mrs. St. Julien Ravenel (wife of the noted physician who eradicated yellow fever from the city), and the comprehensive guide-book by Mazÿck[2]—a descendant of one of the old Huguenot families. In 1800 Charleston was the leading centre of culture on this continent, with graceful institutions and a high level of taste such as no other American region can ever parallel. The social season extended from May to November, when malaria drove the planters to town from their inland estates; and was supplemented by a shorter period around the end of January call'd the "Gay Season". The great social institution of the town, whose meetings and functions determined the recreative life of the greatest families, and whose judgments determin'd the status of every person of consequence, was (and *still is*) an organisation originally of musical purpose, call'd the St. Cecelia Society. The St. Cecelia's Day concerts and balls of this society, and its Thursday functions that began at 9 p.m., soon became bywords of exclusiveness; till at length its musical character was merged in its social dictatorship. Various other dancing assembles were frequented by the gay, and the Philharmonick Concerts were also well thought of. Jockey balls attested the importance of the Sport of Kings, as did the Carnival Race Week, which form'd a sort of Charleston carnival. Business was likewise transacted during the "Gay Season", advantage being taken of the presence of many planters in town. Everyone was generally back in the country by the end of March, not to see Charleston again till May. Jedediah Morse, in his "Geography" (1802), says: "In no part of America are the social blessings enjoy'd more rationally and liberally than in Charleston. Unaffected hospitality, affability, ease in manners and address, and a disposition to make their guests welcome, easy, and pleas'd with themselves, are characteristick of the respectable people of Charleston."[3]

The gentlemen constituting this profound and permanent civilisation were almost without exception planters of rice and cotton—the latter having begun to replace indigo as a major staple. They were probably more maturely and mellowly cultivated than the corresponding class of fox-hunting squires in Virginia—the latter generally taking to civick and political pursuits rather than to the nicer elegancies of learning. This difference was doubtless largely due, as previously hinted, to the long urban season made necessary by the inland fever and malaria. Mercantile pursuits were abandon'd by good families after the Revolution, and left to new men from England and Scotland—a bourgeois class corresponding to that in Richmond which produced the Galts and Allans, amongst whom Poe's childhood was spent. These persons had a separate club and social life of their own, and have not much mixt with the planter class even to this day. Publick education was promoted about this time, tho' scholarship continu'd to have far more of aristocratick individuality than in Boston, New-York, Philadelphia, and other centres where insincere and conventionalised standards had begun to spring up. Favourite authors, besides the dominant Graeco-Roman classicks, were Shakespeare and Montaigne—an happy contrast to the sour-mouth'd and meaningless divines and quibblers pored over by the cramp'd neo-Puritans of the Massachusetts-Bay. Coaches now appear in frequent use, and on every hand we behold the ideal of gentlemanly carelessness (as oppos'd to peasant calculativeness, greed, shrewdness, and practicality) uppermost. No man of culture knew how much he was worth in cash, or indeed saw much actual currency. Trade and calculation were largely left to hirelings from the North, call'd "factors". It was a common jest, that a gentleman cou'd read Homer and explain the constitution, but cou'd not do a sum in vulgar fractions. Personal honour was very carefully guarded, and duelling was frequent despite much sentimental opposition.

In those days the factors' offices and merchants' warehouses form'd a distinct district along Bay St., which faces the Cooper River or principal waterfront. Popular shopping streets were the east ends of Broad, Tradd, and Elliott. General stores carrying all manner of goods were the rule, the jewellery shops forming the main exception. Country trade was conducted by long, white-topt waggons with 4 or 6 horses or mules, pil'd high with cotton-bales, high up in King St. near the present railway station. Most of the town was below, or only slightly above, Calhoun St. (then called Boundary St.); just as before the Revolution it had been mostly below Broad—or at most Queen or Cumberland—St. It shou'd be noted that Charleston is a narrow peninsula like the island of Manhattan, so that urban expansion is invariably northward. There was no one residence section, homes being scatter'd and surrounded by large gardens or tracts of land. The Battery, lower Meeting St., Legare St., and so on, were then as now favour'd for fine dwellings. Indeed, we may say that the social complexion of the town has chang'd but little since those gorgeous days of 1800. The Battery was, as it still is, a favourite place of resort and promenade, tho' the East Battery was not graded and built up till the 1830–1860 period. This sea-wall'd region at the tip of the peninsula was slow to develop because of the autumnal hurricanes. On a wharf from the South Battery was a popular tea-house, and near by was Watson's Botanick Garden.

About "Boundary St." (Calhoun) was the semi-rural region known as "The Neck", abounding in creeks and marshes. St. Paul's and the Second Presbyterian were pioneer churches in this region. The neighbourhood of St. Paul's was known as Radcliffeborough; that below Calhoun, east of Meeting, as Ansonborough; and that around the corner of Meeting and Calhoun as Louisburgh. The western section of this district, along Calhoun and Bull Sts. to Rutledge Ave., was call'd Cannonsborough, and was partly given over to large rice and lumber mills on dammed-up creeks. Below it, along the line of the present Montague St., was the section called Harlestonborough. In this northerly region may be seen still some fine houses of the late eighteenth and early nineteenth century, spar'd by war and disaster; among them the splendid Manigault house (1790), whose unique circular gate lodge is now the ignominious adjunct of a gasoline filling station.

In 1822 the town was alarm'd by reports of a threaten'd insurrection of the numerous blacks, under the incitement of Boston abolitionists. The class affected were not the servants or rural workers, but that stratum of black artisans and mechanicks whose advent is to be traced in the declining level of craftsmanship. Their visible leaders were a free mulatto call'd Denmark Vesey, and an African-born conjurer or witch-doctor call'd Gullah Jack. Fortunately the plot came to nothing, but it put the people on their guard against the empty rantings of Northern abolitionists whose chief inspiration was a complete lack of first-hand knowledge of the negro. Shortly afterward tensity toward the North was increas'd by the tariff troubles culminating in the nullification agitation of 1832–3 et seq. South-Carolina, taking its cue from the rebellion of 1775–83, was ever a stronghold of local independence and separatist sentiment, and was not dispos'd to be trodden upon by Yankees who had set the example for se-cession in 1775 and had threaten'd to repeat it in 1809.

The more ordinary people of Charleston (and even many of the better class), no doubt influenced by the whispers of their black nurses and servants, were richly and picturesquely superstitious; and sponsor'd weird tales and beliefs which deserve the at-tention and literary treatment of the modern fantaisiste. Ghost legends multiply'd be-yond all count, and anecdotes of second-sight and verify'd dreams grew common. Queer signs and omens were universally regarded with seriousness, and odd happen-ings always receiv'd the most mystical possible interpretation. Many of the popular tastes resemble the folklore of the picturesque Narragansett country, in southern Rhode-Island, whose close social resemblance to the South has often been pointed out. There was a belief in a great black dog which loped along a certain highway near the town in the morning and evening twilight; never harming anyone, and absolutely im-pervious to gunshot. Other suggestive narratives (to cite a late case) were developed from the case of an ancient house at Goose Creek, which upon being demolisht by the earthquake of 1886, was found to have a secret tunnel leading from the cellar to the interior of a tomb in a venerable neighbouring graveyard. Taste and literary life con-tinued to flourish; producing such figures as the graceful poet Henry Timrod.

The Civil War naturally produc'd a great impression upon Charleston, tho' it was not the scene of any active land fighting, and was not laid waste by the Federal troops which finally pass'd through it. Secession began in South-Carolina, and the first shots of the war were fired at Fort Sumter in Charleston Harbour. Almost coincident with these events was the Great Fire of 1861, which created a vast burn'd district west of Meeting St. and along and below Broad, although it was of accidental origin and totally uncon-nected with the hostilities. This fire destroyed St. Andrew's Hall in Broad St., formerly the leading place of publick assemblage; and the site has never again been built upon. The whole burn'd district remain'd a desert throughout the war, and even afterward was a long time in getting built up once more. At the period of its greatest extent it virtually divided the city into two parts. Wartime hardships—blockade and siege and all their consequences—pressed heavily upon Charleston, but the population bore these afflic-tions with Spartan fortitude. St. Michael's chimes, sent inland to Columbia for safe-keeping, were destroy'd by the torch of Sherman's vandals; but were later recast in Lon-don to their pristine sweetness and purity of tone, the original moulds being still in exis-tence. On account of the Federal gunfire in the harbour, the antient lower end of Charleston was left almost deserted during the war; the inhabitants congregating in those regions north of the burn'd district. Vegetation and solitude claim'd the most his-torick sections, tho' fortunately they came to no harm. At length the conflict ceas'd, Sherman came and went with less than his usual barbarousness, and the people nor-mally redistributed themselves thro' Charleston's antient lanes. The material prosperity of the town had been destroy'd for ever; but despite external change, the basick civilisa-tion proved too deep to eradicate. The old families still liv'd; and tho' without money, they still had their blood and standards. Good birth and taste depend not on riches; so that for all the visible decay, the ideals of beauty, discrimination, balance, and proud reticence did not depart from the gentlefolk of Charleston. Perspectives and institutions persisted, and the continuity which had withstood the successful rebellion of 1775 again withstood the unsuccessful one of 1861. Charleston endured the nightmare of carpet-baggery without flinching, and emerged with standards unimpaired. At length a limited prosperity began to dawn, and commerce surged back along the ancient ways. Broad St. again bristled with banks, brokers, and barristers, and King St. became a fashionable shopping promenade of the elegant eighties. Meeting St. drove a thriving jobbing trade in dry-goods, clothing, shoes, and crockery, whilst the East Bay St. waterfront buzzed anew with the talk of grocers and ship-chandlers. The rice and cotton industries, however, never reached their former state of opulence.

In 1886 Charleston sustain'd the severest earthquake ever experienc'd on the Atlantick coast; a thing which demolisht many buildings and publick works, and severly injur'd many more—including the splendid old edifice of St. Michael's. Recuperation, however, was very swift; a circumstance testifying to the essential vitality of the antient town.

And so Charleston has come down to our own melancholy age of decay, to meet the greatest test of all as the engulphing barbarism of mechanised life, democratick madness, quantitative standards, and schedule-enslaved uniformity presses in upon it from every side and seeks to stifle whatever of self-respecting humanity and aristocratick individualism remains in the world. Against all the inherited folkways which alone give us enough of the illusion of interest and purpose to make life worth living for men of our civilisation, there now advances a juggernaut of alien and meaningless forms and feelings which cheapens and crushes everything fine and delicate and individual which may lie in its path. Noise—profit—publicity—speed—time-tabled convict regularity—equality—ostentation—size—standardisation—herding. . . . . . The plague has swept all before it, saddling old New England with unassimilable and corrosive barnacles, extinguishing once-proud New York with a foetid flood of swart, cringing Semitism, and sapping even at old Virginia and the Piedmont Carolinas with a tawdry industrial Babbitry all the more blasphemous because working through normal Anglo-Saxons. Values evaporate, perspectives flatten, and interests grow pale beneath the bleaching acid of ennui and meaninglessness. Emotions grow irrelevant, and art ceases to be vital except when functioning through strange forms which may be normal to the alien and recrystallised future, but are blank and void to us of the dying Western civilisation. James Joyce . . . Erik Dorn[4]. . . . Marcel Proust. . . . Brancusi. . . . . Picasso. . . . . . The Waste Land. . . . . Lenin. . . . . Frank Lloyd Wright. . . . . cubes and cogs and circles. . . . segments and squares and shadows. . . . wheels and whirring, whirring and wheels. . . . purring of planes and click of chronographs. . . . . . milling of the rabble and raucous yells of the exhibitionist. . . . "comic" strips. . . . Sunday feature headings. . . . advertisements. . . . sports. . . . tabloids. . . . luxury . . . Palm Beach. . . . "sales talk". . . . . rotogravures. . . . radio. . . . . Babel. . . . . Bedlam. . . . .

But Charleston is still Charleston, and the culture we know and respect is not dead there. Dilution there may be, but in the main there is more alive than in any other place in America. The original families still hold sway—Rhetts, Izards, Pringles, Bulls, Hugers, Ravenels, Manigaults, Draytons, Stoneys, Rutledges, and so on—and still uphold the basic truths and values of a civilisation which is genuine because it represents a settled adjustment betwixt people and landscape, old enough to have created the overtones needful to a sense of interest and significance. Here still dwell men who realise that quality is a matter of emotional adjustment to the external world; and that luxury, ostentation, visibility, and publicity are cheap tricks which a gentleman shuns as he would shun gaudy jewellery or pungent perfumes. Gentlefolk in Charleston still pursue their ways for pleasure and not for show or profit, and are still decently anxious to keep their names and personal affairs *out* of the papers, instead of vulgarly handing them over to low-bred "society editors" to be printed and mouthed over by the swinish herds of tradesfolk, Ford-owners, and bungalow-dwellers. The Charleston dailies are the only ones without a "society column" to spy upon the comings and goings of important people. Here, thank God, gentlemen still maintain a sense of proportion and individuality; and decline to let upstart curs snapshot them and their families for the greedy eyes of impertinent strangers! Testimony is united that Charlestonians are not yet ruin'd by the tendencies of the times. Business is not dehumanised by speed and time-tabling, or denuded of courtesy and leisureliness. Quality, not quantity, is the standard, and there is as yet scant use for the modern fetish of "maximum returns" to be obtain'd even at the sacrifice of everything which makes those returns worth having, or life itself worth preserving. Even the middle classes are not apt to make fools of themselves, for the whole community has a very deeply ingrained sense of real values—appreciating the fact that quiet and modesty and moderation and freedom and leisure and courage are excellent things, and that publicity and show and extravagance and megalomania and noisiness and pointless haste are cheap and inferior and irrelevant and contemptible things. The more one observes of Charleston, the more impress'd is he that he is looking upon the only thoroughly civilised city now remaining in the United States. The streets, of course, teem with blacks; but of the regular population all are hereditary Nordick-Americans of the English tradition. The foreigner, with his disruptive and disintegrative influence, has no place in the life of this genuine civick unit. In the magazine of the *New-York Times* for June 22, 1930, a correspondent writes:

> "Other towns have to make stoves or sell goods for a living; it is enough for Charleston only to be. The tourists who stop there sense at once, as one expressed it, that they are 'back in America'. They stop in increasing numbers and for longer intervals. Some of them stay. Have you noticed that when Americans are able to choose where they shall live they invariably select old places, calm and slow-paced, and when they settle there, as in Charleston, set themselves against change more implacably than the natives? Can it be that all of us in our hearts do not choose to run?"[5]

Literary and artistic life remain in a healthy state, embracing both native aesthetes, and others who have come to enjoy the harmonious milieu. The local poetry society is one of the most important in the country, and has entertain'd the leading figures in contemporary letters. What the future holds, none may say; but one may feel confident that Charleston will stay longest above the flood of neo-American chaos and barbarism, just as Mt. Everest wou'd stay longest above a flood of water ingulphing the whole planet. Just now its prime menace is not so much the lowly immigrant as the wealthy settler from the North—whose coming in large numbers would introduce a jarring note and set up an alien atmosphere.

It remains to speak of the famous *street-cries* of Charleston; rare bits of folklore whose decline in the last 20 years is so great that old residents almost refuse to class the present remnants with the lusty rituals of the great old days. These cries were—and are—confin'd wholly to itinerant negro hucksters, and are most amply heard in the early morning. At their best they had a quality of joyousness and spontaneous balladry about them which prov'd that even the black of Charleston retains a large element of the personal and the decorative in his commercial transactions. Black or white, no human being is so barbarous as to harbour the ideal of "strictly business" in this antient and civilised town.

Typical cries are those of the dawnlight shrimp and crab sellers, who march through the cobbled streets and past the fanlighted doorways singing melodiously: "Swimy raw, raw!", and "She craib! She craib! She craib!"—the latter formula, however, being given something of a yelling, nasal intonation. In 1910 a negro did business in lower King St. under the sign of "Joe Cole and Wife". He look'd like an Indian, limp'd, and us'd his cane as a baton. Whilst selling porgy—a fish ally'd to the chub—he wou'd bellow the following elaborate refrain:

> "Old Joe Cole—good ol' soul—
> Porgy in the summer-time,
> An e whiting in the spring,
> Eight upon a string.
> Don't be late, I'm waitin' at de gate,
> Don't be mad,—here's your shad,
> Old Joe Cole—good ol' soul!"

Another pedestrian merchant used to recite the following:

> "Here's your Little John, Ma'm. I got Hoppen John Peas, Ma'm! I got cabbage—I got yaller turnips, Ma'm, oh, yes, Ma'm!" [Variant: "I got sweet pertater—I got beets—I got spinach!"]

An older vendor used to cry:

> "Load my gun
> Wid Sweet Sugar Plum
> An' shoot dem nung gal
> One by one.
> Border lingo
> Water-million."

The ensuing cry of an aged negress becomes more explicable when we learn that the commodity named is really a very toothsome form of cocoanut and molasses candy:

> "Come on, chilluns, and get yer monkey meat!"

The ebon hind responsible for the following formula wished to call attention to his fresh "yard eggs"—i.e., eggs laid in his own farmyard: "Enny yad aigs terday, my Miss?"

Charleston chimney-sweeps all cultivated the refrain "Roo-roo", and were in consequence sometimes known as "Roo-roo* boys". The charcoal boy with his two-wheeled donkey-cart had a weird, melancholy way of chanting the unadorn'd word "char—coal". There was likewise a whole class of burly negresses known as "Vegetubble Mammas", who had cries such as "Red rose tomaytoes!", "Green Pease! Sugar Pease!", "Straw-*ber*-ry, an e fresh an e fine, an e just off the vine! Straw-*berry*!", and "Sweet Pete ate her!"

These street cries have received much serious study, and an excellent summary of them (with intonations reproduced as written musick) has been made in a small brochure available at the Charleston Publick Library.

---

*or "Ro-ro", as others interpreted the sound.

II. The Architecture of Charleston

Architecturally Charleston is the most remarkable town in the United States; being built up differently from any other in colonial times, and having preserv'd a phenomenal proportion of its early construction. For this preservation three reasons may be assign'd: first, the decline in trade which discourag'd ambitious building projects after the War between the States; second, the native taste and conservatism of a civilised community, which appreciates existing beauty and avoids meaningless change; and third, the unusual excellence, spaciousness, and solidity of the colonial construction itself; this being far beyond the average level for American towns of the eighteenth century. Charleston, as the cultural centre of one of the richest planting districts in the world, was perhaps the foremost of all American cities in taste and civilisation before and just after the Revolution; and its architecture reflected the refinement and competence of its inhabitants.

Of the earliest wave of buildings in Charleston nothing at all survives; but we may conjecture that they were small, plain houses of brick design'd in an European manner (with perhaps more of the continental influence than the houses farther north) and without that system of piazzas typical of later Charleston dwellings. It was not to be expected that a northern European people, settling in this region, wou'd at once work out that rapprochement with their new southerly climate which ultimately gave rise to perfected Charleston architecture. The Charleston of the early eighteenth century, then, may be pictur'd as a compact town of European-like houses, built of brick and stucco in solid blocks, without porches or balconies, and with only the usual northern arrangement of doors and windows. This is borne out by a study of the oldest remaining houses, which date from about 1720, and whose original parts can be readily pick'd out by experts from amidst any such additions as may have cluster'd round them.

From the first, however, Charleston architecture seems to have been very distinctive. Styles were eclectick and vary'd, many experiments seeming to have been try'd and abandon'd before a widespread local type was finally hit upon. There is, for example, one surviving instance of the *gambrel roof* (the pink house in Chalmers St.) which became so universal in New-England, and which generally straggled down the coast as far as Virginia. Evidently the style was try'd, but found impracticable in the warm climate of Charleston and given early abandonment. If any kind of house seems typical of Charleston, it is a plain brick edifice cover'd with stucco, some three storeys tall, and with a fairly steep roof (with or without dormers) slanting up equally on all four sides and culminating in a single central peak. These houses were built both in blocks, directly on the street, and separately, with walled gardens around them—the latter fashion seeming to gain ground after 1740. Tiled roofs were introduced about 1735, and soon became very common and characteristick; the tiles often being given pronounc'd colours such as salmon pink or purple black. Concave curved tiles of local manufacture were most used. In

Typical Charleston Street View
(early type house)

early times shingle and slats were the rule. The stucco covering the brick walls was generally made of burnt oyster-shell lime, and was sometimes given a vivid and unusual colouring such as pink. Occasionally houses would be built of a brick-like composition call'd "Bermuda Stone", "horn-work", "coral-stone", or "tabby" [corrup. *tapia*], and made of lime, coral, and sea or oyster shells. Much of this material is found in old mills, and two finely preserv'd houses near St. Philip's Church are partly built of it. That Charleston has a more *continental* aspect than other colonial towns is universally conceded, and generally laid to the large Huguenot population. This continentalism, however, is distinctly more *Dutch* than *French;* perhaps owing to the long stay of many of the Huguenots in Holland before coming to Carolina. In France, *stone* is the great building medium; but here the Dutch custom of *brick* work holds universal sway. West-Indian influence was also very considerable. Expert architects point out many idiosyncratick features of Charleston building design, notably the tendency of

the steep roof lines to flare up a trifle at the eaves. Many reasons have been assign'd for this; some postulating Dutch influence* and others adducing practical constructional considerations; but it must be admitted that the question is still unsettled. Walls were very thick, and windows often deeply recessed. Mediaeval features in gable and roof line are quite frequent, and include the so-call'd "jerkin head roof" found in seventeenth-century buildings elsewhere in the colonies. This quaint early diversity gives rise to some highly picturesque urban skyline effects; many artists delighting to study and record various groups of huddled roof lines as seen in perspective from sundry choice points of vantage. Chimneys were made very large to allow of frequent and easy sweeping by the "Ro-ro Boys", according to city ordinance. Many of the early houses bore the metal plaques of various insurance companies, as was the custom in Philadelphia. At some unplaced date, about midway in the eighteenth century, the famous and typical Charleston porches and balconies began to appear; marking the gradually perfected adaptation of a northern race to its present subtropical surroundings. Porches ran all the way up the houses, with levels for each storey, on the south or west sides to catch the prevailing

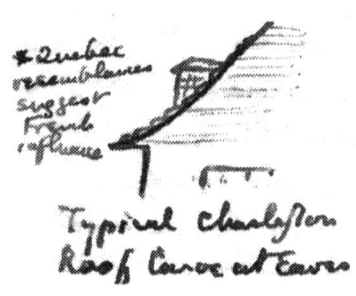

Typical Charleston Roof Curve at Eaves

Charleston: Mediaeval gable & Roof Line

---

*Quebec resemblances suggest French influence.

Charleston:
Typical Urban
group, shewing
jerkin-head Roof
+ added porch on
lower storey —
door opening from
such low piazza
which fronts upon
a wall'd garden
with iron grille-
work Gates.

winds. They faced at right angles to the street, and generally overlook'd a high-wall'd garden. On the end toward the street they generally had a wall, forming an extension of the wall of the house's lower storey, through which was cut a door giving directly on the street. This door, usually with all the typical adornments and accessories of a Georgian doorway, form'd the principal pedestrian entrance to the house and its premises; though the garden wall wou'd generally have a large gate at some other point (sometimes serving as a carriage entrance, as such gates did for large mansions set back from the street), closed by wrought-iron grille-work of the finest craftsmanship. Houses of this piazza'd type may be taken as the most typical form of Charleston domestick architecture; tho' it must be pointed out that all sorts of other designs were occasionally fol-

low'd. After 1760 houses were commonly built higher than before—three storeys and attick at least, and with taller basements—in order to catch as much of the sea breeze as possible. French windows—especially where piazzas or balconies were involv'd—appeared at a date much earlier than in any other towns of America; and became highly characteristick of Charleston houses. All rooms were fully panell'd, and drawing-rooms were on the second storey overlooking the street.

Charleston —
Street View, shewing old
house with Porch — later XVIII
Century. Typical of its period
and later. Note grille-work
Balcony overhanging the Street.

One peculiarity of Charleston architecture in the eighteenth century was the whimsical use of *Gothick* design for casual, homely, or ignominious purposes—coach-houses, slave-quarters, gates, garden-walls, and the like. Such things frequently possess pointed windows or embrasures, and other elements of Gothic ornament, of a highly pleasing pattern; tho' the style was not seriously regarded, and was in no sense a precursor of the widespread revival of Gothick after 1830. Nor is it to be confus'd with the Strawberry-Hill spirit which prompted the construction of a large, fine, and compleatly Gothick church in Archdale St. in 1772. One favourite feature of Charleston architecture, launch'd before the Revolution but gaining greatest ascendancy afterward—and being a cardinal feature of many of Charleston's publick buildings of the 1800 period—was the double entrance flight of steps; railed, often gracefully curving, and having a long top platform under which in the centre an arched tunnel ran beneath the building and contain'd the doorways of the basement apartments. This arrangement has counterparts in the North, and is even remotely akin to the typical double flights of steps of colonial Providence; but nowhere save in Charleston did it receive its fullest development and most widespread use. Another typical Charleston feature is the parapet, or false attick front, extending a few feet above the roof line of many houses of a square, flat-roof'd type. In this are usually set two flattish rectangular horizontal embrasures, or false windows, symmetrical with the real windows below, and faced with iron grille-work.

Many of the architects of Old Charleston are known by name, and venerated by the discriminating. The magnificent Brewton-Pringle mansion (1765) is the work of one Ezra Waite, "Civil Architect, House-Builder in General, and Carver, from London". Other local architects were the Horlbeck brothers, John, Adam, and Peter; masons from Plauen in Saxony, with much European experience, and especially skill'd in the execution of massive or monumental designs. In the late colonial period many British architects came to Charleston, and are responsible for an abundance of fine middle-Georgian and early-Adam-period architecture and decoration. A certain proportion of mansions in brick and wood, without stucco, and wholly transcending the local Charleston type, may be traced with some certainty to them. After the Revolution a leading local architect was the gentleman-planter Gabriel Manigault (pronounc'd

Man´-i-go), a Huguenot of independent means who had study'd in Europe and employ'd Adam designs with the utmost taste and skill. He is responsible for the splendid mansion of his brother Peter, built in 1790 and still to be seen, together with its unique circular gate lodge, at the corner of Ashmead and Meeting Sts. At this period we see panelling disappearing except as wainscots. Piazzas and open galleries multiply, and fix the permanent type of Charleston house which remains dominant till the Civil War. Architects working in Charleston

Typical Neo-Classick Edifice in Charleston, shewing common form of steps in rail'd double flight.

from this period onward are the famous James Holme, and the local men Robert Mills, Col. E. Blake White, Jones and Lee, etc. To these are due that opulent wave of building-up which followed the first cotton prosperity after the invention of the cotton gin in 1793—the wave which produc'd such a wealth of classick publick buildings. Sheer hand *craftsmanship* had begun to decline, but these architects more than atoned for the slight falling-off by the artistick brilliancy of their *general designs.* These men likewise helped to conceal the menace of the nascent machine age by designing the steam rice mills which began to appear after 1817. Most if not all of such mill structures are really beautiful specimens of late Georgian architecture; their parts being functionally justify'd and admirably balanc'd.

It is also in this age that Charleston *wrought-iron work* becomes such an opulent and exquisite thing. Iron-working began before the Revolution with Tunis Tabaut and William Johnson, but it was later that its use became so universal. In 1820 the master craftsman Iusti came from Germany and fashion'd the magnificent gates of St. Michael's churchyard. Werner came, also from Germany, in 1828, and was still working in 1870. Ortmann, from Baden, came in 1847; and his descendants still conduct the exquisite and traditional industry.

We now face the advance of the nineteenth century, which brought so tragic a collapse to architecture throughout the United States. The general order of departure from the Georgian was through classicism to Gothicism and thence to utter disintegrative chaos—but in Charleston we find a marvellous and exceptional retention of sound elder standards. Classicism remained enthroned despite occasional Gothick churches, and in private houses the elements of late-Georgian design linger'd on miraculously into the thick of the Victorian age. Doorway-design, with fanlight and sidelights, remained the same in general essence; and the general house-plan did not greatly alter, notwithstanding a tendency toward the *colossal* and the *monumental,* perhaps induc'd by the expansive agricultural prosperity of the 1840's and 1850's. Houses began to have exaggeratedly lofty rooms, and winding staircases in hemicycles at the end of the hall, with niches at the landings and floor levels (cf. urban architecture elsewhere, especially Bulfinch's later houses on Beacon Hill, Boston). Heavy drapery became the mode, and Adam-period mantels gave place to mantels of dark vein'd marble shaped like Grecian temple-facades. Furniture of the heavy Empire type appear'd, but did not commonly degenerate into the most extream horrors of Victorian haircloth, marble-top, and jigsaw'd black-walnut. Architectural details became heavy and almost crude as negro craftsmen replaced skill'd white carvers, though the good models of the eighteenth century were never wholly lost sight of.

Such was the Charleston—a Charleston still mainly Georgian in its visual as well as social-intellectual aspect—upon which the Civil War descended. Afterward a few ugly Victorian houses were erected in the newer sections and the burnt district; but these were very few indeed, relatively speaking. Cash for building was not plentiful, and local taste always tended to stay above the lower depths in which the rest of America was sunk. Charleston quickly responded to the architectural recuperation of the '90s and early twentieth century, and has recently built nothing in violation of the ancient Georgian tradition. Even the new Francis Marion Hotel is essentially conservative in pattern, and so far there would seem to be no danger of a lapse into the meaningless vortex of "modernistick" theory. Charleston is too profound a civilised entity to be swept off its feet by ephemeral abstraction, and is well aware of the authenticity with which the try'd, familiar forms express and symbolise its priceless history and heritage.

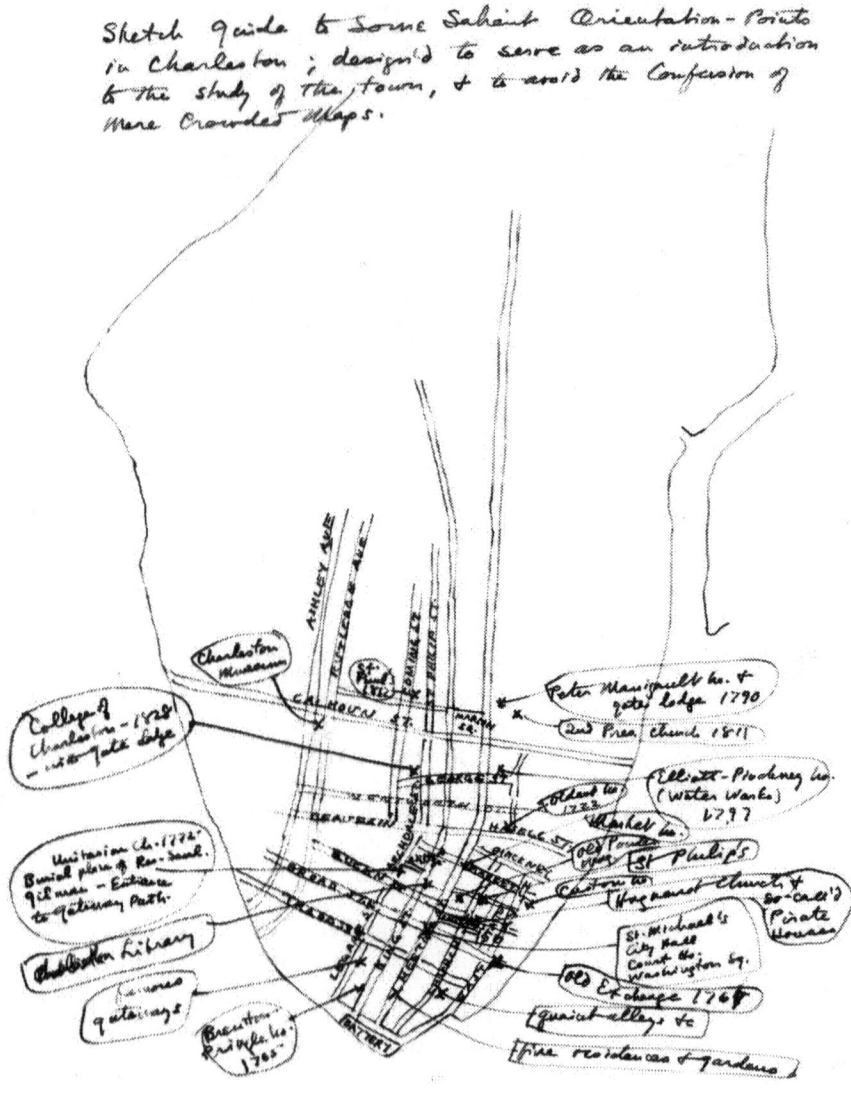

III. The Present State of Charleston, and Modes of Exploring It

Charleston occupies a flat—and originally marshy and creek-threaded—tongue of land betwixt the mouths of the rivers Ashley and Cooper, which here flow into one of the most spacious and notable harbours on the Atlantick coast; a harbour full seven miles across, and separated from the open sea by several islands, of which Sullivan's, containing Fort Moultrie, and the small isle holding Fort Sumter, are the most celebrated. The city is the natural port of a spacious lowland region of subtropical climate and fertility, cut by many rivers and once the seat of most extensive planting. Approaching the district by land from the ugly and barren uplands of Carolina, the traveller is imprest with the sensation of having enter'd an earthly paradise. All the way down from Camden, through Columbia and Orangeburg and Summerville, the genial and exotick character of the country is clearly manifest. Here are gardens of figs, pomegranates, peaches, oranges, oleanders, myrtles, azaleas, camellias, acacias, jujubes, and roses; and outside the towns one beholds the wild rose, the wild yellow jessamine, the magnolia, and the twisted and curious live-oak with festoons of Spanish moss hanging from spectral branches. Vast cathedral-like forests of pine and live-oak are common, and suggest the strange landskips pictur'd in Mons. Chateaubriand's romance of "Atala".[6] The resort town of Summerville, 24 miles from Charleston, lies imbedded in such a forest; and derives therefrom a curious picturesqueness. Amidst such natural beauty, we do not marvel at the fame of Charleston gardens, or at the circumstance that two of our most celebrated flowers, the *poinsettia* and the *gardenia,* were nam'd from gentlemen of Charleston, who cultivated them. The poignant and bristling *palmetto-tree* is very frequently met with, and more clearly than anything else proclaims the nearness of the region to the tropicks. Upon the sensitive imagination, accustom'd only to northern scenes, such sights cannot but produce an extreamly sharp effect; and it is universally allow'd that the literary genius of Mr. Poe, who spent a season at Fort Moultrie on Sullivan's Island, was very strongly influenc'd by this, his only glimpse of an environment other than northern.

Charleston itself lies in N. Latitude 32° 45', and W. Longitude 79° 57'. Approach'd from the sea, its flatness gives it a very curious and engaging aspect; the many spires and roofs seeming to rise directly out of the water, as if forming the topmost pinnacles of a submerg'd Atlantis. St. Michael's and St. Philip's steeples are the dominant and traditional features of the skyline. Owing to the rigid plan of my Ld Ashley, upon which the system of streets was first started, the town has not the maze of tangled lanes which we find in such other antient places as Boston, lower New-York, and Annapolis; yet the great age and diversity of the buildings cause the scene to lack nothing of quaintness. The generall arrangement of the town is much like that of New-York, with cross-streets, and long north and south streets ending in a battery with a sea-wall. The social topography, however, is very different; insomuch as the Battery is a fashionable place of residence and promenade (on account of the cool breezes), whilst business flourishes on the two great north-and-south streets, King and Meeting, about midway in their course. The principal cross-streets, from the Battery upward, are Tradd (a thoroughfare wholly colonial), Broad (the street of bankers and brokers), and Calhoun (which marks the focus of the modern business section, and crosses Meeting and King Sts. at an open park call'd Marion Square). The great north and south streets, from the Cooper River or principal waterfront westward, are East Bay, Church, Meeting, King, Legare (which runs north into Archdale and St. Philip, and which is pronounc'd *Legree ´*), Rutledge Ave., and Ashley Ave. The region below Broad St. is, except for the fringe along the Ashley River, almost wholly colonial. Along the line of Meeting St.

and around the Battery it is exceedingly fashionable and beautiful; whilst east of this, along the line of Church St., it is quaint and homelike, and much given over to artists' studios. As one gets north of Stoll's Alley, a dismal slum district of abandon'd warehouses and negro tenements begins to develop along the Cooper waterfront; but this is well worth exploration because of the age and picturesqueness of the houses. One ought to study this section with a retentive memory, since it is likely to be swept away by a wave of hotel-building before many years have pass'd. Betwixt Broad and Calhoun lies a region which may be call'd *semi-colonial*, and which ought to be pretty thoroughly cover'd by the visitor, since it contains the leading publick edifices. The focal point of this and the older southerly region is the historic intersection of Broad and Meeting Sts., once the principal gate of the original wall'd town, and for two centuries the real civick centre. On the four corners of this intersection will be found antient St. Michael's (1761) (S.E.), the City Hall (1801) (N.E.), the Court House (1788) (N.W.), and the modern but sightly post-office (S.W.). Adjacent to it, and having gates on both Meeting and Broad Sts., is the old City Park or Washington-Square, which lies behind the City Hall and forms the principal down-town resting-place besides the Battery. Here we find an excellent statue of William Pitt, Esq., set up in 1770 and mov'd to the present site from elsewhere; also a monument to the graceful Charleston poet, Henry Timrod, Esq., and one to the Civil War general Pierre Gustave Toutant Beauregard. The park extends through to Chalmers St. on the north, and on the east is bounded by a very picturesque and antient Georgian wall. Encompass'd as it is by venerable publick structures, it forms a highly appropriate spot for the thoughtful visitor's repose and reflection.

In order to behold with intelligence the rich and vary'd antiquities of Charleston, it is advisable first to gain a good idea of the streets from the study of suitable maps. Of these there is no lack, the best available for distribution being those in the booklet issu'd by the street-car company, and in the guide brochure publish'd by W. W. De Renne of Savannah, Ga.[7] Charleston's street plan ought to be master'd with some thoroughness, so that objects and places of interest may be quickly found and identify'd by their location as stated in guide-books or directions. Of course, everything cannot be carry'd in memory; so that it is well always to have a map (preferably that by A. T. S. Stoney in the De Renne booklet) in one's pocket.

Just what to see, if time be limited, must always be a question largely dependent on one's personal taste. To this end the consultation of a good array of guide-books is necessary. Of the free booklets distributed by various interests in Charleston, the following ought to be in the possession of the visitor:

(1) Charleston, America's Most Historic City.
Monthly magazine issued by Charleston Chamber of Commerce. Issue for Dec. 1929 contains the best short itinerary of sights, arranged in good walking order, but without map of city. Has map of Charleston environs, including harbour and islands. This is the most important of the free guide-books.

(2) What to See—Where to Go—in Historic Charleston.
Brochure published by W. W. De Renne, Box 481, Savannah, Ga., and sent free on request. Has excellent guide material, plus the best extant sightseeing map of Charleston. This book *and map* form almost an absolute necessity for the unguided sightseer.

(3) The Lure of Charleston the Historic.
Folder issued by Chamber of Commerce, with small map which points out historic spots by means of guide lines. Excellent, but requires a magnifying-glass for effective use.

(4) See Charleston—Ride by Street Car.
Brochure issued by S.C. Power Co., with excellent map of the city and complete information concerning street-car service. Ought to be carried by all sightseers.

But for the thorough student—or even for the casual visitor if he desires maximum pleasure and convenience—additional material is necessary. The one *indispensable* guide-book to obtain is:[8]

> Street Strolls
> around
> Charleston, South Carolina,
> Giving the
> History, Legends, and Traditions;
> by
> Miriam Bellangee Wilson*

This book is sold at all bookstalls for 75¢, and ought to be obtain'd at the outset. In this book is told practically everything there is to tell about everything of interest in Charleston; walking itineraries being arranged, and every house or site or association along the way described in proper order and with adequate detail and background. The walks are arrang'd as conveniently as possible; with due regard for œconomy of distance, and with a minimum of duplication. The whole city is cover'd; and he who has pursu'd the plan with fulness, may say very truthfully that he knows Charleston almost like a native. A good walker, persistent in his wish to master everything, might fully cover this itinerary in three or four days; tho' not less than a week ought to be given to it. The slower one goes, the better; so that the colour and atmosphere may be imbibed with an intelligent leisure permitting the fullest savouring, digestion, and correlation with one's historical, literary, and imaginative background. If a sort of preface, introduction, or orientation-tour is desired, it is pleasant to take the motor sightseeing trip of the Grey Line[†] before entering on detail'd pedestrian research. In the remarks to follow, it will be assum'd that the reader has the topography of the city at his disposal in the form of maps, and that he has access to suitable guide-book descriptions of the various objects of interest mention'd. Only the most salient things will be touch'd upon, tho' it is to be hoped that the visitor will not confine his inspection to these alone. No attempt will be made to describe the multiplicity of noble objects to be view'd in the rural regions around Charleston. These include many fine plantations, the ancient Goose Creek Church (1711), St. Andrew's Parish Church (1706), and the world-famous Magnolia and Middleton Gardens, which are open to the publick in the early spring. Objects like these deserve a special expedition devoted to them, a thing best accomplisht when one has a coach at his

---

*A flat, grey-cover'd pamphlet; which, once folded, will neatly fit the pocket. It is #2 of a series of Charleston guide-books and maps, later items of which will describe the churches and publick buildings in some detail.

†Offices in Marion-Square, King and Calhoun Sts.

disposal; tho' there is a publick coach service to Magnolia and Middleton Gardens during the season (March and April) they are open.

Arriving in Charleston, the visitor beholds a city that is alive in the fullest sense despite its historick past. Tho' suggesting Salem and Newport in its physical aspect, it has not the languid deadness of those archaick towns; but is indeed the present metropolis of a vast and opulent region, in which it stands alone and unrivall'd. Accordingly, it will be found to possess a variety of urban refinements and facilities, and to harbour a metropolitan self-sufficiency, which wou'd not be found in a town of like size in the North. The population, including the blacks, of which there are a great number, does not much exceed 62,000; yet the general atmosphere is that of a large town of vast assurance and maturity. There are signs of a commercial revival in the near future, and an increasing flood of appreciative tourists heightens the aspect of liveliness during the early spring season. The vast new Cooper River Bridge (a marvellous feat of engineering worth the study of those interested in such matters) serves, in connexion with another bridge over the Ashley, to place Charleston on a new direct coastal route betwixt Florida and the North; a circumstance which may cause it to be more widely frequented by outsiders, yet which one hopes will not serve to destroy its individual and self-contain'd manner of life, or make it self-conscious and exhibitionistick like Cape Cod. Since the decline of rice and cotton prosperity, Charleston's chief industries have been the manufacture of phosphate fertilisers and asbestos products, and the export of vary'd agricultural products. The agricultural trade is very brisk, owing to the excellence and healthfulness of South-Carolina vegetable produce. The local farm products are phenomenally rich in the necessary *iodine* element; a circumstance deem'd so important by local œconomists, that the word "IODINE" has (with somewhat doubtful taste) been plac'd upon the 1930 licence-plates of all South-Carolina motor vehicles.

Seeking a tavern to stop at, the stranger had better be guided by his personal taste and requirements. The ascetick antiquarian, to whom historick impressions are more important than ice-water and push-buttons, will do very well at the Y.M.C.A.; whilst the man who demands an uniform environment of material luxury had better stop at the Francis Marion in Marion-Square, or the Fort-Sumter Hotel on the Battery. An ideal medium, perhaps, is the homelike and old-fashion'd *Timrod Inn*, a neat hostelry of reposeful pre-Civil-War design, with piazzas overhanging the street, which stands at the very centre of things in Meeting St. near Broad, on the eastern side of the street, facing Washington-Square. It is nam'd for the Charleston poet Henry Timrod, Esq., who dy'd in 1867, and is exceedingly well spoken of by a gentleman of the writer's acquaintance who lately stopt there. Its prices are moderate, even cheap—and it is very conveniently situated with respect to ordinaries and eating-saloons (an important matter with many), a good abundance of which are scatter'd along the west side of Meeting St. northward from its doors. These houses of refreshment are not of the one-arm'd sort now so universal in New-England; but remain (in accordance with Charleston conservatism) equipp'd with the old-fashion'd personal service so cherish'd by those accustom'd to Sybaritick refinements and Patersonian luxuries.[9]

Sallying forth from his tavern with map and guide-book in hand, the stranger cannot but note the civilis'd and distinctive atmosphere of the antient city around him. The pace of life is sensible and leisurely, and there is no needless noise or bustle or excitement. Everything essential is accomplish'd without that needless parade of haste, and that criminal sacrifice of beauty and all that makes life worth enduring, which we find so universal amongst the foreign and barbarick industrial centres of the North. The abundance of negroes is picturesque, and now and then the sweet chimes of old St. Michael's can be heard striking the hours, halves, and quarters as they have done since 1774. Odd characters and quaint beggars abound to an extent unheard-of in the "efficient" and de-humanised North. Such misfits are view'd with kindly tolerance and even affection, and are assur'd of a livelihood thro' the bounty of the citizens. They include both white men and blacks, and are an integral part of the local folklore. Around Washington-Square a dreamy bearded man is often seen to loiter, and in the same region one may see Jimmy O'Brien, the idiot newsboy whose malform'd face and great teeth (either in laughter or in anger) are of so hideous a cast as to suggest the most nefandous daemons of the pit. Jimmy is of pure white Irish blood, but his form of physical atavism gives him a yellow Mongoloid cast which causes many to mistake him for a mulatto. His father, whom he resembles, was the town drunkard until delirium tremens removed him from the scene. Another local character is a slightly clouded little old gentleman of the antient planter stock, who dresses immaculately in a tight-fitting blue suit of elder pattern, clutches a neatly roll'd umbrella, and minces about to various shops in the business district asking pointless questions and ordering goods which he does not want and which everyone knows enough not to give him. A good central point to see local characters and hear local folklore is the photograph-shop of *George W. Johnson, 71 Hasell* St.*, where the best actual photographs of Charleston scenes (taken by Mr Johnson personally, and re-tail'd at 5 cents each) may be obtain'd. Mr. Johnson is a man of venerable years, keen intelligence, and hospitable affability; very familiar with old times and old tales, and courteous and genial in his conversations with visitors. The best headquarters for penny postcards, quaint souvenirs, and guide-books of every description, is *Lighthart's Book-store, 322 King St.*, on the east side of the street just below George. Here may be ob-tain'd, likewise, the New-York papers; or if Lighthart is out of them, they can generally be had from a smaller place a few doors down on the same side of the street. Lighthart is open daily till 9 p.m., tho' Mr. Johnson keeps the usual hours.

The stranger cannot but find the climate of Charleston much to his taste; it being mild in winter, and in summer cool'd by the breezes of the neighbouring ocean. The annual mean temperature is 67° Fahrenheit, and there are on the average only six freezing days in a year. The Battery is never warm, and the writer cou'd never endure the cold of it any evening in the early part of May. The sun in Charleston shines more continuously than in any other American city except Los Angeles; and in the writer's sojourn of eleven days there was not a single rainfall or long cloudy period. The one drawback is the tendency toward gales and hurricanes in late August and September; a thing largely offset by stout building construction and massive sea-walls. The beaches of Charleston—Folly Beach, Sullivan's Island, and Isle of Palms—are among the finest in the South; and being directly on the open ocean, ought to be a good source of deep-sea shells and marine vegetation for those who collect such material. Sullivan's Island, with Fort Moultrie (pronounc'd *Moo´-try*), ought in particular to be visited because of its association with Mr. Poe, its part in his celebrated tale, "The Gold-Bug", and its possession of the grave of the unfortunate Seminole chieftain *Osceola*, who was there confin'd. Happily, one of the sightseeing excursions of the Grey Line (offices in Marion Sq.) include all the features of this island. General information about anything in Charleston can be obtain'd from the Chamber of Commerce at the corner of Broad and Church Sts. Its address is 50 Broad St., and its telephone numbers are 440, 240, and 4160. (No local exchange names in Charleston.) Research at the publick library is also desirable, nor should one omit visits to the Museum and the Gibbes Art Gallery.

---

*Pronounc'd *Ha´zel.*

The best way to see Charleston is first to drift aimlessly about the ancient streets below Broad, picking up random impressions of centuried charm and exotic tradition without the psychological hindrance of a preconceiv'd or systematick plan, and then—having reach'd the palmetto-fring'd and live-oak-dotted Battery with its numerous monuments—to begin the regular following up of some stated sightseeing route; preferably the compleat series given in the Wilson guide-book "Street Strolls Around Charleston" (75¢ at Lighthart's or any bookstall), or if this is impossible, one of the briefer schedules outlined in the Chamber of Commerce's magazine, the De Renne brochure (see sheet XIII, p. 2), or the ensuing pages of this description. In the random Batteryward stroll a very good notion of Old Charleston may be secur'd. One will stumble on the quaintest conceivable streets, alleys, and quaint and hidden churchyards, and will encounter the most sumptuous mansions imbedded in wall'd tropical gardens. Along the principal waterfront, that on the Cooper side, he will discern the myriad abandon'd and ruin'd brick warehouses which speak so eloquently of former shipping prosperity. As in Newport and Salem, relatively few of the antient houses are ever demolish'd; tho' there are threats of a vast hotel development amidst the curious old slums of lower East Bay St. The exoticism of the old tiled and stucco'd houses, with their occasionally bright hues, will engage the eye from the outset; suggesting something oddly French, or Latin, or foreign in some obscure way. The great blackness of the numerous negroes will also be remark'd; it being evidently the custom for mulattoes to keep to themselves in the newer far-northern part of the town. Foreign faces are almost wholly absent except in the small Italian quarter around State St.; though there are some Jew merchants and Greek keepers of ordinaries. For the most part Charleston is strictly a Nordick-American town. Here and there a classick, old-fashion'd publick building or church will attract notice; and at all times one is looking for glimpses of the two dominant landmarks, St. Michael's and St. Philip's spires. *Wrought-iron work* produces a deep impression because of its universal profusion—gates, balconies, window grilles, railings, and the like; all of the finest craftsmanship. The gates are especially numerous because of the prevalence of high-wall'd gardens in this land of luxurious flowers, rambling vines, and opulent trees that weave an omnipresent green twilight redolent of perfume and musical with bird-song when the sun goes down. Charlestonians endeavour to secure privacy and the open air at the same time. One tasteful feature of this antient part of the town is the absence of obtrusive street signs; the names of the streets being on bronze plates sett in the sidewalks at the street corners. This custom is becoming universal throughout Charleston.

Having thus absorb'd the general colour of the town, and having form'd a good idea of the general street system—an idea buttress'd by an adequate map in one's pocket—one shou'd next proceed to make a tour of the principal sights* according to a regular plan. The following brief itinerary, beginning at the Battery, is design'd to cover the whole city in a single route with as few repetitions as possible; but is of course merely fragmentary as compar'd with all the sights to be seen. It may be follow'd in one long walk—a full day's pedestrian quota—or taken in sections; and in any order whatsoever. It is not meant to include everything in Old Charleston, and it wou'd be a pity if any reader were to follow it blindly without consulting the guide-books and ascertaining what else is to be seen. Likewise, it leaves to these fuller guide-books the task of supplying ampler descriptions of the few things which are touch'd upon. A map with the course outlined in blue is appended to this itinerary.

---

*Many of the more important houses and sites are mark'd by very convenient historical placards.

Beginning at the *Battery*, the visitor shou'd observe the semi-tropical scenery of that pleasing area, and pay good attention to the mansions fronting on it. Looking down the harbour somewhat eastward, he may behold historick *Fort-Sumter* upon its small island in the distance, and see to the left of it *Fort-Moultrie*, occupying a point of land on *Sullivan's Island.* Turning inland, there is to be seen at No. 8, South-Battery (on the left-hand corner of Church-Street), the elegant private mansion built in 1768 by Tho: Savage, Gent., and in 1785 built by *Col. Wm Washington* of the celebrated Virginia family. If any one now chuse to go up King-St. to N°. 27 and explore the antient *Brewton-Pringle house* (hdqtrs. of H.M. arm'd forces 1780–81), he may well do so; tho' this dwelling will be later encounter'd along the bending line of exploration. If not, it is proper to begin the tour by turning up *Church-Street;* tho' not without carefully looking up *Meeting-Street,* and observing the spacious mansions and estates lining both its sides. Advancing along Church-St., which is here very narrow, we pass by quaint antient houses and stables, and notice the trim dwellings of artists as well across Atlantick-Street. After this we encounter a bend, on the left-hand side of which are some very antient houses. No. 35, once inhabited by the learned author of Johnson's "Traditions of the Revolution",[10] was built in 1745. No. 37 was built before 1733. No. 39, the well-known *George Eveleigh house,* was built in the decade 1743–53, and had a secret stairway to the second floor. All three of these houses once had a secret passage to Vanderhorst Creek, which follow'd the line of the present *Water St.* We now come to Water St., which in its aqueous days was here crost by a bridge. That part of Church St. we have just been traversing, was antiently call'd Fort-Street. The large round object which we see in the sidewalk at this intersection is a *tidal drain,* made necessary by the low and watery nature of the region. Somewhat west of this is the spot where Col. Rhett caused 57 pirates to be hang'd in a single afternoon. Advancing around the bend, we now encounter on our right the entrance to *Stoll's Alley,* lately a slum, but now splendidly restor'd as an habitation for artists. It is to be hop'd, that this colony will remain sacred to the genuine followers of the arts, and not sink to the state of a Greenwich-Village. An exploration of this alley is well worth one's while, nor is it a vain digression to go all the way through the narrow part to *East-Bay St.* In the wider part the Georgian restorations are of the most tasteful and agreeable sort. At East-Bay St. we turn to the left, noting the abandon'd and ruin'd warehouses along the waterfront. We soon come to *Longitude-Lane,* leading back to Church-Street, opposite which, on the water side of the street, is an exceeding sightly edifice of brick, of Adam-period design, and in a pathetick state of desertion and decrepitude. This is *Vanderhorst Row,* put up in the year 1800 and said to be the oldest apartment house in America. Now turning into Longitude-Lane, we pass by the moss-grown brick walls of abandon'd cotton warehouses; noting the cobblestones set for mules' feet, the flagstones for the dray-wheels, and the snubbing-posts at the warehouse doors. One of these posts is an old ship's cannon. To the writer this place has a melancholy charm of a very acute sort. Once back in Church-Street, we look to the left and digress backward a bit to see the entrance of an old warehouse on the eastern side, and the classick facade of the *First Baptist Church* (1822) opposite it. Next the church, and opposite the mouth of Longitude-Lane, is (#69) the *Jacob Motte house,* built in 1760 and having a pink colour which it has borne from the earliest times. Next door—at #71—is the *Robert Brewton house* built in 1740 and forming a fine example of the smaller single houses of early Charleston. Still further along—at #73—is the *Miles Brewton house* (a typical old-Charleston double house) built in 1733. Across the street from it, at #78, is an old house with a fine wrought-iron balcony from which Genl. Washington is reputed to have deliver'd an address. A study of this balcony tends to disprove the tradition, since (although the house itself is antient) the craftsmanship points to a later date than 1791, the period of the General's visit. One singular feature of the house is the symmetrical central position of the doorway; a thing universally met with in Georgian New-England, but very uncommon in the South. We come now to quaint and antient *Tradd St.*, which is so picturesque that it will pay us to stroll down it to the river and return. On both sides we may see very antient houses, built flush with the street and with walls adjoyning, as a protection against the raids of pirates, Spaniards, and Indians. *Bedon's Alley*, a very old and curious byway containing a large three-storey brick house which may possibly be the oldest in Charleston, extends northward from a point half-way to the river; on its western corner being the site once housing the *Carolina Coffee-House*. There, in 1790, the St. Cecelia Society held one of its concerts; and in 1793 the Ugly-Club us'd it as a dining place. At East Bay St. we again behold Vanderhorst Row, and note on the northern corner of Tradd the site of the birthplace of the first white child of the town; Robert Tradd, from whom the street was nam'd. Looking out over the river past *Adger's Wharf*, we behold the island call'd *Castle-Pinckney*; and farther off, the opposite shoar of Mt. Pleasant, and part of Sullivan's Island. Returning now to Church St. and resuming a northerly course, we behold on the left at #87 the *Heyward house*, a fine Georgian mansion of generalised rather than Charlestonian architecture, now under careful restoration by the Society for the Preservation of Old Dwellings and the Charleston Museum. This house was built in the 1770's or before, and was us'd by Genl. Washington during his Charleston visit of May 1791. Adjoining this structure is an old house which in 1791–1810 was the *French Theatre*, afterward the *City Theatre*. The auditorium was in the rear, reach'd by crossing thro' an archway and traversing an inner court. In more recent times, the place was sunk to a slum and used by negroes as a vending-place of vegetables, being commonly known as "Cabbage Row", and presented in the novel "Porgy", by DuBose Heyward, Esq., as "Catfish Row".[11] Very lately it has been reclaim'd to its original elegance and neatness, and is now the abode of art shops. Proceeding onward, we shou'd note the quaint alleys on either side of the street—*St. Michael's Place* to the left, and *Elliott St.* to the right. We now come to *Broad St.*, the leading transverse thoroughfare of the town, and an abode of bankers and brokers. On the northeast corner is the new bank building which has most unfortunately displac'd the old and historic Shepheard's Tavern, where the first Masonick Lodge in America was organised in 1736. On the northwest corner the *Chamber of Commerce* occupies the brick structure erected in 1784 for the Bank of South-Carolina, and used from 1835 to 1914 as a publick library. It will be worth our while to walk down Broad St. to the river and study the antient and remarkable publick building which squarely faces the end of the street. This is the *Old Exchange*, built in 1767 on the site of the old guard post call'd "Half-Moon Bastion", and used as executive headquarters by His Majesty's Forces in 1780–81. It was later a post-office, and is now an headquarters of the D.A.R.—also housing certain clerical federal activities. During the Revolution prisoners were confin'd in the basement of this building; and on the northern end, close to the ground, can still be seen the small square holes, with heavy grating, which afforded scanty light and air to some of the dungeons. The architecture of the building in general is very fine. To the right of the Old Exchange, across a seaward lane and on the water side of East Bay St. at *Nos. 114–116*, will be found *a group of very antient buildings*, two of which have cupolas, or observation-towers. These towers were us'd by observers to watch the incoming shipping and transmit the news to the publick. Ships were first sighted from a tower on Sullivan's Island, whose watchman relay'd the news to these Charleston towers by raising ball signals on a pole—a black ball for a square-rigger, and a white one for a schooner-rigg'd vessel. These signals were repeated by the Charleston watchers, the signal-balls being left up until the ships they represented came to anchor. The small building on the corner (later the British consulate) next the tallest cupola'd building is the old *French Coffee-House or Harris's Tavern*. Beneath this structure may still be found the antient wine-cellars, which form a tunnel extending far out under East Bay St., and then turning toward the Battery in an arm reaching half a block. We now, after a glance at the classick bank facade on the landward side of E. Bay above Broad, turn back along Broad St. for one block; then turning northward into *State St.*, originally call'd *Union St.* Following this to the first intersection, we there turn to the left into antient and picturesque *Chalmers St.*, a broad cobbled thoroughfare, at whose farther end can be seen in the distance the splendid classick pillars of *Hibernian-Hall* (1841) in Meeting St. Almost all the houses along Chalmers St. are colonial. At No. 8, the small, low archway adjoining a pretentiously turreted building, is the *Old Slave Market* at which train'd servants and skill'd artisans were sold—the common field niggers being procurable at "Vendue Range", the foot of Queen St. where the Clyde Line wharves now extend. Nearly opposite the "Slave Mart" is that curious pink-colour'd building which possesses the *only gambrel roof in Charleston*. This is a very old house, and was a tavern before the Revolution. It has three storeys, but only one room to a floor. We are now back at Church St., tho' it wou'd do no harm to walk along Chalmers to Meeting and back in order to observe the antient houses. Turning up Church, we next come to *Queen St.* (formerly Dock St.), at whose southeast corner is the sightly Gothick church (1845) and churchyard of the Huguenots. This is today the only Huguenot church in the country, and deserves the support (which it sorely needs) of every surviving group of Huguenot descendants. Money may be subscrib'd in the name of some bygone Huguenot leader, to whom a memorial tablet will be erected within the edifice. Many such are already in position. Across the street from the church is the deserted and dilapidated ruin of the *Planters' Hotel*, built about 1805, and famous in the great cotton aera as a rendezvous of neighbouring planters and their families. On the northwest corner, and extending a considerable space along Church St., is a group of five small houses built of brick and Bermuda coral-stone, and known to have been standing prior to 1742. These are the so-called *Pirate Houses;* reputed to have received visits at a later from Mr. Poe. Of the truth of these traditions the writer has no opinion to offer. They are now all converted into fashionable shops, and the courtyard betwixt them has been developed as a highly fascinating byway. Beyond these comes the bend in the street, with the fine porticoes and steeple of *St. Philip's* Episcopal Church looming up in the foreground, and sections of the churchyard stretching off on both sides of the way. St. Philip's present edifice does not antedate 1835, but it is a fine late-Georgian specimen whose steeple shares honours with St. Michael's as a landmark of the city, and a welcoming symbol to the mariner approaching the port. The tower, with its triple portico, is very notable. When this fane was built, Church St. did not extend in front of it; the bend being made to accommodate it. The present street cuts the old churchyard in two, separating the larger part (which contains the last mortal resting place of the Hon. John C. Calhoun) from the edifice itself. We now push on to *Cumberland St.*, chusing whether or not we shall stroll down toward the waterfront to see the old house (on the N. side) with the elaborate ironwork, and the wrought-iron emblem of the Iron Workers' Guild—which was probably the residence and shop of a master craftsman. With this side-trip made or omitted, we follow Cumberland west of Church toward Meeting, noting on the left-hand side the *Old Powder Magazine* in its limited but pleasing grounds. This squat, peaked-gabled bit of Cyclopean vaulted masonry is the oldest structure in Charleston, dating from the

1730's and having form'd a bastion of the city wall. It is the only surviving fragment of that wall. The Colonial Dames are in charge of it, and visitors are admitted to the heavily vaulted interior for a shilling. We now follow Cumberland to Meeting and turn northward to *Market St.*, beholding in the middle of that thoroughfare the high classick facade of the *Old Market House*, whose upper part is now a Confederate Museum. This edifice, built in 1841, is typical of Old Charleston publick architecture; having the characterstick double flight of steps with the mouth of an arched tunnel beneath. Behind the building the low-roofed shed of the Market (erected in 1800) extends all the way to the river, along the line of what was once Fish Market Creek. In earlier times the refuse of this market attracted a famous array of buzzards, which became incredibly tame. Following the market shed to East Bay St., after a glance upward along Meeting at the classick facade of the old *Charleston Hotel*, we behold somewhat to the right, and set near the water, the massive and splendid *Custom-House* with its classick architecture, begun in 1850 and finish'd after the Civil War. From the seaward side of this building an impressive view of the harbour may be obtain'd. We now proceed three squares up East Bay to *Hasell St.*, here turning to the left and proceeding again toward Meeting St. On the north or right-hand side, at #54, is what is probably (the claim of the Bedon's Alley house notwithstanding) the *oldest dwelling in Charleston*, built in 1722 or before by the old pirate-fighter William Rhett, and later forming the birthplace of the eminent soldier and statesman, Genl. Wade Hampton. Reaching Meeting St., we may if we wish make a side-trip beyond to see the venerable classick facade of the *Jews' Synagogue* (1841) on the right, and *St. Mary's Romish Church* (1838) on the left. We then turn northward along Meeting toward George, noting on the left the stately columns of *Trinity M. E. Church* (1875), call'd "the youngest church below Calhoun St." At George St. we note on the N.W. corner the fine but dilapidated *King mansion* with its wall'd grounds, built in 1806 and later used as a high-school. Making a side-trip eastward along George, we see on the north side the grounds and building of the local water-works—which is the old *Elliott-Pinckney-Middleton house*, finished in 1797 and forming one of the finest possible specimens of Adam-period architecture. The interior of this mansion, defac'd tho' it is by industrial uses, still retains much fine woodwork and proportioning—especially the circular stairway and the oval room upstairs. Travellers shou'd explore the interior, insomuch as opportunities for seeing Charleston interiors are somewhat limited for strangers without local introductions. The region around this place was once called Ansonborough. Returning now to Meeting St., we follow it northward again till we come to *Calhoun St.* and the easterly end of the open park or parade-ground known successively as *Inspection Square, Citadel Green*, and *Marion Square*. This was formerly the line of the city's northernmost defences, and in the midst of the park may be seen a single remaining bit of the old *"Horn Wall"*—made of a mixture of lime and sea shells—which form'd the fortifications of 1780. On the north side of the green is the long, battlemented line of *The Old Citadel* (1822), which form'd the home of the Military College of S.C. from its foundation in 1842 to its recent removal (1924) to new quarters in the extream northwestern part of the city. The King St. side of the green is the focus of modern business life and the seat of the leading new hotel. The Meeting St. side marks the local district once known as Louisburgh. Continuing along Meeting beyond the Square, we see above Charlotte St. the splendid avenue of approach to the *Second Presbyterian Church*, which was built in 1811. Just beyond this, at the corner of Ashmead St. and much defac'd by an encroaching petrol station, is the fine old *Peter Manigault mansion*, with its striking circular gate lodge (a typical Old Charleston feature, though only two now survive), built in 1790. At times this house is open as a publick museum, tho' it is too often found clos'd. The interior contains a splendid curved staircase, as well as an interesting secret stairway.

We have now reached a logical northerly limit of travel, tho' many may wish to proceed westward thro' Hudson and Vanderhorst Sts. to *Coming St.*, up which, on the right-hand side, is *St. Paul's Episcopal Church*, a spacious fane built in 1810–12. This district was once known as Radcliffeborough. Proceeding south to *Calhoun St.* we may, if we desire, go westward several blocks to *Rutledge Ave.*, in the old Cannonsborough section (south of which lay Harlestonborough), where we will find the *Charleston Museum* with its many antiquarian and other exhibits. Typical Old Charleston rooms and apothecary shops are shewn in the gallery of this celebrated institution. The museum is the oldest in America, having been founded in 1773. Returning along Calhoun to *St. Philip St.*, we see in the next block, on the north side of Calhoun and extending to the new hotel fronting Marion Sq., the spacious grounds and venerable building (1792) of the *Charleston Orphan House.* The early prevalence of cholera, fever, and smallpox in the district left so many orphans that this institution was deem'd a necessity. It still serves its original purpose—tho' the inroads of disease have long since been reduc'd to normal thro' the progress of medical science. Descending St. Philip St. we come, at George St., upon the grounds, edifices, and lodge-gate of the stately and reposeful *College of Charleston*, whose oldest structure was erected in 1828. Proceeding eastward thro' George to King St., we turn to the right and descend that business thoroughfare for many blocks. In the course of our walk we shall see two surviving instances of antient *shop signs;* the *drum clock* over the jewellery shop at #285, betwixt Society and Wentworth Sts. on the western side, and the *plough* over McIntosh's Seed Store next the Masonick Temple on the eastern side betwixt Wentworth and Hasell. At *Clifford St.* we turn to the right, proceeding through to *Archdale St.* (a thoroughfare known for a time, and so designated on signs and maps, as *Charles St.*, which causes considerable confusion). On the southeast corner we behold the ancient edifice and picturesque churchyard of *St. John's Lutheran Church;* which is directly adjoin'd on the south—in Archdale St.—by the Gothick precincts of the famous *Unitarian Church*, where for 40 years preach'd the Revd Sam$^{l.}$ Gilman, of the Province of the Massachusetts-Bay, author of the widely known college hymn, "Fair Harvard". In the tower of this church a Memorial Room has been dedicated to Dr Gilman by Harvard alumni. The edifice is very remarkable as being one of the very few *Gothick* specimens erected in the eighteenth century. It was built in 1772; and tho' badly damag'd by the earthquake of 1886, has been carefully restor'd to pristine strength. Its churchyard, together with the neighbouring churchyard of St. John's, which is virtually one with it, is the supreme epitome of exotick glamorousness; a perfum'd green tropick twilight of twisted-branch'd, overarching live-oaks and hanging vines, with antient slabs and altar-stones peeping thro' a vivid, verdurous undergrowth threaded by curious winding walks. It is truly something out of a dream— such things do not belong to the waking world! Recognising this quality of fascination in the old Archdale St. churchyards, as well as in other churchyards and garden plots to the east, the President of the Charleston Garden Club some time ago form'd the notion of mapping out an idyllic cross-town walk which might include as many as possible of these with a fair degree of continuity. The Unitarian churchyard had already establish'd a walk thro' to King St. opposite the publick library, with a fine wrought-iron gate on the latter thoroughfare; and now a similar walk with gates was provided in the garden area just across the way—extending from the publick library grounds in King St. to the yard of the *Gibbes Art Museum* in Museum St. Still further coöperating, the *Circular Congregational Church* in Meeting St. opposite the Gibbes Art Museum (an ugly Victorian church, but having a delightful Old-Charleston chapel [1867], with classick facade and double entrance flights, in its grounds) open'd its spacious churchyard as a continuation of the garden stroll; being seconded by St. Philip's Church, whose westerly churchyard spreads from Church St. to meet the rear of the Congregational churchyard. Thus the walk is made continuous from Archdale St. across King and Meeting to Church St.; and now there is talk of continuing it through St. Philip's *easterly* churchyard—behind the church, and emerging in Cumberland St. thro' a future gate. Such is the *Gateway Path*, so-call'd; and every visitor to Charleston ought at some time or other to thread its entire length from St. John's to St. Philip's. For our *present* tour, we follow it from the Unitarian churchyard out to King St. and the library; there turning to the right and following King St. southward. On the easterly side of King below Queen, at #138, is the *site of the old Quaker Meeting-House*, enclos'd by a tall iron fence. The first meeting house was built in 1694, but there has been no edifice on the site since the fire of 1861; the Quakers being now extinct in Charleston. The churchyard, however, is own'd and maintain'd in good condition by the central organisation of Quakers in Philadelphia; and two of the antient graves may yet be seen. Having seen this, we advance down to *Broad St.*, making a short side-trip along this thoroughfare to the right to see the *Ralph Izard house* at #110 (1750), *the later Izard house* (#114) (1827) now occupy'd by the Catholick Bishop, *the Rutledge house* (1760), and the still *intact site (#118) of St. Andrew's Hall*, built in 1814 and burn'd in the fire of 1861. It is melancholy to observe the decaying garden walls and the mossy bricks of the long-disused walks. This was, in its day, the principal auditorium of the town, a distinction now falling to Hibernian Hall in Meeting St. The St. Andrew's Society, which built it, was organised in 1729, and is alive in a flourishing state, having celebrated its 200th anniversary in 1929. Genl. Lafayette was entertain'd in the vanisht building in 1825. Beyond this site may be seen the modern *Cathedral of St. John the Divine*, but we must now return eastward; retracing our steps to King St., and proceeding beyond to the important Meeting St. intersection. On the left-hand side of Broad, just back of the Court-House, is a small street known as *Court-House Square*. The large Georgian double house visible at its end, with a peculiarly Charlestonian arrangement of steps, and twin colonial doorways with transoms having double rows of lights, is the house exploited in the novel "Lady Baltimore", by Owen Wister.[12] Approaching this house and proceeding thro' the *green gateway on the left,* we encounter a quasi-rustick lane which leads to a hidden group of idyllically embower'd houses—a sylvan oasis not a stone's throw from the town's civick centre. This is the champion "and where"[13] of all time! Emerging thence to the intersection of Broad and Meeting, we are indeed at the civick heart of things. On the N.W. corner is the *Court House*, built in 1788 on the site of a burn'd down State House in the days of Charleston State Capitalship. Across on the N.E. corner is the *City Hall*, built in 1801 as the United States Bank, and used as a City Hall since 1818. On the S.E. corner is ancient *St. Michael's* (1761) with its glorious steeple, exquisite chimes, and quaint old churchyard with wrought-iron gates by Iusti. And on the S.W. corner is the modern but by no means unsightly *Post Office*. Back of the City Hall is *Washington-Square*, with its walks, benches, Pitt, Timrod, and Beauregard Monuments, and ancient rear wall with arch'd embrasures. In the N.W. corner of the park, on the S.E. corner of Meeting and Chalmers Sts., stands the classick hall of records put up in 1826 and call'd the *Fireproof Building* because it was the first of that type erected in America. It prov'd its worth in the earthquake of 1886, when alone of all the structures in this region it remained uninjur'd. Opposite the park in Meeting St. is the old *Timrod Inn* with its archaick portico extending over the sidewalk. On the same western side of the street opposite the end of

Chalmers is the stately classick facade of *Hibernian Hall* (1841), the city's principal auditorium and the home of a society of gentlemen of Irish descent, who alternately elect a Protestant and a Catholick as their president in their annual elections. Hence proceeding south down Meeting St., we behold on our left, below St. Michael's Place, the splendid edifice of the *South Carolina Society*, built in 1804 and design'd by Gabriel Manigault, Esq. This is a masterpiece in the true Charleston tradition, with double steps flankt by wrought-iron lamps. The colonial portico over the sidewalk is very justly esteem'd, and is of a somewhat later date than the building proper. The society which this building houses, was form'd for charitable purposes in 1736, and is still vigorously flourishing. Descending to Tradd St., we behold on the N.W. corner an antient mansion with a two-storey'd porch (probably of much later date) overshadowing the street. This is the *Governor Branford or Horry House*, built in 1751–57. On the S.W. corner is the old *Scotch or First Presbyterian Church* and churchyard, the present sightly edifice dating from 1814. Just below this, on the same side of the street (#51), is the splendid *Nathaniel Russell mansion* built in 1811 and following general Adam-period designs in its exterior, which is of un-stucco'd brick. Over the doorway the initials "N.R." are woven into the wrought-iron balcony. The interior is very celebrated, and includes a magnificent circular stairway lighted by two vast and unusual windows. Descending Meeting St. still farther, we must not omit to glance down any quaint alleys we may pass. At Water St. we are near the spot where Rhett hanged 57 pirates. Here were antiently the sources of Vanderhorst Creek. All along the street, on both sides, are now seen residences of the greatest beauty and antiquity. *No. 39*, on the right-hand side, was built in 1767. *No. 35* was the residence of Mr. Bull, a Charleston gentleman who was Lieutenant-Governor at the time of the Revolution. Just across the street, at *No. 34*, resided the last lawful Governor of the Province, appointed by the Crown; Ld *William Campbell*, who at length was so threaten'd by seditious mobs that he withdrew secretly, thro' an hidden passage, to a small boat in Vanderhorst Creek, by which he was convey'd to His Maj$^{ty's}$ vessel *Tamar*, then lying in the harbour. We now turn to the right thro' *Ladson St.*, tho' not without a glance down Meeting (to meet the upward glance we made when starting from the Battery) at the many fine mansions and gardens. Proceeding thro' Ladson to its end in King St., we find ourselves at the splendid *Miles Brewton or Pringle house* (#27), a spacious brick mansion with wall'd garden, coach-house, and slave-quarters, built in 1765, and displaying the best British architecture modified for Charleston needs with a two-storey'd portico. It was us'd as an headquarters for His Majesty's officers in 1780–81, and is open to the publick at the rather high admission-fee of one dollar. The interior, from vaulted basement to rafter'd attick, is well worth inspection. All the great rooms are finely decorated and panell'd, and shew early phases of the Adam influence—rare in the colonies as early as 1765. There are some notably fine mantels, and much good furniture is present. The gardens and outbuildings are all highly interesting—especially the *coach-house* fronting on the street just above this house, which displays very fully the whimsical use of Gothick as practic'd in Georgian Charleston. We now proceed southward along King St.; noting, as we cross it, the extream narrowness (on the left-hand side) of *Lamboll-St.*; which despite its alley-like dimensions betwixt Meeting and King, is a residential thoroughfare of the first order. As we approach the Battery, we may well pause to observe #3 *King St.* on our right; this antient house being call'd by guide-books the *narrowest* residence in Charleston, and perhaps in the whole South. Arriv'd at the *Battery*, we turn to the right, or westward; pausing as we do so to reflect that on this spot in 1718 were hang'd the celebrated pirate captain *Stede Bonnet*, and some 40 of his men. It is said, that Colo. Rhett compell'd these malefactors to dig their own graves, so that upon being cut down their bodies fell into them, where they still lye. Another account has it that they were hang'd above the water, and cut down so that the ebb of the tide might carry them away. At all events, it is known that the efforts of Rhett made Charleston reasonably safe from pirates. There is much doubt, confusion, and hearsay in all these tales; and this hanging on the Battery is often mixt up with that other hanging of the 57 over-against Vanderhorst Creek about the same period. Several guide-books declare, that it was *Bonnet's* hanging which took place on the creek; appearing to joyn the facts of two events in one. It is not well to place too much reliance on any statement made concerning these nebulous and traditional matters. We now proceed westward, or toward the Ashley-River, for a single square; then turning to the right up *Legare St.* (pronounc'd *Le-gree ´*). This is equal to lower Meeting St. in the taste and elegance of its dwellings, and is altogether inhabited by families of consequence. Like all places long tenanted by a vivid gentlefolk, it is full of old legends which guide-books still relate; amongst them being that of a duel fought with pistols from opposite upper windows across the street. On every hand are exquisite specimens of wrought-iron work, old granite and cypress hitching-posts (very typical of Charleston), fine polisht knockers, graceful gates and doorways, pleasing house-facades, and wall'd gardens of unutterable charm. At the head of *Gibbes St.* we observe in a wall one of the most famous pairs of *wrought-iron gates* in Charleston. At #14, on the eastern or right-hand side on the street, we come to the *George Edwards* house in its wall'd grounds, noticing the famous *gates* with their pineapple-topt posts, which were erected in 1820. Into the iron-work around the doorway are woven the script initials "G" and "E". The iron-work of the gates is piec'd out with cypress-wood, but so cunningly that the difference cannot be told. Cypress was at one time a great medium of construction in Charleston, many entire houses being built of it. Such an one is now seen, on the left, at *#15 Legare St.;* this being one of the houses from whose upper windows the celebrated duel of tradition was fought. On the right, the *knockers* of the Edwards house and of its neighbour at #16 are deserving of especial notice. We ought also to observe the antient iron lanthorns over the entrance gates, the finest of which will be found at #18. Approaching *Tradd St.,* we see in the brick wall on our right, at #32, the famous *Simonton Sword Gates,* which are perhaps the most beautiful specimens of their kind in Charleston, or in the country. They derive their name from the central horizontal bars of their design, which are in the form of Roman short swords, on which impinge vertical supports in the form of Roman javelins. The scroll-work supplementing these is of the most graceful description, and the whole is topt by a fine lanthorn. Behind the gates are spacious and well-order'd grounds and an old flagston'd avenue of magnolias leading to a mansion built before 1776. The gates are reckon'd of more recent date than this. In the late eighteenth century this estate became a fashionable girls' school conducted by a French gentlewoman, Madame Talvande, who fled hither from the San Domingo massacre. Later the place was own'd by a young gentleman from England, whose revelry and gaming made it a scene of nightly resort for the gayest of Charleston's young bloods. We now reach the corner of *Tradd St.,* and may if we wish digress westward toward the Ashley River to observe some of the old houses and gateways. At *#127,* on the left, is a fine recess'd gate with a curving wall on each side. Next it, at *#131,* is another excellent specimen. Across the street at *#128* is a fine old house built in 1760 and reached by curv'd steps climbing to a high porch. Around the corner, to the right, in *Logan St.* is the antient churchyard of a vanish'd church, old *St. Peter's.* This is in the burn'd district of 1861, hence beyond it most of the houses are new. At *#141 Tradd St.,* however, is a fine old recess'd fence with a splendid gate of cluster-and-arrow ironwork at the inner bend of the curve. Behind it is a deep garden with trees, at the end of which the mansion may be seen at a distance. Now retracing our steps toward Meeting, we re-cross Legare and note some more objects of interest. On our left *Orange St.* runs up to Broad, and we may behold at its end the younger Izard house now occupy'd by the Catholick Bishop. On the N.W. corner, at *#104 Tradd,* is the *Stuart house,* built in 1772 and own'd by a loyalist. At *King St.* we note the fine tiling of the three-storey edifice on the N.W. corner. Beyond this, on our left, we see at *#72–4 Tradd St.* a fine old English double house with steps, built in 1734. Next door, at *#70,* is the Robert Pringle house, built in 1774 and since defaced by the addition of a bay-window. The next corner is *Meeting St.,* with the *Branford-Horry house* on our left and the *South or First Presbyterian Church* on our right. Those we beheld before, when descending Meeting St., and we are at last aware that we have come upon the end of our sightseeing route.

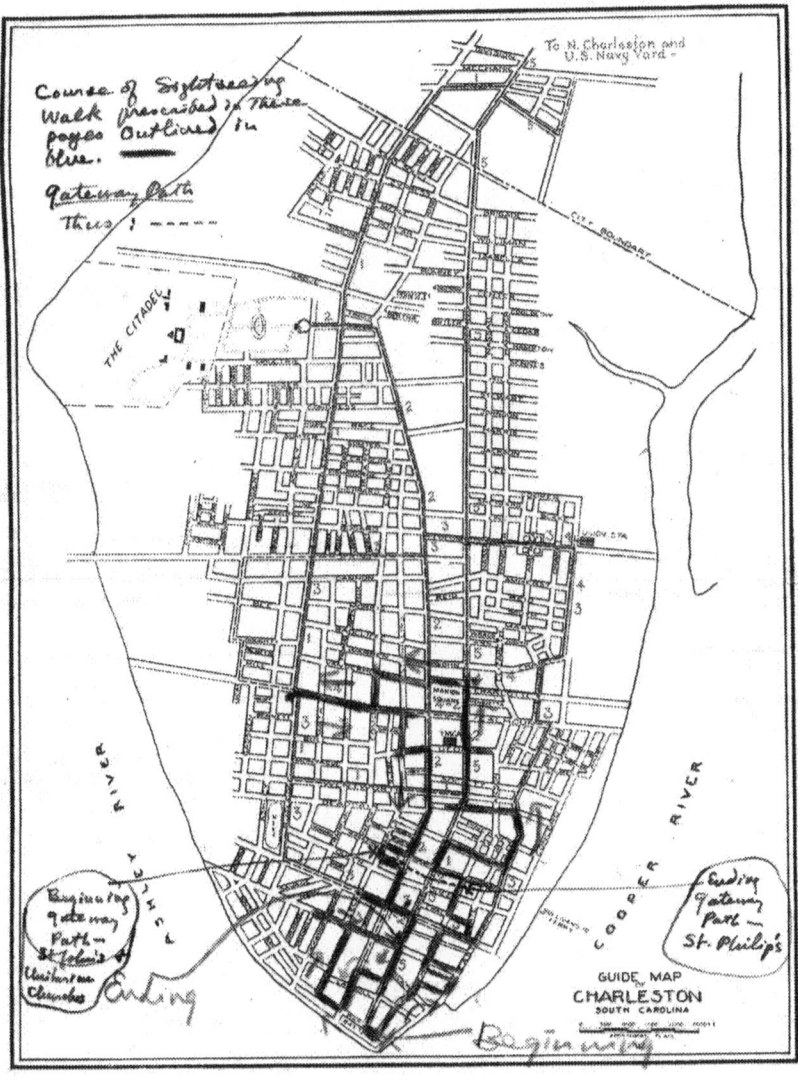

EDITOR'S NOTE   FP: MW 361–406. Text based on the AMS (JHL), dated 17 July 1930. Perhaps the most literarily impressive of HPL's travelogues—a document that not only records the overwhelming impression Charleston made upon him (he came to rank it second only to Providence as his favourite among cities—largely because, in spite of its warmer climate, its architecture is strikingly similar to that of colonial Providence), but also underscores many of his sociopolitical principles (continuity with the past, detestation of modern-day speed, bustle, and conformity, social and intellectual aristocracy, and the like). Like some of the other travelogues, it is marred by touches of crude racism and social snobbery. Because the text exists only in manuscript, HPL does not seem to have circulated it among his colleagues. He did, however, condense it (and remove some of its most piquant features, notably its eighteenth-century diction) in a letter to H. C. Koenig (later revised as an essay), published as *Charleston* (see p. 261). Most of HPL's account of Charleston history was probably derived from local histories and contemporary guidebooks (see nn. 6–7), which provided dates for the houses and other structures HPL describes. Some of the dates have since been somewhat revised, but no effort is made here to correct HPL's errors (or his sources'). Most of the structures HPL saw still exist, but a few have been destroyed. On subsequent trips to the South HPL would return as often as possible (he visited the city again in 1931, 1934, and 1935).

Notes

1. Samuel Galliard Stoney, "Foreword" to *The Octagon Library of Early American Architecture: Volume I—Charleston, South Carolina*, ed. Albert Simons and Samuel Lapham (New York: Press of the American Institute of Architects, Inc., 1927; rpt. 1970), n.p.

2. Mrs St Julien (Harriott Horry) Ravenel (1832–1912), *Charleston: The Place and the People* (1906). Arthur Mazÿck (1850–1914), *Guide to Charleston Illustrated* (1875).

3. Jedidiah Morse (1761–1826), *Geography Made Easy* (1784; rpt. Boston: I. Thomas & E. T. Andrews, 1796), p. 244. HPL misdated the book because he owned an 8th ed. (Boston: I. Thomas & E. T. Andrews, 1802; *LL* 626). He also owned a 19th ed. (1818; *LL* 627).

4. HPL refers to Ben Hecht's avant-garde novel *Erik Dorn* (1921). In a 1927 letter HPL notes: "You can get a fairly good bird's-eye view of literary modernism by reading Ben Hecht's 'Erik Dorn' for prose, and T. S. Eliot's 'The Waste Land' for what purports to be verse" (*SL* 2.96).

5. Anne O'Hare McCormick, "The South: Cities Astride the Centuries," *New York Times Magazine* (22 June 1930): 23.

6. François-René de Chateaubriand (1768–1848), *Atala* (1801), a romance based in large part upon a visit that Chateaubriand had taken to wild and uninhabited regions of the American continent. HPL notes that Chateaubriand also made use of the bluffs of Natchez, Miss., in his novel (see *SL* 4.41).

7. *What to See—Where to Go in Historic Charleston* (Savannah, GA: W. W. De Renne, 1929).

8. Miriam Bellangee Wilson, *Street Strolls Around Charleston, South Carolina* ([Charleston, 1930]). Later editions (e.g., the 5th ed. of 1946) are considerably expanded and revised.

9. An allusion to James F. Morton.

10. Joseph Johnson (1776–1862), *Traditions and Reminiscences, Chiefly of the American Revolution in the South* (Charleston: Walker & James, 1851).

11. DuBose Heyward (1885–1940), *Porgy* (1925). Heyward and his wife, Dorothy Heyward, later turned the novel into a play (produced 1927); George Gershwin then wrote an opera based upon it, *Porgy and Bess* (1935). HPL cites the opera in "Charleston" (p. 271).

12. Owen Wister (1860–1938), *Lady Baltimore* (1906), a humorous love story set in Charleston.

13. On the significance of this phrase see W. Paul Cook's memoir (1941; *LR* 137).

A Description of the Town of Quebeck in New-France, Lately added to His Britannick Majesty's Dominions

By H. Lovecraft, *Armiger*,
of
Providence, in New-England.

Design'd for the Information of the Curious, and for the Guiding of Travellers from His Majesty's New-England and other American Provinces. To which is added, an historical Account of New-France.

With Designs and Maps Illustrative of the Text

———

Contents

PROVIDENCE, in RHODE-ISLAND
Printed by John Carter at Shakespear's-Head in King-street

MDCCCCXXXI.

A DESCRIPTION OF THE
Town of
QUEBECK, in New-France,
Lately added to His Britannick Majefty's Dominions.

By H. Lovecraft, Armiger,
of
Providence, in New-England.

BOOK I. An Historical Account of Quebeck, and of New-France.

(A) Founding and Establishment of New-France

The antient wall'd city of *Quebeck,* in *North-America,* is not only the oldest surviving town upon that continent north of *New-Spain,* but is of all such towns the most retentive of its early aspect. It lyes on a promontory on the north bank of the River *St. Lawrence;* forming a small peninsula with the *St. Lawrence* on the south and east sides, and the confluent River *St. Charles* on the north. Most of this peninsula is a very lofty table-land, rising above a narrow shoar strip in the sheer cliffs of rock. The table-land itself is uneven, having a tendency to slope downwards from the south toward the north, and possessing as its highest point a bold headland on the southern side, near the tip of the peninsula, call'd *Cape-Diamond.* The average height of the cliffs is about 300 feet; corresponding cliffs existing on the other side of the river, where the town of *Lévis* is situate.

The latitude of *Quebeck* is 46° 48 23 N., and its longitude is 71° 12 23 W. It is 400 miles from the Gulph of *St. Lawrence,* into which the river empties, and is 180 miles below the metropolis of *Montreal.* It is about 400 miles north of *Boston,* in *New-England,* and a little over that from *Providence,* as coach-routes are reckon'd. The climate is not thought inclement by those of hardy tastes, tho' the temperature falls as low as -30° in winter. The summers are nearly as warm as those of *New-England,* the temperature often rising to 94°. This peninsula was antiently the site of an Indian village call'd *Stadacona;* the name *Quebeck* (notwithstanding some fanciful false etymologies often advanc'd) being an Indian word signifying *a narrow place in the river,* since the *St. Lawrence* is here narrower than at any other neighbouring place. The generall regional name of *Canada* is the Indian for "a collection of huts".

The history of Quebeck is closely bound up with that of New-France as a whole, insomuch as it was the chief town and seat of governance of the region under both French and English authority till the year 1865, and is still the local capital of the Province of Quebeck. Along its coast, New-France was first seen by the early Northmen; and first in historick times by John Cabot, a Venetian under His Britannick Majesty's flag, in 1497. It was likewise glimpsed by the Portugese Cortereal in 1501, by the Portugese Fagundez in 1520, by Verrazano (that Italian in the French King's pay who first saw *Rhode-Island*) in 1524, and by His Britannick Majesty's naval officer John Rut in 1527. None of these explorers, however, saw the St. Lawrence River; which continued to be undiscover'd notwithstanding the increasing presence of fishing-boats from Europe off the Great Banks. The discovery of the Gulph and River of St. Lawrence was accomplisht in 1534 by the celebrated Jacques Quartier (commonly known as Cartier) of St. Malo in Britanny, acting under the orders of the French King. Capt. Cartier erected, upon the Gaspé peninsula at the mouth of the river, a cross thirty feet high bearing the shield and lilies of France, and with the inscription *Vive le Roy de France*. This form'd the formal seizure of the territory in the French King's name, tho' curious Indians were assur'd it was no more than the setting of a mark for navigators. Jacques Cartier is justly to be reckon'd the real discoverer of New-France, and the first of that line of illustrious Gallick pioneers whose exploits are so well told, for the instruction and entertainment of youth, in the novels of the late Henry Everett McNeil, Esq.[1]

In the year 1535, on a second expedition of three vessels, Jacques Cartier first sail'd up the St. Lawrence and beheld the site of *Quebeck*, being thus the undisputed white discoverer of that spot. Here, at the Indian village of *Stadacona*, whose chieftain Donnacona he found friendly, he left his two larger ships whilst he explored the river's upper reaches in the smallest. It was upon this inland voyage that he beheld and nam'd the island and hill of *Mont-Real*. Capt. Cartier spent the winter at Stadacona on the banks of the St. Charles at the junction with the river Lorette, in the present suburb of Limoilou; but lost so many men from scurvy that he cou'd man only two ships on his return to Europe in the spring. In 1541 Cartier again visited New-France, sail'd to Montreal, and winter'd at Cap Rouge, just above Quebec; this time under the orders of Jean François de la Roque, Sieur de Roberval, who had been appointed by the King as Viceroy of the new land. He return'd home, however, before de Roberval himself arriv'd. The purpose of Cartier himself, like that of the earlier American explorers and many later ones, was merely to find a sea-passage to Asia; a widespread attitude reflected in the ironick naming of the explorer La Salle's seigneury above Montreal, which was called *La Chine*, the French name for China. De Roberval, however, had a design to found a colony; and upon his voyage brought out a load of convicts whom he try'd to settle, in 1542, at Cap Rouge (so call'd from its reddish hue, due to oxide of iron). This colony did not last above a year; scurvy, cold weather, and disorder working the most extream havock with it. Many men were hang'd or imprison'd, and the rest were sent back to France in the autumn of 1543. De Roberval, having return'd with them, was later kill'd in a nocturnal street fight in Paris.

From that time till the opening of the seventeenth century, no attempt was made to colonise New-France; tho' fishermen and explorers continu'd to frequent it. The government of France was kept busy with religious wars, hence had no time to think of colonies till the promulgation of the Edict of Nantes in 1598. In that year the Marquis de la Roche, of Brittany, made an unsuccessful attempt to colonise the Isle de Sable, off the Nova Scotian coast, with some convicts; whilst in 1600, the fur-trading advantages of New-France being made manifest, there began that long series of settlements by royally-granted commercial monopolies which was to lay the permanent structure of the colony. These monopolies, and the colonising enterprises associated with them, were not unlike those of the Dutch and English which settled many of the regions to the southward. In 1600, after the manifest failure of de la Roche, a fur-trading monopoly was granted jointly to Pierre Chauvin, an Huguenot merchant of Honfleur, and to François Gravé, Sieur du Pont, a maritime gentleman of St. Malo. These traders receiv'd their grant on condition of their bringing to New-France not less than fifty colonists per year; a thing which M. Chauvin sought to carry out by establishing a settlement of sixteen men at Tadoussac, on the St. Lawrence below Quebeck, at the mouth of the grim, gorge-like tributary River Saguenay. Most of these men perisht the first winter, and M. Chauvin himself dy'd in 1602. In 1603 the monopoly was transferr'd to a group of maritime merchants under Sieur de Chaste, governor of Dieppe, to whom upon his death in 1604 succeeded the celebrated Pierre du Guast, Sieur de Monts, an Huguenot gentleman holding the governorship of Pons, in Saintonge. De Monts was given a fur monopoly of ten years, but under harder conditions than those formerly impos'd; it being obligatory for him to bring out a full hundred colonists per year, leaving a thousand in the future settlement at the end of the ten-year arrangement.

In April, 1604, De Monts sett sail from Havre, having with him the later illustrious Samuel de Champlain as Geographer Royal, and being follow'd by other vessels bearing many gentlemen of importance, including Gravé, Sieur du Pont—commonly known in history as Pont-Gravé—and two years later by the attorney Marc Lescarbot, who in 1609 writ the history of the enterprise. The spot chosen for settlement was that seaboard region call'd, thro' affectionate classicism, Acadia, or Acadie; and at the advice of Champlain the actual town site was an island at the mouth of the River St. Croix, within the present limits of Maine, in New-England. De Monts may thus with justice be call'd the first white settler, builder of houses, and planter of grain, in New-England; even tho' his colony was not fated to survive, and tho' it was not part of that continuous New-England fabrick which has pass'd into history. In June, 1604, 79 settlers of an heterogeneous sort, both Huguenots and Papists, were landed on the island, and severall houses were built within a palisado. Grain was planted both on the island and on the neighbouring (Maine) mainland, but the soil was found poor, scurvy prevalent, and the colonists turbulent and unmanageable. Of the 79 men only 44 remained alive in the following spring, and in that year of 1605 the settlement was transferr'd to the opposite shoar of the Bay of Fundy, forming that *Port-Royal* (now Annapolis, N.S.) which was (with an interruption which, like that of Tadoussac, prevents it from dethroning Quebec as the oldest continuously settled town) destined to survive and have an eventful history. The ruins of De Monts's settlement were discover'd in 1798 by commissioners negotiating a boundary betwixt Maine and New-Brunswick, and are today mark'd by a tablet put up in 1904, at the tercentenary of the short-lived settlement. The island has been at times the seat of residences, but now holds only a lighthouse belonging to the U. S. government. It is but 900 × 125 feet in dimensions, and is now known as Dockel's Island. Port Royal had actually been settled and named by De Monts's associate, Baron de Poutrincourt, almost as soon as the St. Croix island. In 1606 a new lot of settlers came out under de Poutrincourt's auspices; but in September, 1607, the bulk of the colony return'd to France, and in 1608 de Monts's trading monopoly was revok'd. Enough colonists remain'd, however, (under the direction of Lescarbot) to keep it nominally alive; tho' very few new settlers came out. The final end of the enterprise came in 1612, when a party from His Britannick Majesty's new Dominion of Virginia, under the buccaneer Samuel Argall, wiped it out in the course of a raid made to assert Great-Britain's right to the country by virtue of John Cabot's discovery in 1497. The party of Argall likewise destroy'd the abandon'd buildings of De Monts's first colony on the island in the St. Croix. Of all the men connected with the enterprise, Champlain is the most notable. He had been to New-France in 1603 under De Chaste's auspices, and during his period at St. Croix and Port Royal he made voyages down the coast of New-England, accurately charting all the harbours as far south as Plymouth.

In 1608 Samuel de Champlain, under the auspices of de Monts, founded the town of *Quebeck*. De Monts having chosen the St. Lawrence region for his next venture—a venture undertaken under competitive conditions since his fur monopoly was rescinded—Champlain push'd up the river beyond Tadoussac and establish'd his trading post at the narrow place where Cartier had found the Indian village of Stadacona. On the narrow shoar betwixt the St. Lawrence and the cliff at the easterly tip of the bold peninsula he settled himself and his crew in a well-built and habitable fort which he called *L'Abitation de Quebecq*. Tho' more a post or garrison than a true colony, its success caus'd it to remain; even in spite of the fact that the competition of other fur traders had to be met by de Monts. Champlain was in charge of the post, and in 1613 he succeeded in getting a new monopoly—in his own name—for a company he had organised. This company lasted till 1620, after which time a new company headed by the Huguenot brothers Caën and having Champlain's participation, took over the monopoly; conducting affairs till 1627, when Cardinal Richelieu intervened with ambitious designs of his own.

The permanency and success of the Quebeck settlement are without doubt largely due to the genius and sagacity of Sieur de Champlain. Profiting by the failure of De Monts's other enterprises, and perceiving the need of a potent agent at the French King's court, he conceiv'd the idea of persuading a member of the royal family, the Comte de Soissons, to assume the flattering-sounding post of Lieutenant-Governor or Viceroy. The good effect of this scheme is to be judg'd from the fact that after Comte de Soissons's death Champlain persuaded Prince de Condé to become his viceregal successor, he being follow'd successively by the Ducs de Montmorency and de Ventadour. These viceroys receiv'd a rich share of the fur profits; their honorary position being so lucrative that Duc de Montmorency pay'd the sum of 11,000 crowns to secure his appointment. In the mean time M. de Champlain continu'd to be the actual ruler of the colony, under the title of Commandant. He steadily resided at Quebeck and perform'd prodigies of industry and valour in the service of his settlement. His explorations, made mostly in an effort to find a water route to Asia, are attested by the lake which bears his name; and there is little reason to question that judgment of posterity which honours his memory and accords him the title of "Father of New-France". Errors of judgment he indeed made, but these are more than overshadow'd by his solid achievements. In 1613 Champlain sail'd far up the Ottawa River, and 1615 made a long tour which finally tapped the present province of New-York. Also in 1615 he sent his associate, Étienne Brûlé, on a southward trip of discovery which reach'd as far as Chesapeake Bay. Brûlé also discovered the copper mines of Lake Superior.

The first colonists of Quebeck, being sailors and traders instead of an assemblage of convicts as in many previous cases, were well calculated to secure its survival. Sieur de Champlain, being a Catholick of almost fanatical piety and austerity, early conceiv'd the notion of Christianising the redskin salvages, albeit in a fashion less sanguinary than that practic'd by the Conquistadores in New-Spain. In accordance with this plan he invited into the colony some friars of the Recollet order, four of whom came in 1615, and others at a later date. One of them accompany'd him on his longest expedition inland, and all were soon active in the propagation of their faith. From this time on, we behold the growth of that extream priestly domination which has ever been typical of Quebeck; and which has proved both useful as an influence toward coherence and conservatism, and hurtful as a barrier against intellectual expansion. In 1625 there began to arrive members of the powerful and arrogant Jesuit order, who soon displac'd the Recollets and became a paramount influence in Canada. They made of

Quebeck as much of a mission station as a trading post, and furnish'd those incredibly valiant priestly martyrs whom the Popish church hath lately rais'd to the rank of Saints. The first church in Quebeck was built by Champlain in 1615, close to the *Abitation*; it being but a small chapel.

As an actual colony the growth of Quebeck was relatively slow. The *Abitation* on the shoar in the lee of the cliff consisted of several buildings within a palisado, including the moated "castle" or residence of Champlain himself. The houses seem to have been of the old peaked Gothick sort, with lozenge-paned windows, and with certain French details distinguishing them from the first houses in Virginia and New-England. Of this group of structures no trace now remains, and some doubt exists as to their exact site. It may be said, roughly, that they stood at that point where the short Rue Sous le Fort meets the shoar. They were destroy'd by military operations in 1629, together with the chapel close by which Champlain had built in 1615.

Up to 1617 the population had consisted wholly of traders and priests; but in that year, persuaded by the far-seeing Champlain, there arriv'd the first genuine settler with his family and with the design of prosecuting an agricultural career. This pioneer, to whom a monument is erected, and whose descendants all harbour a just pride, was one Louis Hébert, an apothecary of Paris, who had gone to Acadia in 1606 and whose interest in herbs turn'd him naturally to husbandry. His transference to Quebec, and settlement on the top of the great cliff just above the *Abitation*, was a great event for the colony; and upon the granting of lands to him (on the present site of Laval University, the Basilica, the Seminary, and the houses in Rues Couillard and Hébert) he became the first Seigneur of New-France. The wife of Hébert, Marie Rollet, was the first teacher of children in Quebec; whilst his son-in-law, Guillaume Couillard, was the first to exercise actual tillage of the soil. It is interesting to observe that at the present day—many of the French having penetrated southward into New-England—the junior senator from Rhode-Island to the Federal Congress at Washington is M. Felix Hébert, a scion of this antient line. It may be claim'd with justice, in view of Louis Hébert's migration to Port Royal in 1606, that this is the oldest white family in America north of New-Spain.

In 1620 Champlain (after another experiment on the cliff where the ramparts now are) began constructing a fort and residence, call'd Ft. St. Louis, on the top of the cliff, not far from the edge overlooking the *Abitation*. Within this fort, in 1647, a later governor (Montmagny) built the celebrated castle, Château St. Louis. From the two nuclei— the *Abitation* on the low-lying shoar and the fortress on the lofty table-land near the agricultural acres of Louis Hébert—grew respectively the *Lower Town* and *Upper Town* of the later city of Quebeck. The site of Fort St. Louis is now occupy'd by that sumptuous hostelry, the *Château-Frontenac*, whilst the edge of the cliff at this point is made into that celebrated and magnificent rail'd promenade, *Dufferin Terrace*, (nam'd for one of His Britannick Maj[ty's] governors in the nineteenth century) from which is obtainable one of the finest landskip vistas in all the world—an unparallel'd panorama of lower town, river, distant shoars and cliffs, and remote mountains. Also in 1620 was built the first monastery of the Recollet Fathers, who were a branch of the Franciscan Order. This edifice (bought in 1683 by Bishop St. Valier as an hospital to be conducted by the Nuns of the Hôtel Dieu—an hospital which still survives as the General Hospital) was rear'd on the banks of the River St. Charles, a long way from the earlier settlements, at a site where Champlain had a temporary design of building a city to be call'd *Louisville*. This site now lies at the edge of the St. Sauveur district, at the foot of the Boulevard Langelier, just across the river from Victoria Park. The Jesuits built their fine college (antedating Harvard by a close margin as first seat of higher learning in North-America) on the cliff near the fort in 1635,[2] the antient building surviving till 1878, when it was most regrettably pull'd down to make way for a City Hall—which was not, however, built till considerably later. The Ursuline order of Nuns, together with some nuns of the order of the Hospitalières, came to Quebeck under the leadership of Mme. de la Peltrie in 1639, being first lodg'd in a private house in the lower-town market place near the site of the *Abitation,* but in 1641 founding a convent in the Upper Town near the fort, where it still remains. Their first and second edifices were destroy'd by fire, but the third one, erected in 1686, remains in good preservation. The first church in Quebeck, as previously mention'd, was the small chapel in the lower town near the *Abitation,** built in 1615 by Champlain, and burnt in 1629 in a war with His Britannick Majesty, when our naval forces under Sir David Kirke held the town for a time. Upon the return of Quebeck to the French in 1632, Champlain prepar'd to fulfil a vow by building another church; this one in the upper town near the fort, and to be call'd Notre-Dame de Recouvrance in honour of the recovery of the colony. This he did in the following year; the structure being burnt in 1640, and the site serving in 1647 for the erection of the Parish Church of Notre-Dame, which with many additions, alterations, and restorations has become the present celebrated Basilica or Cathedral.

During the lifetime of Champlain the fur-trade of New-France became very important, tho' the growth of population was slow. An event of ill omen to the French power was the involvement of the colony in the prevailing Indian wars, in which the Hurons and Algonquins† of the Canadian region were ally'd against the powerful and warlike Iroquois or Five Nations of the region later the Province of New-York. In this matter the diplomacy of Sieur de Champlain may well be call'd into question; for without adequate necessity (as most look upon it—tho' some choice between the tribes was doubtless needful, and in this case the nearer faction would naturally be selected) he accompany'd the Hurons in three war-raids on the Iroquois, in 1609, 1610, and 1615; in each case defeating the foe through the use of firearms, then novel to America, but sowing the seeds for a deadly and vindictive Iroquois hatred of the French. This hatred was to result in a never-ceasing hostility of the Iroquois toward New-France; first manifested in sanguinary raids after the Five Nations secur'd firearms for themselves from the Dutch of New-Netherland, and later bearing momentous fruit in the staunch alliance of the Iroquois with His Britannick Majesty's forces after our settlement of New-England, New-York, and the regions southward, and the consequent birth of a relentless finish [sic] struggle betwixt English and French for the mastery of this continent. The Iroquois reprisals first took place against their old Huron foes, together with such French outposts and missions as existed among them. In 1649 they nearly extirpated the Hurons; driving some survivors toward the Detroit region, where they became known as the Wyandots, whilst the residue accepted the protection of the French; encamping for a time on the Place d'Armes in Quebeck's upper town near the fort, and eventually being establish'd in a village call'd Lorette, on the St. Charles River eight miles from Quebeck, where they remain to this day. The protection extended by the French made the Hurons their perpetually grateful allies; so that they acted as a foil to the English-allied Iroquois in the struggles to come. Many of the Indians involv'd in

---

*Probable site—cor. Rue Sous-le-Fort and Petit-Champlain.

†The Hurons were of the same Stock and Language as the Iroquois, this being the most powerful and superior Indian Race in North-America. The Algonquins were of that less develop'd Stock which our *English* Forefathers found in *New-England.*

the sanguinary French raids upon our settlements—Schenectady, Salmon Falls, Haverhill, Deerfield—were Hurons; though some, like the Schenectady raid, involv'd Iroquois who had been Christianis'd by the French, whilst others included the Algonquin tribes of Canada and New-England.

(B) The Company of 100 Associates

In the year 1627, Cardinal Richelieu having acquir'd ascendancy in France, the fur-trading charter of the brothers Caën was revok'd; and a new monopoly set up under the auspices of the royal court. This "Company of New-France", or "Company of One Hundred Associates", formed on the model of such things as the East India Co., the Virginia Co., the Dutch East-India Co., and so on, consisted largely of great Paris merchants, and was much better organis'd than any which had preceded it. Richelieu himself bought the Vice-Royalty of New-France, and allotted that region to the company under feudal tenure, with a right of sub-granting seigniories. In exchange for a permanent monopoly of the fur-trade, and a fifteen-year monopoly of all other colony trade, the company was requir'd to bring to New-France some 200 or 300 men of all trades within a year, and 4000 persons of both sexes during the next fifteen years. Only Roman Catholics cou'd be brought to the colony; a highly unfortunate condition which excluded the fine Huguenot material later emigrating to Rhode-Island, New-York, and South-Carolina, and lay'd the foundations for a popish bigotry and ecclesiasticism often hurtful to the region's progress. The insistence on colonists was a wise one, and help'd greatly to make of Quebeck a real town instead of a meer trading and missionary post. That growth was not swifter was due to the policy of the company, who did not wish a large population to drive off the fur-bearing animals and aggravate the problems of pelt-gathering. It is to be noted, that this hostility of fur-trading companies to a settled population remain'd for more than two centuries a bar to Canadian growth under French and British rule alike. Even in recent Dominion days the influence of the Hudson's Bay Company was thrown against the colonisation of the great prairie region now forming the provinces of Manitoba, Saskatchewan, and Alberta. It seems an universal truth, prov'd by the experience of all colonising nations, that trade monopolies do not promote the growth of that solid settlement needful for provincial progress. Under the Company of New-France, the King appointed a governor nominated by the company, approving him at triennial intervals. No baronies, or any holding greater than a seigniory, cou'd be created but by consent of the Crown. To the post of Governor, Samuel de Champlain was very justly appointed, nor did he leave office till his death in 1635.

In 1629 the rule of Sieur de Champlain was interrupted by the rigours of invasion; France being at war with His Britannick Maj'ty during this period. Our fleet, commanded by Sir David Kirke, had the year before conquer'd the French settlements in Acadia; to which His Majesty had not ceas'd to lay claim, and which had in 1621 been granted to the Scotsman Sir W. Alexander, under the name of Nova-Scotia. Now, in the summer of 1629, Sir David enter'd the St. Lawrence and on July 16 forc'd the surrender of Quebeck, where Champlain had but an hundred men. During the trouble much of the lower town was unfortunately burnt, including the original *Abitation* and the chapel built in 1615. Champlain, returning to Europe, found that peace had been declar'd before the capture; and persuaded the French government to insist on the restoration of Quebeck to France in the ensuing treaty negotiations. This being carry'd out, Quebeck return'd to the French rule in 1632; Champlain resuming his post and building the chapel of Notre Dame de Recouvrance in the upper town in honour of the event. The town had suffer'd greatly from the war, and from the scarcity of good colonists sent out. The peril of the Iroquois remain'd acute, and Champlain was a prey to continual worry. On Christmas Day, 1635, he succumb'd to paralysis; sincerely mourn'd by all who had known him and his work, and assur'd of a place in history as one of the few supreme pioneers of the North-American continent. A gentleman of distinguisht ability and untarnisht virtue, 'tis a pity Samuel de Champlain cou'd not have been an Englishman and a Protestant.

As governor of New-France, Champlain was succeeded by Charles Jacques de Montmagny;[3] the Indian translation of whose name—*Onontio*, or the Great Mountain,—became the common word amongst the salvages to designate the French King's governing agent, as the name of *Caesar* became a common word in Europe for any sort of Emperour. In 1633 a fresh settlement had been made up-stream at Three Rivers. Under Montmagny the colony was further extended by the founding of a town at Hochelaga, or Montreal, by Paul de Chomedey, Sieur de Maisonneuve. This, despite the later growth of Montreal as a fur-trading post, was an enterprise undertaken for the purpose of converting the salvages to Christianity; and involv'd the establishment of an hospital and mission station. Maisonneuve, and his association of gentlemen under the auspices of the Sulpician friars, were in 1642 granted the isle of Montreal under the peculiar mediaeval condition of *frank-almoigne*, whereby the proprietors were obligated, in exchange for the tenure, to offer up prayers for the souls of the donors and their heirs. Against the advice of Montmagny, who realis'd the exposed position of Montreal and the constant peril of the Iroquois, Maisonneuve settled on the island in May, 1642, with a band of pious men and women who at once offer'd up a mass. True to prophecy, the new settlement was repeatedly beset by Iroquois; and in 1660 was sav'd only through the Thermopylae-like[4] sacrifice of a band under Adam Dollard Sieur des Ormeaux, who held the Ottawa Valley at the cost of being slain to the last man. In the end, however, it flourish'd, and became the chief town of Canada. After the accession of Montmagny, the governor gen'l at Quebeck became a less absolute figure; local governors to act under him being appointed at Three Rivers and—after 1644—at Montreal. In the latter case, where the Sulpicians receiv'd authority to select their own local governor, distance from Quebeck made the latter official a well-nigh independent ruler. With great appropriateness, Sieur de Maisonneuve receiv'd this post. In 1647 the governor of Quebeck was supplemented by a consultative council consisting of the ex-governor, when there was one, the Superior of the local Jesuit order, and two of the general inhabitants. Fur profits, at first good, declin'd after a time; trade finally getting into the hands of a dishonest clique at Quebeck. Among the most striking events of this period is the wholesale conversion of the redskins by Jesuit missionaries, who work'd over the whole region and branch'd out into unknown inland domains with fanatical zeal and incredible bravery. Learning the Indian tongue, these heroick fathers endur'd every hardship of the wilderness and in many cases suffer'd martyrdom amidst incredible tortures. For the most part gentlemen by birth, their fortitude possesses a splendour worthy of epick literature; and it is not without reason that their church has lately chosen new saints from amongst them. Their leading field was amongst the Hurons in the region now Ontario, south of Georgian Bay, where they had extensive mission stations. It was when the Iroquois attack'd these settlements that their courage was put to the test. In 1643 Fr. Isaac Jogues was captur'd by the Iroquois, but escap'd to France by way of the Hudson Valley and the Dutch New-Netherland colony. Returning in 1646, he suffer'd martyrdom. In 1649 the Iroquois conducted their great massacre of Hurons, wiping out the Georgian Bay region's mission stations and killing several of the missionaries, including the celebrated Fathers Bréboeuf and Lallemant, (whose osseous reliques are preserv'd in the Hô-

tel-Dieu at Quebeck) amidst tortures of the most barbarick order, which the victims endur'd with a bravery well-nigh transcending imagination. By 1656 the boldness of the
Iroquois had become so great that they plunder'd Quebeck itself, ravaging many houses
in the lower town without opposition. Had it not been for the sacrifice of Dollard's band
in 1660, which convinc'd the redskins of the prodigious valour of the French, it is probable that the colony might have been wholly wiped out. Meanwhile, however, some important exploring had been going on. In 1658 two fur-traders, Pierre Esprit Radisson
and his brother-in-law Médard Chouart, Sieur de Groseilliers, struck into the unknown
west and reached the region now forming Wisconsin—the Galpinian country west of
Green Bay.[5] Their report of a 'great river that divides itself in two' makes it probable
that they were the true discoverers of the Mississippi. In 1659 they reached Lake Superior, and in 1660 brought back to New-France a great wealth of furs which sav'd the In-
dian-ravag'd colony from bankruptcy. On a second expedition in 1661 Radisson and
Groseilliers founded a trading-post at the west tip of Lake Superior, and subsequently
(in all probability) ascended the Albany River to Hudson's Bay. Upon returning to
Quebeck with a prodigious store of furs, they were stript of a great part of their profits by
the governor, on the pretext that they had traded without a licence. Disgusted by this
treatment, they quit New-France and went to London in an effort to interest our British
merchants in the fur-trade; succeeding so well that in 1670 there was form'd that most
historick of monopolies, The Hudson's Bay Company, under the government of H. R. H.
Prince Rupert, nephew of His martyr'd Majesty, Charles the First. They later became
the company's leaders and agents in the regions around Hudson's Bay, which were
claim'd by His Britannick Majesty, Charles the Second, and awarded in feudal tenure to
the company. It is amusing to note that amongst the English MM. Radisson and Groseilliers were known respectively as "Mr. Radishes" and "Mr. Gooseberry", by a kind of
whimsical, good-humour'd colloquial nomenclature.

The town of Quebeck itself remain'd more of a trading-post and mission station
than a city in the fullest and most self-contain'd sense. It was still the centre of all fur-
shipping activities, since Montreal (tho' at the very mouth of the Ottawa River up
which most of the fur-trade lay) was at this date too remote and undefended from the
Iroquois to form a suitable metropolis. The population was scarce more than that of a
village; and the private dwellings, of which none have survived, (the oldest existing
house having been built in 1674) were not of an imposing sort. Emigration to Canada
had been discourag'd by the fur merchants who wish'd to keep it unpopulated, and by
the terrifying accounts of the redskin salvages publisht in the reports or *Relations* of the
Jesuit fathers. In 1647 Gov. Montmagny began the construction of that imposing official castle on the cliff within the fort, *Château St. Louis,* which is so fam'd in history as
a seat of vice-regal power. It was greatly enlarg'd and rebuilt at later dates—in 1694 by
Governor Frontenac and in the early nineteenth century by Sir James Craig—and was
burnt down on Jany. 25, 1834; the site being now occupy'd by the celebrated hostelry,
the Château-Frontenac. Also in 1647 was lay'd the corner-stone of the new church of
Notre-Dame, now the popish Cathedral or Basilica, on the site of Champlain's upper-
town chapel of Notre Dame de Recouvrance, which had burn'd down in 1640. At this
period we may picture Quebeck as a spacious half-rural place; with heights strongly
fortify'd, and with both upper and lower towns built up to a slight extent by small
houses and a few publick edifices like the church, the chateau, the Jesuit College, the
Ursuline nunnery, and so on. The narrow winding streets, unpav'd and rough, had
some indications of their future courses; and there were publick market-places in both
lower and upper towns. The lower-town market-place was close to the site of Cham-

plain's burn'd-down *Abitation* and chapel, in the shadow of the high cliff where the fort and castle were now seen towering aloft. Its upper-town counterpart was adjacent to the Jesuit College; and here in 1647 the first publick tavern in Quebeck was open'd by one Jacques Boisdon at the Sign of the Baril d'Or, or Golden Barrel. Upon this sign was a whimsical motto, *"J'en bois donc"*, (therefore I drink) which form'd a pun upon the tavern-keeper's surname. Boisdon was officially granted the right to serve guests at any time save during mass, sermon, catechism, or vespers—these provisions well illustrating the priest-ridden state of the colony, a condition analogous to that prevailing in the Puritan colonies of New-England. As for fortifications, no attempt cou'd be made to encircle the lower town or the shoar beneath the cliff; but this strip was well guarded by the guns of the fortress above. The upper town was on this side well protected by the cliff and fort. Inland, where the plateau continu'd westward, an earth and wood wall was rear'd at a place which left a good space within, and which marks the line of the present city wall. On the lower level or higher, wherever one of the few avenues of access to the upper town began or continued its steep course, a well-guarded gate was plac'd. Gates were also provided at needful places in the westward wall. Eventually the primitive walls gave place to the strong masonry walls now existing, and fine gates were constructed wherever necessary; this work being carry'd on by the British after the capture of the town. The wall, crossing the plateau from Cape Diamond to the northern edge, is pierc'd on the upper level by the St. Louis Gate at the end of Rue St. Louis, by Kent Gate at Rue Dauphine, and by St. John's Gate at Rue St. Jean. It then descends the sheer precipice to a place where the later French civil governors or "Intendants" had their palace on a higher level of the lower town, and where St. Nicolas or Palace Gate was built. Thence following the rise of the cliff, it intersects the road call'd Canoterie-Hill at Hope Gate, where on both sides the guns of the Ramparts and Grand Battery frown down from their dizzy eminence atop the hill known as St. Famille. From here around the east end of the plateau the cliff itself, with a parapet having many battery emplacements, forms the only needed wall. Close to the fort and chateau, where Mountain Hill or Côte de la Montagne forms the principal link betwixt upper and lower towns, Prescott Gate was built near the upper level. As names indicate, much of this fortification and gate-building was of later date and British origin; but the general plan of the defences is the original one. Of all five gates only two, St. Louis and Kent, now remain; the others having been demolish'd in the middle nineteenth century to meet the exigencies of traffick. Indeed, the present St. Louis and Kent Gates are new ones dating from that period, of a width and height adapted to more contemporary needs. The necessity of most of the changes may be admitted, tho' one feels that Hope-Gate might have been preserv'd—even in its quaint original form—since to this very day the traffick up and down Canoterie-Hill is remarkably slight.

During this middle seventeenth century period, when Montmagny and de Lauzon and d'Argenson and de Courcelles and d'Ailleboust were viceroys, the streets of Quebeck must have had an exceedingly picturesque aspect; being fill'd with painted Indians, buckskin-clad and barbarically trinketed trappers, stocking-capped and booted sailors, cuirassed soldiers, black-robed Jesuits, grey-garb'd Recollets, prim Ursuline nuns, and the gaily-habited populace of the village and adjacent farms. There was undoubtedly much more natural gayety, vivacity, colour, and adventurous zest of living than in the New-England colonies to the southward; and the streets no doubt teem'd with a roystering and brawling to which the towns of those colonies were much less accustom'd. The colonists of New-France, being few in number, of that irresponsible temper engender'd by a despotick government, of a race and religion free from gloomy reflections, and drawn to the colony by an excitement and ambition strong enough to conquer all dread of Indian devastation, were of a very different sort from their sober English neighbours. They came more as traders and adventurers than as every-day settlers, and were not so quickly dispos'd to duplicate the tame industry and prosaick habits of the Old World on the soil of the New. There was in them a spirit of carefree liberation, and a resolve to extract as much enjoyment as possible from the experience of life, which marks them as instinctively civilised in spite of their popish bigotry; and differentiates them very sharply from the morbidly serious victims of the Puritan tradition. We are commonly dispos'd to underestimate their merits by reason of having learn'd about them first from Puritan historians; who naturally held them in disfavour both through disparity of temper and through historick position as military and political foes. In truth, their manner of life was much more rational and sane than that of the Puritan; it being no true evil to remain content with simple living, undevelop'd trade and enterprise, and passiveness in affairs of state. The Puritan, in pursuing a blind urge toward expansion, industry, self-government, and education, strove after things of very doubtful value to him; and lay'd the foundations for that blind worship of size, material progress, speed, wealth, and industry for its own sake, which is today the most serious barrier against civilisation in America. The French-Canadian, on the other hand, strove to seize the moment's quota of joy, light, beauty, and song; and if the process left him poor in an outward way, it more than repay'd him in all that real gratification of natural yearnings which alone forms the criterion of value in the meaningless process call'd life. At the same time it must be made clear, that this civilis'd capacity for enjoyment does not serve to best advantage in solid colonisation. In the founding of new realms, and the quick extension of homeland ways of life over these unpeopled wastes, the dogged British colonist is without anything approaching a rival. Coming in vast numbers, in evenly balanc'd families, and with no intent but to pursue the familiar English occupations of agriculture, trade, and industry on a freer scale, the New-England immigrants at once establish'd a wholly different relationship to the soil from that possess'd by the French. They were settlers, not explorers; and preferr'd to give a small strip of coast a thorough English peopling, both rural and urban, and with all the mild phases and activities of English life reproduced unchanged, rather than penetrate thinly far into the unknown interior and indulge in adventurously unaccustom'd pursuits for the sake of glory, excitement, and possible wealth. As a result, we behold very different conditions in the New-France and New-England of the middle and later seventeenth century. The French had settled the countryside but sparsely, and had no really considerable towns but Quebeck and later Montreal; yet their traders and missionaries had explored and open'd vast stretches of westward territory, so that the French tongue and ways and merchandise were known to remote Indian tribes of whom the English and Dutch had never heard. To this day the place-names of the Middle West and the tribal nomenclature of most Western Indians exhibit a Gallick cast which is a good measure of the extent of French penetration and influence. On the other hand, whilst there was very little territory in Canada at this date which truly resembled France in industry, social order, and degree of settlement; the seaboard of New-England was already the seat of a busy English life surprisingly akin to that of the mother country. By 1660 Salem, Boston, Newport, and New-Amsterdam were all considerable towns, with settled ways, and with a native-born generation almost ready to take the stage of principal activity; whilst the countryside was thickly dotted with farmsteads and till'd with traditional diligence. Even a sea-trade with the West Indes was beginning to spring up. At a date when Quebeck and Canada were still a pioneering experiment, New-England, tho' settled from 12 to 22 years later, was already a well-fill'd country of Englishmen with a solid type of English life and ways completely crystallis'd. This is why New-England towns founded in 1620, 1626, 1630, 1636, 1640, and so on, emphatically seem, and indeed in all practical respects are, distinctly older than Quebeck, notwithstanding the latter's founding in 1608. One salient difference in French and English policy was that respecting relations with the Indians. The French, despite their ceaseless feud with the Iroquois, approach'd the redskin salvages on a basis of acquiescent tact and respectful fraternity; honouring Indian customs and ceremonies in the making of treaties, and using vast diplomacy in the maintenance of missions and trading-posts amongst them. The disinterested enterprise of the Jesuit fathers open'd up paths of intercourse in a pacifick way, and the course of most trappers and traders in taking Indian wives or concubines pav'd the way toward a softening of lines of demarcation. Vast hordes of half-breeds were created, whose descendants still populate much of the Canadian northwest; and many Frenchmen went over altogether to the Indians and dwelt amongst the tribes. One special class of semi-Indianis'd Frenchmen, who wore a half-Indian costume of paint and feathers, had Indian wives, and harbour'd many Indian beliefs, were known as *coureurs de bois,* or rangers of the woods, and are very well describ'd in the fictions of the late Everett McNeil. They dwelt in the wilderness and serv'd as guides for the *voyageurs* or wandering fur-traders from Quebeck, and later Montreal, who paddled their canoes up the Ottawa River and along the labyrinthine streams of the wild sub-arctic regions beyond. But of all pioneers the Jesuit missionaries were the most enterprising. Borne along by a fanatical zeal to Christianise the redskins, they were ideal advance scouts for the traders and settlers who follow'd; since they amicably prepar'd the Indians for the coming of a French influence. Their temporary "conversions", effected through the Indian's love of trinkets and mystical mumblings, had no effect on the life or culture of the Indians; yet the whole missionary process was of the greatest political importance. Only the conquistadores of New-Spain exceeded the French in effecting links with the Indian. These, indeed, carry'd the process as far as an actual hybridism whereby Indian blood enter'd the best Spanish veins; but the French stopp'd short of that. The Gallick half-breeds form'd a separate class, tho' no doubt a small stream of Indian blood did eventually trickle imperceptibly into some of the humbler French *habitants* or peasants—perhaps on a larger scale then ever occurred in the English areas. Our own attitude toward the Indian was the antipodal opposite of the Latin one. The Anglo-Saxon temper cou'd brook no equality with dusky salvages, and accordingly even the best of them were treated with a brusqueness, arrogance, and contempt for their customs, which did not encourage the growth of amity. We despis'd them as something hopelessly different from anything our body-politick cou'd ever contain, and accordingly sought to get their land and push them back in order to enjoy a New-English nation with no inhabitants but ourselves. Cross-breeding, lawful or unlawful, was almost negligible as judg'd by the Latin standard; and indeed our settled type of living was not such as to give our traders and pioneers much contact with the bulk of the redskin population. Then, of course, King Philip's War virtually wip'd out the Indian as a factor in New-England after 1676. After that date there were children in the coast towns who scarce knew what an Indian look'd like; having seen only the few own'd as domestick slaves along with the blacks (which the French never acquir'd) lately imported from the West-Indes. Our parsons, aside from John Eliot, Mr. Roger Williams, and a few others, had no interest in making Christians of the salvages; it having been seen very early how hard it was to produce any real change in their thoughts and ways. Our statesmen, when it was needful to make compacts with the tribes, had none of the suavity, respect, and ingratiating pageantry of the French; but behaved with a scornful aloofness highly irritating to the proud Indian temper. As a result of all this, the redskins were in general always inclin'd toward friendliness with the French, and toward hostility against ourselves. Only the Iroquois, with their special grudge against New-France, form'd an exception to this general rule; and even they at one later time half-waver'd in their attitude—being then kept on our side only through the influence of the celebrated Sir W: Johnson, who dwelt amongst the Mohawks and mingled with them in the French way. He, a singular character among us, would have been in no manner remarkable in Canada.

An event of great importance in the history of New-France was the appointment of an head of the Romish church there; a post of manifestly prodigious importance in a colony so priest-ridden. A bishop there had long been desir'd by the French King, but the papacy was very cautious in responding. In 1659, tho' declining to create an out-right bishoprick, the pope appointed a so-call'd *apostolick vicar* of bishop's rank; one whose title (following the popish custom of giving dignitaries imaginary provinces in the early Christian world) was *Bishop of Petraea in partibus infidelium.*[6] This clerick, whose name has enter'd history as one of the greatest executives of New-France, was the celebrated Monsignieur François de Montmorency-Laval, a gentleman of antient family and brilliant intellect whose organising genius helped to fasten upon Canada that ingrained ecclesiasticism which survives undiminish'd to this day. In 1663 he founded the seminary, still a great institution in the upper town, out of which Laval University grew. In 1670 the Vatican consented to create a Bishoprick of Quebeck, to which as a matter of course Monsignieur de Montmorency-Laval was at once appointed. This see, extending over all of North America except New-Spain, was expressly made independent of the archbishops of France, and subject only to the Vatican itself; a circumstance further promoting the fanatically orthodox and ultra-montane character of its communicants, since it left the region untouch'd by any of the liberalising influences later operative in Old France itself.

(C) New-France as a Royal Province

In 1663 a still more important event occur'd in the form of a cancellation of the rule and monopoly of the Hundred Associates, or Company of New-France. King Louis the Fourteenth, disgusted with the scant progress, slack trade, and thin colonisation achiev'd under the Company, put a period to its charter and resolv'd to erect New-France into a crown colony rul'd by himself through the usual system of royal provincial government. He had learn'd what our British monarchs were even then learning—that commercial or charter government is at best but ill adapted to the needs of any colony of which a populous and settled future is expected. 'Tis notable, that Virginia became a royal province in 1624, New-Hampshire in 1679, Massachusetts in 1684, Maryland in 1690, New-Jersey in 1702, Carolina in 1712, and Georgia in 1752. In this case the Grand Monarch determin'd to make New-France as close a duplicate as possible of the provinces of Old France; giving it as similar a government as conditions wou'd allow. Accordingly, on the French provincial model, it was to be rul'd by a *Governor* or King's representative to form the titular or ceremonial head, plus an *Intendant* or business agent to oversee the actual administration of affairs; these two supplemented by a Sovereign Council (corresponding to the provincial parliaments in Old France) appointed by the King on recommendation of the colonial officials. In this council, *ex officio*, the local Bishop was to serve; thus strengthening the theocratical nature of the colony. In the provinces of France, by virtue of that curious French trait which even now makes the president of the republick a ceremonial figurehead as compared with the premier, the post of *Governor* had become merely decorative, leaving the *Intendant* as sole actual head of affairs. Quebeck did not quite parallel this; for many Governors vigorously asserted themselves, both against the Intendant and against the reigning Bishop. The actual change from company to royal rule was effected by the genius of that celebrated French financial minister Jean-Baptiste Colbert. As a beginning, Daniel de Rémy, Sieur de Courcelles, was appointed Governor, whilst Jean Talon, a relative of Colbert and afterward celebrated for his brilliant executive ability, was made Intendant. The third or clerical post of power was of course in the hands of Monseigneur Montmorency de Laval. Having temporary precedence over all of these officials, in order to give the new province an unify'd start in the manner of a Roman dictator, was Marquis de Tracy, appointed to the newly devis'd temporary post of "Lieutenant-General of the King in North and South America".

The details of provincial policy were all decided in France, and at this period was fashion'd that compleat system of feudal tenure which was pass'd on to the British conquerors; remaining as a legal actuality till 1854, and having effects on the local manners and customs which have not even yet departed. Seigniorial holdings had before been granted now and then, but only now did they multiply to an universal extent. As a royal province, New-France was soon subdivided into a myriad of long, narrow seigniories fronting on the St. Lawrence and Richelieu Rivers; the latter being the stream connecting the former with Lake Champlain. These seigniories were held by gentlemen-colonists—never by absentee landlords—and rented to a suitable number of agricultural *habitants* or tenants. Rents were usually pay'd in produce, tenants ow'd their seigniors military service, and fines were due when a farm chang'd hands. As seigniories were divided, the need for river frontage made the cleavage always longitudinal; so that a much-divided holding became meerly a series of ribbon-like strips—like the old home lots of early Providence, with their necessary frontage on the town street along the waterfront. In Quebeck the institution of feudalism work'd admirably until modernity destroy'd patriarchal society and introduc'd the notion of land as a much-exchang'd commercial commodity. Fees of the seignior to the Crown, and of the tenant to the seignior, were light and equitable; nor was it an hardship that all habitants were oblig'd to use their lord's grist-mill. We have heard this system abus'd by the democratically-prejudic'd historians of New-England, yet must refuse to endorse their complaint as to its social effects. It did indeed breed a docile type of peasant vastly unlike the restless, assertive, and equalitarian Yankee farmer; but not a few will maintain that there is nothing to be censur'd in such a result. The fact is, it is probably better for a nation's culture to have a fabrick of contented peasants whose status enables the superior classes to cultivate the arts of leisure and give refinement to the general spirit. Such a system of squirearchial settledness is to be prais'd and adher'd to *as long as it can be made to work*. When sundry conditions such as moral decadence or the growth of industry and urbanism make it no longer practical, there is no use in trying to save it against the will of the social determinism; but during its heyday, as in the case of seventeenth and eighteenth century Canada, it deserves nothing but commendation. The paternalistick government and feudal organisation of New-France made that region admirably suited to military mobilisation; and the compulsion upon gentlemen to settle genuine tenants on their land was a vast aid to rapid colonisation. Indeed, there are many who look upon the real history of Canada, as a populated and civilis'd province, as beginning in 1663 rather than in 1608. The military advantages of paternalism and feudalism were made strikingly manifest in our wars with New-France, when the enemy's intelligently unify'd action and effective mobilisation contrasted disastrously well with the disjointed and ill-related plans and manoeuvres of our separate and more or less democratical provinces. The Frenchmen, curse 'em, harry'd us most abominably despite our potentially superior numbers; and not even the Albany Convention of 1754, just before the last war, was enough to weld us into a comparably effective unit.[7] That our final victory was due less to any land superiority, or to Gen. Wolfe's memorable taking of Quebeck, than to the earth-wide power of His Britannick Majesty's Navy, is freely affirmed by all who give any intelligent thought to the matter. With good supply communications, the French cou'd have defeated any force such as we then had in America. By cutting 'em off from France we secur'd the dominance of the New World. God Save the King! It remains to add, that feudal ceremonies continu'd to lend picturesqueness to Canada's official life till the final abolition of seigniorage in 1854. American guidebooks of the 'fifties allude to the quaint acts of fealty and homage perform'd with great pomp by the Quebeck seigneurs before His Majesty's Governor.

The actual regeneration of New-France began in 1665, with the belated arrival of the Lieutenant-General, Marquis de Tracy, from the West Indies. His first step was to remove the Iroquois menace, which he did by means of a swift and effective pro-gramme of campaigns and fort-building. He had with him a full regiment of the choic-est veterans of Old France; and after their subjugation of the Iroquois settlements in New-York he settled as many of them as possible as colonists along the Richelieu River; giving seigniories to the officers and making the common soldiers their tenants. To this day the bulk of the population in the Richelieu Valley is descended from the men of this disbanded Carignan-Salières regiment, whilst place-names perpetuate the memory of the officers-seigniors—Sorel, Chambly, Verchères, and so on. Marquis de Tracy return'd to France in 1667, leaving the government in the hands of the perma-nent officials, Governor de Courcelles and Intendant Talon. His wars against the Iro-quois may be said to have done for New-France what King Philip's war did for New-England a decade afterward.

After the sword came the arts of peace; and in the years following 1667 we behold a remarkable œconomick and social growth on the part of New-France, so that within a decade the colony had some 10,000 inhabitants, whereas in 1663 it had had but 2500. Many shiploads of settlers were dispatch'd, including girls of marriageable age whose presence enabled the colonists to found families of pure white blood. In the work of œconomick adjustment, the governor (tho' by no means wanting in civick and military skill) was quite eclips'd by the superlatively brilliant Intendant Talon, whose kinship to Colbert always ensured him the good coöperation and attention of the home government. Talon was the first to see Canada as other than a mere fur-trading centre, and persuaded the French King to look upon it as a potential source of raw materials and market for manufactur'd goods—which it must inevitably become if supply'd with that ample population which the fur monopoly had discourag'd. Besides importing colonists, he put a penalty upon bachelors, gave dowries to new-marry'd couples, and devis'd bounties for all families having twelve children or over. The fecundity he incul-cated, persists to this day; so that at present the French-Canadians are the most rapidly multiplying element in the new world. Not only have they pushed back most of our English settlers who enter'd the province of Quebeck after 1760, but they have over-flow'd into adjacent regions once populated wholly by us—Ontario, and the states of New-England. Today whole sections of Rhode-Island, including such ample cities as Woonsocket and Central Falls, (also Fall River, just across in the Massachusetts-Bay) are as wholly French as Quebec itself; and the population thus overflowing is jealously

tenacious in its retention of French speech and manners, having a wholly different attitude from that of any European foreign group in New-England. This sturdy persistence
of French blood and ways, which we English have scarce been able to equal amidst the
general mongrelisation of the continent, reminds one of nothing so much as the persistence of Greek blood and ways in the antique world despite the spread of Roman dominion and the later mongrelisation of the Empire. It confirms us in the common belief
that the French are the Greeks, as we are the Romans, of the modern world. The quality of the population as encouraged by Talon probably compared favourably with that
of the English colonies as a whole, despite prejudicial disparagements indulg'd in by the
people of Ontario and New-England. There were inferior elements, but perhaps not
more than in the English colonies; although the proportion of actual peasant blood
may have been higher. New-England, whose common populace came from a yeoman
rather than a peasant class, is perhaps the only region where the masses could present a
higher mental and emotional average. The gentry of Canada, tho' not rich, had a pride
and sense of beauty which makes them inferior to none, and which contrasts advantageously with the sharp, tradesmanlike temper of many of our chief men. Today there is
perhaps no town in North-America, except Charleston, in South-Carolina, which has
a tenth of the genuine refinement and sound civilisation of French Quebeck.

Talon, who built a residence call'd Château Talon on the low ground north of the
great cliff (site of the present hotel, Château Champlain), develop'd the trade of New-
France with the utmost assiduity; encouraging the export of raw materials and natural
resources, securing royal aid for shipbuilding at Quebeck, promoting mines and fisheries, importing farm implements and livestock, and stimulating marine commerce with
France, the West Indes, and New-England. In 1668 he erected a brewery near his residence, on the upward slopes of the lower town at the foot of the northern cliffs; which,
after alteration by one of his successors, became a permanent Palace or residence for
the Intendant, rivalling the governor's Château St. Louis on the cliff as a seat of power,
and giving its name to the hill, street, and gate linking it with the upper town. The
building was later twice burnt and repair'd, and in 1775 was utterly demolish'd during
the military operations whereby the rebel General Benedict Arnold, later noted as a
turncoat, sought to take Quebeck in conjunction with Montgomery. Upon its site was
later erected Boswell's Brewery, beneath which the original vaults of Talon's brewery of
1668 are still exhibited with pride. Further acts of Talon were systems of price-fixing
and personal registry and regulation—the latter providing for the existence of a record
or *dossier* of every one in the colony, and being not unlike systems still in use in Old
France and other parts of continental Europe. There can be no question but that
Talon was virtually the founder of Canada as a settled, civilised colony, just as Champlain was its founder as a permanent foothold of French trade and enterprise. Meanwhile the Jesuit missionaries had been pushing westward, in 1669 founding Indian
missions at Mackinaw, Sault Ste. Marie, and Green Bay; regions now included in the
American Middle West.

In 1672, after an administrative period of unbroken harmony with each other,
Talon and de Courcelles return'd to France. This period had been marked by an ascendancy of the Intendant's functions over those of the governor, but in the combination
appointed to succeed them the order was spectacularly revers'd. The Intendant was a
M. Duchesneau; but the governor was that foremost of all rulers of New-France, the
renowned and universally admired Louis de Buade, Comte de Frontenac. Frontenac was
a nobleman of haughty and violent temper whose court career had been spoilt by his
personal arrogance; but his military and civil ability were of the highest, hence upon

coming to Canada to repair his official fortunes he at once became a notable figure in its history. His tact and skill in dealing with the Indians, who call'd him the Great Onontio, were profound and enormous; and by entering into their spirit and recognising their forms and ways he was able to treat them like a stern parent without arousing their enmity. It is related in the works of Parkman, how Count Frontenac us'd to plume and paint like an Indian chief, and joyn in the warlike dancings and shoutings of his salvage allies; a thing absurd to the English mind, yet in truth not at all incompatible with a certain kind of dignity. In the internal affairs of New-France, Frontenac frequently clash'd with the authority of others; beginning in the autumn of his first official year, when Colbert rebuk'd him for convening in a representative way the Estates-General of Canada, a body of nobles, clergy, and commons analogous to the original Estates-General of Old France. It was Colbert's opinion, that this sort of convening was antagonistick to political good order; fit only for emergencies in Old France, and unwise at any time in the colony. Other troubles were conflicts of authority with the Intendant Duchesneau and Bishop Montmorency de Laval; things to be expected in view of Count Frontenac's haughty temper, and the traditionally subordinate nature of the office he held. He did his best to curb the even then noticeable despotism of the Jesuit clique, and might have won had the Intendant sided with him. In one matter Frontenac is scarcely to be commended; this being his wish, on œconomick grounds, to legalise the trading of liquor to the Indians, which Laval and his clergy had outlawed. In 1682 the general cleavage of purpose betwixt the officials became so mark'd that both Frontenac and Duchesneau were recall'd to France, tho' the former was to return in greater glory seven years later. Frontenac founded the wilderness outpost fort which bore his name (now Kingston, Ontario) at the northeast corner of Lake Ontario.

Meanwhile exploration had been progressing at a vast rate, bringing to prominence names now famous in the history of this continent. In 1673 the trader Joliet, born and educated in Quebeck, and the Jesuit Father Marquette, sail'd down the River Wisconsin and discover'd—perhaps for the first time, tho' Radisson and Groseilliers probably encounter'd it before—the broad river Mississippi, known to them before only thro' Indian tales of a great "Father of Waters". Down this vast stream they sail'd, past the Missouri and the Ohio, till they touch'd the region travers'd by the Spaniard De Soto 132 years before. They learn'd that the river extended to Mexique Bay, and wish'd to descend thither; but having stopt at the mouth of the Arkansas to feast with friendly Indians, were warn'd of hostile tribes farther south, and perswaded to return whence they came. In 1669 a memorable series of explorations was begun by that celebrated and pious enthusiast, René Robert Cavelier de la Salle, whose repeated frustrations and courage in the face of vicissitudes are so frequently describ'd. His seigniory near Montreal was facetiously call'd La Chine because of his wish to find a westward route to China; but his main ultimate design, form'd after he learnt from Marquette and Joliet that the Mississippi flows to Mexique Bay, was to extend the French power down the valley of that river and found a southern base to be used as a threat to Spanish dominion in Mexico. His early explorations concern'd the region betwixt the Ohio and the Great Lakes; but in 1679, when commandant at Fort Frontenac on Lake Ontario, he undertook to descend the Mississippi to its mouth for the first time. With Count Frontenac's cordial and unswerving support, he founded a new post at Niagara Falls, built a vessel, and set sail on the Great Lakes for Green Bay, whence he sent back a load of furs as part of his mixed trading and exploring venture. Thereafter, having establish'd a fort at the mouth of the River St. Joseph, (Mich.) he entered the region of the Illinois and endured the perils of hostile Indians, incipient mutiny,

desertion, and loss of the vessel he had sent back to deliver furs and return with supplies. History relates his bold endeavour under these trials. Building a second fort and
leaving his men, he return'd to Canada on foot in the dead of winter amidst all the perils of icy wilderness travel; there finding difficulties rais'd by his enemies, but retaining
the faith and favour of Count Frontenac. Again going westward, he found his Illinois
fort, which he had call'd Crevecoeur, or Heartbreak, deserted;* a thing which compell'd him to return to Canada once more. Frontenac being still well-dispos'd, La Salle
a third time started west; on this occasion meeting the success he deserv'd. Proceeding
to the bottom of Lake Michigan, at the present site of Signor Capone's metropolis of
Chicago, he made a portage of his canoes to the Illinois River, descended that stream
to the Mississippi, and as soon as the February ice conditions permitted, commenc'd
the descent of the Father of Waters with a canoe party of 22 Frenchmen, a Franciscan
missionary, his Italian lieutenant Henri de Tonty, and some Indians—about 50 indi-
viduals in all. On March 13, 1682, having paus'd at the village of the Arkansas Indians, La Salle formally took possession of the Mississippi Valley in the name of the
French King; and on April 6 he reach'd the mouths of the Great River amidst sensations of the most signal triumph. Finding a dry spot amidst the marshy bayou land on
April 8, La Salle the next day erected a cross with the shield and arms of France attach'd, and caus'd pious hymns to be chanted in a ceremonial fashion. Returning
slowly over his route, hamper'd by illness and pausing to arrange posts and Indian affairs, La Salle reach'd Quebeck in November, 1683, only to find that Frontenac had
been recall'd, and that the new governor de la Barre was oppos'd to his ventures. Proceeding, however, to France, La Salle found favour with the son of Colbert, then deceas'd, and receiv'd a commission to found a post at the mouth of the Mississippi to
serve as a base against Spain—with which nation France was then at war, and which
had arbitrarily defin'd Mexique Bay as a clos'd sea under Spanish control. This half-
military, half-colonising expedition, which set sail for Mexique Bay on the 1st of August, 1684, as a squadron of four vessels, involv'd much internal dissension and came
to compleat grief. The full facts seem obscure; but is it known that La Salle miss'd the
mouth of the Mississippi, landed on the Texas coast, built a fort, made some futile expeditions, and in Jany. 1687 set out for Canada with 16 men, having left 20 at the fort.
On the 20th of March he was assassinated by one of a faction of mutineers, who later
fought among themselves in a brawl which cost the murderer his life and caused the
survivors to join a neighbouring band of savages. The faithful residue of the party
push'd on to the Mississippi and reach'd a post, establisht by La Salle's faithful associate De Tonty, on July 27, 1687. The dream of La Salle had at last come to pass; and
France held a vast empire from Mexique Bay to the northern snows, which join'd the
older New-France and form'd a solid barrier to the westward expansion of our English
colonies along the Atlantick seaboard.

At Quebeck the successors of Count Frontenac did not meet with smooth conditions. The Iroquois having made an expedition westward in which they had destroy'd
the Illinois but suffer'd a repulse by the warlike Sioux, again began to harass the French
settlements as they had not done since De Tracy's campaign. Governor de la Barre
mov'd against them, but so feebly and blunderingly that he was recall'd to France. Fever
among his troops was one of the causes of his failure. To de la Barre in 1685 succeeded

---

*The Illinois Indians of that region had been attack'd by the Iroquois, and the French had
had to leave. It was from this fort that Fr. Hennapin made his historick trip up the Mississippi from the mouth of the Illinois. See McNeil's novel, "Tonty of the Iron Hand".

the Marquis de Denonville, a much abler man who led an expedition against the Seneca settlements and destroy'd them in the absence of most of the warriors. He also built a fort at Niagara. In 1689 the Iroquois took their revenge; attacking the settlements of La Chine, at La Salle's old Seigniory near Montreal, on the night of August 25th and massacring most of the inhabitants. They killed some 200 persons with the most extream cruelty, remaining unopposed as masters of the isle of Montreal till the middle of October, when they retired, bearing 120 prisoners. This frightful event threw the entire colony in terror, and it was rumoured that our English colonists in New-England and New-York had instigated the raid, notwithstanding a treaty of 1686 which provided that neither France nor England shou'd employ redskins in time of war. War was indeed now existing, the French King having espoused the cause of our exiled Stuarts against that of His Protestant Majesty, William the Third. Governor Denonville's terror was extream, and he caus'd Fort Frontenac to be abandon'd; thus leaving scarce an outpost of France betwixt Three Rivers and Mackinaw, at the head of Lake Michigan. Of the trouble he had said "God alone could have sav'd Canada this year." At this time he was already under recall, since it was evident that a stronger leader was necessary amidst the complications of Indian attack and future English military operations. Indeed, in June of the same year there had once more been appointed to the governorship of New-France that one man in all the French kingdom competent to deal with the desperate crisis. On the 12th of October, 1689, at the age of 69, there again settled within Château St. Louis, in the fort atop Quebeck's lofty cliff, Louis de Buade, Comte de Frontenac.

The Quebeck to which Count Frontenac return'd was a town of no mean aspect; built up quite thickly with small steep-roof'd French houses having sometimes two tiers of dormer windows. The prevailing materials were then, as now, stone and stucco-cover'd brick. The general topography was much as it is at present; and because of the highly dramatick, unique and unalterable character of the landscape setting, the general atmospherick effect cannot have been greatly different from that at any later period. A flat town may change its appearance overnight, but a town set amidst permanent geographick features of mark'd distinctiveness must always convey a more or less similar impression. In 1689 the lofty Cape Diamond, towering above even the upper town and reached from the level of Fort St. Louis by a steep incline or glacis, already bore the character of a citadel, tho' its fortifications were of wood and demanded frequent repair. Below it cou'd be seen the general surface of the plateau, bristling with the upper town's steep roofs, and glistening as the sun touch'd the tin-coated spires of the churches, convents and college, and seminary. Château St. Louis, adjacent to the fashionable promenade and parade-ground call'd "Place d'Armes", frown'd at the edge of the cliff; behind it was a stone windmill on a hill less lofty than the citadel, and beside it rose the newly rebuilt Ursuline Convent, which has surviv'd to this day. On the present site of the Anglican cathedral near the fort there wou'd soon be finish'd the new Recollet Monastery, the old one on the River St. Charles having been bought in 1683 by Bishop St. Valier, Laval's successor, for the Nuns of the General Hospital. The Jesuit's College rose close by, facing the upper market place, and having attach'd a church built in 1666, and not far from that was the imposing Basilica of Notre-Dame—made a Cathedral in 1664 by Pope Clement, but not yet enlarg'd to its present size. Beside the Cathedral, near the point where the cliff-edge takes a northward turn, rose the spire of the Quebeck Seminary—an edifice since damag'd by fire many times, but still in a sort of Phoenix-like existence. A little way down the cliff along the line of Mountain-Hill, the road to the lower town, stood the splendid palace of the Bishop—where Montmorency Park is now. Near this was the old burying-ground, abandon'd for such use in 1687. Far around the cliff to the northward, on another approach to the lower town, the Hôtel-Dieu convent and hospital, built in 1657, was seen. The lower town itself was not rich in publick edifices; the finest perhaps being the Intendant's Palace on the gentle rise leading up to the northerly face of the cliff where a road ascended to the top. This had recently been made over by the Intendant de Meulles from Talon's old brewery, and the cliff just where it was becoming known as Palace Hill. Nearly opposite it, where the roadway curv'd up the fortyify'd height, Palace or St. Nicolas Gate was about to be constructed. The only other notable lower-town building was the new (and still existing) parish church then called L'Enfant Jesus, built in 1688 on the market place beneath Fort St. Louis near the site of Champlain's *Abitation*, where the Breakneck Steps and upper town road led down to a waterside battery of guns beside the principal wharves. Just up the river from here was the cave call'd Cul de Sac, and the district of Neuville, where Champlain St. now is. Outside the recognis'd limits of the town on the bank of the St. Charles, was the former Récollet Monastery, (where in his first governorship Frontenac wou'd go into "spiritual retreats"—emerging fiercer than ever!) purchased as a General Hospital. The suburbs in general were just beginning to appear—as separate villages which would later be overtaken by the growth of the city outside the walls. St. Roch was on the lower level north of the cliff and west of the Intendant's Palace. Still farther westward, beyond the General Hospital, was St. Sauveur. On the upper level the St. Jean suburb was outside the walls on the road to Ste. Foy and Montreal; St. Louis being on the rather higher ground south of this, nearer the St. Lawrence. Limoilou lay across the St. Charles River, and Sillery was on the St. Lawrence's north shore a few miles above Quebeck. Down the St. Lawrence on the same side as Quebeck lay Beauport, five miles away, where some of the most antient seignioralties were to be found. Still farther along—some nine miles from the city—were the great falls of the Montmorency River, which thunder'd as they do today down a cliff of more than 250 feet into the St. Lawrence; carving, it was rumour'd, a subterraneous passage beneath the great river and rising again off the neighbouring Isle of Orleans at a dangerous spot call'd by boatmen Le Taureau, or The Bull. The Isle of Orleans, a long, large body of land set east of Quebeck at a point where the St. Lawrence widens from a true river into a prodigious estuary, was already dotted with villages and farmsteads; and had enjoy'd several names besides its principal one—"Minego" according to Indian nomenclature, "Isle of Bacchus" according to those early explorers who had noted its abundance of grapes, and "Isle of Sorcerers" according to the superstitious, who fear'd its reputed population of daemons. It is now one of the least modernis'd parts of the country, and is much favour'd for summer travel. On it is the oldest rural convent in Canada. Across the St. Lawrence from Quebeck rose the vast cliffs of Point Levi, now call'd Lévis; as majestick as those of the city itself, and cleft by the spectacular falls of the River Chaudière a little west of this region. A village was already beginning to spring up here. Such was the scene which greeted Count Frontenac upon his second arrival. In the city there had developed a social life of not unpleasing cast; pious and somewhat austere in tone, and more dominated by the clergy than the urban life of Old France. Priests, nuns, and students in the ecclesiastical institutions, were omnipresent; and the presence of an increasing official and seigniorial group lay'd the foundations for amenities perhaps superior to any on this continent north of Virginia. In the streets, as of old, were a motley and colorful throng—soldiers, sailors, voyageurs, merchants, coureurs de bois, habitants, merchants, Indians, half-breeds, friars, and every sort of denizen common to a great French outpost. The Ring, Grande Place, or Place d'Armes beside the fort and

Château St. Louis in the upper town, was the chief scene of publick resort; and besides harbouring military parades and meetings of various sorts, it was the recognis'd promenade for persons of fashion. Even at this early date the upper town, both because of its superior attractiveness and because of its position as a military and governmental centre, had begun to acquire that social preference which it has always since possess'd. The leading street of residence seems to have been the Rue St. Louis, which stretch'd westward from the fort, pass'd the short lane to the Ursuline Convent, and ended at the city wall near the gate named for it, beyond which lay the future suburb of St. Louis and the fertile pastures call'd the Plains of Abraham after their original owner—the Scotsman Abraham Martin, first pilot on the St. Lawrence, to whom a monument has lately been erected on the waterfront. On the river below, an increasing number of masts and sails were seen, both of merchant ships and of the French King's frigates of war. Warehouses, the platform and battery, sea-taverns, shops, and the like, all gave spice to the teeming maritime fringe. A rich body of sailorly legend grew up; and the one jutting part of the cliff, where the ramparts extend north of the fort, became known as *Sault au Matelot,* or the Sailor's Leap, from some event or legend now dim to memory. The narrow street in the lee of this precipice is even today called Rue Sault au Matelot. Meanwhile there arose, some 21 miles east of Quebeck, beyond the Montmorency Falls along that north shore so thickly lay'd out in seigniories, a curious shrine reputed by the Popish church to effect miraculous cures, and to this day famous throughout North-America as the shrine of Ste. Anne de Beaupré. According to legend, this fane was establisht by some Breton sailors, who, being beset by a storm upon the St. Lawrence, made a vow to the patron saint of their native region that they wou'd build her a sanctuary on whatever spot of land she might safely conduct them to. Coming ashore at a place call'd Petit-Cap, they proceeded to fulfil their vow by erecting a small wooden chapel of Ste. Anne; which may be deem'd the fabulous ancestor of all the churches later standing there. In the year 1645 we hear of a missionary priest, Saint-Sauveur, in this region; and the Jesuit fathers quickly follow'd him. Seigniories were here granted from 1650 onward. The district being now well settled, plans were made for a church; and in 1659 its foundations were bless'd by the Sulpician father de Queylus, in company with M. d'Ailleboust, Governor of New-France under the Hundred Associates. At this period all Canada contain'd but ten churches; one at the antient settlement of Tadoussac one at Château-Richer, on the north shoar next to the new Petit-Cap region; one at Montreal; one at Three Rivers; one at Sillery; one at the Jesuit Residences on St. Geneviève Hill just outside the Quebeck limits; and four in Quebeck itself—the parish church of Notre-Dame, where the future explorer Joliet often play'd on the organ; the chapels of the Ursulines and the Jesuits, and that of the original Hôtel-Dieu, built in 1657. This church of St. Anne at Petit-Cap or Beaupré, then, was the eleventh in New-France. During the laying of the foundations, it is claim'd in the *Relations des Jesuites,* one Louis Guimont, a local habitant, sett some stones in place as an act of pious devotion and was at once cur'd of his chronick rheumatism. Later, in 1662, the wife of another farmer who had witness'd this cure was heal'd of a sort of curious paralysis by means of prayers offer'd to "La Bonne Ste. Anne". In the same year, moreover, a neighbouring epileptick profess'd a cure after having made a *novena,* or nine-day prayer, to the kindly saint. A fourth cure, says the Jesuit chronicle, was that of a soldier from the Quebeck garrison in 1667, who wholly lost a total paralysis of one leg on the fifth day of a novena at the shrine. The curative fame of Ste. Anne de Beaupré seems to date from about 1665, and in 1666 and 1667 it was the scene of devotions by the Lieutenant-General Marquis de Tracy, who first subdu'd the Iroquois. Not long afterward, the church was enricht by gifts from the Queen of France; Anne of Austria, mother of the Grand Monarch. In 1694 a steeple and bell were added; which still survive on the chapel built in 1878 from the stones of the old church—the latter having become ruinous and unsafe. This church was not the one whose foundations were lay'd in 1659. Difficulties caus'd the demolition of that structure before completion, and a more permanent structure of wood and stone was erected on a neighbouring spot in 1662. This, in turn, gave way to a stone church in 1676; which with additions was to endure for two centuries. It may be added, that a later church built in 1876 was destroy'd by fire in 1922, and that a fifth edifice is now under construction. The shrine, whose psychological effect upon credulous papists must be prodigiously potent, is now a place of the utmost fame throughout the continent; and is the goal of numberless pious pilgrimages. It is conducted, together with many necessary sacerdotal devices, by the Redemptionist Fathers; and its collections of saintly reliques and antique objects of religious art attract vast and profitable crowds each year; in addition to those who come to make devotions or to invoke the aid of the local goddess in the healing of disease. Of the cures effected by this New-World Lourdes we may say, as of other miracles including Christian-Science, that they involve such functional disorders as never had any real exis- tence, but which were the result of morbidly concentrated attention on the patient's part. A physician skill'd in the science of the mind cou'd shew as high a proportion of similar cures as can the venerable grandmother of the Redeemer. At this shrine, the central curative agent is held to be a statue of St. Anne; burnt in 1922, but now being repro- duced with much fidelity and sanctity. Amusing as these things may appear to the ra- tional, it is truly to be hop'd that they will not altogether pass away. The naive mood of awe, reverence, and credulity underlying such worship is part of mankind's primitive heri- tage, and is assuredly a valuable counteractive to the prosaic standardisation and value- destruction of a mechanical aera. It has the beauty inherent in all ancient and wonder- making things, and works against the disillusion of decadence.

(D) The French-English Struggle for North-America

(1) King William's War.

As we shall soon see, the year 1689 was a major landmark in the history of French and English relations on this continent. Up to this time the natural rivalry of the two civilisations had smouldered, owing to the vastness of the region at stake, which per- mitted each nation to expand unchecked, without much interference from the other. It is true that our claim to the whole Atlantick coast-line, resulting from the discover- ies of John Cabot, sett up a very early rivalry respecting Acadia and parts adjacent; but this was a relatively small matter as compar'd with the tensity produc'd when the French push'd down through the Mississippi valley in 1682 and cut off potential British expansion to the west. As late as 1666 there was amity between French and English; so that in the Province of New-York, whither Sieur de Courcelle's had penetrated in pur- suit of the Iroquois, Canadian troops were very civilly receiv'd and entertain'd at our settlements. The rivalry in Acadia has been previously mention'd. In 1612 the Virgin- ian privateer Argall destroy'd Port-Royal, but French posts were almost immediately reëstablish'd, including Fort Pentagoët, (1613) within the present limits of Maine, in New-England. In 1621 King James the First erected the domain of Nova-Scotia, and granted it to Sir W. Alexander, who sent out a Scottish colony (unfortunately not permanent) to the site of Port-Royal. In 1628 Sir David Kirke captured all the French posts in Acadia and carry'd the proprietor of the colony, Claude de la Tour, to England; though the region was restor'd to France by the treaty of 1632. Internal dissention betwixt M. de la Tour and the Lieutenant-Governor Sieur de Charnisay soon lay'd the region open to aggression from New-England; and in 1654 a body of our troops under Maj. Robert Sedgwick (holding authority from the usurper Cromwell) took possession of the province and install'd as governor the son of de la Tour, who had treasonably taken our side against his own government. In 1667, however, the region was ceded back to France. It is curious to observe that the Dutch had a brief foothold here, occupying Ft. Pentagoët in 1674 till their expulsion shortly afterward. It is at this fort that the Baron de St. Castin settled with his Indian wife; forming a theme for the poetick pens of Whittier and Longfellow,[8] and giving his name to the New England town of *Castine* which later sprang up on the site.

The gravity of the long struggle for the continent was at last perceiv'd with great force by both sides. When, in June of 1689, Count Frontenac was once more appointed governor, he was told to recover for France the Hudson's Bay country, to protect Acadia, and to prepare an army for a descent into New-York, the capture of which wou'd be aided by a French fleet. It was design'd to hold the Province of New-York as a permanent barrier betwixt New-England and the other colonies of Great-Britain; permitting English papists to remain, but banishing all others, as well as all the long-settled Dutch inhabitants, to our territories in New-England and Pennsylvania. As French Governor of this Province, the Sieur de Callières was appointed in advance; a piece of sanguine presumption shewing vast ignorance of the indomitable force of our antient English valour. French privateers were despatch'd to harass our coasts; one fleet consisting of a large barque, a small barque, two sloops, and some smaller craft, becoming a great pest off Southern New-England. In July, 1689, this fleet gain'd access to Rhode-Island waters by employing a renegade Englishman as a decoy to answer hails; and having found upon inquiry that Newport was too strong to attack, seiz'd the outlying isle of Block-Island; holding it for a week amidst the greatest plunder and outrage. This is the only occasion upon which any part of our colony has been held by a foreign foe. Acts of indignity and peculation were extreamly numerous, as is shewn in the case of John Rathbone, Esq., great-great-great-great-great-great-grandfather of the present writer. The Frenchmen, upon hearing that this gentleman was a person of property, conceiv'd the idea of seizing him and extorting from him an account of where his possessions were hid; in the course of which plan they mistakenly seiz'd and tortured his son (the writer's great-great-great-great-great-grandfather) of the same name. This fleet, under one Capt. Piquard, later attempted to harass the coast towns of Connecticut; but was finally driven off to sea by an expedition of two sloops which put out of Newport, commanded by the celebrated privateer Capt. Paine—who, 'tis said, had been associated with the French captain in former marine ventures.

Then, on August 25th, before the arrival of Count Frontenac in New-France, occurr'd the sanguinary massacre of La Chine, as formerly mention'd, conducted by the Iroquois in revenge for Marquis de Denonville's destruction of the Seneca settlements. It does not seem to be conclusively settled, whether our New-England and New-York colonists in any way instigated this atrocious event; which wou'd of course have been in direct violation of the agreement of 1686, that neither nation shou'd employ salvage allies in case of conflict; but in any case the French believ'd such instigation to exist, and accordingly consider'd the agreement abrogated. There had been some previous Indian raids of French instigation upon our outposts along the Maine coast, where the boundary betwixt French and English influence was but ill-defin'd; but now a raiding-programme of far more drastick nature was plann'd. Count Frontenac, upon reaching Quebeck, resolv'd to enlist his Indian allies in a triple descent upon the English provinces; and accordingly sent out early in 1690 three expeditions, one from Montreal, one from Three Rivers, and the other from Quebeck. The Montreal expedition, employing a band of Christian Iroquois favourable to the French, was commanded by three brothers of the celebrated Canadian family of le Moyne; one of whom, the Sieur d'Iberville, was later to become celebrated as the founder of Louisiana. This expedition, after a 22-day journey through the snows, fell just before midnight upon the sleeping village of Schenectady, in New-York, burning all of its houses and massacring such of its English and Dutch inhabitants as did not succeed in escaping to Albany. The Three Rivers expedition, led by the sanguinary Hertel de Rouville (later infamous as the leader of the Deerfield slaying-party) and his sons and nephews, contain'd Indians and coureurs de bois, and descended upon Salmon Falls, on the Piscataqua River in New-Hampshire not far from Dover; where after a severe battle they burn'd houses, barns, and cattle, and bore away 54 captives, mainly women and children, whom they forc'd to carry the loot taken from the settlement. The prisoners eventually became slaves and servants, either of the Indians or of the French to whom they were sold. This practice of bearing off women and children became a settled policy with the French and Indians, and formed one of the chief reasons for our undying hatred of them. It is curious to observe, that one of our chief regrets in this matter was that New-England children shou'd be rear'd amongst the French as idolatrous Papists. The expedition of de Rouville, returning from Salmon Falls, met the outgoing expedition from Quebeck; and having joyn'd forces with it, proceeded to the English settlement of Fort-Royal, on Casco Bay, the present site of the city of Portland, Maine. The fort being captur'd, all the garrison and inhabitants were massacred; and the raiders return'd to New-France unpunish'd.

But in these successes were sown the seeds of France's downfall in the New World; for the response was a decisive and inexorable rousing of that ENGLISH will to conquer and extirpate, which can no more be resisted than the will of the ROMAN PEOPLE of old. GOD SAVE THEIR PROTESTANT MAJESTIES, WILLIAM AND MARY! RULE, BRITANNIA! "It was thought," say'd the wise and venerable Dr. Increase Mather, "that the English subjects in these regions of America, might very properly take this occasion to make an attempt upon the French, and by reducing them under the English government, put an eternal period at once unto all their troubles from the Frenchified Pagans."[9] Accordingly, on April 28, 1690, there set out from Nantasket, near Boston, a naval force of about 700 men, under the command of Sir William Phips, Knt., General and Commander-in-Chief, in and over Their Majesties' Forces of New-England, by Sea and Land. Sir William, later Captain-General and Governor-in-Chief of the Province of the Massachusetts-Bay, and one of the most illustrious figures in the early history of New-England, was man of humble origin; one of the twenty-six children of a gunsmith, and at first a ship's-carpenter by trade, born at a remote settlement on the Kennebeck River, in Maine. Becoming a master of his trade, he mov'd to Boston, learn'd to read and write, marry'd a widow'd gentlewoman of wit and substance, and resolv'd to rise in the world till he shou'd be master of a King's Ship and own a fair brick house in the Green-Lane of North-Boston. Taking to the sea, he gave his attention to the recovery of sunken Spanish treasures; finally obtaining command of a ship, and at last, having brought back to his royal and noble employers the rich contents of a founder'd West-India galleon, being made a Knight by King James the Second. On this occasion Sir William with his fleet proceeded to Port-Royal, in

Nova-Scotia, which he reach'd on the 11th of May and which quickly surrender'd to the authority of our English crown. Demolishing the fort, administering to the inhabitants an oath of loyalty to Their Britannick Majesties, and setting up a provisional government under the authority of the Massachusetts-Bay, Sir William return'd to Boston and endeavour'd to rouse the people of New-England to further measures against the French. "As Cato," saith the old Magnalia Christi Americana, "could make no speech in the Senate without that conclusion, Delenda est Carthago, so it was the general conclusion of all that argued sensibly about the safety of that country, [New-England] Canada must be reduced. It then became the concurring resolution of all New-England, with New-York, to make a vigorous attack upon Canada at once, both by sea and by land."[10] There was much conference among all the colonies upon the subject.

The attack by land was to be made upon Montreal, with a view to diverting the energies of the enemy whilst our fleet might make a successful siege of Quebeck. It was to consist of a thousand Englishmen from New-York, Albany, and Connecticut, together with 1500 Indians; and had it reach'd its goal, wou'd have almost certainly have brought us victory, thus greatly changing the course of New-French history. Canoes, however, were lacking for water transportation over Lake Champlain and the Richelieu River; and the Indians fell away from the project; so that in the end the English turn'd back and abandon'd the venture. Upon hearing of this, Count Frontenac concentrated all his defences at Quebeck.

The sea-force, under Sir W: Phips, consisted of 32 ships and tenders, of which the Admiral's vessel was the largest, having 44 great guns and 200 men. It set sail from Hull, near Boston, on the 9th of August (O.S.)[11] 1690, and thro' skilful navigation reach'd the Isle of Orleans, over-against Quebeck, in excellent order on the 5th of October. On Monday, the 6th, Sir William sent to Count Frontenac a summons demanding the surrender of Quebeck, giving as provocation the French and Indian raids upon New-England. In the name of Their Majesties William and Mary, and with the authority of the Massachuset-Colony, he ask'd of the French governor "a present surrender of all your forts and castles, undemolished, and the King's and other stores, unimbezzled, with a seasonable delivery of all captives, together with a surrender of all your persons and estates to my dispose"; in return promising mercy and security, and adding: "Your answer positive in an hour, return'd by your own trumpet, with the return of mine, is required, upon the peril that will ensue."

But for once Sir William had met a worthy adversary, tho' a Frenchman; for Count Frontenac, adopting the French position of favour toward the depos'd Stuarts, and exercising that native haughtiness characteristick of him responded in this way:

> 'That Sir William Phips, and those with him, were hereticks and traitors to their King, and had taken up with that usurper, the Prince of Orange; and had made a revolution, which if it had not been made, New-England and the French had been all one; and that no other answer was to be expected from him, but what shou'd be from the mouth of his cannon.'

On the 7th the siege began in earnest, but the difficulties of landing, the nearness of the hellish northern winter, and the prevalence of smallpox in the fleet, were all against our success. With great difficulty, a landing was made at Beauport, on the north shoar east of Quebeck, but from this point the troops were dislodg'd by a French force under Capt. Pierre Carré, since call'd by his countrymen "The Hero of Beaupré". In this dislodgment the battel was really lost; but the intrepid Phips, being unwilling to accept defeat, sail'd close up to the fortify'd cliffs of Quebeck and fir'd boldly upon them despite their return fire and generally impregnable nature. On Mt. Carmel, behind the Château St. Louis, the French placed a battery in a stout stone windmill; inflicting much damage with it upon our ships. To this day a ruin'd stone redoubt remains upon the spot, bearing a bronze tablet and having the name "Le Cavalier du Moulin". It was the design of Sir William to prosecute the siege as long as possible, in the hope of reducing Quebeck by starving if not by assault; but

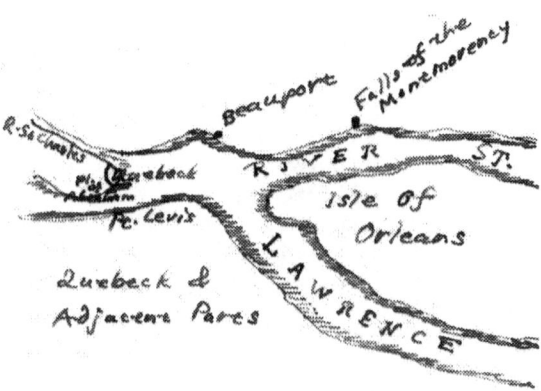

the coming of a great storm soon scatter'd the fleet so badly that such action cou'd not be taken. There was nothing to do but return to Boston, hence on Octr. 11th the siege was given over amidst the encreasing cold and snow. The bulk of the fleet reach'd Boston in safety on the 19th of November, but one brigantine, with 60 men under Capt. John Rainsford, was stranded upon the "desolate and hideous" island of Anticosti, at the mouth of the St. Lawrence; subjecting the castaways to every horror and rigour of freezing and famine. The unfortunate men, having built huts of trees, and planks from their shatter'd vessel, pass'd the entire winter on the bleak island; a few of them escaping in a small boat on March 26, 1691, and after incredible perils reaching Boston Harbour on the 9th of May and arranging for the early rescue of their companions. Sir William ever regretted the failure of his project: the more so, as even his earlier victory was annull'd by the French recapture of Port-Royal in 1691. He vainly sought authority for another expedition against Quebeck; and it was said of him, that *Canada* was writ upon his heart, as *Calais* was upon Queen Mary's.[12] Sir William, being in London at the time Dr. Increase Mather was there in quest of a new charter for the Massachusetts-Bay, lent his voice to that of the Boston clerick; and in the course of negotiations receiv'd royal appointment as the first governor of the reorganis'd Province of Massachusetts-Bay. Assuming this office in 1691, he was sorely vext by the Salem witch disorders of the following year; being not a little blam'd for the vigour of his prosecutions. He dy'd whilst in London on the 18th of February, 1695 O.S., receiving universal lamentations throughout New-England, and being made the subject of a poetick elegy in Cotton Mather's Magnalia, which begins thus:

> "Rejoice Messieurs; Netops rejoice; 'tis true,
> Ye Philistines, none will rejoice but You:
> Loving of All He Dy'd; who Love him not
> Now, have the Grace of Publicans forgot.
> Our Almanacks foretold a great Eclipse,
> This they foresaw not, of our great PHIPS."[13]

Meanwhile the "Messieurs" in Quebeck were indeed rejoicing in the most fervent fashion over the escape of their town from surrender. The newly-built (1688) chapel of L'Enfant Jesus, on the market place in the lower town, was rededicated to the Virgin Mary in honour of the deliverance; being now call'd *Notre-Dame de la Victoire*; whilst the guns and standards captur'd from our men at Beauport were ceremoniously distributed as martial trophies. In 1691, as before related, the French regain'd Port-Royal; and thereafter they continu'd to lead the Indians in raids upon our settlements. In January, 1692, they took the town of York, in Maine, and offer'd the inhabitants a choice betwixt death and captivity. In 1693, the conquest of Canada having been resolv'd on in London, a fleet was despatch'd to effect it; but after an unsuccessful encounter off Martinique the yellow fever work'd havock with the crews, so that when it put into Boston it was in no shape to proceed further. In this year also was a French and Indian raid upon Oyster River in New-Hampshire, where some 94 persons were kill'd or carry'd away. These forays along the coast were wholly instigated by the Jesuit missionaries, who boast of the matter in their Relations. At this period of the war our only successes were in the western theatre of action. Here, in 1691, the Albany Dutchman Schuyler made a foray into the Sorel country and effected a safe retreat, whilst in 1692 a French raid into the Seneca territory was dearly pay'd for. The Iroquois repeatedly harass'd the French in the Richelieu Valley above Lake Champlain, laying waste the countryside and besieging the forts and stockades. In the autumn of 1692 they laid siege to the fort at Verchères, near the mouth of the Richelieu; but were almost miraculously held off despite the absence of the usual defenders, the Sieur de Verchères' fourteen-year-old daughter, assisted only by two soldiers, an aged man, and her two small brothers, keeping the fort till help arriv'd. In 1693 Count Frontenac did damage to the Mohawk settlements, and in 1695 reoccupy'd Fort Frontenac on Lake Ontario, which Marquis de Denonville had abandon'd. In 1696, borne on a litter because of the feebleness of advancing years, he led a great punitive expedition into the lands of the Oneidas and Onondagas. Meanwhile La Motte Cadillac, the governor at Mackinac, (in 1705 founder of Detroit) confirm'd the friendship of the more westerly Indians. The Iroquois felt that they were sustaining more than their share of the struggle; and altogether the outlook was not bright for us. In 1696 the fort at Pemaquid, Maine, was taken by the French. In March, 1697, the Indians descended upon Haverhill, in the Massachusetts-Bay; slaying and capturing as usual, but receiving one severe reverse through the boldness of Mrs. Hannah Duston, since regarded as the prime heroine of her region, and honour'd by a very sumptuous monument in the main square of Haverhill. Mrs. Duston was sett upon by the salvages in her home, with a new-born infant and nurse and seven other children, whilst her husband was absent in the fields. The older children, escaping to the woods, were met and guided to safety by their returning father, who kept off the redskins with a musket; but Mrs. Duston was taken, the house burnt, and the brains of the new-born infant dash'd out against a tree. Later, Mrs. Duston and the nurse being carry'd north by the Indians to an island in the Merrimack above the present site of Concord, N.H., this intrepid matron plann'd and executed the reprisal for which she is famous. Inciting a fellow-prisoner, a young boy from Worcester, to learn from the Indians how scalping was accomplisht, she and the nurse in turn learn'd from him; and in the night all three sett about scalping their sleeping captors. Having kill'd 10 or 11 Indians, all those in their immediate wigwam, Mrs. Duston, the nurse, and the boy escap'd down the Merrimack in a bark canoe, and at length came once more to Haverhill. It is pleasing to relate, that Mrs. Duston liv'd to a ripe and peaceful age, leaving behind a numerous and worthy posterity well represented in Haverhill to this day.

This war, known to us in New-England as King William's War, nominally ended at the Peace of Ryswick in 1697; tho' boundary questions were left unsettled, and the status of the Iroquois made a matter of great dispute. Sieur d'Iberville, greatest of the brothers Le Moyne, continu'd to harass us in the Hudson's Bay Country, in Newfoundland, and in the West Indes, and in truth no one on either side consider'd the struggle as truly over. Finish'd it could never be till either we or the French had undisputed supremacy of the continent. The French were at this time greatly expanding in the west and down the Mississippi. Daniel Greysolon du Lhut, after whom the town of Duluth was later nam'd, founded a trading post on Lake Superior and explor'd the wilderness as far north and west as Lake Winnipeg. In June, 1701, Cadillac founded the town of Detroit with a Jesuit missionary and 100 Frenchmen. Illinois now contain'd many French posts, and in 1702 Vincennes, now in Indiana, was settled. In October 1698 Sieur d'Iberville brought a band of settlers by sea to the lower Mississippi region, looking for a colony site on the Gulf Coast west of the Spanish province of Florida, whose western outpost was Pensacola. After considerable exploration, a fort was built at Biloxi, in what is now the state of Mississippi; this forming the French seat of local government till 1702, when the chief fortress was transferr'd to the mouth of the Mobile River—a second and shorter transfer to the present site of the town of Mobile, Alabama, taking place in 1711. English counter-claims to the Mississippi Valley were made from 1698 onward, but never develop'd to any decisive degree. Sieur d'Iberville dy'd in 1706, universally lamented amongst his people, and generally allow'd to have been one of the greatest of the French officers and explorers—the true father of Louisiana. To him, as leader of the southern French colony, there succeeded the royal governor La Motte de Cadillac, founder of Detroit; after whom came d'Iberville's much younger brother Jean Baptiste Le Moyne, Sieur de Bienville (1680–1768). Upon his appointment in 1718, under the Royal authority and in connexion with that inflated trading monopoly of the Scotsman John Law soon to be known as the Mississippi Bubble, Bienville founded the town of New Orleans, destin'd to have so mighty a future.

(2) Queen Anne's War.

Meanwhile, in 1702, actual war broke out again; this being the conflict call'd in New-England "Queen Anne's War", but in reality forming an American phase of the War of the Spanish Succession, whereby England oppos'd that consolidation of Bourbon and popish interests which wou'd have ensu'd had the French King, as now came about through dynastick succession, been able to claim for his family the throne of Spain. Our conflict being this time with both France and Spain, two of our colonial areas were involv'd in warfare; New-England, bordering upon New-France, and Carolina, adjacent to the Spanish territory in Florida. Count Frontenac, a noble enemy great in years and honours, had departed this life in 1698; and the Governor of New-France was now the elder Marquis de Vaudreuil. In the South, the Carolinians did well against both Spaniards and French fleets; the Huguenots of Charleston fighting eagerly against their popish kinsfolk. New-England, however, has mostly disaster to relate. The Iroquois being neutral, New-York was let alone; but in 1703 the coast of Maine was aflame with French and Indian massacre. In February 1704 the town of Deerfield, on the Connecticut River in western Massachusetts, was set upon by the sanguinary Hertel de Rouville and a party of 200 French and 142 redskin salvages in a midnight raid and massacre; the houses being burnt, and 47 persons kill'd. 112 persons, including the Rev^d Mr. Williams and his family, were taken into captivity; many, however, being ransom'd. Mr. Williams' youngest daughter, aged 7, could not be ransom'd in any way; but grew up a papist in an Indian village near Montreal, later marrying a Caughnawaga chieftain. Years afterward she visited Deerfield in Indian dress, but profest no wish to return permanently to the race from which she came. From 1705 onward, French and Indian raids on New-England became too numerous to chronicle; perhaps the worst being that of August 1708 upon Haverhill, (then a frontier town set against the wilderness) led by the infamous de Rouville and Sieur des Chaillons. In this outrage the Rev^d Mr. Rolfe was beaten to death, and his wife and infant otherwise slaughter'd; whilst others in the town far'd no better. As the barbarians return'd, their force was harass'd by a smaller local force under the heroick Samuel Ayer, and several captives were rescu'd.

At sea, New-England made many efforts against the French, but succeeded only in capturing Acadia, or Nova-Scotia. The fleet which accomplisht this, consisting of 6 ships from England under Nicholson and 30 from New-England, with 4 New-England regiments, sett sail from Boston in Septr. 1710; reaching Port-Royal in 6 days, and on the 16th of October (N.S.) receiving the honourable surrender of M. Subercase, the French governor. The flag of old England, rais'd over the town, has never since been lower'd; and by the grace of God and our British strength never shall be. In honour of Her reigning Majesty, Queen Anne, the name of Port-Royal was chang'd to *Annapolis,* which it still bears.

Efforts were now made to interest the London government in a decisive conquest of Canada; it being made clear in an appeal from the legislature of New-York that the French were hemming all our colonies in and making alliances everywhere with our potential Indian foes. At this period the redoubtable Peter Schuyler took a party of five Iroquois chieftains to England for an audience with the Queen; their picturesque aspect exciting the notice of everyone in London, and giving rise to some witty reflections in literature, particularly certain essays by Mr. Addison.[14] In the end, an ambitious plan of campaign was foster'd thro' the influence of the Secretary of State— the brilliant Henry St. John, afterward Viscount Bolingbroke, and celebrated philosophick friend of Mr. Pope. A fleet of 15 warships and 40 transports, commanded by Sir Hovenden Walker and mann'd with the pickt veterans of the immortal MARLBOROUGH's campaigns, was sent to Boston for an expedition against Quebeck; whilst a great land force of New-England and New-York Englishmen, Palatine immigrants, and 600 Iroquois, was assembled at Albany for an attack on Montreal, now a place of vast importance as a military post and fur-trading centre. Even as far west as Wisconsin the Fox nation of Indians was expected to coöperate against the French. But all this came to naught in that gloomy year of 1711. The French, greatly alarm'd, strengthen'd their Indian alliances and prepar'd to defend Quebeck with supreme desperation; yet found no attackers in view. French peasants on the coast had in August seen British vessels at sea; yet after weeks of watching nothing appear'd to the sentinels on Quebeck's high ramparts. At length the truth became known: that the ambitious fleet of Sir Hovenden Walker had been wreck'd thro' poor judgment and seamanship near the mouth of the St. Lawrence; making the sea assault on Quebeck impossible, and cancelling the design for a land assault on Montreal. Even the Fox Indians, who attempted to burn Detroit, came to grief; failing, and being subject to fierce French reprisals. It was a dismal hour for us, and a great one for New-France. At Quebeck that lower-town church which had been renam'd *Notre-Dame de la Victoire* in 1690, after Phips's repulse, was now still further renamed *Notre-Dame des Victoires;* it being assum'd that the Virgin Mary had in two cases given France a victory through the dispersal of her enemies. The church still bears its name of 1711, tho' now on soil gloriously added to the dominions of His Britannick Majesty.

The fortunes of the war were at last decided by the glorious arms of BRITANNIA on the European continent, and in 1713 the treaty of Utrecht was sign'd in a manner advantageous to Great-Britain. In the New World we retain'd Nova-Scotia, New-foundland, and the Hudson's Bay country; and France agreed never to molest the Iroquois. Canada and Louisiana, however, remain'd French; and the question of boundaries was still a sore spot. For many years no open warfare existed, though there were local troubles such as that caus'd by the French artist and ascetick Sebastian Rasles, who, independently of New-France, organis'd a settlement of devout Popish Abenaki Indians in Maine and had much friction with the New-Englanders from 1717 till his death in battle in 1724. One great source of misunderstanding was the question of the Lake Champlain region, claim'd by both France and England. In 1731 the French establish'd a garrison (Ft. St. Frederic) on the lake which develop'd into the fortress of Crown Point; yet New-England settlers were swiftly penetrating the Green Mountain region, then call'd the New-Hampshire Grants, tho' claim'd by New-York as well as by that colony. In 1735 Fort Dummer was built on the site of Brattleboro, Vermont, this region then being thought within the limits of the Massachusetts-Bay. Clearly, the expansion of both French and English was bringing them into ominous contact. Parkman well says, "The English hunter, in the lonely wilderness of Vermont, as by the warm glow of sunset he piled the spruce boughs for his woodland bed, started as a deep, low sound struck faintly on his ear, the evening gun of Fort Frederic, booming over lake and forest."[15] Cape Breton Island, adjoining Nova-Scotia, being retain'd by France, a strong fortress was built upon it to serve as a guardian for the mouth of the St. Lawrence River. This stronghold, call'd *Louisbourg* in honour of the French King, was recognis'd to be a vast menace to our colonies in time of war, by reason of the ready harbourage it afforded for hostile privateers; so that its reduction was look'd upon as a necessary early feat of any coming conflict. Acadia itself, tho' under British dominion, remain'd almost totally French in race, language, and manners; English colonists being at first very slow to enter it.

At this period the westward vista of New-France was prodigiously enlarg'd by the intrepid explorations of Pierre Gaultier de Varennes, Sieur de la Vérendrye, and his dauntless sons Jean, Pierre, and François. Sieur de la Vérendrye, a gentleman of Canadian birth, was in 1728–30 station'd in a military capacity at the lone western post of Nipigon on Lake Superior, where he heard from Indians many tales of a great westward-flowing river, and a vast, flat, timberless country with large herds of cattle. Being desirous, like all others of his time and before, to find a westward water route to the Pacifick, and thinking this a possible opportunity, La Vérendrye proceeded to Quebeck and obtain'd the authority of Governor and merchants for a combin'd trading and exploring expedition in the remote and unknown west. In 1732 he started; proceeding cautiously and establishing a chain of trading-posts, each one of which form'd a safe base for further penetrations westward. As he proceeded, he met the untam'd Sioux Indians, by whom some of his men, including his eldest son Jean, were slain. One of his trading-posts occupy'd the site of the present city of Winnipeg, Manitoba. Another was at the site of the Portage la Prairie, whence he hop'd to be able to reach the Pacifick. Not succeeding in this aim, but establishing other posts and conducting desultory explorations, La Vérendrye was in 1740 forc'd to return to Montreal to make adjustments with his creditors. During his absence his sons Pierre and François prest westward across the plains through the country of the Mandan Indians, and in 1743 discover'd the foothills of the Rocky Mountains. Pierre de la Vérendrye, with a party of Indians, reach'd the main range of the Rockies; but cou'd not go on toward the Pacifick, from which he was indeed a thousand miles distant. The later fortunes of the La Vérendryes reveal much ingratitude on the part of New-France; the father indeed being for a time supplanted in his command of the western posts by a favourite of the Governor. Tho' at length restor'd, he was worn out by his experiences and dy'd in the year 1749; the claims of his sons being subsequently ignor'd. As openers of the American continent the Vérendryes rank very high; part of their extream western route being later us'd as a section of the celebrated "Oregon Trail".

(3) King George's War.

In the year 1741, England having for 2 years been at war with Spain,* there broke out in Europe the War of the Austrian Succession, in which France sought to prevent the accession of Maria Theresa upon the death of her father, Emperor Charles VI. England was ally'd with Austria, and Spain with France; and it was but natural for the Anglo-French conflict, which open'd in 1744, to have its echoes in the New World, where the increasing expansion of France in the Mississippi Valley made plain the sharp rivalry of that nation with the English for control of the North-American continent. An event of great advantage to us was a treaty made with the Iroquois at Lancaster, Pennsylvania, by representatives of Pennsylvania, Virginia, and Maryland; by which the British claim to the Ohio Valley and to disputed northern frontiers was strengthen'd by Indian support. The Iroquois were now stronger than ever, having lately become the *Six Nations* through the admission of the Tuscaroras to the original confederation of Mohawks, Senecas, Oneidas, Cayugas, and Onondagas. It was clear that from now on, our wars with the French must involve our western as well as northern boundaries. France had been sending agents eastward from the Mississippi, whilst we had been gradually spreading westward to meet them. In 1716 Governor Spottswood of Virginia, with a mounted party of Virginia gentlemen guided by rangers and Indians, crossed the Blue Ridge and open'd up the Shenandoah Valley; his expedition being call'd "The Knights of the Golden Horseshoe" from the fact that its horses were the first in Virginia to be shod. From this time onward, the plan of settling the Ohio Valley was a fixt Virginian ambition; of which we shall soon see substantial developments. Meanwhile, however, the plan of immediate campaign in the present war had a far different objective; namely, that of capturing the mighty fortress of Louisburg on Cape Breton Island, which was generally recognis'd as France's strongest outpost in the New World, and which serv'd as a nest for pirates and privateers injurious to New-England commerce. This enterprise, conducted almost solely by New-England men, was led by the Honble William Shirley, Gent., His Majesty's Governor of the Province of ye Massachusetts-Bay, an executive of vast courage and activity who was to play a great part in the final struggles against the French. Gov. Shirley, upon the decision in Jany. 1745 to move against Louisburg, was exceedingly diligent in securing the best advice and support; and conducted important correspondence with the Governors of New-York, Pennsylvania, and the several colonies of New-England.[16] As a general for the expedition, there was appointed the capable and intelligent merchant William Pepperrell, of Kittery, Maine; and recruiting activities of profound extensiveness were everywhere conducted. On the 24th of March, 1745, the fleet with its arm'd troops sett out from Boston, being soon joyn'd by a fleet from Gt. Britain under Admiral Sir Peter Warren (who later settled in Greenwich-Village, close to the city of New-York.) From that time till July the anxiety of New-England concerning the expedition was very great. One vessell was sent back during the siege, containing important French prisoners taken at sea and outside the wall of Louisburg, who assur'd the inhabitants of Boston that Louisburg was far too stout ever to be storm'd with success. And in truth the task was of Herculean proportions, for the walls of the vast fort were of solid masonry, 30

---

*In this war, Gen. Oglethorpe of Georgia harass'd Florida.

feet in height, 40 feet thick at the base, and surrounded by a 50-foot ditch. At times, owing to the strength of the fortress and the wild and marshy nature of the surrounding country, the taking of the place was despair'd of; but New-England ingenuity found various ways of circumventing the several obstacles, and the ships in the harbour arrang'd a cannonade which well supplemented the assaults of the land batteries. At length the discontent of the French garrison, and the incapacity of their commander Duchambon, became increasingly apparent; and on the 17th of June the seemingly impregnable stronghold capitulated to the arms of His Britannick Majesty. God Save the King! The news of this glorious victory was receiv'd with the wildest joy throughout New-England, church-bells being rung, and cannon fired, in every village of the land. Boston's rejoycing was particularly keen, and is to this day perpetuated by the name of *Louisburg-Square*, that exquisite Georgian backwater on antient Beacon-Hill. Gen[l] Pepperrell was, for his feat, made a baronet; the first native of New-England so to be honour'd. His portrait, shewing him in scarlet uniform before Louisburg's embattled walls, is to this day to be seen upon the walls of the Essex-Institute in Salem. Scarce any other feat of New-England arms has ever equall'd this. Of the difficulty of the siege we may form some notion by reflecting that even the sage Dr. Franklin, of Philadelphia, thought it a fruitless effort when it was first propos'd. Rhode-Island's contribution to this expedition was the 26-gun sloop-of-war *Tartar* (built in 1740 for service against Spain) under Capt. Daniel Fones. Tho' the vessel was sold at auction in 1748, one of its cannon is still preserv'd on Washington-Parade, in Newport. As matters turn'd out, the taking of Louisburg was (aside from the privateering in which RHODE-ISLAND was prominent) the sole actual event of this war—which has become known in history as "King George's War". Other operations, however, were anticipated, including a conquest of Canada by Shirley and Pepperrell; and the coast of New-England was strongly fortify'd by such defences as Fort Sewell, at Marblehead, which still survives as a park. What chang'd the plans of New-England was news of a great French armada under the Duc d'Anville, which had put to sea in 1746 to retake Louisburg and ravage our coast. The strength of this fleet—40 ships of war and additional transports—was such as to occasion the greatest alarm for the safety of our colonies; but chance almost miraculously remov'd the peril thro' the agency of storm, disaster, and shipwreck. The batter'd French fleet was forc'd to turn back, and its commander dy'd (nominally of apoplexy) under circumstances which strongly indicated suicide by poison. His immediate subordinate, like Brutus of old, kill'd himself by falling upon his sword. "This," says the gifted Nath: Hawthorne, Esq., "was as great a deliverance for New-England as that which Old England had experienc'd in the days of Queen Elizabeth, when the Spanish Armada was wreckt upon her coast."[17] GOD SAVE THE KING! Peace was made in 1748, and it was a matter of regret to New-Englanders that, as a minor phase in the negotiations, and exchanges attendant upon the conclusion of a great war, (the Peace of Aix-la-Chapelle) the return of Louisburg to France was provided for (in exchange for Madras, in India.) However, the confidence of the French in their fortress had been shaken; so that it no longer represented the menace it had once been. Its second taking—in 1758, by Amherst and Wolfe—was by no means so difficult as the original siege of Pepperrell and Warren. In the Hudson Valley, King George's War was markt by a French and Indian raid upon Saratoga (now Schuylerville) in November, 1745, in which the houses were burnt, and many persons kill'd or taken as prisoners to Quebeck. There were also some later raids in the same region.

(4) The Old French War.

The few years of nominal peace following 1748 were actually fill'd with great tension betwixt France and England in North-America, insomuch as the inevitability of a death-struggle for the continent was by everyone clearly perceiv'd. For this struggle the contestants were quite evenly match'd; our preponderance of population (15 to 1) being offset by the strategick hold of the French upon the country—the great line of forts and posts dominating the St. Lawrence and Mississippi valleys, and this completely enclosing and limiting our own territory. The wise choice of sites for these French outposts is well shewn by the greatness of the towns into which many of them developed—or which sprang up on their sites—these including Detroit, Chicago, Vincennes, St. Louis, Natchez, and New Orleans. To neutralise this encirclement, plans were push'd forward for English expansion in the Ohio Valley; a group of Virginians forming the Ohio Company, of which Lawrence Washington, Esq. was chief manager, in 1748, with a view to planting a colony on the east bank of the upper Ohio, in territory now included in West Virginia and southwestern Pennsylvania. Upon learning of this design, the Governor of New-France, La Galissonnière, made a counter-move in 1749; sending to the Ohio Valley an expedition of 300 men under Céleron de Bienville, to claim the country in the name of the French King, and to record possession by burying inscribed leaden plates at the mouths of all the principal creeks. Before long a new line of French forts was constructed in this region, extending southward from Lake Erie (at Erie, Pa.) to where the junction of the Alleghany and Monongahela Rivers forms the Ohio; (Pittsburgh, Pa.) whilst in the north, the ambitious La Galissonnière pursu'd a design of influencing the French inhabitants of Acadia—now British soil, and with a population dedicated to neutrality despite their French blood—to flock to the disputed border of their province in order to form a barrier against further English expansion. At this time the English settlements in Nova-Scotia were few and small; Halifax having been founded as recently as June, 1749, by disbanded officers, soldiers, and marines, and their families, to the number of 1400. The new town, which in 6 months grew to the extent of 300 houses, was named from my Ld Halifax, whose vigour and intelligence inspir'd the enterprise. About this time, at Quebeck, La Galissonnière was replac'd as Governor by the less imperialistick La Jonquière; but the former's influence continu'd to operate in the national rivalry, by reason of his appointment to the French commission engag'd in drawing boundaries. The Ohio Company, operating from Virginia, combin'd to send explorers west of the Alleghanies; and in 1753 the Scotsman Robt Dinwiddie, His Majesty's Governor of Virginia, sent a messenger to warn off the French whose new forts were multiplying so swiftly. This messenger was instructed to proceed to the French fort at Venango, presenting the petition of His Britannick Maj$^{ty's}$ Government, whereby the Ohio Valley was claim'd by right of purchase from the Iroquois. As a messenger was selected the young half-brother of the Ohio Company's first manager lately deceas'd—George Washington, Esq., a surveyor of great skill and courage and Adjt. Genl of Virginia militia, whose later fortunes and eminence fill so large a place in history. Mr. Washington was receiv'd with civility at the French posts, being referr'd by the officers at Venango to the commandant, at the more northerly Fort Le Boeuf. This gentleman promis'd Mr. Washington with great courtesy to transmit the message of Govr Dinwiddie to his Governor-General, Marquis Duquesne, at Quebeck; after which the young envoy return'd with but a single companion to Virginia, enduring all the rigours of a midwinter wilderness. Despite the urbanity of the French officers, it was made plain that no relinquishment of the Ohio Valley was to be expected; hence the Ohio Company prepar'd to assert its right to the region by force of arms. In the spring of 1754 a new-rais'd company of Virginia backwoodsmen under Capt. Wm. Trent began to build a fort at the important strategick junction of the Alleghany and Monongahela (Pittsburgh), but were interrupted and driven off by a large party of Frenchmen and Indians, who completed the fort for themselves, under the name of Ft. Duquesne. At the time of this reverse, Major Washington was advancing with another company; but upon hearing of Trent's repulse decided to pause and build another fort on the Monongahela, (in the region known as "Great Meadows") awaiting the arrival of further troops. This small post, call'd Ft. Necessity, lay about 40 miles south of Ft. Duquesne; and the French, upon hearing of it, sent a scouting party under M. de Jumonville to watch the operations there. Maj. Washington, hearing of this, secured the aid of friendly Indians and set upon the French party under cover of a dark, rainy night; opening fire whilst the Frenchmen were reaching for their arms. In the ensuing action of a quarter of an hour, ten of the French, including de Jumonville himself, were kill'd, and 21 were taken prisoners. The dead were scalp'd by the Indian allies. This was Maj. Washington's first experience under fire, and in a letter to his brother he said, "I heard the bullets whistle, and, believe me, there is something charming in the sound." This observation being reported to King George the Second—himself a man of the greatest courage and a hero of Dettingen—His Maj[ty] dryly observ'd, "He wou'd not say so, if he had been us'd to hear many." The massacre of de Jumonville's expedition hath ever been held by the French to have constituted a gravely treacherous crime; it being their claim, that the party was approaching as a friendly embassy. To this day the same opinion exists amongst them, so that a travel folder of the year 1929, in explaining the name of Rue de Jumonville in Quebeck, speaks of the unfortunate officer as "assassinated under Washington." Washington himself was sensible of the charge levell'd against him, but display'd M. de Jumonville's captur'd instructions as proof that the delegation was no open embassy, but in truth a scouting-party. After this engagement, hearing that a large body of Frenchmen was about to attack him in reprisal, Maj. Washington retir'd to Ft. Necessity and defended himself for an entire day. In the evening, however, he was oblig'd to surrender to a force of 900 French and Indians commanded by the brother of de Jumonville. Being offer'd fair terms, Maj. Washington retir'd to Virginia in good order; leaving the Ohio Valley, for the time, in French hands.

Open war now being highly imminent, representatives of the northern colonies met at Albany to discuss plans for defence against the French. Delegates from the Iroquois were also present, warning the colonists that it was the intention of France to drive every Englishman out of the country. It was at this Albany convention of 1754 that the learned Dr. Franklin of Philad[a.] propos'd the first systematick plan of colonial union; a plan, however, which suffer'd defeat. The only other delegate who fully supported this plan was the eminent Stephen Hopkins, of PROVIDENCE in RHODE-ISLAND. By the early part of 1755, it was clear that war wou'd occur at any moment. Pacifick negotiations betwixt the English and French courts still continu'd, yet strong armies were sent out to the New World from both countries—the British commanded by the bold but stupid and tasteless Edward Braddock, and the French by the experienced veteran Baron Dieskau. Braddock safely arriv'd in Chesapeake Bay, proceeding thereafter to Williamsburg, Annapolis, and Alexandria. In Alexandria he occupy'd the old Carlisle house, still standing, and held an important convocation of colonial governors, whilst recruits for an Ohio campaign were assembled. The old tavern in Alexandria where Mr. Washington, as a Colonel of Virginia militia, obtain'd recruits for this (or the 1759) campaign, is still standing and mark'd by a tablet. Baron Dieskau's fleet, however, was intercepted at sea by a squadron of His Britannick Maj[ty's] vessels under Adm[l] Boscawen; who, notwithstanding the absence of any declaration of war, captur'd two of the French ships and sent great alarm through the rest. In June Baron Dieskau reach'd Quebeck, bringing with him a new governor to succeed Marquis Duquesne. This gentleman was the younger Marquis de Vaudreuil, himself born in New-France, who had seen Canadian service and had been a governor of Louisiana. From now onward, His Maj[ty's] vessels harass'd the ships of France to the utmost possible extent; till at length the French ambassador, Marquis de Mirepoix, left the court of London in recognition that war had actually begun. Thus commenc'd the struggle known in America as the "Old French War" or "French and Indian War", and in Europe as the "Seven Years' War"—though an actual declaration did not take place till May of the year 1756. The European phase of this conflict was markt by our alliance with the Prussian King, Frederick the Great, and its Asiatick echoes included the exploits of the great CLIVE in India. Our plan of campaign in America, in addition to much privateering in which RHODE-ISLAND took a great part, provided for a simultaneous push on all fronts, design'd to dislodge the French from those outposts where they most encroach'd upon the territory claim'd by us. One army under Col. Monckton was to operate in Acadia where the French disputed our frontiers. Another, under Gen. Wm. Johnson (the friend of the Iroquois), was to take Crown Point on Lake Champlain, where the enemy had establisht a wedge betwixt our New-York and New-England dominions. A third under Gov. Shirley of Massachusetts was to take Ft. Niagara. And fourth, the present active theatre of dissention was to be attended to by Genl. Braddock himself, when with two regiments of British regulars, plus as strong a force of Virginia militia as possible, was to capture Ft. Duquesne and drive the French from the Ohio Valley. Of all these operations, the fourth was obviously of greatest immediate importance; and Braddock took pains to collect and train a great force, with ample supplies, at Ft. Cumberland (nam'd for H. R. H. the Duke of Cumberland, Captain-Gen[l] of His Maj[ty's] forces) in the extream west of Maryland just east of the Alleghanies.

The melancholy fate of Braddock and his army, commemorated by a special postage-stamp in the U.S. in 1930, is one of the most celebrated tragedies of history. Early in June, 1755, he set forth into the untrodden wilderness; with axemen hewing a path, and heavy supply wagons heaving and rumbling through swamps and over stump-clogged swaths. With the Virginia militia was Col. George Washington, who cou'd have given valuable advice on the strategy to use in forest warfare against a largely Indian enemy. Braddock, however, had a great and irrational prejudice against the outwardly awkward provincials; and insisted on following the conventional methods of European warfare. Also in the party were Horatio and Tho: Gage, destin'd to serve on opposite sides of a later war. The Monongahela was twice forded with great difficulty; and the French at Ft. Duquesne, learning of the approaching column, were thrown into great dismay. Contrecoeur, the commandant, actually thought of retreat, but a bold captain of the garrison, Beaujeu, offer'd to lead a party of French and Indians to attack the column on its line of march. The Indians were of varied sources; some of them from Canada, including the Hurons settled at Lorette, near Quebeck. It was only with difficulty that Beaujeu could obtain followers; but once he had persuaded his men to go, they began to work themselves up to a great pitch of martial ardour. The attack was made whilst Braddock's column was in a dense stretch of forest, and was an ambush of the most sudden and successful sort. The Indians, yelling savagely, fell upon the unprepar'd column with a murderous musket fire; throwing the season'd troops from Britain into a fearsome panick. Beaujeu himself was kill'd by the first volley from our troops, but his subordinate Dumas capably took his place. Our regulars, bewilder'd and ignorant how to proceed in so unaccustom'd a situation, were slaughter'd like sheep; and Braddock himself, five horses having been shot from under him, receiv'd a mortal wound. Whilst on the field he did more harm than good, insomuch as he stopt the ingenious Virginians from successfully adopting the Indian mode of shooting from behind trees—forcing them to form in conventional platoons and perish beneath the bullets of hidden adversaries. After three hours of this nightmare fighting, during which Colo: Washington had two horses shot from under him and received four bullets in his cloaths, (tho' escaping unwounded) the survivors of the column spontaneously broke into a wild generall flight toward the Monongahela. The Virginia militia was the least precipitate and disorganis'd, and it was Col. Washington who bury'd Gen. Braddock upon his death a few days after. The regulars shew'd the greatest fright of all; and in generall, the bulk of the army fled to Philadelphia without thought of the unprotected settlers left to the fury of their salvage pursuers.

Meanwhile the Monckton expedition charg'd with the conquest of Acadia—that is, the reduction of the French forts in those boundary regions still claim'd by France—had a very easy victory. Moreover, three thousand men from the Province of the Massachusetts-Bay, under Genl Winslow, brought the whole disputed region (including those mainland regions distinct from the peninsula of Nova-Scotia, now forming the province of New-Brunswick) most completely under His Maj$^{ty's}$ authority, where it hath ever since remain'd without dispute. A stern and unfortunate incident connected with this victory is the memorable deportation of all the French inhabitants of Acadia to other parts of the British dominions in America; an event forming the theme of Prof. Longfellow's celebrated sentimental poem intitul'd "Evangeline". This drastick step was deem'd necessary by reason of the partiality of these inhabitants toward the French cause, notwithstanding their position as British subjects since 1713. It is very probable that partiality did exist to a troublesome extent; for the ties of blood are strong, and the simple habitants cannot have felt any great change when their region pass'd from the sphere of the French crown. French priests under the jurisdiction of the Bishop of Quebeck undoubtedly urg'd the people to refrain from swearing allegiance to His Britannick Majesty, and we have seen how the ambitious Governor La Galissonnière sought to concentrate them along the disputed border and secure their coöperation against British expansion. They certainly supply'd their French kinsfolk with provisions, and sometimes took part in French and Indian raids on our settlements—tho' they alleg'd that they did the latter only under intimidation from the Micmacs, the Indians of the region. In 1713 they had been given a choice of leaving Acadia or taking our oath, but had done neither. It must be admitted that we sought to discourage their emigration; insomuch as we did not wish our new province depopulated, or the neighbouring French provinces strengthen'd by an influx. Most of the Acadians were honest and simple folk who probably wish'd to remain on their old lands in a state of neutrality. Had they been let alone by their kinsfolk under the French King, it is likely that they wou'd have given us no trouble. Now, in the midst of this desperate war, it was necessary to remove every obstacle; and the opinion gain'd ground that it wou'd be better to let Nova-Scotia become a free field for British settlement and civilisation. Accordingly it was decided to scatter the 7000 Acadians throughout our other colonies, where they might neither aid the French nor form centres of disaffection on His Maj$^{ty's}$ soil. In the end they were collected, told that their lands and possessions were forfeited to the crown, and sent aboard transports bound for various parts of the colonies. In certain cases families were separated by accident, and in almost all cases melancholy and suffering form'd the lot of the refugees; who were deliver'd penniless to lands where the language and manners were unknown to them. Many vainly try'd to return, and others suffer'd much hostility from the populations amongst whom they were deposited. Those in Boston often sank to the state of servants and paupers. In Georgia, after a vain attempt to return to Acadia, they develop'd into a distinct element having the corrupted name of '*Cajins.* Some in the south manag'd to filter across the border to French-speaking Louisiana. But the main purpose of the deportation succeeded, so that Nova-Scotia is today a thoroughly English-speaking province. God Save the King.

Governor Shirley's expedition against Niagara came to nothing, owing to the danger of a French attack on his base at Ft. Oswego, in New-York. Despite his courage, it is possible that he was but a poor strategist; and in 1756 he was depriv'd of his command.

More successful was the expedition against the French around Lake Champlain, headed by the redoubtable Genl. W$^{m.}$ Johnson. Johnson was a native of Ireland and a nephew of the naval victor of Louisburg, Admiral Sir Peter Warren. Coming to the Province of New-York in 1734, he at once took charge of a great tract of wild land belonging to his uncle in the northern country of the Mohawks. There he liv'd in feudal state; building two great mansions and acquiring unlimited influence over the neighbouring Iroquois, with whom he was on terms of the closest intimacy—taking for his second wife a sister of the celebrated Mohawk war-chief Joseph Brant. On this occasion the troops from New-York and all the New-England colonies were muster'd at Albany; Genl. Johnson's force against Crown Point consisting chiefly of Connecticut and Massachusetts militia, plus 500 New-Hampshire foresters, and 4 companies from RHODE-ISLAND in the form of a miniature regiment. The enemy, resolv'd to hold Crown Point at any cost, summon'd to active service every able-body'd man in the Montreal district; so that at harvest time reapers had to be brought from Three Rivers and Quebeck.

Early in August 1755 the New-England troops, under Maj-Genl Phinakas Lyman, built Fort-Edward at the 12-mile portage betwixt the Hudson and the chain of lakes and rivers emptying into the St. Lawrence. Later in the month Genl Johnson led an untrain'd force of 3400, including Indians, across the portage to the wilderness lake below Champlain which the French had call'd "Holy Sacrament". This he renam'd Lake-George, in honour of His Britannick Maj^{ty}; and upon its southern shoar the expedition made an unfortify'd camp—later Ft. William Henry. Meanwhile, in Quebeck, Marquis de Vaudreuil had heard of the operations in this region; and had order'd Baron Dieskau to abandon the contemplated attack on Oswego—moving against the new Ft. Edward instead. This the Baron did, with 600 Canadian Iroquois, 600 French-Canadians, and 200 regulars from France. Mistaking his way, however, he ultimately found himself near Lake-George. Here the Indian allies profest willingness to attack the unfortify'd camp, tho' they refus'd to storm Ft. Edward. At midnight of Septr. 7 Genl Johnson heard of the enemy's approach, and at dawn sent out a thousand men to reconnoitre. These were defeated with a loss of both English and Indian leaders* after encountering an ambuscade; but being shrewd provincials and Indians, unhamper'd by the conventional military notions which had prov'd Braddock's undoing, they made a slow, steady, fighting retreat with a widening front which work'd gradual havock amongst their pursuers. At last reinforcements came from the camp, and the pursuit was check'd. Meanwhile the camp had been rudely fortify'd with a log breastwork, so

---

*Col. Ephraim Williams of Deerfield, and the corpulent old Mohawk chieftain Hendrick.

that it afforded a good haven for the defeated party, and presented a less hopeless front against the inevitable attack of Baron Dieskau's troops. In the end, the tables were completely turned. Dieskau made no rush of assault, but meerly kept up a steady fire against the camp. After several hours our troops, abandoning the defensive, burst out of the camp in a sudden attack on the enemy which turn'd out to be a compleat victory. Dieskau himself was wounded and captur'd, whilst the fleeing bulk of the army were utterly routed and dispers'd by a party of New-York and New-Hampshire rangers from Ft. Edward. For this victory Gen[l] Johnson was made a baronet and appointed superintendent of Indian affairs for the northern tribes. Many, however, assign chief credit to Gen. Lyman, and the brave New-England troops. His subsequent career was one of great honour and usefulness, but was sadden'd by the approaching differences betwixt the colonists and their Sovereign. He dy'd suddenly in the summer of 1774, and there are not lacking those who attribute his death to a suicide brought on by the political tension of the times. Sir William Johnson had his crudenesses and vanities, but he must ever be reckon'd one of the greatest figures of our colonial history.

A large part of the events of this war centre around the same region of Lake-George, in the Province of New-York. At the northern point of the lake—or rather, on Lake Champlain but near the northern point of Lake George—the French now planted the mighty fortress of Carillon (later Ticonderoga); whilst Johnson built Fort William Henry (nam'd for the Duke of Cumberland) at the lake's southern point, near the camp at which he had defeated Dieskau. It is unfortunate that Johnson did not, as Gov[r] Shirley advis'd, follow up his victory by a pursuit of the French; for as it was, the plan of campaign cannot be said to have been fulfill'd. Not only was Crown Point not taken, but a new French stronghold had arisen still farther south. Thus ended the 1755 chapter of this most complex and extensive of all the French wars in North-America. In 1756 the French cause was strengthen'd by the sending of that mighty and illustrious warrior, Field-Marshal Louis Joseph, Marquis de Montcalm de St. Véran, as commander of the army in Canada. Marquis de Montcalm, a gentleman of the highest genius and cultivation, and of the widest attainments in military science, was amongst the noblest adversaries with whom we have ever had to contend; and but for the failure of Marquis de Vaudreuil to work in harmony with him, might have secur'd the French successes of which he just fell short. His reputation had preceded him; and the Indians were astonisht to behold a man of meerly medium height, when they had expected to encounter a giant. "We thought," they said, "his head would have been lost in the clouds." Later, imprest by his qualities, an antient chief said to him, "When I look into your eyes I see the height of the pine and the wings of the eagle." Montcalm himself, in writing to his Sovereign, declar'd—"I will save New-France or perish in the attempt." History relates how tragically this prophecy was fulfill'd.

The immediately following years of the war were highly unfavourable for us, due largely to the genius of Marquis de Montcalm. An ambitious plan of parallel campaigns, like that of the preceding season, was propos'd by a congress of colonial governors at New-York in December, 1855; but never reach'd the point of adoption. In England, the Earl of Loudon, a friend of my L[d] Halifax, was appointed commander-in-chief over all His Maj[ty's] armies in continental America; with my L[d] Abercrombie as second in command. Of these new commanders, Abercrombie arriv'd in Albany in June, and Loudon in July. Ft. Oswego, in New-York on the southern shoar of Lake Ontario, was then badly menac'd by a French army, yet no quick defensive step was taken. In mid-August Montcalm mov'd against Oswego and captur'd it without any siege beyond a preliminary skirmish and some wall-rending gunfire. The fortress was levell'd to the ground, and a great number of prisoners, besides captur'd supplies, borne down the St. Lawrence to Quebeck. The colours of the defeated garrison were given as trophies to the churches of Montreal, Three Rivers, and Quebec, and the omnipresent Jesuits planted a triumphal cross on the site of the fort.

In the period following this event the French (tho' opprest by a famine in Canada, due to lack of ploughing and planting amidst the rigours of war) greatly strengthen'd their standing amongst the Indians, seriously rivalling the attempts of Sir W: Johnson to hold them as our allies. The next summer witnest a tremendous reverse for our arms; namely, the famous capture and massacre of Ft. William Henry. Montcalm, with a great force of 6000 Frenchmen and 2000 Indians assembled from every part of Canada, descended to Lake George in August and besieg'd our fortress with irresistible strength. With him was the son of the Governor, Vaudreuil; and his spirits were high from his having just receiv'd the red ribbon of the Order of St. Louis from the French King. Ft. William Henry was commanded by the intrepid Lt. Col. Monro, who had but a slight force. At Ft. Edward was the pusillanimous Webb with the force of 4000; but so great was his cowardice, that instead of arranging to help Monro, he sent him a note exaggerating the size of the French force and advising him to surrender. Montcalm captur'd this note, but sent it on to its destination since it favour'd rather than acted against the French purpose. On Aug^r 4th, 1757, Montcalm had urg'd Monro to surrender, but receiv'd a defiant answer. After about a week's siege, the hopelessness of defence having been made plain by the note from Webb, the brave commandant at last capitulated, and march'd his men out of the fort with full honours, under a pledge that they wou'd not serve against the French for 18 months. Montcalm, in granting this honourable surrender, had urged upon his Indian allies the need of helping him fulfil its liberal obligations, and had taken care to keep all intoxicating liquors from them. The salvages, however, somehow obtaining liquor, held a nocturnal session of revelry; and at dawn attack'd the defeated garrison in a general massacre, tomahawking and scalping with wild fury despite the efforts of the French to stop them. In view of the great number of French soldiers present, some have disputed the sincerity of Montcalm's attempt to check the treacherous carnage. It is certain, however, that he and other officers dash'd amongst the salvages at great personal risk, trying in vain to restrain them. He is said to have cry'd out, "Kill me, but spare the English who are under my protection." Montcalm destroy'd the fortress and bore off abundant supplies. Of his own men, only 53 had been killed or wounded. In their subsequent plans both Genl Webb and Ld Loudon display'd a most reprehensible timidity; but their alarum was in vain, since Montcalm retir'd to Ft. Carillon, or Ticonderoga, without following up his victory. The effect of the massacre upon the population of this region was prodigious, and the calamity never ceas'd to be talk'd about. A friend of the present writer—Jonathan E. Hoag, Esqr of Greenwich, in New-York, who dy'd in 1927 at the age of 96—was in his youth told of it at first-hand by his great-aunt, (who liv'd to be 106) who was a child at the time of the massacre.[18]

Our fortunes in the war were now at their lowest ebb, largely owing to the incompetent ministry in power at home. In 1758, the wise and eminent William Pitt, Earl of Chatham, came to the helm; and immediately a more intelligent plan of campaign and selection of leaders develop'd. Pitt addrest the colonial governors in a letter promising a large force from England and urging them to raise as many local troops as possible, and there was outlin'd a tripartite mode of attack upon the French: first, a taking of Louisburg, repeating the old feat of 1745; second, an assault on Ticonderoga; and third, the capture, at last, of Fort Duquesne in the Ohio Valley. Meanwhile His Maj$^{ty's}$ navy was helping to keep supplies from the French at Quebeck; with such success that Montcalm confess'd a state of partial famine, and even spoke despondingly of the ultimate issue. It is perhaps true, that Britannia's rule of the waves was in the end a more potently decisive factor in the conquest of Canada than any of the famous operations by land. Gradually it became impossible for any adequate communication to exist between Quebeck and Old France; a condition aggravated by the loss of Louisburg. Pitt's choice of commanders was almost invariable wise; and it is at this stage that we behold the advent of such men as Sir Jeffrey Amherst and the immortal JAMES WOLFE, the latter 31 years of age, and a veteran of the European fields of Dettingen, Fontenoy, and Laffeldt. Gen. Wolfe, brave, kindly, modest, and exemplary in all the relations of life, was a person of slight frame and ailing constitution whose military genius and courage kept him to the fore when others would have lapsed into obscurity under equal burthens. To Amherst and Wolfe was entrusted the capture of Louisburg, the naval support of A$^{dm.}$ Boscawen being given them. Genl. Forbes was to attend to the Ohio Valley, whilst my Ld Howe and Genl Abercrombie were to take Ticonderoga and Crown Point.

Amherst and Wolfe reach'd Halifax, in Nova-Scotia, on the 28th of May, 1758. On June 8 the expedition landed on Cape Breton Island near Louisburg, beginning the siege on the same day. Various outer works were gradually captur'd, till at length the heroick French commander, Chevalier de Drucour, was forc'd to surrender. On July 27th His Maj$^{ty's}$ forces occupy'd Louisburg, and in consequence became masters of Cape Breton and Prince Edward's Islands, over which the banner of ENGLAND has never since ceas'd to float. God Save the King! In the conduct of the siege—a much less arduous one than that of 1745—Adm^l Boscawen gave adequate support, for which he receiv'd an unanimous tribute from the House of Commons. In the land forces, Maj. Isaac Barré and Lieut. Richd Montgomery achiev'd enviable distinction. Trophies were deposited in St. Paul's Cathedral, London, and all New-England rejoyc'd anew, as it had done in 1745. France's greatest seaboard fortress in the New World had fallen, and thenceforward the Old and New France cou'd communicate only with difficulty. There had been vague thoughts of an attack upon Quebeck itself—mighty citadel of citadels and centre of all French life in America—but the season was now too far advanc'd for the planning of a siege, whilst the aid of the great Amherst was needed in the operations around Lake-George. In the taking of Louisburg we employ'd an army of 14,000, and a fleet of 20 ships of the line and 18 frigates. From the French were taken 5737 prisoners and 120 cannon; their naval loss being 5 ships of the line and 4 frigates.

In the operations around Lake-George, this great victory was unhappily offset by disaster. The incompetent Ld Loudon having return'd to England, Genl Ld Abercrombie remain'd as Commander-in-Chief. He, with my Ld Howe, now assembled the greatest arm'd body of Europeans ever muster'd upon this continent in an attempt to take Ft. Ticonderoga. In all there were 16,000 men, of whom 9000 were provincials; and these were aided by a great train of artillery. Sailing up Lake George on a July morning in an armada of 1035 boats, the glittering army afforded an example of impressive pageantry which no participant or spectator ever forgot. Later, however, disaster ensued. Incompetent guidance and imperfect knowledge of the fortress caus'd the troops to reach their goal in poor formation for attack, and a rash assault without artillery was order'd. In that brave but futile attempt, which lasted upward of four hours, we lost full 2000 men in kill'd and wounded. In the end there was a precipitate retreat in boats across Lake George, and an end of the summer's hopes in this region. In this engagement my Ld Howe was kill'd.

What sav'd this campaign from compleat ignominy was its brilliant sequel; when Colo: Bradstreet secur'd my Ld Abercrombie's permission to take 3000 men for an expedition against Ft. Frontenac (now Kingston) on the north side of Lake Ontario, that antient outpost about which so much military and exploring history has revolv'd. This expedition sail'd in open boats across Lake Ontario, landed within a mile of the fort, and in two days compell'd the French commandant to surrender. There were here captur'd 9 arm'd vessels, 60 cannon, 16 mortars, and a great amount of ammunition and other supplies. God Save the King! Meanwhile Genl Amherst, hearing of Ld Abercrombie's disaster, hasten'd from Louisburg with four regiments to ensure the safety of the Lake George region. Abercrombie return'd to England in November, but escap'd censure for his poor campaigns and general incapacity. He had never been a great commander, and for the success of the Ticonderoga campaign Ld Howe had really been rely'd upon. Other officers in that campaign were Capt. John Stark of New-Hampshire and Major Israel Putnam; both prominent in the subsequent lamentable rebellion against His Maj$^{ty's}$ authority.

The campaign of Gen. Jas. Forbes against Ft. Duquesne was intrusted to the provincials of the central and southern colonies. Maryland, Pennsylvania, Virginia, and South-Carolina contributed troops, and among the later-celebrated persons participating were the painter Benj: West, Anthony Wayne, and Colo: G^e Washington. Its prosecution was greatly delay'd by reason of the serious illness of Genl Forbes, and from the desire to make the route of the army—the same that was follow'd by Braddock's ill-fated column—a well-built road to serve as a future generall approach to the West; but it none the less mov'd steadily on; very largely owing to the skill of Col. Washington as a guide and leader. In September a reconnoitring detachment which had gone on ahead without orders was captur'd by the garrison of Ft. Duquesne, which amounted to not more than 800 men, including Indians. In November, when only half the distance had been cover'd, it was decided to advance no further that season; but Col. Washington, having learn'd from prisoners of the garrison's weakness, secur'd permission to go on with 2500 pick'd men. This he did with much rapidity; so that the Frenchmen, hearing of his approach, set fire to the fort and retreated down the Ohio. Washington, with the veteran Armstrong who had joyn'd him with 1000 men, enter'd the ruins of the vacant fort on the evening of Saturday, Nov. 25th, 1758. The flag of His Britannick Maj^{ty} was rais'd by Armstrong's own hand and the place was, at the suggestion of Genl Forbes, renam'd Fort Pitt—later Pittsburgh—in honour of William Pitt; an apellation which still designated the vast city which arose there. Despite the failure at Ticonderoga, the year 1758 had prov'd a favourable one for our arms, and arous'd the hope that all of New-France might yet be conquer'd. The French, on their side, likewise saw that the tide had turn'd; and Marquis de Montcalm wrote to his government of the impending doom, which only some miracle, or some vast error on our part, cou'd avert. The population of Canada was not above 82,000, of whom only 7000 were able to bear arms. Food was scarce because of untill'd fields, livestock was meagre, soldiers were unpaid, and financial corruption was undermining the local government. At the last, however, desperation arous'd the people to a dogged resistance; and they resolv'd to defend themselves to the utmost. Prayers were offer'd up in the churches, and the priests us'd all their exaggerated influence to stir the people to action. There were masses and penances to avert divine wrath from the colony, and even old men, women and children were order'd into the fields to reap the gravely needed harvest.

For the year 1759 a quadruple campaign was plann'd. Genl. Stanwix was to complete the British hold on the Ohio Valley forts, from Pittsburgh to Erie. Genl. Prideaux, with Sir W: Johnson, was to attack the French at Ft. Niagara, repeating the earlier frustrated design of Govr Shirley. Genl Amherst was to move against Ticonderoga and Crown Point, in the central and most sanguinary region of the war. And foremost of all, Genl. Wolfe was to threaten the very centre and nucleus of the French power—the cliff-guarded and seemingly impregnable fortress of QUEBECK itself. By these three campaigns, it was thought likely that all Canada might be reduc'd.

Ft. Niagara, first built by La Salle and strongly fortify'd by Denonville, was invested in July; the expedition having sail'd along Lake Ontario. During the siege Genl Prideaux was kill'd by the bursting of a cohorn, and Sir W: Johnson succeeded to the command. French reinforcements, marching up from the nearest forts, (Detroit, Presqu'Isle, Le Boeuf, and Venango) were defeated and put to flight; and on July 25 the garrison of 600 capitulated. The province of New-York extended its territory to the Niagara River and Lake Erie; Genl Stanwix having meanwhile taken the whole line of Ohio forts— Venango, Le Boeuf, and Presqu'Isle. At this point the French became very apprehensive about the safety of Montreal; and Montcalm's second in command, Chevalier de Lévis Leran, sought to occupy the passes of the St. Lawrence (Mt. Ogdensburg, N.Y.) in protection of it, coming from Quebeck with a very meagre force. Amherst ordered Lt. Col. Gage to forestall this move, but the latter (now successor to Prideaux) neglected to do so.

At the tragick old Lake George battle-ground, conditions had so chang'd that operations savour'd of anticlimax. Amherst reach'd Ticonderoga with one division on July 22nd; but most of the garrison had retir'd to Crown Point and the rest soon surrender'd. After refortifying Ticonderoga for our own use, Amherst march'd north to Crown Point—Ft. St. Frederic—but found that place already deserted. Seizing and strengthening the empty fort,* Gen. Amherst wish'd to follow the French to their new stronghold on the Isle aux Noix, at the north end of Lake Champlain—a powerful camp of 3500 men and adequate artillery—but was prevented by lack of naval equipment.

The stage was now sett for the climax of the drama—the great mass'd attack upon QUEBECK itself—a stronghold which had defy'd the strength of Phips, and had been the vain hope of Sir Hovenden Walker; a fortress whose invincible might had become a legend, and whose precipitous cliffs had known no conqueror since the early days of Sir David Kirke. Always dream'd of as the final key to the conquest of New-France, its reduction was now to be seriously attempted. Yet even in view of the weaken'd state of the French, 'tis not likely we wou'd have taken it in this campaign, but for the genius of that illustrious warrior and gentleman who lay'd down his life in the accomplishment of the Herculean feat—the immortal JAMES WOLFE, whom posterity has enshrin'd as one of the glories of ENGLAND and of mankind.

(5) The Fall of New-France.

Steps toward the conquest of Quebeck had begun as soon as the season permitted; Wolfe making Louisburg his base for planning his campaign and assembling his forces. His army compris'd 8 regiments, 2 battalions of royal Americans, 3 companies of rangers, artillery, and a brigade of engineers; forming in all about 8000 men. The fleet—22 ships of the line, 22 frigates and arm'd vessels, and 119 transports—was commanded by Adm^l Saunders, whose grave in Westminster-Abbey (he dy'd in 1775) is about to be adorn'd with a memorial offer'd to the Dean of Westminster in 1930 by Prime-Minister Bennett

---

*He had been criticis'd for doing this, since the now certain conquest of Canada wou'd surely render it useless. Amherst was a brave and noble officer, but wanting in supreme genius.

of the Dominion of Canada. Among those on the ships were Jervis, afterward L^d St. Vincent, and Capt. James Cook, later fam'd as a navigator and explorer, and a lineal ancestor of the linguist and musician Alfred Galpin. Of the land forces, some of the commanders were Robt Monckton, later Govr of N Y and conqueror of Martinique, George Townshend, the statesman, Genl. James Murray, Isaac Barré, Col. Guy Carleton, and Lt. Col. (later Sir Wm.) Howe. History will have more to say of all of these men.

On June 26, 1759, this armada, after a safe trip up the St. Lawrence, for which great credit is due to Adm^l Saunders, arriv'd at the Isle of Orleans, near Quebeck, and made a camp. The French, meanwhile, under Montcalm, were strongly fortify'd at Beauport, on the northern shoar, where in 1690 a landing-party of Sir W. Phips was defeated; their intrenchments extending from the St. Charles River, close to the city, on the west, to the Great Falls of the Montmorency on the east. Above Quebeck, for the space of over nine miles, every known landing place was guarded. At first the French vainly try'd to harass our fleet with fire-ships, but it soon became clear that we had full command of the river. On the night of June 29 Monckton occupy'd Pt. Lévis, the great cliff region across the river from Quebeck, and no attempt to dislodge him was found practicable. Gunfire from this point considerably damaged Quebeck's lower town—almost, indeed, destroying it—and even the upper town was not safe from shells. Seeing that the east bank of the Montmorency was higher than the ground where the French were array'd, Wolfe cross'd thither and camp'd; the farmhouse inhabited by him being still in existence and in good condition. He also sail'd up the river beyond Quebeck, looking for landing-places and wondering how the precipitous cliff might be scaled. Once on the plateau containing the upper town, his army wou'd be assur'd of success. On the last day of July a landing was made just west of the Montmorency, in front of the French lines, but the impetuosity of the advance detachments brought on a disorder leading to a repulse. Attempts were made, thro' Genl Murray, to communicate with Amherst; but no success attended this step. The fall of Niagara and the abandonment of Ticonderoga and Crown Point were learn'd of, but Amherst made no real attempt to conquer the 3000 French at Isle-aux-Noix and proceed against Quebeck. As when Phips had vainly expected help by land, Wolfe was forc'd to act single handed. At this stage his health, undermin'd by fever, gravel, and rheumatism, was also a vast obstacle to the enterprise.

Thus for weeks the siege remain'd at a virtual deadlock—proud Quebeck being ever visible on its heav'n-scaling height; so near and yet so far; a perpetual goal, symbol, and tantalisation. Seen in the morning light with its frowning batteries and bastions, its red roofs and glistening silver steeples, and its great citadel on the Cape Diamond promontory towering above all the rest, it form'd a spectacle of almost supernatural loveliness and impressiveness—as indeed it has done at all stages of its history. The great stone fortress, convents, and churches presented much the same aspect as in Phips's time; though there were many more houses, and a somewhat greater sprinkling of spires. At some time in August, whilst Wolfe lay ill in the white-walled, curving-eaved farmhouse at Montmorency, Gens. Monckton, Townshend, and Murray held a council at which was adopted the plan of campaign that actually succeeded. The idea was to divide the army; leaving a part where it was to hold the enemy's attention by false attacks, whilst another force quietly ascended the river by night, climb perilously up the cliff behind the city, and draw Montcalm into a fight on the plateau.

Early in September this design was put into execution, Adm^l Holmes passing up the river with ships and transports whilst a force of 5000 march'd in the same direction along the southern or Lévis shore. Montcalm, half-suspecting the plan, dispatch'd Bougainville to watch their movements and guard the northern shoar. On the night of the 12th, which was clear, calm, and moonless, 30 boats with 1600 men put out from the southern shoar some two hours before dawn; drifting across the river on the ebb tide (for the St. L. at this point is really an arm of the sea rather than a river) without the noise of rowing. Genl. Wolfe, having improv'd somewhat in health, commanded in person; and during the passage discuss'd with other officers the celebrated Elegy by Mr. Gray, which he had lately seen for the first time. Having recited the lines—including that which ran, with such melancholy prophecy, "The paths of glory lead but to the grave"[19]—the general observ'd, that he wou'd rather have written that poem than take Quebeck on the morrow. Approaching the northern shoar, the boats were hail'd by a French sentry; but a captain of Fraser's Highlanders, knowing French like a native, was able to answer without arousing his suspicion. A landing was safely made some distance above the city—the place being now known as Wolfe's Cove—at a point where a steep narrow path or defile led up the face of the vast precipice. Wolfe was at first sceptical about the possibility of ascent; but it was indeed found feasable, and attempted at once. A small guard at the top was quickly overcome; and before dawn all the boats had landed; their occupants swarming up the cliff and forming in battle array on the plateau above. Montcalm, of course, soon heard of the move; and hasten'd across the St. Charles to the Quebeck shoar. His troops were greatly reduc'd through dispersal, disaffection, and famine, but he resolv'd to do the best he cou'd with 7500 men—5 battalions from France plus some arm'd local habitants. It was, of course, a vast disappointment to him that he had not been able to hold our troops off until winter; when the cold wou'd have hamper'd an attack. Climbing to the upper-town level, Montcalm led his men west of the city walls to the region now built over and known as the St. Louis suburb, but then open pasture land, and known as the "Plains of Abraham" from its having been once own'd by the famous early river pilot, the Scotsman Abraham Martin. Meanwhile Wolfe's troops—season'd Englishmen, kilted Highlanders, and hardy provincials—had march'd across the open region now occupy'd by Battlefield Park and drawn up on a line approximately the present Rue de Salaberry. Ignoring the desultory fire from French sharpshooters station'd in the surrounding woods and cornfields, Wolfe waited for the close advance of Montcalm's main divisions. Not till the enemy was within 40 yards was the command to fire issued. Then indeed the British musketry blaz'd forth in a single titanick fusilade, wreaking almost indescribable havock amongst the paralysed French ranks. At the second British volley the enemy shrank back with unmistakable fear, yet still continued for a few moments to return the fire. Then, amidst a wild and triumphant cheering, our men began to advance and press the French back—sweeping all before them and finally bursting into a Berserk run and orgy of slaughter. The Highlanders hack'd through whole rows of Frenchmen, pursuing the killing till the very walls of the city (the present line of walls, now far within the settled urban area) were reach'd. "Never," says Parkman, "was a victory more quick or more decisive."[20] The enemy had lost 1500 men, kill'd wounded, and captur'd; the residue either escaping within the walls or fleeing across the St. Charles to the main encampment. At last our own lines re-form'd themselves on the plain; a rear attack by Bougainville having been abandon'd when the strength and preparedness of our force was perceiv'd by him. God Save the King! Yet in this glorious victory we had lost the greatest armament of our army, and the man who made the victory itself a reality; for in the midst of the charge the immortal WOLFE receiv'd his fatal wounds. Hit first in the wrist, later in the side, and finally in the chest, the commander fell at the head of his grenadiers and was borne to the rear by four soldiers. He knew he could not survive, and refus'd the services of a chirurgeon. Those around him, sadden'd tho' they were, cou'd not help observing with pride and satisfaction the victory that was occurring. "See how they run!" cry'd an officer; whereat Gen¹ Wolfe, opening eyes already closed by approaching death, ask'd "Who run?" "The enemy, Sir," he was told, "they give way everywhere." Dying tho' he was, Wolfe was still the general. "Then," he said, "tell Col. Burton to march Webb's regiment down to Charles River to cut off their retreat from the bridge. Now, God be praised, I will die in peace." These were his last words. A moment later, the illustrious JAMES WOLFE was no more.

In the same fight, and almost at the same instant, there likewise fell the eminent leader of the enemy, Marquis de Montcalm. Mortally wounded, he was rushed to the ancient General Hospital (still standing) on the banks of the St. Charles, and later transferr'd to the residence of Dr. Arnoux, Jun. (still standing) at 59 St. Louis St. within the city. His last hours, protracted longer than Gen. Wolfe's few dying moments, were mark'd by equal evidences of nobility of mind. He express'd disgust at the poor support afforded him in his campaigns, and prais'd the valour of his adversaries. At one time he wrote a letter to our commander, urging clemency toward the French prisoners of war. When told that he had but a short time to live, he rejoic'd that he wou'd not behold the surrender of Quebeck. He outlin'd a plan for a concentration of troops and a fresh attack upon us, and urg'd the commander of the city garrison to remember the honour of France. At the very end he busy'd himself with the ceremonies of religion, dying peacefully at five the next morning. Thus perish'd Louis Joseph, Marquis de Montcalm de St. Véran, a commander and gentleman of the highest qualities and attainments, and not unworthy to be compar'd with his illustrious adversary. He was bury'd in the Ursuline Convent and his skull is to this day preserv'd there in a glass case. The joint death of these two leaders gave to the battle a particularly dramatick element which combines with its actual decisive importance to make it memorable. Intrinsically, it may be said to have decided the fate of this continent with respect to its linguistick and cultural control; destroying the French dream of empire and assuring the North-American world an Anglo-Saxon dominance. Editors include it in new editions of Creasy's "Fifteen Decisive Battles of the World."[21] It did not end the war, but it decided how the war wou'd end; for no one longer believ'd in the ability of the French to hold out. News of the victory, though temper'd by the sad tidings of Wolfe's death, was receiv'd with the wildest acclaim throughout America and England. In America the bell-ringings, illuminations, bonfires, sermons, political addresses, and so on, suggested the uproar of 1745 at the first taking of Louisburg. Septr. 13, 1759 was indeed an unforgotten day. Four days later, before siege batteries were constructed, the city of Quebeck formally surrender'd—M. de Ramezay, the commandant, having been advis'd to do so in a letter from Governor Vaudreuil, who was at Montreal. In the final council of decision, only one French officer advocated a longer resistance.

Of His Maj^{ty's} surviving commanders at Quebeck, Gen¹ Monckton had been severely wounded in the lungs, leaving only Murray and Townshend with a capacity for active service. Gen¹ Murray assum'd charge of the army, and settled down at Quebeck as a military governor. Relations betwixt the soldiery and the French population prov'd surprisingly peaceful and even friendly; many French women knitting leggins to cover the bare knees of Fraser's Highlanders, who were quarter'd in the old Ursuline Convent, and who suffer'd prodigiously from the bitter Quebeck winter. His Maj^{ty's} officers, employing as aids and agents the French-Canadian captains of militia, ably, justly, and generously administer'd the laws of the region; scrupulously respecting French manners and customs, and in truth giving the townspeople a far better government than they had ever known before. In the Ursuline Convent is still shewn a table on which our officers sign'd their first death-warrant as civil administrators—that of one Mme. Dodier, a murderess who had poison'd her husband. The Jesuits' College on the Upper Town Market Place was seiz'd and us'd as a barracks. Most of the officers dwelt at the citadel, high on the Cape Diamond promontory. Others inhabited the house of Dr. Arnoux, in Rue St. Louis, where Montcalm had dy'd; this being just downhill from the citadel on the inland side, and very convenient to it. It is still employ'd, together with its next-door neighbour, in connexion with the local military establishment. This next house is dubiously famous as the home of Mme. de Péan, mistress of the Intendant Bigot, whose plundering corruption help'd to bring about the downfall of New-France. Bigot organis'd a storehouse or trading company in connexion with certain henchmen, including Cadet, who held the contract to supply all the French posts in Canada with goods. Seizing grain without payment from the people, he sold it back to them at piratical prices; and likewise charg'd the government ten times too much for the supplies furnish'd by Cadet. Whether Marquis de Vaudreuil was in league with him, is not yet known; but Montcalm was utterly disgusted by the state of things, writing home— "What a country, where rogues grow rich and honest men are ruined!" The people commonly call'd Bigot's corporation, whose offices and storehouses were in Rue St. Paul, Lower Town, "La Friponne", or "The Cheat". Bigot had been conducting his operations for a long time, and had greatly antagonised the local merchants. One of the most celebrated legends of Old Quebeck concerns one Nicolas Jacques dit Philibert, whose mercantile house stood near the Place d'Armes, on the site of the present post-office. The building (as shewn by a lead marker attach'd to the corner stone) was put up by M. Philibert in 1735, and soon became a seat of much prosperity. Bigot's oppressive activities, however, in time caus'd the good merchant much harassment; hence, being deny'd legal or overt redress, M. Philibert put up a sign in which his feelings found veil'd expression. This was a quaintly carv'd and gilded dog gnawing a bone, accompany'd by the following rhym'd inscription:

"Je suis un chien qui ronge l'os,
 En le rongeant je prends mon repos,
 Un temps viendras qui n'est pas venu,
 Que je mordray qui m'aura mordu."

[I am a dog who gnaws a bone
 I crouch and gnaw it all alone;
 A time must come, which is not yet,
 When I'll bite him who me has bit!]

The idea of such a sign was not new, another example having been found in the south of France. M. Philibert at times try'd to circumvent the frauds of Bigot, but that official retaliated by quartering troops upon him at the Chien d'Or, as the establishment became known from its sign. At length matters burst into open warfare, and after a violent quarrel or duel M. Philibert was kill'd by one of Bigot's henchmen or companions, M. de la Repentigny. Repentigny fled to Acadia, but return'd after a pardon from the French King. When Quebeck fell to His Maj[ty's] troops in 1759, the Bigot clique was forc'd to take flight, and M. de la Repentigny went to Pondicherry, in India. Here, according to legend, he met the son of his old victim, and was kill'd by him in a duel. The Chien d'Or has been made the subject of a well-known historical romance by Kirby.[22] After our seizure of Quebeck, the building was us'd as an inn by one Miles Prentice, a sergeant in Wolfe's 78th regiment, under the name of the Masonick Hall. The sign of the Golden Dog is still preserv'd in the facade of the Post Office now occupying the site. Bigot, who of course dwelt in the Intendant's palace at the foot of Palace Hill, had a sumptuous and imposing country-seat in the foothills of the Laurentians near the village of Charlesbourg—a village which, during our siege of Quebeck, form'd a refuge for many of the women and children of the city. This country-seat, call'd *Beaumanoir* or The Hermitage, was a place of feudal magnitude and solidity, and had many intricate secret passages. Here were held orgies and revels of the most extravagant description, usually in connexion with the hunting-parties of which Bigot was exceedingly fond. Many dark tales are told of what occur'd there, and today the vine-grown ruins of the chateau are view'd with melancholy and aversion.

Quebeck itself, as compar'd with its aspect when Phips saw it from afar in 1690, had grown considerably; tho' its population was less than 9000. There were more silver spires and red roofs, and to the small steep-roof'd houses had been added many of a maturer sort. There were also some fine artillery barracks* built in 1750 on the west side of the Rue du Palais at Palace Gate and towering just above the high city wall opposite the Intendant's palace. French architectural modes, of course, were universal; and the newer houses presented many features—such as curv'd eaves and certain outlines of gable-ends—like those of the early houses of Charleston, in South-Carolina, which had been built under Huguenot influence. A little later—perhaps in the early nineteenth century—we shall see the development of certain features probably more purely Canadian—among these being a kind of gambrel roof with steep, curv'd lower pitch, (tho' unlike the Dutch) flattened dormers, and heavily projecting cornices. Windows, upon abandoning the mediaeval diamond pane, do not seem to have assum'd very often the English form with many square panes. Instead, they follow'd a French model in which the casements have a heavy vertical dividing bar cross'd by two lighter horizontal muntins. Over these windows were frequently blinds or shutters horizontally divided like a Dutch door as well as vertically divided; only the lower parts being thrown open. Statues in niches in front of buildings, usually the signs of shops or taverns, were not uncommon. One of Neptune—the sign of the Neptune Inn at the foot of Mountain Hill—is still in existence. Another of Jupiter—on a tavern in Rue St. Jean in the upper town when that thoroughfare was a fashionable promenade—is now vanish'd. In old times this tavern was far from the built-up section, and form'd the traditional boundary for the unsupervis'd strolls of children—who were told by their mothers 'not to go beyond the Great Jupiter'. In later years (1774) a wooden statue of Gen[l] Wolfe was sett up in front of the tavern at St. Jean and Palace Sts., where a duplicate of it (the original having been carry'd off by sportive man-of-war's-men and plac'd in the Que. Lit. and Hist. Soc. library upon its restoration to the city) is still to be found. Several fine mansions existed in the upper town, such as the de Léry manor house (now destroy'd) built in 1726 on an easterly part of the cliff, near the Seminary, known as St. Famille hill. The most fashionable places of residence—all in the upper town, of course—were Rue St. Louis, which stretch'd westward to its gate from the old Château and Fort, and the ramparts, at the edge of the cliff on St. Famille hill. Montcalm's residence, whilst in Quebec, was in a house on the Ramparts near the corner of Rue Hamel opposite Hope Gate. The fort, Château St. Louis, Churches, Hospitals, Schools, and Convents—most then already venerable—still dominated the scene; and of course priests, monks, and nuns form'd a vast and influential share of the population, as indeed they do today. Wealth and fashion were not absent, and well-curl'd periwigs under three-corner'd hats throng'd the narrow streets, which likewise glow'd with the scarlet uniforms of His Maj[ty's] soldiers. The principal mode of conveyance was the *calèche*, of which many still remain for the delight of tourists—a one-horse, two-

---

*Now us'd as Dominion Arsenal, and presenting a highly impressive aspect from outside the walls.

wheel'd vehicle well adapted to the steep and tortuous topography of the town. The social life was brilliant, mellow, and cultivated; aesthetick and traditional rather than intellectual, because of the mediaeval dominance of the clergy. In short, Quebeck was in 1759 a very quaint, stately and beautiful provincial French garrison town; with the added colour imparted by occasional Indians, trappers, traders, coureurs de bois, sailors, soldiers of assorted kinds, and prisoners from the English and Dutch areas of North-America. The cannonade of the siege had naturally caus'd vast damage to houses and publick buildings alike—virtually destroying the lower town on the sides expos'd to the river. In that area, the only building of importance sav'd was the old church of Notre Dame des Victoires—whose injuries were capable of repair, and which stands to this day as a monument to antient days. In the upper town, the Jesuit Church and Seminary were almost wholly wreck'd, whilst the great Basilica was burnt so badly as to require extensive rebuilding—tho' the walls, pillars, arches, and belfry remain'd firm. As we have seen, two of the vast ecclesiastical institutions were us'd for military purposes—the Jesuit College for barracks and the Ursuline Convent for Fraser's Highlanders—whilst many soldiers of both sides were bury'd in the graveyard of the old General Hospital by the St. Charles. The artillery barracks at Palace Gate were us'd for their original purpose, whilst at King's Wharf, in the lee of Cape Diamond, His Maj$^{ty's}$ Custom-House was establish'd near where King Louis XVth had open'd a naval ship-yard in 1746. The uneven and still uninhabited Cove Fields, on the plateau just west of the Citadel, remain'd much as before; their highest point, Buttes à Neveu, (now Perrault's Hill) serving as in French times as a place of publick execution. The Citadel and city walls were put in good repair and subjected to occasional improvements and reconstructions which have since given them an altogether new cast. It is pleasing to observe how well our troops and government got on with the French; a warmer cordiality springing up at once, and increasing as the mildness and fairness of Genl. Murray became more and more manifest. Some 450 Englishmen of low grade flock'd into Quebeck in the wake of the army, and made some highly arrogant demands; but Genl. Murray whenever possible favour'd the native inhabitants. His opinion of the Canadian French was very high, and he wrote of them as "perhaps the bravest of the best race upon the Globe, a race, who cou'd they be indulged with a few privileges which the Laws of England deny to Roman Catholicks at home, wou'd soon get the better of every National Antipathy to their Conquerors and become the most faithful and useful set of men in this American Empire." Another reason for cordiality was the wretchedness of the French administration which our conquest displac'd. Even the most ancestrally patriotick Canadians cou'd not help seeing and blessing the vast improvement in social and political conditions brought about by the rule of His Britannick Majesty. In the ensuing years friction and rivalry of a sort have sometimes occur'd, yet at no time is it likely that any thoughtful Frenchman in Canada wou'd have willingly consider'd a return to the colonial Empire of France. The eminent Parkman has truly written: "A happier calamity never befel a people than the conquest of Canada by British arms."[23] *God Save the King!!*

However, as we have said, the fall of Quebeck did not wholly end the Old French War. Our southern colonies were at this time greatly harass'd by a war with the Cherokees, independent of the main conflict; but in the north the campaigns of former years were brought to a conclusion. In the Quebeck region, Chevalier de Lévis, Montcalm's successor, open'd the season of 1760 by leading an army from Montreal to retake the antient capital. On April 28 Murray march'd out of the city toward him, meeting the French troops west of the city at Sillery Wood, where the village of Ste.

Foy was springing up. The result of this battle was a defeat for our troops, and Murray was forc'd to retire within the walls. Lévis now lay'd siege to Quebeck, but our garrison prepar'd for a dogged resistance. Meanwhile at home Wm. Pitt was prompt in sending naval aid; so that on May 15 a British squadron reach'd the beleaguer'd town and destroy'd all the French ships lying off it. On the 17th the enemy rais'd the siege, marching away and abandoning 40 cannon. God Save the King! The French, proud of the courage of Lévis, have since apply'd his name to the region across the river from Quebeck, which formerly bore the very similar designation of Point-Levi. They have likewise rais'd a monument to Lévis and his men (tho' of course including Murray's forces also) on the site of Genl. Murray's repulse—about a mile from Quebeck on the Ste. Foy road, near the intersection of the present Belvedere Rd. or Ave. des Braves. That they have been permitted to do so, is a good evidence of the enlighten'd liberality of His Majesty's rule.

Meanwhile Genl Amherst, now commander-in-chief, was rous'd at last to the need of taking *Montreal*, last remaining stronghold of the enemy, and now the seat of the French Governor-general Vaudreuil. Sending Genl. Haviland by way of Ticonderoga and Crown Point, he himself went with 10,000 men to Oswego, thence sailing down Lake Ontario and the St. Lawrence. Murray, order'd from Quebeck, met Amherst Sept. 6 directly before Montreal, and the next day Haviland arriv'd from Crown Point. Resistance being obviously useless, Vaudreuil capitulated without a siege; on Sept. 8 delivering up to His Britannick Maj$^{ty's}$ authority the whole of Canada, including the French posts at Detroit and Michillimackinac. Five days later Genl. Rogers, with 200 American rangers, started thro' the wilderness to take over the western posts for His Majesty. In this expedition—the first occasion upon which any great number of Englishmen had sail'd on Lake Erie—the Rogers party encounter'd the arrogant imperiousness of the Ottawa chieftain *Pontiack;* who refus'd to acknowledge any authority over the region save that of the Indians, and suffer'd them to pass only as a reigning sovereign might extend hospitality to strangers. In the ensuing years this same Pontiack was to lead that great and historick conspiracy, a worthy successor to the designs of old King Philip in New-England, which form'd the last generall uprising of the red men against the whites upon this continent.

Thus was extinguish'd the power of France upon the continent of America. In 1763 the Treaty of Paris defin'd the permanent allocation of territories; an allocation complicated by the fact that we had also been at war with Spain and had taken Havana in 1762. In the final generall peace France ceded to us all of her Louisiana territory east of the Mississippi, having secretly ceded the area west of the Mississippi to Spain. Spain, in exchange for the return of Havana, turn'd over Florida to His Maj$^{ty's}$ Government. Thus the continent was left wholly in English and Spanish hands, tho' France retain'd her rich West-India possessions, plus two tiny islands—St. Pierre and Miquelon—off Newfoundland as a base for her Grand Banks fisheries. These isles today represent all that is left of France's North-American realm.

(E) Canada Under His Brittanick Majesty's Government

Upon the establishment of peace in 1763, His Maj^{ty} George the Third, who had in 1760 succeeded to the throne, proclaim'd a provisional civil government for Canada, to remain in effect till the enactment of more permanent legislative measures. As first civil governor, there was kept in office that valiant, able and upright Scotsman, Genl. James Murray, who had so well serv'd as Military Governor since 1759. Murray was, as we have seen, a vast admirer of the French-Canadians; and not at all dispos'd to cater to the somewhat low-grade English population which had filter'd into the region in the wake of the army. These latter he call'd "four hundred and fifty contemptible sutlers and traders". In 1766, through the influence of this trading class (which had powerful connexions in London) Gen. Murray was recall'd, and Col. Guy Carleton, another of Wolfe's officers in the old days, appointed in his stead. Carleton, later knighted and rais'd to the peerage as Ld Dorchester, was probably the greatest figure in the early history of British Canada. To the French he was as favourable as Murray, and his honesty was such that he refus'd to accept any of the fees and perquisites attach'd to his office. It was at that time thought by some that the region wou'd soon become Anglicis'd; but Carleton, looking deeply into the problem, recognis'd the tenacity of the Gallick culture, and wrote what has turn'd out to be true so far as the area now forming the province of Quebeck is concern'd; namely—"This country must, to the end of time, be peopled by the Canadian race, who have already taken such firm root . . . that any new stock transplanted will be totally hid, and imperceptible amongst them, except in the towns of Quebeck and Montreal." Carleton's policy was to hasten the extension of all possible privileges to this conquer'd stock which he deem'd the normal population. In 1766, upon his accession to the governorship, he permitted them to sit on juries, and made the French language legal in the courts. In 1767 he confirm'd the old land laws of New-France. In 1774 there was pass'd by His Maj$^{ty's}$ parliament the Quebeck-Act, superseding the proclamation of 1763, erecting New-France into the "Province of Quebeck", and providing a permanent government which lasted till 1791.* This act was wholly in favour of the French; and provided for the retention of the old French civil law though the milder criminal code of England was establisht with full local consent and approval. The region was to be administer'd by a Royal Governor and appointed Council; there being no representative assembly because Catholicks could not by English law sit on a legislative body. Had a legislature been establisht, only the handful of "Old Subjects" (as the English Canadians were call'd) cou'd have sat upon it; a condition manifestly unfair to the French or "New Subjects". As much as possible was conceded to the Popish church, which had so obvious a hold over the New Subjects. The Romish Bishop of Quebeck was informally recognis'd, and even the payment of church tithes by papists was enforc'd by law—the law of Protestant England! The result of the Quebeck Act was to ensure the French culture a perpetual survival in the St. Lawrence Valley; and likewise to conciliate the French so greatly that they have ever since stood faithfully by the British Empire despite the greatest temptations to desert. Indeed, the immediate result of the act was to antagonise the Old Subjects; who had expected to enjoy British institutions in Canada, yet found themselves under conditions surviving from the ancient French regime. The general life both of the countryside and of the towns remain'd essentially French—Quebeck perhaps more thoroughly than Montreal. All the houses erected were of the French sort, so that even today there are very few structures of really English architecture in the whole region.

There now broke out—in 1775—that unhappy warfare betwixt His Maj$^{ty's}$ thirteen more southerly colonies and the home government; which culminated in the loss of those colonies to the Empire, and which may in times to come bring about their tragicall ingulphment in a new and alien barbarism of mongrel and autochthonous origin, in which all the standards of civilisation will be lost in a brainless worship of size, speed, wealth, success, and luxury, sad chapter to record! The rebels of 1775 were not insensi-

---

*In the western part of the new Province, which included the long disputed Ohio Valley, there was a serious conflict of title with his Maj$^{ty's}$ Dominion of Virginia.

ble of the advantage they wou'd gain by stirring up a like sedition in Canada; and rely'd upon the racial differences of the French, plus the discontent of the new British population at the preservation of French laws, to turn both elements against their rightful government. They hop'd to joyn Canada in their confederation, thereby weakening the strength of His Maj$^{ty's}$ forces on this continent, and removing the peril of a northerly attack upon themselves. Much correspondence was exchang'd betwixt men of the rebel faction and certain sympathisers in Canada, and it was generally thought that a successful rebel expedition into the country wou'd bring most of the population to the rebel standards. Severall plans having been propos'd and rejected, it was finally decided by the rebels to send two expeditions into Canada to meet before Quebeck; one along Lake Champlain, where both Ticonderoga and Crown Point had fallen into their hands, and the other through the district of Maine, up the Kennebec River and across the wilderness to the neighbouring head-waters of the Chaudière, which flows north into the St. Lawrence near Quebeck. For the first expedition, the celebrated Genl Schuyler was chosen leader; but owing to his illness the command devolv'd upon Genl. Richd Montgomery, an Irish gentleman who had come with His Maj$^{ty's}$ army for service in the Old French War, but who, disappointed of promotion, had resign'd, settled down in the Province of New-York at Rhinebeck, on the Hudson, and marry'd a daughter of the celebrated house of Livingston. Genl. Montgomery, now 39 years of age, was a person of the highest character, apart from his rebel sentiments, and of extreamly great ability. To command the Kennebeck-Chaudière expedition there was selected that bold, fiery, and unstable Connecticut apothecary and West-India horse-dealer, Col. Benedict Arnold, whose later treachery toward the rebel cause hath gain'd him the disesteem of both sides. Col. Arnold, a man of some pompousness, yet of vast ability and inflexible determination, was then 35 years of age. At Quebeck, Govr Carleton was given the generall command over all His Maj$^{ty's}$ forces in America; taking the field, and leaving the civill administration in the hands of the Lieutenant-Govr Cramabé. One of his aides-de-camp was the eldest son of the great William Pitt, Ld Chatham; but he soon resign'd from a reluctance to fight against those colonies whose earlier and reasonable demands his father had favour'd. The most southerly post of our loyal forces along the Champlain route contemplated by Schuyler and Montgomery was St. John's, on the Richelieu River betwixt the lake and the St. Lawrence. This Genl Carleton wish'd to defend, and for that purpose assembled near 900 men at Montreal. The attempt, however, was futile; and on Novr 3d the rebels took the fort. Nine days later Montgomery occupy'd Montreal without opposition, and Govr Carleton was oblig'd to resort to a peasant's disguise in order to get down the river and reënter Quebeck. The expedition of Arnold, starting from the rebel hdqrs. at Cambridge and comprising 10 companies of New-England infantry, 2 Pennsylvania companies, and a company of Virginia riflemen under the celebrated Danl Morgan, included such figures as Lt: Colo: Christopher Greene of Rhode-Island, and the young Aaron Burr, later destin'd to such vivid and vary'd fortunes. It sail'd from Newburyport, in Massachusetts-Bay, on the 19th of September, and the next day enter'd the Kennebeck River in Maine. Securing small boats, the party proceeded up the river through a picturesque wilderness; on Octr. 10th carrying their bateaux amidst great hardships to the Dead River, which they follow'd for 83 miles with frequent portages. At this period letters were sent ahead by messengers to the other rebel army and to private persons in Quebeck; which, falling into the hands of His Maj$^{ty's}$ authorities thro' Indian duplicity, inform'd us what to expect in the way of invasion. Also at this stage one Lt. Col. Roger Enos led back to Massachusetts, without permission, the three companies under him; for which he was later court-martiall'd but acquitted. Autumn was now advancing, and snow began to beset the sub-arctick wilderness. Shoes and clothing suffer'd, and hunger became so great that the party began to eat the dogs that attended them. After a terrifick struggle over the carrying-place from the Dead River, the party finally reach'd Lake Megantick, from which the Chaudière flows. Crossing the lake and entering the river, they were much troubled by falls and rapids; but finally reach'd the French village of Sertigan. Here they were well receiv'd by the simple peasantry, amongst whom they distributed proclamations printed in French, presenting the rebel arguments in highly persuasive form. Following the river onward thro' the French countryside with its curving-eav'd, whitewashed houses, curious village steeples, and quaint popish wayside shrines, Arnold at length reach'd the great St. Lawrence and proceeded on the night of Novr 13th to ferry his men across to Wolfe's Cove from Point Lévis. Meanwhile His Maj[ty's] forces in Quebeck were making ready for the invader; Lt. Govr Cramabé putting the walls in good condition by means of 100 carpenters fetch'd from Newfoundland. On Nov. 12, the town was reinforced by 170 Scottish Highlanders—disbanded veterans who had settled in Canada and who were now collected by Colo: Allan MacLean. All the merchant seamen in port were muster'd for the town's defence, and there lay in the harbour two of His Maj[ty's] ships-of-war, the Lizard and the Hunter. At most, the garrison finally number'd some 1800 men. Arnold succeeded in ferrying across some 500 of his 650 remaining men, the residue being perforce left behind because of discovery at dawn. The old route of Wolfe up the Heights of Abraham was follow'd without disaster; and having reach'd the plateau, the troops march'd to within 800 yards of the city walls. Here, with vast bombast and pompousness, Arnold sent a threatening demand for surrender to the Lt. Gov[r]; meanwhile hoping that a large number of the inhabitants of Quebeck, especially the French natives, wou'd desert to his side. Naturally this boastful message from a scanty force was receiv'd with disdain; tho' the ignorant populace felt some terror at the appearance of these warlike strangers (especially Morgan's queerly shirted Virginians) from the unknown wilderness. Arnold, now perceiving the weakness of his force and the adequate defences of the town, withdrew to Point aux Trembles, 20 miles up the river, to await aid from Montgomery, whose capture of Montreal had become known. At this point Govr. Carleton reach'd Quebeck by stealth, the fact early becoming known to Arnold. Realising that one of the leading reasons for Quebeck's fall in 1759 was the fact that Montcalm had fought outside the walls, Carleton adopted an opposite course and resolv'd to let the enemy wear themselves out against closed gates till a very late and opportune moment. News of Montgomery's success at Montreal, and of his probable juncture with Arnold before Quebeck, at one period induc'd a disaffected element within the walls to advocate a surrender; to which the wise and upright Carleton responded by ordering all who would not defend the town to leave it in four days. When all such persons had withdrawn, there were left in Quebeck some 300 regular British troops, 330 English Canadian soldiers, 543 French-Canadians, 485 sailors and marines, and 125 able-body'd workmen capable of military service. On Novr. 26 Montgomery set out from Montreal with 300 men, provisions, and artillery—which latter Arnold had totally lack'd. Arnold had by this time muster'd a few more men, and on Dec. 3[d] Montgomery reach'd him; giving the half-frozen soldiers a supply of more suitable clothing. The combined rebel forces now number'd something under a thousand men, to whom were added a body of 200 French-Canadian volunteers. Advancing on Quebec, with Genl. Montgomery in command, the rebels braved the hellish cold of a northern winter and flounder'd as best they might thro' an increasing snowfall. Quebeck was reach'd on Decr. 5th, and the troops took up their quarters in the suburb of St. Roch, which lyes at the northern foot of the vast cliff, adjoining the lower town and stretching westward from Palace Gate. Arnold occupy'd a house there, whilst Montgomery dwelt on the St. Foye Rd. upon the plateau. Since the enlistments of the New-England men expir'd at the end of the year, it was necessary for the rebels to act quickly; to which end Genl. Montgomery sent Gov. Carleton various wild threats and demands for surrender—devices which not only fail'd of their object, but actually strengthen'd the morale of the defenders by making the struggle seem more equal, and the need for strong precautions correspondingly greater. There now follow'd a long period of deadlock'd waiting, during which the rebels conducted some occasional shelling from small mortars—a shelling which was wholly powerless to injure the garrison within the walls, but which did much damage to the buildings of St. Roch and the adjacent parts of the Quebeck lower town. It was amidst this shelling that the great Intendant's Palace just outside Palace Gate was demolish'd; only the vaults of the original Talon brewery of 1668 remaining. In later years a new brewery—the celebrated and still existent Boswell's—was rais'd over these vaults, and they are to this day us'd for their first purpose and shewn upon request to the curious. On Decr. 15th, after the construction of a battery on the plateau facing St. John's Gate in the upper town, Montgomery again sought to send demands to Govr Carleton, but was told that His Maj$^{ty's}$ representative wou'd hold no parley with rebels. It now became apparent to the besiegers, that they cou'd never take the town but by storm; and accordingly they revolv'd plans for a desperate attempt toward that end. Some disaffection amongst Col. Arnold's officers made evident the need of haste, and on Christmas Day Montgomery addrest the troops, held a council, and resolv'd upon a nocturnal assault against the lower town at the first good opportunity—when it might be dark and cloudy, and not too cold for action. This information being carry'd within the walls by a deserter, the garrison adopted tactics of constant vigilance; even Gov. Carleton sleeping in his clothes in order to be ready for defence at any moment. The chosen night—dark and cloudy, with snow and hail—was the last of the year 1775. According to Genl Montgomery's plan, the garrison's attention was to be diverted by two feign'd attacks on the plateau level—one upon St. John's Gate, and the other up Cape-Diamond, where the citadel stands high over the riverward cliffs. The real attacks, to be launched at a rocket signal from the feinting party on the high Cape Diamond terrain, were to be upon the lower town; Montgomery leading a detachment down the cliff to the narrow shore of the St. Lawrence and approaching from under Cape Diamond, whilst Arnold operated from St. Roch, skirting the cliff east of Palace Gate, and marching through the lower-town streets as far as Mountain Hill. At the latter place—the principal approach to the upper town, guarded near the top by Prescott Gate—the two detachments hoped to meet; storming Prescott Gate and perhaps forcing a way through. Montgomery, leading somewhat under 300 "Yorkers" including the young Aaron Burr and the two able aides-de-camp Majors Cheeseman and Macpherson, descended by Wolfe's route to the shore; and thereafter scrambled along the narrow and perilous margin betwixt the towering cliff and the icy river—all the while harass'd by the bitter cold, northeast wind, driving hail, and icily insecure footing. The premature sending of the rocket signal occasion'd some separation and confusion, and at times barriers were encounter'd, which carpenters had to saw and tear away. At last, having reach'd the defile marking the location of Champlain St., below Cape-Diamond, the advance party with Montgomery, Burr, Cheeseman, and Macpherson encounter'd a log blockhouse set directly in the road, from which no sign of animation proceeded. In this structure were some 50 men of the defending force under a transport-captain nam'd Barusfare, and a marine officer nam'd Coffin. The cannon were mann'd by expert seamen, and the gunners were on the alert to discharge their pieces as soon as order'd. Montgomery, when about 60 of his force had caught up with him, cry'd out—"Men of New-York, you will not fear to follow where your general leads; push on, brave boys! Quebeck is ours!" Pressing instantly forward, he was answer'd by a volley of grapeshot from the defenders—which at once wrought the gravest havock amongst the rebels. Montgomery, Cheeseman, and Macpherson, with ten others, fell dead at the first fusilade; though Aaron Burr escap'd without even a wound. The residue, under Donald Campbell, at once retreated to Wolfe's Cove; there resting without any attempt to discover how Col. Arnold's attack on the other side of the town had progress'd. Meanwhile Arnold, in the St. Roch suburb with twice the number of Montgomery's troops, found his path impeded by masses of ice thrown up by the River St. Charles. Finally reaching Palace Gate, the rebels heard the bells of the city ring out in concert with a generall alarum of drums, whilst a cannonade from the defenders began. Proceeding in single file, with lower'd head and guns protected from the storm by their coats, the attackers proceeded to round the cliff under the Ramparts to the eastern side; abandoning the field-piece which they had sought to take along. At the Sault au Matelot, in Rue Sault au Matelot at the foot of Dog Hill, the defenders had their first barricade or battery. Col. Arnold had just been severely wounded in the lower leg by sailors firing from behind the walls of the Hotel Dieu convent, so that he had to be convey'd back to the antient General Hospital on the banks of the St. Charles. (At that place he was much depress'd by learning of the death of Genl Montgomery.) The rebels, however, persisted in their attack; being commanded by the celebrated Virginia rifleman Danl Morgan. After an hour of terrifick battle they carry'd the Sault au Matelot defences and rush'd along the narrow Rue Sault au Matelot to the second barrier at the corner of Rue St. James, where Rue St. Pierre approaches so closely as to form a virtual junction. Here a very heroick attempt to take the defences was made by the intrepid Colo: Greene of RHODE-ISLAND; but all in vain, since His Maj$^{ty's}$ troops stood behind the barricade with fixt bayonets, whilst sharpshooters from the houses on both sides of the street kept up an unceasing and effective fire. The casualties on both sides were heavy; the rebel artillery leader Capt. Lamb having his jaw partly shot away, so that he had to be borne from the field, and the Pennsylvanian Hendricks, who had accompany'd Arnold thro' the wilderness, being shot dead in the act of aiming his rifle. Scaling ladders were apply'd to the barricade, but it soon became manifest that retreat was all that remain'd for the rebels. Some took shelter in stone houses whose defensive possibilities seem'd good, whilst others escap'd over the ice on the St. Charles River. The majority, however, were fated for capture; since Govr Carleton, reliev'd of the need of reckoning with Montgomery, was now giving full attention to the Arnold party. Suddenly sending a force of 200 from Palace Gate, he overwhelm'd the rebel force under Capt. Dearborn that was left to guard Arnold's rear from surprises; thus completely trapping the main force of attackers within the narrow, tortuous streets of the lower town. Morgan of Virginia proposed a desperate fight for egress; but soberer counsels prevail'd, so that at 10 o'clock on the 1st of January, 1776, a rebel force of some 450 surrender'd to the arm'd might of His Britannick Majesty. Thus ended the last attempt ever made to take the great citadel of the North by storm. God Save the King! In the night's battle the rebels had lost 160, kill'd and wounded, whilst the losses of the defenders did not exceed 20. Govr Carleton exercised toward the prisoners a magnanimity and consideration distinguish'd in the annals of warfare; sending an officer on parade to the rebel camp to get clothing and supplies needed by them, and quartering them in the antient Quebeck Seminary. The shoar beneath Cape-Diamond was search'd for the rebel dead, 13 bodies being found, including those of Montgomery, Cheeseman, and

Macpherson. Montgomery's body was taken to the house of a cooper nam'd Gaubert in Rue St. Louis near the corner of St. Ursule, (lately demolish'd) and 3 days later was bury'd with honour, together with the bodies of Cheeseman and Macpherson, in the yard of the old Military Prison—now a military storehouse—of Citadel Hill next the corner of Rue St. Louis. The site is today markt by a small boulder. Lt. Govr Cramabé, for the sake of security, permitted the burial to be made within a wall enclosing a powder-magazine. Shortly afterward word was relay'd to Govr Carleton by the rebel Arnold that Montgomery's widow wish'd the watch the slain leader had worn; and tho' Arnold offer'd almost any sum for the relique, Carleton promptly sent it with a refusal to receive anything in return. Forty-two years later, in June, 1818, His Maj$^{ty's}$ Government yielded up the body to Montgomery's still-surviving widow; so that it was transferr'd to New-York and interr'd with military honours from the rebel Federal government in the churchyard of antient St. Paul's, in Broadway at the corner of Vesey-Street, where it rests to this day. Generations later the bodies of Cheeseman and Macpherson were exhum'd during excavations in the yard of the old military storehouse, and preserv'd for exhibition in a glass coffin by one Patrick Lewis, one of the workmen at the storehouse. Mr. Lewis later—in 1894—identify'd the burial-place of the other rebels slain with Montgomery; these being reinterr'd near the same spot, and their grave mark'd by a suitable tablet. The scenes of both battles are markt by tablets, one being on the cliff over Près-de-Ville (as the site of Montgomery's fall, near the antient Neuville, is now call'd) and the other in the lower town at the corner of Rues St. Pierre and St. James. These tablets read, respectively,

HERE STOOD	HERE STOOD
THE UNDAUNTED FIFTY	HER OLD AND NEW DEFENDERS
SAFEGUARDING	UNITING GUARDING SAVING
CANADA	CANADA
DEFEATING MONTGOMERY	DEFEATING ARNOLD
AT THE PRES-DE-VILLE BARRICADE	AT THE SAULT-AU-MATELOT BARRICADE
ON THE LAST DAY OF	ON THE LAST DAY OF
1775	1775
GUY CARLETON	GUY CARLETON
COMMANDING AT	COMMANDING AT
QUEBEC	QUEBEC

In the first tablet the word "undaunted" refers to the threats of dire vengeance in case of non-surrender flung into the city by Arnold and Montgomery before the battle. In the second, the term "old and new defenders" refers to the fact that the old French stood side by side with the Englishmen, Irishmen, Scotsmen, Welshmen, Channel Islanders, and Newfoundlanders in the defence of the town. God Save the King! In ensuing years the narrow shore under the cliff at Près-de-Ville and beyond toward Wolfe's Cove became considerably develop'd as a waterfront; wharves and houses being erected, and the thoroughfare being consider'd an extension of Rue Champlain. It was tenanted by an Irish population, and became the seat of the Quebeck Hibernian Club. Far out toward Wolfe's Cove a French marine village sprang up at Cap Blanc, and here was erected the maritime chapel (still us'd) of Notre-Dame de la Garde. In later years the region fell to the condition of a slum; and in 1889, at a spot betwixt the old King's Wharf (end of the antient Lower Town) and the site of Montgomery's death, a terrifick landslide on the cliff occurr'd; wrecking all the houses beneath it and killing many of the slum denizens. No houses have since been built at this point, and the face of the cliff is here smoothly wall'd up with cemented stones. The effect of this is to make of the remaining Champlain St. slum a detach'd and somewhat sinister suburb. On walking around the cliff from the original lower town, one comes to a seemingly deserted region with only ruin'd wharves and foundation-walls; and fancies that the urban district here ends. Only perseverance will induce one to proceed farther and witness the resumption of the interrupted lines of slum houses. They are today in a fearsome state of decrepitude; many being wholly abandon'd, and vast gaps existing where edifices have collaps'd or suffer'd demolition. Near the old Hibernian Club an interminable flight of wooden steps leads one up to the ancient Cove Fields behind the Citadel, and across these fields a boardwalk leads to the inhabited region around the St. Louis road on the plateau.

The delicacy and consideration of His Majesty's officers after the capture of the rebels is illustrated by many anecdotes. One officer (he who years afterward identify'd Montgomery's body upon its exhumation) wore the sword of Montgomery in his belt, but remov'd it upon perceiving what melancholy it produc'd amongst the rebel prisoners. Montgomery himself was prais'd in parliament by many speakers, including Mr. Burke and the veteran Barré, who had serv'd with him in the Old French War. Ld North, however, went so far as to say, "Curse on his virtues—they've undone his country!"

After this crushing defeat, Arnold (recovering somewhat from his wound) assum'd command of the 800 rebels left near Quebeck; having been made a Brigadier-General by the rebel Congress for his gallantry in the futile attack. He now receiv'd reinforcements from New-England, who reach'd Quebeck on snowshoes, carrying their own provisions. Entrenching himself three miles from the city, he enforc'd as tight a blockade as he cou'd; tho' it was vain to hope that he might keep the St. Lawrence clos'd against ships from England in the spring. On the 1st of April old Genl Wooster of New Haven, Conn. came down from Montreal and superseded Arnold in the command; the force now standing at about 2500, tho' greatly ravag'd by smallpox. Wooster, conscientious but by no means capable, erected batteries on the Plains of Abraham and on the Lévis cliffs across the river, but the cannonading had no effect on the town. Arnold, falling from his horse, re-injur'd his wounded leg and was forc'd to retire to Montreal. Wooster, at his own request, was now superseded by Genl Thomas of Massachusetts; who, however, dy'd of small-pox a month later. Spring was not far advanc'd, and reinforcements were constantly reaching Quebeck from Nova-Scotia and England. Thomas had order'd a retreat on May 5th, and the retreating rebels were attack'd by two sallying parties from St. John's and St. Louis Gates, so that they fled in confusion to Deschambault, 48 miles above Quebeck. Those wounded were car'd for by Canadian peasants, and later welcom'd to Quebeck's antient general hospital, where the supremely magnanimous Carleton provided for their treatment and free release to return home upon their recovery. Pursu'd from Quebeck, the disorganis'd rebel army now retreated to Sorel, where the Richelieu River (from Lake Champlain) empties into the St. Lawrence. There Thomas died—and meanwhile the main body of British reinforcements under Gen. Burgoyne, including the Brunswick mercenaries under Baron Riedesel, had reach'd Quebeck. God Save the King! A further rebel retreat from Sorel was now check'd by the newly-arriv'd commander Genl Sullivan, who turn'd it into an advance toward Quebeck as far as Three Rivers. Here, however, some fresh troops from Europe (whose transports had by Carleton's orders proceeded on past Quebeck without a pause) defeated the rebels under Genl. Anthony Wayne and forc'd them to retreat again to Sorel. Meanwhile Genl. Arnold, commanding at Montreal, found the whole rebel hold on Canada steadily weakening. The French natives did not take

kindly to the Yankees and the civil institutions they set up, whilst the omnipotent popish clergy and the old nobility were unreservedly on the side of His Majesty's lawful
cause. In May mixt troops of English, Iroquois, and Canadians defeated the rebels at a
post on the St. Lawrence's north bank; and at last, after the final rebel retreat to Sorel,
it became manifest that the enemy must soon quit Canada. Arnold tarry'd at Montreal
as long as he cou'd, but finally—when the Sorel troops began a retreat along the
Richelieu toward Lake Champlain—he joyn'd them and assisted Genl. Sullivan in
managing matters. It being impossible to persuade the troops to make a stand at St.
John's, on the Richelieu, the commanders proceeded to the Isle aux Noix in Lake
Champlain; Arnold subsequently going to Albany for a council of generals, and Sullivan retreating still farther south to Crown Point and Ticonderoga, successively. Carleton, at Quebeck, now order'd a fleet to be built at St. John's for the purpose of
combating the rebels on Lake Champlain; this being met by a rebel fleet under Genl.
Arnold, who had commanded ships when in the West-India trade. In the ensuing engagement, which took place Octr. 11th, honours rested with His Maj$^{ty's}$ vessels; but
there was no serious attempt to dislodge the rebels from Ticonderoga. The mild winter
of 1776–77 was fill'd with plans for moving southward against the rebels; it being decided (tho' not without protests from those sensible of the asperities of salvage barbarism) to employ the Iroquois as allies. These tribes were greatly sway'd by the civilis'd
Mohawk chieftain Joseph Brant, whose sister had wed the celebrated Sir W: Johnson.
Sir William had dy'd (possibly by his own hand) in 1774, but his sons were powerful,
and his heir Sir John Johnson had succeeded to the paternal post of Superintendent of
Indian Affairs for the North. Govr Carleton wish'd to lead an army of ten thousand
into the southern colonies, and was in this wish upheld by Genl Burgoyne; but the
home government, upon the recommendation of Sir W^m and Adm^l Howe, defeated the
project. In May 1777 Burgoyne, after an absence, return'd to Quebeck; and at this time
Carleton was depriv'd of the conduct of any future campaign beyond the borders of
Canada. Burgoyne, taking charge of the propos'd expedition, had as assistants the capable Genl. Phillips, the noted Highlander Genl Fraser, and the German Baron Riedesel. The design, develop'd carefully in London by Ld George Germain and his advisers,
(including Ld Amherst) was to follow the old Lake Champlain route and effect a junction with Sir W: Howe, who held New-York; and besides the main advance there was
to be a smaller western force under Lt. Col. St. Leger, landing at Oswego and proceeding down the Mohawk Valley toward the Hudson for an eventual union with Burgoyne
near Albany. Genl. Burgoyne advanc'd from St. John's, on the Richelieu, on June 15th;
and the next day camp'd just north of Crown Point, where he addrest a council of his
Indian allies—comprising 400 Iroquois, Algonquins, and Ottawas. Early in July His
Maj$^{ty's}$ forces approach'd Ticonderoga, the nearest rebel post, and made preparations
for a siege. Unable to get reinforcements, the rebel commander St. Clair evacuated the
fortress and retir'd to Ft. Edward, where Genl Schuyler had command. Later Ft. Edward was likewise abandon'd by the rebels, who retreated south four miles to Moss
Creek, and there put up defences. Burgoyne took up his position at Ft. Ann, some distance below Lake Champlain. At this point he wish'd Govr Carleton to send more
troops from Canada to hold Ticonderoga, but the latter consider'd that his loss of authority outside the Province of Quebeck prevented him from so doing. The position of
Burgoyne was attended with much difficulty; and great local indignation was excited
by the barbarity of his Indian allies, who were led by the sanguinary and vindictive
Frenchman (arrested by the rebels when they held Montreal) La Carne St. Luc. The
chief incident occasioning this resentment was the savage murder and scalping of Miss

Jane McCrea, a young local gentlewoman betroth'd to an officer in His Maj[ty's] forces, on July 27th; this atrocious happening being ever afterward a leading tale in the folklore of the region. The present writer has a snuff-box made in 1853 from the wood of the great tree (which dy'd in 1849) under which Miss McCrea was slain. She herself lyes bury'd in a suitably mark'd grave near Ft. Edward. Only fear of defection amongst the Indians induc'd Gen[l] Burgoyne to pardon the assassin. On July 28th Burgoyne occupy'd Ft. Edward, whilst the rebels retir'd to Stillwater. Meanwhile St. Leger had started from Oswego, and on Aug. 3[d] reach'd the carrying-place where the lake-emptying waters approach the Hudson-emptying waters of the Mohawk. Here was situate Ft. Schuyler, formerly Ft. Stanwix, held by a rebel garrison of 700, to whose aid a reinforcing army under Gen[l] Herkimer was marching. St. Leger lay'd siege to the fort and defeated Herkimer's party 8 miles away, at Oriskany; but was frighten'd into a retreat later in the month, before the fort fell, by a small rebel party under the resourceful Benedict Arnold, who sent ahead a pretended deserter to delude the besiegers into thinking that he had 2000 men. In the main theatre of action Burgoyne, to increase his supplies, sent out a side expedition of 1000 to capture reported stores at Bennington, in the newly organis'd region of Vermont; but on August 16 this force was badly defeated by the rebels under Col. John Stark at the battle of Bennington. Amongst the rebels Schuyler was now superseded by Genl. Horatio Gates; and on Sept[r] 19th the two armies met in a major engagement at Bemis Heights, west of the Hudson; Genl. Arnold and the Virginian Dan[l] Morgan being the leading figures on the enemy's side. This conflict was indecisive; our forces losing about 500 whilst the rebels lost 300. On Oct[r] 7th there was fought in the same region the Battle of Saratoga, near Stillwater, south of Bemis Heights. This, too, had no instant result; but Genl. Fraser was slain, and so unfavourable to our forces did conditions appear, that Genl. Burgoyne began a retreat. Pursuit was instituted by the rebels, and it soon became manifest that no way out of the region was left—and likewise that no communication could be had with His Maj[ty's] forces in the town of New-York. Accordingly, on the 17th of October, at Saratoga, near an old fort of Baron Dieskau's, Genl. Burgoyne surrender'd to the rebels under honourable circumstances; yielding up 6000 men, who were march'd across country to Cambridge under an agreement to be return'd to England after pledges to serve no more against the American rebels. This agreement was dishonourably broken by the rebel congress, so that the prisoners were finally sent to Virginia. The defeat cost us a third of our total forces in America, and was probably the turning-point of the war. Creasy includes it in his Fifteen Decisive Battles of the World. The conquest of this northern region clos'd the direct share of Quebeck in the current hostilities. In 1778 Carleton (who in 1781 replac'd Clinton as head of the army in America, taking up headquarters in New-York) was superseded as Governor of Quebeck by Genl Sir Frederick Haldimand, who built a fine Georgian mansion (still in existence, with additions, as a publick hostelry) at the falls of the Montmorency River, and in 1784 built a mansion over the old military defences beside the Château St. Louis, which he call'd Château Haldimand. This was demolish'd in 1892 to make way for the massive Château Frontenac hotel. The military status of the old fortress-capital was unchang'd, and it knew the presence of many a celebrated figure of army and navy. Here, at the Masonick Hall Inn conducted by Miles Prentice in the old building that had housed M. Philibert's Chien d'Or, young Capt. Nelson (afterward Admiral L[d] Nelson of immortal fame) paid court to Prentice's niece in 1782, and was prevented from wedding her only by being forcibly carry'd aboard his vessel. Here also—at the same famous inn—the young naval Duke of Clarence, later King William the Fourth, was chastis'd by a gentleman of Quebeck, to whose daughter he had pay'd unwelcome attentions. It was Mrs. Prentice, the inn-keeper's wife, incidentally, who identify'd the corpse of the rebel general Montgomery after the battle of Decr. 31, 1775. In 1784 Haldimand, having dy'd, was succeeded as Governor of Quebeck by Thomas Carleton, brother of Sir Guy—who was also Governor of Nova-Scotia, and of the new province of New-Brunswick, created in 1784 from the Acadian mainland contiguous to Maine, in New-England.

Up to this period the British population of Canada had been relatively slight; consisting mainly of petty traders in the large towns of Quebeck and Montreal, plus the military and civil persons connected with the garrisons. No part of the country was thickly settled save the original French region of the St. Lawrence Valley betwixt Montreal and the sea, and only in the towns was there anything like English-speaking life. Notwithstanding this, English newspapers had been founded in both Quebeck and Montreal—these being the first newspapers of any sort in Canada. The old Quebeck Gazette had its office in the lower town at the foot of Mountain Hill, on the side toward the cliff. Only much later, oddly enough, was any French paper founded in this antient French region—and even today an English daily Chronicle-Telegraph, which claims lineal descent from the old Gazette—is the leading publication of overwhelmingly French Quebeck.

In 1783 a vast and sudden change came as a result of the unfavourable termination of the American War. The thirteen southerly colonies being lost, about a third of their population—the element faithful to their rightful King—were driven into exile because of their refusal to swear fealty to the rebel government; and these loyal and noble subjects, men of the finest type in heritage and in devotion to a lofty standard, found a haven in the neighbouring lands still faithful to His Majesty, where they were given lands in recompense for what they had lost. The southerners went chiefly to the West Indes, where today their descendants are among the choicest of the population. The Northerners, on the other hand, moved more northward still—taking lands in Nova-Scotia, New-Brunswick, Prince-Edward Island, and those westerly parts of Canada above the St. Lawrence and the Great Lakes and inland beyond Montreal. About 30,000 New-England men of the most superior sort peopled the maritime provinces of the old Acadian region, whilst over 10,000 settled in upper Canada. Virile, capable, highly civilised, energetick, and used to the free and equitable institutions of Englishmen, this tremendous wave of loyal Americans swept tumultuously into the vacant parts of British North America like a transforming miracle. In a moment the anciently seated French population became reduced from a virtual Canadian totality to a mere section of a dual nation, of which the other section had the advantage of sharing the race, language, and institutions of the governing Empire. A new balance of forces and a new set of conditions had arisen—for English Canada had been born overnight. Halifax and St. John, in Acadia, became important towns, with Rhode-Island and other good old Yankee names on their records and eventually in their churchyards. In upper Canada the new town of York on the N. shore of Lake Ontario—now Toronto—grew rapidly in size and importance. Clamour arose at once for new laws and a new local government, since free Englishmen of such standing and in such numbers could not be expected to exist under the crude and archaick French system establish'd for the benefit of the French population by the Quebeck-Act. At home the need was acknowledg'd as soon as a provisional county system establish'd by Gov. Tho: Carleton had fail'd. Of course, it was recognis'd that if representative government be given the English, it must be given the French too; so that the old bar against the representation of Catholicks must be abandon'd. Nova-Scotia, Prince-Edward Island, and New-Brunswick, being outside the region affected by the old Quebeck-Act, offer'd no problems; these being separate English provinces from the start. But Canada proper, or the so-call'd Province of Quebeck, demanded fresh and radical action by His Majesty's Parliament. Accordingly in 1791 there was enacted the Quebec Government Bill, or Constitutional Act, by which the old Province of Quebeck was divided into *Upper-Canada,* the British region now call'd Ontario, and *Lower-Canada,* the old French area now call'd the Province of Quebeck. Upper-Canada, settled by United Empire Loyalists from the lost colonies, was to have English laws and institutions; whilst in Lower-Canada the old French institutions legalised by the 1774 Quebeck-Act were to be continu'd. Over both Provinces a Governor-General was to reign by Crown appointment, and under him each province was to have a separate Lieutenant-Governor and executive council, also appointed by the Crown. The Governor-General was to reside in Lower-Canada, of which Quebeck was still capital, and there were to be bicameral representative legislatures—the Upper Chambers of Legislative Councils being appointed by the Crown whilst the Lower Houses or Legislative Assemblies were to be elected by the people. Upper Canada, whose capital was in 1796 fixt at York, (Toronto) soon became in practice quite independent of the Governor-General; the Crown's Lieutenant Governor being virtually without supervision in local affairs. Thus the races of England and France in the New World were still kept separate; the only persons at a disadvantage being the English minority in Lower Canada, who had to submit to old French laws and institutions. These were mainly in Montreal, which at one period was quite Anglo-Saxon in tone, in Quebeck City, and in the so-call'd Eastern Townships, southeast of Montreal and just across the line from the New-England states of Vermont and New-Hampshire. (Place-names like Granby, Sherbrooke, Lennoxville, etc. attest this Englishry.) This French-swamped English element, never large except in Montreal, is now rapidly disappearing because of emigration to other provinces, and through the greater fecundity of the French. Today there are below 5000 English in Quebeck City. In practice, the government of both Canadian provinces soon became a select oligarchy of certain members of the Executive and Legislative Councils, known (after 1828) in Upper Canada as the "Family Compact", and in Lower Canada as the "Château Clique". Dissatisfaction naturally resulted from this, so that in both provinces there were constant anti-government agitations—the Scotsmen Robert Gourlay and William Lyon Mackenzie in Upper Canada, and Louis Joseph Papineau in the French area. In 1806, during a dispute over Lower-Canada taxes in which the English minority of traders wished land taxation whilst the French agricultural majority wished trade taxation, the French in Quebeck City founded *Le Canadien,* the first *French* newspaper in Canada. Some of the editors of this journal being arrested by the Lieutenant-Governor, Sir James Craig, that official's regime is still known amongst the Canadian French as "The Reign of Terror". In 1837 there were actual rebellions against the government in both Canadas, instigated by Papineau and Mackenzie, who later fled to the United States. That in Lower Canada was naturally the more serious, tho' hostilities occur'd in only two places—St. Eustache, north of Montreal, and the valley of the Richelieu. Upon the consequent suspension of the Constitution for three years, the capable Ld Durham straighten'd matters out as Governor-General; advocating the reunion of the two Canadas in order to give the dominant English their just proportion of power, and recommending a locally responsible government in all matters not involving imperial interests. In 1841 much of this advice was taken, there being set up an united Canada under a Crown Governor-General, a Crown Executive Council, and a Legislature with a Crown upper house and elective lower house. Successive governors at this period were Sydenham, Bigot, and Metcalfe. In 1847 Ld Durham's son-in-law Ld Elgin suc-ceeded Metcalfe as Governor-General, and endeavour'd to inaugurate a more locally responsible form of government. He invited the English and French Liberal leaders, Baldwin and La Fontaine, to form a government; and refus'd to veto a locally-enacted bill of the French (indemnifying persons who had suffer'd loss in the 1837 rebellion) which was highly repugnant to the English; this refusal being firmly given in the face of vast unpopularity and even mob violence in Montreal (where the legislature was then sitting). It was Ld Elgin who reaffirm'd the old dictum of Govr. Guy Carleton (1766), that the local French cou'd never be stript of their antient language and manners and made into Englishmen; writing, "I for one am deeply convinced of the impolicy of all such attempts [as suggested by Ld Durham] to denationalise the French. . . . You may perhaps *Americanise*, but, depend upon it, by methods of this description, you will never *Anglicise* the French inhabitants of the province. Let them feel, on the other hand, that their religion, their habits, their prepossessions, their prejudices, if you will, are more considered and respected here than in other portions of this vast continent, who will venture to say that the last hand which waves the British flag on American ground may not be that of a French-Canadian?"

The 1841 Act of Union met with some obstacles in operation, since the English in Upper Canada did not wish to be dominated by the more populous Lower Canada, of whose governing majority the French would certainly be the chief electors. Accord-ingly a plan was hit upon to have each province, despite this unequal population, send an equal number of representatives to the legislative assembly; and to require any given vote to command a separate majority in each of these equal local delegations (42 members each) in order to be carry'd. Dualism, French and English, crept into all appointments and administrations; and many questions like that of ecclesiastical funds and the old French seignioral tenure caus'd acute trouble. The greatest leader of this period was the Scotsman John Alexander Macdonald, (later knighted) who united many oppos'd parties and prov'd a vast conciliator. By 1851 an ironick situation had develop'd regarding the equal-representation principle of the English and French prov-inces; since rapidly growing Upper Canada—now call'd Canada West and receiving vast accretions from the British Isles—especially Scotland—had become more popu-lous than Lower Canada—or Canada East—so that the principle no longer protected an English minority but actually depriv'd an English majority of the power they might otherwise have. In the 1860's the idea of a union of all the various British Provinces in North-America began to be talk'd of; and even the French, led by their capable statesman Georges-Etienne Cartier, became reconcil'd to the prospect. All the prov-inces sent representatives to a Conference held at Quebeck in Octr 1864, which even-tually propos'd a plan of union to be ratify'd by the several legislatures. Of these legislatures, those of Newfoundland and Prince-Edward Island refus'd to ratify the plan; whilst in Nova Scotia there was ineffective popular opposition. The others acted favourably, so that Canada, New Brunswick, and Nova-Scotia sent delegates to Eng-land to arrange for the new united colony. Imperial authorities approved the design; and on July 1, 1867, Her Maj^ty's Parliament pass'd the British North-America Act, whereby there came into being that puissant branch of our English Empire which today flourishes in ever-increasing splendour despite the rigours of its inclement climate— the proud and self-sufficient DOMINION OF CANADA. The Dominion has a Gov-ernor-General appointed by the Crown, an Executive Council, and two elective Houses of Parliament—a Senate and House of Commons. Each Province has a sepa-rate representative government under a Lieutenant-Governor appointed by the Dominion government, an Executive Council, and an elective legislature in some cases unicameral and in some cases bicameral. The capital has from the first been Ottawa, on the Ottawa river which separates Upper and Lower Canada—from this time onward separate provinces under the names of Ontario and Quebeck. Into this great Dominion has come all of British North America except Newfoundland and the strip of Laborador belonging to it. The great Canadian West, its boundary with the United States being adjusted in 1846, gradually became explored, penetrated by fur traders of the great monopolies, and finally settled. Little by little it was form'd into provinces and territories having a place in the Dominion; the government having purchas'd title to the land in 1869 from the Hudson's Bay Company. From Ontario westward along to the Pacifick Coast now stretch the provinces of Manitoba (1870), Saskatchewan (1905), Alberta (1905), and British Columbia (a crown colony after 1858) (1871); the first two wholly given to wheat-raising, the third to agriculture and ranching, and the last to agriculture, mining, fisheries, and commerce. The boundaries of all the provinces were in 1905 push'd greatly northward, tho' above the western ones still remains a great zone of arctic territory unsuited to regular habitation. The icy isles of the Arctic Ocean are also parts of the Dominion. Prince Edward Island in 1873 revers'd its earlier decision and joyn'd the united fabrick. Since the formation of the Dominion, its degree of independence from the Empire has increas'd to a mark'd extent, till it is now a virtually separate political entity. It is not likely, however, that any disloyal repudiation of the hereditary tie will ever take place. God Save the King! Canada's part in all the important wars of Old England is a matter of history. Old Quebeck, no longer capital of Canada as a whole, has remain'd the capital of Lower-Canada, or the Province of Quebeck; so that it still serves its ancient function of immediate governmental centre of the French population of the New World. Canada's arms are those of G^t Britain, with the lions of England, the lion of Scotland, the harp of Ireland, the lilies of France, and the maple-leaf of Canada, itself quarter'd in the field. The motto is "A MARI USQUE AD MARE."[24]

Meanwhile the differences with the revolted southern colonies were not quite settled. In the western part of New-France, the Ohio and Illinois country claim'd by Quebeck, there were many campaigns betwixt the rebels and the troops at the posts; the chief rebel marauder being the celebrated George Rogers Clark of Virginia. In 1779, at Vincennes, (now in Indiana) Clark captur'd Col. Henry Hamilton, His Maj$^{ty's}$ commander at Detroit. The reason the rebels did not again attack Canada proper, was that they had ally'd themselves with the French, and did not wish to give France a renew'd foothold in the New-World. The mulcting and expulsion of loyal subjects after the success of the rebels, and in defiance of treaty promises, caus'd His Maj$^{ty's}$ government to retain hold of the Western posts—Michillimackinac, Detroit, Niagara, Ft. Erie, (opp. Buffalo) Oswego, and Oswegatchie (Ogdensburg)—until the year 1796.

In the war of 1812, primarily started by American resentment of the seizure of seamen by His Maj$^{ty's}$ vessels, one of the major Yankee ambitions was the conquest of Canada. This war was oppos'd by a great part of the American nation, especially New-England; hence did not prove as disastrous to old Quebeck as it might otherwise have done. Most of the military events took place in the West, and in English Upper Canada; where some recent settlers from the United States had created the nucleus of a disloyal element, and arous'd in the invaders the hope of aid from within. Early in July Gen. Hull took 2000 Americans from Detroit across the strait to Canadian soil, issuing a bombastick proclamation in the role of a rescuer from British tyranny. Genl. Isaac Brock, His Maj$^{ty's}$ commander, added to a small English force a detachment of Indians under the great Shawnee chieftain Tecumseh; and drove the invader back to Detroit, after which he prepar'd to besiege the town. Hull, before the attack truly began, surrender'd his fortress despite his command of 2500 men and 25 pieces of ordinance against a force of only 700 English and 600 Indians.* After an armistice the Americans made another attempt on Canada, attempting to land at Queenston, just across the Niagara River from New-York. Here Genl Brock was kill'd, but the invaders fail'd to effect their purpose because of the refusal of some of the Yankee troops to leave American soil. In 1813 the Americans plann'd a threefold campaign against Canada—much as our old colonial forces us'd to plan campaigns against New France in the loyal days of the 1750s. Detroit, Niagara, and Montreal were the three objectives. The Detroit campaign met with varying fortunes; Americans and British occasionally pushing the engagements upon their enemies' respective soils. In September the Rhode-Island Commodore Oliver Hazard Perry destroy'd a flotilla of His Maj^{ty} on Lake-Erie, which open'd up Upper Canada to American invasion and precipitated a battle in which Chief Tecumseh (he whose Indian conspiracy against the whites was put down at Tippicanoe in 1811 by Genl. Harrison) was kill'd. The Niagara campaign open'd successfully for the invaders, and gave them possession of the Niagara peninsula. Commodore Chauncey, with a small American fleet, obtain'd control of Lake-Ontario; and in April Genl. Dearborn took the town of York (Toronto) and burn'd the publick buildings—in revenge for which Adm^l Cockburn later burn'd the Yankee publick buildings at Washington. In June, however, His Maj$^{ty's}$ forces succeeded against the invaders at Stony Creek, near the west end of Lake Ontario; and by the end of 1813 had not only driven them from Canada but invaded their own soil as well. But the most serious operations, and those most closely connected with the historick region of New-France, were the moves in the American campaign against Montreal . . . whose real and ultimate objective was Kingston—the old Fort Frontenac—with its important shipyards. This attack was to be twofold; Genl. Wilkinson starting from Sackett's Harbour, on Lake Ontario, and Genl. Wade Hampton of South-Carolina (grandfather of the illustrious Confederate general) following the historick Lake Champlain route; the expeditions meeting at the mouth of the river Châteauguay and thence swooping jointly upon Montreal by way of La Chine—La Salle's seignioral region. Wilkinson was defeated at Chrystler's Farm in Upper Canada on Novr. 11. Genl. Hampton, having enter'd Lower Canada on Septr. 20, reach'd the junction of the rivers Châteauguay and Outard; and there encounter'd a force of 300 French-Canadians under Col. de Salaberry, which on Octr. 25 was reinforc'd by 600 English under Col. Macdonnell. In the resulting battle the small Franco-English army of 900 utterly routed Hampton's 3000 invaders, causing them to retreat to their own soil. This brilliant victory did much to give spiritual union to the French and English in Canada, and the name of de Salaberry is now given to one of the principal streets of Quebeck—on the plain of Abraham where the town has overflow'd the walls. It is notable that Quebeck's Rue de Salaberry marks very closely the immortal battle-line of WOLFE in 1759. In 1814 a new American attack on Canada was begun; Genl. Jacob Brown expelling the Canadians from the New-York region opposite Niagara, crossing the river and taking Ft. Erie through a victory at Chippewa, but finally being check'd at Lundy's Lane. He was induc'd to retire at last thro' failure to receive naval coöperation, and thro' hearing of veteran British reinforcements at Montreal. Upper Canada being now free of the invader, His Maj$^{ty's}$ Governor-General,

---

*The American prisoners at Detroit were lodg'd at Quebeck in the old Union Club Bldg.—still standing—in Rue St. Louis.

Sir George Prevost, began a personally led offensive on American soil; driving the Americans toward Plattsburg, on the western side of Lake Champlain. Meanwhile the insufficient flotilla on the lake was defeated by the American fleet under Capt. Tho: Macdonough, so that in the end Prevost return'd without taking Plattsburg. This was the end of Canadian operations in the war. The later land campaigns were around Chesapeake Bay and Washington, and in the region near New Orleans; the war itself ending with the Treaty of Ghent, Decr. 24, 1814, before the final New Orleans fight of Jackson and Pakenham, who had not heard of the treaty. From that time to this there have been no hostilities betwixt the still loyal and the revolted colonies of His Maj^{ty}; whilst on the fields of Europe in 1917 and 1918 the two factions fought side by side. Thus may it ever be—and may some day the conservative forces in the revolted area help to bring back the wanderer to His Majesty's fold, thus checking the wretched quantitative barbarism of commerce and time-tables which is wrecking American civilisation. God Save the King! Minor disputes betwixt Canada and the United States have concern'd the northern boundary of Maine, and the partition of the vast Oregon territory on the Pacifick Coast; both long subject to international litigation, but fairly settled prior to 1850. Other irritations have been due to American filibustering aid given to Canadian rebels in 1837–8, and to Irish-Fenian raids in the Niagara Peninsula in 1866. At times, small elements in Canada have desir'd annexation to the United-States; moves of such sentiment being perciptible in 1775, 1812, 1837, and 1849.

All this time the antient fortress-town of Quebeck frown'd down from its beetling cliff unthreaten'd. The mighty fortifications—city walls, Grand Battery, Ramparts, gates, and Citadel atop dizzy Cape Diamond—were gradually put into their present form according to plans prepar'd in 1775 by the eminent French engineer Chaussegros de Léry, who had enlarg'd the Basilica to its present form in 1744. The walls and gates were fairly well advanc'd before the close of the eighteenth century, but the present Citadel was not built till 1822–23; the Duke of Wellington having meanwhile approv'd the de Léry plans for this work. At this same period the gates were largely reconstructed. The Quebeck Citadel, reach'd by a steep ascent from Rue St Louis, is still the most imposing and picturesque piece of fortification on this continent. With its walls, parades, batteries, bastions, casemated barracks, magazines, and officers' quarters covering 40 acres, it contains a square at the easterly end, overlooking the river, where the Governor-General of Canada maintains a summer residence, and where an excellent Artillery Museum is situate. From the King's Bastion, 300 feet above the river, is obtain'd what is probably the most impressive panoramick view in the Western Hemisphere. Walls and citadel have lately been repair'd by my Ld Willingdon, retiring Governor-Genl of Canada; and two of the gates, St. Louis and Kent, were reconstructed for permanent preservation in the middle nineteenth century. Unfortunately St. John's, Palace, Hope, and Prescott Gates have been demolish'd—all in the middle nineteenth century. Three great forts were also built on the heights of Lévis, across the river; so that in all probability Quebeck is still the most strongly defended town in the New World. In the same period that the other important works were undertaken—1820—a government storehouse was erected near the custom-house (pres. loc. Marine and Fisheries Bldg.) at King's Wharf; this remaining one of the very few buildings of English-Georgian architecture in Quebeck. Meanwhile the town was extending far beyond its antient walls, especially along Rue St. Jean. Rue Claire Fontaine is about the westward limit of Georgian Quebeck.

In 1791—remaining till 1794—as commander of the 7th Royal Fusiliers, there came to Quebeck H. R. H. the Duke of Kent, in later years father of Her Majesty,

Queen Victoria. As a town house he took the Chartiers de Lotbinière house on Rue St. Louis (#23) near the old Fort, which still stands, tho' in alter'd shape. For a country-seat he purchas'd the commodious mansion of the late Sir Fred'k Haldimand, K. C. B.—former Governor-General—at Montmorency Falls, having seen it advertis'd in the Quebec Gazette of Dec. 1, 1791. This building, now a resort hostelry known as "Kent House", still exists in greatly enlarg'd form. The Duke entertain'd with much lavishness there, assisted by Baroness de Fortissan. In 1792 the first Canadian parliament was open'd in the old palace of Bishop St. Valier near the top of the Mountain Hill, where Montmorency Park now is, and in 1793 the Church of England was seated in Quebeck—a Bishoprick under Dr. Jacob Mountain being establish'd. Popery of course remain'd dominant, but it now had a competitor. The Jesuit property had long been actually confiscated; and in 1800 dy'd Fr. Casault, last of the order in Canada, after which the Govt. formally took over the college edifices (us'd as barracks). The arrogance of the Jesuits in civil concernments well earn'd them suppression, tho' in 1889 they were financially reimburs'd for all property seiz'd by His Majesty. In 1807 the remains of the Jesuit Seminary Chapel, wreck'd by the bombardment of 1759, were demolish'd. The antient church and convent of the Recollet Fathers beside the Rue St. Anne near the Place d'Armes having been burn'd in 1796, the site was purchas'd by His Maj$^{ty's}$ government for an Anglican Cathedral. Previously, Anglican services had been held in the Recollet church by permission of the Fathers. The new Cathedral—still standing as one of the few specimens of English Georgian architecture in Quebeck—was consecrated in 1804, and is of a very fine and commodious Ionick type. The churchyards and Georgian steeples of these old English fanes form pleasing reminders of home to the visitor from England or the English colonies. In 1805 there was erected in the Place d'Armes near the Cathedral the so-called Union Bldg., on the site of old Gov. d'Ailleboust's residence of 1649. Here were held the genial festivities of the Baron's Club (1808 et seq.) and here for a time the Upper Canadian Parliament maintain'd government offices. It was in this building—still in good condition—that defensive measures against the Americans in 1812 were plann'd. In 1812, under the threat of war, 4 Martello towers were constructed outside the city on the plateau—2 in the southerly Cove fields, and 2 on the northerly cliff. Of these three now remain—those in the fields, and one bet. Rues Racine and Marchands, on the N. cliff opposite the point where Rue St. Jean blends with the Ste. Foy Rd. In 1815 occur'd a great waterfront fire, one of the many destructive holocausts which this antient town has had to endure. The unusual predisposition toward sweeping fires manifested by Quebeck is perhaps due to the intense winter heating made necessary by the frigid climate. St. Matthew's Anglican Church (tho' not the present building) dates from about this time, and in its churchyard is interr'd (together with other military men of that period) Thomas Scott, Esq., brother of Sir Walter, who resided in Canada as paymaster for His Maj$^{ty's}$ 70th Regiment from 1814 to his death in 1823. The regiment was at first quarter'd in Upper Canada, but it finally came to old Quebeck; and in that town dy'd also Mr. Scott's young daughter Barbara, on Octr. 3, 1821, at the age of eight. St. Matthew's is situate in Rue St. Jean, beyond the walls at the corner of Rue St. Augustin, in what was once call'd the St. John Suburb. In 1824 were built the Anglican chapel of Holy Trinity, in Rue St. Stanislas, and the Scotch church of St. Andrew in Rue St. Anne; the latter still standing in good shape. In 1827 a fine monument to Wolfe and Montcalm was erected in the Governor's Garden near the old Fort and Château—this being still in good condition after restoration in 1871. It bears the motto, "Mortem Virtus Communem, Famam Historia, Monumentum Posteritas Dedit."[25] In 1832 and '34 (and also in 1849, 1851, 1852, and 1854) Quebeck was visited by a frightful outbreak of Asiatick cholera; victims of which are bury'd in the old Cholera Burying Ground on the Plain of Abraham—off the Grand Allée (continuation of Rue St. Louis) at the head of the Rue de Salaberry, Wolfe's old battle line. In 1832 Quebeck, formerly a *town*, was made a *city* by Royal decree; and in that year also the first Irish Catholick Church, St. Patrick's, was built. The fane still remains—in McMahon St. (nam'd for the Irish priest)—formerly Rue St. Hélène, off Palace Hill. In 1833 there was launch'd at Quebeck the Royal William, first steamship to cross the Atlantick under its own steam. In 1834, on the night of Jany. 23, and at an hellish nightmare temperature of 22 below zero, there was destroy'd by fire the mighty Château St. Louis, antient seat of the French Royal power, which had been enlarg'd under Sir James Craig, and which was now tenanted by my Ld Aylmer. This vast feudal pile, of an area 210 × 40 feet, and beetling out over the lower town at a dizzy height of 200 feet, had been one of the most majestick, fascinating, and even terrible sights of old Quebeck; its bulk recalling the days when it had harbour'd such menaces to our British safety on this continent. The fire was a spectacle of vast grandeur and danger; and burning fragments menac'd the lower town by falling over the cliff. For many years the stately blacken'd ruins were one of the picturesque sights of Quebeck, but eventually they were remov'd to make way for the beginning of a magnificent 1500 foot promenade along the cliff-edge—at first call'd Durham Terrace, after Ld Durham, but later renam'd Dufferin Terrace from the subsequent Viceroy who greatly enlarg'd and improv'd it. The vast hotel Château Frontenac marks the approximate site of the old fort and chateau, and some of the ruin'd foundations still exist beneath the planks of Dufferin Terrace. In 1837 Quebeck was agitated by the Canadian revolutionary disturbances; and five agitators, including the American adventurers Theller and Dodge, were imprison'd in the mighty citadel. From this stronghold, with almost incredible daring and enterprise, these two Americans actually succeeded in escaping; letting themselves down the precipitous walls of the flagstaff bastion, and later getting outside the city gates undetected, to reach eventual safety in the United States. In 1844 the first police force was organis'd; order formerly having been enforc'd by the military—under both French and English regimes. 1845 will ever be remember'd as Quebeck's hideous year of flame, the St. Roch suburb being then visited on May 28 by a conflagration which nearly wip'd it out; whilst on June 28, exactly a month later, the upper-town suburbs of St. John and St. Louis were scarcely less disastrously afflicted. In the year following, the theatre adjoining the ruins of Château St. Louis—a former riding-school—was burn'd down during a performance with a loss of 45 lives. In 1852, as an adjunct of the ancient Seminary, there was founded Laval University, which has become the foremost Catholick institution of learning in North-America, with a famous library, and a branch in Montreal. The Seminary itself was founded by Bishop Laval in 1663, and open'd classes in 1666, in the house formerly occupy'd by Hébert's son-in-law Couillard on St. Famille hill, near the site of the edifice it was itself erecting. The first class contain'd 8 French boys, 6 Hurons, and some Algonquins; but it was later found impossible to educate the Indians. The Seminary was enlarg'd in 1677, burnt in 1701 and 1705, wreck'd by the shell-fire of 1759, and subsequently restor'd. Its chapel, built in 1690, was burnt in 1750 and restor'd—and has since been burnt in 1889, and supplanted in 1891 by a new chapel. The imposing new university building, built solidly contiguous to the Seminary and extending out to where the Grand Battery runs along the cliff-top, was erected in 1857, and has a belfry forming a salient point of the Quebeck skyline. It overlooks almost the precise spot in the lower town where in 1775 the invaders were finally defeated at the second Sault-au-Matelot barricade, where the tablet now is. In 1854 the old Bishop's Palace, housing the Parliament, a library, and a museum, was burnt down; so that the legislators were forc'd to remove to the new church of the Grey Nuns—which in turn fell a prey to the flames. Sittings were then held in Musick Hall, in Rue St. Louis (which was in later years—March 17, 1900—burnt). In 1859, however, a new Parliament House of the Ionick order, with dome and lanthorn like those of the Boston state house, was erected on the site of the old. This soon prov'd unsatisfactory; and in 1878 (after the formation of the Dominion) there was commenc'd that sumptuous (tho' lamentably Victorian) Provincial Parliament House on the north side of the Grande Allée, just outside St. Louis Gate, which is still the pride of Quebeck. Betwixt this imposing edifice and the city wall is a park-like expanse cut by the Ave. Dufferin and having a picturesque circle in the centre. Just inside the wall at this point is the Esplanade, a former parade ground now a publick park. The broad, turf-topt wall itself can be walk'd upon on this western side; from the citadel on the south, across St. Louis and Kent Gates, to a point just short of the demolisht St. John's Gate. On the eastern side of the Esplanade, which extends from St. Louis to Kent Gate, runs the Rue d'Auteuil. The new Parliament House was begun none too soon, for in 1883 the building of 1859 burn'd down. It was in this older edifice that the famous Quebeck Conference leading to the formation of the Dominion of Canada was held in 1864. The site of the old Bishop's Palace and Parliament House on Mountain Hill is now a restful cliff-edge park call'd Montmorency Park. It may be added that the newer Archbishop's Palace, a highly tasteful structure of Adam-period atmosphere, stands just across Rue Port-Dauphin from there. In 1860 the Prince of Wales, later King Edward VII, pay'd Quebeck a memorable visit, and in that same year there was dedicated the Monument aux Braves on the Ste. Foy Rd., in memory of de Lévis's attempt to retake Quebeck a century before. In 1864 came the famous Conference, and in 1866 there dy'd at his home, 14 Rue St. Flavien, the eminent Canadian historian, M. François-Xavier Garneau. It may be remark'd, that the profound and urbane culture of French Quebeck hath produc'd a great number of accomplisht littérateurs, poets, historians, and genealogists; local history and genealogy indeed being there pursu'd to an extent unrivall'd in North-America. Also in 1866 was a disastrous fire in the St. Roch and St. Sauveur suburbs—and in this year a municipal fire department was establish'd. In 1867 came the Dominion, and the establishment of a Provincial Lieutenant-Governor at Quebeck. The latter has a residential seat (a low, rambling mansion like a southern plantation house) call'd Spencer Wood, in the midst of an extensive park on the wild plateau west of the town beyond Wolfe's Cove, reach'd by a winding drive from the St. Louis Road. In 1869–70 the Duke of Connaught, later Governor-General of Canada, serv'd with his regiment at Quebeck, and in 1870 another terrifick fire occurr'd, consuming 500 houses. Other fires were in 1876, when 9 churches and 7 hotels were burnt in the St. John suburb, and 1881, when 600 houses were destroy'd. In 1879 Dufferin Terrace (formerly Durham Terrace) was open'd in its present form by Ld Dufferin. In 1884 the Prince of Wales visited Quebeck. In 1889 a terrifick fire ravag'd St. Sauveur, destroying 700 houses. These fires have cost Quebeck a vast number of her antient buildings, and it is indeed a wonder that so many do survive. In 1889 also came the great landslide at Cape Diamond, destroying 7 dwellings in Champlain St. and killing 66 persons. In 1890 the Duke and Duchess of Connaught visited Quebeck. In 1898 Quebeck's troops went forth to the Boer War. In 1900 there was laid the cornerstone of a long-wish'd bridge across the St. Lawrence west of Quebeck, connecting the region with the territories to the south; but in 1907 the steel work collaps'd, taking 80 lives. In 1901 their present Majesties visited Quebeck, as heirs to the throne. In 1905 Quebeck became the summer port of the CPR's transcontinental steamships. In 1908 the antient town celebrated the tercentenary of its founding by Champlain; the Prince of Wales— His present Maj^{ty} George the Fifth—and Field Marshal Ld Roberts being present. On this occasion the open country west of the built-over Plain of Abraham and the Cove Fields, on the cliff-edge reaching to Wolfe's Cove south of St. Louis Road,—a former race-course—was dedicated to the heroes of 1759 as Battlefields Park, and is now a pleasing and favourite place of resort, with ramparts, walks, and a museum soon to be open'd. In 1914 came the sinking of the steamer Empress of Ireland, with the loss of 1024 lives, and the departure of the first troops for World War service. In 1915 more troops left. In 1916 the new bridge again collaps'd, but was completed next year. Meanwhile an era of monument-building had begun; important memorials in all parts of the town being dedicated from time to time. In 1919 there dy'd Sir Wilfrid Laurier, the eminent French-Canadian statesman. In 1922 the Basilica was gravely damag'd by fire, and in 1923 a destructive fire devastated St. Roch. Also in 1923 the present Prince of Wales[26] visited Quebeck. In 1926 the great hotel Château Frontenac, erected on the site of Ft. St. Louis, was damag'd by fire. In 1928 Quebeck was visited by H. R. H. Prince George, youngest son of their present Majesties. Also about this period the walls and citadels were extensively repair'd by the Governor-General, Ld Willingdon. During the nineteenth century Montreal outstript Quebeck as the Canadian metropolis, and the antient capital is now the fourth, fifth, or sixth (as the new census will determine) city in the Dominion; places like Toronto, Winnipeg, Ottawa, etc. having forg'd ahead. By annexing suburbs, including Limoilou across the St. Charles but excluding Lévis across the St. Lawrence, modern Quebec shews a population figure not far from 130,000, of whom very few are foreigners, and of whom only about 5000 are English. A vast number of the dominant French, however, are fluently familiar with the English language. The motto of Quebeck is "Natura fortis, industria crescit";[27] and in order to live up to the latter half, the town has lately made great efforts to compete with Montreal as a centre of trade. It is to be hop'd that this commercial ambition (already responsible for one terrac'd skyscraper, the Price Bldg.) will not lead to the destruction or vitiation of local quaintness. Education is largely controll'd by the Romish Church, tho' there are separate schools for the Protestant minority. No general free publick library exists, but many of the educational and religious institutions have good libraries, both French and English, available under suitable conditions; the number totalling 9. Quebeck has 1 University, 1 Seminary, 1 Commercial Academy, 1 Technical School, 1 Art School, 24 commercial schools, 6 Business Colleges, and 2 Protestant high schools. There are 24 charitable institutions, 46 Popish churches, 4 Anglican churches, and 5 Dissenting meeting-houses. Gas, water, electricity, tramway, railway, and omnibus service, mercantile establishments, etc. etc. etc. all reflect a settled and prosperous modern civilisation. There are 2129 retail shops, 205 wholesale houses and 215 manufactories, and the town is a trading centre for a region 75 miles W. and S., and 100 miles N. and E. Harbour developments have been extensive. The choice upper-town shopping district centres around Rues Buade, Fabrique, and St. Jean. In the lower town retailing centres around Rues St. Joseph, St. Valier, and de la Couronne, in the St. Roch ward. The old lower town is the wholesale and financial district—St. Peter St. being the local Wall St. As a whole, Quebeck has about 12,000 edifices, 425 streets totalling 101.6 miles, 47 banks, 4 daily papers, (1 English) 22 other periodicals, (2 English) 11 theatres, (cinemas) and 24 parks (9 main ones).

BOOK II. The Present State of Quebeck; design'd for the Information of the New-England Traveller.

(A) The Province of Quebeck, and Approaches to Quebeck-City.

For the New-England traveller, the best approach to Quebeck is from Boston, by a route involving the Boston and Maine, Central Vermont (Canadian Pacifick), and Quebeck Central railways. The rail-road cars leave the North-Station in Causeway-St., proceeding to Lowell, on the Merrimack River, and thence up that stream past the New-Hampshire factory towns of Nashua, Manchester, Concord, Laconia, and Plymouth. At Woodsville the route crosses the Connecticut-River into the colony of Vermont, formerly His Maj$^{ty's}$ New-Hampshire Grants; thence proceeding northward thro' excellent northern New-England scenery from Wells River thro' Passumpsick, St. Johnsbury, Lyndonville, and Newport. In this northerly region the topography and architecture are still typically Novanglian, but many publick notices—as of fairs at Sherbrooke, and the like—proclaim the close relationship of the inhabitants to the northward and still loyal province of Quebeck. At Derby Line Vermont soil is left behind, and the traveller is made sensible that he is at last speeding over the actual present domains of His Britannick Majesty. GOD SAVE THE KING!!

Those parts of Quebeck Province near the Vermont border—the English-settled Eastern Townships—have an Anglo-Saxon nomenclature and do not differ substantially in aspect and atmosphere from those of old New-England. Beebe Junction— Boynton—Ayers' Cliff—Massawippi—Woodland Bay—North Hatley—Eustis— Capelton—Lennoxville—Sherbrooke—all these sound like New-England, and *are* like it. Only in subtle ways—the use of the word "Imperial" in the names of products advertised on posters and billboards, and so on—does one realise that the rebel colonies are left behind. God Save the King! For a moment one feels a touch of homesickness in the knowledge that one is soon to pass from among familiar English sights and ways. Sherbrooke is a small city of very pleasing aspect, not unlike the average place of corresponding size in the United States. Its hotels and streets have good Anglo-Saxon names—New Sherbrooke House—Grand Central—New Wellington—Albion— American House—King George—King St.—Depot St.—Wellington St.—Aberdeen St.—Minto St.—etc.—and only when one catches the word "Rue" on an obscure street-sign does one realise that French is the dominant legal language of the province. Beyond Sherbrooke the atmosphere begins to exhibit subtle differences—both as regards the face of Nature, and as regards the creations of mankind. French signs and advertisements begin to appear in the villages, though the names and architecture are still English—Ascot—East Angus—Bishop's Crossing—Marbleton—and so on. This is obviously a region first settled by us, and subsequently overrun by the southward-flowing French, like the manufacturing towns of Rhode-Island and other New-England states. In visual aspect the country is often highly impressive, with great sweeps of rolling terrain affording magnificent vistas of wooded valley and river-bends. To a Southern-New-Englander the vegetation seems sparse and meagre; a thing one notices to a lesser degree in Vermont. Along the river-banks, however, it is darker and thicker. Frequently one beholds evidences that this is a lumbering country; the rivers being in many places jamm'd thick with logs, while deforested stump areas are numerous. The farther we go, the more unlike New-England the region seems. There are here absolutely no stone walls, but crooked rail fences of the antient Virginia type. The barns resemble New-England's, but the houses are more like cheap Victorian suburban cottages than like New-England farmhouses. This is doubtless because this particular belt of country was not settled thickly till the Victorian age—if indeed it may be call'd really *thickly* settled even now. There are great tenantless stretches, and not very much visible agriculture. We do not find here the much-prais'd beauty and quaintness of antient French cottages, as occurring in the older parts of the province, but merely a kind of squalor and dinginess much like that of foreigners in New-England. There are, however—as Sherbrooke falls farther and farther behind—some pleasantly curious village churches built in a manner distinctly French; and another notable thing is the profusion of bright flowers (if one, as wisdom dictates, travel in summer) even around some of the most squalid hovels. The squalor reminds one of the barren sandy uplands of the Piedmont Carolinas, and indeed many of the French cottages are not much better than nigger cabins. There are even a few *log* huts, and huts of half-hewn timbers. Sundry touches of the unfamiliar are supply'd by certain of the telegraph or telephone poles, which are of an European type not seen in New-England. If the traveller, as very frequently, chances to make this trip during a misty but clearing dawn; he will behold vivid evidences of the subtly northern realm he is entering. In the south the skies are hard and decided; and transitions from light to darkness, darkness to light, clearness to cloud, and cloud to clearness, are accomplisht suddenly—without delicate and imagination-stirring gradations. As a possible result, the races of the south are sharp and realistic in the moods; and but little given to the ingrain'd brooding, phantasy, and mysticism of the northern, forest-nurtured Teutons and Celts, who have for uncounted millennia watch'd and wonder'd at the gradual, elusively provocative, and sometimes supernal and apocalyptick mutations of earth and sea and sky around them. Here in boreal Quebeck an advancing morning of dissolving mist is food for any fancy; the grotesque and ethereal forms of the haunted vapours, and the strange tricks they play with the sunlight as they churn and spiral upward from the horizon, forming something wholly unprecedented for the untravell'd Southern New-Englander. Especially exotick is the vast abundance of denuded forest land displaying endless reaches of withering stumps; a melancholy and even sinister sight. And to complete the exoticism in a less dismal way, one beholds striking and omnipresent evidences of the French-Canadian agricultural custom of making endless rows of *very small haystacks;* things not an eighth of the size of those which the Yankee farmer makes, or us'd to make. After a time the train reaches a grey and ugly area—Thetford Mines—containing the world's largest asbestos mine—an area wholly given over to this industry, and abominably depressing in consequence. From the windows one beholds stupendous and Cyclopean quarry-pits—one of which seems to shatter all records for its kind. Upon leaving Thetford Mines behind, the traveller is glad to find himself in a distinctly older part of the province—the older parts naturally being those toward Quebeck City. The landskip becomes extreamly magnificent; involving in many places bold hills and glimpses of river valley like the Connecticut-Valley or Shenandoah regions, and in other places flattish expanses and gently rolling hills enabling the eye to span seemingly limitless leagues of sunlit verdure and zigzag rail fences. This region is *rocky*—exactly like New England—but has singularly few *trees* of any sort; its bareness in this respect reminding one of rural Ohio. Here, also, we begin to encounter typical old-time French farmhouses—genuine outgrowths of the historic native building tradition. They are not the really *oldest* edifices, for the early farming land was on the north side of the St. Lawrence; but they probably date from the late eighteenth and early nineteenth centuries, and are authentick developments of the original style—made of wood instead of stone. Among the most

distinctive features is the *curving roof-line,* which to the superficial eye suggests the Dutch curve so familiar in the Province of New-York. A representative survey, however, shews that most of them are differently proportion'd—there being no gambrels, and the long downward sweep being perfectly straight except at the eaves, as in the accompanying sketch. This idiosyncrasy, soon found to be the typical mark of an old French cottage, closely resembles a kindred curve found in the oldest urban houses of Charleston, in His Maj[ty's] Province of South-Carolina; and suggests that the Charlestonian usage was imported by the numerous Huguenot settlers who exercis'd so much influence there. An important work on architecture obstinately maintains that the Charleston custom is Dutch—pick'd up by the Huguenots during their stay in Leyden—but the evidence of Quebeck is all to contrary. Another distinctive French feature of these old houses—which we shall likewise find universal in urban Quebeck—is the type of *window,* especially (as regards the farmhouses) in the gable ends. It is of the hing'd casement type, and has the French horizontal cross-bars instead of the small panes of our old houses. The trims and lintels, also, are distinctive (*see sketch*). This window type is *not* found in Charleston, nor has the present writer observ'd it elsewhere in the United States. Another typically French manifestation is the *slender spire sometimes surmounting the old barns*—which are otherwise quite like New-England colonial barns. The prevailing type of needle-like spire and small cupola tends to suggest the Old Ship Church at Hingham, in His Maj[ty's] Province of the Massachusetts-Bay. In general, these houses and

farm buildings are arrang'd much like those of a New-England farm. Were it not for the local and national variations here mention'd, and for the total lack of trees and stone walls, one might well imagine himself in New-England when viewing one of the typical landskips near Quebeck City. Only when a typically French village steeple is glimps'd across the meadows, does the dominant impression become violently exotick. These ornate steeples, however, with their frequent coating of tin, are wholly alien in atmosphere when contrasted with our white Georgian village spires embower'd in greenery. It may be added that the eaves of the old Quebeck houses—both rustic and urban—all have a tendency to project; the roof overhanging the walls on all four sides. At Beauce Junction the train encounters the River Chaudière, famous for Arnold's expedition of 1775; after which the scenery becomes steadily more and more picturesque—many slender French steeples revealing the presence of villages here and there. As the train nears the St. Lawrence, on the high ground betwixt Diamond and Charny, there is a suspicion of a view of distant QUEBECK itself, far off across the river; and one strains to test the reality of the steep-roof'd, battlemented and headland-perch'd silhouette which hovers so magically and alluringly on the borderline of ethereal phantasy. Thus it must have been glimps'd by Arnold and his men as they near'd the end of their gruelling voyage thro' the wilderness—its mirage-like doubtfulness half-symbolising the failure to which their bold enterprise was destin'd. The train crosses the Chaudière basin at a vast height, but does not afford a view of the celebrated falls marking the confluence of this stream with the St. Lawrence. Charny, the last village encounter'd on the St. Lawrence's southern shoar, gives one an appetising welcome to Old World feudal antiquity by displaying a picturesque and quite unparallel'd cluster of typical French steeples. Then comes the great Quebeck Bridge—that vast feat of engineering whose completion was accomplisht only after two disastrous failures. He who sees the titanick river from its dizzying height for the first time, is given an impression which time is powerless to efface. Tho' the great stream is here at its narrowest, so far as its lower course is concern'd, an impression of prodigious breadth is convey'd by looking eastward. The sensation is that of a lake or sea, and the suggestion of dreamlike exoticism is intensify'd by the strange, slender spires which rise on every hand—Sillery Church lower down on the shore ahead, and the bristling steeples of Lévis and Charny on the high cliffs we are leaving behind. For a moment it is hard to connect this breathless vista with unmagical reality, or to realise that one is not being wafted bodily into the midst of some vast picture vivid with adventurous expectancy. The headland on the north shoar to which the bridge finally takes us, is Cap-Rouge, fam'd as the wintering place of Jacques Cartier's third (1541) expedition, and as the seat of Sieur de Roberval's unsuccessful convict colony of 1542. It is still wholly rural, and as we gain and penetrate the land we find this northerly region more forested, topographically diversified, and generally like New-England than the Chaudière Valley we have left behind. The train crosses the Quebeck peninsula toward the narrow St. Charles, passing not far from the antient village and church of Ste. Foy, and the Huron village of Lorette, and remaining on the lower level of ground. As it turns eastward to follow the right bank of the St. Charles, the increasingly precipitous upper-town plateau looms up on the right, topped by the ever-thickening roofs and spires of the ancient city. The sight is moving beyond belief; yet the view toward the left is scarcely less alluring—expanses of pleasant green countryside, with the mystical purple peaks of the Laurentian Mountains looming austerely in the far background. At length the St. Sauveur and St. Roch Suburbs press closely against the tracks on our right; the archaick general hospital almost touching us as we pass it. On our left, at the same point, we see Victoria Park beyond a picturesque loop in the St. Charles. A moment later we are skirting Rue Prince Edward in the St. Roch slums, and beholding the quaint and distinctive architecture of the old French houses there. The oldest part of the upper town is now fairly close, and we can distinguish many of the silver-shining steeples and the towering Norman roof of the colossal Château Frontenac. The majesty of the great cliff and climbing down begins to ingulph us—and at last the train stops, in a park-fronted station not far from where old lanes climb toward and beyond the ancient Palace Gate.

Emerging from the station, we are struck by the overpowering archaick spell of the beautiful old town. On our left, a row of mellow antient buildings lines one side of the vista toward the city; whilst straight ahead looms the titanick cliff and the labyrinth of centuried roofs and steeples and curving lanes climbing and crowning it. Running along the base of the moderate rise which leads up from the level plain to the foot of the cliff proper is the broad trunk thoroughfare Rue St. Paul, on which we may discern the great hotel Château Champlain, marking the site of the mansion built and tenanted by the illustrious Intendant Jean Talon. High above the roofs of the houses in Rue St. Paul we behold the Cyclopean masonry of a colossal heavenward rampart which seems to hint of exotick mysteries remote in space and time. This, we shall learn, is where the city wall descends the cliff from the west to Palace Gate, and is surmounted by the upward continuation forming the wall of the ancient artillery barracks, (1750) now the Dominion Arsenal. To the left of this the roofs of the rambling Hôtel Dieu hospital rise, while high up—in the far distance over all the rest of the picture—the park of the Château Frontenac can be glimps'd. Here and there a curious silver spire provokes the imagination; and the curving lines of the curious uphill lanes which lead to the demolish'd Palace Gate and beyond—Rue St. Nicolas on the right and Rue Lacroix on the left—beckon with an antique, mystical charm well-nigh impossible to resist.

Before viewing the antient town, however, it may be well to obtain a somewhat fuller picture of its rural background; to which end a fleeting glimpse of the venerable North Shore countryside toward Montmorency Falls and beyond is advisable. For this purpose one may, upon leaving the tasteful and traditionally steep-roof'd Union Station and advancing to St. Paul St., turn to the left for a single block and board an electrick train of the Quebeck Railway, Light, and Power Co., which traverses the region in question, often close to the shoar, and passes the foot of the great Montmorency cataract in a way affording a magnificent view. The train, upon setting out, crosses the St. Charles on a railway bridge built in 1890, and enters the somewhat colourless suburb and junction-point of Limoilou. Turning eastward, it soon shakes off the urban penumbra and enters a countryside of intense beauty, quite comparable to some of the finest regions of New-England in general topography. Ancient houses are not as numerous as one might expect, but many distinctively French specimens exist—especially a characteristic type also found in the urban part of Quebec and probably dating from the early nineteenth century, with gambrel roof having a steep, curved lower pitch, flattish dormers, and heavily projecting cornices. There are also new houses, some of them embodying architectural features peculiar to the locality. What old houses one does behold, are of the choicest and most picturesque sort, with curve-eav'd, projecting roof, whitewash'd stone sides, end chimneys, dormers, and other earmarks of early French construction. Such cottages are generally low—a story and a half. (*see sketch*) All houses in the region—new and old, nearly without exception—have the French type of casemate window. Now and then—but oftener from the highway than trom the train—a wayside shrine with Cross and bleeding Saviour, or Madonna and Child, is to be seen; and occasional village  steeples and church towns add to the quaintness of the idyllick landskip. In this region one finds many surviving examples of the small dog-drawn carts used in France and the Low Countries for transporting milk and other rural products. Though much affected by modern change and urban proximity, the countryside is still extremely archaic in its life, customs, and institutions; affording a hint of the quaint and idyllick conditions undoubtedly existing in the less accessible parts of the province. This is the region where in 1759 Montcalm had his battle line, remnants of the redoubts being still visible near the beach. Montcalm had his headquarters in the antient Giffard manor-house, ruins of which still remain. From the tower of the church at Beauport Govr Vaudreuil watch'd the French troops send out fire-ships in a vain attempt to destroy His Maj$^{ty's}$ fleet. After the taking of Quebeck, this Beauport region was overrun by our troops, whose conduct was more savage than necessity call'd for. The divisions perpetrating this vindictive occupation, oddly enough, were commended by Col. Alexander Montgomery, brother of the gallant officer who sided with the rebels in 1775 and was kill'd at Près-de-Ville barricade. The Beauport or Côte de Beaupré region, antiently call'd Côte des Pères, (after the Jesuit fathers who once held much of the land) was a seat of many important seigniories. As the train progresses, the quaintness of the scenery is enhanc'd by the several shore towns encounter'd—fishing villages like St. Gregoire, with curious parish steeple towering above clusters of archaick roofs, and with glimpses of picturesque lanes and strips of beach. History again intervenes to remind us that it was here that Phips made his attempt to secure a land foothold in 1690, only to suffer repulse. The political unit hereabouts, we may note, is the *parish* (as in most French regions, including Louisiana); those east of Quebeck, in the Côte de Beaupré region, being Giffard, Beauport, St. Gregoire, Boischatel, L'Ange Gardien, Château Richer, Ste. Anne de Beaupré, Beaupré, and St. Joachim. Here, as elsewhere, the overshadowing influence of the Popish religion amongst a simple populace is everywhere manifest. At length we come to a tract of flat beach land, with station and park in the foreground, and with a vast line of lofty cliffs, comparable to the Quebec and Lévis cliffs, or the Palisades of New-Jersey, rising a few rods inland, on our left. Over this cliff-line, from a height of 270 feet, in plain sight of the train, there thunders the rushing bulk of the Montmorency River—plunging from its pine-grown plateau to the flats of the St. Lawerence level in a mass of tumultuous foam. To one who has never before seen a great cataract, the effect of this natural wonder is stupendous and awe-inspiring—an effect which increases as one approaches it and hears the full magnitude of its cosmic roar. An ingenious elevator conveys one to the summit of the vast cliff—the upper level on which the highways and general Montmorency countryside are located. Here we behold the old Georgian mansion built by Gen[l] Haldimand and later inhabited by the Duke of Kent—now enlarg'd and open as a publick hostelry under the name of Kent House. Here also we find the antient and typical whitewash'd stone cottage of old French design which the immortal WOLFE us'd as an headquarters, and within which, from a sick-bed of pain and peril, he plann'd that glorious campaign whereby Quebeck became ours. God Save the King! In 1759 the Montmorency River—boundary betwixt the parishes of Beauport and L'Ange Gardien—form'd the frontier betwixt Montcalm's lines and our own. Beyond Montmorency Falls we see the brick works now forming Quebeck's leading industry, and later encounter some fine countryside around L'Ange Gardien and Château Richer. Finally the train reaches quaint and curious Ste. Anne de Beaupré, whose popish shrine has made it one of the most celebrated spots on the continent. With its many chapels, spectacles, and monuments, its famous reliques and art objects, and its rapidly progressing new Basilica, this place is well worthy of a day's exploration. The so-call'd Old Chapel on the hillside is built of the materials of the demolish'd church of 1676—the steeple and ball being the same that were added to the antient fane in 1694. Beyond the village lie Beaupré, Queylus, St. Joachim, lofty (2000 ft) Cap Tourmente, (where the water becomes salt) and eventually Murray Bay, Tadoussac with its antient settlement, and the mouth of the gloomy and impressive River Saguenay, which flows down from Lac St. Jean and Chicoutimi betwixt great cliffs and headlands. It is not possible, however, to survey the whole Province of Quebeck in a single tour of ordinary magnitude; hence we must limit ourselves to a consideration of that which serves a direct setting for the ancient capital. The Province in general is probably the most remarkable bit of the Old World to be found in America. Agriculture, dairying, fisheries, and forestry still form leading industries; and the simple habitant population, under the sway of their priests, live both physically and mentally in a seventeenth century atmosphere. The French are very prolifick, causing the population to double every 29 years; but instead of remaining congested in urban and suburban zones, they tend to spread rapidly—overflowing into the Eastern Townships, Ontario, and New-England, as well as pushing north around Lac St. Jean and in the subarctic parts of the Province. Some immigration from France has occurred—especially of members of expell'd religious orders—but in general immigration has not been a major factor in Quebeck history. There are probably fewer foreigners in Quebeck than in any other American city of any prominence save Charleston. The Popish church is a supreme governing influence; controlling education and having the payment of tithes by members enforc'd by civil law. The local government is wholly in the hands of the French, and nowadays there is but little friction with the English; who, tho' a minority population, are still in control of financial, commercial, and railway interests. The rural dialect is an archaic Norman-Breton patois, and the civil law of the province is based on the old Custom of Paris, the pre-Revolutionary code of antient Bourbon France.

(B) The Aspect and Architecture of Quebeck.

(1) Architecture.

Urban Quebeck, the most antient, exquisitely lovely, historically glamorous and mystically picturesque city in the northern part of America, deserves the closest study from every historian, architect, and devotee of beauty and phantasy. With its fortress-crown'd green headland jutting skyward from the mile-wide St. Lawrence, its mediaeval city walls and gates, its endless tiers of steep roofs, red or glittering with silver, climbing a grim, grey cliff-line, its numberless silver spires catching the rays of the sun, its impressive glimpses of ancient ramparts and battlements, its labyrinth of quaint, centuried houses huddled along winding lanes and scaling precipices at impossible angles, its rambling flights of steps from plain to upper town, its grey, archaick churches and convents, its urbane, kindly throngs with their sprinkling of black-rob'd monks and priests, its hordes of horse-drawn calèches, its breath-taking and unexpected vistas of urban quaintness, landscape and river grandeur, and distant mountain-wonder, its restful squares, its curious old facades, doorways, and windows, its park-like sweeps of hillside up to the citadel, its air of civilised leisure, and its general allegiance to a background-linked, Old-World order which has largely pass'd away on this continent . . . . . with all these things, Quebeck seems scarcely part of the waking world at all; but rather a miraculously crystallis'd fragment of one of those vague, elusive dreams where all our memories of art and literature and experience fuse tantalisingly into some momentary panorama of luminous ultimate wonder and beauty corresponding to nothing in objective existence, but underlying all our conceptions of supernal paradises, transcendental memories, and gateways of sunset magic and adventurous expectancy. Sir Michael Sadler of Oxford, whose opinions are bas'd upon extensive travel and sensitive appreciation, places Quebeck amongst the twenty most beautiful cities of the world[28]—a list so rigorously compiled as to exclude all other towns of North and South America, and to reject even antient London with its spires and domes and memories. Sir Michael's twenty most beautiful towns are the following: Rome, Florence, Venice, Vienna, Constantinople, Paris, Stockholm, The Hague, Budapest, Nuremburg, Gothenburg, Ob-der-Tanbau, Dijon, Angouleme, QUEBECK, Agra, Benares, Edinburgh, Bath, and Oxford. The best single view of Quebeck is probably that to be had from the cliffs of Point Lévis, across the St. Lawrence, or from boats and ferries plying that majestick stream. Thus seen, the antient town is a marvel of enchantment and loveliness beyond the power of men to describe. With half-closed eyes and fancy withdrawn from realistick detail, we glimpse the whole fabrick of headland, cliff, citadel, roofs, and spires as a solid exotick carving, of which the natural and artificial features blend imperceptibly into one another. The effect is curiously like that of lower New-York city as seen from the heights of Brooklyn. In that marvellous vista, we are led to confuse the peaks of the vast sky-

scrapers with the spires of some haunted hill town, and to think of the windowed terraces that climb the sky as terraces of strange houses climbing the earth. Here we have
the reality which New-York imitates—an actual hill town where nothing is merely false
or illusory and where solid background, enchanted antiquity, and continuous racial tradition and habitancy are actual living realities. Looking more sharply and closely, we see
individual colours and contours and features begin to stand out. The ancient waterfront
with quays, warehouses, classick customs-house, and ships riding at anchor—the irregular lines of ramparts and climbing streets—the tiers of steep slant roofs, the green of foliage, and the lighter tones of great publick edifices—the dizzy height of Cape Diamond
with its citadel of frowning bastions, and the glorious ensign of BRITANNIA floating
over all—the towering Norman roof of the mighty Château Frontenac—the grey abut-
ments of Dufferin Terrace—the gleaming walls and golden dome of the post office—the
silver spires of churches and convents—the blue of a northern sky over the pale grey of
the citadel, the dark, rust-streak'd grey of the cliffs, and the patches of green mingling
with the grey—the commanding bulk and imperious steeple of Laval University where
the landscape-line drops precipitously to the Lower Town at the turn of the gigantick
cliff—the blue of the river, the chequer'd and undulant green of the roof-and-steeple-
dotted countryside beyond—the lone steeple of Sillery up the river—the purple, mystical Laurentians toward the north, looming hazily like the serrated edge of an unknown
planet rising beyond the horizon—all these things unite to make of Quebeck's totality a
sight more gorgeous, alluring, dream-like, and potentially adventurous than anything
else the New-World imagination can conceive. But the most marvellous thing of all is
that there is no disillusion behind this mirage-like glamour. The picture is not the elusive and insubstantial dream which we instinctively fear it to be. Indeed, a close approach and exploration not only does not detract from the spell, but actually intensifies
and doubles it. Quebec is a realisation of that always-beckoning and bitterly-tantalising
conception of imaginative infancy—a fairy-tale picture into which one can actually
walk, and whose outspread wonders one can actually touch and savour and sample.

The buildings of Quebeck, notwithstanding the frequent great fires and occasional
cases of ill-advised destruction, (as of the Jesuits' College near the upper-town market-
place, the de Léry manor in the Seminary grounds, etc.) still include a marvellous proportion of seventeenth and eighteenth century specimens; and the town's archaick air is in-
tensified by the conservative persistence of antient architectural traditions. Some ugly
Victorian atrocities occur; but few of them are as bad as corresponding examples in the
United States, whilst nearly all of them are subordinated by their harmonious old French
setting. English Georgian edifices are very few in number—outstanding examples being
the English Cathedral, St Andrew's Church, and the government storehouse at King's
Wharf. Fanlighted Geor-
gian doors are rare, but
not wholly absent. The
most antient type of pri-
vate house (*see sketch*)
as represented by the
Montcalm headquarters
at Rues St. Louis and
Desjardins (oldest house
in Quebeck—1641) is
of a single full story with
two attick stories, has an

exaggeratedly steep roof like the rare Colonial "lightning splitters" of Providence, and is distinguish'd by ponderously overhanging cornice and *double rows of dormers*—a feature, in America, quite peculiar to French Canada. Steep roofs and double rows of dormers also distinguish the antient publick buildings, tho' in this case the roofs are balanc'd in the manner suitable to their more ambitious purpose. Solid blocks seem to have been the custom from a very early period, and the dominant building materials were stone and stucco'd brick, as in most towns of continental European heritage. Houses of the second period—the early eighteenth century—are more like the brick town houses—with slant roof and dormers—of the English colonies of the same period, save that their roofs are steeper, and that their end chimneys are very broad and thin (*see sketch*).

Others are more like the rural cottages, with curving eaves like those found in Charleston. Some of these differ in having two full stories and often two atticks with typical double dormer tiers of urban Quebeck (*see lower sketch*). The roofs of these, on the average, are rather sharper than the rural roofs. In all these cases there is a heavy cornice overhang suggesting the cornices of Newport, R.I., which may have arisen from French Huguenot influence. Many of the best specimens of these older roofs are found in slums of the most dismal description. We may note in passing, that in cases of double dormer rows the upper ones are almost invariably the smaller. This accords with the French custom of gracefully diminishing the height of windows on successively ascending stories—a custom found in late-Georgian and early-Victorian English and American houses, and coincident with a copying of French modes.

The windows of the earliest houses were undoubtedly of the early type with leaded diamond panes, but no specimens now remain in situ. There is a possibility that small square panes of the English type were experimented with at the end of the seventeenth century, but they could never have obtained any genuine foothold. Broadly speaking, the eighteenth century transition was to the French type of vertically halved casement window with heavy vertical bars closing into one broad centre bar, and with two lighter horizontal bars in each half (*see sketch*). The type seems to be quite universal; both

in urban edifices of every description, publick and private, and in all the rural cottages. Dividing bars were and are generally painted white. This type of window seems to have persisted to the present with very little interruption of use. A common tendency of early gable ends is to contain the chimney and to exceed the outline of the edifice in size, thus forming a sort of flange or false side. This occurs elsewhere, but in Quebec the discrepancies betwixt house and gable in size and even shape appear to be given an unique latitude (*see sketch on right*). There are many cases of a quasi-mediaeval gable end (*see sketch on left*) strongly like a type found with extreme rarity in Charleston—naturally sug-

gesting the Huguenot origin of the latter. Indeed, the visual resemblances betwixt the local street scenes of Quebeck and those of Charleston are—allowing for differences in terrain and occasional subtropical variants in the latter town—exceedingly numerous and well-mark'd. In the middle and later eighteenth-century, types of Quebeck domestick architecture seem to have become more sumptuous and vary'd. There were some square houses, with roof-slopes meeting in a point (*see small sketch*); the less steep-roof'd ones being not unlike the English Georgian models of the period (cf. Boswell's Brewery). More frequent, however, were tall, slant roof'd houses of a Parisian type—or at least, of types common in the best French provincial towns. Of these tall, slant-roof'd houses the choicest specimens are to be found along the Rue St. Louis, and in other streets near the old fort like Avenue St. Denis. In them we see many of the characteristics found in older and

smaller houses—such as flange-like gable ends, (tho' in these cases the flange effect is generally confin'd to the roof, not extending to the facade proper) steep roof lines, etc. The windows frequently have iron grilles or balconies—especially the lower ones. The doors are of a characteristic French type unlike our Georgian forms—tall and narrow, with high, rectangular pediments which, together with the jambs, frequently bear elaborate carving of Gallick renaissance of pseudo-classick baroque or rococo design. Flights of steps and railings are not frequent, steps being generally inside the street doors, just as in many old Boston houses the steps leading to the door are recessed inside open archways flush with the sidewalk-line. The tallness of these French doorways is sometimes very conspicuous—the door opening on the street from the sidewalk level, and the top of the pediment reaching as high as the top of the ground-floor tier of windows (*see sketch on right*). Doors were often double—vertically divided, as in Colonial Philadelphia. Tall French windows reaching to the floor are not uncommon on the ground story, and the upper windows frequently possess the French half-opening blinds common to Quebeck—blinds divided both vertically and horizontally like Dutch doors, so that the lower halves can be flung open whilst the upper halves remain clos'd. This sort of blind is so characteristick of every kind of Quebeck building—old or later, large or small, publick or private—that it deserves to be noted with particular attention. (*see sketch*). Another feature of some of the fine houses of this later eighteenth century period—especially brick houses—is the presence of vast shallow embrasures in the facades, sometimes surrounding a single window, and sometimes a group of two windows. This is a thing not absolutely peculiar to Quebeck, but follow'd there

to an extent making it typical. In general, the tasteful mansion of the Rue St. Louis may be said to tend toward height and narrowness; with steep roof, end chimneys, tall front doors, tall, floor-reaching, ground-story windows with outside grilles, half-blinds on upper windows, and (sometimes) large shallow embrasures in the facades. Coming into the nineteenth century, we find on every hand—and especially where the old town overflowed its eighteenth century limits, or was rebuilt after a conflagration—an overwhelmingly characteristic type of old-Quebeck small house or cottage, whose use also spread like wildfire to the adjacent villages. This type has a gambrel roof of tremendously steep lower pitch, like the antient Swedish houses of Delaware; but with that pitch curv'd—tho' not at all in the familiar Dutch manner. The type of curvature may be compar'd to that of the all-too-familiar "French roof" of American houses of 1870. In this steep curved lower pitch are (necessarily flattish) dormers; and sometimes there are dormers—small ones, and of naturally opposite proportions—in the upper, non-curv'd, and more horizontal pitch; thus sustaining the tradition of the French double rows of dormers. Virtually all the houses of this description have only one full story, tho' the steepness of the lower gambrel pitch makes the nominal half-story above virtually a second full story. In the case of the larger cottages with two rows of dormers, there is of course a second and very shallow upper story or attick. These houses all

have very heavily projecting eaves, sometimes supported by a line of prominent corbels (*see sketch at right*). The best and most frequent specimens with double dormer rows are to be found in the quaint old streets of the St. John suburb, leading uphill

toward the south from Rue St. Jean (*see sketch on left*). It seems probable that houses of this type were built quite late into the nineteenth century, in accordance with typical Quebeck conservatism, for the number of ugly and typically Victorian dwellings is relatively slight. The more recent houses of the city—including those now under construction—are of a peculiar and unique description, tho' not without resemblances to older Quebeck architecture; and are characterised in many cases by broad piazzas. They tend toward basements and more or less high flights of steps; and generally—when of the two-family sort—have a long curving outside flight of steps leading to the upstairs piazza and front door. Another type of house—probably suburban or semi-rustick when

built, as judg'd by style and location—resembles the trim New England suburban cottages of about 1830, and has a front doorway with sidelights and transom. The distinctive feature is the great proportionate *width* of the sidelights, plus the fact that they are often set with *shutters*. Transoms with shutters are also fairly frequent— and the general use of shutters on sidelights and transoms does not seem to be entirely confined to the type

of house just mention'd. The publick buildings of Quebeck are vary'd in style, an unfortunately large number being of Victorian date. They are not, however, among the worst specimens of their period; and their general Gallo-renaissance designs accord better with the prevailing old French architecture than they would with the Georgian architecture of an old New England town. Some of them attempt to reproduce old French forms of monumental design, and it cannot be said that such piles as the Château Frontenac and the Union Station are wholly unsuccessful. Among the more frankly Victorian edifices are the vast Parliament House, the City Hall, the Court House, and various commercial edifices. The post office, with its renaissance-classick leaning and golden dome, is much more meritorious; whilst the classick custom-house, profoundly British in conception, is really attractive. It is notable that *domes* are very infrequent things in Quebeck; those of the Post Office and Custom House being the only prominent specimens one can recall off-hand. Of recent-American terraced functional architecture there is fortunately only one specimen as yet—the tall Price Bldg. in the upper town. Even this has adopted the steep Norman roof in order not to clash too violently with the dominant architecture of the city. The really old publick buildings— Ursuline Convent, Hôtel-Dieu, (old part) Seminary, General Hospital, etc.—are admirably tasteful edifices, and reflect the highest credit on the seventeenth century architecture of the French. The accompanying sketch shews the earliest and best preserv'd

specimen — the General Hospital by the St. Charles, to which both Montcalm and Benedict Arnold were taken after their respective battle injuries. Many of these old buildings— especially the Hôtel-Dieu— have been plac'd at a disadvantage by ugly Victorian additions, and so far there has been no tendency toward restorations. Quebec, indeed, tho' noted for its historical scholarship, is not dispos'd to regard its antient monuments in a museum spirit; but continues to use them for their original purposes, adding such auxiliaries as are necessary to adapt them to current requirements. This is no doubt a result of that pronounc'd continuity of atmosphere which makes antient, conservative towns like Quebeck and Charleston so unique and fascinating. In such places, there is a lack of antiquarian care for the past because there is no sense of departure from the past. We do not try to recapture something which we are not conscious of losing, and in Quebeck the original cultural impulse and original set of folkways still function. One Quebeck building which deserves especial mention is the Archbishop's Palace at the head of Mountain Hill. Though apparently of Victorian date, chronologically, it is of a splendid eighteenth century design; without the least hint of the vitiated taste of the post-1830 period. As we have seen, there is very little British Georgian material in Quebeck; the only prominent surviving specimen, aside from the English churches, being the government storehouse at King's Wharf, erected in 1820. The city gates and towers of Quebeck belong to the 1870 period, and unhappily shew it. At a suitable distance, however, they loom up with ineffable charm.

The churches of Quebeck, in general, follow antient French traditions; having either tall slender steeples or less soaring belfries of rather open or skeletonic construction. Those belfry-steeples, which in urban Quebeck vastly outnumber the tall spires, have some resemblance to the less lofty steeples of Sir Christopher Wren, (his actual London work, and not the tapering later-Georgian spires erroneously attributed to him) and to the high, slender belfries of American churches, academies, and halls in the early Republican period. Their form is a very antient one, and has chang'd but little since the seventeenth century, as is attested by specimens (like that on the old chapel at Ste. Anne de Beaupré) which have surviv'd from that period. What makes them especially distinctive in Quebeck—aside from their immense numerousness, which results from the priest-ridden psychology of French Canada—is the antient local practice of surfacing them with gleaming tin; so that they glisten mystically and allusively in the sun, like the pinnacles and minarets of a fabulous silver dream-city. This custom of tinning extends to the roofs of other types of buildings; but nowhere is its effect so exotic, breath-taking, and fancy-stirring, as when it appears in connexion with a belfry-steeple—whether of a church, a seminary, a convent, an hospital, or any other sort of edifice. It is almost impossible to conceive of any urban vista more provocative of imaginative ecstasy, and of the sense of magical gateways opening on adventurous dream-worlds of exotick wonder, than a chance glimpse of one of these silver spires at the end of an ancient uphill or downhill street; ending with a touch of lunar necromancy a perspective laden with the mystery of years and forgotten secrets. Of such vistas, the town affords a very great number; especially in the western districts outside the walls or just within them. Particularly striking examples are the steeple of the Men's Congregational Church in Rue d'Auteuil (or Dauphine), seen from Rue St. Jean at St.

John's gate, crowning a breathless uphill prospect of antient roofs and city walls; that of the Sisters of Charity Church at Rues Richelieu and Glacis, seen downhill from Rue St. Jean through Rues Glacis or d'Youville; that of St. Jean Baptiste in Rue St. Jean, seen down Rue Claire Fontaine from any point high above St. Jean; and that of St. Roch, at Rues St. Joseph and de l'Eglise from many points in the St. John upper-town suburb. The great Basilica in the upper town has an impressive facade added about 1845, with towers as mismated as those of St. Sulpice in Paris, tho' in no way suggesting the latter. Of these towers one is crown'd by a belfry-steeple of the old French type. It would be impossible to enumerate all the picturesque belfry-steeples in a town fairly bristling with such objects; and one may add that part of their very charm lies in this dense and unidentifiable profusion—a profusion which adds an element of uncertainty, mysticism, and adventurous exoticism to many of the random glimpses we obtain. Of the slender, needle-like spires,

the oldest and most typical is perhaps that of antient Notre-Dame des Victoires (1688) at the original market-place in the lower town. This archaick fane, whose traditional setting has been well preserv'd, gives an exceedingly vivid idea of one phase of early French chapel architecture (*see sketch at left*). In urban Quebeck one does not see relatively many of the tall and somewhat grotesque steeples—obviously of nineteenth century origin—so typical of the smaller French-Canadian villages. Distant village spires visible from Quebeck and adding vastly to the loveliness of the landskip are those on the high Lévis cliffs across the river, that of Sillery, low down on a point near the shoar, as one looks up the St. Lawrence's north bank beyond Battlefield Park and Spencerwood, and those of Limoilou on the distant northward plain across the St. Charles. Of the English churches, the Cathedral of 1804 is by far the finest—a splendid and commodious Georgian fane whose stately spire would be eminently in place in any New-England town. St. Andrew's Scottish Church (1824) has another very tasteful old steeple. Chalmer's Church, in St. Ursula off St. Louis, up the hill toward the Citadel, is of Victorian Gothick design; but is by no means offensive. The interiors of many of the churches are of famous magnificence; tho' the French specimens generally seem too ornate, gilt-bedeck'd, and highly colour'd to suit English taste. St. Matthew's Anglican Church at the corner of Rues St. Jean and St. Augustin is a Victorian replacement, but has a fascinating old English churchyard containing the graves of His Maj$^{ty's}$ officers and executives, including the brother of Sir Walter Scott.

(2) Atmosphere and Topography.

Quebeck is a town which ought, if possible, to be seen at leisure, and in a gradual, rambling way; since its complex and manifold charm has a multiplicity of new subtleties to reward each new angle of observation. The general environmental keynote is one of antique loveliness, continuity, urbanity, and repose; with architectural grace join'd to a rural background whose influence is never absent. The rural setting is enhanc'd by the fact that the river and countryside are never remote from visibility. In the upper town there is no escaping the hinterland panorama, since every cliffward street ends in a broad vista of distant landskip. The sojourner in Quebeck is never lacking in orientation, for at all times he has around him a familiar setting of green hills and cliffs, blue sky and river, and distant purple mountains. Northward the farm-and-village dotted fields always stretch off toward the mystical Laurentians, with the bristling roofs and steeples of St. Roch or the lower town as a foreground. And on the south there is always the mile-broad river, with Lévis' frowning cliffs and picturesque roofs on the horizon. Loitering about the archaick streets, we begin to absorb impressions which in time seem to us characteristick of Quebeck. Clatter of horses' hooves—sweet bells from silver steeples—repose and cour-tesy—civilised, easy-going ways—symbols of His Maj$^{ty's}$ glorious and unbroken rule in the form of flags, the royal arms on post boxes, red-painted mail-collecting gigs, government shops, and shops in general—signs of sacerdotal supremacy—saints' names for most of the streets—constant encounters with black-rob'd priests and monks, and children in the black uniforms of convent and other popish schools—horse-drawn vehicles—antient calèches and delivery-wagons—watering-troughs—frequent use of *boards* for sidewalks and esplanades—glimpses of walls and gates—old men of courtly grace in old-fashion'd tail-coats and standing collars—policemen in tall white helmets—young men wearing low-crown'd derby or bowler hats like those of Jew comedians—profusion of low-pric'd restaurants along Rue St. Jean within the walls—absence of cafeterias and "one-arm" lunches—bi-lingual official signs—

Prenez garde	ARRET	Gardez la droite	NE STATIONNEZ
aux chars	DE	Keep to the Right	PAS ICI
DANGER	TRAMWAYS		NO PARKING HERE
Look out for cars	STOP*		

—street-signs in French, but without word "Rue"—car signs which translate French street names—

---

*Us'd in place of familiar New-England "white pole".

AVE. DES ERABLES
MAPLE AVENUE

—red modern tramcars, no opens—abundant lines—Gallick influence easily dominant in shop signs—"Reg'd", "Enrg.", L^{td} or L^{tee}, instead of "Inc."—Canadian stamps and currency—occasional English shops, especially in lower St. John, Fabrique, and Buade Sts. near the Château Frontenac and other first-class hotels—crowds of obvious tourists—sightseeing calèches, char-à-bancs, and roofless tram-cars—souvenirs everywhere obtainable—chain stores—Woolworth—Kresge—clerks sometimes speak no English—St. Roch and St. Sauveur wholly French—faded French grandeur in old mansions along Rues St. Louis, St. Denis, etc.—Château Frontenac roof always a landmark—hackmen at Lévis ferry greet incoming passengers in a row with pointed fingers, crying "Taxi! Taxi!" as predecessors used to line up and cry "Have a hack! Have a hack!" at New England railway stations long ago—cheap lunchrooms around Union Station—obvious lumbermen loitering on corners near the station, clad in gay Mackinac shirts or blouses—what American town north of Mexico has more of quaintness or distinctiveness to offer?

The more we study Quebeck in architecture and mood, the more we tend to compare it with Charleston as one of the sadly few remaining American strongholds of continuous tradition and social coherence. Topographically, however, it is level, regular, foreplann'd Charleston's utter antithesis; being virtually one mass of tangled and complex curves and unevenesses. Tho' mainly of two levels, the strip of shoar and the cliff-rais'd plateau, each of these levels has mark'd differences within itself. North of the cliff, the terrain of the lower town and of St. Roch slopes very considerably upward from the River St. Charles before it strikes the base of the real precipice; whilst the upper town slopes steadily up from north to south, making the general level the Rue St. Jean and the St. John extra-mural district substantially below that of the Rue St. Louis and Grande Allée. Continuing to climb, the plateau of course gains its summit on the extream south; where Cape Diamond forms a stupendous headland guarding the river, and bears upon its peak the fam'd and impregnable Citadel. From the grassy ramparts surrounding the citadel, the view is of indescribable impressiveness; enabling one to look down upon even the tallest spires of the Upper Town. One may climb up this turf slope from Dufferin Terrace near the cliff, and continue around toward Citadel Hill, where the main approach to the fortress stretches upward from Rue St. Louis just inside the walls. From a certain salient betwixt these two points, there is obtainable the most intoxicatingly beautiful view of Quebeck which can possibly be obtained—perhaps the most intoxicatingly beautiful view of any kind upon the North-American continent. On the extreme left, rising above a screen of foliage which softens and ex-oticises their Victorian lines, loom the colossal towers of the Parliament-House. Next to them snatches of ancient city wall and the turret of St. Louis Gate can be spy'd; and from this point to the extreme right of the view the foreground is one suburban sweep of wide, down-sloping turf border'd by a line of verdure which at the centre takes the form of a stately and exquisite row of tall poplars. The view ends on the right, just past the towering Château Frontenac, in the steeply-climbing height of Cape Diamond itself; with the grim outer-works of the citadel standing out against the sky. Betwixt these two extremes—the Parliament towers on the left, and the high citadel on the right—and above and beyond the foreground of turf and frame of poplars and other trees, stretches of the most marvellous urban and landskip panorama which the Western Hemisphere can afford. Tangles of steep antient roofs bristling with magical silver

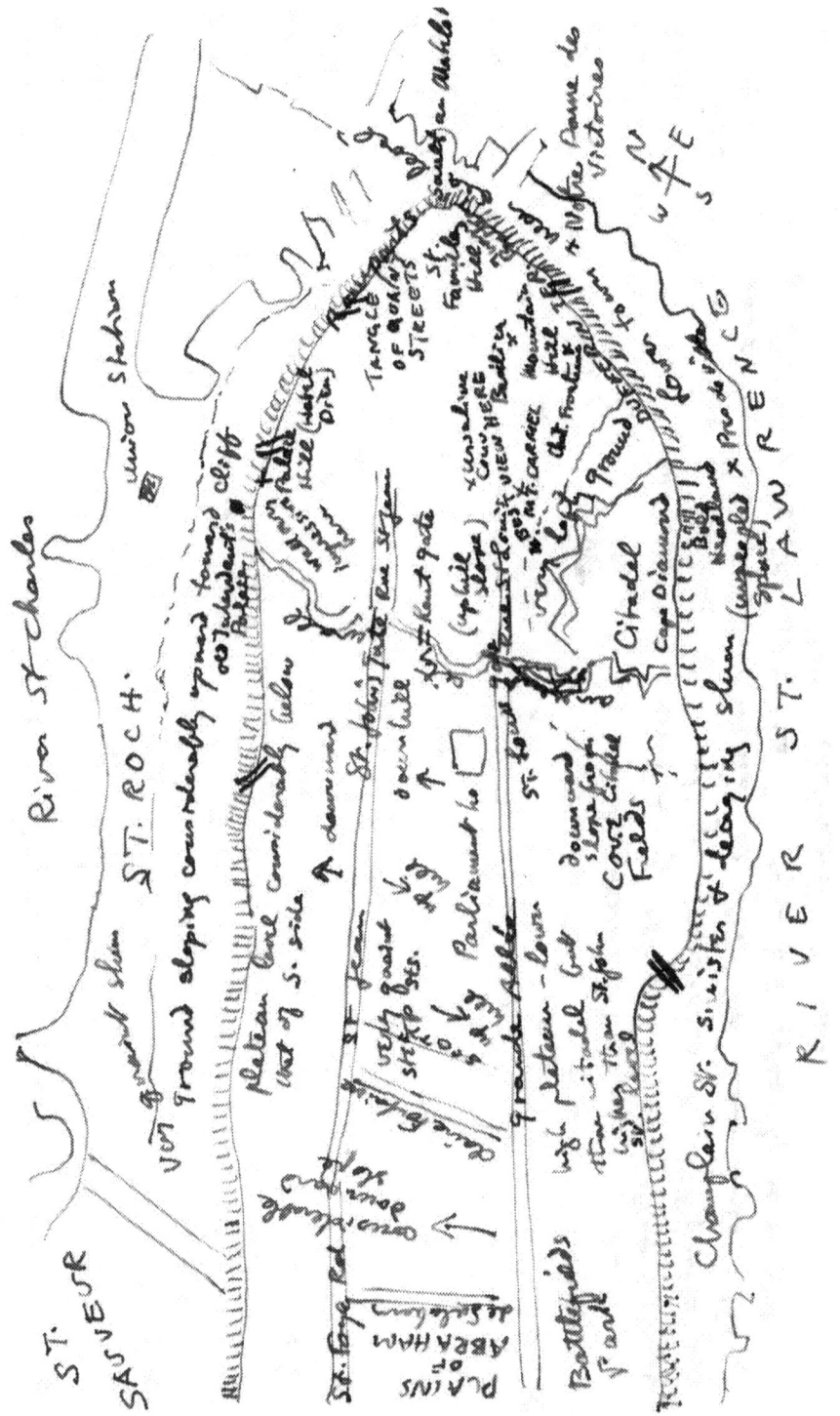

spires and belfries—seas of curious chimney-pots splashed with reds, silvers, greys, browns, and yellows—tall individual steeples and peaked roofs and towers—patches of alluring verdure at unexpected points—dizzy depths below depths, where the cliff drops sheerly to the labyrinth of lower-town roofs and spires—and beyond all the rest the dreamlike background of outspread blue river and green steeple-dotted country-side; land blending into water in graceful points and curves, and the whole vista bounded by the cosmic uncertainties of the purple, ethereal Laurentians and the cloud-dotted vault of heaven. The only jarring note—and even this is a minor discord because of its redeemingly archaick roof—is the skyscraping Price Bldg., built in 1929; but with a little care we may find a spot where this is almost wholly conceal'd by the spire of Chalmers' Church, leaving the vista absolutely traditional, and exquisite beyond imagination. The cliff edge in general, at different points, is arbitrarily divided into different "hills"—the principal ones being Palace Hill, above Palace Gate on the north edge, St. Famille Hill, at the Sault au Matelot, on the east point of the cliff where Laval University stands, and Mountain Hill, just south of this, where the main old road from the lower town climbs. Inland hills include Mt. Carmel, just back of old Ft. St. Louis and the present Château Frontenac; and Citadel Hill, the slope upward from Rue St. Louis and the Grande Allée toward the peak of Cape Diamond. Access from the lower town (Basse Ville) to the upper town (Haute Ville) is obtainable at several points by means of steps and ingeniously sloped or winding roadways, of which those near the old fort (Mountain Hill Street and the Breakneck Steps which rise from the head of Little Champlain and Sous-le-Fort St.'s in the lower town to the great bend in the street about ¾ of the way to the top) and near the old Intendant's Palace (Palace Hill) are the most ancient. Other connecting roads are Côte Sauvageau, which connects the St. Sauveur district with the upper town; Côte d'Abraham, which performs a like office for St. Roch; Rue Cicoton, which links St. Roch to the St. John suburb just outside the walls at Glacis St.; next comes Palace Hill and Canoterie-Hill and Rue Dambourges, which connect the old lower town with the ramparts of St. Famille Hill at the site of the old Hope Gate, one sloping down northward toward Palace Gate, whilst the other, beginning about ¾ way up its mate, slopes in the opposite direction, and is supplemented by a flight of steps by which the pedestrian can cut off the detour down Canoterie Hill which vehicles must take in order to strike Rue Dambourges. Next comes Mountain Hill, which is the last upward roadway. Flights of steps can be found at Rue de la Couronne, (St. Roch) leading to the upper town; at the foot of St. Augustin St. (upper town) descending to a point on Rue St. Valier (St. Roch) near the street (Bridge St.) leading to the highway bridge (Dorchester Bridge) to Limoilou; at Mountain Hill, (Breakneck Steps); and around on the south shore where an interminable flight of rickety wooden steps leads up from the crumbling Champlain St. slum near the old Hibernian Club to a board walk on the plateau which stretches across the still wild cove fields to a point on Ave. Laurier in the St. Louis suburb. There are also approaches of a sort at Battlefields Park, and the old scene of Wolfe's perilous ascent. At various other parts of the town shorter flights of steps serve to accommodate the picturesquely irregular terrain to the needs of the pedestrian. There is a passenger elevator (fare, 6¢) which ascends from the head of Rues Petit-Champlain and Sous-le-Fort (foot of Breakneck Steps) to a point on Dufferin Terrace near the hotel Château Frontenac.

(C.) Modes of Observing Quebeck

1. General Considerations

Upon landing on the Quebeck Union Station, the stranger is urg'd to adopt a systematick plan of sightseeing at once; in order to master in the shortest possible time the salient aspects of this antient and complex town. Only when the visitor knows his way about, is he fully at ease to enjoy the various antiquities and savour them at leisure. The first step is a good map and guide-book, and this combination can fortunately be purchas'd at the news stand of the station itself for the modest sum of 35¢. It is

Carrel's Illustrated Guide and Map of Quebec

publish'd by the Chronicle-Telegraph Company.[29] A careful study of the map will do much to enlighten the traveller on how he may reach the various points of interest. He will see that the stupendous cliff ahead of him, with its heights of Cyclopean masonry, its bristling roofs and spires and towers, and its antient climbing ways, is the logical goal for his first steps—the seat of all the most desirable taverns, shops, and tourist starting places. Accordingly, guided by the map, he will plunge adventurously into the past up the archaick slope of narrow Rue Lacroix; continuing up Côte du Palais as it curves at the left of a sky-reaching fortress-rampart, and finally passing at the top, where an ancient tavern-statue of Genl WOLFE peers down from a venerable carven facade upon the leading business intersection. This is Rue St. Jean or St. John St., the seat of the principal shops and restaurants. The Victoria Hotel at this very corner is an excellent stopping-place, tho' more sumptuous accommodations can be had at the celebrated Château Frontenac whose peaked Norman tower can be seen beckoning farther ahead. On the left we see a broadening of Rue St. Jean, where it divides into other thoroughfares the most extensive right-hand bend being Rue Fabrique, a broad continuation of the shopping district represented by St. Jean. This is the way to the Château Frontenac and the old Place d'Armes—the tourist centre. To reach the Place and Château one follows Fabrique to its end in Basilica Place—where the facade of the old Popish Cathedral marks the antient upper-town market—and crosses the square to Rue Buade, which roughly continues the line of Fabrique. After a block or two in Buade, a right turn into Rue du Fort (or its predecessor) takes us toward the Place d'Armes—which we reach after traversing another block. Slightly uphill, across a quaint small park, we see the main facade of the great Château Frontenac; whilst all around us are tourist offices and sightseeing vehicles—ancient horse calèches, motor char-à-bancs, and the clever roofless tramcars of the local street railway.

It is advisable, however, to become fortify'd with more guidebooks before attempting the conquest of Quebeck; hence the visitor who has just ascended Palace Hill to St. John St. may well look west along that thoroughfare—to the right. Here, largely on the north side, will be found the greatest profusion of moderate-pric'd restaurants; and here, too, after walking three squares, we come to antient St. John's Gate—or rather the site of it. This is a rather spacious open area, with an ineffably mystical and alluring vista on the left uphill where the great city wall rears for its southward stretch and the tapering silver spire of a church soars above the antient roofs of Rue d'Auteuil. On our right is the Y.M.C.A.; and after passing the wall and following the curve around the Auditorium Theatre we come upon a broader reach of Rue St. Jean—where it penetrates, still as a main street, the extra-mural St. John suburb. Here, downhill toward the northern cliff-edge on our right, we glimpse another silver spire in mystically alluring perspective—foretaste of sights to come. Proceeding along extramural St. John St., we soon encounter on our right the Woolworth and Kresge shops; where inexpensive souvenirs, pictures, and penny scenick postcards can be obtain'd in amazing variety. Among our purchases here shou'd be the fifteen-cent

Souvenir Guide of Quebec in Colours,[30]

which has splendidly concise and available information, fine views, and a map of the most antient upper and lower town districts on a larger scale, and in more conveniently consultable form, than the folding map of the whole town in Carrel's Guide. It is well, for the sake of convenience and unduplicated information, to procure a third guidebook also; for which purpose we continue along Rue St. Jean (either on foot or by Ave. des Erables/Maple Avenue street car) past St. Matthew's old Anglican churchyard (beyond a low bank wall on the left at the corner of Rue St. Augustin) and the impressive silver-belfried church of St. Jean Baptiste (on our right at the corner of the Rue Deligny). Betwixt these two churches the uphill street vistas on our left are especially deserving of attention because of the age of the houses, the quaintness of the steep streets with their occasional steps in the sidewalk, and the general collocation of ancient roofs and topographical features. This group of streets—Côte Ste. Genevieve, Scott, Claire Fontaine, etc.—deserve a later detail'd exploration. The downhill streets on the right also merit attention; since the bristling roofs and steeples of St. Roch below the cliff-edge, and the background of distant countryside and ethereal mountains, form an exquisite and unforgettable picture. At length Rue St. Jean forms a junction with Rue d'Aiguillon, which has been running parallel a block to the north, and changes its name to *St. Foye Road.* At No. 890—on the left-hand side—is the Quebec Information Bureau, design'd for tourists, where for 25¢ our third desiderate guidebook—

Quebec, Canada, How to See It—

may be obtain'd.[31] This has conveniently available statistics and information, useful maps, and a fine aërial view of the Place d'Armes section which will later assist in our orientation. This bureau will also give information concerning good inexpensive lodgings. If we wish to avoid a trip so far out of the city at the outset, we may previously order our guidebook by mail. The address of the Quebec Information Bureau is 890 St. Foye Rd., or P.O. Box 55, Quebec, P.Q., and its telephone number is 2-2655. If we are making our trip by motor, it is very convenient to approach Quebeck past this bureau. The route from Montreal is naturally the St. Foye Road; whilst if we come from New-England over the great Quebec Bridge, we shall come thro' Sillery and the St. Louis Road, farther south—reaching the St. Foye Rd. by making a left turn thro' Ave. des Braves, or Belvedere Road, which emerges at the park and Monument aux Braves dedicated to the heroes of Chevalier de Lévis's attack in 1760. If we prefer—and especially if we have a car to be lodg'd—we may secure rooms at some of the many cheap but comfortable tourist lodgings along the St. Foye Rd., of which the Maple Leaf House at #105 (cor. Bougainville) is an excellent specimen. The only disadvantage of this is the pedestrian distance from town—tho' this is offset by street-car service from Ave. des Erables, (not far in from where most of the lodgings are) and by the fact that distance from town means all the greater nearness to Battlefields Park and Wolfe's Cove. The maps in the guide books will shew how walks of varying length to Wolfe's Cove, the Governor's estate of Spencerwood, and even picturesque Sillery can be arrang'd from an headquarters on the St. Foye Road.

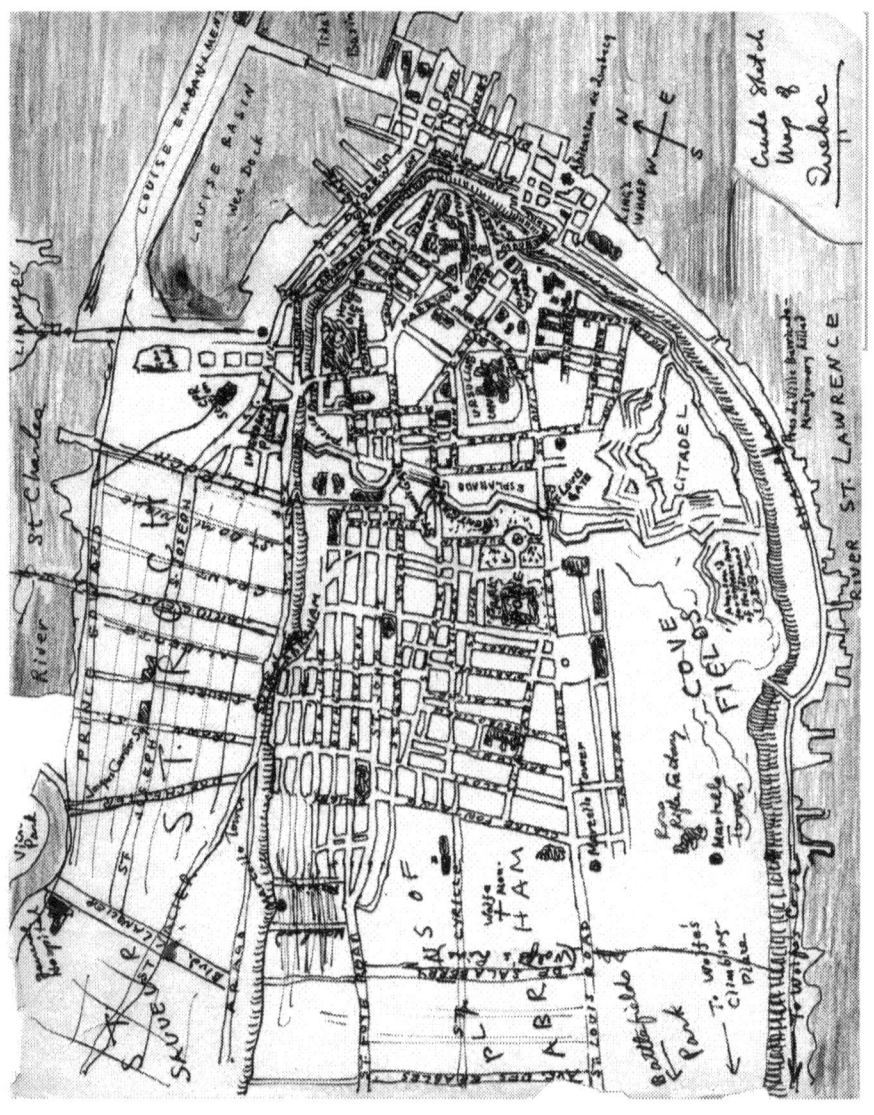

It is now in order to perform one or more orientation-tours in order to grasp the general geography of the town, the relative distances from place to place, and the juxta-position of the leading sights and landmarks, preparatory to a detail'd pedestrian explora-tion of the particular quarters which merit such. For this sort of preliminary touring, the standardised service of the various motor-coach sightseeing companies, and of the street-railway corporation, is strongly recommended as the cheapest and most comprehensive method. All the tours begin at the Place d'Armes—the coaches generally waiting on the lower or northern edge of the park whilst the roofless trolley-car waits higher up near the Champlain Monument and the end of Dufferin Terrace. The route of the various coach companies—Gray Line, Royal Blue Line, etc.—is identical, and the fare is $1.00 for the city trip of 1½ hours. (Their folders should be study'd for information on their longer suburban tours to historick spots.) The trolley company runs its roofless sightseeing cars over virtually all the trackage in the city at a cost of 50¢ per trip of $1^h 45^m$—with a special night sightseeing service (45 minute trip) at only 25¢. All cars and coaches have compe-tent lecturers, so that this service gives one a valuable introduction to the central town as an objective reality. The stranger is advis'd to take *both* coach and trolley trips despite the identity of much of the route. The repetition will be usefully instructive, whilst the unique parts of each trip will be valuable from any standpoint. The coach traverses many interesting places devoid of tracks, whilst the trolley covers a considerably greater area. Parts of these routes, of course, will be cover'd again when detail'd pedestrian explora-tions are made; but many of the less antient and important sections—the modern wharves, the lower-town suburbs of St. Roch and St. Sauveur, and the western part of the upper town—will not necessarily demand such a return—hence the tourist is urg'd to pay close attention to the discourse of the coach and trolley lecturers in order to grasp what is being pass'd. Sightseeing on the run is always unsatisfactory except for orientation purposes; but it is better than nothing, and a valuable aid in acquiring general impres-sions of districts not worth studying more closely. The coach makes stops to permit tour-ists to see the interior of old Notre-Dame des Victoires and the Franciscan Sisters' Church in the Grand Allée, but the trolley—as a rail'd vehicle on ordinary routes of traf-fick—naturally cannot do this. For the visitor of ample means, no mode of sightseeing is so good as a trip in a hir'd calèche; great numbers of which antient vehicles can be seen waiting in the Place d'Armes, mostly on the side toward the Anglican churchyard. The drivers are generally old men very familiar with the subtle traditions and folkways of Quebeck, and the individual nature of the service permits of digressions, reproportion-ings, leisurely assimilations, and the like which no standardised service cou'd provide. Persons with a vehicle may obtain the services of an individual guide (a competent driver) to accompany them and point out places and objects of interest—these being fur-nish'd by the Quebeck Information Bureau above mention'd, from which private motor vehicles for sightseeing may also be hired.

2. An Orientation-Tour of Quebeck

It is well to note here the salient points touch'd in the average Quebeck sightseeing tour. Starting from the Place d'Armes by way of Rue Ste. Anne, past the homelike An-glican Cathedral we turn to the right down the first intersection; (site of the house and store of the Company of One Hundred Associates) where (on our left after the turn) the garden of the great quasi-Victorian City Hall (site of old Jesuits' College) combines with Basilica Place just ahead to form a large open space. Basilica Place, where Rues Desjardins, (which we are traversing) Buade, St. Famille, and Fabrique converge, was the antient upper-town Market Place. On our left in the City Hall Garden is a vast

Monument to Louis Hébert the pioneer, and his family; the work of the French-Canadian sculptor Alfred Laliberté. In the middle of Basilica Place ahead (also call'd City Hall Square) is a circular park area, and here, placed asymmetrically, occurs a statue of Cardinal Taschereau, a late nineteenth century prelate who was Canada's first Cardinal. As we enter Basilica Place we turn a sharp corner to the right from Desjardins into Buade St., noting as we do so the great two-tower'd facade of the Basilica on the eastern side of the square, on our left. Beyond this, giving us a glimpse of the venerable edifice, is the entrance to the old Seminary. Proceeding along Buade for a double block (the same route that we travers'd in getting from the station to Place d'Armes), we come to the corner of Rue du Fort; where considerable space opens up, and we see the top of Mountain Hill—site of old Prescott Gate—ahead. Also in the vista is the great monument to Laval, first Bishop of Quebeck, which stands in front of the not unhandsome domed Post Office looming on the farther right-hand corner. On the left there is an obtuse-angled turn behind the Basilica, which we take; seeing on our left the handsome palace of the Archbishop, and on our right the restful expanse of Montmorency Park with its statue of the nineteenth century statesman Georges-Etienne Cartier, where the older Bishop's Palace, later serving as a Parliament house, and the second Parliament House, us'd to be—and where still earlier the settlement graveyard was situate. Montmorency Park leads off to the battlemented edge of the cliff, and on its right we see the drop of Mountain Hill—the park edge being a bank wall. Looking back at the P.O., we see in the main facade, over the door, the famous Golden Dog sign taken from the Philibert store formerly occupying the site. Proceeding toward the cliff-edge at the left of Montmorency Park, we note the ancient cannon rang'd along the parapet. This is the Grand Battery, and marks the beginning of a line of fortification which extends all the way around the cliff-point till it descends at Palace Gate. On our left is the wall of the antient seminary, to which is now added Laval University. We shall explore this later in detail. The quaint steeple of the University building is a notable Quebeck landmark. As we round the first corner of the Seminary wall we come close to the cliff-edge; viewing the distant river, countryside, and mountains, peering at the dizzying sea of tangled roofs and chimney-pots below, and noting the increas'd rusticity of our surroundings. Soon we turn sharply to the left at the Sault au Matelot, leaving the Seminary wall behind us. Next comes the descent of Canoterie-Hill—old Hope Gate—on our right, and we note the numerous embrasures in the cliff-edge parapet with old guns standing guard. We are now on the Ramparts, and the houses on our left were once among the most fashionable in Quebeck. At #40, near the corner of the Rue Hamel, Montcalm once liv'd. The road now becomes a steep descent, and there appears on our left the high wall of the venerable Hôtel Dieu, which we shall later revisit. Soon we are at Palace Gate, on the higher level of the lower town at the foot of the cliff; and the Cyclopean height of the city wall topped by the antient Artillery Barracks (now the Dominion Arsenal, where munitions for the Canadian Army are made) looms up ahead on our left. This is the most impressive of all possible aspects of the artificial defences of Quebeck. On our right, where two steep streets lead down to the neighbourhood of the Union Station, we see an old corner building with a newer one next it. This is Boswell's brewery, on the site of the famous Intendant's Palace, which we shall inspect later. We now make a precarious hairpin turn into Rue St. Charles, doubling back in general direction and skirting the lower edge of the cliff as we have been skirting the upper edge. This is the scene of Benedict Arnold's attack on the lower town, his severe knee-wound having occurr'd here. Rue St. Charles meets Rue St. Paul at the foot of Canoterie-Hill; and we now turn into St. Paul, an wholesale thoroughfare of no great charm. As we pass the foot of Rue Dambourges, a descent contributory to Canoterie-Hill, we see (on our right, of course) the entrance to a very narrow lane in the lee of the cliff which leads off from Dambourges to run onward parallel to our own course in Rue St. Paul, and separating us a trifle from the great beetling precipice from which the guns and embrasures of the Ramparts frown down. This is the celebrated Rue Sous-le-Cap, "narrowest street in Canada", and we shall study it later tho' the sightseeing vehicles do not commonly enter it. Soon we reach the point just below the Sault au Matelot, noting the turn of the cliff and the opening of the narrow Rue Sault au Matelot—which Arnold's men storm'd in 1775—on our right. In another moment we ourselves turn to the right into St. Peter St., which continues the trunk route along the base of the cliff. A short block brings us to St. James St.; where there is a considerable confluence of ways as Rue Sault au Matelot touches St. Peter on its parallel course, and as narrow Rue Sous-le-Cap finally ends its tortuous length by emptying into St. James. This is the scene of the invader's defeat and capture in 1775, and a bronze tablet on Molson's Bank commemorates the event. St. Peter St. is the financial section of Quebeck, and here the U.S. Consulate may be found. At Rue des Soeurs we make a jog to the right into the narrow and picturesquely antient Rue Notre-Dame, which shortly spreads out into a small quiet square lined by ancient houses, having a circular grass plot and fountain in the centre, and bounded on the farther side by an old steep-roof'd chapel with graceful, needle-like spire. This is the original market place of the lower town, tho' long obsolete as such; and the church is the celebrated Notre-Dame des Victoires, built in 1688. The coaches stop here to permit tourists to visit the interior, which is well adorn'd and supply'd with works of art. We shall return to this spot in later explorations. Proceeding ahead, at the right of the church, we emerge from the square and turn to the right up narrow, picturesque Rue Sous-le-Fort, near which Champlain had his original 1608 Abitation. The cliff, here crown'd by the stately Château Frontenac and the beginning of Dufferin Terrace, looms up ahead with ineffable grandeur. As we reach the cliff itself and turn to skirt its bottom, we see on our right the foot of Breakneck Steps, which lead up to the former Prescott Gate near the top of Mountain Hill. Here Champlain had his original chapel of 1615, and here, according to some, he was buried. The old settlement spring was also here. The street into which we make a left turn to skirt the cliff-base is narrow, ancient Rue Petit-Champlain; which has no sidewalks, and which (but for its slum decay) would well represent a typical lower-town thoroughfare of the old French regime. The right-hand row of archaic houses is solid, and presses close against the cliff. On the left there are occasional gaps with short flights of steps leading down to a parallel street which runs near by at a slightly lower level. Mendicant children add to the Neapolitan picturesqueness of the scene. Finally we come out at what seems the end of the town—nothing but cliff rounding away on our right, and nothing but abandon'd wharfage and the river appearing on our left. We shall later learn that more does indeed exist around that deserted and mysterious cliff-bend, but for the present we double back over the slightly lower-levell'd street which here rises to form a junction with Petit-Champlain. As we turn, we note the vast increase of height of the cliff ahead. This is Cape Diamond, from which the Citadel frowns down. Houses once existed at this point, but they were wip'd out by a landslide in 1889 which kill'd 66 persons. Farther around the bend is the site of Genl. Montgomery's death on Dec. 31, 1775, at Près-de-Ville barricade. Doubling back, we follow Champlain St., which is nearest the water. On our right the Marine and Fisheries building marks the site of the old King's Wharf and Louis XV's Royal Naval Shipyard of 1746. Here is the old British government storehouse of 1820, one of the few truly Georgian-design'd edifices in Quebeck. To the left the omnipresent

cliff looms up, its sides somewhat cover'd with verdure—a sight of unparallel'd magnificence in its sweep from the lofty citadel behind us to the tower of the Château Frontenac ahead—with the antient roofs of the houses far below the rampart-line of Dufferin
Terrace. Now and then we can see the gaps or alleys which lead up a few steps into Rue
Petit-Champlain, and which we saw before from the other side. After a moment the
buildings on our right cease, leaving only a railing between the street and the wharves.
Ahead is a sharp right turn to the east which takes us out away from the cliff for two
squares' distance. Then a left turn back to our original northward direction, and in a
moment we are on that broad waterfront plaza forming the present publick market—
Champlain Market, whither the farmers bring their produce each Tuesday and Saturday. We are now on the main local waterfront from which the Lévis and Orleans ferries,
and all the river steamers—for Montreal, Thousand Islands, and Toronto up stream,
and the Saguenay down stream—leave. Later it will be well to cross to Lévis and view
the Quebec skyline from there. This is the general region of Champlain's landing and
site of his Abitation de Quebecq. Proceeding along Dalhousie St., we come at length to
the classick Custom-House near the water's edge, but turn to the left into St. Andrew
St. before getting a good front view of the pillar'd facade. On our right we now see the
recent harbour developments—Louise Basin, the docks of the ocean liners, the Grain
Elevator, and the immigration buildings. We shall not detour to visit the monument to
Abraham Martin the Scotsman—first river pilot and owner of the land west of the town
later call'd the "Plains of Abraham"—which stands on Louise Embankment beyond the
Basin. We now draw landward again, taking a general westerly direction as St. Andrew
joins Rue St. Paul and leads us past the familiar Norman roof'd Union Station. The station is on our right; whilst our left is the same stupendous panorama of climbing roofs,
bristling towers and steeples, and Cyclopean city and arsenal wall which so impress'd us
upon our first entry to the town. Also on the left is the hotel Château Champlain, on
the site of the Intendant Talon's residence. Rue St. Paul is very broad and spacious here,
and we follow it till it makes a slight left bend on crossing Rue St. Roch, after which it
takes the name St. Joseph and becomes a busy shopping district. We have just enter'd
the suburb of St. Roch, now a part of the city, which form'd the seat of Benedict Arnold's encampment of 1775. Old buildings are rare, except in certain parts, since this
district has been repeatedly swept by prodigious fires. At Rue du Pont we see on our
right the great Dorchester Bridge which takes all highway traffick to Limoilou, Beauport, and the antient north shore generally. St. Joseph is St. Roch's main longitudinal
business street, and contains some notable establishments—such as the Laliberté fur
shop on our left, founded in 1867—to which the tourist lecturers call attention.
St. Roch is not quite equal to the upper town in tone, and very little English is spoken in
it. On our right, at the corner of Rue de l'Eglise, we see the enormous bulk of St. Roch
church with its silver belfry; and in the next block on the same side we behold St. Roch
Convent. We are now at the corner of Crown St., or Rue de la Couronne, which is
St. Roch's main transverse business street. This intersection, known as Jacques-Cartier
Square, contains the Hôtel St. Roch (right) and the Jacques-Cartier Monument (right).
At this point some of the coaches turn directly up Rue de la Couronne to the left toward the cliff—thro' a shoemaking district—but others continue out St. Joseph to the
broad Boulevard Langelier, which marks the boundary of St. Roch and the beginning of
the St. Sauveur suburb, now a part of the city. This suburb was nam'd for the early cleric
St. Sauveur. If we turn'd down the Boulevard to the St. Charles we would come upon
the antient General Hospital, which we must later explore in detail; but unfortunately
the coach turns southward, to the left in the direction of the cliff. The usual route here

is to turn again toward the left into Rue St. Valier (nam'd from the 2nd Bishop of Quebeck), which takes a diagonal course toward the cliff. Or the Rue St. Colomb, with a subsequent jog, may be used. This is one of the few remaining antient sections of St. Roch—never prosperous, and now a picturesque slum. Some very quaint houses can be seen, and throngs of mendicant children are usually visible, pleading for "pennies" (the one English word they know) from the passengers of the sightseeing vehicles. St. Valier reaches the cliff at the head of Dorchester St.—nam'd for Genl Sir Guy Carleton, Ld Dorchester—whilst St. Colomb ends in Rue Belleau, which leads into Rue Arago; the latter the cliffside street west of Dorchester, where it forms a junction with St. Valier. If we were to alight and stroll down Dorchester as far as Rue St. Hélène, we would see in the latter—next the NE corner of Dorchester—an obviously old house which presents a puzzle in the strongly New-Englandish cast of its architecture. Marks on another building some distance along St. Hélène suggest that this was once one of three. It is a 1½ story gambrel-roofer of astonishingly Yankeefied type, like the now demolisht Peter Randall house in Providence; the roof lines being of distinctly Novanglian proportions, the doorway having fluted pilasters and a plain transom. Of its history no record seems to be available; but it is difficult to believe that it and its vanish'd fellows were not built by some New England immigrant in the years following the conquest of Canada by His Maj$^{ty's}$ arms. We shall not, of course, see this if we remain on the coach; but it is certainly worth a special visit (as long as it is permitted to stand) from every New England traveller.* The coach now approaches the head of Rue de la Couronne, where on our right a dizzy flight of steps scales the cliff to the St. John district on the plateau. In our vehicle, however, we ascend the gradual glacis known as Côte d'Abraham—recently enlarg'd—gaining the upper level near the foot of Rue St. Augustin. On the left there is considerable open space, and we glimpse the Patronage orphanage for boys, and the more distant silver belfry-steeple of the Sisters of Charity church. Now gaining St. John St. and turning westward—to the right—we see on the SW corner of St. Augustin the antient churchyard of St. Andrews, with the grave of Thomas Scott. This is the district which we have possibly traversed before, in seeking the Quebec Information Bureau; but it will pay us to glance again to the left for the quaint uphill street vistas, and to the right toward the cliff for glamorous glimpses of lower town, distant countryside, and hazy Laurentian Mountains. Of the left-hand uphill streets, Ste. Geneviève, Scott, and Claire Fontaine most merit inspection. Here we find houses of the abundant early XIX century French type, with gambrel roofs having a steep lower pitch and mark'd overhang. Passing the church of St. Jean Baptiste on the right we follow the increasingly unpicturesque St. John westward beyond the junction where it becomes the Ste. Foye Rd. If we now digress down Rues Racine or Marchand to the cliff-edge, we shall see one of the Martello Towers. At Rue de Salaberry our course passes the north end of Wolfe's battle-line of 1759. Beyond Ave. des Erables, on the left, we see the large edifice and extensive grounds of the wayside church—Notre-Dame des Chemins. This is a region of sacerdotal and charitable institutions, and we see many embower'd in spacious grounds amidst the quiet suburban atmosphere where pleasing maples line the way and prove the right of Canada to her national symbol. Here, also, are the roadside tourist lodgings previously mention'd. Some distance beyond Notre-Dame des Chemins, in what is still largely open country, we reach the scene of the Battle of Ste. Foye in 1760, when Chevalier de Lévis forc'd Genl Murray to retire behind the city walls. Here, on the right, is a small park containing the Monument aux Braves, a fluted Dorick column sur-

---

*This interesting edifice now (1933) demolished.

mounted by a statue of Bellona, created in 1860 to the memory of the combatants. If our course allows for a digression to the cliff-edge, we may thence obtain a marvellous panorama of St. Sauveur's bristling roofs and spires, of the distant church at the Huron village of Lorette, and of the always mystical line of ethereal Laurentians on the ultimate horizon. This is the western limit of our trip. The Ste. Foy Rd. continues 180 miles to Montreal, but we now turn south—to the left—into Belvedere Rd. or Ave. des Braves, traversing a recent real estate development and entering the St. Louis Rd., which leads westward to Sillery and the Quebec Bridge. Our first town is to the left— eastward—toward the city—but we presently make a right turn into Battlefields Park; a former race course which in 1908, at Quebeck's tercentenary, was dedicated to the contending armies of 1759, and which contains several guns then captur'd from the French. This park forms the southern edge of the plateau just east of Wolfe's Cove and climbing-place; and is therefore on the route travers'd by Wolfe toward his final battle-line on the now built-over Plains of Abraham. The cliff-edge is form'd into a promenade and driveway with convenient parapets, known as Earl Gray Terrace (from the Gov. General at time of dedication), and from this place of vantage may be obtain'd some marvellous vistas. Looking westward—to the right as one faces outward toward the cliff-edge and river—we may see Wolfe's old-time point of ascent not far off, mark'd by a small round white house. In the same direction, embower'd in a spacious wooded park, we may descry the low, rambling white mansion of the Lieutenant Governor—Spencer Wood or Spencerwood—which bears a curious resemblance to a Virginia plantation-house. Farther away—on a point of land jutting out into the river and marking a lowering of the plateau level—we may see the lone, picturesque spire of Sillery Church silhouetted in tall grace against the water. Across the river rise the bold cliffs of Lévis, exact counterparts of those on which we are standing; and beyond them can be glimps'd the dim purple peaks of the Allegheny Range. Facing east toward the city, we see at the farther end of the park the stately column of the Wolfe monument, marking the spot where that hero fell, and the gleaming marble facade of the new museum—still incomplete. Just beyond the park limits are the district gaol—straight ahead—and the Quebeck Observatory Tower, somewhat to the right. Proceeding onward, we pass to the right of the Wolfe Monument, and finally turn back into the St. Louis Road—which from this point to St. Louis Gate is called the Grande Allée, and forms the most fashionable residence street of the modern city. This broad, well-shaded avenue is, of course, roughly parallel with the more northerly arterial line of St. John St. and the Ste. Foy Road, and forms its counterpart as a trunk thoroughfare. As we proceed, we behold evidences of the slow conquest of modern Quebeck by the apartment-house—tho' all the local specimens seem to make sound concessions to the old French architectural tradition. The vast Château St. Louis (left) is so far the largest apartment building in the city, but we shall shortly encounter another nearly as large. At Rue de Salaberry we cross Wolfe's old battle-line, seeing on the left St. Bridget's church—in the rear of which, on ground now occupy'd by St. Patrick's School and the Redemptorist Monastery, was the old cholera burying-ground. At about this point—or a little before—we can glimpse on our right the Quebeck observatory tower; and presently, in the same direction, the Ross Rifle Factory, now a Canadian Ordnance Depot. Nearer than the factory, but at about the same point in our vista to the right, (encounter'd perhaps a trifle sooner) is one of the 1812 Martello Towers, which has a still-existing underground passage to the distant citadel. About opposite this tower—on our left at the corner of Rue Claire Fontaine—(which form'd the approximate limit of Georgian or early XIX century Quebeck) is the well-known chapel and convent of the Franciscan or White Sisters, whose custodians have needlework and various ecclesiastical articles for sale. A stop is generally made here by the sightseeing coaches. Proceeding onward, we see on our left (cor. Scott St.) the new church of Saint-Coeur de Marie—one of many sacerdotal and charitable institutions in this neighbourhood. On the other side of the street is the spot where Montcalm was mortally wounded, and where we now behold a monument dedicated to him in 1911. Looking again to the left, we see the Grande Allée Apartments, second only to the Château St. Louis in size. The right-hand vista now opens out into a small square park recently nam'd Place George V in honour of His reigning Majesty, at the back of which extends the broad facade of the Drill Hall or Armouries. In this park is the monument to Short and Wallick, the soldiers who lost their lives bravely fighting the St. Sauveur fire of 1889. On the left there now appears the parklike square in which is set the great Parliament house of 1878. On the grounds before the street facade is a fine statue and monument to the eminent historian F. X. Garneau, author of the "Histoire du Canada"[32] whilst a little farther along, in the landscaped space beyond this facade, is a monument to the nineteenth century statesman Mercier. The main facade of the building is that facing the city at right angles to the Grande Allée; and by looking back we can appreciate its tower'd stateliness as it looms above the parklike expanse separating it from the city wall. The view ahead is now alluringly picturesque, the turreted and parapeted arch of St. Louis Gate giving a massive mediaeval frame to the huddle of steep roofs and facades marking the older intramural town within. Just before we enter the old town we see on the right a grassy uphill slope next to the ancient wall. Here stands the white and graceful Cross of Sacrifice erected to the memory of Quebec soldiers who fell in the World War. Inside the walls we see on the right the uphill road to the citadel, with the fashionable Garrison Club on the farther corner. A little way up this road, on the side next the wall, is the old military storehouse where Montgomery, Cheeseman, and Macpherson were buried. On our left is the esplanade, once a parade-ground, with the Boer War monument not far from the street. Just beyond it the single row of ancient houses in Rue d'Auteuil, facing westward, slopes gently downward toward the north; the steep roofs, chimney-pots, and traditional French facades affording a picture of the most fancy-stirring sort. Along that row, as it begins to dip more steeply in the distance, the alluring silver spire of a church rises up to add a touch of ethereal unreality. We are now in Rue St. Louis—of which the Grande Allée is the extra-mural prolongation—which in old times was the fashionable residence street of Quebeck. The neighbourhood is now genteelly decay'd—small retail shops and lodging-houses punctuating the residence more and more thickly as we approach the Place d'Armes. The houses are nearly all fine old French mansions; and most of them are still in excellent structural condition, so that a study of their details will amply repay the antiquarian. On our right, behind the steep roofs and chimney-pots, rises the spacious green slope toward the citadel; which beyond the Rue Ste. Ursule receives the name of Mont Carmel. At the NW corner of St. Louis and Ste. Ursule is the site of the old City Hall, and approximately of the house where Montgomery's body was taken. Looking up Ste. Ursule, we see the Gothick spire of Chalmers Church outlin'd against the green of the hillside. Advancing along St. Louis, we soon see on our right an old stone double house with broad flat chimney—#s 59 and 57. Half of this was, in the earlier eighteenth century, the home of Intendant Bigot's mistress Mme. de Péan, whilst the other half (#57) nearer the city, was the doctor's house where Montcalm dy'd. Buildings along this row are largely connected with the Canadian army. Just below this stone house, we find the Military Hospital. We now see, on the left-hand side, the opening of a short street leading to the ancient Ursuline Convent; which we shall later revisit, and where Montcalm's mortal remains are deposited. Just beyond on the same side is the precipitously steep-roof'd old house—1674, the oldest in Quebec—where Montcalm had his headquarters. Across the street and ahead on our right is the old Lotbinières house, inhabited 1791–4 by H. R. H. the Duke of Kent, father of Queen Victoria. This virtually brings us back to the Place d'Armes, and we see the elaborate Court House on the farther left-hand corner. On the right near corner is the imposing hotel Château Frontenac, on the site of the old Fort and Castle St. Louis, and of the Château Haldimand of 1784. Rounding the corner past the Château's main facade, we come to the Champlain Monument and beginning of Dufferin Terrace with its unequall'd view. Once more we are in the Place d'Armes, convenient as a centre from which to take more detail'd and observant pedestrian trips.

3. A Series of Pedestrian Explorations

The general fountain-head of sightseeing interest in Quebeck is, unmistakably, the region of the old Fort and Place d'Armes—of the modern Château Frontenac and Dufferin Terrace—in the upper town. This being the centre of things in old French times, it has retain'd the greatest crowding of historick reliquiae; as well as possessing the finest vistas of the St. Lawrence, the Lévis cliffs, and the countryside as a whole. Near by are the Basilica and old Market Place, the antient houses of Rue St. Louis, the old Ursuline Convent, the Seminary, the head of Mountain Hill—a burying-ground from 1606 to 1687, and later the location of formidable Prescott Gate and the old Bishop's Palace which became a Parliament-House, (present Montmorency Park) the English Cathedral, the Governor's Gardens with Wolfe and Montcalm monument, Mt. Carmel, and the steep grassy ascent to the all-crowning citadel. Over the sheer edges of the precipice bristle the gables and chimney-pots of the Lower Town, with the slim, needle-like spire of old Notre-Dame des Victoires standing out as a focus of attention. It will repay the visitor to cover this section very fully, using the Place d'Armes as the hub of a wheel whose spokes are brief tours of exploration.

The Place d'Armes

The Place d'Armes itself, an attractive square with a park in the centre having walks, trees, benches, and a central Monument to Faith (commemorating the first missionaries), slopes gently downward from south to north. Eastward there is an open sweep of vision toward the cliff and the river where the great Monument to Champlain (er. 1896) stands near the beginning of Dufferin Terrace. This square is the concourse of all sightseeing vehicles and enterprises—calèches, omnibuses, roofless trolley-cars, and the like; and often echoes to the shouts of rival tour-conductors. It was antiently a scene of battles with the encroaching Iroquois—before the building of the city walls—and subsequently form'd the camping-place of the remnant of the Hurons after the annihilation of their nation and before their settlement at Lorette. Still later it was a military parade-ground and promenade of fashionables under the French governors—being then known as the Grande Place. Here the French finally surrender'd their arms to Murray in 1759. On the higher or southern side, at the beginning of Rue St. Louis and marking the site of the old fort and Château St. Louis of Champlain (1620) and Montmagny (1647), (burn'd 1834) and of the 1784 Château Haldimand, stands the massive and imposing hotel of the Canadian Pacific Railway, the Château Frontenac. This vast and rambling pile, with an old-fashion'd central courtyard having archways on Rues St. Louis (Place d'Armes also) and Mont Carmel, was begun in 1892, later added to, and restor'd after a disastrous fire in 1926. Its great Norman tower with corner turrets is a landmark visible from all over the city, and still dominates the skyline despite the erection of the Price Bldg. Despite its Victorian date this structure has real beauty, and succeeds in giving a suggestion of the glamorous seventeenth century. On the archway fronting Rue St. Louis and the Place d'Armes is a keystone bearing a Maltese Cross and the date 1647. This is thought to have been prepar'd by Govr Montmagny, who was a Knight of Malta, for a priory of that order in Quebeck, which for some reason was never built. Betwixt the Château and the river is the beginning of Dufferin Terrace, a broad wooden promenade on the cliff-edge which extends for 1500 feet toward the Citadel and connects with a walk taking the pedestrian completely around Cape Diamond to the Cove Fields. The average width is 60 feet, and at intervals along the edge are kiosks or pavilions where band concerts are sometimes held. The terrace is suitably rail'd, and benches are placed for those who wish to enjoy the magnificent view of the river, the Lévis cliffs, and the Isle of Orleans—perhaps the finest view in North-America save that obtainable from the still greater height of adjacent Citadel Hill. It is a fashionable promenade for residents and visitors alike, and is of course clos'd to vehicles. Seen from below, its foundations are tremendously impressive. 160 feet of this terrace were constructed by Ld Durham during his regime, the original name being Durham Terrace. In 1854 it was prolong'd to 276 feet; and in 1879, under the auspices of Ld Dufferin, it was extended to its present length and receiv'd its present name. The beginning—where the great Champlain Monument now rises close to the Château Frontenac—is built over the foundations of part of the antient Château St. Louis, where that formidable and historic edifice beetled over the sheer 200-foot precipice. On the north or lower side of the Place d'Armes—across the park and opposite the Château Frontenac—still stands the steep-roof'd Union Bldg. (#12 Rue St. Anne) erected in 1805 on the site of the old Govr. d'Ailleboust's residence of 1649. Here, as previously mention'd, the Barons' Club held its festivities in the years following 1808; and here too the Parliament of Lower-Canada for a time had government offices. In this building defensive measures against the invaders of 1812 were plann'd. On the west side of the Place d'Armes, where Rue St. Anne leads out of it, we behold the rear of the Anglican Cathedral built in 1804 and forming a homelike touch of English Georgian amidst this predominantly Gallick environment. The site of this fane, and of the antient Court House, was in 1650 occupy'd by the Court of La Senéchausée, and in 1683 was purchas'd by Mgr. de St. Valier, second Popish Bishop of Quebeck, as a site for a new Récollet Monastery, since he wish'd to use the old one on the St. Charles River as a General Hospital to be conducted by nuns from the Hôtel Dieu. The new Récollet Friar's Convent and Church were finish'd in 1693; and tho' technically confiscated (along with other popish property) by His Britannick Majesty's Government upon the acquisition of New-France, were not in fact taken from the monastick tenants. Upon the establishment of an Anglican Bishoprick in Quebeck under the Revd Jacob Mountain in 1793, the Récollets permitted its services to be held in their church; and when in 1796 both convent and church burn'd down, His Maj$^{ty's}$ government decided to utilise the area. A court-house (burn'd in 1873 and replac'd by the present one) was built upon the more southerly half, adjoining Rue St. Louis, in 1800; whilst upon the northerly half adjoining Rue St. Anne the present splendid Ionick edifice was rais'd in 1804. In the north gallery of this church is the Governor's Pew, where have worshipp'd not only the various representatives of His Majesty, but many members of the Royal Family itself. There are several reliques of notable interest, including the antient colours of His Maj$^{ty's}$ 69th Regiment, which for a time garrison'd Quebeck. Adjoining the churchyard and occupying the corner of Rue St. Louis just across from the Château Frontenac is the Supreme Court House or Palais de Justice, a Victorian relique which is perhaps not as bad as contemporary structures in the U.S.

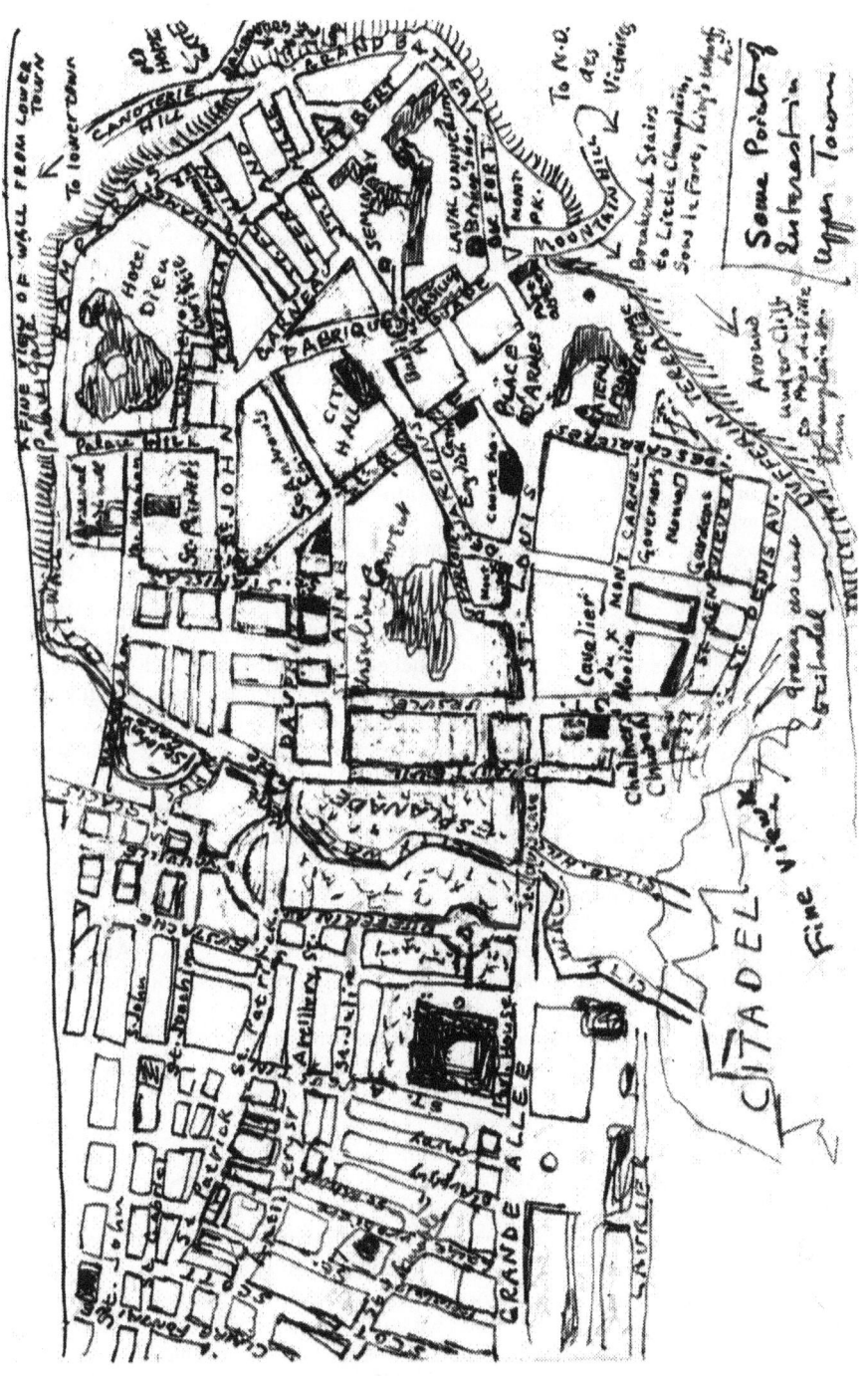

Mount Carmel and Rue St. Louis

Having completed a survey of the Place d'Armes, we may well undertake our excursions therefrom, starting with the inland region behind the Château Frontenac represented by the slope toward the citadel and the length of Rue St. Louis. Rounding to
the rear or southern side of the Château, we see Rue Mont Carmel ascending an incline away from Dufferin Terrace, and having as its first intersecting street the Rue des
Carrières, which runs beside the Terrace at a higher level, separated from it by a bank
wall. Extending back from des Carrières and running beside Mont Carmel on our left is
the pleasing old park known as the Governor's Gardens, toward the front of which
stands the granite obelisk erected in 1828 (repair'd 1871) to the memory of Wolfe and
Montcalm. "Mortem virtus communem, famam historia, monumentum posteritas,
dedit." As we proceed past the Governor's Gardens, we find the aspect of Rue Mont
Carmel growing more and more rustick; till finally the houses on our right end and give
place to a bank wall and declivity, within which are the remains of an old stone redoubt. Ahead, a gate bars our way, but reveals alluring semi-rusticity beyond. A tablet
informs us that this is the site of Le Cavalier du Moulin—the stone mill whence Phips
was bombarded in 1690. This region—Mount Carmel—is one of the loveliest in all
Quebeck, with fragrant and graceful lilacs, and picturesque vines and greenery draping
the antique ruins. It was once, according to tradition, an Indian cemetery. We now
return to Rue des Carrières and walk along it past the front of the Governor's Gardens,
continuing to the last street which ascends the slope before the steeper rise to the
Citadel on the south ends the urban section. This final street—Ave. St. Denis—has
some of the finest old French houses in Quebeck—as indeed has Ave. Ste. Geneviève
which precedes it and bounds the Governor's Gardens on the south. Ascending either
Ste. Geneviève or St. Denis, we emerge on the southern end of Rue Ste. Ursule, into
which we make a right-hand turn. As we pass northward—downhill again and away
from the citadel—we have on our left the modern but not unpleasing facade and steeple of Chalmers' Church. Soon we emerge upon Rue St. Louis, once the most fashionable of all Quebec residence streets, and still containing traces of departed grandeur in
buildings long since given over to light commerce and shabby-genteel lodgings. Many
of the old French mansions along this thoroughfare are fine architectural specimens,
and deserve the most careful study of the antiquarian; though their condition does not
average so good as that of the houses in St. Denis and Ste. Geneviève. At the intersection of St. Ursule where we emerge, the old City Hall once stood on the NW corner,
close by the house of the cooper Gaubert, to which the body of Genl. Montgomery was
taken on the morning after his death. This house was demolish'd only in recent times,
to make way for a more pretentious residence—for Rue St. Louis here emerges from its
decay'd phase and prepares for its aristocratic status as the Grande Allée beyond St.
Louis Gate. Turning to the left into St. Louis and proceeding westward toward the
gate, we come upon the Esplanade—a former parade-ground just within the walls on
our right, now a publick park. Here stands the monument to Quebeck soldiers who fell
in the Boer War. Ahead looms the stately St. Louis Gate with its tower, turret, and
steps; on either side of which the great turf embankment of the city wall stretches away
and bends into angled bastions. On our left Citadel Hill climbs southward to the main
or Dalhousie Gate of the Citadel—now permanently tenanted by the 22nd Canadian
Regiment—where, if we have the time, we can secure permission to explore the great
fortress under guidance; beholding the various bastions and buildings, gates, vaults,
cells, and underground passages, and such reliques as a cannon captur'd from the re-

bels in 1775 at Bunker Hill, and another taken from Montgomery's invading force. The S.E. corner of Citadel Hill and Rue St. Louis contains the tasteful edifice of the Garrison Club, Quebeck's most exclusive social organisation. Just above this, on the other side of the roadway next the wall, is the old military storehouse which in 1776 was a military prison—and in whose yard the bodies of Montgomery, Cheeseman, and Macpherson were interr'd. Cheeseman and Macpherson still rest there after exhumation and reinterment, and a bronze tablet marks the spot. Just beyond the St. Louis Gate, on the north side of the Grande Allée, (prolongation of Rue St. Louis) stands the great Parliament House of 1878; an imposing Victorian pile whose main facade fronts the ancient wall, from which it is separated by a well-landscaped park expanse. If we wish to inspect this, now is the time. The building, with interior court, forms a perfect square with facades of 300 feet; 4 stories tall, with mansards and towers at each corner. The main tower on the front or cityward facade is the crowning feature, and affords an unrivall'd view. Before the main entrance is a bronze Indian group by the Canadian sculptor Hébert (descendant of the pioneer), whilst in niches on the facade are heroick statues of the great men of Canadian history—Frs. Bréboeuf and Viel, martyr missionaries; La Vérendrye, the explorer; Intendant Talon; Gov. Boucher; Count Frontenac; WOLFE; Montcalm and Lévis; De Salaberry; Lord Elgin; Sir H. Lafontaine; Baldwin; Guy Carleton, Ld Dorchester, etc. etc. On the grounds are monuments to the historian Garneau (situate before the Grande Allée facade) and the statesman Mercier (on the front plot at the corner of the Grande Allée). Across the Grande Allée just west of the Parliament house is Place George V, an open area at the rear of which is the local drill hall or Armouries, and in whose centre is the Short-Wallick monument, dedicated to the two soldiers who lost their lives whilst bravely fighting a fire in St. Sauveur in 1889. Behind the Drill Hall are the Cove Fields, and by looking far to the right we may glimpse one of the Martello Towers. Saving more westward objects for a separate excursion, we now return to St. Louis Gate; noting the Cross of Sacrifice just outside the wall uphill on the right—dedicated to the Quebeck soldiers who fell in the World War. Passing inside the walls thro' the small right-hand sidewalk and under the gate tower, and proceeding along Rue St. Louis, we retrace our former course to Rue Ste. Ursule—after crossing which we reach territory not travers'd before. Here we keep watch on the right-hand side for historick buildings. Many of the structures here—including the military hospital—are connected with the Canadian army. One of the buildings—the old Union Club—was the place of confinement of U.S. prisoners taken at Detroit in the War of 1812. Behind them rises the green and lovely slope of Mt. Carmel, much the same now as in the old days. At Nos. 59 and 57 we find an ancient double house of stone, of two and a half stories with broad, thin, gable-end chimneys and a long row of dormers. Both halves of this house—despite some ambiguities of identification—seem to be historically connected; for #59 was the abode of Intendant Bigot's mistress Mme. de Péan, whilst #57 was the home of Dr. Arnoux the younger, garrison surgeon for the French army at the time of Wolfe's siege—and the place where the illustrious Montcalm breath'd his last. After 1759 both halves were us'd as quarters for His Maj$^{ty's}$ officers.

We now see, across the street on our left, the beginning of short, bending Rue du Parloir; which, before its termination in Rue Desjardins, leads to the entrance of the fam'd old Ursuline Convent, from whose *parlour* it was nam'd. This celebrated institution deserves a visit from us; hence we shall digress in order to pay it. The street bends toward the right, and the convent entrance is plainly discernible. The grounds are enormous, extending back to Rue Ste. Ursule and across to Rue Ste. Anne; and the wings of the rambling, composite stone building are all steep-roof'd, double-dormer'd affairs of the antient French pattern. On the chapel is a pleasing belfry of the old traditional sort. The Ursuline nuns, headed by the Venerable Mother Marie de l'Incarnation and accompany'd by their patroness Mme. de la Peltrie, arriv'd in Quebeck in 1639 and stopt provisionally at the house of Noël Juchereau in the lower-town Market-Place (present square in front of N. D. des Victoires). Later they were transferr'd to Sillery, and finally, in 1641, to their present location. The first monastery was burnt in 1650, and rebuilt. The present one, burnt in 1685, was rebuilt in 1687 and enlarg'd three times during the present century (1900–12–15). The first chapel, on land presented by the Co. of 100 Associates, (also formerly containing the house built for Mme. de la Peltrie in 1644 and occupy'd 1650–61 by Bishop Laval—replaced by a school bldg.) was built in 1656 and burnt in 1686. The second chapel was built in 1720, and enlarg'd in 1901. Very fortunately, the additions have sustain'd the spirit of the original—instead of taking tawdry and inharmonious forms as in the case of the Hôtel Dieu. This convent is fam'd as a seat of education for the daughters of Catholick gentlemen, both of Canada and of the United-States. The founder, Mother de l'Incarnation, who lyes entomb'd in the cloister, was a woman of great sagacity and ability; often consulted by the governing authorities, and a truly prominent factor in the early development of New-France. In 1759 the illustrious Montcalm was here interr'd by the sisters—one of whom, Esther Wheelwright, was curiously enough of the race and nation of his conquerors; a Wheelwright of the old New England line, great-granddaughter of that Revd John Wheelwright who founded Exeter, in His Maj$^{ty's}$ Province of New-Hampshire, in 1638. She had been stolen from the frontier post of Wells, in Maine, in 1703, at the age of seven; her French and Indian captors taking her to Quebeck as was so often the custom with prisoners.* Here she was adopted by the French Governor and converted to the Popish faith; finally becoming an Ursuline nun.† At the time of Montcalm's burial, some of her very close kinsfolk were amongst the conquering legions of WOLFE; tho' both she and they were insensible of the circumstance. Later on this gentlewoman rose to be Mother Superior of the Convent— the only English person ever to hold that important distinction. She dy'd in the year 1780, aetat 84. In the winter following the taking of Quebeck, this convent form'd the barracks of Fraser's Highlanders; and official measures of importance were here transacted. In 1783 the body of Montcalm was brought to light during repairs to a wall; being reinterr'd all but the skull, which has since been preserv'd in a glass case and is exhibited to visitors. In the convent are many ecclesiastical reliques—a suppos'd skeleton of St. Clements, brought from the Roman catacombs in 1687; the reputed skull of one of St. Ursula's companions, brought in 1675; the alleg'd skull of St. Justus, brought in 1662; one of the numberless pieces of the singularly extensive and durable True Cross, brought in 1667; and a choice portion of the Crown of Thorns brought from Paris in 1830. The convent likewise has a library of 12,000 volumes, and a plenitude of ecclesiastical paintings of great merit. There are many important memorials, and a votive lamp which has been lighted since 1717. Returning to Rue St. Louis as we came, we continue toward the city another square. There—at #32½—on the nearer left-hand corner of the down-sloping Rue Desjardins, we behold the ancient "lightning

---

*Her father, learning of her fate, left her £100 in his will, to be given her if she return'd to New England—which she never did.

†In 1754 she was (by special permission of the Bishop) visited by her nephew, Maj. Nath: Wheelwright, who gave her a miniature of her mother, Mary (still at the convent), and gave the convent some fine linen and a silver flagon, knife, fork, and spoon.

splitter" where Montcalm had his headquarters, and which is by good authorities consider'd the oldest house in Quebeck, having a date of 1674. This edifice—now housing the Hwaiking Oriental Shops—is worthy of careful study, as affording a clue to the general aspect of the Quebeck of the Frontenac period. Its rambling juncture with its neighbours on both streets is highly picturesque. On the other or right-hand side of Rue St. Louis, somewhat nearer to Place d'Armes—at #23—we now behold the Chartier de Lotbinière house, inhabited from 1791 to 1794 by H. R. H. the Duke of Kent, father of Queen Victoria, who was in Canada as Commander of the 7th Royal Fusiliers. This was his town house—his country-seat having been, as we have seen, the former mansion of Genl Haldimand at the falls of the Montmorency. The edifice, which stands a little back from the sidewalk-line, is now commercially us'd; and has been rais'd a story since His Royal Highness's time. We now take a few more steps into the Place d'Armes beside the Château Frontenac, and are ready for explorations in another direction. This time we shall take a long ramble thro' many connexion sections, including the antient lower town.

Mountain Hill

Next we proceed northward, out of the lower end of the Place d'Armes, along Rue du Fort, to where the way opens out at the top of Mountain Hill, and the end of the domed Renaissance Post Office rises up on our right. Turning the right hand corner into Buade St., we have on our right the main facade of the P.O., and on our left the great Laval Monument—beyond which, across Mountain Hill, the restful expanse of Montmorency Pk., with the monument to the statesman Georges-Etienne Cartier, stretches off to the battlemented cliff-edge. This is the site of old Prescott Gate—or rather, that site is somewhat below—just before Breakneck Steps leave Mountain Hill. From the end of Buade St.—at the far corner of the P.O.—a flight of steps descends to Mt. Hill to cut off a long corner around the Laval Monument. Looking backward toward the left beyond the Laval Monument, we see, facing the top of Mt. Hill, the tasteful palace of the Archbishop and the beginning of the Seminary wall. Ahead, Mountain Hill slopes down and turns a gentle corner to the left, preparatory to turning another very sharp leftward corner as it performs its swerve to the north—finally to strike the lower-town level at the joint heads of Rues des Soeurs and Notre-Dame, where the old Quebeck Gazette was printed in the eighteenth century. This is the main artery betwixt upper and lower towns in their oldest parts. At the middle stretch betwixt the gentle and the sharp turns, the top of Breakneck Steps, leading to the joint heads of Rues Sous-le-Fort and Petit-Champlain, opens narrowly on the right. To the left of Mt. Hill Montmorency Park extends—its stone retaining wall growing higher and higher as the hill accelerates its drop. This park marks the site of the first graveyard (1608–1687) of the old palace of Archbishop de St. Valier, used as a Parliament-House from 1791 to its burning in 1854, and of the second dom'd Parliament House built in 1859 and burnt in 1883. The P.O.* is on the site of the old Philibert store built in 1735, (as shewn by a cornerstone found when the edifice was demolish'd) and has set in its major facade the famous gilded store sign—the Chien d'Or or Golden Dog, which the proprietor plac'd on the old building to signify his resentful feelings toward the rapacious Intendant Bigot and his cheating monopoly La Friponne. (See sheet X.1.) A study of this old sign—whose story Kirby has told in the novel "The Golden

---

*The main fort of the Hurons, who camp'd around the Place d'Armes in 1658, was about here.

Dog"—will amply repay us. At a later date the old house was kept by the British ex-soldier Miles Prentice as the Masonick Hall Sun. Now crossing to Montmorency Park, we note the warlike parapets and old cannon at the cliff-edge. This is the beginning of the Grand Battery, which extends around the top of the cliff for an ample distance. At the end of Mont. Pk. is a modern platform with benches where we may sit at the for-tify'd cliff-edge and enjoy the magnificent view of river, lower town, and distant coun-tryside and mountains. On our left the Seminary and University wall approaches the cliff and turns a corner to run parallel to it. If we now follow the gentle declivity of the Grand Battery and wall around the tip of St. Famille Hill past the Sault au Matelot—above the spot where Arnold's troops were repuls'd in 1775—we shall soon come upon the Ramparts, at the site of Hope Gate where Canoterie Hill and Rue Dambourges de-scend to the lower town; where, too, Montcalm once dwelt. Streets leading inland from these Ramparts strike an exceedingly quaint and ancient district; which is also conveniently approachable from the main business junction at the tip of Palace Hill, where Rue St. Jean forks into wide Fabrique St. (extending to the right uphill to the Basilica and forming a continuation of the high-class business section) and narrow Rue Couillard, that curves along to the left into picturesque antiquity. This district deserves the most minute study from the artist and the antiquarian, for it is the best surviving example of an old French neighbourhood, with the houses still unalter'd and in such quantity as to give each one its perfect original setting and environmental atmosphere. Perhaps the best way to approach this ancient quarter is through either end of its cen-tral trunk artery—Rue Couillard winding mysteriously eastward from the end of St. John St., or Rue Hébert penetrating inland beside the Seminary wall from the Grand Battery at Sault au Matelot. Rues Couillard and Hébert are sections of the same thor-oughfare, such changes of name being common in all old towns of Europe and Amer-ica, tho' nowhere else surviving to such an extent as in Quebeck. To see this quarter at its best, one must walk slowly along Rue Couillard-Hébert, glancing up and down every cross street in both directions, and occasionally exploring one of them. The cream of this district is along the Couillard section of the thoroughfare, where the cross streets lead upward (on the right if we proceed eastward from St. Jean, as is perhaps preferable from the standpoint of dramatick unfolding) to Rue Garneau, and downward to the Ramparts, with the vista ending in the remote blue of the harbour, with its warehouses and shipping. These streets, in order from the end of St. Jean along Couillard, are Christie, Hamel, St. Flavien, Ferland, St. Famille, and St. Monique. St. Famille is the last which ascends to Rue Garneau, and it is well to follow this up to the latter, so that one may return to St. Jean along Garneau, looking down along all the streets to the right (Seminary wall on left) in order to see them in a fresh perspective. Garneau itself is exceedingly quaint. This neighbourhood was once very fine, the eminent French-Canadian historian F. X. Garneau having lived and dy'd at 14 Rue St. Flavien, which is mark'd by a tablet. At 22 Rue Ferland the first French newspaper in Quebeck was pub-lish'd—*Le Canadien*, 1806—the office being raided by the troops of Lt. Gov. Craig be-cause of its political policy. The Ramparts, at the foot of these streets, form'd a very fashionable place of residence in the eighteenth century; Montcalm having liv'd at No. 40 (at foot of Hamel), where a tablet marks his house. Houses hereabouts are of the dominant eighteenth century French type, with half-opening blinds, tall doors, casement windows, chimney-pots, and all the accustom'd attributes in untainted form. The streets are still neat and well kept, tho' the neighbourhood has declined to a re-gion in which hotels and rented rooms are frequent. This is, in general, the seat of the residences of the pioneer Louis Hébert and his son-in-law Guillaume Couillard, as street-names indicate. The house of Couillard form'd the first house of the Seminary, and stood in the grounds of the latter. Tho' this region is neglected by guidebooks, it is not unknown to artists of taste and discrimination; many of whom can sometimes be found sketching in the streets.

The Old Lower Town

The antient lower town which fringes the bottom of the cliff from Palace Gate on the north, around the Sault au Matelot to King's Wharf, beneath Fort St. Louis (Château Frontenac) on the south, is worthy of long and careful exploration. One may conveniently descend from the Ramparts (foot of Rue St. Famille) by means of Rue Dambourges, cutting down the steps from Canoterie Hill in order to save distance. The lower level thus gain'd is built up with old houses—the same, in many cases, that Benedict Arnold's men saw in 1775—and beneath some of these are the vaults of still more antient commercial buildings. Rue St. Paul, a wholesale mercantile street which curves from the foot of Palace Hill to follow the turn of the cliff, was the seat of the rapacious Bigot's stores—La Friponne—and is the chief lower-town thoroughfare from the north until the eastward point of the cliff is reach'd. It then digresses into a wharf, and gives place to the southward intersecting Rue St. Pierre or St. Peter St. (French and English street names seem to be us'd quite indifferently throughout Quebeck) as

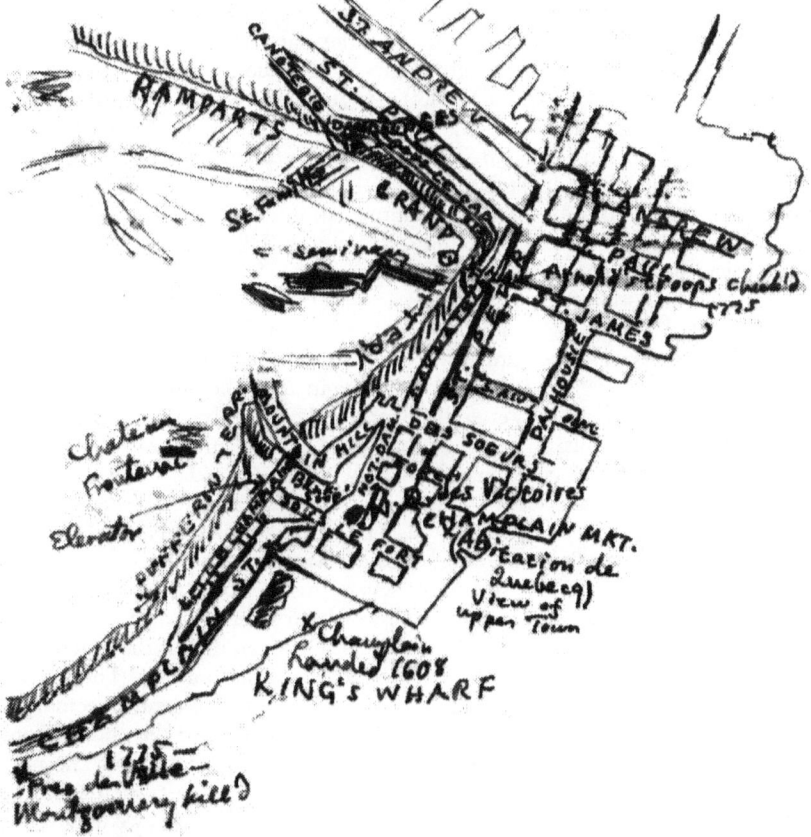

the dominant trunk-line prolongation. St. Peter St. is a financial thoroughfare, and is especially rich in English banking firms. Though St. Paul and St. Peter Sts. roughly follow the foot of the cliff, they are not actually the closest streets to it; there being another line of narrow streets or alleys directly under the damp stone precipice. The first which we encounter in descending Rue Dambourges is the famous Rue Sous-le-Cap, widely advertis'd in guidebooks as the "narrowest street in Canada". This opens to the right, off Rue Dambourges just before St. Paul is reach'd; and is a slum of mark'd squalor, tho' it was once a commercial street of standing. With the houses of its inner side press'd close against the rough stone of the cliff—which occasionally shews its moss-crusted surface betwixt and high above them—this narrow and tortuous lane is always in a damp, sinister twilight; a condition intensify'd by the custom of building houses across the street from upper story to upper story, which makes the sidewalkless board highway a virtual tunnel. Some of the decrepit and malodorous houses of Sous-le-Cap have rickety wooden outside staircases by which second and even third stories are reach'd; these sometimes leading to the overhead bridges across the roadway. In width, Sous-le-Cap is barely large enough to admit one vehicle. The width is variable, owing to irregular building lines and occasionally projecting steps; but in no place could two ordinary vehicles pass. After two sharp bends corresponding to the eastern tip of the abutting cliff, Sous-le-Cap makes a right-angled left turn at the Sault au Matelot and comes out at the point where Arnold's troops were repuls'd in 1775—the place where narrow Rue Sault au Matelot and broader Rue St. Pierre run parallel and nearly contiguously, (parallel to the cliff, and to the last lap of Sous-le-Cap before the right-angle turn) and are intersected at right angles by the Rue St. James (which latter prolongs the line of Sous-le-Cap's final outlet). At this general concourse of ways a bronze tablet on a building (Molson's Bank, cor. St Peter and St. James) marks the repulse of the invader. God Save the King! We may now proceed down Rue Sault au Matelot, which from this point onward replaces Sous-le-Cap as the closest under-cliff street. It is antient throughout its length, and affords an interesting study for the antiquarian. At Rue des Soeurs we strike the foot of Mountain Hill, which bends upward to the upper town around the bank wall of Montmorency Park and past the site of Prescott Gate. Here, in one of the old houses against the cliff, the antient Quebeck Gazette was publish'd. Beyond Rue des Soeurs the line of Rue Sault-au-Matelot is roughly (with a jog to the right) continu'd by Rue Notre-Dame, which leads to the antient lower-town market place (no longer such) where in 1639 the newly-arriv'd Ursuline and Hôtel-Dieu nuns, with the Venerable Mother Marie de l'Incarnation and with their patroness Mme. de la Peltrie, lodg'd at the house of Noël Juchereau des Chatelets, a relative of the first seigniors of Beauport, and where in 1688 the stone Chapel of L'Enfant Jésus (now Notre-Dame des Victoires) was built. Here, also, Intendant de Champigny erected a bronze statue of Louis XI. The church, renam'd Notre-Dame de la Victoire in 1690 after Phips' defeat, and N. D. des Victoires after the wreck of Sir Hovenden Walker's fleet in 1711, is still (after several restorations) in fine condition, with steep roof and needle-like spire; and is well worth an interior inspection. It contains some celebrated works of ecclesiastical art, including a painting of the crucifixion supposedly by Rubens, and one of St. Geneviève attributed to Van Loo. The houses around the former Market Place are mostly antient ones, and in the centre, facing the church, is a grassy mound bearing a bronze bust of Louis XIV. Behind the church from shore to cliff runs quaint old Rue Sous le Fort. Following this (or better still, the narrow Rue La Place which precedes it) to the shore, we strike the vast open space of Champlain Market—the present publick market. Looking up to the cliff, we obtain the most impressive possible vista of the Château Frontenac and Dufferin Terrace towering dizzily over the lower town's steep roofs and the green and grey cliffs. Near this market was Champlain's original 1608 Abitation. From here, also, the modern ferries and steamers largely leave. At the head of Sous-le-Fort, under the cliff, was the old chapel of 1615 (burnt during the Kirby siege of 1629)—and also the settlement's spring. Proceeding up to this, we find on our right the dizzy iron flight of Breakneck Steps, leading to the bend near the top of Mountain Hill. The steps—originally of stone, were formerly much more winding, steep, and picturesque; but middle nineteenth century alteration gave them their present form.* Against the cliff we see the great elevator leading to Dufferin Terrace above and can imagine the grandeur of the scene when old Ft. St. Louis beetled over the brink, as it did prior to 1834. On the left the narrow, sidewalkless and antient Rue Petit-Champlain, with its steep roofs, broad, thin chimneys, and crumbling dormers leads along under the edge of the cliff. Following the latter, we behold a street as quaint as any in Marblehead or Charleston; with mendicant children reminding one of the small Italian boys in Boston's North End. The right-hand side is a solid row of houses against the cliff. On the left, there are occasional gaps with short flights of wooden steps leading down to the closely parallel street which runs at a slightly lower level. Eventually we reach a junction with this street not much beyond the old King's Wharf, where in 1746 King Louis XV establish'd a Royal Naval Shipyard, and where Marine and Fisheries Hdqrs. now are. Some distance back to the left we see the old Government storehouse built in 1820 and bearing the date with the magick initials G. R.[33]—one of the few British Georgian buildings in Quebeck. Ahead, along the shore under the cliff, a compleat absence of all buildings seems to indicate the ending of the town. Proceeding onward and looking more closely, however, we discover the foundations of edifices which once were there; and presently we notice that the cliff on our right is wall'd up to a considerable extent by artificial masonry. This is the scene of the great landslide of 1889, when a portion of the cliff fell upon the houses then standing, killing 66 persons. Continuing along the deserted roadway—Champlain St.—we presently see a tablet on the cliff marking the site of the Près-de-Ville barricade, where Montgomery was kill'd in 1775. At length, after traversing a distance equal to several city squares, we come upon houses again; and find something almost spectral in this disjoin'd and half-forgotten district whose existence so few land travellers to Quebeck ever suspect. As we grasp more details, our impression of the spectral and the macabre increases; for we see that this suburb indeed has something of death about it, in that all of its houses are mere shells of immemorial decay, whilst frequent gaps in the rows on both sides tell where buildings have been demolish'd or have collaps'd under their own weight. Squalor everywhere reigns, and many of the still-standing houses are deserted; either tightly boarded up or gaping open with sashless windows and empty doorways. The bare cliff, here towering up to a stupendous altitude, since we are now at Cape Diamond below the lofty citadel, has an especially malign and terrifying aspect when glimps'd through the gaps caus'd by the vanish'd houses; and we come to weave disquieting dreams wherein we connect some hideous, palaeogean rock-sentience and evil purposiveness with the slaying of the 66 so many years ago, and with the general blight and disintegration which have fallen upon the whole district. There were houses below Cape Diamond at a very early date, forming the section call'd Neuville; but these do not seem to have reach'd as far as Près-de-

---

*In 1866 a vault was found at the foot of this flight—thought by some to be Champlain's tomb, tho' doubtful.

Ville, since accounts of Montgomery's attack speak of the wild and narrow nature of the shore path from Wolfe's Cove. The present structures, however, must have been built not long afterward; since their architecture is of a very early type. We first hear of this district as inhabited by Irish families, of whom (as attested by the building of commodious St. Patrick's in 1832) there were once a great number in Quebeck. At a bend in the road, where the cliff juts out beyond the citadel in bow-window fashion, we may still see the commodious building of the Quebeck Hibernian Club; now in a dingy state tho' not in actual disrepair. Close to this, an endless flight of rickety wooden steps leads up to the Cove Fields, beside some abandon'd fortifications built by Gen¹ Haldimand in 1783, and connects with a board walk stretching to Laurier Ave. and the Grande Allée. Looking sharply to the left from this walk we may see (near Ross Rifle Factory) one of the Martello Towers; another being visible nearer the Grande Allée. The Champlain St. district, by the time of the 1889 landslide, had sunk to a slum, and it has probably retrograded still further since then. The present population, which seems as much French as Irish in all places, and wholly French as one proceeds farther along the shoar, seems to be engaged mostly in fishing if one can judge by the wharves and boats that line the water. Beyond the steps and the Hibernian Club the houses thin, but soon thicken again as we reach what is evidently the distinct French fishing village of Cap Blanc. Here, at the water's edge, and reach'd from the road thro' a picturesque yard with flagg'd walk, is the quaint seaman's chapel of Notre Dame de la Garde. Beyond Cap Blanc there is access to Wolfe's Cove and Sillery along the shoar, tho' the region is but little settled. The Champlain St. district, sever'd tho' it is from the city proper, is nevertheless reach'd by an omnibus line. One section of it is locally known as Les Foulons, perhaps because of some long-vanish'd fulling-mill.

A Circuit of the City Walls

The antient *city walls* of Quebeck deserve a study by themselves; and the wise visitor will not omit a compleat circumnavigation of them—walking along their summit when possible. They remain virtually compleat, except for the demolish'd St. John's, Palace, Hope, and Prescott Gates; and do not seem to be at all threaten'd by modern "progress". The walls as a whole enclose a liberal area of the upper town, and were so wisely plann'd that urban growth did not cause them to be overflow'd by solidly compact streets till the later eighteenth century; tho' the suburb of St. John had early develop'd outside St. John's Gate on the principal road to Three Rivers, Montreal, and the upper St. Lawrence Valley generally. This is in strong contrast to the case of Charleston, whose meagre wall'd area, lay'd out in 1680 and re-fortify'd in 1703, was so inadequate to future needs that the town had far transcended it by 1720—causing the walls to be demolish'd bit by bit from then onward, till shortly nothing but one of the pointed bastions remain'd (still surviving as the "Old Powder Magazine" in Cumberland St.). The Quebeck city wall begins—reckoning from the southwest—at the Citadel, and forms a continuation of the outer works of that stronghold. It crosses the plateau to the northern rim as a towering rampart of earth-fill'd masonry rising sheer from the downward-sloping ground-level, and having four projecting casemated bastions along its course. Along this western stretch are three gates—St. Louis Gate, still existing after reconstruction in the 1870's, where Rue St. Louis passes outside the walls and becomes the now-fashionable Grande Allée; Kent Gate, also surviving in reconstructed form, where Rue Dauphine forms an egress, and changes into St. Patrick St; and St. John's Gate, now demolish'd, where the great arterial business street, Rue

St. Jean, leaves the wall'd area. An exploration of the walls may well begin at the cita-del—forming a continuation of an observation-stroll on that elevation, or of a walk along Rue St. Louis, or of a tour of the sinister Champlain St. slum, in which latter case we gain the plateau by means of the steps behind the Hibernian Club, and reach the citadel over the Cove Fields plank walk and the easterly end of Ave. Laurier. From the citadel northward we may walk along the broad turf top of the wall; an excellent path, supplemented by planks and bridges where necessary, being provided for the purpose. As we follow the angles of the bastions we may obtain some excellent vistas, not only of the town, but of other parts of the wall itself. Crossing over St. Louis gate with its stone steps, platform, parapets, and towers, we find ourselves on a stretch flank'd on either side by open park-like areas—the Esplanade, an abandon'd parade-ground, on our right within the walls, and extending to the rising line of Rue d'Auteuil with its picturesque antient houses; while on our left is the park attach'd to the House of Parliament, penetrated by Ave. Dufferin, and having an handsome circle opposite the entrance of the great edifice. The general view from this point is impressive in the extream; involving the bristling roofs and spires of the intra-mural town, with the gleaming silver of the Men's Church in the foreground, and the suggestion of distant river, countryside, and mountains in the background. Intimations of St. Roch's roofs and steeples below the northward cliff likewise add to the picture. Following the angles of a very large bastion, we come at length to Kent Gate, (close to the silver-steepled church) which resembles that of St. Louis, and which we cross in the same manner. There was a gate here as early as 1663. These two are the only surviving gates of the original five. The wall has by this time closely approach'd Rue d'Auteuil, and we may descend the steps to that picturesque street if we wish; but if we wish otherwise, we may continue to a point near Rue St. Jean, where the wall abruptly ends at the site of the demolish'd St. John's Gate. Scrambling down the grassy bank to Rue d'Auteuil, we follow the descent of that hill street for a few yards and come upon the great St. John thoroughfare. This ends our walk on the walls proper; for we shall not be able to ascend them for the rest of their western stretch, whilst later on they cease to be actual walls, but coincide with the cliff-edge as ramparts and batteries. From the open square where St. John St. curves around from its intra-mural to its extra-mural section, we may advantageously look up the hill we have descended; for the vista is picturesque and archaick in the extream, despite the demolition of the gate proper. The rising ground seems to us the entrance to some elder and alluring mystery—some archaick world or crystallis'd mirage preserv'd for our delectation—and the effect is immeasurably enhanc'd by the steep antient roofs of Rue d'Auteuil, topp'd mystically by the tapering silver spire of the Men's Church. St. John's Gate is one of the principal urban centres, containing the Y.M.C.A. and the leading theatre. We now proceed down Rue Glacis, first of the extra-mural streets, noting the mystical spire of the Sisters of Charity Church. The wall, on our right, is now largely hidden by intervening buildings. A recent extension of McMahon St. would enable us to turn east within the walls thro' a new breach, and gain Palace Gate by a route passing St. Patrick's 1832 church; but for our present purpose it is better to continue outside the walls down Glacis St., past what seems to be a convent or monastery, and descend the cliff to St. Roch by way of the zigzag Rue Cicoton. Or if we prefer, we may add a detour into McMahon St.; where, before returning, we may again get close to the wall at a point on our right where a bastion turns east before resuming the general northward trend in the convent garden on our left. Our descent of the Rue Cicoton deposits us in St. Roch at a section of St. Valier St. a square and a half beyond the walls. Turning eastward—to our right—down

St. Valier we soon come upon the wall again; crowning the dizzy precipice on our right, far overhead, but commencing a gradual and picturesque descent of the cliff as it extends ahead toward the east. As we proceed, this drop begins to be compensated for by the increasing height of the vast rampart; since the old artillery barracks (1756—now Dominion Arsenal where munitions for the Canadian Army are made) are situate here just inside the wall, so that their fortress-like outer surface forms a continuous upward prolongation of the wall itself. It is this stupendous and mediaeval sight—the most grimly impressive vista of its kind in America—which the traveller beholds from a lower level as he enters the town by way of the Union Station. Presently we see the Cyclopean wall turn a corner to the north, where a steep street with sidewalk-railing climbs upward to the plateau in the lee of the overpowering masonry. This is Côte du Palais, or Palace Hill, and we are made aware that we have reach'd the site of old Palace or St. Nicolas Gate—built 1691, improv'd 1720, reimprov'd 1790, rebuilt 1823–33, and finally demolish'd in 1864. The gate itself was somewhat up the hill. On our left, two streets beginning quite close together—Rues St. Nicolas and Lacroix—descend to the level of Rue St. Paul and the railway station. Also on our left—at the NW corner of St. Valier and St. Nicolas—we see a late eighteenth century building flank'd on the left by a taller and more modern business block. These form the celebrated Boswell's Brewery, and occupy the site of the old Intendant's Palace, which in turn replac'd Talon's old brewery of 1668. This return to the original purpose is somewhat picturesque. The subterraneous vaults of the old 1668 brewery still exist, and will be shewn to visitors upon request. The old Talon brewery was chang'd to a palace by the Intendant de Meulles in 1686. It was burnt in 1713 under the infamous Intendant Bigot, and repair'd by him. Another fire—ever the bane of old Quebeck—damag'd it in 1726, but Dupuy restor'd it in 1727. As we have seen, the old palace was eventually destroy'd in 1775 by the batteries of the invader Benedict Arnold in St. Roch. Across Palace Hill on the farther right-hand corner—with the curve of that street on its right and the rising glacis for the Ramparts on its left—we see the wall of the rambling Hôtel Dieu, which we shall visit in detail later on. The city wall, save in connexion with the Arsenal and demolish'd gate, does not ascend Palace Hill; but becomes identify'd with the cliff-edge as it rises beyond Palace Gate. It here receives the name of The Ramparts, and its inner side becomes a parapet along the edge of the precipice, with a street bordering it. The top of the thick parapet slopes downward toward the outside, and has a covering of boards. Salient terraces at various points contain old-fashion'd cannon which frown down on the lower town and harbour in truly formidable style. As we stand at Palace Gate, we have a choice of walking below the wall thro' Rue St. Charles (which here forms a continuation of St. Valier), or following it upward on the inside along the Rampart street. We have been along both routes before during our orientation tour, and this time it is probably wiser to choose the upward course. We curve up with the wall of the Hôtel Dieu on our right, and the fortify'd brink of the ever-rising precipice on our left. The view of lower town, waterfront, and distant landscape becomes more and more impressive; and finally we reach the lofty plateau level, veering gently toward the right as the cliff-edge turns. There now spreads out one of the boldest of the gun platforms, while ahead we see a pleasing urban landskip—the foot of Rue Hamel on our right, just beyond it the square, point-roof'd house once inhabited by Montcalm, and in the distance, over other roofs, the curious French steeple of Laval University—which is one of the most pronounc'd of all Quebeck landmarks. Over the cliff-edge on our left we see the point where, in the lower town, Rue St. Charles runs into St. Paul, and Canoterie-Hill begins to climb the cliff from the junction of the two.

The ascending houses in Canoterie-Hill form a quaint and pleasing sight with their steep roofs and antient facades. Of those only an outer row exists; the inside of the street being close against the fortify'd cliff. As we advance to meet the point where this glacis will reach the top, we see the steep Rue Dambourges opening off it toward the other side of the lower town. It is from the foot of this descent, we recall, that narrow Rue Sous-le-Cap begins—past whose roofs we shall now stroll. Passing the Montcalm house, we reach the top of Canoterie-Hill, just below which old Hope Gate once stood. So slight is the traffick on the hill, that the removal was really needless and unfortunate; and it is to be wish'd that a reproduction of the antient gate might be install'd. Leading inland from this point are the narrow and picturesque streets of St. Famille hill which we have previously explor'd. As we reach Rue Hébert—where the cliff-edge makes its sharp turn at the Sault au Matelot—we encounter on our left the Seminary walls with the bulky University building towering just above it, and enter upon that section of the cliff-defences known as the Grand Battery. The roofs immediately below us are now those of Rue Sault au Matelot; and as we proceed, we find the old guns rang'd along the parapet much more thickly and continuously than in the earlier stages of our course. The road, which has a pleasing semi-rusticity of aspect and which affords a magnificent view, now ascends gently toward Mountain Hill and Montmorency Park; where the cliff-line leaves the road and forms the outer boundary of a pleasant and restful expanse of grass and trees—where the older Bishop's Palace and Parliament House used to be. It will pay to follow the parapet with its antient cannon along a somewhat irregular course to where, near the Cartier Monument and the bastion of old Prescott Gate, the zigzag glacis of Mountain Hill cuts through the cliff and intersects our path at the foot of a masonry embankment. Across the street, on the rising level below us, the occasionally quaint and oldish houses of Mountain Hill climb in a curving line; broken just below us by the head of Breakneck Steps, which lead down to the joint beginning of Rues Sous-le-Fort and Petit-Champlain. We may reconstruct the scene, in imagination, as it was when frowning Prescott Gate existed. This was not constructed in its formal fashion and with its historick name till 1797. It was rebuilt, along with others, in 1823, but succumb'd to the demands of traffick in 1871. Our journey is now broken by the need to ascend to Buade St., proceed around the post office, and reach the cliff-edge again at the beginning of Dufferin Terrace. Here, antiently, the beetling masonry of Fort St. Louis us'd to frown out over the lower town; even now the fort's foundations exist under the boards of the terrace. From here to Cape Diamond, of course, the cliff-edge forms the natural line of defence; hence the rest of our course is merely a stroll to the end of the terrace, with the lower town below us, and the magnificent landscape of river, countryside, and Lévis cliffs forming a background. We may now, if we wish, climb the steep grass slope to the citadel, or continue around the face of Cape Diamond to the Cove Fields by way of the Citadel Walk and King's Bastion. At any rate, our circuit is now perform'd, and we have a better notion than before of the extent and topography of the old fortify'd upper town.

The Northern Upper Town

Another necessary walk of exploration includes the important historick antiquities of the civick centre in the northern upper town. Leaving the Place d'Armes as we did on our first orientation tour, we proceed along Rue Ste. Anne past the Anglican Cathedral to Rue Desjardins, where on the corner we find a tablet marking the site of the house or store of the old Company of 100 Associates. (It is well to note that many of the historick sites and edifices are so mark'd, and to adopt a policy of reading the descriptive tablets whenever possible.) This house was also us'd as a parish church and residence of the Jesuits from 1640 to 1687. A pleasant stream, now cover'd up in the course of urbanisation, once flow'd thro' the meadows at this point, and was cross'd by a small bridge. Continuing to repeat our orientation tour, we turn to the right down Desjardins and once more note Basilica Place or City Hall Square—the former upper-town Market Place. Here, on the nearer or southern side, (line of Buade St.) Quebeck's first tavern—the Baril d'Or or Golden Barrell—was open'd by Jacques Boisdon, who had on his sign a motto, "J'en bois donc", which form'd a pun on his name. We have seen that Boisdon was officially granted the right to serve guests at any time except during mass, catechism, or vespers—such being the regulations of a distinctly theocratic colony. So strict was the popish grip, as we have noted, that no Protestants were allow'd in Canada. In 1685 the noted Huguenot Gabriel Bernon sought to establish a home here, but was deported back to France and imprison'd—so that eventually he sought the more liberal atmosphere of His Britannick Maj$^{ty's}$ Rhode-Island Colony, there becoming one of the most illustrious citizens, and the founder of King's Church (now St. John's) in Providence. It is amusing to reflect, that the site of the Baril d'Or is even now occupy'd by a restaurant. Antiently this side of the square was much higher than the opposite or northern side, so that a really steep terrace descended to the market area betwixt the Cathedral and Jesuit's College. The inequality has been very much lessen'd and graded in later years yet is still very apparent in the tilt of Basilica Place, and of its central grassy circle containing the Taschereau Monument. On our left as we enter the Place is the City Hall; its garden, containing the Hébert Monument, stretching back to Rue Ste. Anne. This edifice occupies the site of the antient Jesuit's College, built in 1635, and antedating Harvard by a year as the first institution of higher learning on this continent. Here taught some of the most famous of the early Canadian priests, including the martyrs Lallemant, Bréboeuf, Noué, Jogues, Daniel, and Vincent, who fell victims to Iroquois barbarism. It was here, we are inform'd, that Marquette form'd his plans for exploring the Mississippi Valley—whilst his companion Joliet play'd on the organ in the Cathedral across the square. The antient building, a splendid example of steep-roof'd French architecture on a massive scale, design'd by the Jesuit Jean Ligeois, who was bury'd under it, was in the form of a hollow square; and in 1759 was seiz'd by His Maj$^{ty's}$ forces, clos'd as a college, and turned into a barracks. The chapel attach'd to it, endow'd by a son of Marquis de Mammache who enter'd the Jesuit order, was ruin'd by the bombardment of 1759 and finally demolish'd in 1807. The college remain'd as a barracks till 1878, when it was very unwisely demolish'd to make way for a City Hall. So massive was its construction, that the stone walls cou'd be destroy'd only with difficulty; and it is an eternal pity that it was not preserv'd and remodell'd for City Hall use. Beneath it were found the graves of the architect, Bro. Jean Ligeois, of Fr. de Quen, founder of the Tadoussac Mission and discoverer of Lac St. Jean at the head of the Saguenay, and of Fr. François du Peron, one of the most eminent of the missionaries amongst the Hurons. Ligeois was kill'd, decapitated, and scalp'd by the Iroquois at Sillery in 1655. All three skeletons thus found were finally (1891) reinterr'd at the Ursuline Convent. The City Hall was not erected till later—1900–1906—and is a quasi-Norman affair of great size and depressingly Victorian atmosphere. An annex is about to be added. On the north side of Basilica Place is a brick business building (shop of S. Fisher and Sons) marking the site of the home of Genl. Brock, who serv'd so ably and met his death so nobly in the war of 1812. Opposite the City Hall on the eastern side of the square is the great and celebrated Basilica of

Notre-Dame with its mismated towers—the right-hand one of which bears a splendid and highly typical Quebeck belfry-steeple. This distinguish'd fane is approximately on the site of its predecessor, the Chapel of Nôtre-Dame de la Recouvrance; which Champlain built in 1633 as the result of a vow, and which commemorated the recovery of Quebeck from His Britannick Maj^{ty's} power thro' the treaty of St. Germain-en-Laye. This chapel was burnt in 1640; and in 1647, under Montmagny, the cornerstone of the present church was lay'd by the Jesuit Father Vimont. In 1650 it was sufficiently compleat to permit of masses, and in 1658 it receiv'd its first bell—one of 1000 lbs., presented by Robert Hudon. The first organ, given by Bishop Laval, was play'd by the explorer Joliet. In 1664 the edifice was made a Cathedral by brief of Pope Clement, and in 1697 it was enlarg'd from 100 × 33 to 150 × 38 feet. In 1744 the eminent engineer Chaussegros de Léry—who later design'd the Citadel and fortifications under His Britannick Majesty's government—made radical alterations, built the side aisles, lengthen'd the structure 60 feet, and in general gave the Cathedral its present outline. In 1759 fire and bombardment greatly damag'd the edifice; but the structural supports and walls remain'd intact, so that restoration in 1768 was entirely practicable. An extension of 22 feet brought it to its exact present size of 216 × 94 feet. In the late eighteenth and earlier nineteenth century both exterior and interior were greatly embellish'd by three members of the celebrated engineering family of Baillargé. François Baillargé added a baldachin in 1793, and new statues and decorations were supply'd. A new belfry was built by Jean Baillargé. In 1820 the roof was tinn'd and a new organ provided, and in 1829 a sacristy was built. In 1844 Thomas Baillargé supply'd the present facade, thus creating the typical appearance manifest today. In 1874 a papal decree made the cathedral a Basilica, and in 1921 a complete restoration was undertaken. Late in 1922 a disastrous fire destroy'd everything but the external structure—including valuable antiquities and paintings. Only materials in the vaults were saved. Restoration was undertaken at once, following the old designs; and in 1925 the Basilica was again in shape and made fireproof. The interior was reconstructed with great taste, eighteenth century French designs predominating. Architects of the general rebuilding were Tanguay and Chênevert, whilst in the finer details Chênevert was assisted by Roisin of Paris. The baldachin and certain other details are by Vermare of Paris. New collections of ecclesiastical paintings and antiquities are in process of assembling; France having donated six fine canvasses. Beneath the Basilica are bury'd nearly all the popish Bishops of Quebeck, and four of the French governors—Frontenac, de Callières, the elder Vaudreuil, and de Jonquières [sic]. Immediately adjoining the Basilica, and forming the northeast corner of Basilica Place, beside which Rue St. Famille stretches out toward the Ramparts, is the gateway to the extensive grounds of the ancient Seminary and Laval University. Just inside, on the left, is the modest and sightly Seminary Chapel—built in 1891 to replace one built by Frontenac in 1690, burnt in 1750 and restor'd, and finally burnt in 1889. Here are a number of ecclesiastical art objects, and several impressive reliques including portions of the inexhaustible Cross, remnants of the extensive Crown of Thorns, and scraps of the voluminous Seamless Robe. Among the objets d'art is a heavily jewelled reliquary, presented by Leo XIII and valued at $50,000. Beneath the Chapel is interr'd Bishop Laval himself, ceremoniously transferr'd thither from the Basilica in 1838. The antient Seminary itself, whose stone walls and steep double-dormer'd roof may be seen thro' the gate from the square, was built in 1663 by Bishop de Laval (enlarg'd 1677) and in 1775 form'd the place of imprisonment of the rebel officers of Arnold's invading force. Fires, as usual, have wrought havock with the edifice; it having been burnt and restored in 1701 and again in 1705. The siege of 1759 nearly demolish'd it; but restoration follow'd, and it was enlarg'd in 1822 and thereafter, and has since been made fireproof. This ground was originally the estate of Guillaume Couillard, son-in-law of the pioneer Hébert, and was purchas'd from his widow in 1663. Classes were first held in the house of Couillard; which stood on the grounds till long after the completion of the main edifice, and whose site is now mark'd by a tablet. The first class, held in 1666, contain'd 8 French boys, 6 Hurons, and few Algonquins; but it was soon found impossible to educate the Indians—these northern tribes being found more resistant to European ways than the civilis'd Mexicans encounter'd and assimilated by the Spanish conquistadores. Today the Seminary offers courses in general education and in divinity—60 professors and 1000 students in the former, and 12 professors and 200 students in the latter. The tortuous interior of the antient building and its additions, with underground corridors, endless steps and turnings, and galleries of dark-rob'd priests, might well suggest to the alert imagination some such venerable establishment as Dr. Bransby's in Stoke-Newington, well describ'd by Poe in "William Wilson". The Seminary now has a 5-story annex with all modern improvements, extending toward Hébert St., which will later be link'd with the main group. It is on land once us'd as a hop field for the brewing of beer for the students. Its construction unfortunately entail'd the destruction of the antient de Léry manor house, land for which was sold to the de Lérys in 1726, and repurchased in recent years. Attach'd to the Seminary and extending out to the Ramparts at Sault au Matelot is the great 6-story Victorian bulk of Laval University, redeem'd from the commonplace by a quaint and curious spire of archaick French design which forms a salient object on the Quebeck skyline. Laval University, the foremost Popish institution of learning in North-America, was founded in 1852—the edifice having been erected in 1857. It is an outgrowth of the Seminary, and has courses in medicine, law, geodesy, forestry, and the general arts and sciences essential to a liberal education. There are four chairs—Theology, Law, Medicine, and Art,—and the personnel numbers 125 professors and over 600 students. There is a branch in Montreal, and over 26 other colleges and seminaries are affiliated with it. The building, so impressively rising from the edge of the great cliff, houses notable halls and museums; and an art gallery with exceedingly valuable paintings—including 2 Van Dycks, 1 Poussin, 1 Lesueur, 1 Tintoretto, 1 David, 2 Parrocels, 1 Paget, 1 Vernet, and 4 Salvador Rosas. The library is one of the finest in Canada. On the roof is a promenade offering marvellous vistas of the countryside up the St. Charles and down the St. Lawrence.

Having now completed our round of the Seminary grounds, we reëmerge into Basilica Place and start down the slope of broad Fabrique St., which forms a northwestward prolongation of the square. This is a thoroughfare of the highest class of shops, and we shortly come to its broad junction with quaint and ancient Rue Garneau, which joins it from the right. This is one of the curious byways of St. Famille Hill which we have previously noticed. One square farther down the slope, and we come to the open space where Couillard St.—archaick and picturesque, comes in from the right, whilst St. John St.—a continuation of the main business district—goes on to the left. This is the end of Fabrique, but a narrow byway opposite the end leads down to the secluded backwater of Rue Charlevoix, whose single row of antient houses faces the venerable wall of the Hôtel Dieu. This venerable convent and hospital is probably best reachable from Palace Hill—a square to the left along Charlevoix—where some new construction is even now progressing. It was founded in 1639 by the Duchess d'Aiguillon, niece of Cardinal Richelieu, and the first nuns came to Quebeck with the Ursulines. The full name is "L'Hôtel Dieu du Précieux Sang". The original edifice was constructed in 1657, but has since been many times burnt and restored. Victorian additions have overshadow'd the fine, steep-roof'd old building with their atrocious bulk, but the veteran still survives, and can be seen in the rear of the hodge-podge. The old chapel also exists, and houses some notable paintings—as well as the bones of the famous Jesuit martyrs Bréboeuf and Lallemant. From Hôtel Dieu we may, if we wish, descend Palace Hill and revisit the old Artillery Barracks—present Dominion Arsenal, where Canada's munitions of war are made. We may also enter McMahon St., which opens off Palace Hill to the left a block below where Charlevoix opens to the right, and view on the southern or left-hand side the dignify'd facade of St. Patrick's church, erected in 1832 for the Irish Catholicks of Quebeck, and now conducted by the Redemptionist Fathers—who also control the new St. Patrick's in the Grande Allée, and the celebrated shrine of Ste. Anne de Beaupré. Now turning and ascending Palace Hill to St. John—our route on arriving in Quebeck at the Union Station—we note the old building—formerly a tavern—on the N.W. corner, with the quaint Genl. Wolfe statue in a niche overlooking the intersection. This, as we have seen, is a reproduction of the original tavern sign; which was carried off by sailors as a practical joke, and plac'd in the library of the Quebeck Lit. and Hist. Soc. upon its ultimate restoration. It is notable that this is still a prominent tavern corner, the well-known Victoria Hotel being here and having entrances on both St. John and Palace Sts. Turning westward into St. John, we traverse it one square; then turning southward—to the left—into St. Stanislas;[34] which we follow to the quaint open square where a homelike English Georgian steeple—the only one in Quebeck besides the Anglican Cathedral's—rises in simple tastefulness. God Save the King! This is St. Andrew's Scotch Church, built in 1824 and still in excellent condition. Close by is Morin College, occupying a remodell'd gaol building, a Presbyterian institution affiliated with McGill University of Montreal. This institution is a sort of intellectual centre for Quebeck's Anglo-Saxon minority, and contains the library of the Quebeck Literary and Historical Society. It is nam'd from a former mayor of the city. Also in this neighbourhood is the house (65 Ste. Anne) inhabited in 1873 by that mild and correct old lady William Dean Howells of Boston, who here writ his book, "A Chance Acquaintance".[35] Now returning to the Place d'Armes by way of Rue Ste. Anne, we re-pass the site of the Hundred Associates' store at the corner of Desjardins, and have on our right the fine churchyard of the Anglican Cathedral—which faces us as we advance. On the left for the balance of the way we see many tourist and souvenir centres—both across from the Cathedral, and on the north side of the Place d'Armes.

Westward Regions

At least one detail'd pedestrian journey shou'd be taken in the western part of the city; especially the St. John suburb, where we have mention'd the quaint streets leading uphill on the left from extra-mural St. John St. The route from the intra-mural centre, of course, is along Rue St. Jean; and as we advance we must not fail to note again the ethereal and alluring vistas we have seen before—the rising lines of St. Stanislas, St. Angela and St. Ursule Sts.; the silver spire of the Men's Congregational Church over the ancient climbing roofs of Rue d'Auteuil on our left just before we pass through St. John's Gate; the glimpses of the Sisters of Charity belfry-steeple downhill on our right shortly after we have pass'd through the gate; the quaint ascending lines of Rues d'Youville and St. Eustache on our left; the picturesque old churchyard of St. Matthew's on our left at the S.W. corner of Rue St. Augustin; the glimpses of St. Roch's roofs and the distant countryside and mountains at the end of the downhill streets leading to the cliff-edge on our right, etc. etc. etc. It is beyond St. Augustin that the quaintest uphill streets on our left begin, and these are so rich in archaick atmosphere that they deserve particular exploration—for the downhill vistas from above, and some of the vistas along lateral streets wholly hidden from St. John, are of the greatest quaintness and beauty. The dominant type of house in this quarter—which was probably built up in the early nineteenth century—is the characteristick French gambrel with heavily overhanging cornice and steep, curved lower pitch; and sometimes with double tiers of dormers. Houses are generally of a story and a half—with sometimes an extra attick story to which the upper dormers admit light. They tend to be of brick—often painted yellow. Some have doorways like New England 1830-period houses—with transom and sidelights—though these transoms and sidelights tend to have shutters. The sidelights tend to be broader than those of New England. As we have said, the compact part of old Georgian Quebeck seems to have extended west about as far as Rue Claire Fontaine—which was nam'd from a spring on Abraham Martin's old property. If one were to ascend Côte St. Geneviève to St. Patrick and turn to the right, one would come upon Rue St. Michel—where in antient days the extra-mural defence of Ft. Pique was situate. The choicest route, however—if one is to make a digression from St. John—is up Scott to Rue Plessis, through Plessis, to the right, to Claire Fontaine, and thence down to St. John again along Claire Fontaine; at all times glancing appreciatively thro' the cross streets for quaint architectural vistas. This neighbourhood represents the early nineteenth century in Quebeck, just as St. Famille hill represents the eighteenth. In its prime, of course, it was the suburb of St. John, and not an official part of the city. At present it is rather seedy, but not a downright slum. Indeed, the actual slums of Quebeck (Sous-le-Cap, Petit-Champlain, Champlain, and places in St. Roch) are by no means so offensive as the corresponding slums of U.S. towns; probably because of the homogeneity and long-seatedness of the population. As we ascend the very steep gradient of Scott St. (presumably nam'd for Sir Walter's brother Thomas, who lyes bury'd in St. Matthew's Churchyard) we note the presence of occasional steps in the sidewalk to break the steepness. These sidewalk-steps are characteristic of the uphill streets in this region. Our sensation in penetrating this airy realm of old brick facades and curving roofs is that of walking bodily into a fantastick picture, for the perfect archaism of Scott St. is comparable to that of Tradd St. in Charleston. At St. Gabriel—the next up from St. John—Scott St. makes a considerable jog to the left—this being one of the sources of its especial picturesqueness as view'd from below. Above this jog the grade is less steep. Continuing to Rue Plessis we turn to the right and strike Claire Fontaine; then turning once more to the right and proceeding down the steep incline of Claire Fontaine to St. John again. This descent of Claire Fontaine, with its many sidewalk steps, (more than in Scott) old painted brick facades, curved gambrel roofs, heavy cornices, double dormer rows, etc. etc. shou'd be accomplisht in a leisurely, observant way permitting the full savouring of all the archaick details. The sidewalk steps, it may be noted, occur most thickly in the steepest part immediately above St. John. During the whole of this downhill stroll the glamour of the scene is enhanc'd by the exquisite silver belfry-steeple which looms up below, where the quaint lines of curving roofs converge. This is attach'd to the large church of St. Jean-Baptiste in St. John St. Beyond it, from the high parts of the street, we may see over the housetops the St. Roch suburb beyond the cliff-edge, and the distant countryside and mountains.

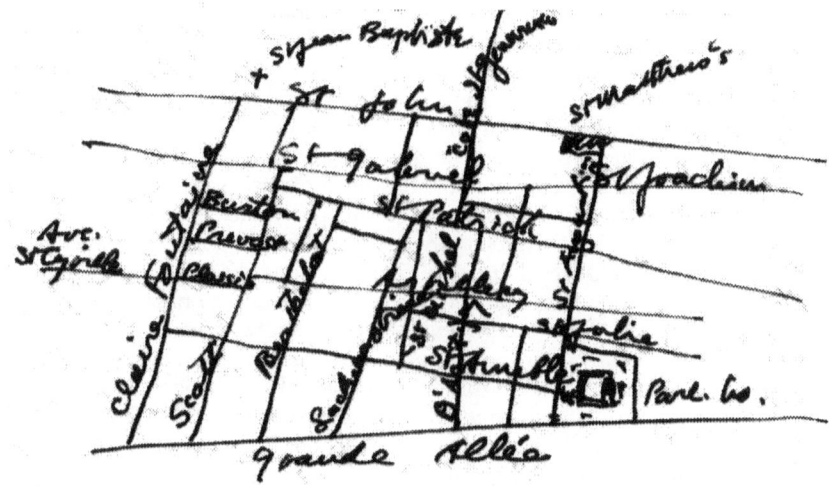

If we now have a wish for compleatness, and feel equal to a substantial further walk, it wou'd pay us to round out our urban exploration by descending to St. Roch and visiting the antient General Hospital on the banks of the St. Charles. Before doing this, however, we may wish to stroll out St. John to its union with the Ste. Foy Road; thereafter descending either Racine or Marchand to Latourelle—where, betwixt the first-mention'd two, one of the remaining 1812 Martello Towers stands in excellent condition on the cliff-edge. In any case, we seek the steep flight of steps descending to the head of Crown St. (de la Couronne) in St. Roch; which we reach by following La-tourelle east from the Martello Tower and turning to the left down Ste. Claire, or—if we have not visited the tower—simply by following Ste. Claire (a virtual continuation of Scott St. down to the northern cliff-edge) down to its end from St. John. Descend-ing to Crown St., we may advantageously turn to the left along St. Valier to its junc-tion with Arago; then turning to the right along Dorchester; where, as previously mention'd, we behold on the NE corner of Ste. Hélène a gambrel-roof'd cottage (once one of three) of surprisingly Novanglian aspect. Continuing to St. Joseph—St. Roch's main street—we turn to the left and follow St. Joseph to the broad expanse of Boule-vard Langelier; which separates the district of St. Roch and St. Sauveur, and beyond which we can see the great bulk of St. Sauveur church looming up in the distance. The parts of St. Roch just east and south of this point are very quaint and old, as we saw during our orientation-tour; and if we wish to visit them again we may vary our pro-gramme by retracing Dorchester to St. Valier and proceeding to Boulevard Langelier either by that thoroughfare or by Rue St. Colombe, which can be reached from St. Valier by turning to the left a block down short Rue Belleau. But whatever be our mode of reaching the Boulevard, our next step is to follow it completely down to its northern ending on the narrow loop of the St. Charles River, where we shall find the famous and antient General Hospital. In reaching this we shall pass the celebrated Technical School of the Provincial Government, whose tall, ornate tower we have no doubt previously noted as one of the landmarks of the northwestward vista from the plateau. The school looms on our left. Just beyond, on the same left-hand side of the Boulevard, there rises the high wall of the Hospital; above which we can descry archa-ick gables, and the curiously graceful steeple of the Hospital Chapel. Entering the grounds, we note the tasteful landscaping and the marvellous picturesqueness of the steep-roof'd, double-dormer'd edifices. These fine old buildings are the least alter'd of any of the antient publick structures of Quebeck, having never suffer'd damage by fire; and close study of them will give one an idea of the original aspect of such places as the Seminary, Ursuline Convent, and Hôtel Dieu. There is an old windmill nearby bearing the date 1607; but this latter is certainly erroneous or spurious in view of the history of the settlement. This mill was us'd as a fort for the convent. Across the narrow river-bend are great vaults us'd in French times for storing provisions. As we have noted, the General Hospital was built as a monastery for the Récollet Order, a branch of the Franciscans who came to Quebeck in 1615, thus preceding the more arrogant and en-terprising Jesuits, who soon swept all before them. Their first monastery was built on this site in 1620—its relation to the present edifice, itself obviously very antient, being obscure to the present writer. It was the intention of the Récollets to found a seminary for both French and Indian boys, but this did not materialise. The location of the mon-astery at this point is attributed to an intention of Champlain's to found a city there—to be call'd Louisville—which was subsequently abandon'd in favour of the original Quebeck site. The present hospital buildings are those of the Récollet Monastery, as is the antient church. The old cloister of the friars is still in good condition, and contains an interesting monastick cell. We may also behold the rooms tenanted by Count Fron-tenac when, during his first governing period, he us'd to come hither for an annual spiri-tual retreat. He was an especial patron of the Récollets; but it is said that he usually emerg'd from his retreat periods more violent and cholerick than when he enter'd upon them. In 1683 Bishop St. Valier purchas'd the monastery for use as an hospital (special-ising in incurables) and retreat for the aged, to be conducted by nuns as a branch of the Hôtel Dieu; whereupon the Récollets built a new monastery and church (1693) in the upper town, on the site of the Seneschal's Court next the Place d'Armes, where the An-glican Cathedral now stands. The hospital, once establish'd as such, has never alter'd its nature or management; tho' its nuns were separated from those of Hôtel Dieu in 1701, and tho' the feature of old-age refuge did not permanently materialise. In 1759 many of the wounded from Plains of Abraham—of both armies—were treated here; amongst them being the fatally stricken Montcalm, who was later transferr'd to the house of Dr. Arnoux in the upper town. Many of the dead from this battle, and from the Ste. Foy fight of the following year, are interr'd in the hospital's graveyard. In 1775 it was to this hospital that Benedict Arnold was taken after his knee was shatter'd in the fighting near Palace Gate. The antient hospital buildings are very rambling, and cover much ground; and he is indeed fortunate who secures time and permission to inspect all of them. The gracefulness of the group, with venerable steeple and landscap'd grounds, is such as to excite the admiration of the artist. Whilst in this part of Quebeck, the traveller may well seek one of the bridges to graceful Victoria Park, across the narrow bend of the river Charles, where an excellent statue of Montmagny exists.

(4). Suburban Pilgrimages.

Point Lévis

Having now well cover'd the urban part of Quebeck, and having still earlier ex-plor'd the adjacent north shoar of the St. Lawrence as part of the process of absorbing provincial colour; we may now round out our Quebeck survey by briefly visiting certain close suburbs where material of historick interest is available. Foremost of all comes

Quebeck — from Levis, across the St. Lawrence. (skyscrapers omitted)

Lévis, to which we must cross on the ferry (foot of Rue La Place, rear N. D. des Victoires, Breakneck Steps, and elevator to Dufferin Terrace) for an exquisite view of the entire urban skyline. Splendid glimpses may be had from the ferry itself, but to obtain the most advantageous view one must land in Lévis and ascend to the cliff-top there; either by a dizzy flight of steps a square or two to the left of the ferry landing, or by a trolley-car which may be boarded opposite the landing itself. Lévis, like Quebeck, has an upper and lower town; but is by no means an antient place. Its buildings seem to be mostly of Victorian date, and resemble building of the corresponding period in Quebeck—with French window-casements and other characteristick features. On the heights are some churches whose spires resemble the tall provincial specimens rather than those of Quebeck City, and three old forts; from which Wolfe's troops shell'd Quebeck in 1759. The best view of Quebeck is to be had from the head of the steps from the lower town; and to see this at its best one ought to choose the sunrise, when all the old town's steep roofs and silver belfries are touch'd with dawn-fire, or at sunset, when the frowning citadel, grim Château tower, and grotesque university steeple are darkly silhouetted against the flaming red and orange mystery of the west. The whole skyline sweep—from bold Cape Diamond on the left to the steepled turn of the cliff at Sault au Matelot on the right—is magnificent beyond description against a background of sky and a side setting of green countryside with mystical purple Laurentians on the horizon. An excellent trolley trip from Lévis is along the shoar westward to the great Quebeck Bridge at Charny, across the Chaudière Basin.

Isle of Orleans

The traveller should most certainly take the long ferry sail to the Isle of Orleans eastward in the St. Lawrence from Quebeck (Indian, *Minego*) antiently known as the Isle of Bacchus because of its grapes, and as the Isle of Sorcerers because of its reputed evil spirits.* Here, according to most travellers, the provincial countryside may be seen in a state more antient and unspoil'd than on the northern mainland shoar. Fortunately there are sightseeing coaches from the Place d'Armes which tour this island in a very ample and satisfactory manner. It is on this island, we recall, that Wolfe had his main encampment in 1759. Here may still be seen the quaint old villages of Ste. Petronille, St. Pierre, Ste. Famille, St. Jean, St. Laurent, and St. François; many of them having antient and notable churches. There exist here also Canada's oldest rural

---

*The distant bobbing lanthorns of the Orleans fisherfolk at night, as seen from Quebeck, are thought to have been mistaken for the torches of evil spirits in infernal dances—hence the reputation and name.

convent, seignieural mills, typical French* farmhouses, and the like. From many points, also, magnificent views in all directions are to be had.

Charlesbourg Road

If the traveller be equipt with a vehicle, he had better drive across Dorchester Bridge to the Charlesbourg Road; following it to the point where, about a mile distant from the city in Limoilou, a (cross) monument marks the spot (at the confluence of the St. Charles and the small Lairet) where Jacques Cartier spent the winter of 1535–6 with the crews of the Petite-Hermine and Grande Hermine. Here was the Indian village of Stadacona, of which Donnacona was the chief or Agohanna. Over-against it Cartier erected a fort, and on May 3,1536, three days before his return to France, he here plac'd a cross (of which the present one is a duplicate) 35 feet high inscrib'd with the arms of the French King and the inscription "Franciscus Primus Dei Gratia Francorum Rex Regnat."[36] Splendid views of Quebeck can be obtain'd from the Charlesbourg Road, and many may wish to continue to the village of Charlesbourg itself, on the first foothills of the Laurentians, where many of the women and children were sent for safety during Wolfe's siege of Quebeck. Four miles east of this, in the mountains, may be found the ruins of the hunting-lodge or country seat—Beaumanoir—of the vicious Intendant Bigot.

Lorette

The Huron Indian village of Lorette, eight miles northwest of Quebeck near the falls of the St. Charles, is eminently worthy of a visit. It may be reach'd by railway, or by road vehicle along either the Charlesbourg or the Little River road. It is here that the remnants of the Iroquois-massacred Huron nation were finally settled (1697) after a long period of camping in the upper town and elsewhere. They are here still—using the language and religion of the French and occupying themselves with the manufacture of such typical Indian goods as moccasins, beaded slippers, snowshoes, and canoes. Much of their handiwork is sold in the shops of Quebeck. They have a virtual monopoly in this especial field, and work and live precisely in the manner of their ancestors. There is now, of course, much white blood in their veins. To view these warrior-scions in their village tranquillity, and to think at the same time of the once potent Iroquois on their reservations in northern New-York, is to arouse a train of historick and philosophick reflection not soon to be banish'd. The falls of the St. Charles at Lorette, with a drop of 150 feet, are very sightly, and betwixt them and Quebeck the fleet canoes of the Hurons us'd often to ply. There is a large tannery at which leather for the Huron manufactures is drest. The church or chapel at Lorette is above 200 years old; and is well worth visiting not only for its own sake but because of the important reliques of the past therein deposited. Lorette is about a half-hour's trip by rail from the Union Station.

Sillery

The village of Sillery, whose church-steeple on a point jutting into the St. Lawrence just above Quebeck is so prominent a landmark in the adjacent countryside, and so alluring a background-feature of the vista from Battlefields Park, is well worth a visit

---

*Some see a *Scandinavian* influence in these old Norman cottages.

from the traveller. It may be reach'd from Quebeck on a stroll along the shoar beyond Wolfe's Cove, by the St. Louis Road, and by an electrick trolley line. In proceeding thither we may behold the gubernatorial estate of Spencerwood, beyond Battlefields Park—a low, Southern-looking manor-house once inhabited by the Governors-General of Canada, and now by the Lt. Governors of Quebeck Province. Two well-kept cemeteries also lie along the route. Detouring to the left at the proper spot from the St. Louis Road, we come upon Sillery itself, with its convent and church of St. Columba on a river headland forming a lower part of the plateau. This locality was very early a seat of Jesuit missionary enterprise amongst the Algonquins; and in 1637 St. Michel's church and the Residence of St. Joseph were built, around which an Indian village sprang up. In 1640 the Ursuline nuns were quarter'd here, before the building of their Quebeck Convent on its present site. Here Canada's first missionary Massé dy'd in 1640, earning a bronze memorial tablet in 1646 and (upon the rediscovery of his bones) a stone monument in 1870. Hence departed the martyr Jesuits Jogues, Bré-boeuf, and Lallemant, upon their fatal missions in the Iroquois-haunted wilderness. Noël Brulart de Sillery, (b. 1577) Commander of the Knights of Malta and (after 1642) a missionary priest, was the leading spirit in the establishment of these ecclesiastical enterprises. St. Michel's church no longer exists except as ruin'd foundations, but the Residence of St. Joseph still survives as the oldest house in the Province of Quebeck, and probably in the Dominion of Canada. It is a simple edifice of gray stone, with red window shutters; and has an underground passage which runs east from the front of the building opposite the door—the latter undoubtedly for purposes of escape in case of hostile Indian attack. St. Columba's modern church, whose steeple is such a land-mark, is of the Irish Catholick variety. For those who wish to go beyond Sillery, Cap Rouge is a worthy objective. Here the St. Louis and Ste. Foy roads unite in a region (glimps'd from the train coming over Quebeck Bridge) affording the most significant possible views of the St. Charles and St. Lawrence valleys. It was here, we recall, that Jacques Cartier's third expedition (1541) winter'd; and here that Sieur de Roberval unsuccessfully attempted to found a convict colony in 1542. The name is deriv'd from the ruddy colour of the soil and rock at this point, a phenomenon arising from the presence of oxide of iron.

THE END

Quebeck visited—Aug.–Sept. 1930.
Description finish'd—Jany . 14, 1931.

APPENDIX

Place-names in Quebeck which differ substantially in form according to common French and English usage.

Côte de la Montagne	Mountain Hill
Côte du Palais	Palace Hill
Rue de la Couronne	Crown St.
Rue de la Reine	Queen St.
Rue de l'Eglise	Church St.
Ave. des Erables	Maple Ave.

```
Rue Desjardins ................................................. Garden St.
Rue du Pont ....................................................... Bridge St.
Rue du Roi ........................................................... King St.
Parc des Champs de Batailles ................. Battlefields Park
Rue Petit Champlain ........................ Little Champlain St.
Rue St. André ............................................. St. Andrew St.
Rue St. Jean ..................................................... St. John St.
Rue St. Pierre ................................................. St. Peter St.
```

Origins of Place Names

Canada	Ind. Kanata, a Collection of Huts
Lauzon (west of Lévis)	Mem. Jean de Lauzon, Governor of New-France, 1651–6.
Lévis	Mem. François Gaston, Chevalier Lévis Leran, General under Montcalm, and after him Commander. Victor at Ste. Foy 1760. Name changed from Point Levi.
Montmorency (river and falls)	Mem. Henri de Montmorency, Viceroy of New-France 1620–24. Name given by Champlain.
Montreal	Royal Mountain—named by Jacques Cartier.
Quebeck	Indian Kébek, a narrow strait.
Sillery	Mem. Noël Brulart de Sillery, Knight of Malta, who became a priest and Indian missionary 1642.
Three Rivers (bet. Quebeck and Montreal)	City at confluence of St. Lawrence and two others.

Origin of Street Names

Buade	Louis de Buade, Comte de Palluau et de Frontenac. Govr. New-France 1672 et seq.
Carillon	Battle by Lake Champlain, where Montcalm distinguish'd himself. Carillon was original name of Ft. Ticonderoga.
Champlain	Samuel de Champlain. Founder of Quebeck.
Charlevoix	Jesuit Historian of New-France.
Châteauguay	Battle, War of 1812. Genl. Wade Hampton repuls'd near Montreal.
Claire Fontaine	Spring on prop. of Abraham Martin, 1st river pilot.
Collins	Surveyor—late XVIII cent.
Côte d'Abraham	Abraham Martin, Scotsman, 1st St. L. Pilot, own'd land nr. here.
Couillard	son-in-law of Pioneer Hébert
d'Aiguillon	Duchesse d'Aiguillon, niece [of] Richilieu—founder of Hôtel Dieu.

d'Argenson	Pierre Voyer, Vicomte d'Argenson, Gvr. 1658.
d'Artigny	noted Quebeck family.
de Courcelles	Governor 1655.
de Jumonville	French officer in Ohio Valley, kill'd 1754 by party under Lt. Col. Washington at Ft. Necessity, on the Monongahela.
de l'Eglise	nr. St. Roch Church.
de Salaberry	French-Canadian Colonel, hero of Châteauguay (1814).
Dorchester	Gen. Sir Guy Carleton, Govr. Canada 1766 et seq. later Ld Dorchester.
Dufferin	Marquis of Dufferin—Gov. Canada 1846.
du Fort	road to Ft. St. Louis.
du Palais	hill road from Intendant's Palace.
du Parloir	road to parlour of Ursuline Convent.
du Pont	street to Dorchester Bridge, St. Roch.
du Tresor	Treas. of Marine liv'd here.
Elgin	Gov. Gen. Canada, XIX cent.
Ferland	Priest-Historian of Canada.
Garneau	F. X. Garneau, eminent Canadian historian.
Haldimand	Genl. Sir Fred'k Haldimand, Gov. Gen. 1781.
Hébert	Louis Hébert, first settled landholder of Quebeck.
Lallemant	Jesuit priest—martyr among Iroquois.
Laval	1st Archbishop of Quebeck.
Laurier	Sir Wilfrid Laurier, XX cent. statesman.
MacMahon	1st priest of St. Patrick's Church.
St. Valier	2nd Bishop of Quebeck.
Sault au Matelot	Sailor here jump'd from cliff.
Scott	Thos. Scott (bro. Walter) military paymaster at Quebeck.
Sous-le-Cap	narrow street under the cliff.
Sous-le-Fort	street leads to cliff beneath old Ft. St. Louis.
Talon	First Intendant of New-France under Royal Govt.

EDITOR'S NOTE FP: In *To Quebec and the Stars*, ed. L. Sprague de Camp (West Kingston, RI: Donald M. Grant, 1976), pp. 111–309. Text based on the AMS (JHL). HPL's longest travelogue, and the longest single work he ever wrote: at 78,000 words, it is half again as long as *The Case of Charles Dexter Ward* (51,500 words). HPL's first trip to Quebec in late summer 1930 was a spur-of-the-moment affair: he had discovered a remarkably cheap $12.00 excursion fare to Quebec, and accordingly boarded a train on 30 August; he stayed only three days, but saw virtually everything there was to see. By mid-October he was announcing to James F. Morton that he was "*trying* to devise a *Quebeck* travelogue of some sort, which you shall behold upon its completion" (*SL* 3.197); by late December he had reached page 65 (*SL* 3.249), and by mid-January he told Morton: "Well, Sir, I have the honour to state, that I last Wednesday [14 January] compleated the following work, design'd solely for my own perusal and for the crystallisation of my recollections, in 136 pages of this crabbed cacography" (*SL* 3.266). HPL never made any attempt to type the work and does not appear to have shown it to anyone.

HPL's historical section ("Book I") is extraordinarily lengthy as compared to similar sections in other travelogues, not only because he found the three centuries–long history of Quebec of unusual interest but also because it allowed him to express his Anglophilia in portraying the eventual conquest of Canada by the British. HPL notes in October 1930 that "it took more study than I thought to assemble the necessary historick background" (*SL* 3.197), but he does not specify what works he consulted in assembling this background. Presumably the guidebooks he obtained in Quebec would not have been sufficient for the purpose. Among the leading histories of Quebec in English to which HPL may have had access are Robert Christie, *A History of the Late Province of Lower Canada* (18448–66; 6 vols.); J. M. Le Moine, *Historical and Sporting Notes on Quebec and Its Environs* (1889); Gilbert Parker and Claude G. Bryan, *Old Quebec, the Fortress of New France* (1903); and Benjamin Sulte, C. E. Fryer, and L. O. David, *A History of Quebec: Its Resources and People* (1908; 2 vols.). As the text itself reveals, HPL liberally consulted Francis Parkman's *Conspiracy of Pontiac* (see n. 15) for the period of the French and Indian Wars. Of actual guidebooks, HPL cites three (see nn. 29–31).

HPL visited Quebec again in 1932 and 1933.

Notes

1. Everett McNeil (1861–1929), author of boys' books and friend of HPL; living in the Hell's Kitchen district of west-central Manhattan during the period of HPL's residence in Brooklyn (1924–26), he was a member of the Kalem Club. Among his historical novels dealing with Canada or neighbouring regions are *Tonty of the Iron Hand* (1925), *Daniel Du Luth; or, Adventuring on the Great Lakes* (1926), and *The Shores of Adventure; or, Exploring in the New World with Jacques Cartier* (1929).

2. Harvard was founded in 1636.

3. Cf. a fictitious "Frenchman of Louis XIII's time named Pierre-Louis Montmagny" cited in "The Shadow out of Time" (1934–35): *The Shadow out of Time*, ed. S. T. Joshi and David E. Schultz (New York: Hippocampus Press, 2003), p. 57. Previous texts (e.g., *DH* 396) have read "Montagny."

4. At the battle of Thermopylae (480 B.C.E.), a narrow pass linking Greece with Thessaly, the Greeks under Leonidas inflicted heavy losses on the invading Persians and, with an army of 300 Spartans, died heroically to the last man.

5. Alfred Galpin had attended Lawrence College in Appleton, Wis., about 40 miles southwest of Green Bay. In 1932 he returned to Lawrence College as an instructor.

6. "Bishop of Petraea in the lands of the infidels."

7. HPL means the Albany Congress, a meeting of the representatives of seven of the British colonies in North America held in June–July 1754 in Albany, New York, to plan military, political, and economic strategy in preparation for the Seven Years' War (French and Indian War), 1756–63. He cites it also in "The Lurking Fear" (1922; *D* 191).

8. See Whittier's "St. John" (1841) and Longfellow's "The Student's Second Tale: The Baron of St. Castine" (*Tales of a Wayside Inn*).

9. Increase Mather (1639–1723). The quotation has not been identified.

10. Cotton Mather (1663–1728), *Magnalia Christi Americana* (1702), Book VII, Appendix, Article VIII. HPL owned a first edition (*LL* 598). *Delenda est Carthago* ("Carthage must be destroyed") was repeatedly uttered by Cato the Elder (Marcus Porcius Cato, 234–149 B.C.E.) in the course of the Punic Wars, which ended in 202 B.C.E. with Carthage's defeat (but not its destruction).

11. "Old Style (Calendar)," referring to the fact that Great Britain did not convert to the Gregorian calendar (which was eleven days ahead of the Julian calendar and began the new year on 1January rather than on 25 March) until 1752. Cf. *The Case of Charles Dexter Ward* (*MM* 149).

12. The French city of Calais, conquered by the English in 1347, became the last remaining piece of French territory controlled by England. It fell to French forces in 1558. Queen Mary ruled from 1553 to 1558.

13. Mather, *Magnalia*, Book II, Appendix ("Pietas in Patriam").

14. See Joseph Addison, *Spectator* No. 50 (27 April 1711).

15. Francis Parkman (1823–1893), *The Conspiracy of Pontiac* (1851), ch. 5. HPL owned this landmark work by a leading American historian (LL 674).

16. See William Shirley (1694–1771), *Correspondence of William Shirley, Governor of Massachusetts and Military Commander in America, 1731–1760* (1912; LL 801).

17. Nathaniel Hawthorne (1804–1864), "Famous Old People" (Section VIII), *Grandfather's Chair: A History for Youth* (1841; LL 401).

18. HPL repeats this anecdote about Jonathan E. Hoag (see "Observations on Several Parts of America," n. 17) at SL 5.372.

19. Gray, *Elegy* (1751), l. 36.

20. Parkman, *Conspiracy of Pontiac*, ch. 5.

21. Sir Edward Shepherd Creasy (1812–1878), *The Fifteen Decisive Battles of the World, from Marathon to Waterloo* (1851). HPL owned a 1908 ed. (LL 208), which included descriptions of several more battles, including Quebec, written by an anonymous historian.

22. William Kirby (1817–1906), *The Golden Dog (Le Chien d'Or): A Romance of the Days of Louis Quinze in Quebec* (1897).

23. Parkman, Parkman, *The Old Regimé in Canada* (1874), ch. 24.

24. "From sea to sea."

25. "Courage gave [them] a joint death, history gave [them] fame, posterity gave [them] a monument."

26. Later Edward VIII (1894–1972; r. 1936), who abdicated in order to marry a divorcée, Mrs. Wallis Simpson, thereby becoming the Duke of Windsor. His visit to Quebec occurred in 1919, not 1923.

27. "[Quebec is] strong by nature, [and it] grows by industry."

28. Sir Michael Ernest Sadler (1861–1943), British educational pioneer and master of University College, Oxford (1923–34). His remark has not been located.

29. Frank Carrel (1870–1940), *Guide to the City of Québec* (1899). The 1929 edition, which HPL probably consulted, gives *Carrel's Illustrated Guide and Map of Québec* on the cover.

30. Not located.

31. *Quebec (Canada): How to See It.* A 1933 edition has been located, but earlier editions probably exist.

32. François-Xavier Garneau (1809–1866), the greatest writer of nineteenth-century French Canada and its leading historian. His *Histoire du Canada* was published in 3 volumes in 1845–48; a supplement was issued in 1852.

33. I.e., "Georgius Rex" (King George [IV]).

34. A St. Stanislaus' church is mentioned as being in Arkham in "The Dreams in the Witch House" (1932; MM 271, 298).

35. William Dean Howells (1837–1920), *A Chance Acquaintance* (1873), a novel telling in part of a boat trip along the St. Lawrence and into Quebec.

36. "Francis I, King of the French, rules by the grace of God."

EUROPEAN GLIMPSES

The glamour of an old world trip begins before familiar shores are left behind. On the evening of Tuesday, July 19, 1932, I boarded the great Southampton-bound liner *Europa* at the foot of Christopher Street, New York City, and saw on every hand the excitement and marks of adventurous expectancy which attend a plunge toward another and older world. It was to be my first adult journey abroad—with England, Germany, and France as my goals—and as I noted the noise, confusion, and emotional farewells I could feel that this crowded pier, so close to home in a geographical sense, was indeed a gateway to the distant lands ahead, if not an actual outpost of their historic charm.

At 11:30 a bugle sent visitors ashore, but crowds on the wharf continued to wave and roar. At midnight a deafening blast of the ship's whistle announced the sorting, and presently the wharf with its milling shouters began to recede. The light-starred silhouette of Manhattan's fantastic towers, pyramids, and minarets took on a shadowy, dream-like aspect and stood out in diminishing perspective. The harbour unfolded in sombre grandeur, guarded by the blazing and Cyclopean bulk of the Statue of Liberty. A powerful searchlight beam shot forth from somewhere and followed the ship till every other link with the shore had vanished—slowly spinning itself out to a faint, golden spider-thread and finally fading away altogether. Then we were alone with sea and sky, flooded with pale radiance from a rounded, gibbous moon two days in the wane.

The voyage as a whole was smooth, pleasant, and uneventful, with little differentiation between the various days. Cuisine was uniformly excellent, with luncheon comparable to dinner in amplitude and elaborateness, and with tea at four o'clock each afternoon. Music and dancing were provided for those desiring them, a cinema show was presented daily, and there were other amusement devices including a miniature horse-race in which the movements of puppet horses were determined by casts of dice. My own time was spent largely on deck, where one might enjoy the varying effects of ocean and cloud-dappled sky. The sunsets were particularly fine, their foreground of unbroken sea lending them an impressiveness seldom found on land. Some of the combinations of crimson, mauve, and gold were highly unusual, and full of that vague suggestion of half-inaccessible wonders which a sunset always possesses to a greater or lesser extent.

It is difficult to describe the sensations afforded by a first sight of the Old World's misty shores. Dreams seem to be taking a tangible form, and legend to be crystallising into fact. The ancient cliffs of England breathe a homecoming, and we feel close to the source and focus of our civilisation. Southampton remains in memory as a scene of bustle and excitement—of customs inspection, and of embarkation on the London-bound train, so tiny to American eyes. From the train-window one might see the delectable English landscape outspread in rich summer greenness—the fields, hills, and hedgerows of that Mother Land which shaped our thoughts and imaginations through centuries of continuous life. Here and there a graceful country seat or village spire was glimpsed amid the hills or caught outlined against the sky, and one could not but note the many vestiges of mediaevalism inherent in the aspect of the cottages and in the fortress-like architecture of the older manor-houses.

London

At last the outflung suburbs of Greater London straggled into view, and after a debarkation full of expectant excitement came a trip through historic streets to the hotel chosen for the Cook's Tour group of which I formed a part. It was cosy, comfortable, and unobtrusive, and the meal offered at tea-time was a typically English one—menu, servants, and atmosphere—consisting of roast beef, two vegetables, thin bread and butter, and a sweet; delightfully and daintily prepared and served, and obviously much enjoyed by all the guests. My presence in the great metropolitan centre of Anglo-Saxon cultural life seemed hardly credible at first, but in the evening I telephoned friends and was shewn about the city in a kind of orientation tour. There was a gentle rain, but I was somehow glad of the fact; finding in the damp greyness something vaguely home-like and reminiscent and characteristic of the land.

The next day—Monday, July 25—was likewise rainy, but the Cook party was not deterred from its motor-bus sightseeing trip. The route included all the London "high spots" usually sought by rapid tourists, and was probably more closely packed with significant sights and revivified memories than any other day's trip on this planet could possibly be.

Naturally the Tower of London with its gory memories, suggestions of the Middle Ages, and sumptuous crown jewels figured prominently in the itinerary. The reality is much like its widely known pictures, so that one has an odd sense of treading on familiar ground. The sense of the past is tremendous as one walks through massive vaulted gateways and into ponderous Romanesque aisles, and it is impossible not to think of the hapless prisoners who walked here centuries ago, only to perish on the executioner's block. Anne Boleyn, Sir Thomas More, Lady Jane Grey, Raleigh, Strafford, Laud, the Jacobites of 1745—the list is long and illustrious. Many of the victims of the axe lie buried beneath the chapel of St. Peter ad Vincula, within the Tower's precincts, and some of the walls of the various dungeons bear scrawled inscriptions made by captives of every rank. It was a relief to turn from such marks of menace and death to the glittering regalia in Wakefield Tower—gold and precious stones on a scale scarcely to be dreamed of, and full of memories of the long line of sovereigns who have worn them. This is the greatest single collection of jewels in existence. The Yeomen of the Guard and other forces connected with the Tower are dressed in curious Elizabethan costumes—which were, however, adopted in the time of Charles II as conscious archaisms.

From the Tower we proceeded to St. Paul's—that magnificent apex of Anglo-Classic architecture whose dome has crowned the London skyline for nearly two centuries and a half. It was appropriate for one's first sight of Wren's masterpiece and tomb (for he is buried here) to occur in the year of his tri-centennial, and as I viewed it I reflected on the vast extent to which his methods influenced the architecture of colonial America. St. Paul's is the third largest church in the world, but I found an almost equal charm in some of the many smaller churches (over fifty) with which Wren dotted London after the Great Fire. St. Bride's in Fleet Street, built in 1701, has a spire strongly suggesting those of the next generation in America; while the bells of St. Mary le Bow, in Cheapside—the "Bow Bells" of tradition—are as famous as the exquisite steeple in which they ring.

Westminster Abbey—shrine of the British nation and of the entire Anglo-Saxon race—needs no description from any casual hand. As at the Tower, the visitor is overwhelmed by a mounting consciousness of the centuries; though here the impression is tinctured with beauty and mystery rather than with terror and gloom. The bulk of the church dates from the thirteenth century; though the Norman Undercroft goes back to 1066, while the Chapel of Henry V, in a late and ornate form of Gothic, is of the sixteenth century. It is unfortunate that the popular conception of the Abbey—based on salient externals—is derived from the relatively modern Western Towers, planned by Wren and completed by Hawkesmoor (1745) in an age unsympathetic toward the Gothic tradition. In leaving the cloistral twilight of the famous fane one carries away a curious variety of reflections. The illustrious dead—the greatness of the race—the continuity of tradition—all these thoughts crowd to the fore, and reduce the present moment to insignificance. Every English sovereign since Edward the Confessor has been crowned in this awesome edifice, and not the least of its treasures is the Coronation Chair with its celebrated Stone of Scone.

My closest and most revealing views of Old London—the London of Addison and Steele, Defoe and Newton, Johnson, Goldsmith, and Boswell—were obtained apart from the touring group in a series of excursions, largely on foot, under the guidance of friends. To speak of all I saw and absorbed would be impossible in anything short of a full-length book, but certain memories remain especially vivid and dominant. Among these is the house of Newton in the tiny street now named for him—a building at present remodelled as a school, but containing a perfect restoration of the white doorway through which the sage so often passed.

On one occasion I had supper at the old Cheshire Cheese tavern in Wine-Office Court off Fleet Street, in the heart of the region made memorable by Dr. Johnson, Goldsmith, Boswell, Garrick, and the rest of the old Literary Club. Of the several inns closely associated with Johnson, this alone has survived in its original form; and it has for generations been a famous literary rendezvous. The edifice was reconstructed in its present aspect in 1667, after the Great Fire, but the vaulted wine-cellar beneath plainly bespeaks a still greater antiquity. Relics of the past are very much in evidence here. In the front entry a parrot said to be lineally descended from that which tenanted the same cage (or one precisely like it) in Dr. Johnson's time greets the guest with raucous hospitality, while the lexicographer's original pipe still hangs in a corner over his favourite table. I was served the same sort of toothsome beef pie which he relished in his day, and the mugs at the tables are exact copies of those from which he quenched his Gargantuan thirst. Duplicates of these mugs are for sale, and form especially apt mementoes of the place and its illustrious frequenter. Appropriately enough, a life-like painting of the doctor hangs in his chosen corner. A little way up the Court is the house where Goldsmith wrote "The Vicar of Wakefield", while farther along is Gough Square, where Johnson composed his dictionary. Not very far away along Fleet Street is Bolt Court, the scene of Johnson's later years. It was here that he died in 1784.

Additional memories are of the Temple and other quaint Inns of Court, of the stately Houses of Parliament, and of numberless little streets near the waterside, tangled, crooked, and circuitous, many of whose houses antedate the Great Fire. Victoria Embankment along the north side of the Thames proved extremely fascinating. At one point the Temple gardens add to its beauty, while against a nearby wall is fixed a large plaque with the features of Victoria, marking (as did once the vanished Temple Bar between Fleet Street and the Strand) the boundary which separates the extra-mural "liberties" of the ancient City of London from the mediaeval Borough of Westminster. The Albert Embankment on the river's southern shore is also a pleasant promenade; while all the bridges—especially graceful Waterloo Bridge, dating from 1819 and now the oldest—captivate the eye.

In the three days spent in London I did not neglect High Holborn, the Strand, and the West End. Buckingham Palace, home of the Sovereigns, is of great size and impressiveness; while the ancient ceremony of changing the guards, enacted before it each morning, is one of the most vivid pieces of pageantry which our increasingly dull-grey and devitalised world affords. It is impossible not to be thrilled by the red coats of the men, and the imperious voice of the bugle. St. James's Palace, now the home of the Prince of Wales, is of much greater age and interest than Buckingham; its earliest portions dating back to the reign of Henry VIII.

Charing Cross and Trafalgar Square; Pall Mall and Piccadilly; Regent Street, Bond Street, Oxford Street, and Oxford Circus; Portland Place, Berkeley, Grosvenor, and Cavendish Squares; Mayfair and Marylebone (the latter name, sometimes corrupted to "Marrowbone", really represents *Marie le Bonne*)—each of these has its own type of appeal, as do the numberless bye-streets of infinite quaintness and antiquity, known to very few tourists, and scarcely to be recalled by name. The parks of London really deserve a chapter to themselves—St. James's Park, famous in Restoration comedy, Green Park, Hyde Park with its Marble Arch and Rotten Row (Route en Roi), Kensington Gardens and the Serpentine, and Regent's Park, the largest of all.

In Hyde Park I beheld the nightly swarm of amateur orators whose soap-box eloquence provides so ample a safety-valve for social and governmental discontent. Around these hoarse and excited expounders of political, religious, ethical, economic, philosophic, and divers other doctrines there gathers regularly a hungry, ragged, argumentative horde such as Hogarth would have loved to draw. Each ardent prophet has his own private solution for his country's ills and those of the world in general, and no two will commonly be found to offer anything like the same panacea. All, however, have their respective (if sometimes less than respectful) audiences, with whom they usually share a complete ignorance of the problems they discuss. No limit is placed on their radicalism of utterance, since it is a traditional British belief that free speech affords the safest possible vent for disturbed emotions and bewildered brains. The staring, listening crowds are mostly indifferent and apathetic; saying little, and evidently seeking free entertainment more than anything else. Though unemployed and helpless, they seem to sense obscurely that not much real aid for a troubled planet will ever come from these passionate, self-chosen Messiahs, each of whom is a never-ceasing fountain of unfulfilled promises.

"He who is weary of London," said Dr. Johnson, "is weary of life"[1]—and it was with reluctance that I moved onward in compliance with my touring schedule. I had hoped to see something of the placid and beautiful countryside with its ancient manors, churches, and villages; of Oxford and Cambridge; of the great cathedral towns, the Shakespeare district, and mystic and primordial Stonehenge; and of the quaint seaports and fishing hamlets of the coast; but unforeseen obstacles forced a speeding up of my itinerary, and a direct dash for my next goal—Wiesbaden, in Germany on the storied Rhine.

After an all-too-tantalising trip through hoary Kent—with Rochester and immortal Canterbury flashing by with tragic brevity—I embarked at Dover on a channel boat for Ostend, Belgium, where a train for Cologne was waiting. The English-speaking world now left behind, I observed with keen interest the level, sleepy Belgian meadows through which the train presently took me. The villages seemed quaint, drowsy, and delightful, and the farms were all of neat and enterprising aspect though devoid of any signs of vast abundance or striking success. At length came the German frontier, a run through the fertile Rhineland district and a final approach to the splendid cathedral spires of Cologne, on the Rhine itself.

The Rhine

The lordly Rhine, bordered by ancient towns and castle-crowned hills, and winding with majestic breadth, amply merits its high place in folklore and general admiration. It is the custom to compare it with the Hudson, but so akin are its golden-tinted waters to those of our Southern rivers that I would consider the meandering and bluff-bordered Tennessee—as it coils past Chattanooga—a closer American parallel. The Rhineland region is the oldest part of Germany in point of civilised life, it having been the only Teutonic region to fall within the Roman domain. Caesar twice crossed the Rhine—in 55 and 53 B.C.—and in A.D. 13 and afterward the territory was permanently conquered by Drusus Claudius Nero—stepson of Augustus, brother of Tiberius, father of Claudius and of the celebrated Germanicus, grandfather of Caligula, and great-grandfather of the young Ahenobarbus who later disgraced the honourable name of Nero. This imperially connected conqueror built no less than fifty forts along the Rhine, nearly all of which survive to this day as cities and towns.

Cologne—to whose peerless cathedral and wealth of other notable antiquities I could not devote as much time as I wished—is even older than the Roman occupation, being originally the chief town of the Ubii. It became a Roman colony in A.D. 51, when the Emperor Claudius sent out settlers and named it *Colonia Agrippina* in honour of his wife—also his niece—the infamous Younger Agrippina, daughter of Germanicus and mother of the Emperor Nero.

The charm of a voyage up the Rhine is past all adequate description except by a poet—the only flaw in my case being my inability to stop at each of the tantalisingly beautiful towns along its shore, or to linger near each of the awesome and impressive castles—some converted to museums and the rest in various stages of picturesque ruin—that crown the alluring green slopes. Every inch of the twisting stream is rich in brooding legend—spectre, elf, and Lorelei—and the play of sunlight and shadow conjures up a thousand overtones of dream, wonder, and mystical expectancy as vista on vista unfolds in an endless series of breath-taking surprises. Sunset beyond the spires of some millennial city or the ivied remains of some bygone hilltop stronghold is a spectacle more of phantasy than of reality. Mist—twilight—dusk—all the familiar phenomena of Nature take on a new significance in this strange, haunted, and altogether exquisite materialisation of fairyland.

Bonn—originally the camp of the Sixth Roman Legion—is a splendid old university town containing the birthplace of Beethoven. Nearby are the Godesburg—an ancient sacred place of the Ubii—and the stupendously lovely crag of Drachenfels, topped by one of the most appealing old ruins I have ever seen.

Coblentz (the Roman *Confluentes*) is one of the old forts of Drusus Nero, and stands where the vineyard-bordered Moselle—so nobly sung by the Gallo-Roman poet Ausonius[2]—empties into the Rhine. Across the great river rises the castle-crowned slope of Ehrenbreitstein. Then in magical succession come Stolzenfels—tall, machicolated towers at a dizzy height above the stream—the Marksburg with its massive masonry frowning over Braubach; Rheinfels silhouetted starkly against the sky; the fatal rock of the Lorelei, where amidst gloomy cliffs the mariner of old was lured to his death; the compactly turreted Pfalz on its tiny islet; the lofty steeple and Gothic ruins of Bacharach; Rheinstein on its vertiginous crag of barren granite; bleak, brooding Ehrenfels; the legended Mouse-Tower of Bishop Hatto sung by Longfellow;[3] and the spreading roofs of Bingen—another of Drusus Nero's old forts—where the Nahe (Roman Nava) flows into the Rhine. The ancient stone bridge across the Nahe erected by Drusus still survives and most incongruously bears a railway line. Mayence is another fine old town originating as a camp of Drusus.

Wiesbaden

Finally came Wiesbaden, my destination. This is now the largest curative spa in Germany, and is a place of singular charm and natural beauty despite its baroque architecture and lack of visible antiquities. It lies at a healthful altitude in a Rhine-watered valley enclosed by the Taunus Hills, with the green and lovely Neroburg (probably named for Drusus Nero) rising directly behind it. The present population, including annexe and suburbs, is 154,000. Twenty-seven hot mineral springs of medicinal value give the city its chief fame, and make it a perennial focus for health-seekers. It was largely frequented in Roman times when it bore the name of Fontes Mattiaci or Aquae Mattiacae, referring to a local tribe of Germans.

The terrain of Wiesbaden is well landscaped, and rich in graceful verdure. Its most pretentious edifice is the new Kurhaus, completed in 1907 and set in the midst of an exceptionally fine park. The architecture of this building is Roman on an almost florid and grandiose scale, and its functions include those of a concert hall, reading room, and restaurant. The neighbouring State Theatre, also finely landscaped, is very ambitious in its sumptuousness, though of a less purely classical design. Much of the curative bathing is done at the finely appointed Kaiser Friedrich Baths and at the pretentiously housed hot spring known as the Kochbrunnen.

The streets and squares are laid out with much taste, and some of the public buildings are impressive. Among the latter are the Museum, the Town Hall, the High School, the Post Office, and the Lesser State Theatre. The "Paulinenschlosser" or edifice of assembly halls is an unfortunate example of that meaningless "functional" architecture of recent years, to which Germany has become so regrettably addicted. In the Museum are many interesting reliques of the Roman period, including some well-preserved stelae and statuary. The city is full of sumptuous and picturesquely steepled churches, and presents a magnificent sight when seen from certain vantage-points. Sidewalks are laid out in a curious geometrical mosaic pattern of which irregular semi-circles form the chief motif.

The standard of municipal neatness is very high, trim wire receptacles for rubbish being attached to the lamp posts. Traffic is light, and relatively few taxicabs or private motors are to be seen. Motor buses form the chief public mode of transit, though there is a sprinkling of horse-drawn vehicles—landaus—for hire. Bicycles are numerous, and workhorses and delivery motors are occasionally to be seen. Many streets are named from celebrated German musicians; Wagner, Haydn, and Mozart being represented. The shops are small and extremely tasteful—especially those devoted to art. Despite the immaculateness of streets and houses, personal attire is apt to be somewhat negligent and unfashionable.

One curious feature of Wiesbaden is the reduced canine population, with a tremendous scarcity of puppies and young dogs and a corresponding preponderance of aged and decrepit specimens. Scarcely any but old dogs are seen on the streets—an effect which strikes the casual traveller as distinctly bizarre and almost depressing. Upon inquiry I found this condition to be a consequence of the monthly tax of 5 marks on each dog kept in the city—a measure enacted some time ago, but not made applicable to dogs already owned at the period of its adoption. As a result, the poorer families—who account for most of the dogs commonly seen at large—cling to their ancient and tax-free pets, but refrain from acquiring new ones.

In the residential districts, especially toward the hills, there are many spacious villas rising tier on tier; each terrace covered with richly glowing gardens and adorned with well-distributed shade trees at both front and rear of the houses. Throughout the gardens there are luxuriously shaded tables and seats, the latter usually made of cleverly twisted branches. There is at least one hideously modernistic house, but it is to be hoped that the number will not increase.

The Neroburg is a favourite place of public resort, its steep slope being traversed by a cable railway. Many persons regularly frequent this eminence each afternoon, enjoying the music and beverages purveyed there for their benefit. High up stands the picturesque and bulbous-domed Greek Orthodox Chapel, erected by Russian residents in 1857. My visit to the mountain took place in the afternoon, and the sunset view of the outspread city below was magnificent and fancy-stirring beyond description. Spires and domes, roofs and chimney-pots lay transfigured in a mauve mist, while beyond them the golden thread of the Rhine shimmered in the sun's last rays. In the distance loomed the mountains, green, majestic, and shadowy, looking down on the peaceful valley like kindly protecting spirits.

The smaller hotels in Wiesbaden are, like most of those on the Continent, cleanly though somewhat primitive. Running water is on tap only at certain points, and baths must be brought by attendants and paid for. No tea or coffee is served at dinner and supper, though such may be obtained at any of the numerous restaurants or sidewalk cafes. Wine, beer, and cordials are in common use, though I encountered no visible cases of drunkenness. As in the rest of Europe, ice-water is extremely rare. Beer and champagne are served cold, but all other unheated beverages come at the prevailing temperature of the air. Hotel attendants are extremely neat and courteous, and I found the housemaid at the villa where I stopped a person of exceptional refinement, conscientiousness, unobtrusiveness, and good manners.

The climate of Wiesbaden is of unusual mildness for its latitude, so that it has many winter visitors. Spring and autumn, however, are the main tourist seasons. For the benefit of both natives and transients a great variety of musical, dramatic, and other cultural activities is provided, while well-organised sports and amusements are also maintained. Dances, fireworks, fêtes, Rhine boating, tours of the Taunus Hills, aviation, golf, tennis, motor racing, athletic competitions, swimming, sailing regattas, skating, skiing, and toboganing are among the regular diversions available. The influx of travellers is excellently handled by the various transportation facilities, which include railways, Rhine steamboats, and aeroplane lines. Excursions to neighbouring points of scenic and historic interest are common—the whole Rhine country, with its lovely wooded hills and vales, castled crags, steepled villages, and picturesque ruins, being within easy reach.

It is hard to make these dry, factual paragraphs convey to the full the peculiar charm of Wiesbaden. Undoubtedly, the scenery forms of core of that charm—the mountains, the trees, the streams, the flowers, and the exquisite system of parks. The latter are developed on an almost unprecedented scale, stretching solidly from the Kurhaus to the distant magical woodlands of the Taunus. The variety of bewitchingly beautiful rural and sylvan walks is virtually unlimited. Qualitatively, the landscaping displays a vivid and subtle imagination—as if the gardeners had read Poe's "Domain of Arnheim".[4] Unusual shrubs and trees are selected and allocated with artistic delicacy, and lakelets are woven sensitively into the general picture. The effect is vaguely exotic and redolent of dream, leaving an impression which no lapse of time serves to dissipate.

During my stay of five days in Wiesbaden I had opportunities to observe the disturbed political state of Germany, and the constant squabbles between various dismally uniformed factions of would-be patriots. Of all the self-appointed leaders, Hitler[5] alone seems to retain a cohesive and enthusiastic following; his sheer magnetism and force of will serving—in spite of his deficiencies in true social insight—to charm, drug, or hypnotise the hordes of youthful "Nazis" who blindly revere and obey him. Without possessing any clear-cut or well-founded programme for Germany's economic reconstruction, he plays theatrically on the younger generation's military emotions and sense of national pride; urging them to overthrow the restrictive provisions of the Versailles treaty and reassert the strength and supremacy of the German people. He is fond of such phrases as: "Germany, awaken and take your rightful heritage with your own strong hands!"—and when speaking of elections usually intimates that in case of defeat he will consider an armed march on Berlin corresponding to Mussolini's Roman coup d'état of 1922.

Hitler's lack of clear, concrete objectives seems to lose him nothing with the crowd; and when—during my stay—he was scheduled to speak in Wiesbaden, the Kurpark was crowded fully two hours before the event by a throng whose quiet seriousness was almost funereal. The contrast with America's jocose and apathetic election crowds was striking. When the leader finally appeared—his right hand lifted in an approved Fascist salute—the crowd shouted *"Heil!"* three times, and then subsided into an attentive silence devoid alike of applause, heckling, or hissing. The general spirit of the address was that of Cato's *"Delenda est Carthago"*[6]—though one could not feel quite sure what particular Carthage, material or psychological, "Handsome Adolf" was trying to single out for anathema.

After the conclusion the crowd respectfully opened a path for his departure, and he left in his car as quietly as he had arrived—the only sound being a shout of farewell from his followers. Then—silently, though perhaps with the general muffled discontent of the period—the kindly burghers dispersed to their not quite happy homes. At the time of this speech Hitler's tactics hinted of a "back to the Monarchy" movement; and Prince August Wilhelm, son of the ex-Kaiser, was a brief supplementary speaker. The royal scion, however, failed to overshadow the would-be dictator in the popular emotions.

The waste of energy and widespread chaos caused by the incessant conflict of no less than thirty-six separate parties—of which three may be called major ones—is the most distressing phenomenon in modern Germany; yet no one seems able to reconcile the various shades of opinion and feeling which cause this confusing diversity. Taxes are exorbitant, unemployment terrific, and general confidence at a very low ebb. The people of Wiesbaden have lately come to call their habitat "the city without a smile", though the same might be said for almost any city in the Reich. Passport restrictions are very stringent, including both visas and police registration; and the tourist is taxed nine pfennigs a day during his sojourn in the country. Yet the German people as a whole, apart from the governmental meshes in which they are entangled, are perhaps the most kindly and affable beings I have ever met. They are gracious, courteous, and delightful; and seem to radiate a really cordial glow devoid of hollowness or superficiality. They perform their duties with an almost military precision and effectiveness, and when once led out of their present chaos will undoubtedly resume their place of importance in the world. One hopes that a suitable leader may arise before the existing misery increases.

At last the pressure of time forced me to leave Wiesbaden—with many regrets, though with keen anticipations of Paris, which lay at the end of a pleasant rail journey from Mayence, across the river. At the Lorraine frontier one crosses into territory reconquered by France in the Great War, and becomes aware of the change in environment. Metz is a fine old cathedral town at which there was no time to pause. Finally the outskirts of Paris hove in sight, and I realised that I was at last in the great centre of Continental culture—the heart of that France which is without doubt the modern counterpart of shining Hellas, just as our own Anglo-Saxon world is the counterpart of all-conquering Rome.

France and Its Drawbacks

There are, however, obstacles to enjoyment in France—as I discovered immediately upon disembarking at the railway station. The French trading classes, with proverbial thrift and hardness, see in every American a potential source of revenue; and are determined to improve their opportunities to the limit of possibility. The most persistent nuisance is the short-changing made easy by the nature of French currency. Though outwardly very simple, the Gallic decimal system puzzles the Americans because of the smallness of its units—especially since the post-war deflation of the franc. A franc now represents no more than four cents; yet it is divided into 100 centimes, and many small copper pieces of only a few centimes' value are in general circulation. When equipped with the usual exchange supply of 5, 10, 20, 50, and 100 franc notes, the tourist cannot but be confused by the change-making operations which flood his pockets with tiny coins whose appearance and value he has had no time to learn. Shopkeepers are aware of this confusion, and sometimes have no hesitancy about turning it to their own financial advantage. One has to exercise superhuman vigilance in every transaction, great or small.

My welcome to Paris was an amusingly stormy one. No sooner had the Cook's Tour group been led from the station by its appointed guide than a violent altercation broke out between this functionary on the one hand and, on the other hand, the porter carrying our luggage and the chauffeur of the waiting taxicab; an altercation which, though I could not decipher its purport, quickly attracted an excited and gesticulating crowd. Words passed into action as the guide angrily seized the valises which the porter had placed in the cab, and the stream of evident abuse continued to increase in volume, vehemence, and speed—each side clearly intent on breaking all records for rapid-fire billingsgate. Just as I was wondering whether the whole party would be taken to an hotel or to gaol, the porter proceeded to summon a gendarme—a grave, ponderous person who may or may not have heard the disjointed tales which all three combatants tried to pour simultaneously into his ears. Finally the guardian of public order strolled away with a philosophic shrug of his huge shoulders, leaving us all exactly as we were before.

As the battle continued, some of our group displayed justifiable signs of impatience; but despite cries of "Let's go", there was no movement except of tongues, hands, shoulders, and eyes. Meanwhile the crowd of spectators grew. Our final deliverer was an English-speaking gendarme who, perceiving the nationality of the party, asked us at large, in our own language, "What is the trouble?" I took it upon myself to answer him—or rather, appeal to him, since I knew as little of the cause as he—remarking that Paris's welcome to Americans seemed somewhat less gentle than America's welcome to Parisians would be likely to be, and urging him to do his official duty and lead us to safety. This second warden of the nation's peace did not fail us, and by his aid we obtained another cab and rolled away with our guide, leaving the porter, the first chauffeur, and the amused spectators to liquidate the performance as best they might.

Our guide then told us in very doubtful English just what it was all about. It appears that the porter and the first chauffeur were in collusion, the latter planning to overcharge his passengers and divide the spoils with the former in exchange for the steering of the victims to his vehicle. The man from Cook's had been quick to detect the manoeuvre, and had accordingly refused to patronise the piratical cab—hence the conflict which brought so much amusement to the audience, and so much delay to our group.

That this policy of extortion is quite general, later events forbade me to doubt. Toward the end of my stay in Paris I suffered from a gastric ailment induced by the drinking water, and found that medical service forms no exception to the rules of plunder. When the doctor (secured after great delay because of the week-end suspension of all activities in Paris) and nurse decided that my illness would be a matter of several days, they consented to my transfer to the American Hospital at Neuilly-sur-Seine (just west of the city proper) and there I met with Gallic banditry at its subtlest apex.

Though relief from pain came quickly, the aftermath of weakness prevented immediate departure, and I arranged for the cheapest private room at a rate which the receiving clerk told me would be $3.20—three dollars and twenty cents in American money, the equivalent of 80 francs—per day; this room to be abandoned for a cheaper public ward as soon as possible on account of the depleted state of my purse. As time passed, my removal was not accomplished; and on the third day I was presented with a bill for 960 francs, purporting to cover three days at a rate of 320 francs ($12.80) each—a deliberate confusion of this latter figure with the $3.20 in American money (80 francs) which I had agreed to pay. When I protested that I had not enough cash with me to meet such a charge, the nurse became somewhat alarmed; and at length the superintendent authorised my transfer to a ward—which proved to be a pleasant sun-porch with only one other occupant. This, I was told, would be only $2.80 (70 francs) per day.

The "racket" now took a fresh turn—this time hinging on delay. Day after day I announced myself able to go, but was repeatedly told that my temperature, or lung congestion, or heart action demanded a longer sojourn. Others, I soon learned, had been subjected to the same experience; one woman being still a patient after seven weeks of practical recovery, while another had met French extortion by taking "French leave". Only the approaching sailing of my homeward boat put an end to this buccaneering. Even then the clerk tried to induce me to let her exchange my ticket for a later one, but for once I was firm. Eventually I was allowed to depart—but only after being faced with a bill which did not correct the original 320-franc error, and which added an extra 450 francs for some mythical "laboratory work", plus 250 more for "treatment". When I summoned the superintendent he apologised for the "error"— quite in line with the general French policy of shrewd and systematic overcharges, with apologies and corrections offered only when the victim detects the fraud himself and demands an accounting. To crown the matter, I later learned why the clerk had been so anxious to help me exchange my steamship ticket. It seems that this service would have involved an extra charge, part of which would have come to her as a fee.

And yet this hospital is undeniably the finest institution of its kind that I have ever seen, with splendid facilities and the highest type of medical service. It is, I am told, in a state of bankruptcy because of the decreasing numbers of Americans and English in Paris; and it really deserves a generous endowment to enable it to carry on its work without "going native" in its financial treatment of patients. If I have been tedious in this digression, it is only because my experiences furnish so typical an example of what all Americans in France must prepare themselves to meet. The notion that everyone from the western hemisphere must be a gullible plutocrat is something which sticks naively and childishly in the common European mind along with the parallel notion that all Americans are blatant barbarians with cheap tastes and undeveloped mentality. Both impressions doubtless come from the fact that the mass of Europeans usually notice only the cheaper outgrowths of American life—the noisy, illiterate, and ostentatious parvenu tourist, the inane and tawdry cinema film, the raucous strains of jazz, and the reports of sensational crime and rampant commercialism which drift across the Atlantic. Only the better classes of the Old World know of the America which still holds to its heritage of colonial culture—the America of Harvard University, *Harper's Magazine*, and the traditions of New England, Virginia, and Charleston.

But lest I be grouped with the blatant, querulous-minded, and the unappreciative tourists so properly condemned, let me hasten to say that the material difficulties just mentioned did not in the least prevent me from revelling in the loveliness and historic glamour of ancient France. My great regret is that I could not see more, and what I did see will remain long and vividly in my memory.

Paris

Paris is probably the most beautiful of all the large cities I have ever seen. London is mellower and richer in overtones, Manhattan more spectacular, but La Ville Lumière surpasses both in sheer grace and classic perfection of form—and this despite the architectural heterogeneity of which Victor Hugo complained. Baroque structures which would elsewhere be garish and obtrusive seem here to lose their individual defects in a larger harmonious design. The broad avenues and boulevards, the columned and statued squares, the vast geometrical vistas, and the eternal keynote of the Seine with its finely walled and landscaped banks and its exquisite bridges, all conduce to a highly distinctive charm impossible to escape and subtly suggestive of the Graeco-Roman.

No other city affords such utterly glamorous, dream-provoking panoramas as does this brooding heir of the centuries with its tangled roofs, towers, spires, and domes, and its picturesque heights—Montmartre, La Villette, and Butte Chaumont on the north, and the Pantheon region and Montparnasse on the south. There are innumerable views of awesome loveliness, from the various hill sections and from the towers of the great churches; and the spectacle of a sunset beyond the dome of the Invalides, the facade of St. Sulpice, or the shimmering line of the river and its endless bridges, is a mystic and memorable thing which opens gateways of fancy to illimitable spheres of flaming wonder. Nor is anything on earth more utterly fairy-like and Dunsanian than the shimmering, many-domed pallor of fantastic Sacre-Coeur as it looms wraith-like in the distance atop Montmartre.

I saw relatively little of the modern city—though the Eiffel Tower, Rue de la Paix, Opera House, and other nineteenth-century features were glimpsed in passing—but concentrated on the old Paris of Balzac, Dumas, and Hugo. Despite all modernisations, a surprising amount of the ancient town is left, and it is easy to reconstruct in memory the Paris of Philip Augustus, of Louis XI, of Louis XIV, and of the Revolution—with the three main regions, City (Ile de la Cité, the original Gallic village), Town (north or right bank of the Seine), and University (south or left bank) clearly defined. In many local areas—notably the squalid Marais on the right bank north and east of the pretentious Hotel de Ville, the dingy Rue Mouffetard and its neighbourhood on the left bank sloping down eastward of the Pantheon, and certain tumbledown parts of Montmartre—the narrow streets retain a very mediaeval aspect, and conceal many buildings of tremendous age with quaint inner courts. In the Marais there are the blighted remnants of several ancient mansions, with hanging turrets at the corners in the true style of the Middle Ages.

Despite its intellectual progressiveness—or perhaps because of it—Paris holds more of the past than any other metropolis today. Here and there are touches of the primitive—a moss-grown street near the Pantheon, a flock of goats led by a piping herdsman, open-air bookstalls on the Quais, a row of silent fishermen beside the Seine, a garden, an apiary, or a hay-cart—which well symbolise the traditional soil-boundness of the real Frenchman—a quality which will serve him well in a world plunging into chaos through mechanisation. I was also impressed by the home-like plenitude of cats and dogs. Street names are notably picturesque, including such specimens as *Rue Gît-le-Coeur* (Street Where the Heart Lies), *Rue Chat-qui-Peche* (Street of the Fishing Cat—probably named from a bygone shop sign), *Rue de l'Arbre Sec* (Street of the Dry Trees), and so on. This quaint nomenclature is typically French, and is paralleled in other towns of France, and in Quebec on our own continent. Many streets are likewise named for the illustrious dead—not only statesmen and warriors, but men distinguished in the arts—a practice also common in Germany, but in America followed only in Boston. Thus a splendid park-like thoroughfare near the Eiffel Tower has recently been renamed Avenue Anatole France. One rather confusing attribute of Paris streets is their old-fashioned habit of changing names at various points along their course—a thing still common elsewhere in Europe, but decreasingly so in the U.S. Of the fame and importance of Paris's galleries and museums it is scarcely necessary to speak; and one of my great regrets is that I was unable, on account of the illness which cut short my sojourn, to explore the treasure-filled alcoves of the Louvre and Luxembourg.

My tours around the city included a very fair number of typical sights, some of which left a deep impression on me. The ancient Ile de la Cité—seat of the primal Gallic village of Lutetia Parisiorum and focus of the Roman town—is rich in famous antiquities. The Palais de Justice includes the famous Conciergerie prison and a fourteenth-century clock tower—the latter the oldest in France. Some parts go back to the twelfth century, when Philip Augustus first erected the structure as a fortified palace. Nearby is the narrow but exquisite Sainte-Chapelle—with gorgeously bejewelled interior—built in the thirteenth century by Saint Louis and somehow more fascinating to me than any other one thing in Paris. Victor Hugo speaks of its rising above the surrounding roofs "like an elephant's back with a tower on it—only that here the place of the elephant's tower was occupied by the boldest, openest, airiest, most notched and ornamented spire that ever shewed the sky through its lacework cone."[7] What impressed me especially were the huge Gothic windows—including the magnificent fifteenth-century rose window in the facade—which take most of the space in three out of the chapel's four sides. These still contain the original stained glass, treated by a process whose secret is now lost. Sainte-Chapelle forms a distinctive object in most Parisian vistas.

At the opposite end of La Cité is the massive cathedral of Notre-Dame—famous in art and literature for centuries, and attesting its age through the time-buried state of its lower steps. It was built in the twelfth century, but extensively restored in Victorian times by Viollet-le-Duc, whose antiquarian skill was similarly employed on most of the old Paris buildings standing in his day. Many consider Notre-Dame the finest object in Paris, and it surely deserves to be surveyed from every possible angle. To me the rear or apse end seems most beautiful, especially when glimpsed from the bookstall-lined Quai de la Tourville on the left bank. The vaulted interior is majestic and mystical—always suffused with a subdued glow, as if the great windows did not so much transmit as absorb and reëmit the light of outer day. To some the infinitely grotesque and often monstrously horrible chimaeras or gargoyles on the exterior are the chief attractions of Notre-Dame. These loathsome hybrid brooders and watchers that leer grimly over parapets and doubtfully survey the outspread city—dog-men, ape-men, cat-men, devourers of nameless repasts and thinkers of nameless thoughts—by far transcend the average waterspout-figures of mediaeval churches. They illustrate the slumbering terror and sardonic humour of the Gothic imagination—even though many of the present specimens are parts of Viollet-le-Duc's restoration.

The left bank just across from the Ile contains the overflow of the Roman town. The ancient church of St. Julien le Pauvre—oldest in Paris, with a classic architecture not debased into Romanesque—dates from a Merovingian time when Latin was still spoken, while the foundations of a Roman arena can be seen in the Rue Monge. Adjoining the Cluny Museum are the ruined baths and palace of the Emperor Julian, who greatly favoured Paris as a place of residence. It is well known that Gaul was really the most cultivated part of the Empire after the third century A.D.

The Hôtel de Cluny or Cluny Museum deserves a treatise of its own. Built in the fifteenth century by Jacques d'Amboise as a mansion for the abbots of Cluny, it is a splendidly picturesque specimen of Gothic design. Its high wall and courtyard—with an ancient well—add to its charm; and the adjacent wooded garden, where mystical statues lurk in a perpetual green twilight, and sunshine adds glamour and expectancy as it filters down through the leaves of gnarled old trees, is a bit of the Middle Ages where peace and wonder reign unhampered and urban clamour seems very far away in time and space. The nearest American analogue is the garden of the George Grey Barnard cloisters on Washington Heights in New York City owned by the Metropolitan Museum.[8] Nearby are the Roman baths of Julian, which complete one's sense of linkage to limitless antiquity. The museum itself houses a highly important collection of decorative objects and architectural details of the Gothic and Romanesque periods.

Just above the Cluny is the Sorbonne, oldest university in the world and determinant focus of left-bank Paris—the Latin Quarter—while higher up the hill is that imposing standby of the urban skyline—the Pantheon, Soufflot's great domed masterpiece of the later eighteenth century. It is impossible not to be impressed by the colossal classic structure, though there are many who oddly prefer the older and more modest Church of St. Étienne du Mort just behind it—a curious hybrid of Gothic and Renaissance design begun under Francis I but not finished till the time of Louis XIII. St. Étienne's rood-loft and shrine of Ste. Genevieve are especially famous. Other notable old left-bank churches are St. Germain-des-Prés and St. Severin on the lower ground, and the celebrated but not very beautiful St. Sulpice—just below the Luxembourg—whose classic design and mismated towers typify the French taste of the middle eighteenth century. Downhill behind the Pantheon and St. Étienne is the shabby and picturesque ancient quarter whose chief street is the Rue Mouffetard, while near the Seine is the famous Jardin des Plantes.

I took care not to miss the splendid Luxembourg Gardens—reminiscent of Remy de Gourmont[9] and countless other writers—which lie across the Boulevard St. Michel from the Pantheon region. Though possessed of a strong Latin formality, this sylvan retreat has a charm all its own—its graceful vistas, delicately poised statues, stately terraces, urns, and flights of steps, impressive palace, classic fountains (notably the Fontaine Medicis), and occasional glimpses of the Pantheon's lordly dome through masses of foliage, combining to form a peculiarly potent imaginative stimulant. Time was lacking for an exploration of the Palais de Luxembourg—a gallery of art second only to the Louvre in importance.

Farther west in left-bank Paris is the great golden-domed Hôtel des Invalides, built by Mansard in the time of Louis XIV and now containing the tomb of Napoleon. Think what one may of his conquests, it is impossible to remain unmoved before the final resting-place of modernity's only counterpart of Alexander and Caesar. He has left his stamp on France more emphatically than any other one person in history. Nearer the river at the Quai d'Orsay is the celebrated Chamber of Deputies, from which a bridge reaches to the Place de la Concorde on the right bank, affording a splendid view of the Egyptian obelisk (corresponding to those on London's Victoria Embankment and in Manhattan's Central Park), the classic buildings of Gabriel, and the more distant Madeleine—together with the far-off, hazy heights of Montmartre, crowned by the pale, dream-like Church of the Sacred Heart.

Westward along the Quai d'Orsay is the spacious Champ de Mars with the famous Ecole Militaire at its upper end, and the ugly steel Eiffel Tower at its riverfront end. The Eiffel Tower, built in 1889 as part of the Exposition Universelle, may be demolished in the course of time. It is 986 feet high, and until the erection of New York's almost equally ugly Empire State Building was the tallest structure in the world. Across the river one sees the park and palace of the Trocadéro, the latter a large and tasteless pseudo-Moorish structure put up in connexion with the exposition of 1878. Its neighbourhood is now one of Paris's finest residential districts. At sunset the twin towers of the Trocadéro form a marvellously glamorous spectacle when seen in the distance.

On the right bank I found the massive rococo Opera House—the work of Charles Garnier—of some interest, and enjoyed the busy and fashionable shopping streets around it, especially the Rue de la Paix. The Place Vendôme, with its massive Napoleonic column patterned after Trajan's Column in Rome, is highly stirring; as is the classic bulk of the Madeleine, which formed the pattern for so many Grecian buildings in America a century ago. From the Madeleine eastward, in a semicircle ending at the Place de la Bastille, runs the most famous chain of boulevards, following an ancient line of city walls. Riverward is the stately Place de la Concorde, from which the splendid Avenue des Champs Elysées stretches west past the Elysée Palace (residence of the French President) to the magnificent Place de l'Étoile and Arc de Triomphe (the largest triumphal arch in the world), with the tomb of the Unknown Soldier. Southwest from the Étoile is the Avenue Foch—once the Avenue du Bois de Boulogne, most famous of promenades—which leads to the finest of Paris's parks, the celebrated Bois de Boulogne, with its Auteuil and Longchemin racecourses. Northeast the Avenue Hoche leads to the small and lovely Parc Monceau, with its ruined eighteenth-century colonnade, which lies in the midst of a very fashionable neighbourhood.

Eastward from the Place de la Concorde I found the Gardens of the Tuileries fully worthy of their fame. Opposite them the sidewalks of the Napoleonic Rue de Rivoli are arcaded like many in cities of America's extreme South. The Louvre with its central court affords what is without question the finest urban perspective in the world—the westward stretch of the Tuileries and Avenue des Champs Elysées from the Place du Carrousel with its triple triumphal arch past the Place de la Concorde and its obelisk to the distant and misty outline of the great Arc de Triomphe in the Place de l'Étoile. One could spend hours enjoying this breath-taking vista despite its familiarity in pictures, for the reality has something which pen, brush, and camera can never quite capture.

East of the Louvre, where the Boulevard Sébastopol comes down from the north to join the Rue de Palais on the Ile and the Boulevard St. Michel on the left bank, stands the lone and exquisite Tour St. Jacques, last of the city's Gothic masterpieces. Farther on is the great Hôtel de Ville, rebuilt in 1878 as an enlarged copy of the original structure of 1553, which was burned during the Commune of 1871. Just east of it is the Church of St. Gervais, hit in 1918 by a German shell from the famous "Big Bertha" 72 miles away. Inland from this region is the squalid but fascinating Marais with its ruinous mediaeval mansions. Eastward are the few stones left from the Bastille, and the spacious Place de la Bastille—with its column commemorating the revolution of 1848—laid out on the famous prison's site and forming the easterly end of the Grands Boulevards system. From this point my explorations followed the boulevards north and west, past the Place de la République and the great gates of St. Denis and St. Martin, which stood at the limits of the town three centuries ago.

I later explored the lofty northern heights of Montmartre, determined to see at close range that shimmering and alluring modern marvel, the many-domed Church of the Sacred Heart, which enchants the spectator at a distance from every part of Paris. Perched on the city's highest point, its close aspect is by no means a disillusionment; though one might wish it followed a more classically conservative design. Its sheer size almost overawes the beholder. The streets nearby—long the seat of a decadent pseudo-artistic life like that of New York's Greenwich Village—are of vast quaintness and antiquity, though they are unfortunately succumbing to a poisonous modernisation including the erection of dwellings in freakish "functional" patterns. Meanwhile the convivial poseurs are migrating to Montparnasse, at the opposite end of the town beyond the university quarter. On my trip to Montparnasse I saw little to warrant permanent recording.

Malmaison and Versailles

My glimpses of the smaller towns and of the French countryside were unfortunately rather limited, but a few pleasant trips left a lasting impression. One of these took me out of Paris by the Porte de Neuilly—on the west, just above the Bois de Boulogne—to Malmaison, whose modest chateau formed a summer residence of Napoleon, and the home of Josephine after the divorce. On the way thither I saw the tombs of Josephine and her daughter Hortense (Queen of Holland and mother of Napoleon III) at Rueil. Malmaison is restored to the exact appearance which it had in Josephine's time, and the chateau and gardens proved worthy of a careful survey. It is here that one may see most perfectly embodied the furniture and decorative scheme known as "Empire". Farther on I saw Marly, a summer home of Louis XIV and site of the ancient machines supplying the fountains of Versailles with water.

But the high spot of the trip was Versailles—11 miles southwest of Paris—famous throughout the world and woven importantly into the history of three centuries. It is needless to repeat details concerning this universally known palace and its appurtenances—built by Mansard for Louis XIV in the late seventeenth century, and with what are perhaps the finest formal gardens in the world, laid out by Le Notre and containing terraces, ornate fountains, lakes, canals, statues and groups of statuary, rockeries, hedges, colonnades, and an exquisite orangery. The great palace itself lies east of the gardens and fronts the principal square of the now thriving town which grew up in connexion with it. Its numberless rooms and halls—including the famous Glass Gallery or Hall of Mirrors—are associated alike with the splendour of the Grand Monarque, the decadent luxury of Louis XV, and the tragic career of Louis XVI and Marie-Antoinette. Here in 1783 was signed the treaty of peace between England and the seceded American colonies forming the United States. Since Louis-Philippe's time Versailles has been an historical museum and seat of important public convocations. Here the invading Prussians proclaimed the birth of the German Empire in 1871, and here that same Reich was humbled after the World War by the Peace Conference of 1919. The chapel of the palace is especially fine, and forms the last work of Mansard.

Near the great palace and gardens are two subsidiary residences, the Grand and Petit Trianons; the former built in 1687 by Mansard for Louis XIV, and the latter—more a pavilion than a palace—built in 1766 by Gabriel for Louis XV. Both are now museums. The Petit Trianon was a favourite abode of Marie-Antoinette; who surrounded it with a hamlet, dairy, and garden imitating the idyllic English countryside, and who there played at peasant life in the affected manner of the age of Rousseau. I saw both the great palace and the Trianons, and drank deeply of the dream-stirring loveliness of the gardens. Unfortunately I could not, either on this or a later visit, see the famous fountains in action.

Another interesting thing seen briefly in passing was the small town of Sèvres, famous in the history of ceramics. On the return trip I passed through the picturesque hillside village of St. Cloud, on the left bank of the Seine seven miles west of Paris. From this vantage-point is obtained one of the most enchanting panoramas in all France—the blue, bending river, the wide verdant stretch of the Bois de Boulogne, and the vast outspread expanse of the metropolis with its bristling towers and steeples, its glittering domes and huddled roofs, and its open spaces, monuments, arches, and bridges. Subsequently I entered the city through the lovely sylvan drives of the Bois de Boulogne.

Barbizon and Fontainebleau

Another trip took me through the Port d'Italie on the left bank and across an exquisitely undulating countryside to the village of Barbizon, where in the nineteenth century dwelt an important group of landscape and genre painters, including Corot and Millet. In the town, whose main street is of extreme quaintness and beauty, the studios of many of the artists are still pointed out; that of Millet being restored as a public museum. Nearby is a field which guides point out as that depicted in the famous "Angelus".[10] Barbizon, which lies picturesquely at the edge of the Forest of Fountainebleau, is now in danger of being overrun with sophisticated Parisians and sharing the fate of such quaint American towns as Rockport, Provincetown, and Santa Fé.

On this trip I was driven through the exquisite forest, whose ancient, brooding trees, tangled, shadowy thickets, rocky retreats, unexpected green slopes, and weird, desolate gorges stir the imagination to an acute and almost disturbing degree. In the midst of the wood lies the prospering town of Fontainebleau, 37 miles southeast of Paris. Close to the town, and bordering on a splendid pond filled with carp, is the rambling royal chateau whose size, ornateness, and historic importance have made it so famous.

This palace is now a museum, and I had the good fortune to explore it with considerable thoroughness. It was begun by Francis I on the site of a much older royal castle or manor-house, and greatly enlarged and altered by subsequent monarchs, especially Henri IV. The architecture, planned by the Italian Primaticcio, is typical of the French Renaissance; and the enormous rooms are decorated in a lavish, glittering fashion involving much gilt and varied colours. Leonardo da Vinci, Andrea del Sarto, and Benvenuto Cellini coöperated in the adornment. So vast is the congeries of buildings forming the palace that they are said to cover 14 acres. Five great courts are involved in the final design.

It would be tedious to enumerate all the royal personages who have sojourned at Fontainebleau, and all the historic events which have occurred there. It is the birthplace of Louis XIII, and besides the French sovereigns it has harboured such guests as James V of Scotland, Christina of Sweden, Peter the Great of Prussia, and Pope Pius VII. Here in 1685 was signed the Revocation of the Edict of Nantes which sent so many Huguenots to England and America, and here too Napoleon abdicated in 1815. Napoleon was very fond of Fontainebleau and left a strong imprint on it. Among the ornate chambers pointed out today are many connected with Francis I, Henry II, Louis XIII, Mme. de Maintenon, Diane de Poitiers, Marie-Antoinette, Napoleon, and Pius VII. Furnishings of all ages from the Renaissance to the Napoleonic Era are to be found—including splendid tapestries and silk draperies. For sheer lavishness and almost barbaric splendour Fontainebleau is scarcely to be equalled.

Rambouillet and Chartres

One of the pleasantest of my excursions was that which extended beyond Versailles and the ruined Abbey of Port-Royal to the beautiful Valley of Chevreuse with its woods and hills and winding roads. Here—30 miles southwest of Paris and beyond the Guises' Château de Dampierre—I beheld the ancient and castellated Château de Rambouillet and its delectable park and forest, once the tarrying-place of royalty and now the summer home of the French President. By a fortunate circumstance I was able to explore this venerable edifice, though it is not a freely open museum like the other royal palaces. The original parts, including the great machicolated tower, have a very high antiquity, and were built by the great family of D'Angennes, who received this domain in the fourteenth century. It was to this family that the celebrated Marquise Catherine de Rambouillet—whose Paris abode was such a famous literary salon in the seventeenth century—belonged. Kings of France were frequent guests at Rambouillet, and Francis I died there. In the eighteenth century Louis XVI purchased the estate and turned it into a model sheep-farm. Here Marie-Antoinette, continuing the idyllic mock-pastoralism of the Trianon, built the artistic dairy still visible in the great park. Napoleon used the palace as a hunting-lodge, and it is here that Charles X, last absolutist king, abdicated in 1830.

Most of the existing chateau is of Renaissance design. The interior has splendid and spacious chambers in various styles of decoration, with tapestries and carved woodwork of marvellous artistry. I have never seen any tapestries comparable to those of Rambouillet—specimens at Versailles, Malmaison, and Fontainebleau being perhaps next in order. They represent Renaissance art at its best, and have no trace of Gothic grotesqueness. So fine is their execution that one might almost think them paintings. The woodwork, too, is incomparably fine and delicate—to my eye even beyond any achievement of Grinling Gibbons. It is impossible for any picture to convey the full magic of the lace-like garlands and spider-web-traceries which cover the panels of the reception-hall, council chamber, boudoir of Marie-Antoinette, and other apartments. Among the apartments is the graciously tiled bathroom of Marie-Antoinette—which did not, it appears, prove new and large enough for Napoleon, despite his actually smaller stature. The Napoleonic bathroom is a highly imposing affair of neo-classic design with an arched niche and decorated panels. The park at Rambouillet—including the dairy, the rustic hermitage, the shell-work pavilion, and the rock grotto—is worth a whole day's exploration. A link with America is furnished by the avenue of Louisiana cypresses, reminiscent of France's great eighteenth-century colonising experiment.

From Rambouillet my route led past the Château de Maintenon, presented by Louis XIV to his celebrated morganatic wife, and finally reached the old cathedral town of Chartres, 55 miles southwest of Paris on the river Eure. Few places are more crowded with quaint antiquities than this delightful provincial backwater, which was a village of the Carnutes, and later the Roman town of Autricum. Picturesque gables loom on every hand, and the spiral Gothic stairway of Queen Bertha, once part of a great mansion, attracts wide notice. The great Porte-Guillaume takes one back to Merovingian times.

But of course the stately cathedral of Notre-Dame—so much admired by Henry Adams[11]—is the salient feature of Chartres. It is a Gothic edifice of vast extent, dating largely from the thirteenth century and having twin towers and steeples of dissimilar design. Its crowning charm lies in the surviving members of a series of magnificent thirteenth-century stained glass windows; others of which were destroyed by the fire of 1830 and kindred causes. It is related that during the Franco-Prussian war, when Chartres was seized by the Germans and one of the cathedral windows was broken, a workman climbed up at great peril to his life and saved the remaining pieces of stained glass—whose art was beyond duplication. For this act he consistently refused all reward, nor would he permit his name to become known. The window in question is now filled with ordinary glass. Of particular interest today are the exquisite rose windows and the very distinctive portals. Under the cathedral is an eleventh-century crypt, and the site is reputed to have been a Druid grotto.

Other churches in Chartres are those of St. Pierre and St. André. In one I beheld a series of exceedingly rare enamel paintings of the apostles, produced by a process now wholly lost, and of virtually incalculable value. Fabulous sums offered for these treasures by millionaires and museums have been refused, even though the countryside is greatly in need of money. The enamels are kept locked behind iron grates, and exhibited only for a few minutes at a time.

But the wonders of Chartres are quite limitless. Beneath one of the churches are crypts dating back to Carolingian days, while a deep Roman well is vaguely reputed to have been a receptacle for the bodies of early Christian martyrs. I moved on with extreme reluctance, though the return route to Paris was not without its delights. Saint-Cyr, 2½ miles west of Versailles, contains the famous military academy housed in what was once Mme. de Maintenon's convent school for the daughters of indigent noblemen—with the semi-royal foundress still buried in its chapel. In St. Germain-en-Laye is an old castle of tremendous interest, and a terrace affording magnificent views of the Seine valley and its hills, and of Paris 13 miles to the east. It is here that James II found refuge after the revolution of 1688 in England.

World War Battlefields and Rheims

A trip combining remote with immediate history was that which included many of the battlefields of the Great War. I passed through Claye, Trilbardoux, and Meaux, crossed the Marne at Triport, and soon entered the still scarred and upheaved region covered by the first battle of the Marne. At La Ferte-sous-Juarre is an imposing monument to the 4000 British regulars who bravely fell at the outset of the conflict. Later I encountered scenes of American action in 1918—at Veaux, which still shews the effects of shell-fire.

Belleau Wood was the scene of especially severe fighting by the 2nd, 3d, and 26th American divisions, and marks the beginning of the Germans' final retreat. It contains an American military cemetery and other points of interest. Another high spot is Château-Thierry, birthplace of the fabulist La Fontaine and seat of a notable and difficult victory by the American marines in 1918. A monument marks the latter event. At Darmans there is a fine allied monument, while Bligny contains an Italian military cemetery. Hill 408 marks repeated mine explosions, being on the famous Hindenberg Line. Rheims—which I visited and duly absorbed—is in this vicinity.

Along the now historic Chemin des Dames—65 miles northeast of Paris—is Soissons with its fine cathedral of the twelfth and thirteenth centuries, its twelfth-century churches of St. Pierre and St. Léger, and its ruined abbey. This ancient town of the Suessiones was probably the *Noviodunum* mentioned by Caesar. In Roman times it was called *Augusta Suessionum* and Suessiona, and was an important centre of military roads. When the Empire fell it became the chief Roman town of northern Gaul, and it was here that Syagrius the last proconsul lived before his final defeat by Clovis's Franks in A.D. 486. Battles have repeatedly raged around and over it, the Great War forming no exception.

South of Soissons is Rethondes, where the armistice was signed in 1918—now graced by an impressive monument. Circling toward Paris I passed through Senlis, partly burned by the retreating Germans in 1914. This village figures vividly in Manuel Komroff's recent novel "Coronet".[12] Still nearer Paris I saw the famous airport of Le Bourget, where Lindbergh landed in 1927.

In some parts of the battlefields trenches and dugouts still exist, awesomely reminding one of the tremendous cosmic forces of destruction—so seemingly futile yet so inevitable—which have raged over the land, using helpless human beings as part of their expression. Many trenches are quite intact, and in one region there is a log cabin museum housing such relics as rusty machine-guns, helmets, hand-grenades, and mouldy shoes. The most interesting thing of all is a great steel and concrete subterranean vault of prodigious strength constructed by German officers as a recreational centre. The top is covered by an enormous flat slab of stone held in place by massive girders, beneath one side of which is the entrance—a small opening leading down some steps to the great concrete floor, now partly covered in the process of refilling. In this luxurious crypt the "Boche" officers took their ease whenever they could— spacious and comfortable living-rooms, libraries, baths, swimming-pools, billiard-rooms, and every other possible accessory of indoor recreation and diversion being provided

for their benefit. There is a suggestion of weirdness in the notion of this relaxation going on under the earth, beneath the shell-torn region of death and devastation. Some
fear exists among the authorities that unexploded powder or bombs may lurk in this
strange retreat, hence matches, smoking, and the like are prohibited to visitors. It is
said that the place will be left intact for a century to provide for the natural disintegration of any remaining explosives, after which the entire catacomb will be destroyed—
unless, indeed, future wars dictate other fortunes for it.

But it was the ancient and royal city of Rheims, 81 miles northeast of Paris, which
left the greatest impression. Originally an important centre of the Remi—called Duro-
cortorum—it submitted voluntarily to Roman rule and became the no less important
town of Remi. After the fall of Roman power Clovis was baptised there, and it formed
the scene of the consecration of later kings—every one, in fact, from Philip Augustus
to Charles X and the end of the Bourbon kingdom. In the tenth century Rheims was a
noted seat of monkish learning, and subsequently it has suffered much through the
many wars which have raged around it. It is now a good-sized industrial city, specialis-
ing in woollen textiles and champagne.

Of course the partly ruined cathedral—a victim of the World War—took my eye
first of all. Restoration progresses slowly, and the great towers still have a ruggedness
which they will eventually lose; but in spite of all damage it is easy to understand why
so many consider this venerable structure the noblest cathedral ever built by man.
Erected in the thirteenth century on the site of Clovis's baptism, it has a facade in
harmonious style though dating a century later. It once had spires, but these perished
in a fire in 1481. The cream of the edifice is its marvellous facade, with great pointed
portals, magnificent rose window, and statue-bearing Gothic niches. The towers are
267 feet high.

The archbishop's palace dates from about 1500, and the Renaissance Hôtel de
Ville from the seventeenth century. Ancient and curious houses exist on every hand,
and there are champagne vaults far underground whose quasi-Romanesque vaultings
and icy temperature make one forget their lack of historic antiquity. Fine monuments
are especially numerous, those of Louis XV, Marshal d'Erlon, Joan of Arc, and the
French soldiers being notable. In the centre of the broad Place d'Erlon is a splendid
fountain. Of the old circumvallation, several gates still exist, the finest being the Porte
de Paris in the Rue de Vesle, erected at the coronation of Louis XVI.

But to some the most fascinating object in Rheims is the finely preserved Porte
Mars near the railway station on the road to Rome—a genuine relic of classical antiquity. It is a triple triumphal arch of the Corinthian order, built in the Augustan age by
the loyal Remi to honour Caesar and Augustus, and to celebrate the construction of
the great road system of M. Vipsanius Agrippa. The name comes from a temple of
Mars which stood near by. Its genuinely Roman (even though provincial) outlines well
attest the rapidity with which the Gauls assumed the manners and culture of their
conquerors.

* * * * * * * *

To leave a world of such fascinating historical vestiges is hard, but at last—
accelerated by my illness—the parting had to come. Hospital, boat train, glimpses of
ancient countryside, spires of Rouen—and finally the limitless Atlantic and the topless
towers of Manhattan once more.

There may be those who will think my modest jaunt a sadly hackneyed coursing in the beaten paths, but to them I can only reply that no path is truly purged of its glamour so long as any ancient memories or overtones of fancy still cling around its sights and impressions. Europe's common sights, imbibed for the first time, have enchanted me with the magic of such memories and such overtones; hence I have no apologies to make, except so far as I have failed to transmit the magic in these inevitably prosy and inadequate notes. Only the veriest clod could remain unmoved before the familiar ancestral shrines of modern Western civilisation.

EDITOR'S NOTE FP: *European Glimpses* (West Warwick, RI: Necronomicon Press, 1988). Text based on the AMS (JHL), dated 19 December 1932. This is certainly the most unusual of HPL's travelogues, in that it is an account of a trip he himself did not undertake. Instead, it is a revision of a work written by his ex-wife, Sonia H. Greene (1883–1972), three years after her divorce from HPL. As she notes in her memoir: "in 1932 I went to Europe. . . . I sent a travelogue to H. P. which he revised for me" (*The Private Life of H. P. Lovecraft* [West Warwick, RI: Necronomicon Press, 1985], p. 17). Sonia gives an account of the places she visits that tallies exactly with the sites described in the essay. In HPL's one surviving discussion of the work, he writes (in a letter to Alfred Galpin, 4 November 1933) that it was "a ghost-writing job for a goof who wanted to be publicly eloquent about a trip from which he [*sic*] was apparently unable to extract any concrete first-hand impressions" (*Letters to Alfred Galpin*, pp. 196–97). HPL may have disguised the identity of his revision-client to Galpin because he did not wish to reveal that he was still doing work for his ex-wife. The only significant passage in the work is Sonia's witnessing of a Nazi rally in which Hitler spoke.

Notes

1. Quoted by James Boswell in *Life of Johnson* (1791; LL 113), s.d. 20 September 1777. Johnson said "tired," not "weary."

2. D. Magnus Ausonius (310?–393?), *Mosella*.

3. Longfellow, "The Children's Hour." The legend of Bishop Hatto is also told in S. Baring-Gould's *Curious Myths of the Middle Ages* (1866; LL 66), in a passage that manifestly inspired HPL's "The Rats in the Walls" (1923). See Steven J. Mariconda, "*Curious Myths of the Middle Ages* and 'The Rats in the Walls,'" in *On the Emergence of "Cthulhu" and Other Observations* (West Warwick, RI: Necronomicon Press, 1995), pp. 53–56.

4. Poe's sketch "The Domain of Arnheim" (1847) is an expansion of an earlier work, "The Landscape Garden" (1842). When HPL saw Richmond's Maymont Park in 1930, he believed it to represent "Poe's 'Domain of Arnheim' and 'Island of the Fay' all rolled into one—with mine own Cathuria and gardens of Yin added for good measure" (SL 3.149).

5. At this time Hitler was vigorously promoting his Nazi party. In April he had lost narrowly to Paul von Hindenburg in the presidential election, but the Nazi party polled a surprising 37.2% of the vote in July elections. In January 1933, Hindenburg appointed Hitler chancellor, paving the way to his rise to power.

6. See "A Description of the Town of Quebeck," n. 10.

7. Victor Hugo, *The Hunchback of Notre-Dame* (1831), Book III, ch. II ("A Bird's-Eye View of Paris").

8. HPL visited the Cloisters (now a branch of the Metropolitan Museum of Art) on several occasions, the first in 1922, before it was fully completed.

9. HPL refers to Remy de Gourmont (1858–1915), *Une Nuit au Luxembourg* (1906); Eng. trans. by Arthur Ransome as *A Night in the Luxembourg* (1912). See *SL* 1.250.

10. Jean François Millet (1814–1875), French painter whose "Angelus" (1857–59), depicting a peasant couple praying in the fields, became one of the most reproduced paintings of the nineteenth century.

11. See Henry Adams (1838–1918), *Mont St. Michel and Chartres* (1904).

12. Manuel Komroff (1890–1974), *Coronet* (1929), an epic romance about the decay of the aristocracy in Europe.

SOME DUTCH FOOTPRINTS IN NEW ENGLAND

Devotees of the Dutch Colonial tradition do not commonly look upon New England as within their field. If they think of it at all, it is largely as the foe whose outposts on the Connecticut River called forth certain steps from the mountainous Wouter van Twiller—the building of an armed fort on the site of Hartford in 1633, and the fruitless despatch of a force of seventy soldiers in the following year. The Dutch, it will be remembered, claimed all the territory up to the Connecticut's west bank (notwithstanding the counter-claim of England to all the Atlantic coast region); and it is by no means certain that they were not the discoverers of that river. Vaguer Dutch claims extended all the way to Cape Cod.

It is not true, however, that this boundary dispute formed the sole link of Holland with Novanglian history; for a fairly close survey reveals a multitude of Dutch footprints in New England. The record begins in 1614 with Adriaen Block, whose expedition in the New Netherland-built ship *Onrust* explored the New England coast as far as Cape Cod; charting the principal features and applying a nomenclature which includes several still-surviving names. Not only does Block Island preserve his memory, but he is probably responsible (notwithstanding contrary hypotheses) for the name of the distinguished State of Rhode Island; since his account of a small reddish island (*een rodtlich Eylandken*) in Narragansett Bay seems to have caused later settlers to apply that designation by mistake to the larger island of Aquidneck, on which Newport stands, and thence to the colony established there. It is a little-known fact that the Dutch nomenclature of Block persisted quite generally on charts of Narragansett Bay until the very close of the seventeenth century.

Rhode Island has another Dutch link on its southern coast; where a ruinous old fortification, long attributed to the Indians and known as Fort Ninigret, is now quite generally considered of Dutch origin. Dutch artifacts including Delft ware, clay pipes, and items for Indian trade have been found on this site; and it seems highly probable that the fort was one of several along the New England coast, with which the Dutch sought to establish a title to the region. Its probable date is 1627, a conjecture supported by a letter of the Dutch ambassador to England in 1631. In 1637 the Dutch acquired an island in that western part of Narragansett Bay which Block had named "Sloop Bay", and built a trading post upon it; causing it to become known to later generations as "Dutch Island".

Still another Dutch–Rhode Island link is afforded by Roger Williams, who had studied the Dutch language at Cambridge through his belief in Holland's importance as a factor in religious freedom. He had long associated with Anabaptists and Mennonites of

Dutch origin in England, and in the new world his relations with New Netherland were especially cordial. In June, 1643, when in New Amsterdam for the purpose of embarking for England, Mr. Williams was able to perform notable service in mediating between the Dutch and the warring Indians of Long Island. Later, on his second visit to England in 1652 and 1653, occurred his well-known service of instructing Milton in Dutch.

Rhode Islanders, whose long-standing differences with the Massachusetts Bay Colony made Boston an uncongenial port for them, employed New Amsterdam more than once as a place of embarkation for the old world. It was from there that Samuel Gorton, second only to Williams as a champion of liberty, sailed for Holland and thence for England in 1645. A further Netherlandish link with Rhode Island is afforded by the Holland education of Dr. John Clark, the eminent physician and clergyman who founded the Baptist church in Newport and secured for the colony its charter of 1663.

More surprising to the layman than the connexion of southern New England with the Dutch is the fact that a part of Maine's rocky coast has known the rule of the States-General. Such, however, is the case; for the ancient fortress and trading post of Pentagoët at Castine (founded by the French in 1613, and by some claimed to be the oldest permanent settlement in New England) was held by the Dutch from 1674 to 1676. On August 10, 1674, the French garrison under Captain de Chambly was overcome after an hour's hot fighting by a force from the Dutch privateer the *Flying Horse,* commanded by Captain Jurriaen Aernouts and piloted by an Englishman from Boston. The visitors disarmed the fort and removed the cannon, taking Captain de Chambly to Boston, whence he was later ransomed for a thousand beaver-skins. The bulk of the French colonists, who had settled there in 1671, submitted to the invaders. In November, 1676, two years after the second and peaceable transfer of New Netherland to the English by the Treaty of Westminster (October 31, 1674), a French force under Baron de St. Castin recaptured the stronghold, expelling the settlers because of their readily granted allegiance to the Dutch. Thus for more than twenty-four months after the treaty with England by which the Netherlands nominally resigned all claim to North American soil in exchange for a recognition of their rights in the West Indies and in Surinam, an actual Dutch hold on this continent existed.

Certain older historians have tended to dismiss this capture of Pentagoët as a mere buccaneering incident, though the old Jesuit chronicler Charlevoix speaks of Captain Aernouts as having a commission from the Prince of Orange. Others, however, have always recognised the official nature of the Dutch hold on Pentagoët; and in recent years this recognition has become quite general. On the site of Fort Pentagoët—in Perkins Street, Castine—there is now a tablet whose inscription relates, among other things, that the post "became the seat of government . . . of the Province of New Holland, the capture of which by Baron de St. Castin—November, 1676— ended the Dutch authority in America".

That Plymouth should possess many Dutch connexions is only natural in view of the long sojourn of the Pilgrims in Holland. Correspondence between Pieter Minuit and Governor Bradford was courteous and friendly; and in 1627 Minuit's secretary Isaac de Rasieres spent some time in Plymouth, being very cordially received and establishing fruitful and long-enduring trade relations between that colony and New Netherland. It is from a letter of de Rasieres that we derive the best of all descriptions of early Plymouth. Less generally known is the fact that the Pilgrims picked up several Dutch expressions during their stay in Leyden, several of which retained currency in the new colony. Chief among these is "meerstead", applied to the plots of land assigned to each member of the colony.

That the Dutch gave New England several of its choicest strains of blood is no news to those who recall the famous name of Wendell. Another noted line of this sort is that of the Rhode Island Updikes, planters and gentry in the old Narragansett country, and derived from a New Netherland ancestor, Dr. Gysbert op Dyck.

It would be hard to catalogue the various Dutch influences manifest to a greater or less extent in New England folkways. There is considerable evidence that the gambrel roof is of New Netherland origin, despite the different form which it took throughout the Yankee countryside; while the popularity of Dutch scriptural titles around New England fireplaces speaks for itself. Dutch culinary and linguistic influences certainly filtered eastward from the Hudson Valley at a very early date; as attested on the one hand by the doughnut, and on the other hand by such words as cookie, stoop (small porch), span (of horses), pit (stone of fruit), boss, scow, waffle, and hook (point of land).

The currency of Dutch coins—along with those of other nations—in colonial New England is of course a matter of common knowledge; this circumstance oddly surviving in the name Guilder Street, applied to a quaint alley along the ancient waterfront of Providence.[1]

Thus we realise that the old New Netherland civilisation is one which the seemingly alien Yankee cannot look upon as wholly detached from his own background. Between New England and its Dutch neighbour were all the ties of proximity, and of kindred settlement, purpose, and modes of life; hence today their respective sons cannot but look back together upon a substantial fund of common memories, prides, and institutions.

EDITOR'S NOTE FP: *De Halve Maen* 9, No. 1 (18 October 1933): 2, 4. Text based on the TMS (JHL) (AMS also extant). The essay was written in July 1933 at the behest of Wilfred B. Talman, editor of *De Halve Maen* (The Half Moon), a paper published by the Holland Society of New York. In his memoir, *The Normal Lovecraft* (Saddle River, NJ: Gerry de la Ree, 1973), Talman notes that he engaged in lengthy debates over stylistic niceties in the essay as a kind of revenge for what he felt was HPL's heavy-handed revision of "Two Black Bottles" (1926). The essay is a routine discussion of remnants of Dutch influence in New England, specifically Rhode Island.

Notes

1. The street is cited in *The Case of Charles Dexter Ward* (1927). It no longer exists.

HOMES AND SHRINES OF POE

When amateurs visit the Fossil Library in its new Philadelphia home,[1] it is to be hoped that they will not overlook another literary landmark of the colonial metropolis, also opened during the past few months. This is the neat brick cottage at North Seventh and Spring Garden Streets, where from 1842 to 1844 lived Edgar Allan Poe, the greatest author our country has so far produced.

Because of Poe's migratory life, the number of houses and sites associated with him is very great. Many are known, but only a few are properly marked or restored as shrines. The site of the cheap boarding-house in Boston's South End, where in 1809 he was born to a pair of strolling players, bears a bronze tablet with the simple facts; and at one time the junction near it—Broadway and Carver Street—was named "Edgar Allan Poe Square".

In 1811 Poe's mother, then acting in Richmond, died and left him to be adopted by the wealthy local merchant John Allan. She was then stopping at a small brick cottage in the rear of the theatrical boarding-house on the northwest corner of Main and 23rd Streets. This cottage (and the boarding-house as well) is still standing though unmarked. The district, inhabited by negroes, is very squalid. Mrs. Poe was buried in St. John's churchyard at Broad and 24th Streets, and her grave was suitably marked in 1928.

The Allan home into which the child was taken, a three-story brick house at 14th Street and Tobacco Alley, is still standing, though long ago converted into a shop and now deserted and unmarked.

The Poe sites in England and Scotland, where young Edgar was taken by his foster-parents and where he remained from 1815 to 1820, are not marked or generally known. The school at Stoke-Newington, so vividly described in the story "William Wilson", has long been demolished.

When the Allans returned to Richmond their first permanent home—after a summer at the bygone and uncommemorated house of Mr. Allan's partner at Franklin and Second Streets—was at Clay and Fifth Streets. This house has vanished, and the site is unmarked. In 1825 Mr. Allan purchased the mansion called "Moldavia" at Main and Fifth Streets, and it is there that the most important crisis in Poe's life occurred. This house also is demolished without the marking of the site.

Poe's brief period at the University of Virginia in Charlottesville is, fortunately, well commemorated. His room at 13 West Range is fitted up as it was during his tenancy, and above the door is a plaque reading "EDGAR ALLAN POE—MDCCCXXVI—DOMUS PARVA MAGNI POETAE".[2]

After Poe's breach with his guardian he entered the army as a common soldier; and many of the military landmarks connected with him—Fort Independence in Boston Harbour, Fort Moultrie on Sullivan's Island in Charleston Harbour, and Fortress Monroe, Virginia—survive, though without Poe tablets.

Discharged from the army, Poe stayed for a time with his blood-relatives in Baltimore. The house was in Mechanics Row, Milk Street, and has vanished without commemoration. In 1830, after a brief reinstatement in the Allan home, Poe went to West Point; but no marker remains to record his sojourn in Room 28, South Barracks. After he prematurely left the Academy he returned to the Milk Street house in Baltimore. Thence, in the autumn of 1832, he removed with his relatives to a dormer-windowed brick house at 3 Amity Street, which is still standing though unmarked.

In 1835 Poe went to Richmond with his aunt Mrs. Clemm and her daughter Virginia, having married the latter. The family lived at a boarding-house in Bank Street, Capitol Square, which has disappeared and whose site is unmarked.

Early in 1837 Poe and his family migrated to New York City, living at the corner of Sixth Avenue and Waverly Place in Greenwich Village, where no trace of his tenancy remains. In the spring he moved to 13½ Carmine Street, a site still commonly associated with him, though neither house nor marker exists.

In August, 1838, the family began its six years' residence in Philadelphia. The first two stopping-places were boarding-houses situated respectively at Twelfth Street above Arch, and on the northeast corner of Fourth and Arch; neither site now possessing the original house or any tablet. In September they moved to a small house—also gone and uncommemorated—in 16th Street near Locust. Late in 1839 or early in 1840 another move was made—to a brick house of three stories at the junction of Coates Street and

Fairmount Drive, overlooking the Schuylkill. Though without a marker, this building is still standing unless very recently destroyed.

Some time before the end of May, 1842, Poe transferred his household to the cottage now restored and opened as a shrine. Here, amidst an environment then village-like and semi-rural, he performed considerable work of importance. When he left in the spring of 1844, it was to go to New York once more for the final phase of his tragically brief career.

The first haven in Poe's second New York period was Morrison's boarding-house on the northwest corner of Greenwich and Albany Streets; an ancient brick building which had once been the Planter's Hotel, favoured by Southern visitors. This structure still exists in good condition as a restaurant; though there is no tablet to indicate Poe's connexion with it. The poet himself soon resigned the Greenwich Street quarters exclusively to his wife and aunt; taking a room of his own at 4 Ann Street, where all traces of his presence are swept away.

When summer came the family was reunited in the rustic Bloomingdale region then far north of the compact town; boarding at a farmhouse which stood on a knoll near what is now the busy intersection of Broadway and 84th Street. The house has of course long vanished, nor does any marker amidst the babel of shops and apartments attest the fact that "The Raven" was completed on that spot.[3]

In November Poe left the country and took quarters in a Greenwich Village rooming-house at 15 Amity Street. Neither the house nor any marker exists at present. In May, 1845, a removal to 195 Broadway was effected. There the whole family lived in extreme poverty, sharing a single back room in a run-down tenement long ago destroyed and forgotten. By midsummer a change for the better was made—a return to Amity Street, this time to No. 85, which like so many other Poe abodes has sunk without a trace. In the spring of 1846 the family returned briefly to the Bloomingdale farmhouse, moving later to another rural boarding-house at Turtle Bay, where the present 47th Street meets the East River. This was a large farmhouse, of which no vestige or memorial now survives.

The next and final move—near the end of May, 1846—was to the famous Fordham cottage. This small but shapely farmhouse, of an early nineteenth-century type common in the region, was in Poe's time situated amidst a countryside of the greatest possible beauty. Here, early in 1847, Poe's wife died; and it was still the family home when the poet himself expired in 1849. In time the expanding metropolis engulfed the district, and the cottage was hemmed in by new buildings. In 1913 the city purchased the edifice as a public museum and moved it northward about 450 feet to the crossing of the Grand Concourse and Kingsbridge Road, in a small park named for Poe. By 1921 its restoration was complete, and the surrounding landscape was made to resemble its original setting as closely as possible. It is furnished just as it was in Poe's time; three articles—a rocking-chair, a bedstead, and a mirror—being actually the ones he owned and used. Various relics of Poe are present, and there is a notable collection of different editions of his works.

Poe died in Baltimore October 7, 1849, and two days later was buried among his relatives there in a corner of Westminster Presbyterian Churchyard. A stone prepared by a cousin was accidentally destroyed before being set in place; so that for twenty-five years the poet's grave remained unmarked. In November, 1875, a marble monument was placed beside the grave by admirers; this forming the first of Poe's public shrines. Today the churchyard is in a decaying section, but within its walls dignity still reigns.

The grave is adorned with green vines, and those who come to pay tribute feel that this last of the weary, wayworn wanderer's many homes is not the least appropriate.

In Richmond, which he always regarded as his real home, Poe's memory is perpetuated through a shrine unconnected with any actual dwelling of his, though not far from where his mother died. The nucleus of this shrine is a venerable stone house on Main Street near 19th, undoubtedly the oldest building in Richmond. Just east of it is a fireproof structure in the ancient manner, having built into it two architectural features—the staircase and the mantel of Poe's room—from the old Allan home at 14th Street and Tobacco Alley. Behind the house is an exquisite garden with a loggie built of bricks from the demolished magazine office where Poe worked. The shrine as a whole—which was dedicated in the early 1920's—contains one of the best Poe collections in existence.

The newly opened Philadelphia house is unique in being the only Poe dwelling on its original site to become a memorial museum. It is a pleasant brick cottage of three stories in the rear of a larger house at 530 North Seventh Street; evidently built early in the nineteenth century and perhaps originally forming servants' quarters. Around it is a small and tasteful garden, now restored as in Poe's time except that a great pear tree which he loved is missing. The front yard opens on an alley extending in from Seventh Street, with the dreary width of Spring Garden Street just beyond. It is hard to visualise the secluded, almost rustic neighbourhood that the poet knew.

Once in the garden or house, however, we step out of the present. The cottage has lasted well, and no structural alterations have ever been made. The small-paned windows, harmonious mantels, and panelled doors all bespeak the quiet grace of Georgian architecture. There are only two rooms to a floor, and all are furnished just as during Poe's tenancy; though only a desk and a chair are actual Poe relics. Eastward on the ground floor is the parlour with its attractive fireplace, piano-forte, sofa, and book-closet. Across a narrow hall is the kitchen, where the family also ate. On the second floor is Poe's bedroom, with a neat black slate mantel; while across the hall is a smaller study. Here can be found his desk, with appropriate books of the period along the top. On the low-ceiled third floor are the rooms of Poe's wife and aunt, with modest fireplaces and small casement windows. Everything is neatly kept—curtains, flowers, plants, pictures, china, and linen—just as it was in Poe's time.

In the large adjoining house, which has a connecting door, is a notable Poe collection. Here are copies of magazines containing the first appearance of most of the tales and poems, and other associative items too numerous to record.

Of the Poe houses still standing, none comes to life more vividly as a typical home than this unpretentious cottage. Its recent restoration and opening to the public, made possible through the generosity of the Philadelphia merchant Richard Gimbel, form an event at which devotees of Poe and of American letters cannot sufficiently rejoice. Though heretofore surprisingly little known, this shrine is likely to become, as time passes, a leading place of pilgrimage for those who revere genius and admire one of the greatest and unhappiest of its exemplars.

EDITOR'S NOTE FP: *Californian* 2, No. 3 (Winter 1934): 8–10. An essay on all extant and non-extant Poe residences in New York, Philadelphia, Richmond, and elsewhere, most of which HPL had personally visited. The essay was written around July 1934 at the urging of Hyman Bradofsky, editor of the *Californian*, an amateur journal of the National Amateur Press Association. The journal offered unprecedented space for lengthy contributions, and Bradofsky wanted a two-thousand-word article, as HPL notes in a letter to Edward H. Cole

(22 January [1935]): "I didn't want to write anything in the first place, but Hymie esk me I shood mek it an article too-t'ousand voidts longk en ah hurry . . . & you behold the dire result. Ordinarily I never write anything unless I have something to say. This time, without anything to say, but wishing to encourage Brother Hymie's long-prose policy, I allowed myself to sink to the level of the schoolboy essayist or embryonic amateur who simply sits down with a resolution to 'write something'" (ms., JHL).

Notes

1. The Fossil Library (a large collection of amateur journals assembled largely by Edwin Hadley Smith and placed under the aegis of the Fossils, the alumni organisation of amateur journalism) was placed in the Franklin Institute in Philadelphia on 6 April 1935.
2. "The small home of a great poet."
3. There is now such a marker.

THE UNKNOWN CITY IN THE OCEAN

There are few trips in which one travels through time as well as through space, finding at the end a veritable surviving bit of some elder scene and way of life. Quebec, Marblehead, Annapolis, Charleston, and Natchez[1] are reached by such trips. So, too, is Nantucket—that island outpost of New England which some have called "America's bowsprit", and which stands as a sort of meeting-place or boundary between the familiar world we know and the mysterious outer realm of unfathomed water distance.

Thirty miles out from the nearest mainland—Cape Cod—and fifty-four miles from the ancient whaling port of Bedford, Nantucket has lingered in the past, almost untouched by the changes and confusions of today. Even its throngs of summer visitors have helped to confirm rather than destroy its antiquity. The voyage from the continent is a pleasant one—past verdant Martha's Vineyard, and for a moment out of sight of all land. Then, after the modern world has been wholly cast off, the low line of the ancient island rises ahead. And when the ship rounds Brant Point and enters the great harbour, there looms up a skyline of venerable wharves and roofs, topped by white-style and old belfries, which belongs altogether to the brighter, vanished world of a century or more ago.

Nantucket is about fifteen by seven miles in extent, with its principal town (of the same name, but called Sherburne prior to 1795) on the northern shore. In some respects this town is the best-preserved fragment of the elder America in existence today—having cobble-stoned streets lined with colonial houses; horse-blocks, hitching-posts, and great silver doorplates; picturesque lanes and waterfront; a windmill built in 1746; archaic churches with galleries and box pews; whaling and historical museums—everything, in short, that the antiquarian could ask.

The town rises from the water's edge, and the tangle of centuried streets climbs several distinct hills. Its numberless gardens and fine old mansions are luxuriant, while its aged wooden houses and great Georgian mansions bear suggestions of Salem. Many architectural features are essentially local, particularly the railed platform or "walk" for marine observation found on most of the roofs. This island metropolis dates back only to about 1720, the first settlement having lain somewhat westward, on a smaller harbour which closed up around 1700. One of the principal features today is the Maria

Mitchell Observatory in Vestal Street, which adjoins the birthplace of the celebrated astronomer whose name it bears.[2]

Nantucket was first described by Gosnold in 1602, and first settled by Massachusetts men about 1660. It had a fair-sized Indian population, with whom the whites dealt honourably. In 1664, the island was incorporated in the Province of New York, but in 1692 was transferred to Massachusetts, to which it has ever since belonged. Its great prosperity came from whaling, which began about 1670. Whales were first killed off shore from small boats; but when they grew locally scarce, the Nantucketers began to equip large whaling vessels and scour the high seas. By 1730 they covered west of the Atlantic, and after 1791 they rounded Cape Horn and made the Pacific their own. Though greatly retarded by the Revolution and the War of 1812, Nantucket whaling reached its apex around 1842, when the island teemed with wealth and supported a population of about 10,000. Then whales grew scarcer and the demand for whale oil fell off through the discovery of petroleum. Decline set in, and the last Nantucket whaler came back to port in 1870.

After the end of whaling, Nantucket fell into great poverty, from which the summer-resort industry finally pulled it. It is now mostly a summer colony, with the fine old houses appreciatively maintained by the visitors. The permanent population—some 3,800—largely descend from the original settlers, and when not in the summer real-estate business conduct a slim and precarious whaling industry. Typical island surnames are Macy, Coffin, Starbuck, Folger, Ray, Gardner, and Hussey. Benjamin Franklin's mother was a Nantucket Folger, and a fountain in her honour now stands near the town beside a main highway. At one time Quakerism was dominant in Nantucket, but it is now extinct there, the last Friend having died around 1900. The islanders have a sturdy and distinctive character of their own and use several idioms peculiar to their remote domain.

The surface of Nantucket Island consists mainly of low, rolling moors; almost without stones, and treeless except for some struggling pines planted in 1847. Fresh ponds abound, and the great amount of pure ground water puzzles physiographers. The contour of the coast is frequently altered by the sea, which washes land away in one place and deposits sand in another. Climatically, Nantucket is like all islands very equable, with cool summers and warm winters. It is nearer the Gulf Stream than any other part of New England.

Aside from Nantucket Town, the principal settlement is Siasconset (locally pronounced "Sconset") on the southeast coast—an ineffably quaint quondam fishing village settled in 1690 and now wholly a summer resort. Siasconset's rustic, garden-bordered lanes, restored and occupied, form a sight not easily forgotten.

But Nantucket's full charm is something much too elusive for words. It includes a curious apartness—a sense of timeless suspension and closeness to other ages and other worlds—which no mainland region could possibly duplicate, and which defies all the influences of vacationers and art colonists. When we tread the curving, cobbled ways of the town, we see around us the actual unchanged substance of a whaling port of the past. That such a thing can continue to exist is a perennial astonishment and revelation. Daniel Webster, visiting Nantucket Town in 1835, called it with typical orotundity "the unknown city in the ocean". Today no more graphic phrase can be found to suggest its quenchless surprises and ineradicable touch of wonder.

EDITOR'S NOTE FP: *Perspective Review*, Winter 1934, pp. 7–8. HPL's ecstatic description of Nantucket island, off the coast of Massachusetts, which he visited for the first time during a week-long stay on 31 August–6 September 1934. The essay was presumably written shortly thereafter. Its title purportedly is based (as HPL notes in the final paragraph) on a comment by Daniel Webster, but it has not been located.

Notes

1. HPL visited all these cities.
2. Maria Mitchell (1818–1889), American astronomer who taught at Vassar (1861–88) and made numerous astronomical discoveries.

CHARLESTON

Of all the cities of the United States, Charleston is probably the most distinctive and unforgettable. Nowhere else does the atmosphere of the original America so strongly survive. Nowhere else can the past be so concretely visualised. Today the ancient South Carolina metropolis is increasingly a goal of tourists, who find its unique charm and eighteenth-century spirit a source of unending delight.

A full, appreciative enjoyment of Charleston depends on judicious observation plus adequate background knowledge, and facilities for both are more and more easily obtainable. Superficial glances—very useful for orientation purposes—may be gained through the standard sightseeing coaches operated from Marion Square; but for a really intelligent acquaintance, a pedestrian tour is necessary. This, fortunately, can be arranged quite readily, with a map of the city (procurable free at the Chamber of Commerce, Broad and Church Sts.; a cruder specimen, with route outlined, is appended to the present brochure) as a basis. The traveller with more than a day or two in Charleston would do well to secure a full guide-book, such as Miriam Bellangee Wilson's "Street Strolls around Charleston, S.C." (75¢ at any good stationery store, like Lighthart's on the east side of King Street just below George). This volume not only points out all essential features of interest, but relates the history and traditions centreing around everything described. Its itineraries could be covered in three or four days, though to receive justice they ought to have at least a week of unhurried attention.

Charleston was first founded in 1670 on a site somewhat removed (across the Ashley River) from its present peninsular location. The colony of Carolina was chartered by Charles II in 1663, though then containing only some straggling settlements of Virginian and West Indian planters in its northern parts. In its government, the enterprise adopted a very formal and oligarchical plan called the "Grand Model", derived from the philosophical ideas of John Locke, and providing for fixed ranks (landgrave, cassique, baron) dependent upon land tenure. These distinctions were never clear and finally fell into desuetude. The first new colonists—a group of 160 in two ships under Capt. Wm. Sayle—were sent out in 1669 to build a "Towne of Trade" and in 1670 settled at their first location. The two great rivers, *Kiawah* and *Wando,* were renamed respectively *Ashley* and *Cooper* in honour of the greatest of the Lords Proprietors (who never visited the colony)—Anthony Ashley Cooper, later first Earl of Shaftesbury. Within a year of the settlement many persons questioned the wisdom of the site and after 1672 a sprinkling of colonists began to drift across to "Oyster Point", the peninsula betwixt the Ashley and Cooper. By 1679 a change of site was agreed on and in 1680 the new *Charles-Town* (like the first named from Charles II, though *Carolina* was named from Charles IX of France because of abortive Huguenot settlements in 1562–5) was laid out according to a carefully preconceived plan. From this second planting the real history of Charleston dates. For protection against Spaniards and Indians the town was fortified with strong breastworks which soon developed into city walls, with bastions, salients, and guard posts at the gates. Under these influences the town soon developed into a narrow parallelogram four squares long and three wide, fronting on the Cooper River and bounded on the south by Vanderhorst's Creek—now filled in and forming the line of Water Street. The western boundary corresponded to the present Meeting Street, having here a wall, gate, and drawbridge. Places were reserved for a church, a town hall, and a parade-ground. The north and south streets were Church and Meeting; the east and west ones, from the south boundary up, were Tradd (named for the first white child born in the town), Elliott, Broad, and Dock (later Queen).

The town soon outgrew its walls, and by 1700 had spread westward desultorily to the Ashley River. The decade 1679–1689 brought heavy immigration, especially of dissenters after the accession of James II. West Indian planters also flocked in, founding families still in existence. In 1693 the culture of *rice* was introduced and soon became the leading pursuit of the inhabitants. In 1741 the introduction of indigo provided another major industry—both lasting until the nineteenth-century age of cotton.

Churches very early appeared—Anglican, Baptist, Presbyterian, Quaker, and Huguenot. The Charleston Quakers are now extinct, but an Huguenot church still exists at Church and Queen Sts.—the only one surviving in the U.S. The Huguenots—so influential in Charleston history—came mostly between 1680 and 1688, uprooted by oppression in France. Some Dutch from Nieuw Nederland also appeared, followed by Germans and Swiss who established the wrought-iron industry. Buildings of a good type were erected, though no specimens earlier than 1722 survive.

Early Carolina history was turbulent. In 1686 the Spanish from St. Augustine destroyed a Scottish settlement farther down the coast—Port Royal—and went unpunished only because of religious discord in the colony. This discord eventually led to the abolition of the proprietary government and the establishment of Carolina as a royal province in 1719. In 1699 fever, hurricane, and flood ravaged the colony. These scourges recur all down the centuries, though modern medical science has stamped out yellow fever, while eighteenth-century engineering provided stouter sea-walls and better houses to resist the September tempests.

It was in the eighteenth century that the ripe culture of old Charles-Town fully flowered. Architecture flourished and all the attributes of a mellow civilisation appeared. In 1702 Gov. Moore led an expedition against the Florida Spaniards, holding all of St. Augustine except the fort for a time. Indians and pirates also harassed the colony. At one time Col. Rhett hanged 57 of the latter at once on a spot near the tip of the peninsula, where Church and Water now intersect. In 1719 the colony became a royal province and a decade later its present division into North and South Carolina was made. By 1720 Charles-Town had largely overflowed its walls and these barriers now began to be demolished bit by bit. Today only a fragment of them remains—the ancient bastion in Cumberland Street, built in 1703 and now called the "Old Powder Magazine".

At this period the city began to assume much of its present aspect. Houses as early as the 1730's are still very numerous; and we still see the town, so far as general impressions go, as it was in the middle and later Georgian era. Block on block of the ancient edifices may still be descried in the region below Broad Street—to an extent not duplicated in any other American city. Roof-tiling—a rare thing in early American houses—was introduced about 1735, and gave to the steep gables of the houses their characteristic aspect. Early experiments with porches were suggested by the warm climate, and before the end of the eighteenth century we see Charleston as a town of outdoor living . . . with great verandahs on all three storeys of the south and west sides of the houses, opening on exquisite walled gardens which passers-by might glimpse through gates of magnificent wrought-iron grille-work. The brick-and-stucco houses generally followed Georgian models, but in an individual and localised way; so that no other colonial city looks just like Charleston. We find the city's gardens first mentioned about 1740. In 1748 the present proprietary library was founded, attesting to the good scholarship of a people more urban than the Virginians because of the heat and fever which drove them from their inland plantations to their town houses during a great part of the summer. Theatres appear about the middle of the eighteenth century (the first in 1736) or before—the principal one being at the corner of Dock (Queen) and Church Streets. In 1752 a great storm damaged the town and produced much rebuilding—giving the streets a good deal of their present form.

Charles-Town weathered the revolution with considerable poise, though largely rebel in sympathies. It was defended by a strong fort on Sullivan's Island, commanded by Col. Moultrie and later named for him. On June 28th, 1776, occurred that attack by His Majesty's fleet during which the rebel sergeant Jasper leapt outside the breastworks and saved his colours under fire. Charles-Town held out under the rebels till 1780, when the forces of Sir Henry Clinton and Lord Rawdon moved in and took up headquarters at the splendid Brewton-Pringle mansion in lower King Street—a place still standing and open as a museum for the exorbitant fee of a full dollar. There was some friction between troops and populace, for which blame seems evenly divided. Charles-Town was used as a base of supplies by the regulars during most of the Southern campaign—a campaign in which the chief obstacles were the Rhode Island General Nathanael Greene and the local South Carolina guerrillas Francis Marion, Sumter, and Pickens. After the disaster to Lord Cornwallis's army in October 1781 the town was evacuated—the troops bearing away the chimes of St. Michael's church to London, whence they were afterward regained by purchase.

In 1783 the city's name was officially changed from *Charles-Town* to its exact present form of *Charleston*. Its general culture had been very little impaired by the upheavals of war, and the old social order continued to flourish. In 1792 the negro uprisings in St. Domingo sent to Charleston a great number of French gentlefolk who were instantly made welcome, and who formed a highly civilising influence. About this time Charleston was superseded by the inland town of *Columbia* as capital of South Carolina—the new place being laid out especially for that purpose.

This age—the late eighteenth and early nineteenth centuries—marks the heyday of Charleston's social glory and material prosperity. Culture was promoted by isolation from the hinterland and free communication with Europe—so that to this day the town avoids the characteristic negroid accent of the South. Eighteenth-century taste survived with remarkable tenacity, and classic revival architecture flourished with more than normal vigour. Victorian decadence was longer postponed than it was anywhere else. In 1800 Charleston was the leading centre of culture on this continent, with graceful institutions and a high level of taste such as no other American region is ever likely to parallel. The social season extended from May to November, when malaria drove the planters to town from their inland estates; and was supplemented by a shorter period around the end of January called the "Gay Season". The great social institution of the town whose meetings and functions determined the recreative life of the greatest families, and whose judgments determined the status of every person of consequence, was (and still is) an organisation originally of musical purpose, called the St. Cecelia Society. The St. Cecelia's Day concerts and balls of this society and its Thursday functions that began at 9 p.m. soon became by-words of exclusiveness, till at length its musical character was merged in its social dictatorship. Various other dancing assemblies were frequented by the gay, and the Philharmonic Concerts were also well attended. Jockey balls attested the importance of racing, as did the Annual Race Week, which formed a sort of Charleston carnival. Much of this atmosphere is reflected in DuBose Heyward's fairly recent novel "Peter Ashley".[1] Business was transacted during the "Gay Season"—advantage being taken of the presence of many planters in town. Everyone was generally back in the country by the end of March, not to see Charleston again till May.

The gentry comprising this civilisation were almost all planters of rice and cotton—the latter having replaced indigo as a major staple. Their cultivation greatly exceeded that of the Virginians, and they left mercantile pursuits to a bourgeois class largely from England and Scotland. Public education increased and individual taste developed. Favourite authors, apart from the omnipresent Graeco-Roman classics, were Shakespeare and Montaigne. Coaches now appear in frequent use, and on every hand we behold the ideal of gentlemanly carelessness uppermost. No man knew how much he was worth in cash—trade and calculation being left to hired "factors" from the North. Personal honour was very carefully guarded, and duelling was frequent.

In those days the factors' and merchants' warehouses formed a distinct district along Bay Street, which faces the Cooper River or principal waterfront. Popular shopping streets were the east ends of Broad and Tradd and Elliott. General stores carrying all manner of goods were the rule, the jewellery shops forming the main exception. Country trade was conducted by long, white-topped wagons with four or six horses or mules, piled high with cotton-bales, high up in King Street near the present railway station. Most of the town was below, or only slightly above, Calhoun (then called Boundary) Street; just as before the Revolution it had been largely below Broad—or at most Queen or Cumberland. It should be noted that Charleston is a narrow peninsula like the island of Manhattan, so that urban expansion (checked by marshes on the western or Ashley River side) is invariably northward. There was no one residence section, homes being scattered and surrounded by large gardens or tracts of land. The Battery, lower Meeting St., Legare St., and so on, were then as now favoured by fine dwellings. Indeed, we may say that the social complexion of the town has changed but little in the 136 years since those gorgeous days of 1800. The Battery (or White Point Gardens) was, as it still is, a chosen place of promenade.

In 1822 a threatened negro insurrection alarmed the town, but the plot came to nothing. Shortly afterward tension with the North was increased by the tariff troubles culminating in the nullification agitation of 1832 et seq. Slaves were in general very well treated, so that to this day the blacks of Charleston are orderly and well disposed. Much African superstition was picked up from them, and the region still abounds in weird folklore. Arts and literary life continued to flourish, producing such figures as the graceful poet Henry Timrod.

The Civil War naturally harassed Charleston greatly, though no actual land fighting occurred there. Secession began in South Carolina, and the first shots of the war were fired at Fort Sumter in Charleston Harbour. Almost coincident with these events was the local fire of 1861, which created a vast burned district west of Meeting St. and above and below Broad, although it was of accidental origin and totally unconnected with the conflict. The fire destroyed St. Andrew's Hall in Broad St., formerly the leading place of public assemblage; and the site has never been built upon. The whole burned district remained a desert for years—dividing the town into two parts.

Wartime hardships—blockades and siege and all their consequences—pressed heavily upon Charleston, but the population carried on well. Because of Federal gunfire in the harbour, the lower end of town was left almost deserted during the hostilities—the inhabitants congregating north of the burned district. With the war went Charleston's material prosperity, but despite external change the basic civilisation proved too deep to eradicate. Perspectives and institutions persisted, and the nightmare of "reconstruction" was weathered without flinching. At length a limited prosperity began to dawn. Broad Street again bristled with banks, brokers, and barristers, and King Street became a fashionable shopping promenade of the elegant '80's. Meeting Street drove a thriving jobbing trade in dry-goods, clothing, shoes, and crockery, whilst the East Bay Street waterfront buzzed anew with the bulk of grocers and shipchandlers. The rice and cotton industries, however, never reached their former state of opulence.

In 1886 Charleston experienced the severest earthquake ever known on the Atlantic coast—a thing which destroyed many buildings and public works, and severely impaired many more, including the splendid old edifice of St. Michael's Church. Recuperation, however, was very swift.

Today Charleston is probably the most civilised spot in the United States—the place where genuine values most amply survive, and where the false glitter and confusion of mechanised barbarism are least to be found. The original families still hold sway—Rhetts, Izards, Pringles, Bulls, Hugers, Ravenels, Manigaults, Draytons, Stoneys, Pinckneys, Rutledges, Middletons, and so on—and still uphold the basic truths and standards of a civilisation which is genuine because it represents a settled adjustment betwixt people and landscape, old enough to have created the overtones useful to a sense of interest and significance. Gentlefolk in Charleston still pursue their ways for pleasure and not for show or profit, and are still decently anxious to keep their names and personal affairs out of the papers. The Charleston dailies are the only ones without a vulgar "society column" to spy upon the comings and goings of important people.

Foreigners are not numerous, though Italian and Jewish colonies exist. Blacks, of course, abound, but they are extremely civil and obliging. The street cries of Charleston, all uttered by negro vendors, were once very famous, but are now declining despite artificial efforts to revive them. The town contains many wealthy Northerners who have bought old estates, but so far the newcomers have been very appreciative and assimilable. There is the nucleus of an "art colony" in and around lower Church Street, but fortunately no large-scale "Greenwich Village" has developed.

Architecturally, Charleston is the most remarkable town in the U.S.—possessing unique colonial features and having retained an astonishing proportion of early buildings. West Indian and French Huguenot features, plus native climatic adaptations, produce striking variants of English Georgian architecture—hence the tiers of verandahs, the gay tiles, the painted stucco over brickwork, the peculiar Gallic gables, the curved eaves, the deeply recessed windows, and the occasional jerkin-head roofs. No one, having seen a Charleston house, can ever mistake the type. The side verandahs with their classical doorways opening on the street are utterly characteristic of the place—as are the wrought-iron grilles and gates, and the great walled gardens. Railed double flights of steps curving above an arched passageway—a pleasant Renaissance effect—are nowhere else as numerous as here. In classic revival architecture Charleston excels. She bred the eminent architect Robert Mills, and much of his work is to be found in his native place. There were, too, great numbers of amateur or gentlemen architects like Gabriel Manigault. As the nineteenth century advanced, Charleston largely escaped the general collapse of architectural taste, though a certain heaviness and decadence are visible in later buildings. Some of the coarseness in details can be attributed to the replacement of expert white cabinet-makers by unskilled negro labourers. Today Charleston is refreshingly free from "modernistic" architecture, and seems like Providence determined to remain true to its own heritage. During the past few years there has been an encouraging reclamation of deserted and half-ruinous landmarks (like the splendid Georgian Vanderhorst Row (1802) in East Bay Street and the historic Planter's Hotel at Church and Queen) in connexion with CWA, ERA, PWA, and WPA projects—a work which one hopes may not be interrupted by any reactionary political move.

Charleston occupies a flat—and originally marshy and creek-threaded—tongue of land betwixt the mouths of two great rivers which here flow into one of the most spacious harbours on the Atlantic coast—a harbour seven miles across and separated from the open sea by several islands. The city is the natural part of a spacious inland region of subtropical climate and fertility, cut by many rivers and once the seat of extensive plantations. Here are gardens of figs, pomegranates, peaches, oranges, oleanders, myrtles, azaleas, camellias, acacias, jujubes, and roses; and outside the town one beholds the wild-rose, the wild yellow jessamine, the magnolia, and the twisted and curious live-oak with festoons of grey Spanish moss hanging from spectral branches. Observing Charleston horticulture, one does not wonder at its fame, or at the circumstance that two of our most celebrated flowers, the poinsettia and the gardenia, were named from gentlemen of Charleston, who cultivated them. The piquant and bristling palmetto-tree is very frequently met with, and more clearly than anything else proclaims our nearness to the tropics.

The city lies in N. Latitude 32° 45′ and W. Longitude 79° 57′. Approached from the sea, its flatness gives it a very curious and engaging aspect; the many spires and roofs seeming to rise directly out of the water, as if forming the topmost pinnacles of some submerged Atlantis. St. Michael's and St. Philip's steeples are dominant and traditional features of the skyline. The general arrangement of the streets is like that of New York—with cross streets and long north and south streets ending at the Battery with a sea-wall. The social topography, however, is very different; inasmuch as the Battery and vicinity form a sumptuous residential section (on account of the cool breezes) while business flourishes on the two great north and south streets (King and Meeting), about midway in their course. The principal cross streets, from the Battery up, are Tradd (a thoroughfare wholly colonial), Broad (the street of bankers and brokers), and Calhoun (which marks the focus of the main business section, and crosses Meeting and King at an open park called Marion Square). The great north and south streets, from the Cooper River or principal waterfront westward, are East Bay, Church, Meeting, King, Legare (which runs north into Archdale and St. Philip), Rutledge Avenue, and Ashley Avenue. The region below Broad Street is very largely colonial. Along the line of Meeting Street and around the Battery it is exceedingly fashionable and beautiful; whilst east of this, along the line of Church Street, it is quaint and home-like except for occasional book shops and artists' studios. As one gets north of Stoll's Alley, a dismal slum district of abandoned warehouses and dirty tenements begins to develop along the Cooper waterfront; but this is well worth exploration because of the age and picturesqueness of the houses. Between Broad and Calhoun lies a region which may be called *semi-colonial,* and which ought to be thoroughly covered by the visitor, since it contains the leading public edifices. The focal point of this and the older southerly region is the historic intersection of Broad and Meeting Streets, once the principal gate of the original walled town, and for two centuries the real civic centre. On the four corners of this intersection will be found ancient St. Michael's Church (1761) (S.E.), the City Hall (1801) (N.E.), the Court House (1788) (N.W.), and the modern but sightly post office (S.W.). Adjacent to it, and having gates on both Meeting and Broad Streets (as well as on Chalmers St. to the north), is the old City Park or Washington Square, which lies behind the City Hall and forms the principal downtown resting-place besides the Battery. Here we find an excellent statue of William Pitt, Esq., set up in 1770 and moved to the present site from elsewhere; also a monument to the graceful Charleston poet Henry Timrod, and one to the great Confederate General Pierre Gustave Toutant Beauregard. The park extends through to Chalmers Street on the north, and on the east is bounded by a very picturesque and ancient Georgian wall.

We now come to consider the actual observation of the city, for which a good map is eminently desirable. The slower one can go, the better, since colour and atmosphere can be best absorbed if one has leisure to savour and digest each sight to the fullest extent—correlating it with one's historical, literary, and imaginative background. If a preliminary orientation is desired as a preface to real exploration, that offered by the Gray Line sightseeing coaches will be found excellent. Before beginning any actual trip, it would be wise to prepare in advance for what one is to see—either through this hasty sketch, or through the Wilson guide-book previously mentioned. A minimum of time will then be lost. In this sketch only the most salient things will be touched upon. No attempt will be made to describe the multiplicity of *rural* sights around Charleston—sights which include many fine plantations, the ancient Goose Creek Church (1711), St. Andrew's Parish Church (1706), and the famous Magnolia, Middleton, and Cypress Gardens, which are open to the public in the early spring. These latter, however, deserve a special expedition.

Arriving in Charleston, the visitor beholds a city which is alive in every sense despite the omnipresent aura of the past. Though suggesting Salem and Newport in its physical aspect, it has not the somnolence of those venerable towns, but is indeed the present metropolis of a large and opulent region, in which it stands alone and unchallenged. Accordingly, it will be found to contain a variety of urban refinements and facilities, and to harbour a metropolitan self-sufficiency, which would not be found in a northern town of equal size. The population, including the blacks, does not much exceed 62,000; yet the general atmosphere is that of a large town of vast assurance and maturity. There are—allowing for the depression—signs of a commercial revival in the immediate future; and an increasing flow of appreciative tourists heightens the aspect of liveliness during the early spring season. The great Cooper River bridge serves, in connexion with another bridge over the Ashley, to place Charleston on a direct coastal route betwixt Florida and the North; a circumstance very favourable to its economic outlook. Charleston's chief industries have latterly been the manufacture of phosphate fertilisers and asbestos products, and the export of varied agricultural commodities. The agricultural trade is very brisk, owing to the excellence and healthfulness of South Carolina vegetable produce—the fruit of a soil rich in the dietetically necessary element of iodine.

Regarding hotel accommodations, the traveller of modest needs will be very well served by the excellent Y.M.C.A. on the north side of George Street between King and Meeting, and not far from the 'bus station in Marion Square. Those desiring a degree less of austerity may try the home-like Timrod Inn in Meeting Street near Broad—just across the street from ancient City Park. More modern hotel facilities are provided by the well-appointed Francis Marion Hotel in Marion Square, while still greater luxury can be had at the Fort Sumter—a definitely vacationist hostelry on the Battery at the foot of King Street. Most aristocratic of all, perhaps, is the Villa Margharita, a made-over private mansion in South Battery St.—the street running just north of the park and overlooking the harbour.

Issuing forth to observe his environment, the stranger cannot but note the civilised and distinctive atmosphere of the city around him. The pace of life is sensible and leisurely, and there is no needless noise or bustle or excitement. The abundance of negroes is picturesque, and now and then the sweet chimes of old St. Michael's can be heard striking the hours, halves, and quarters as they have done since 1779. Odd characters and quaint beggars abound to an extent unheard of in the efficient and dehumanised North. As for climate, most cannot but find it very much to their taste; it being mild in winter, and in summer cooled by the breezes of the neighbouring ocean. The annual mean temperature is 67° F., and there are on the average only six freezing days in a year. The Battery is never warm enough to justify coatlessness. The sun in Charleston shines more continuously than in any other American city except Los Angeles. The one drawback is the tendency toward gales and hurricanes in late August and September, a thing largely offset by stout building construction and massive seawalls. The beaches of Charleston—Folly Beach, Sullivan's Island, and the Isle of Palms—are among the finest in the South. Sullivan's Island, with Fort Moultrie, ought certainly to be visited because of its association with Poe (who served in the army there) and its part in his celebrated tale "The Gold-Bug"; and its possession of the grave of the unfortunate Seminole chieftain Osceola, who was confined to the dungeons of the fort. One of the Gray Line tours includes Sullivan's Island.

The best way to see Charleston is first to drift aimlessly about the ancient streets below Broad, picking up random impressions of centuried charm and exotic tradition without the psychological hindrance of a preconceived or systematic plan, and then—having reached the palmetto-fringed and live-oak-dotted Battery with its numerous monuments—to begin the regular following of some stated sightseeing route. In the random Batteryward stroll a very good idea of Old Charleston may be secured. One will stumble on the quaintest conceivable streets, alleys, squares, and hidden courtyards, and will encounter the most sumptuous mansions embedded in walled tropical gardens. Along the principal waterfront, that on the Cooper side, he will discern the many abandoned and ruined brick warehouses which speak so eloquently of former shipping prosperity. As in Newport and Salem, relatively few of the ancient houses are ever demolished; though many are in a state of desertion and decrepitude. The architecture of the old tiled and stuccoed buildings, with their occasionally bright hues, will engage the eye from the outset; suggesting something oddly French or Latin or foreign in some obscure way. The great blackness of most of the negroes will be remarked; it being evidently the custom for mulattoes to keep to themselves in the new far-northern part of the town. Foreign faces, except for a sprinkling of Greeks, Jews, and Italians, are very seldom noticeable; the city being obviously still dominated by the old Nordic stock. Now and then a classic, old-fashioned public building or church will attract notice; and at all times one is looking for glimpses of the two dominant landmarks—St. Michael's and St. Philip's spires. Wrought-iron work produces a deep impression because of its universal profusion—gates, balconies, window grilles, railings, and the like; all of the finest craftsmanship. The *gates* are especially numerous because of the prevalence of high-walled gardens in this land of luxurious flowers, rambling vines, and opulent trees that weave an omnipresent green twilight redolent of perfume and musical with bird-song when the sun goes down. Bronze street signs set in the sidewalk at intersections are a typical feature of modern Charleston. Most important buildings and historic sites are marked by tablets or placards.

We are now ready for our systematic itinerary. The route about to be outlined, beginning at the Battery, is designed to cover the whole city in a single walk with as few repetitions as possible; but it is of course merely fragmentary as compared with all the sites to be seen. It may be followed in one long tramp—a full day's pedestrian quota—or taken in sections; and in any order whatsoever. It is not meant to include everything in Old Charleston, and it would be a pity if one were to follow it blindly without consulting the guide-books, and ascertaining what else is to be seen. Likewise, it leaves to these fuller guide-books the task of supplying ampler descriptions of the few things which are touched upon. For a detailed knowledge of Charleston history and traditions one should consult volumes at the excellent library in King Street, betwixt Clifford and Queen. Those by Mazÿck and Mrs. St. Julien Ravenel (wife of the noted physician who eradicated yellow fever from the city) are especially good. On the following crude map, the route is shewn in red.

Especially important thoroughfares underlined.[2]

Principal north and south Charleston streets or lines of streets, reading east to west from Cooper River front toward the Ashley: East Bay St.; Church St.; *Meeting* St.; *King* St.; Legare—Archdale—St. Philip; Lockwood—Logan—Mazÿck—Coming; Franklin—Pitt; Smith St.; *Rutledge* Ave.; Ashley Ave.; President St.

Principal cross streets or lines of streets of Charleston, reading north from the Battery: *South Battery;* Lamboll—Atlantic; Ladson—Water; *Tradd; Broad;* Queen; Clifford—Horlbeck—Cumberland; Market; Beaufain—Hasell; *Wentworth;* George; *Calhoun;* Vanderhorst—Charlotte; Morris—Mary; Cannon; *Spring;* Bogard—*Columbus.*

Principal Squares: Marion Square or Citadel Green: Calhoun, King, and Meeting Streets; *City Park or Washington Square:* Meeting, Broad, and Chalmers Streets; *Battery or White Point Gardens:* foot of King, Meeting, Church, and East Bay Streets.

Beginning at the *Battery,* the visitor should observe the semi-tropical scenery of that pleasing area, and pay good attention to the mansions fronting on it. Looking down the harbour somewhat eastward, he may behold historic Fort Sumter upon a small island in the distance, and see to the left of it *Fort Moultrie,* occupying a point of land on *Sullivan's Island.* Turning inland, there is to be seen at #8 South Battery (on the left-hand corner of Church St.) the elegant private mansion built in 1768 by Thos. Savage, Esq., and in 1785 bought by *Col. Wm. Washington* of the celebrated Virginia family. If one choose to go up *King St.* to #27, and explore the ancient Brewton-Pringle house (headquarters of His Majesty's forces 1780–81), he may well do so; though this edifice will be encountered later in the circuitous route. If not, it is advisable to begin the tour by turning up Church St., though not without looking carefully up Meeting St., and observing the spacious mansions and estates lining both sides.

Advancing along Church St., which is very narrow, we pass by quaint ancient houses and stables, and notice the trim dwellings of artists as we cross Atlantic St. After this we encounter a bend, on the left-hand side of which are some very ancient houses. No. 35, once inhabited by a local historian, was built in 1745. No 37 was built before 1733. No. 39, the well-known *George Eveleigh house*, was built in the decade 1743–53, and had a secret stairway to the second floor. All three of these houses once had a secret passage to Vanderhorst Creek, which followed the line of the present *Water St.* We now come to Water St., which in its aqueous days was crossed by a bridge. That part of Church St. we have just been traversing was anciently called Fort St. The large round object in the sidewalk at this intersection is a *tidal drain,* made necessary by the low and watery nature of the region. Somewhat west of this is the spot where Col. Rhett caused 57 pirates to be hanged in a single afternoon. Advancing around the bend, we now encounter on our right the entrance to Stoll's Alley, once a slum, but now tastefully restored as an habitation for artists. It is to be hoped that this colony will not sink to the status of a Greenwich Village. An exploration of Stoll's Alley is well worth one's while, nor is it a vain digression to go all the way through the narrow part to *East Bay St.* In the wider part the Georgian restorations are very clever and agreeable, though their artificiality is manifest. At East Bay St. we turn to the left, noting the abandoned and ruined warehouses along the waterfront. We soon come to *Longitude Lane,* leading back to Church St., opposite which—on the water side of the street—is an exceedingly sightly edifice of brick, of Adam-period design, and in a pathetic state of desertion and decrepitude until its recent PWA restoration. This is *Vanderhorst Row,* put up in 1802 and said to be the oldest apartment-house in America. Now turning into Longitude Lane, we pass by the moss-grown brick walls of half-abandoned cotton warehouses; noting the cobble-stones set for mules' feet, the flag-stones for the dray-wheels, and the snubbing-posts at the warehouse doors. One of these posts is an old ship's cannon. Once back in Church St., we look to the left and digress backward to see the entrance of an old warehouse on the eastern side, and the classic facade of the *First Baptist Church* (1822—designed by Robert Mills) opposite it. Next the church and opposite the mouth of Longitude Lane is #69, the *Jacob Motte house,* built in 1760 and having a pink colour which it has borne since the earliest times. Next door—at #71—is the *Robert Brewton house,* built in 1740 and forming a fine example of the smaller "single" houses of early Charleston. Still farther along—at #73—is the *Miles Brewton house* (1733—a typical Old Charleston "double" house). Across the street from it, at #78, is an old house with a fine wrought-iron balcony from which General Washington is reputed to have given an address. A study of this balcony tends to disprove the tradition, since (although the house is ancient) the craftsmanship points to a later date than 1791, the period of the general's visit. One singular thing about the house is the symmetrical *central* position of the doorway; a thing universally met with in Georgian New England, but very uncommon in the South. We come now to quaint and ancient *Tradd St.,* which is so picturesque that it will pay us to stroll down it to the river and return. On both sides we may see very ancient houses, built flush with the street and with walls adjoining, as a protection (says local tradition) against the raids of pirates, Spaniards, and Indians. *Bedon's Alley,* a very old and curious by-way containing a large three-storey brick house which may possibly be the oldest in Charleston, extends northward from a point half-way to the river; on its western corner being the site once holding the *Carolina Coffee-House.* Here, in 1790, the St. Cecilia Society held one of its concerts; and in 1793 the Ugly Club (which must have had its inspiration in Mr. Steele's *Spectator* papers,[3] and to which the present writer would have enjoyed belonging) used it as a dining-place. At East Bay St. we again behold Vanderhorst Row and note on the northern corner of Tradd St. the site of the birthplace of the first white child in the town—Robert Tradd, from whom the street was named. Looking out over the river past *Adger's Wharf*, we behold the island called Castle-Pinckney, and farther off, the opposite shore of Mt. Pleasant and part of *Sullivan's Island*. Returning now to Church St. and resuming a northerly course, we behold on the left at #87 the *Heyward house*, a fine brick Georgian mansion of generalised rather than Charlestonian architecture, some time ago restored as a public museum. This house was built in the 1770's or before, and was used by General Washington during his Charleston visit of May 1791. Adjoining this structure is an old house which in 1791–1810 was the *French Theatre*, afterward the *City Theatre*. The auditorium was in the rear, reached by crossing through an archway and traversing an inner court. In more recent times, the place had sunk to a slum and was used by negroes as a vending-place of vegetables, being commonly known as *"Cabbage Row"* and presented in the novel "Porgy" by DuBose Heyward as *"Catfish Row"*. The interior court of this building is now familiar to northern audiences through the stage setting of the opera "Porgy and Bess". Some years ago it was restored to its original neatness, and it has at times housed various art and book shops. Proceeding onward, we should note the quaint alleys on either side of the street—*St. Michael's Place* to the left, and *Elliott St.* to the right. We now come to *Broad St.*, the leading transverse thoroughfare of the town, and an abode of bankers and brokers. On the northeast corner is the modern bank building which has most unfortunately replaced the old and historic *Shepheard's Tavern*, where the first Masonic Lodge in America was organised in 1736. On the northwest corner, the *Chamber of Commerce* occupies the brick structure erected in 1784 for the Bank of South Carolina and used from 1835 to 1914 as a library. It will be worth our while to walk down Broad St. to the river and study the ancient and remarkable public building which squarely faces the end of the street. This is the *Old Exchange*, built in 1767 on the site of the old guard post called "Half-Moon Bastion", and used as executive headquarters by His Majesty's forces in 1780–81. It was later a post-office, and is now an headquarters of the D.A.R.—open as a museum and also housing certain federal clerical activities. During the Revolution prisoners were confined in the basement of this building; and on the northern end, close to the ground, can still be seen the small square hole, with heavy grating, which afforded scanty light and air to some of the dungeons. The architecture of the building in general is very fine. To the right of the Old Exchange, across a seaward lane and [on] the water side of East Bay St. at #114–116, will be found *a group of very ancient buildings*, two of which have cupolas or observation-towers. These towers were used by observers to watch the incoming shipping and transmit the news to the public. Ships were first sighted from a tower on Sullivan's Island, whose watchman relayed the news to these urban towers by raising ball signals on a pole—a black ball for a square rigger, and a white ball for a schooner-rigged vessel. These signals were repeated by the urban watchers, the signal balls being left up until the ships they represented came to anchor. The small building on the corner, next the tall cupola'd building, is the old *French Coffee-House*, or Harris's Tavern. Beneath this structure may still be found the ancient wine-cellars, which form a tunnel extending far out under East Bay St., and then turning toward the Battery in an arm reaching half a block. We now, after a glance at the classic bank facade on the landward side of East Bay above Broad, turn back along Broad St. for one block; then turning northward into *State St.*, originally called Union St. Following this to the first intersection, we there turn to the left into ancient and picturesque *Chalmers St.*, a broad cobblestoned thoroughfare, at whose farther end can be seen in the distance the splendid classic pillars of Hibernian Hall (1841) in Meeting St. Almost all the houses along Chalmers St. are colonial. At #8, the small, low archway adjoining a pretentiously turreted building is the *Old Slave Market* at which trained servants and skilled artisans were sold—the common field negroes being procurable at "Vendue Range", the foot of Queen St. where the Clyde Line wharves now extend. Nearly opposite the "Slave Mart" is that curious *pink-coloured building* which possesses (perhaps) the only *gambrel roof* in Charleston. This is a very old house and was a tavern before the Revolution. It has three storeys, but only one room to a floor. We are now back at Church St., though it would do no harm to walk along Chalmers to Meeting and back in order to observe the ancient houses. Turning up Church, we next come to *Queen St.* (formerly Dock St.), at whose southeast corner is the sightly Gothic church (1845) and churchyard of the Huguenots. This is today the only *Huguenot church* in the country, and deserves the support (which it sorely needs) of every surviving group of Huguenot descendants. Across the street from the church is the deserted and long dilapidated shell of the *Planter's Hotel,* built in 1805 and famous in the great cotton era as a rendezvous of neighbouring planters and their families. It is now under restoration as a WPA project. On the northwest corner, and extending a considerable space along Church St., is a group of five small houses built of brick and Bermuda coral-stone, and known to have been standing prior to 1742. These are the so-called "Pirate Houses"; reputed to have been the haunt of freebooters in the old days, and said to have received visits at a later date from Poe. They are now all converted into fashionable shops, and the courtyard behind them has been developed as a highly fascinating by-way. Beyond these comes the bend in the street, with the fine porticoes and steeple of *St. Philip's Episcopal Church* looming up in the foreground, and sections of the churchyard stretching off on both sides of the way. St. Philip's present edifice does not antedate 1835, but it is a fine late-Georgian specimen whose steeple shares honours with St. Michael's as a landmark of the city and a welcoming symbol to the mariner approaching the port. The tower, with its triple portico, is very notable. When this fane was built, Church St. did not extend in front of it, the bend being made to accommodate it. The present street cuts the old churchyard in two, separating the larger part (which contains the grave of John C. Calhoun) from the edifice itself. We now push on to *Cumberland St.,* choosing whether or not we shall stroll down toward the waterfront to see the old house (on the north side) with the elaborate ironwork and the wrought-iron emblem of the Iron Workers Guild—which was probably the residence and shop of a master craftsman. With this side-trip made or omitted, we follow Cumberland St. west of Church toward Meeting, noting on the left-hand side the *Old Powder Magazine* in its limited but pleasing grounds. This squat, peaked-gabled bit of Cyclopean vaulted masonry is the oldest structure in Charleston, dating from 1703 and having formed a bastion of the city wall. It is the only surviving fragment of that wall. The Colonial Dames are in charge of it, and visitors are admitted to the heavily vaulted interior for a 25¢ fee. We now follow Cumberland to Meeting and turn northward to *Market St.,* beholding in the middle of that thoroughfare the high classic facade of the old *Market House,* whose upper part is now a Confederate Museum. This edifice, built in 1841, is typical of Old Charleston public architecture; having the characteristic double flight of steps with the mouth of an arched tunnel beneath. Behind the building the low-roofed shed of the Market (erected in 1800) extends all the way to the river, along the line of what was once Fish Market

Creek. In earlier times the refuse of this market attracted a famous array of buzzards, which became incredibly tame. Following the market shed to East Bay St. after a glance upward along Meeting St. at the classic facade of the old *Charleston Hotel*, we behold—somewhat to the right and set near the water—the massive and splendid *Custom House* with its classic architecture, begun in 1850 and finished after the Civil War. From the seaward side of this building an impressive view of the harbour may be obtained. We now proceed three squares up East Bay to *Hasell St.*, here turning to the left and proceeding again toward Meeting St. On the north or right-hand side, at #54, is what is perhaps (the claim of the Bedon's Alley house notwithstanding) the *oldest dwelling in Charleston*, built in 1722 or before by the old pirate-fighter Col. Wm. Rhett, and later forming the birthplace of the eminent soldier and statesman General Wade Hampton. Reaching Meeting St., we may if we wish make a side-trip beyond to see the venerable classic facade of the *Jews' Synagogue* (1841) on the right and *St. Mary's Catholic Church* (1838) on the left. We then turn northward along Meeting toward George, passing on the left the stately columns of *Trinity Methodist Episcopal Church* (1875), called "the youngest church below Calhoun St." At George St. we note on the northwest corner the fine but dilapidated *King mansion* with its walled grounds, built in 1806 and later used as a high-school. Making a side-trip eastward along George, we see on the north side the grounds and building of the local water works—which is the old *Elliott-Pinckney-Middleton house*, finished in 1797 and forming one of the finest possible specimens of Adam-period architecture. The interior, defaced though it is by industrial uses, still retains much fine woodwork and proportioning—especially the circular stairway and the oval room upstairs. Travellers should explore this mansion, since opportunities for seeing Charleston interiors are somewhat limited for strangers without local introductions. The section immediately around it was once known as "Anson Borough" (still commemorated in Anson St.)—most of the northerly and erstwhile suburban parts of Charleston having such individual local names. Returning now to Meeting St., we follow it northward again till we come to Calhoun St. (formerly Boundary St.) and the easterly end of the open park or parade-ground known successively as Inspection Square, Citadel Green, and Marion Square. This was formerly the line of the city's northernmost defences, and in the midst of the park may be seen a single remaining bit of the old "Horn Wall"—made of a mixture of lime and sea-shells—which formed the fortifications of 1780. On the north side of the green is the long, battlemented line of the old Citadel (1822) which formed the home of the Military College of South Carolina from its foundation in 1842 to its removal (1924) to new quarters in the extreme northwestern part of the city. The building still houses military activities. The King St. side of the green is the focus of modern mercantile life and the seat of the principal hotel. The Meeting St. side marks the local district once known as Louisburgh. Continuing along Meeting St. beyond the square, we see above Charlotte St. the splendid avenue of approach to the Second Presbyterian Church, which was built in 1811. Just beyond this, at the corner of Ashmead St., and now defaced by an encroaching filling-station, is the fine old Peter Manigault mansion, with its striking circular gate-lodge (a typical Old Charleston feature, though only two now survive), built in 1790. We have now reached a logical northerly limit of travel, though we may wish to proceed westward through Hudson and Vanderhorst Sts. to Coming St., up which, on the right-hand side, is St. Paul's Episcopal Church, a spacious fane built in 1810–12. This district was once known as Radcliffeborough. Proceeding south to Calhoun St. we may, if we desire, go westward several blocks to Rutledge Ave. in the old Cannonsborough district (south of which lay Harlestonborough), where we will find the Charleston Museum with its many antiquarian and other exhibits. Typical Old Charleston rooms and apothecary shops are shewn in the gallery of this celebrated institution. The museum is the oldest in America, having been founded in 1778. Returning along Calhoun St. to St. Philip St., we see in the next block, on the north side of Calhoun and extending to the Francis Marion Hotel, the spacious grounds and venerable building (1792) of the Charleston Orphan Home. The early prevalence of cholera, fever, and smallpox in the district left so many orphans that this institution was deemed a necessity. It still serves its original purpose—though the inroads of disease have long since been reduced to normal proportions through the progress of medical science. Descending St. Philip St. we come, at George St., upon the grounds, edifices, and gate-lodge (the latter the only surviving specimen of the kind save that of the Manigault house aforementioned) of the stately and reposeful College of Charleston, whose oldest structure was erected in 1828. Proceeding eastward through George to King St., we turn to the right and descend that business thoroughfare for many blocks. In the course of our walk we shall see two surviving instances of ancient shop signs; the drum clock over the jewellery shop at #285, betwixt Society and Wentworth Sts. on the western side, and the plough over McIntosh's Seed Store next the Masonic Temple on the eastern side betwixt Wentworth and Hasell. At Clifford St. we turn to the right, proceeding through to Archdale St. (a thoroughfare known for a time, and so designated on many signs and maps, as *Charles St.*, which causes considerable confusion). On the southeast corner we behold the ancient edifice (1817) and picturesque churchyard of *St. John's Lutheran Church;* which is directly adjoined on the south—in Archdale St.—by the Gothic precincts of the famous *Unitarian Church* (1772). This edifice is very remarkable as being one of the few serious Gothic specimens erected in the eighteenth century. Its churchyard, together with the neighbouring churchyard of St. John's, which is virtually one with it, is the supreme epitome of exotic glamour; a perfumed green tropic twilight of twisted-branched, overarching live-oaks and hanging vines, with ancient slabs and altar-stones peeping through a vivid, verdurous undergrowth threaded by curious winding walks. It is truly something out of a dream— such things do not belong to the waking world! Recognising this quality of fascination in the old Archdale St. churchyard, as well as in other churchyards and garden plots to the east, the president of the Charleston Garden Club some years ago formed the notion of mapping out an idyllic cross-town walk which might include as many as possible of them with a fair degree of continuity. The Unitarian churchyard had already established a walk though to King St., opposite the library, with a fine wrought-iron gate on the latter thoroughfare; and now a similar walk with gates was provided in the garden area just across the way—extending from the library grounds in King St. to the yard of the *Gibbes Art Gallery* in Meeting St. Still further coöperating, the *Circular Congregational Church* in Meeting St. opposite the Gibbes Gallery (an ugly pseudo-Romanesque Victorian church, but having a delightful Old Charleston chapel (1867), with classic facade and double entrance flights, in its grounds) opened its spacious churchyard as a continuation of the garden stroll; being seconded by St. Philip's Church, whose westerly churchyard spreads from Church St. (as before mentioned) to meet the rear of the Congregational churchyard. Thus the walk is made continuous from Archdale St. across King and Meeting to Church St.; and now there is some talk of continuing it through St. Philip's easterly churchyard behind the church, and emerging in Cumberland St. through a future gate. Such is the *Gateway Path* or *Gateway Walk*, so-called; and every visitor to Charleston ought at some time or other

to thread its entire length from St. John's to St. Philip's. For our *present* tour, we follow it from the Unitarian churchyard out to King St. and the library; there turning to
the right and following King St. southward. On the easterly side of King below
Queen, at #138, is the *site of the old Quaker Meeting-House*, enclosed by a tall iron
fence. The first meeting-house was built in 1694, but there has been no edifice on the
site since the fire of 1861; the Quakers being extinct in Charleston. The churchyard,
however, is owned and kept in good condition by the central organisation of Friends
in Philadelphia, and two of the ancient graves may yet be seen. Having inspected the
place, we advance down to *Broad St.*, making a short side-trip down that thoroughfare
to the right to see the *Robert Izard house* at #110 (1750), the later Izard house (1827)
at #114 (now occupied by the Catholic Bishop), the *Rutledge house* (1760), and the
still vacant site (#118) of St. Andrew's Hall, built in 1814 and burned in the fire of
1861. It is melancholy to observe the decaying garden walls and the mossy bricks of
the long-disused walks. This was, in its day, the principal auditorium of the town; a
distinction now falling to Hibernian Hall in Meeting St. The St. Andrew's Society,
which built it, was organised by Caledonians in 1729, and is still in a flourishing
state—having ceremoniously observed its 200th anniversary a few years ago. General
Lafayette was entertained in this vanished building in 1825. Beyond this site may be
seen the modern Catholic *Cathedral of St. John the Divine*, but we must now return
eastward, retracing our steps to King St. (on the northwest corner of which is the oldest pharmacy in America) and proceeding beyond to the important Meeting St. intersection. On the left-hand side of Broad, just back of the Court-House, is a small street
known as *Court-House Square*. The *large Georgian double house* visible at the end, with
a peculiarly Charlestonian arrangement of steps, and twin colonial doorways with
transoms having double rows of lights, is the house exploited in the novel "Lady Baltimore" by Owen Wister. Approaching this house and proceeding through the *green
gateway on the left*, we encounter a quasi-rustic lane which leads to a hidden group of
idyllically embowered houses—a sylvan oasis not a stone's throw from the busy civic
centre of the city. Emerging thence to the intersection of Broad and Meeting, we are
indeed at the very heart of Charleston. On the northwest corner is the *Court-House*,
built in 1788 on the site of the burned-down state-house in the days of Charleston's
state capitalship. Across on the northeast corner is the *City Hall*, built in 1801 as the
United States Bank, and used as a city hall since 1818. On the southeast corner is ancient *St. Michael's Episcopal Church* (1761), with its glorious steeple, exquisite chimes,
and quaint old churchyard with wrought-iron gates by Iusti. And on the southwest
corner is the modern but not unsightly *Post-Office*. Back of the City Hall is *City Park*
or *Washington-Square*, with its walks, benches, Pitt, Timrod, and Beauregard monuments, and ancient rear wall with arched embrasures. In the northwest corner of the
park, on the southeast corner of Meeting and Chalmers Sts., stands the classic hall of
records; put up in 1826 and called the *Fireproof Building* because it was the first of that
type erected in America. The work of Robert Mills, it proved its worth in the earthquake of 1886, when—alone of all the structures in this region—it remained unin-
jured. Opposite the park in Meeting St. is the home-like old Timrod Inn with its
archaic portico extending over the sidewalk. On the same western side of the street
opposite the end of Chalmers is the stately classic facade of *Hibernian Hall* (1841), the
city's principal auditorium and the home of a society of gentlemen of Irish descent
who alternately elect a Protestant and a Catholic as president in their annual ballot-
ing. Hence, proceeding south down Meeting St., we behold on our left, below St. Michael's Place, the splendid edifice of the *South Carolina Society*, built in 1804 and

designed by Gabriel Manigault. This is a masterpiece in the true Charleston tradition, with double steps flanked by wrought-iron lamps. The colossal portico over the sidewalk is very justly esteemed, and is of a somewhat later date than the building proper. The society which this building houses was formed for charitable purposes in 1736, and still vigorously flourishing. Descending to Tradd St., we behold on the northwest corner an ancient mansion with a two-storeyed porch (probably of much later date) overshadowing the street. This is the *Governor Branford* or *Horry house,* built in 1751–7. On the southwest corner is the old *South* or *First Presbyterian Church* and churchyard, the present sightly edifice dating from 1819. Just below this, on the same side of the street at #51, is the splendid *Nathaniel Russell mansion* of un-stuccoed brick. Over the doorway the initials "N. R." are woven into the wrought-iron balcony. The interior (not open to the public, alas!) is very celebrated and includes a magnificent circular stairway lighted by two vast and unusual windows (externally visible on the north side). Descending Meeting St. still farther, we must not neglect to glance into any quaint alleys we may pass. At Water St. we are again near the spot where Rhett hanged his 57 pirates. Here were anciently the sources of Vanderhorst Creek. All along the street, on both sides, are now seen residences of the greatest beauty and antiquity. No. 39, on the right-hand side, was built in 1767. No. 35 was the residence of Wm. Bull, a Charleston gentleman who was Lieutenant-Governor of the Province at the time of the Revolution. Just across the street, at #34, resided the last Royal Governor of the Province, Lord Wm. Campbell, who at length was so threatened by seditious mobs that he withdrew secretly, through a hidden passage, to a small boat in Vanderhorst Creek, by which he was conveyed to His Majesty's vessel *Tamar,* then lying in the harbour. We now turn to the right through Ladson St., though not without a glance down Meeting (to meet the upward glance we made when starting from the Battery) at the many fine mansions and gardens. Proceeding through Ladson to its end in King St., we find ourselves at the sumptuous *Miles Brewton* (his second home, built after he left the house in Church St. previously mentioned) or *Pringle house* (#27), a spacious brick mansion with walled garden, coach-house, and slave-quarters, built in 1765 and displaying the best British architecture modified for Charleston needs with a two-storeyed portico. It was used as an headquarters for His Majesty's officers in 1780–81, and is open to the public for the somewhat excessive fee of one dollar. The interior, from vaulted basement to raftered attic, is well worth inspection. All the great rooms are finely decorated and panelled, and shew early phases of the Adam influence—rare in the colonies as early as 1765. There are some notably fine mantels, and much good furniture is present. The gardens and outbuildings are all highly interesting—especially the *coach-house* fronting on the street just above the mansion, which displays very fully that curious whimsical use of Gothic architecture for ignominious purposes (doghouses, coach-houses, etc.) which prevailed in eighteenth-century Charleston. We now proceed southward along King St.; noting, as we cross it, the extreme narrowness (on the left-hand side) of Lamboll St., which despite its alley-like dimensions betwixt Meeting and King, is a residential thoroughfare of the first order. As we approach the Battery, we may well pause to observe *#3 King St.* on our right; this ancient house being called by guide-books the *narrowest* residence in Charleston, and perhaps in the whole South. Arrived at the Battery, we turn to the right, or westward; pausing as we do so to reflect that on this spot in 1718 were hanged the celebrated pirate Stede Bonnet, and some 40 of his men. It is said that the invincible Col. Rhett compelled these malefactors to dig their own graves, so that upon being cut down their bodies fell into them, where they still lie. Another account has it that they were hanged above the water, and cut down so that the ebb of the tide might carry them away. At all events, it is certain that Col. Rhett's efforts made Charleston remarkably free from pirates. There is much doubt, confusion, and hearsay in all these tales; and this hanging on the Battery is often mixed up with that other hanging of the 57 near Vanderhorst Creek at about the same time. Several guide-books declare that it was Capt. Bonnet's hanging which took place on the creek; appearing to join the facts of the two events in one. It is not well to place too much reliance on any statement concerning these traditional matters. We now proceed westward, or toward the Ashley River, for a single square; there turning to the right up *Legare St.* This is equal to lower Manning St. in the taste and elegance of its dwellings, and is altogether inhabited by families of consequence. Like all places long tenanted by a vivid gentry, it is full of old legends which guide-books still relate; amongst them being that of a duel fought with pistols from opposite upper windows across the street. On every hand are exquisite specimens of wrought-iron work, old granite hitching-posts (very typical of Charleston), fine polished knockers, graceful gates and doorways, pleasing house-facades, and walled gardens of unutterable charm. At the head of *Gibbes St.* we observe in a wall one of the most famous pairs of *wrought-iron gates* in Charleston. At #19, on the eastern or right-hand side of the street, we come to the *George Edwards house* in its walled grounds, noticing the famous gates with their pineapple-topped posts, which were erected in 1820. Into the ironwork around the doorway are woven the script initials "G" and "E". The ironwork of the gate is pieced out with cypress-wood, but so cunningly that the difference cannot be told. Cypress was at one time a great medium of construction in Charleston, many entire houses being built of it. Such an one is now seen on the left at #15 Legare St., this being one of the houses figuring in the duel just mentioned. On the right, the *knockers* of the Edwards house and of its neighbour at #16 are deserving of special notice. We ought also to observe the ancient iron lanterns over the entrance gates, the finest of which will be found at #18. Approaching *Tradd St.*, we see in the high brick wall on our right, at #32, the famous *Simonton Sword gates,* which are perhaps the most beautiful specimens of their kind in Charleston, or in the country. They derive their name from the central horizontal bars of their design, which are in the form of Roman short swords, on which are vertical supports in the form of Roman javelins. The scroll work supplementing these is of the most graceful description, and the whole is topped by a fine lantern. Behind the gates—which date from about 1820—are spacious and well-ordered grounds, and an old-fashioned avenue of magnolias leading to a mansion built before 1776. In the late eighteenth century this estate became a fashionable girls' school conducted by a French gentlewoman, Mme. Talvande, who fled hither from the San Domingo massacre. Later the place was owned by a young Englishman whose revelry and gaming made it a scene of nightly resort for Charleston's gayest young bloods. We now reach the corner of Tradd St., and may if we wish digress westward toward the Ashley River to observe some of the old houses and gateways. At No. 129, on the left, is a fine recessed gate with a curving wall on either side. Next to it, at #131, is another excellent specimen. Across the street at #128 is a fine old house built in 1760 and reached by curved steps climbing to a high porch. Around the corner, to the right, in *Logan St.* is the ancient churchyard of a vanished church—old St. Peter's. This is the burned district of 1861, hence beyond it most of the houses are new. At *#141 Tradd St.,* however, is a fine old recessed fence with a splendid gate of cluster-and-arrow ironwork at the inner bend of the curve. Behind it is a deep garden with trees, at the end of which the mansion may be seen at a distance. Now retracing our steps toward Meeting, we re-cross Legare and note some more objects of interest. On our left *Orange St.* runs up to Broad, and we may behold at its end the previously mentioned younger Izard house now tenanted by the Catholic Bishop. On the northwest corner, at *#104 Tradd,* is the *Stuart house,* built in 1772 and owned by a Royalist. At *King St.* we note the fine tiling of the three-storey edifice on the northwest corner. Beyond this, on our left, we see at *#72 Tradd St.* a fine old English double house with steps, built in 1734, and now inhabited by Miss Eola P. Willis, artist and historian of the Charleston stage.[4] Next door, at #70, is the *Robert Pringle house,* built in 1774 and since defaced by the addition of a bay-window. The next corner is Meeting Street with the Branford-Horry house on our left and the First Presbyterian Church on our right. These we beheld before, and we are at last aware that the end of our sightseeing route has been reached.

Such, in briefest and most inadequate outline, is Old Charleston. It remains to add a partial list of some odd local pronunciations of proper names consistently met with: Fraser, fra'-zier; Hasell, ha'-zel; Huger, yu-jee'; Legare, le-gree'; Manigault, mān'-i-go; Moultrie, moo'-tri; Vanderhorst, van-drorst' or van-drost'. Mispronunciation of these names marks one very definitely as a stranger in Charleston. So far as general language is concerned, the speech of Charleston does not differ greatly from that of New England—contact with England and isolation from the rest of the South having prevented the growth of a typical "Southern accent". Local idiosyncrasies are very slight and subtle, involving minutiae of cadence and quantity. Among the humbler classes, largely derived from Georgia and the Carolina interior, a "Southern accent" does exist.

List of Principal Sights in Preceding Itinerary

*Battery—Ft. Sumter—Ft. Moultrie—Wm. Washington house (Brewton-Pringle house, 27 King St.)
Old houses at bend in Church St.
*Stoll's Alley and Longitude Lane—Vanderhorst Row
Old houses (71, 73, 78) in Church St.
*Tradd St. houses
*Heyward house (87 Church), Cabbage Row
*Old Exchange, foot of Broad St. Adjacent old buildings
Slave Market, 8 Chalmers St. Pink Tavern opposite
View of Hibernian Hall through Chalmers
*Huguenot Church and Planter's Hotel—Pirate houses (Church and Queen)
*St. Philip's
*Powder House in Cumberland St.
*Market House, Meeting and Market
Old Wade Hampton birthplace—Hasell east of Meeting
Water works in George St. east of Meeting
2nd Pres. Ch. and Manigault ho.—Meeting above Marion Sq.
St. Paul's—Coming and Vanderhorst
Museum (if possible), Calhoun and Rutledge
Orphan House—Calhoun near Marion Sq.
*College of Charleston—George and St. Philip

*Especially notable or absolutely indispensable.

Signs along King St.
*St. John's Lutheran and Unitarian Churches—Archdale below Clifford
*Gateway Path
*Court House Sq., Broad and Meeting—Hibernian Hall up Meeting
*Court House, City Hall, Fireproof Bldg., City Park
St. Michael's—Broad and Meeting
*S. C. Society Hall—Meeting below Broad
*Horry house—1st Presbyterian Church—Meeting and Tradd
*Russell house—Meeting below Tradd
*Brewton-Pringle house—27 King
*Houses and gateways in Legare below Tradd

Charleston Itinerary (Pedestrian)

From
Battery up Church St. to Stoll's Alley.
Through Alley to E. Bay and back via Longitude Lane.
Up Church to Tradd St.
Down Tradd to E. Bay and back.
Up Church to Broad
Down Broad to E. Bay and back to State.
Up State to Chalmers
Along Chalmers to Church
Up Church to Cumberland (Cumberland to E. Bay and back?)
Through Cumberland to Meeting
Up Meeting to Market
Down Market to E. Bay
Up E. Bay to Hasell
Up Hasell to Meeting or beyond
Up Meeting to George
George to water works and back
Up Meeting to Charlotte and Ashmead
Through Hudson and Vanderhorst to Coming
Down Coming to Calhoun
Out Calhoun to Rutledge Ave. and back beyond St. Philip
Down St. Philip to George
George to King
Down King to Clifford
Clifford to Archdale
Unitarian Churchyard through to King (or back via Clifford if yard is closed)
Down King to Broad then out Broad to Legare and back
Along Broad Court House Sq. and Meeting
Down Meeting to Ladson
Through Ladson to King
Down King to S. Battery
S. Battery to Legare
Up Legare to Tradd
Through Tradd to Logan and back past Logan to Meeting.

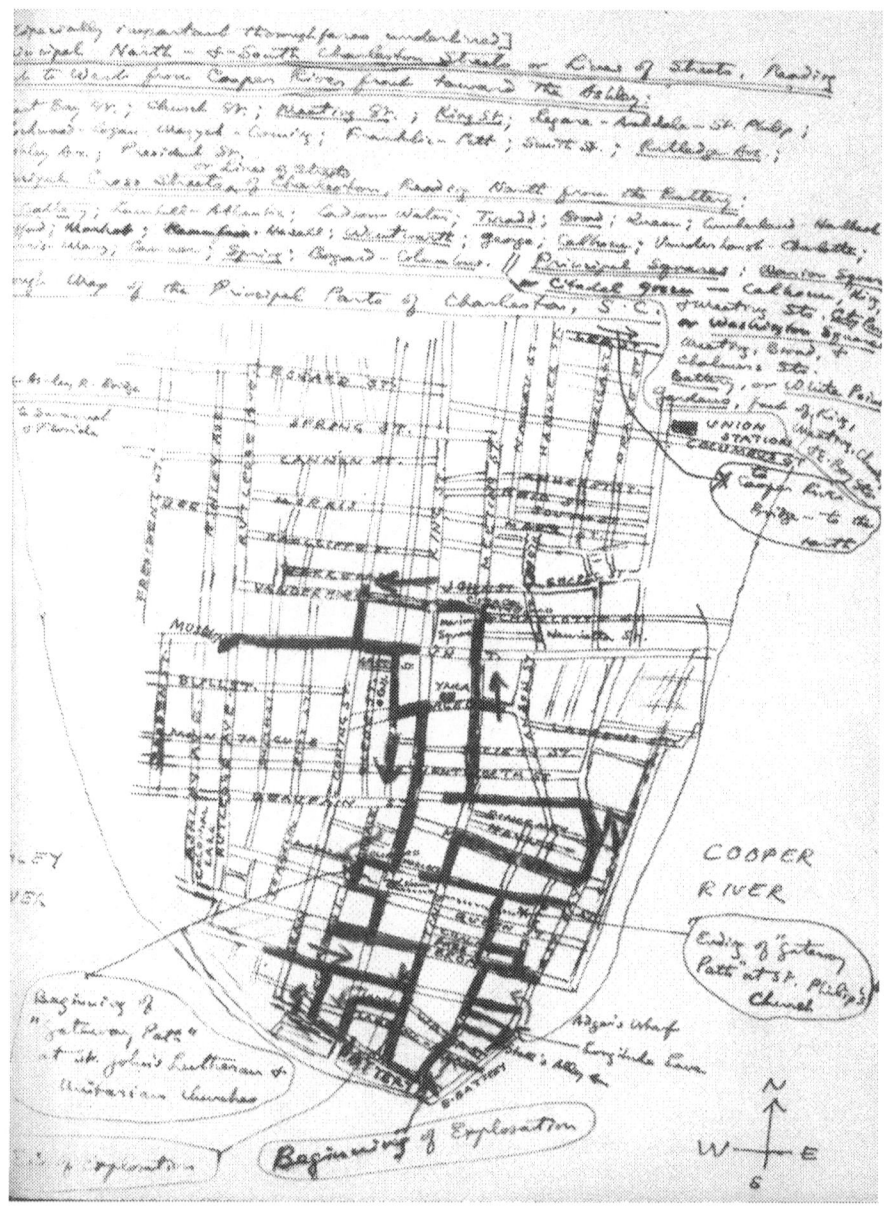

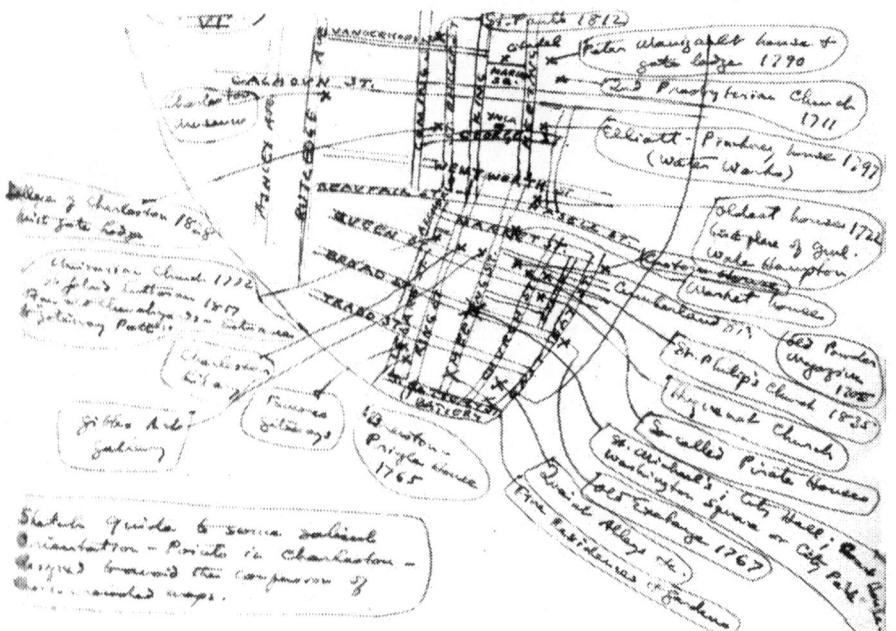

EDITOR'S NOTE FP: *Charleston* (New York: H. C. Koenig, 1936; 2nd ed. 1936). In early 1936 HPL's friend Herman C. Koenig (1893–1959) was planning a trip to Charleston. Evidently knowing that HPL had visited the place, he asked him for a brief guide to the city. HPL, never one to speak compressedly about the city he had come to love second only to his native Providence, unearthed his unpublished "An Account of Charleston" (p. 70) and wrote a letter transcribing much of it in condensed form, removing most of the archaisms of diction and adding a few new details. Koenig, who used the letter to visit Charleston, was so impressed with it that he published it in mimeographed form. This is the "first edition" of *Charleston* (c. January 1936). When HPL saw the published work, he noted that Koenig had committed a number of transcriptional errors (no doubt HPL had written his letter [now non-extant] in longhand), and both Koenig and HPL decided that the work should be rewritten as an essay. HPL performed the revision and Koenig then issued the "second edition" of *Charleston* around February, in an edition of probably 30 to 50 mimeographed copies. It was enclosed in a paper folder that also contained separate sheets on which HPL's drawings of Charleston sites were reproduced as photostats. Many of the most piquant features of "An Account of Charleston" have been suppressed, but the essay is nonetheless a convenient and lively guide to the city.

Notes

1. DuBose Heyward, *Peter Ashley* (1932), a novel of Charleston in the Civil War.

2. These thoroughfares are here rendered in italics.

3. Sir Richard Steele's papers on the Ugly Club can be found in *Spectator* No. 17 (20 March 1711), No. 32 (6 April 1711), No. 48 (25 April 1711), No. 78 (30 May 1711), and No. 87 (9 June 1711).

4. Eola P. Willis, author of *The Charleston Stage in the XVIII Century* (1924).

APPENDIX

For one whose knowledge of the subterranean world has hitherto been confined wholly to dreams and fiction, there are probably few experiences as thoroughly moving and satisfying as an exploration of the endless caverns in Virginia. Though not among the vastest of earth's hidden chambers, this profound labyrinth of night has a wealth of formations and dramatic vistas which can scarcely be paralleled elsewhere; so that it forms a perfect realisation of our wildest and most fantastic infernal visions.

The long railway journey from Washington to New Market, the nearest town to the caves, is through a region made richly historic by the Civil War—beginning with Manassas and ending with the scene of Sheridan's Ride—but the terrain does not become wild and vivid until the latter half of the trip, when the mountains are reached. Then one observes bold landscapes much like those of the Connecticut Valley—rugged ridges of hills and splendid prospects of valleys and distant towns. The agricultural state of the country seems more prosperous than that of New England, though none of the farms approach the typical Yankee homestead in neatness and beauty. Zigzag rail fences of the Southern type serve generally, instead of stone walls, to divide the fields; though a few of the latter are not absent.

New Market is reached after a four-hour ride, and a coach conveys the traveler to the mouth of the caverns, some six miles away. These open from a pleasant spot just at the base of a great hill, where the owners have built an office and laid out suitable grounds. Purchasing a ticket, one enters a building covering the actual gate of the abyss, and is assigned to a party dominated by two guides, a lecture-leader, and a rear guard to save stragglers from the nameless perils of loss in the gulfs of blackness.

Proceeding down steep stone steps to a region whose uniform temperature contrasts oddly with the shifting thermal values outside, the subterranean novice knows he is at last in a real cavern, and that he is about to sample in objective fact those secrets of earth's ultimate core which he has heretofore traversed only in dreams and in literature. It is a great moment; and as the first of the wide gulfs yawns up before the explorer, he feels that something out of phantasy has come earthward to meet him and give substance to his profoundest imaginings.

There is no exaggeration in all the awed and marvel-filled accounts of the caves which have been published. As deep gives place to deep, gallery to gallery, and chamber to chamber, one feels transported to the strangest regions of nocturnal fancy. Grotesque formations leer on every hand, and the ever-sinking level apprises one of the stupendous depth he is attaining. Glimpses of far black vistas beyond the radius of the lights—sheer drops of incalculable depth to unknown chasms, or arcades beckoning laterally to mysteries yet untasted by human eye—bring one's soul close to the frightful and obscure frontiers of the material world, and conjure up suspicions of vague and unhallowed dimensions whose formless beings lurk ever close to the visible world of man's five senses. Buried aeras—submerged civilisations—subterranean universes and unsuspected orders of entities and influences that haunt the sightless depths—all these flit through an imagination confronted by the actual presence of soundless and eternal night. One regrets the uniform illumination of the visited parts of the cave, and lags behind the party as much as the rear guide will let one, in order to imbibe the stupendous spectacle without excessive human cluttering.

The crystal formations at several points are of a fantastic beauty so poignant that all sensations of horror are momentarily forgotten. Water, limestone, and quartz have done strange and exquisite things at the behest of the infernal deities, and under the play of carefully arranged lights the stalactitic, stalagmitic, and other effects are grotesque and exotic with cosmic, interplanetary suggestions. Words cannot describe the utter, supernal loveliness of those formations known as the Diamond Lake and Oriental Room—they are not of this earth, but are sheer fragments of the narcotic rhapsodies of hasheesh-eaters, and the inspired visions of those few rare artists in words and colours who have had glimpses of realms beyond starry space.

And at the bottom of all—far, far down—still trickles the waters that carved the whole chain of gulfs out of the primal soluble limestone. Whence it comes and whither it trickles—to what awesome deeps of Tartarean nighted horror it bears the doom-fraught messages of the hoary hills—no being of human mould can say. Only They which gibber Down There can answer.

EDITOR'S NOTE FP: *Bacon's Essays* 2, No. 2 (Summer 1929): 8. A minimally altered version of one section of "Observations on Several Parts of America" (pp. 28–29). *Bacon's Essays* was an amateur journal edited by Victor E. Bacon.

SLEEPY HOLLOW TO-DAY

Not the least of my pleasures was a trip up the Hudson's east bank to Tarrytown, Sleepy Hollow, and the Washington Irving country in general. Tarrytown is an exquisite village perched on a cliff whose steepness and height make Providence's hill seem like a prairie. At Sleepy Hollow is an ancient Dutch church built in 1685, which with the exception of the Old Ship Church at Hingham (1681) is the oldest house of public worship, continuously used, in these colonies. It stands high on a terrace dominating the post road, and its churchyard has expanded into that enormous Sleepy Hollow Cemetery where the mortal remains of Mr. Irving repose. Sleepy Hollow itself, one of the finest wooded river gorges I have ever seen, is within the domain of the cemetery, no doubt forming a place of convocation for the numerous ghosts attendant upon the subterranean population. I was every moment on the watch for the Headless Horseman, but was denied that sight by reason of the strength of the daylight. In returning to Flatbush, I stopped off the stagecoach at Irvington from a desire to visit Mr. Irving's country-seat of Sunnyside. Here, however, I met with disappointment, for though I descended the bank to the level of the grounds, I was informed by a lodge keeper that the present proprietors do not admit spectators.

EDITOR'S NOTE FP: In *Junior Literature: Book Two*, ed. Sterling Leonard and Harold Y. Moffett (New York: Macmillan, 1930), pp. 545–46. An excerpt from "Observations on Several Parts of America" (pp. 18–19) made by Maurice W. Moe, who was acting as assistant to Leonard and Moffett in the compilation of this reader for seventh-graders. HPL professed to be flattered by the inclusion (the extract was placed in the appendix to the volume, as supplementary reading to Washington Irving's "The Legend of Sleepy Hollow"), writing: "it is rather amusing in a mild way to think of oneself as a real 'classic' permanently represented in a standard school reader!" (*SL* 2.250). How "permanent" HPL's inclusion was is questionable: the volume was reprinted in 1936, but apparently went out of print some years thereafter and has not been reissued since then. The text presented here is a literal transcription of the *Junior Literature* text, in which some of HPL's archaisms have been modernised.